Fairs, Cities and Merchants

SpatioTemporality / RaumZeitlichkeit

Practices – Concepts – Media /
Praktiken – Konzepte – Medien

Edited by / Herausgegeben von
Sebastian Dorsch, Bärbel Frischmann, Holt Meyer,
Susanne Rau, Sabine Schmolinsky,
Katharina Waldner

Volume / Band 19

Fairs, Cities and Merchants

Spatiotemporal Analyses (14th–17th century)

Edited by
Jean-Louis Gaulin and Susanne Rau

DE GRUYTER
OLDENBOURG

Funded by the Deutsche Forschungsgemeinschaft (DFG, German Research Foundation) – Project number 430627254.

Open Access edition supported by Open Access funds of the University of Erfurt.

ISBN: 978-3-11-162083-1
e-ISBN (PDF) 978-3-11-162129-6
e-ISBN (EPUB) 978-3-11-162137-1
ISSN 2365-3221
DOI https://doi.org/10.1515/9783111621296

Library of Congress Control Number: 2024950407

Bibliographic information published by the Deutsche Nationalbibliothek
The Deutsche Nationalbibliothek lists this publication in the Deutsche Nationalbibliografie; detailed bibliographic data are available on the internet at http://dnb.dnb.de.

Cover image: Anonymous. The Cloth Market, ‘s-Hertogenbosch, c. 1530, oil on panel, 126 x 67 cm, collection Het Noordbrabants Museum, ‘s-Hertogenbosch. Photo Peter Cox.
Typesetting: Integra Software Services Pvt. Ltd.
Printing and binding: CPI books GmbH, Leck

www.degruyter.com
Questions about General Product Safety Regulation:
productsafety@degruyterbrill.com

FSC www.fsc.org MIX Papier | Fördert gute Waldnutzung FSC® C083411

Contents

Jean-Louis Gaulin and Susanne Rau

Configuration of European fairs: an introduction

Why a history of fairs? A starting point from the present

Anyone interested in the origins of products for sale on the market today—whether in shops, boutiques, or supermarkets, physical or online—will easily be able to identify where they came from, either because various regulations require the origin or place of production to be indicated, or because such labelling may have tax advantages. Moreover, we often come across labels stating that the products come from the region close to the point of purchase or that they are a contribution to sustainability. These are not signs of nostalgia—a belief that things in the past were better—nor a reversal of the globalisation of trade in goods. On the contrary, the public at large has grown more and more aware of the fact that the availability of all products or goods at all times and in all places (for instance, fresh grapes from the southern hemisphere that are available in a supermarket in Germany or France in January) is not a simple luxury: consumption of such products can have several detrimental effects on the environment and society. There are still no import bans in place, but ethical considerations are becoming increasingly important —for both buyers and sellers. Of course, this leads to different behaviours. Just as there is a growing tendency to buy local or regional rather than global products, shopping in large supermarkets (*hypermarché* in French) in the urban periphery is being questioned, and shopping in smaller shops in the city centre or at the weekly market is becoming attractive again. This has created a new tension between globalisation and regionality. This potent vector of globalisation produced by the great liberalisation of economies over time has been thrown into question, as noted by the French economist Thomas Piketty: "Commerce must become again what it should never have ceased being: a means to higher goals."[1]

If we want to understand the origins of the current configuration of international trade in more detail, it is necessary to ask questions about the relationship

1 On the metamorphoses of capital since the eighteenth century, produced not only by the market but also by income and inherited wealth, see the book by Thomas Piketty and the debate surrounding it: Thomas Piketty. *Le capital au XXIe siècle*. Paris: Éditions du Seuil, 2013. This quote is taken from his blog: https://www.lemonde.fr/blog/piketty/2016/11/15/pour-une-autre-mondialisation/ (14 August 2024).

https://doi.org/10.1515/9783111621296-001

between the spatiality and temporality of commerce. This is the subject of the French-German research project *Configurations of European Fairs. Merchants, Objects, Routes (1350–1600)* (CoMOR).[2] From the perspective of a long-term history of markets and consumption, criticism of the near-universal availability of goods is a relatively recent phenomenon. The coronavirus pandemic and the disruption of global and local supply chains it entailed brought new challenges to the narrative of liberal economics.

If we consider the long history of economic exchange and consumption and the organisation of long-distance trade before the Industrial Revolution and the rise of the liberal economy, we inevitably come to the often-overlooked historical subject of markets and fairs (as opposed to the subject of *economics*). As the backbone of trade, payments, and commercial communication, fairs have played a key role over several centuries by mediating (along with the long-distance traders) between distant lands (and the products and financial instruments hailing from them) as well as local merchants and consumers. They were places where merchants had to go to buy large quantities of goods brought from afar and where they settled their accounts (debts), often with complex financial instruments. At fairs, traders could learn about products, establish contacts, and build up the trust that underpinned the exchanges which often incurred debts entailing multiple layers of transactions in place and time. These fairs were much larger than the weekly local markets, and yet they took place in the city or very close to it and were integrated into local cultural life. Like the local markets, they were far from the anonymous interactions that we have come to experience in the modern liberal market economy. Even well before the nineteenth century, however, these commercial exchanges not only took place in geographically defined places—the physical fair locations—they had already created connections across great distances and, after the development of cashless transactions with ledgers of periodic reconciliation, resulted in virtual, invisible spaces by bringing several currency zones into exchange with one another. Incidentally, it was not only an ethical or moral economy that protected against the anonymity of markets typical

2 Funded by the Agence nationale de la recherche (ANR-19-FRAL-0001) and the Deutsche Forschungsgemeinschaft (DFG project number 430627254), the project "Configurations of European fairs: Merchants, objects, routes, 1350–1600" (CoMOR) was also supported by several teaching and research institutions. Our thanks go to the Universities of Erfurt and Leipzig and, in Lyon, to the CIHAM-UMR 5648 and the École normale supérieure. Special thanks go to Ulf Christian Ewert and Heinrich Lang for reading an earlier version of this introduction and providing important feedback. Jean-Paul Rehr translated the French parts of the original version into English and proofread the entire text. We are deeply grateful to him for his commitment to the CoMOR project.

of our modern era but also the so-called "economy of privilege": the holding of markets or fairs was usually granted or formally instituted by a sovereign ruler.[3]

The starting point of CoMOR's research agenda was the rich literature in the economic history of trade fairs. The traditional approach of this economic history has been to concentrate on institutions, with attempts at integrating the spatial and temporal dimensions of fairs into their analysis.[4] CoMOR's focus in particular is on researching the relations between space, time, and social connections in relation to the commercial exchanges at fairs. There are advantages to describing and analysing the historical development of trade fairs in more detail from a spatial and temporal perspective. This raises questions such as how places and spaces of economic exchange were created; what role was played by proximity or locality; how distances were overcome; how temporal sequences in exchange were created and used; which institutions and trade practices influenced the configuration of economic exchange; and which techniques of space-time management contributed to generating economic profits.[5] This scheme of questions is instrumental to our analysis for two reasons: first, the tangled, layered interplay of agents, institutions, and locations of commercial exchange can be examined; second, commercial spaces can be reconstructed not only on a geographical basis—as done in former approaches—but it is now also possible to take agents' relationships into account, and thus to reconstruct commercial space on a relational basis.

To better understand the pre-modern configuration of periodic markets and their own inherent dynamics, we must first go further back in history and ask the contemporaries what they understood as 'markets' or 'fairs.' In the course of research done by the CoMOR project, a number of historical figures stood out for their ability to express what fairs meant to them. Here, we look briefly at four of

---

3 Markus A. Denzel (ed.). *Europäische Messegeschichte 9.–19. Jahrhundert.* Cologne, Weimar, Vienna: Böhlau, 2018; Guillaume Garner (ed.). *Die Ökonomie des Privilegs, Westeuropa 16.–19. Jahrhundert/L'économie du privilège, Europe occidentale XVIe–XIXe siècles.* Frankfurt: Klostermann, 2016; Douglass C. North. *Institutions, Institutional Design and Economic Performance.* Cambridge: Cambridge University Press, 1990.

4 Examples can be found in the following works: Simonetta Cavaciocchi (ed.). *Fiere e mercati nella integrazione delle economie europee secc. XIII–XVIII.* Florence: Le Monnier, 2001; Franz Irsigler, Michel Pauly (eds.). *Messen, Jahrmärkte und Stadtentwicklung in Europa/Foires, marchés annuels et développement urbain en Europe.* Trier: Porta Alba, 2007.

5 For an introduction to historical spatial analysis, see Susanne Rau. *History, space, and place.* New York: Routledge, 2019, esp. 100–104 on trade and spaces. https://www.routledge.com/History-Space-and-Place/Rau/p/book/9780367660307/ (15 August 2024); for the German version, see Susanne Rau. *Räume. Konzepte—Wahrnehmungen—Nutzungen.* 2nd ed. Frankfurt: Campus, 2017, 157–164, esp. the chapter "Handel: Interaktionsbeziehungen, die Räume hervorbringen."

them who lived between the fourteenth and seventeenth centuries: the Florentine Francesco Pegolotti, famous for his *Pratica di Mercatura*; the Marquis (and novelist) Tommaso di Saluzzo, author of the courtly novel *Le livre du Chevalier errant*; the Nuremberg merchant and arithmetician Lorenz Meder, compiler of the first known merchant manual printed in German, the *Handel Buch* (which is also the first known merchant manual printed in German); and lastly, Andreas Ryff, a modest merchant from Basel who recorded his business travels in a rare diary.

Fairs and markets: testimonials from the past

The Florentine Francesco di Balduccio Pegolotti, agent of the Bardi company at Anvers, London, and Cyprus, owes his fame to a work he created around 1340, the so-called *Pratica della Mercatura*. In this work, he complied various types of information useful to conducting commerce across a vast space, extending from the trading posts at La Tana on the Azov Sea to the western Mediterranean, from Morocco to northern Europe via Atlantic routes. Yet, before detailing the merchant haunts with which he was familiar, Pegolotti established a nomenclature of the places of commerce (*luogora*) for himself and his readers:

> Mercato in Toscana, e
> Piazza in più lingue.
> Bazarra e raba in genovesco.
> Fondaco in più lingue.
> Fonda in Cipri.
> Alla in fiammingo.
> Sugo in saracinesco.
> Fiera in Toscana e in più linguaggi.
> Panichiero in grechesco.[6]

These terms indicating the locations of markets come from the regions familiar to the great Tuscan trading companies of the period—Tuscany itself, Liguria, Flanders, the Maghreb, the Byzantine world, and Cyprus. Some among them, according to Pegolotti, were easily understandable "in many languages," such as *piazza*, *mercato*, *fondaco*, as well as *fiera*. Others—more rare—were known to the Florentine merchant in the Genoise language, such as *bazarra* and *raba*—the latter per-

6 Francesco Balducci Pegolotti. *La pratica della mercatura*, Allan Evans (ed.). Cambridge, MA: Medieval Academy of America, 1936, 17; Maria Elisa Soldani. Pegolotti, Francesco di Balduccio di. In *Dizionario Biografico degli Italiani*. Rome: Treccani, 82 (2015): 86–89. https://www.treccani.it/enciclopedia/francesco-balducci-pegolotti/ (04 September 2023).

haps related to the Arab *ribāṭ*[7]—or through Byzantine Greek, such *panichierio*, which likely stems from the antique 'panegyric.' Pegolotti adds that these places of mercantile activity are of two types: some function continually (*continuamente*), while others are periodic and follow a weekly or monthly rhythm (*a certi tempi ordinati della settimana o vero mesi dell'anno*). In the pages that follow, Pegolotti reviews those places where profitable business can be made in particular. For each one, he details those products (*mercantie*) that can be acquired there, with the weights and measures in force, the monies accepted, and indicates from time to time the customs and practices which a merchant may find useful. Moreover, Pegolotti provides his readers with conversion tables of those weights and measures used by the different merchant locations in such detail that one can reconstitute the spaces of exchange, with their places and their routes, that composed his mercantile worldview.

Of course, the Florentine author makes mention of the *fiere*. Although by this point they had begun their decline, the famous Champagne Fairs were still in a good position relative to those of Flanders, as well as those of Chalon-sur-Saône which, in particular, had a bright future ahead of them. Shifting focus to an entirely different zone, Pegolotti recounts the numerous fairs of the Kingdom of Naples, in Campania, and Puglia. For each of these fairs, he indicates the dates of the year on which they take place—indispensable calendars for merchants. In the same vein, his manual contains an Easter table for the years 1340 to 1465 (with a few errors).[8]

Despite Pegolotti's belief that the term *fiera* was widely known, other words were available to designate the great periodic markets. Aside from the scientific discussion between historians on how to define a fair, the question of the vocabulary used in medieval and early modern sources is worthy of merit and thus central to our research. In the learned language of the period, Latin, '*nundinae*' is the term of reference. In a reversal of meaning over time, this term, which originally designated the weekly markets in ancient Rome, came to indicate meetings of re-

7 In the Genoese context, '*raba*' in the Middle Ages indicated the sole marketplace where the sale of grains was permitted. See https://www.gdli.it/sala-lettura/vol/15?seq=183 (07 October 2024). Although the *Grande dizionario della lingua italiana* suggests that '*raba*' refers to the French '*rève*' (tax at the border), the term may be more related to the Arabic term '*ribāṭ*' which, in the early days of Islam, designated a small fortification built along a border. *Ribāṭ*—which lent its name to Rabat, capital of Morocco—also means 'hospice', 'inn', 'retreat.' We are grateful to Lahcen Daaïf (Université Lyon 2) for sharing his linguistic expertise.

8 Pegolotti, *Pratica, ad indicem*. The fair at Chalon is mentioned without dates ("fiere di Celona in Borgogna", foires de Chalon: 232). The "Tavola della Pasqua" can be found on pages 324–325.

duced frequency, once or twice, maybe four times per year.[9] '*Mercatum,*' on the other hand, was either a general term for a market among jurists (*ius mercati*), or the simpler weekly rural or urban market. Yet, the term '*nundinae*' did not pass into the vernacular languages whose vocabulary most often borrowed the Latin '*feria,*'[10] from which are derived 'fair', 'foire', 'fiera', 'feria,' among others. In German, the word '*Messe*' became the usual term—another reminder of the link between religious celebrations and commercial activity—but not exclusively, with the terms '*meß,*' '*marckt,*' or '*jarmarckt*' being used without much differentiation in official documentation. In the same fashion, Old Dutch had the word '*kermis*' (or '*kermes*'), which resulted from a contraction of '*kerk*' (church) and '*mis*' (holy mass).[11]

Half a century after the merchant Pegolotti, in an entirely different context, the noble marquis Tommaso III di Saluzzo evidenced a clear understanding of the details of fairs as the great periodic markets that animated urban life. Whether his work, the *Livre du chevalier errant,* written in French, was undertaken while the author was a prisoner of the Count of Savoy in Turin in 1394 or written (perhaps completed) when the author was in Paris where he found himself at the beginning of the fifteenth century, is of secondary interest to us. The most important—and also unexpected—event is the incorporation of an episode in which the scene is set in a "noble and beautiful city" hosting a fair into the knight's various rites of passage, where he is accompanied by Love, Fortune, and Knowledge. The author, who colours his narration with a panoply of elements, delivers a very personal and effective description of the fair's characteristics: the multitudes, the diversity of their geographic origins, the duration of sojourns (several days which require overnight stays), and the variety of merchandise.[12] Tommaso even fea-

9 On the roman periodical markets, see: Lukas de Ligt. *Fairs and Markets in the Roman Empire. Economic and Social Aspects of Periodic Trade in a Preindustrial Society*. Amsterdam: Giesen, 1993; Jörg Rüpke. Nundinae: Kalendarische Koordination im republikanischen Rom. In *Kommunikation in politischen und kultischen Gemeinschaften. Stätten und Formen der Kommunikation im Altertum V*, Gerhard Binder, Konrad Ehlich (eds.). Trier: Wissenschaftlicher Verlag Trier, 1996, 75–98; Elio Lo Cascio (ed.). *Mercati permanenti e mercati periodici nel mondo romano. Atti degli Incontri capresi di storia dell'economia antica, Capri 13-15 ottobre 1997*. Bari: Edipuglia, 2000; Jörg Rüpke. L'histoire des *fasti* romains: aspects médiatiques et politiques. *Revue historique de droit français et étranger* 81 (2003): 125-140.

10 *Feast day* in classical Latin, because markets were often held during religious festivals.

11 Kermis. Etymologiebank.nl: https://etymologiebank.nl/trefwoord/kermis (07 October 2024).

12 "En alant par nos journées venismez herbergier en une cité noble et belle. Et viz la multitude des gens qui la estoient, car la estoient gens de divers pays pour une foire qui la estoit [. . .]. Lors avint que quant nous feusmes la sejornez environ .iiij. jours, la foire se partoit et chascun aloit a ses besoingnez [. . .]." The text then goes on to describe a festival in which the actors "estoient

tures brokers (*courretiers*), who we know played an intermediary role between local and foreign merchants, at least for certain fairs.[13] The main manuscript of this text, currently held at the *Bibliothèque nationale de France*, illustrates this episode with an illumination emblematic of a medieval fair. Under the watch of the narrator-knight and his mentor, Lady Fortune, a great public place is laid out, at the centre of which are found a cross, the traders and attendees, and merchandise (animals, fabrics, and so on).[14]

While literary sources with their typifying descriptions of cities and fair traders bear witness to the fact that fairs were part of the standard repertoire of European economic institutions at the time, the new printed books of the sixteenth century contributed to disseminating the specialised knowledge required for doing business at trade fairs.[15] A merchants' handbook published in Nuremberg clearly indicates the dual function of contemporary trade fairs—namely, as commodity markets (for the exchange of merchandise) as well as money markets (for exchange and financial transactions).

The *Handel Buch* was published in 1558 by the Nuremberg citizen Lorenz Meder (d. 1561).[16] It was an important working tool for the merchants of upper

---

tous les courretiers [. . .]." See Thomas III. von Saluzzo. *Le livre du Chevalier errant*, Robert Fajen (ed.). Wiesbaden: Reichert, 2019, 491. For another edition, see Tommaso III di Saluzzo. *Il Libro del Cavaliere Errante (BnF ms. 12559)*, Marco Picat (ed.). Boves: Araba Fenice, 2008. In this edition, one can find a useful contribution by Renato Bordone. Une tres noble jouste. In *Il Libro del Cavaliere*, Picat (ed.), 27–35.

13 On market brokers, see Kathryn L. Reyerson. *The Art of the Deal: Intermediaries of Trade in Medieval Montpellier*. Leiden, Boston, Cologne: Brill, 2002; Sandrine Lavaud. Le courtier dans l'Aquitaine médiéval, un officier de la commune. In *Vendre le vin de l'Antiquité à nos jours*, Sandrine Lavaud (ed.). Bordeaux: Editions Féret, 2012, 237–254; Vincent Demont, Anne Wegener Sleeswijk, Mathieu Scherman (eds.). *Le pouvoir des courtiers. Univers marchand et acteurs du courtage en Europe* (*XIV*^e^-*XVIII*^e^ s.). Paris: Éditions Rue d'Ulm, 2018.

14 On the manuscript and its illumination, see *Paris 1400. Les arts sous Charles VI, Catalogue de l'exposition, Paris, Musée du Louvre, 22 mars–12 juillet 2004*. Paris: Réunion des musées nationaux, Fayard, 2004, catalogue no. 131. Reproduction: https://fairs-in-history.huma-num.fr/expo/online/gallery?object=thomas_saluces (07 October 2024).

15 See the important analytical bibliography by Jochen Hoock, Pierre Jeannin, Wolfgang Kaiser (eds.). *Ars mercatoria. Eine analytische Bibliographie*. 3 vols. Paderborn, Munich: Schöningh, 1991–2001.

16 Lorenz Meder. *Handel-Buch darin angezeigt wird, welcher Gestalt inn den fürnembsten Hendelstetten Europe, allerley Wahren anfencklich kaufft, dieselbig wider mit Nutz verkaufft, wie die Wechsel gemacht, Pfund, Ellen, unnd Müntz uberal verglichen, und zu welcher zeit die Merckten gewönlich gehalten werden*. Nuremberg: Johann vom Berg und Ulrich Neuber, 1558 [VD16 M 1856].

Germany and can be considered a standard work of the time[17] due to the scope and level of detail in the knowledge it contained about trading practices.[18] In the subtitle, Meder outlines the content that awaited the reader: knowledge about the purchase and profitable sale of goods, knowledge about bills of exchange, knowledge of the various weights, measures, and coins, and information about where and when markets and fairs were usually held. The book was aimed at those involved in trade—young merchants in particular. An index is highlighted in red lettering,[19] thus suggesting that the book was expressly designed to quickly look up or access important subjects. The preface emphasises the pioneering and instructional nature of the handbook once again, especially for fairs in foreign countries, for which one would then have to be able to compare coins, measures, weights, and prices.[20] According to Meder, all of this was essential for successful trading. Such merchant handbooks and special calendars of fair dates not only existed in the Holy Roman Empire but were also published in other European countries as of the early sixteenth century.

Meder's first chapter deals in detail with trade in Venice, whose prominent position is explained by the importance of this trading city for the merchants of upper Germany. It does not only present typical goods, but also the payment methods—with the recommendation that such methods should be discussed with the seller beforehand. The recommendation is to pay in gold ducats, as a profit

17 Hans Welser of Nuremberg was the original owner of the manuscript. See Hermann Kellenbenz (ed.). *Handelsbräuche des 16. Jahrhunderts. Das Medersche Handelsbuch und die Welserschen Nachträge*. Wiesbaden: Steiner, 1974, 75–76.

18 Markus A. Denzel. Handelspraktiken als wirtschaftshistorische Quellengattung vom Mittelalter bis in das frühe 20. Jahrhundert. Eine Einführung. In *Kaufmannsbücher und Handelspraktiken vom Spätmittelalter bis zum 20. Jahrhundert/Merchant's Books and Mercantile Practice from the Late Middle Ages to the Beginnings of the 20th Century*, Markus A. Denzel, Jean-Claude Hocquet, Harald Witthöft (eds.). Stuttgart: Franz Steiner, 2002, 11–45, here: 20; Ulf Christian Ewert, Susanne Rau, Leif Scheuermann. Räumliche Konfigurationen des Messehandels im frühneuzeitlichen Europa. Gedruckte Messekalender des 16. und 17. Jahrhunderts und ihre computergestützte Analyse. *Vierteljahrschrift für Sozial- und Wirtschaftsgeschichte* 110:4 (2023): 494–541, here: 497. https://doi.org/10.25162/vswg-2023-0012.

19 See Meder, *Handel-Buch*, frontispiece: "Allen Handthierern / und Jungen Kauffleuten / gantz nützlich und dienstlich. Mit einem Register." The letters u and v were rendered according to their phonetic value.

20 Meder, *Handel-Buch*, Vorrede, [1]: "Dann dises Buch / gleich wie ein Register / Handbuch / Wegweyser / unnd anleytung ist / inn alle Hendel / kauff unnd rechenschafften etc. Dann es zeygt und lehret was der gebrauch / nit allein in Teutschen / sonder auch aller anderer lender / Jarmärckten / unnd handlen seye / Was für unkosten auff jede Wahren gehen / Wie sich allerley Müntzen / Eln / massen / Gewichten etc. gegen einander vergleychen."

(on the exchange) can then be expected.[21] This is followed by chapters on trade with, amongst others and to name but a few, England, Apulia,[22] the Spanish court, Lisbon,[23] Nuremberg, Bolzano, and other regions in northern Italy. About halfway through the book, Meder turns to the city of Lyon with its four fairs. Here it becomes clear that the author and his contemporary readership (the merchants, but certainly a wider urban elite as well) must have been aware of the distinction between the periods of trade in goods and the periods of settlement of payments.[24] This indicates clearly that the trade in goods and the exchange trading were decoupled: the purchase, delivery, and financing of goods traded at fairs took place at different times.

In his presentation of Lyon as a trans-shipment centre for saffron from southern France and Aragon with exports to Nuremberg, domestic interests come to the fore.[25] However, the pages that follow also explain to the target audience the precise mechanics of the payment of these goods. The merchants use bills of exchange to finance their transactions. The bills of exchange purchased at the Epiphany Fair in Lyon are drawn on Villalón at the Lent Fair and honoured there.[26] In the opposite direction, the bills of exchange collected at the Lent Fair in Villalón are remitted at the Easter Fair in Lyon. From there, the bills are drawn

---

21 Meder, *Handel-Buch*, Venediger Handlung, Bescheyd der Bezalung, V^v: "In Venedig sind gemeiniglich allezeyt 3 oder 4 Wechsselbenck / darinn man zalung thun mag. Und so denn einer in Venedig was kaufft, und im kauff nichts sonderlichs wird außgedingt bar zuzalen / so mag einer wol in den bencken zalung thun. [. . .] Item / Wenn einer ein kauff in Venedig thun will / so muß er zuvor mit dem Verkauffer außdingen / Wie im einer bezalen will / mit Duc[aten] oder Fl[orentiner]."

22 The Welsers had a branch in Bari around 1500. See Peter Geffcken, Mark Häberlein (eds.). *Rechnungsfragmente der Augsburger Welser-Gesellschaft (1496–1551). Oberdeutscher Fernhandel am Beginn der neuzeitlichen Weltwirtschaft.* Stuttgart: Franz Steiner, 2014.

23 Due to the Charta of Tordesillas, the Portuguese Crown was the sovereign to lease the contracts for the importation of products from India. See Ron Harris. *Going the Distance: Eurasian Trade and the Rise of the Business Corporation, 1400–1700.* Princeton: Princeton University Press, 2020, 226–248. https://doi.org/10.23943/princeton/9780691150772.003.0009.

24 Meder, *Handel-Buch*, Leoner Handlung betreffend, LIII: "Zu Leon hat es alle jar 4 freye Meß / da nun vil volcks unnd aller hand Kauffmanschatz dahin kommet. [. . .] Unnd jegklicher Meß freyheyt / weret 15 wercktag. [. . .] Darnach fehet die bezalung an / und weret 8 tag oder 10 tag / oder noch lenger."

25 Kurt Weissen. Safran für Deutschland. Kontinuität und Diskontinuität mittelalterlicher und frühneuzeitlicher Warenbeschaffungsstrukturen. In *Beschaffungs- und Absatzmärkte oberdeutscher Firmen im Zeitalter der Welser und Fugger*, Angelika Westermann, Stefanie von Welser (eds.). Husum: Matthiesen, 2011, 61–78.

26 Markus A. Denzel. *Das System des bargeldlosen Zahlungsverkehrs europäischer Prägung vom Mittelalter bis 1914.* Stuttgart: Steiner, 2008, 147.

at the May Fair in Medina del Campo, where payment of Lyon bills is possible until June 15 to 20. The bills acquired at the Spanish May Fair are exchanged and then paid at the Lyon August Fair; bills accepted at the Lyon August Fair are drawn at Medina del Campo for the October Fair, where the bill redemption period runs from October 25 to November 25. This almost completes the annual cycle, as the other bills of exchange from Castile (an August Fair) can only be redeemed at the Lyon Epiphany Fair, while the bills of exchange from the Lyon All Saints Fair can be drawn at the Lent Fair in Villalón.[27]

Using the example of the saffron trade, Meder clearly describes that the exchange trade had to take place via two places at minimum, belonging to different currency zones (Lyon on the one hand, Villalón and Medina del Campo on the other). The Castilian fairs represent a special case here in that Villalón and Medina del Campo were two separate places which alternated their fair locations within one currency zone—that is, the same fair currency (the 'book currency' for settling transactions) was used at both fairs. The merchandise itself was only financially settled in Lyon and travelled as a commodity to a third place, principally—but not exclusively—Nuremberg. To summarise, only the saffron was transported, while the money itself did not 'move.' This configuration of commodity and financial transactions between Lyon and the Castilian fairs was by no means just an example invented by Meder for didactic purposes, but is also reflected in all other trade books, such as those of the Spanish fair traders, to whom Hilario Casado Alonso has devoted a large number of studies.[28]

In addition to these two functions of the fairs, described as commodity fairs and exchange fairs, there was a third—that of financing the 'state.' A striking example is found in Armand Jamme's contribution to this volume wherein he demonstrates that the levying of ecclesiastical taxes was linked to the great fairs in thirteenth- and fourteenth-century Christendom. Although this link does not appear strongly documented in subsequent centuries, other political powers in turn took advantage of the availability of money generated by the fairs and the presence of merchant-bankers at the most important fairs to meet their extraordinary

---

27 Meder concludes by pointing out the potential for profit in the business of bills of exchange. See Meder, *Handel-Buch*, Leoner Handlung, LIII^{V}: "Item alle die obgemelten wechssel / bezalt man Duc Doro, oder oro de Pexo Campa, iusta walutha. Und fura die Campio ist 6 / je 7 oder 8 p [er] Milier besser / dann inn Campi / darumb muß mans inn brieffen bestimmen / ob man abschrieto die Campo / oder darumb bezalen sol."

28 Hilario Casado Alonso. Les relations entre les foires de Castille et les foires de Lyon au XVIe siècle. In *Lyon vu/e d'ailleurs (1245–1800): Échanges, compétitions et perceptions*, Jean-Louis Gaulin, Susanne Rau (eds.). Lyon: Presses universitaires de Lyon, 2009, 91–108.

financial needs. A good case representing this aspect is the role of the Lyon fairs in financing the Italian wars of the kings of France in the sixteenth century which resulted in a loan known under the name the *Grand Parti.*[29]

But fairs were not only a funding source for rulers. The functioning of commodity and exchange fairs is also reflected in one of the rare surviving travel diaries of a Basel merchant from the end of the sixteenth century. The increasing significance of the bill of exchange did not mean that payments were no longer made in cash or by basic credit instruments. The activities of the Basel merchant Andreas Ryff (1550–1603) bear witness to this. The travel diary of this merchant, who visited markets and trade fairs in his region for 30 years during the second half of the sixteenth century, reveals that he travelled to Frankfurt a total of 53 times—that is, to one of the major international trade fairs of the time.[30] Unlike Meder, Andreas Ryff did not write a guide (or manual) for a wider audience, but only for himself and his family, and perhaps for anonymous posterity. In addition to his travel diary, in which he recounts his experiences on various journeys throughout his life, he also wrote an autobiography. Again, there are no definitions of either 'market' or 'fair,' but he explains why it was important for him to travel to the fairs in his region (that is, at Strasbourg and Frankfurt), noting that they had an important function in the payment of previously purchased goods. These were rarely paid for directly—that is, at the same fair, but only at the next instance, or any subsequent one—either because a loan was taken out for them and had to be paid off or because a bill of exchange had to be honoured. When Ryff writes that he had to go to the Frankfurt Autumn Fair "because of the payment,"[31] this meant that the payment was settled at the fair or offset against another transaction in a process that is known as 'clearing.'

---

29 Angela Orlandi. *Le Grand Parti. Fiorentini a Lione e il debito pubblico francese nel XVI secolo.* Florence: Leo S. Olschki, 2002. See also the contribution of Heinrich Lang on the Salviati and the lending of money to the French monarchy in the current volume.

30 "Also hab ich, gönstiger läser, alle die strossen von Basel gehn Franckfort zimlicher mossen erklärt, hab dieselben alle woll geiebt und gebroucht, dan ich hab sidt anno 1569, do ich mein erste reiß dohin gethon, biß uff anno 1597 in eigner person *53 messen besuocht und do erschinen.*" Friedrich Meyer. Andreas Ryff (1550–1603), Reisebüchlein. *Basler Zeitschrift für Geschichte und Altertumskunde* 72 (1972): 40.

31 "Ich bin auch fir daß hin in alle beide Strosburger, Johanne- und wienechtmessen, auch in beide Franckforter, Herbst- und vastenmessen, gefahren; dan die handlung nam durch den segen Gottes deglich zuo und ervordert auch der handel von wegen der bezalungen, daß ich die messen brouchen muoste." Andreas Heusler. Andreas Ryff, Selbstbiographie (bis 1574). *Beiträge zur vaterländischen Geschichte* 9 (1870): 79.

Periodicity and interruptions

From the testimonies it becomes clear that the medieval and early modern fairs were commercial meetings sufficiently extraordinary in the context of a yearly rhythm of urban environments that they were carefully inscribed in calendars and were the object of external communication in order to attract and establish 'regulars.' Yet, the 'established' and regular nature of these meetings, anchored in urban commercial practices, also made them somewhat vulnerable to unforeseen events.

Rhythms enacted in fair privileges

The number of fairs (once per year or more) and their dates formed the central components of the privileges that instituted fairs. More often than not, the dates of the liturgical calendar, holy days, and feast days lent their name to the fairs, both in Latin and in the various vernaculars. Towards 1585, the draughtsman and engraver Jost Amman composed at Nuremburg an allegory of commerce, of which the upper half is taken up by a remarkable calendar of fairs. To the left and right of the figure of Mercury, Amman arranged across six rows 171 fairs which were held in 122 towns, each identified by their name and their coat of arms. The fair dates—some of which are not given by the author—cover the period from the beginning of January to the end of December and reference feast and holy days—from "Leon. Epiphan." (a fair at Lyon on Epiphany, January 6) to "Wintherthur. Thome." (a fair held at Winterthur on the Feast Day of Saint Thomas the Apostle, December 21).[32] Care must be taken with interpreting these dates as they are not necessarily indicative of the exact opening date of a given fair. The fair may very well have opened on the same date as the holiday (generally after vespers) or perhaps shifted a few days afterwards. For example, the letters of franchise granted to Lyon by Louis IX 1463 make clear that the fair called "the Kings' Fair" would begin on the first Monday after Epiphany, meaning that the fair would open, not on a fixed date but, following the liturgical calendar of the given year, anywhere between January 7 and 13.[33] The question of opening and closing dates of a given fair were an important matter as they had a significant consequence from the privileges, notably the fiscal exemptions, if any, and

32 Gallerie—online, Jost Amman, Fairs in History. https://fairs-in-history.huma-num.fr/expo/online/gallery?object=allegorie (07 October 2024).
33 Marc Brésard. *Les foires de Lyon aux XVe et XVIe siècles*. Paris: Éditions Picard, 1914, 21.

those special judicial considerations (*extra ordinem*) demanded by merchants to cover their transactions during that period.

The fair organisers, lay or ecclesiastical lords, and municipal powers were tied to the local calendar in religious, commercial, and popular terms as part of a town's identity, showcasing their city with regularity. In an attempt to increase the fame of these events, they were sometimes even tempted to date its creation back to antiquity. To take one example, the fairs of Saint-Denis, outside Paris, saw a tradition forged in the eleventh century which linked the fairs to the legendary voyage of Charlemagne to Jerusalem from whence came the relics kept by the royal abbey in the town.[34] In another example, the sixteenth-century canon Guillaume Paradin, who surely knew the municipal records and the royal privileges bestowed upon the city of Lyon well, reckoned that the fairs there existed since "time immemorial" because the ancient geographer Strabo had already referred to the city of Lyon as an *emporium.*[35]

Interruptions

Contrary to the impression of regularity prescribed by the franchises of the fair privileges and compiled in fair calendars and of a deep historical continuity constructed in legends, case studies reveal the various risks for periodic markets to be temporarily or permanently interrupted.

Our research could hardly ignore the historical role of epidemics, as our work began at exactly the same time that the COVID-19 pandemic paralysed the European continent. The CoMOR launch meeting, which would have brought the whole team physically together in Lyon, took place on 18 and 19 June 2020—by video conference! All the more so because the epoch covered by the project—from the fourteenth to the seventeenth century—saw frequent returns of the plague after its first traumatic appearance in 1348. Numerous monographs have already underlined the effects of the plague on commercial activities. At Geneva, for example, the location of the covered markets which lodged the fair of Saint-Pierre-aux-Liens (August 1) yielded nothing in 1458 and 1459 *propter pestem.*[36]

34 See Rolf Große. Reliques du Christ et foires de Saint-Denis au XIe siècle. A propos de la *Descriptio clavi et corone domini. Revue d'histoire de l'Église de France* 87 (2001): 357–375 and the article of Nicolas Sarzeaud in this volume.

35 Guillaume Paradin. *Mémoires de l'histoire de Lyon.* Lyon: S. Gryphe, 1573, 12–15.

36 Frédéric Borel. *Les Foires de Genève au XVe siècle.* Geneva: H. Georg, 1892, 223; Jean-François Bergier. *Genève et l'économie européenne de la Renaissance.* Paris: S.EV.P.E.N., 1963, "peste" *ad indicem.*

The archives reveal their share of similar episodes, like the release from confinement authorised by the consuls of the city of Lyon in February 1631. Believing that the great epidemic that raged in 1630 was over, the consulate issued certificates to merchants who had made purchases at the Kings' Fair, authorising them to resume their activities. The bales and containers holding their goods bore the mark of each merchant, marks that were copied with the certificate in the register of the city's council minutes.[37]

Often appearing in chronicles in the same category as the plague for their devastating effects, public insecurity and wars also impacted the holding of fairs. According to the account of the chronicler Thomas Basin, in 1470, French and Burgundian merchants bore the brunt of one of numerous conflicts between King Louis XI and Duke Charles the Bold.

> The fairs of Pentecost were just about to take place at Anvers. The Duke issued at that moment general edicts and had all the property and merchandise identified as belonging to the subjects of the King of France sequestered in that city. Descriptive inventories were taken and entrusted to reliable guardians. When the King of France learned of this, he did not act any differently regarding the property of the subjects of the Duke of Burgundy discovered at the general fair of Saint-Denis, commonly called *le Lendit* [. . .].[38]

Another example in this vein is the military campaign waged in Provence by the imperial governor Antonio de Leyva in the summer of 1536 that caused a notable reduction in traffic to the August Fair at Lyon due to the closed roads. However, the army itself was decimated by the epidemic, and the interruption of the fairs at Lyon was short-lived, quickly recovering lost business.[39]

And yet, analyses based on archival data allow us to put these narrative sources into some perspective. In his book on the fairs of Chalon-sur-Saône, Henri Dubois concluded that despite the near-endemic insecurity that characterised the years 1352 to 1445, the two annual fairs of Chalon took place as normal. Only

---

37 Olivier Zeller. Les marques des marchands suisses enregistrées à Lyon (XVIIe–XVIIIe siècles): usages et morphologie. *Revue suisse d'Histoire* 73:3 (2023): 243–272. We thank Olivier Zeller for signalling this document: https://fairs-in-history.huma-num.fr/expo/online/gallery?object=marques_marchands_lyonnais (07 October 2024).

38 Thomas Basin. *Histoire de Louis XI*, vol. II, Charles Samaran, Monique-Cécile Garand (eds. and trans.). Paris: Les Belles Lettres, 1966, 13. The English translation is done by Jean-Paul Rehr.

39 Heinrich Lang. Seide für Lyon. Der Seidenzoll an der Rhône als Indikator für die Strukturen von Märkten einer europäischen Handelsmetropole in der Mitte des 16. Jahrhunderts. In *Wiegen—Zählen—Registrieren. Handelsgeschichtliche Massenquellen und die Erforschung mitteleuropäischer Märkte (13.–18. Jahrhundert)*, Peter Rauscher, Andrea Serles (eds). Innsbruck, Vienna, Bolzano: Studien, 2015, 387–409, 395–396.

ten merchant get-togethers were cancelled out of the 188 scheduled.[40] A similar conclusion was reached in a study of the Thirty Years' War in Swabia and neighbouring regions. The military conflict did not systematically lead to the closure or cancellation of fairs, but the places where fairs were held—such as Nördlingen—were sometimes difficult to access and could become less attractive, prompting merchants to stay away.[41]

Competition

To such external interruptions of commercial activity should be added the competition between the fairs themselves. The Champagne Fairs owed their attractiveness in part to their well-timed calendar organised by the comital power as of the end of the twelfth century—six fairs in four locations spread between January and November (two each in Troyes and Provins, and one each in Lagny and Bar-sur-Aube).[42] More generally, the work of Franz Irsigler has highlighted the existence of several regional systems of fairs that developed between the twelfth and fifteenth centuries. Each of these systems was based, as in Champagne, on a calendar of fairs that formed an annual cycle. From the twelfth century onwards, such a cycle already coordinated the fairs of the towns in the lower valleys of the Meuse and the Rhine as well as the cities of Aachen, Cologne, Duisburg, and Utrecht. In the fourteenth and fifteenth centuries fairs continued to operate in a coordinated system at a regional level so as to allow merchants to frequent the greatest number possible.[43]

---

40 Dubois, *Les foires de Chalon*, 252–253.

41 Wolfgang Wüst. Süddeutsche Städte unter schwedischer Besatzung. In *Der Dreißigjährige Krieg in Schwaben und seinen historischen Nachbarregionen: 1618–1648–2018. Ergebnisse einer interdisziplinären Tagung in Augsburg vom 1. bis 3. März 2018,* Wolfgang Wüst (ed.). Augsburg: Wißner, 2018, 78.

42 Michel Bur. Champagnemessen. In *Lexikon des Mittelalters*, 1983, vol. II, col. 1685–1689; Franz Irsigler, Winfried Reichert. Les foires de Champagne. In *Messen, Jahrmärkte und Stadtentwicklung* Irsigler, Pauly (eds.), 89–105.

43 See the clarification contained in Michel Pauly. Vom regionalen Messesystem zum internationalen Netz von Messestädten. In *Netzwerke im europäischen Handel des Mittelalters*, Gerhard Fouquet, Hans-Jörg Gilomen (eds.) Ostfildern: Jan Thorbecke, 2010, 49–100, esp. 51 for a map of regional trade fair systems. For a more recent period, see Jürgen Schneider, Markus A. Denzel. Foires et marchés en Allemagne à l'époque moderne. In *Foires et marché dans les campagnes de l'Europe médiévale et moderne (Flaran, XIV)*, Christian Desplat (ed.). Toulouse: Presses universitaires du Mirail, 1996, 137–152.

Yet the proliferation of fairs and the spirit of competition often worked to opposite effect. In Languedoc, where commercial growth was supported by the cloth industry as of the thirteenth century, attempts to establish new fairs (Pézenas, Montagnac, then Avignonet, Béziers, Beaucaire, etc.), which met with varying degrees of success, underscore the competitive situations which royal power was unable to regulate. In 1488, Charles VIII proclaimed that "all localities to which fairs had been granted could hold them, on condition that there were no two fairs on the same day," a recognition that the coordination of a regional system of fairs was a vexing issue.[44]

When the Lyon fairs, which were strongly supported by the royal power (in privileges of 1420, 1444, 1463) took off, they became the target of a coalition of cities from the centre of the French kingdom (Bourges, Tours) and of Languedoc. Shortly after the death of Louis XI, during the meeting of the Estates General at Tours at the beginning of 1484, criticisms were levelled against the Lyon fairs on the grounds that they would encourage the outflow of cash from the kingdom because it was a city on the frontier, the entry point for Italian silks, and because foreign exchange activities carried out there benefited foreign currencies. These complaints convinced the three orders (representatives of the clergy, nobility, and towns) and the royal council, and the privileges of the Lyon fairs were subsequently cancelled. The consulate of Lyon consequently endeavoured to "defend its fairs" with the support of foreign merchants who refused to desert the city—in particular, the merchants of the cities of southern Germany, from the Upper Rhine to the Swiss plateau. In two stages (1487 and 1494), the city managed to regain its four fairs.[45]

Fairs in the Holy Roman Empire saw competition as well, as can be seen with the rather late establishment of a fair at Ulm (1429). Originally scheduled at a date close to the Whitsun Fairs of Nördlingen and Zurzach—both of which played an important commercial and financial role for all of upper Germany—the new fair at Ulm did not succeed because merchants could not attend it alongside one of the two well-established Whitsun Fairs, which resulted in several rescheduled dates.[46]

---

44 Jean Combes. Les foires en Languedoc au moyen âge. *Annales E.S.C.* 13:2 (1958): 259.

45 Jean-Louis Gaulin, Susanne Rau. Rétablissement de deux foires à Lyon (mai 1487). In *Lyon, entre Empire et Royaume (843–1601). Textes et documents,* Alexis Charansonnet, Jean-Louis Gaulin, Pascale Mounier, Susanne Rau (eds.). Paris: Classiques Garnier, 2015, 523–528.

46 See the contribution of Ulf Christian Ewert in this volume.

The research project CoMOR

All these questions, reflecting a spatio-temporal approach to fairs, the places, and the calendars, both theoretical and real, are at the heart of the CoMOR project. Although the public health crisis would come to envelop the start of the project, during the development phase of the project (2018–2019), we had a different crisis on our minds: the 2008 financial crisis and its global impact. In the academic world, this crisis contributed to re-invigorating research in economic and financial history and reviving studies of markets over long periods, despite the relatively brief nature of the crisis. Moreover, attacks against structures which have governed modern international commerce have thrown institutional studies on the related institutions into doubt and provoked questions about the very future of those liberal, globalised markets.

It is within the context of these issues that the CoMOR project took up the history of European fairs from the perspective of "market integration." Towards the end of the Middle Ages, the fairs formed a system that rested on a tightly organised schedule ("calendar of fairs"), permitting merchants to meet in specific places on specific dates known well in advance. At the same time, these fairs facilitated the interconnection between local and regional markets (rural as much as urban) and the trans-regional commercial networks. During the sixteenth century, a decoupling occurred between merchandise and financial fairs, linked to the shift from financing products to pure money markets. The chronological boundaries of the project have thus been chosen in order to best account for these major transformations: from the decline of the old fair systems at Champagne around 1320, through a cycle dominated by the fairs at Lyon, to the decline of the fairs at Besançon around 1630.

The CoMOR project was particularly interested in studying the relational aspects (and their changes) of these gatherings of merchants, the roles assumed by the participants, and their customs and behaviours. Fair data (including places, routes, and exchanges) have been collected for the first time in their spatial and temporal dimensions through an integrated database application which presents the data encoded with historical social and exchange networks founded on over 3,000 historical geographic coordinates. With this, we can trace the merchants through their fairs, commodities and monies, itineraries, and rhythms. The investigation is centred on France, southern Germany, and northern Italy (the specialties of the core consortium researchers), with extensions into neighbouring economic and cultural regions.

This research also has a historiographical dimension. Based on collaboration between German and French researchers, with a significant presence of Italian scholars as well, the team aimed to bring together different academic traditions.

In France, the emphasis is on social history and economic sociology, while in Germany the tradition of '*Handelsgeschichte*' and the history of finance is prevalent.

Sources

The question of sources useful to the production of a history of fairs is paradoxical. Fairs were instituted by sovereign rulers, organised by towns and cities, attended by merchants near and far, and organised by host cities. They were also regarded as "festive" in the conjunction of cultures, local and distant. All of this leads to medieval and early modern fairs having been documented in a great variety of sources. On the other hand, precisely because they developed as temporary moments and places of exchange between princes, cities, and merchants, these fairs did not truly produce a single or unified archival memory of their own as merchant associations and confraternities did. Writing the history of medieval and early modern fairs therefore requires an exploration of multiple archival collections containing many types of sources. In the following section, the principal types of available sources are presented with respect to the agents of their production: sovereign powers, cities, and commercial actors.[47]

The earliest attempts at historical research on European fairs were based on official documents through which these large periodic markets were established—that is, where there is a fair, there must be fair privileges. This official act of granting a fair by a sovereign power set the "rules" for a fair on a case-by-case basis, authorising with a charter the benefiting town to hold one or more fairs per year according to a pre-established frequency and schedule. Tax exemptions for professional attendees as well as the terms for settling disputes arising from their commercial activities were an integral part of fair privileges. Intended to promote trade, the privileges of large fairs also promised security or "safe conduct" to merchants on both their inbound and outbound journeys. Indeed, the safe conducts established by Count Thibaud II as of the middle of the twelfth century were one of the reasons for the Champagne Fairs' success. Numerous other examples can be found in the archives.[48] Fair franchises were implicitly granted 'for life,' but it was

---

47 An interesting anthology of sources for the history of fairs from an Italian perspective is found in Alberto Grohmann. *Fiere e mercati nell'Europa occidentale*. Milan, Turin: B. Mondadori, 2011.

48 Example of Frankfurt: https://fairs-in-history.huma-num.fr/expo/online/gallery?object=sauf-conduit.

common to request a renewal when there was a change in regnal power or in political control.

Fair privileges reflect the numerous holders of *ius mercati* in late medieval Europe: the emperor, kings, princes, lay and ecclesiastical lords, and finally, cities once they had gained a significant level of autonomy. On the contrary, the Papacy, which was an active agent in the creation of fairs until the thirteenth century, ceased to play a direct role in the fairs. This volume presents two studies on the granting of fairs: the privileges for the "new" fairs in the Holy Roman Empire, and the institution of two annual fairs in the Piedmontese city of Asti in 1468 by the Duchess Marie of Cleves, widow of the poet Charles of Orléans, lord of the same city.

The preambles of fair privileges rely on the concept of 'good government' of the time. The reasons invoked in them combine, with variation, the munificence of the sovereign, the loyalty of the subjects rewarded by the granting of such fairs, the desire to populate or repopulate the towns and cities and to support their activity, as well as geographical and/or historical considerations. In reality, the contents of the privileges were the subject of negotiations between the sovereigns, the cities, and the merchants, at times evidenced by other sources. From this, a background of competition between cities and competing powers emerged. This could lead to conflict because fairs were also used as a kind of an 'economic weapon,' as mentioned above.

As recipients of these valuable privileges, the cities carefully preserved the documentation related to them, and as organisers of the fairs, they naturally had to make decisions and incur expenses through public offices, both of which also left traces in various sources. More broadly, city dwellers evoked the fairs which so suddenly animated urban life for a brief period, both in writings of a historical or moralising nature, or with which they intended to glorify their 'homeland.'

With respect to the category of sources produced by municipalities, we find among them letters, memoranda, and other official documentation prepared by urban officeholders and aimed at sovereign powers in order to obtain and defend fair privileges. This 'commercial urban diplomacy' is known (often euphemistically) from municipal deliberations and also through urban account books that record expenses for envoys and embassies, as well as gifts and "donations" demanded by the issuers of privileges. These same accounts also furnish data on the cities' expenses incurred in communicating their fairs—that is, sending messengers to other cities with which they were already in commercial relations or with which they wished to establish new ones.

As much as fairs appear in the expense column of the urban accounts, they were a clear source of revenue and profit as well. The sudden influx of merchants, horses, and other beasts of burden provided work for innkeepers, lodgers, and all the trades that kept them fed. The craftsmen of the fair towns were called upon to build or repair the stands or other parts of infrastructure. The professionals of writing—notaries and scribes—as well as guides and interpreters found a wealthy clientele among the merchants. In principle, this increase in wealth for the towns, produced by holding fairs, was very real but difficult to quantify in all its myriad expressions, and would likely have been offset by an expected decrease in tax revenues. Of course, the towns sometimes collected rental fees for stands from the merchants, as shown by the beautiful *Messestandsregister* of the Whitsun Fair in Nördlingen, the most important fair in southern Germany through the fourteenth and fifteenth centuries.[49] However, tax exemption was a strong argument in the eyes of merchants and was an integral part of the privileges granted to cities by sovereign rulers. Depending on the extent of these exemptions (at 'free' fairs, merchants were treated as totally exempt), the loss of tax income was more or less offset by the increase in economic activities for city dwellers (and thus taxpayers) provoked by the fairs.

Eyewitness accounts of those city dwellers help illustrate how the fairs were perceived by contemporaries. There are sometimes short entries in urban chronicles, which—as with the aforementioned canon Guillaume Paradin at Lyon—can carry a moralising tone. Very rare but all the more valuable sources are the travelogues and diary entries by fair traders themselves.[50]

Already well known to economic historians, the documents produced by the merchants at the fairs—and in connection to the trader's business in general—have been central to our research. Even though third-party notaries still drafted extensive acts during fairs in the sixteenth century (one thinks here of the register of the August Fair kept by the Lyon notary, Nicolas Dorlin during the work to consolidate the aforementioned royal debt known as the *Grand Parti*), merchants themselves authored the practical records of their business from at least the thirtheenth century. Contributions on this topic in the current volume contain numerous references to such sources, which allow us, for example, to reconstruct the relations between the Augsburg merchant David Gauger and his correspondent in Bolzano, David Wagner. Active in Lyon during the first half of the sixteenth century, the Salviati company, through the extraordinary wealth of its

49 Gallerie—online, Registre, Fairs in history. https://fairs-in-history.huma-num.fr/expo/online/gallery?object=registre_stands_nordlingen (7 October 2024). See Ulf Christian Ewert. Handelsräume der vormodernen Stadt. Raumzeitliche Aspekte des Messehandels am Beispiel der Nördlinger Pfingstmesse. *Moderne Stadtgeschichte* 2 (2023): 147–172. See also https://shs.hal.science/halshs-03876815/file/CoMOR-Projektvorstellung-HistSem-27-10-22-Folien.pdf.
50 See Susanne Rau's article in this volume.

archives, offers a privileged field of study to understand the role of the Lyon fairs for the Tuscan and German companies of the period. Beyond the usual—if massive—books of accounts, a rich correspondence between merchants of the company survives in the archives, in addition to price and exchange lists produced for their agents and operators in the field.

Besides the letters and books of accounts produced under the auspices of mercantile activity, there are also (to take up the distinction formulated by Federigo Melis[51]) those texts whose origins were in preparing future merchants for their career and to assist professionals in the mercantile world in handling various practical situations. We have already cited the manual by the Florentine Pegolotti as a remarkable early example of this. Numerous other texts containing pragmatic and practical information, including fair calendars, were composed in many vernacular languages and circulated in Europe, first as manuscripts and then as printed works issued from the new printing presses at the end of the medieval era.[52]

Transactions at fairs were not the exclusive domain of professional merchants. Sources produced by the buyers—when they can be located—provide information on commodities, prices, and the intermediaries in transactions. The examples of the papal court and the House of Savoy are developed in detail in this volume. For these 'institutional buyers' (to use a modern term), expenditures at fairs represented only a fraction of the purchases made over the course of a year. These purchases perhaps may have had a special meaning (abundance of products, trusted sellers, possibility of purchasing on credit, etc.) as they were recorded specifically in princely books of accounts.

Another range of sources, financial and legal in nature, produced in the context of settling disputes between merchants during fairs, promise much research potential even if, due to lack of time, the CoMOR project could only begin to consult them.[53]

---

51 Federigo Melis. Presentazione. In *La "pratica di mercatura" datiniana (secolo XIV)*, Cesare Ciano (ed.). Milan: Giuffrè, 1964, V–XII. For the Italian domain, see Franco Franceschi, Richard A. Goldthwaite, Reinhold C. Mueller (eds.). *Il Rinascimento italiano e l'Europa*, vol. 4: *Commercio e cultura mercantile*. Treviso: Angelo Colla, 2007.

52 See the opening example on Meder's manual and Ewert, Rau, Scheuermann, Konfigurationen.

53 Elena Maccioni, Sergio Tognetti. *Tribunali di mercanti e giustizia mercantile nel tardo Medioevo*. Florence: Olschki, 2016; Christoph Jeggle. Privilegierte Rechtsprechung: die Gründung des Merkantilmagistrats in Bozen im 17. Jahrhundert. In *Die Ökonomie des Privilegs: Westeuropa 16.–19. Jahrhundert*, Guillaume Garner (ed.). Frankfurt: Vittorio Klostermann, 2016, 197–223.

Another field with corresponding sources which the project could only approach marginally due to the specific skills required to work with them are the truly literary and iconographic sources. Nevertheless, several such sources were necessarily consulted, such as the *Livre du chevalier errant* by Tommaso di Saluzzo discussed in the beginning of this introduction, or the celebrated *Dit du Lendit*.[54] We know that fairs have been a rich subject for literary inventiveness and use. One of the most famous farces, that of Maître Pathelin, begins with a dialogue between the penniless judge and his wife Guillemette, who wonders how he is going to buy woollens "à la foire." As the history of theatre and spectacles touch another research discipline distant from fairs, we must leave the exploration of those links between commercial history and the history of theatre to future projects of a more multidisciplinary nature.[55]

There would not appear to be many iconographic representations of fairs that have come down to us—or perhaps the term 'fair' and other related words are not used frequently by image indexers, which would make them easy to locate in image and illumination databases. Medieval illuminated manuscripts do contain market-like scenes, often serving as backdrops for liturgical or legal motifs.[56] Rural markets in the sixteenth and seventeenth centuries seem to have inspired painters—especially the Dutch artists—more than urban fairs. When it came to depicting commerce in urban settings, the trade-related buildings (market halls, exchange houses) attracted more attention than the modest, ephemeral stalls that sheltered traders and their customers.[57] The Beaucaire Fair, or Madeleine Fair, as drawn with its rows of stalls and lively scenes by François Cléric in the early eighteenth century, is a marvellous exception.

As is so often the case, there are also sources that provide information about—and insight into—the fairs that one would not have thought of and that surprise at the archive. However, as a reflection of the very nature of fairs as meeting places,

54 We thank Beate Langenbruch (École normale supérieure de Lyon) for her expertise on this text and as well as the German translation she authored. See Gallerie—online, Dit du Lendit, Fairs in History. https://fairs-in-history.huma-num.fr/expo/online/gallery?object=dit_lendit (07 October 2024).

55 Jean Dufournet (ed.). *La Farce de maître Pathelin.* Paris: Garnier Flammarion, 2005. In a rapidly expanding bibliography, we point to an anthology: Darwin Smith, Gabriella Parussa, Olivier Halévy (eds). *Le Théâtre français du Moyen Âge et de la Renaissance—histoire, textes choisis, mise en scène.* Paris: Éditions L'Avant-scène théâtre, 2014 and to a case study: Marie Bouhaïk-Gironès. *Le mystère de Romans. 1509, une cité en spectacle.* Paris: Éditions de l'EHESS, 2023.

56 We have chosen the most beautiful of these for the exhibition posters and the book cover.

57 See, for instance, Der Vladislav-Saal des Prager Hradschins während des Jahrmarktes 1607, Nuremberg, Germanisches Nationalmuseum, K12245. https://fairs-in-history.huma-num.fr/expo/online/gallery?object=foire_salle_prague# (07 October 2024).

an experience shared by the researchers should also be mentioned here: not only are the archives very heterogeneous when it comes to the documentation of fairs, but sources relating to a particular town's fairs are never to be found solely in that town's own archives. Due to the trans-regional nature of these events, the sources have to be sought out in multiple places. A fair was not only a matter for the archives of the host town! This places high research demands on any study simply dedicated to the fairs of a single city.[58]

'Fairs in History': data and database

One of the principal goals of the CoMOR project was the development of a database drawing from the sources—published or unpublished—consulted by the team members. The database's construction needed to address three desires: first, from a scientific point of view, to create a database in which to store information about the dates and locations of fairs, merchants, goods, and monies traded, and the commercial itineraries; second, with respect to the project timeline, the pilot database needed to be operational as early as possible to allow researchers to test it with real-world data and sources, with a goal to be production-ready by the end of the first year of the project; finally, the database had to adhere to the standards of Open Science.[59]

The database and the website that enables online access to it—known as the application *Fairs in History* (https://fairs-in-history.huma-num.fr)—were developed in Lyon by Jean-Paul Rehr (engineer, October 2020–March 2021). Using historic maps, Leif Scheuermann (Mercator Fellow at Erfurt, July–August 2020 and March–June 2021) produced a geographic database required for encoding CoMOR data, which was subsequently integrated into the *Fairs in History* application. The application also automatically incorporates the bibliography produced by the researchers in conjunction with source analysis using Zotero, aided by Alain Marois (Lyon) and Simon Franzen (Erfurt).

58 On the importance of "translocal dimensions" of towns, see Jean-Louis Gaulin, Susanne Rau (eds.). Introduction: Lyon vu/e d'ailleurs. Une autre perspective sur l'histoire lyonnaise. In *Lyon vu/e d'ailleurs (1245–1800). Échanges, compétitions et perceptions*. Lyon: Presses universitaires de Lyon, 2009, 13–23.

59 Following the requirements of the ANR, three versions of the Data Management Plan were issued (October 2020, February 2022, October 2023); Jean-Paul Rehr, Jean-Louis Gaulin, Susanne Rau, Ulf Christian Ewert. *The CoMOR Data Management Plan*. 2019–2023. DOI: 10.34847/nkl.8ceekn2a. A data paper is in progress.

The database is structured around three levels of data.[60] The top level is a "collection" of sources identified and grouped by the researcher: a register, a series of connected documents, a merchant's manual, etc. The collection contains "sources" which make it up: an act in a register in a series of documents, a section of a manuscript, etc. Finally, the fundamental level of analysis for the database are the "events" which capture the relations between people, groups, and institutions, in a specific location, on a particular date(s) for a particular activity. Each event thus establishes a nexus between actors, places, dates and then qualifies their interaction with a verb (predicate).

A series of collections (that is, sets of data constituted into a corpus by a researcher) can already be consulted online and are freely downloadable in various formats. Thanks to *Fairs in History*, it has been possible to carry out unprecedented analyses—for example, by using data from Francesco Pegolotti's handbook, from reports about the Villeneuve toll on the shores of Lake Geneva, from the *Libro di fiera* kept in Lyon by the Salviati company at Easter 1508, from the diary of Andreas Ryff, and many others.[61]

As an active database, *Fairs in History* is continuing to receive new data gathered by team members. It will also be enriched for years to come by new collaborations between researchers and the CoMOR team. Michel Pauly, invitee of the final colloquium in Turin, kindly allowed and encouraged us to add the list of fairs in the Duchy of Luxembourg to the database based on his extracts from *Historia Luxemburgensis* by Abt Bertel (c. 1600).[62] The *Fairs in History* database is thus not simply a project with a fixed horizon, but welcomes contributions of data produced by researchers working on medieval and modern fairs.

Exhibitions and the general public

The *Fairs in History* web application is also home to a section called 'Fair Exhibition' which gathers resources aimed at a broader and more general public than the database. From its very conception, the project intended to present the re-

60 For an in-depth explanation of how the database responds to the diversity of project sources, see the contribution to this volume by Noémie Lacroix, Jean-Paul Rehr, and Leif Scheuermann.

61 All these collections are accessible on the *Fairs in History* website: https://fairs-in-history.huma-num.fr/about (07 October 2024).

62 Susanne Rau, Marisa Holzer. Archives nationales du Grand-Duché de Luxembourg, A-XIX-1 renseignements divers, 1575–1793, foires et marchés (COL0103). In *Configurations of European Fairs: Merchants, Objects, Routes (ca. 1350–1600)*, Jean-Louis Gaulin, Susanne Rau (eds.). https://fairs-in-history.huma-num.fr/collection/COL0103 (25 July 2024)—to quote just one example here.

search via an exhibition to be shown at Lyon, Erfurt or Leipzig, and Asti. This was successfully executed as "Foires, villes et marchands/Messe, Städte und Kaufleute/Fiere, città e mercanti (1350–1600)," adapted individually to each site. At Lyon (30 Mar–30 June 2023), the exhibition was realised thanks to a partnership with the *Archives du département du Rhône et de la métropole de Lyon*, for which we are indebted to the director, Bruno Galland. At Leipzig, the *Stadtgeschichtliches Museum Leipzig* welcomed the exhibition (1 September–15 October 2023). A final stop was made in Asti at the *Archivio storico del Comune di Asti* from 20 September to 5 November 2024.

In place of printed catalogues, the project opted for a digital solution to present the documents and texts on display. The resulting application was developed for mobile devices and was structured by Anaïs James (Avignon Université), with interfaces by Martin Roček and the database by Jean-Paul Rehr. Such an application would be useless without content, and here Noémie Lacroix and Ulf Christian Ewert played an extensive role in the collective effort of assembling and organising the materials. A sub-section of the application was created by Noémie Lacroix which has been launched for the public, particularly aimed at teachers and students in middle and high school as new resources for teaching and learning about history.

Our work, both in its scientific research and its public engagement, has managed to attract the interest of professionals in the fairs and exhibition business. Even if the function of current fairs is very different from the medieval and early modern antecedents, the questions that the profession is asking today are not entirely disconnected from those with which their 'predecessors' were confronted: the balancing of calendars and schedules, the pleasures and inconveniences of travel, the interest in face-to-face contact despite modern tools appearing to make them redundant, and so on.

This volume

This book is the result of the international research project described above, which was funded over three-and-a-half years and whose members met every six months between 2019 and 2023, alternating between Erfurt and Lyon, and once in Leipzig for two-day workshops. This constant exchange of ideas faced two difficulties: depending on the situation regarding the pandemic, individual workshops took place online or in hybrid mode; and depending on their work group membership status (full or associate) and their individual work packages, the members were able to devote themselves to the project with varying degrees of intensity. In June 2023, the entire research team met in Turin—the symbolic centre of the transalpine orientation of the CoMOR project—for a final conference, to discuss the results of individual studies, especially as related to the initial hypotheses of the project. Once again, everyone was able to benefit from the comments of the experts present. Invited speakers from outside the working group were able to expand our previous horizons with new thematic aspects or the geographical focus: Nicolas Sarzeaud, who had just completed his dissertation on the subject of the holy shrines of Christ venerated at the end of the Middle Ages; Boglárka Weisz, a specialist in urban and economic history of medieval Hungary; and François Gipouloux, a specialist in the economic history of China and the beginnings of globalisation in east Asia. Pauline Gomes, who wrote her master's thesis on the de Pierrevive family at the ENS de Lyon, also joined the group.

The thematically organised chapters that follow this introduction centre on the core geographical focus of the project, with this focus expanding in Chapter IV to include eastern Europe and even Asia. The volume concludes with a joint essay by Noémie Lacroix, Jean-Paul Rehr, and Leif Scheuermann presenting the project's website and database.

Chapter I (Creating, defining, and attending fairs) starts with a contribution by Ulf Christian Ewert on the use of different German terms for markets and fairs, especially in the phase when 'new' fairs were granted in the Holy Roman Empire between the fourteenth and sixteenth centuries. He demonstrates that the granting of privileges by sovereign rulers was necessary to create a coordinated network of markets with a legitimised spatio-temporal structure—one which would not have emerged without third-party enforcement. Using the example of Besançon, Nicolas Sarzeaud points out a connection between the dates of the fairs and the dates for the exhibition of the holy shrouds that has been little observed until now. The proximity of religion and economy thus extends far beyond the fact that fair dates are frequently named after the liturgical calendar. Indeed, the cities would also have benefited economically when they scheduled a trade fair on the date of a religious feast that attracted many pilgrims. Starting from accounting documentation of the former Savoyard States held at the *Archivio di Stato di Torino*, Jean-Louis Gaulin shows how, at the time of Duke Amadeus VIII, the court of Savoy was well connected to commercial networks as well as to the credit markets via the Geneva fairs. Given that the Savoyard States were crisscrossed by trade routes frequented by merchants from both sides of the Alps, the study seeks to understand the motives behind purchases made explicitly at Geneva's fairs.

The contributions in Chapter II (Credit and financial techniques) deal with the financial functions of fairs. To start with, Armand Jamme provides a comprehensive overview of the role of the papal court in European finance. Through his research using original sources, he demonstrates that the Roman Curia was a powerful economic player in long-distance trade by the fourteenth century at the latest. The Roman Curia sent its representatives to the European fairs, and their tax collectors used the fairs to collect church taxes throughout Europe. In a chronologically wide-ranging overview, Ezio Claudio Pia examines the pan-European role of the small town of Asti and its territory. Mainly known beyond the Alps in the twelfth and thirteenth centuries as moneychangers and bankers—the so-called Lombards—the merchants of Asti also contributed to making their city an interface between Mediterranean (Genoa, Savona) and northwest Europe. This role was further strengthened by a trade fair privilege granted by the Duchess Mary of Cleves in 1468. Pia's research in the local archives demonstrates that in the early seventeenth century, some companies from Asti, by managing large sums of money, were part of an extensive system of relations that involved trading centres such as Frankfurt, Cologne, St. Gallen, Lyon, Nuremberg, Lille, Turin, and Genoa. Through the insights gleaned from the outstanding bookkeeping practices of the Florentine Salviati company, which have come down to us in a massive corpus of documentation, Heinrich Lang's study presents us with another point of view: here, the perspective is from the single company trading with their south German partners at the Lyon fairs in the first half of the sixteenth century. A detailed study of several of the Salviati *Libri di fiera* shows the clear predominance of payments via bills of exchange (cash payments were marginal) and a marked interest in the central European silver trade. In his article, Claudio Marsilio focuses on the special type of exchange fair as a first attempt at integration of the European monetary and financial markets in the early modern period. Written and printed exchange lists (*listini*), preserved in large numbers for the seventeenth-century Italian exchange fairs in Piacenza, Novi, Verona, and Bolzano, are an essential source for the history of the European payment system—a system already disconnected from 'real places'—as it developed with the great exchange fairs, first in Besançon in the sixteenth century. Proceeding from a talk he gave at our workshop in January 2022, Markus Denzel has developed a text which summarises the fair functions discussed in this introduction: the major international trade fairs were also money, credit, and exchange fairs. The more innovations—such as discounting in cashless payment and credit transactions—had become established, the more the traditional commodity fairs became obsolete.

Chapter III (Merchants at fairs) looks at merchants and merchant groups at fairs. Clément Lenoble follows the Pazzi (or Passis) family from Florence to the Lyon and Geneva fairs and analyses the shifting economic geography of the late fifteenth century. His hypothesis is that Louis XI, King of France, wanted to encourage Tuscan merchant families like the Pazzis to settle in Lyon, a city loyal to French royalty, rather than in Avignon or Geneva. Pauline Gomes pursues a similar question by following the relocation of the Pietraviva family from Chieri in

Piedmont to Lyon, where they—known as Pierrevive in French documents—were active in the fair trade, especially in the import of spices as revealed by the town's tax records (*garbeaux*). Her research in archives on both sides of the Alps has enabled her to demonstrate that the merchant family was firmly anchored in the respective urban societies. In contrast, Marta Gravela follows in the footsteps of the French Lyon merchants who helped to shape the early fairs. Her article focuses on the group of merchants and moneylenders active in the city and beyond up to the mid-fifteenth century. After identifying the merchants from fiscal lists (*nommées*), she examines their economic and political role and measures the impact of the city's growth on this social group. In the last article of this chapter, Matthias Baumgartl analyses the liquidity management of the merchant David Gauger at Augsburg and David Wagner at Bolzano at the end of the sixteenth century. Employees of these financial service providers attended trade fairs for bill of exchange redemption dates as well as to obtain access to capital markets.

Chapter IV (Europe and beyond: time and space of fairs) addresses questions about temporality and spatiality of trade fairs on different levels—from micro to macro. Drawing on a travel book and an autobiography, Susanne Rau analyses the experience of a Basel merchant while visiting fairs. She proposes a rhythm-analytical approach to analysing fair dates because the fair calendars are normative, and no single trade fair merchant could possibly have visited all of them. The question, therefore, is: which trade fairs were visited by an individual trader and for what reasons? Which routes and means of transport did he use? How much time was required for the journey? Such a rhythm-analytical and spatio-temporal approach can reveal how the micro and macro perspectives were linked.

The Kingdom of Hungary was a special case in that there were virtually no fairs of the type known in western Europe in the late Middle Ages. The article by Boglárka Weisz deals with the emergence of a new trade route to Hungary, which connected the Rhineland (Cologne) with Hungary. In her study, she presents the history of this route from the perspective of the merchant groups—the routes they used to reach the Kingdom of Hungary and their trading activities.[63] François Gipouloux's contribution takes us to Late Imperial China, highlighting the prevalence of the rural fairs and the timing and duration of temple fairs. While temple fairs served as a link between the merchant economy of the countryside and a more complex urban economy—namely, as meeting points and

63 On markets in eastern Europe, see also Katalin Szende, Erika Szívós, Boglárka Weisz (eds.). *Cities and Economy in Europe: Markets and Trade on the Margins from the Middle Ages to the Present*. London, New York: Routledge, 2024.

hubs of the long-distance trade network—the local sources are silent about a potential dissociation of commodity fairs and exchange fairs observed at the same time in western Europe. Markus Denzel concludes this chapter with a study of the commercial meeting points in Poland and Muscovy up to the seventeenth century. The specific nature of the bigger markets in eastern Europe—regionally important but playing almost no role in European high finance—leads him to suggest categorising them as "great annual markets."

Chapter V (Presentation of the CoMOR website/database) concludes the volume with an article co-authored by Noémie Lacroix, Jean-Paul Rehr, and Leif Scheuermann on the *Fairs in History* database and application. Far from a technical review, the authors look at the application from the perspective of historians concerned with capturing and using as much data from sources as possible and in a way that allows different types of documentation to interact and inform each other. The subjects are thus practical and range from describing user interfaces that facilitate non-technical users entering data to describing the tools for research, to concerns about assuring data quality to facilitate the interconnection of sources, to the ready-made outputs for citation and different analyses, from spatio-geographic to networks of people, places, and objects. The chapter concludes with a few brief case studies demonstrating through the outputs the different ways that the merchant and fair data may be easily used.

Special acknowledgements

Special thanks go to Heinrich Lang, co-responsible of the research project, and Marta Gravela, who hosted us at her new university in Turin for the final project conference. We would also like to thank the invited speakers for their commitment at the previous CoMOR workshops (Ulla Kypta, Michael Rothmann, Pierre-Cyrille Hautcœur, Stephan Nicolussi-Köhler, Ulrich Pfister, and Edoardo Demo) as well as the chairs and discussants in Turin (Alma Poloni, Andrea Nicolotti, Alessio Fiore, Francesco Guidi-Bruscoli, and Michel Pauly) who all took part in our fair adventure. Finally, we would like to thank Adina Eckart for the conference report.[64] Before all the articles could be handed over to the publisher, they had to undergo proofreading by Suzanne Amy Foxley, to whom we are also greatly indebted for this Herculean task. With this, we leave this book to readers who want to delve into the historical world of fairs in their many dimensions.

---

64 Her report will be published in the *Annales Mercaturae* 9 (2023).

Bibliography

Primary Sources

Heusler, Andreas (ed.). Andreas Ryff, Selbstbiographie (bis 1574). *Beiträge zur vaterländischen Geschichte* 9 (1870): 37–121.

Kellenbenz, Hermann (ed.). *Handelsbräuche des 16. Jahrhunderts. Das Medersche Handelsbuch und die Welserschen Nachträge*. Wiesbaden: Steiner, 1974.

La Farce de maître Pathelin, Jean Dufournet (ed. and trans.). Paris: Garnier Flammarion, 2005.

Meder, Lorenz. *Handel-Buch darin angezeigt wird, welcher Gestalt inn den fürnembsten Hendelstetten Europe, allerley Wahren anfencklich kaufft, dieselbig wider mit Nutz verkaufft, wie die Wechsel gemacht, Pfund, Ellen, unnd Müntz uberal verglichen, und zu welcher zeit die Merckten gewönlich gehalten werden*. Nuremberg: Johann vom Berg und Ulrich Neuber, 1558 [VD16 M 1856].

Meyer, Friedrich (ed.). Andreas Ryff (1550–1603), Reisebüchlein. *Basler Zeitschrift für Geschichte und Altertumskunde* 72 (1972): 5–135.

Paradin, Guillaume. *Mémoires de l'histoire de Lyon*. Lyon: S. Gryphe, 1573.

Pegolotti, Francesco Balducci. *La pratica della mercatura*, Allan Evans (ed.). Cambridge, MA: Medieval Academy of America, 1936.

Thomas Basin. *Histoire de Louis XI*, vol. II. Charles Samaran, Monique-Cécile Garand (eds. and trans.). Paris: Les Belles Lettres, 1966.

Thomas III di Saluzzo. *Il Libro del Cavaliere Errante (BnF ms. 12559)*. Marco Picat (ed.). Boves: Araba Fenice, 2008.

Thomas III. von Saluzzo. *Le livre du Chevalier errant*. Robert Fajen (ed.). Wiesbaden: Reichert, 2019.

Literature

Bergier, Jean-François. *Genève et l'économie européenne de la Renaissance*. Paris: S.E.V.P.E.N., 1963.

Bordone, Renato. Une tres noble jouste. In *Il Libro del Cavaliere*, Marco Picat (ed.). Boves: Araba Fenice, 2008, 27–35.

Borel, Frédéric. *Les Foires de Genève au XVe siècle*. Geneva: H. Georg, 1892.

Börner, Lars, John William Hatfield. The Design of Debt-Clearing Markets: Clearinghouse Mechanisms in Preindustrial Europe. *Journal of Political Economy* 125:6 (2017): 1991–2037.

Bouhaïk-Gironès, Marie. *Le mystère de Romans. 1509, une cité en spectacle*. Paris: Éditions de l'EHESS, 2023.

Brésard, Marc. *Les foires de Lyon aux XVe et XVIe siècles*. Paris: Éditions Picard, 1914.

Bur, Michel. Champagnemessen. In *Lexikon des Mittelalters*, 1983, vol. II, col. 1685–1689.

Casado Alonso, Hilario. Les relations entre les foires de Castille et les foires de Lyon au XVIe siècle. In *Lyon vu/e d'ailleurs (1245–1800): Échanges, compétitions et perceptions*, Jean-Louis Gaulin, Susanne Rau (eds.). Lyon: Presses universitaires de Lyon, 2009, 91–108.

Cavaciocchi, Simonetta (ed.). *Fiere e mercati nella integrazione delle economie europee secc. XIII–XVIII*. Florence: Le Monnier, 2001.

Combes, Jean. Les foires en Languedoc au moyen âge. *Annales E.S.C.* 13:2 (1958): 231–259.

Demont, Vincent, Anne Wegener Sleeswijk, Mathieu Scherman (eds.). *Le pouvoir des courtiers. Univers marchand et acteurs du courtage en Europe (XIVe-XVIIIe s.)*. Paris: Éditions Rue d'Ulm, 2018.

Denzel, Markus A. (ed.). *Europäische Messegeschichte 9.–19. Jahrhundert.* Cologne, Weimar, Vienna: Böhlau, 2018.

Denzel, Markus A. *Das System des bargeldlosen Zahlungsverkehrs europäischer Prägung vom Mittelalter bis 1914.* Stuttgart: Steiner, 2008.

Denzel, Markus A. Handelspraktiken als wirtschaftshistorische Quellengattung vom Mittelalter bis in das frühe 20. Jahrhundert. Eine Einführung. In *Kaufmannsbücher und Handelspraktiken vom Spätmittelalter bis zum 20. Jahrhundert/Merchant's Books and Mercantile Practice from the Late Middle Ages to the Beginnings of the 20th Century*, Markus A. Denzel, Jean-Claude Hocquet, Harald Witthöft (eds.). Stuttgart: Franz Steiner, 2002, 11–45.

Dubois, Henri. *Les foires de Chalon et le commerce dans la vallée de la Saône à la fin du moyen âge (vers 1280–vers 1430).* Paris: Publications de la Sorbonne, 1976.

Ewert, Ulf Christian, Susanne Rau, Leif Scheuermann. Räumliche Konfigurationen des Messehandels im frühneuzeitlichen Europa. Gedruckte Messekalender des 16. und 17. Jahrhunderts und ihre computergestützte Analyse. *Vierteljahrschrift für Sozial- und Wirtschaftsgeschichte* 110:4 (2023): 494–541. https://doi.org/10.25162/vswg-2023-0012.

Ewert, Ulf Christian. Handelsräume der vormodernen Stadt. Raumzeitliche Aspekte des Messehandels am Beispiel der Nördlinger Pfingstmesse. *Moderne Stadtgeschichte* 2 (2023): 147–172.

Franceschi, Franco, Richard A. Goldthwaite, Reinhold C. Mueller (eds.). *Il Rinascimento italiano e l'Europa*, vol. 4: *Commercio e cultura mercantile*. Treviso: Angelo Colla, 2007.

Garner, Guillaume (ed.). *Die Ökonomie des Privilegs, Westeuropa 16.–19. Jahrhundert/L'économie du privilège, Europe occidentale XVIe–XIXe siècles*. Frankfurt: Klostermann, 2016.

Gaulin, Jean-Louis, Susanne Rau (eds.). Introduction: Lyon vu/e d'ailleurs. Une autre perspective sur l'histoire lyonnaise. In *Lyon vu/e d'ailleurs (1245–1800): Échanges, compétitions et perceptions*, Jean-Louis Gaulin, Susanne Rau (eds.). Lyon: Presses universitaires de Lyon, 2009, 13–23.

Gaulin, Jean-Louis, Susanne Rau. Rétablissement de deux foires à Lyon (mai 1487). In *Lyon, entre Empire et Royaume (843–1601). Textes et documents*, Alexis Charansonnet, Jean-Louis Gaulin, Pascale Mounier, Susanne Rau (eds.). Paris: Classiques Garnier, 2015, 523–528.

Geffcken, Peter, Mark Häberlein (eds.). *Rechnungsfragmente der Augsburger Welser-Gesellschaft (1496–1551). Oberdeutscher Fernhandel am Beginn der neuzeitlichen Weltwirtschaft*. Stuttgart: Franz Steiner, 2014.

Gentil Da Silva, José. *Banque et crédit en Italie au XVIIe siècle. Tome I: Les foires de change et la dépréciation monétaire*. Paris: Klincksieck, 1969.

Grohmann, Alberto. *Fiere e mercati nell'Europa occidentale*. Milan, Turin: B. Mondadori, 2011.

Große, Rolf. Reliques du Christ et foires de Saint-Denis au XIe siècle. A propos de la *Descriptio clavi et corone domini*. *Revue d'histoire de l'Église de France* 87 (2001): 357–375.

Harris, Ron. *Going the Distance: Eurasian Trade and the Rise of the Business Corporation, 1400–1700*. Princeton: Princeton University Press, 2020. https://doi.org/10.23943/princeton/9780691150772.003.0009

Hook, Jochen, Pierre Jeannin, Wolfgang Kaiser (eds.). *Ars mercatoria. Eine analytische Bibliographie*. 3 vols. Paderborn, Munich: Schöningh, 1991–2001.

Irsigler, Franz, Michel Pauly (eds.). *Messen, Jahrmärkte und Stadtentwicklung in Europa/Foires, marchés annuels et développement urbain en Europe*. Trier: Porta Alba, 2007.

Irsigler, Franz, Winfried Reichert. Les foires de Champagne. In *Messen, Jahrmärkte und Stadtentwicklung*, Irsigler, Pauly (eds.), 89–105.

Jeggle, Christoph. Privilegierte Rechtsprechung: die Gründung des Merkantilmagistrats in Bozen im 17. Jahrhundert. In *Die Ökonomie des Privilegs: Westeuropa 16.–19. Jahrhundert*, Guillaume Garner (ed.). Frankfurt: Vittorio Klostermann, 2016, 197–223.

Lang, Heinrich. Seide für Lyon. Der Seidenzoll an der Rhône als Indikator für die Strukturen von Märkten einer europäischen Handelsmetropole in der Mitte des 16. Jahrhunderts. In *Wiegen—Zählen—Registrieren. Handelsgeschichtliche Massenquellen und die Erforschung mitteleuropäischer Märkte (13.–18. Jahrhundert)*, Peter Rauscher, Andrea Serles (eds). Innsbruck, Vienna, Bolzano: Studien, 2015, 387–409.

Lavaud, Sandrine. Le courtier dans l'Aquitaine médiéval, un officier de la commune. In *Vendre le vin de l'Antiquité à nos jours*, Sandrine Lavaud (ed.). Bordeaux: Éditions Féret, 2012, 237–254.

Ligt, Lukas de. *Fairs and Markets in the Roman Empire. Economic and Social Aspects of Periodic Trade in a Preindustrial Society*. Amsterdam: Giesen, 1993.

Lo Cascio, Elio (ed.). *Mercati permanenti e mercati periodici nel mondo romano. Atti degli Incontri capresi di storia dell'economia antica, Capri 13-15 ottobre 1997.* Bari: Edipuglia, 2000.

Maccioni, Elena, Sergio Tognetti. *Tribunali di mercanti e giustizia mercantile nel tardo Medioevo*. Florence: Olschki, 2016.

Melis, Federigo. Presentazione. In *La "pratica di mercatura" datiniana (secolo XIV)*, Cesare Ciano (ed.). Milan: Giuffrè, 1964, V–XII.

North, Douglass C. *Institutions, Institutional Design and Economic Performance*. Cambridge: Cambridge University Press, 1990.

Orlandi, Angela. *Le Grand Parti. Fiorentini a Lione e il debito pubblico francese nel XVI secolo*. Florence: Leo S. Olschki, 2002.

Paris 1400. Les arts sous Charles VI, Catalogue de l'exposition, Paris, Musée du Louvre, 22 mars–12 juillet 2004. Paris: Réunion des musées nationaux, Fayard, 2004.

Pauly, Michel. Vom regionalen Messesystem zum internationalen Netz von Messestädten. In *Netzwerke im europäischen Handel des Mittelalters*, Gerhard Fouquet, Hans-Jörg Gilomen (eds.). Ostfildern: Jan Thorbecke, 2010, 49–100.

Piketty, Thomas. *Le capital au XXIe siècle*. Paris: Éditions du Seuil, 2013.

Rau, Susanne. *History, space, and place*. New York: Routledge, 2019.

Rau, Susanne. *Räume. Konzepte—Wahrnehmungen—Nutzungen*. 2nd ed. Frankfurt: Campus, 2017.

Rehr, Jean-Paul, Jean-Louis Gaulin, Susanne Rau, Ulf Christian Ewert. *The CoMOR Data Management Plan*. 2019–2023. https://doi.org/10.34847/NKL.8CEEKN2A.

Reyerson, Kathryn L. *The Art of the Deal: Intermediaries of Trade in Medieval Montpellier*. Leiden, Boston, Cologne: Brill, 2002.

Rüpke, Jörg. Nundinae: Kalendarische Koordination im republikanischen Rom. In *Kommunikation in politischen und kultischen Gemeinschaften. Stätten und Formen der Kommunikation im Altertum V*, Gerhard Binder, Konrad Ehlich (eds.). Trier: Wissenschaftlicher Verlag Trier, 1996, 75–98.

Rüpke, Jörg. L'histoire des *fasti* romains: aspects médiatiques et politiques. *Revue historique de droit français et étranger* 81 (2003): 125-140.

Schneider, Jürgen, Markus A. Denzel. Foires et marchés en Allemagne à l'époque moderne. In *Foires et marché dans les campagnes de l'Europe médiévale et moderne (Flaran, XIV)*, Christian Desplat (ed.). Toulouse: Presses universitaires du Mirail, 1996, 137–152.

Smith, Darwin, Gabriella Parussa, Olivier Halévy (eds.). *Le Théâtre français du Moyen Âge et de la Renaissance—histoire, textes choisis, mise en scène*. Paris: Éditions L'Avant-scène théâtre, 2014.

Soldani, Maria Elisa. Pegolotti, Francesco di Balduccio di. In *Dizionario Biografico degli Italiani* 82 (2015): 86–89. https://www.treccani.it/enciclopedia/francesco-balducci-pegolotti/ (04 September 2023).

Szende, Katalin, Erika Szívós, Boglárka Weisz (eds.). *Cities and Economy in Europe: Markets and Trade on the Margins from the Middle Ages to the Present.* London, New York: Routledge, 2024.
Weissen, Kurt. Safran für Deutschland. Kontinuität und Diskontinuität mittelalterlicher und frühneuzeitlicher Warenbeschaffungsstrukturen. In *Beschaffungs- und Absatzmärkte oberdeutscher Firmen im Zeitalter der Welser und Fugger*, Angelika Westermann, Stefanie on Welser (eds.). Husum: Matthiesen, 2011, 61–78.
Wüst, Wolfgang. Süddeutsche Städte unter schwedischer Besatzung. In *Der Dreißigjährige Krieg in Schwaben und seinen historischen Nachbarregionen: 1618–1648–2018. Ergebnisse einer interdisziplinären Tagung in Augsburg vom 1. bis 3. März 2018*, Wolfgang Wüst (ed.). Augsburg: Wißner, 2018, 63–80.
Zeller, Olivier. Les marques des marchands suisses enregistrées à Lyon (XVIIe–XVIIIe siècles): usages et morphologie. *Revue suisse d'Histoire* 73:3 (2023): 243–272.

Related CoMOR-Collections:

Rau, Susanne, Marisa Holzer. Archives nationales du Grand-Duché de Luxembourg, A-XIX-1 renseignements divers, 1575–1793, foires et marchés (COL0103). In *Configurations of European Fairs: Merchants, Objects, Routes (ca. 1350–1600)*, Jean-Louis Gaulin, Susanne Rau (eds.). https://fairs-in-history.huma-num.fr/collection/COL0103 (25 July 2024).

Chapter I: **Creating, defining, and attending fairs**

Ulf Christian Ewert

The privileging of ‘new’ fairs in the late medieval Holy Roman Empire: coordination of fairs by means of privileges

Summary: The Holy Roman Empire experienced a trade fair boom in the Late Middle Ages. Numerous ‘new’ fairs were granted by either the king or emperor, or regional rulers. This encompassed not only fairs that were actually new, but also fairs with a long-standing tradition of only being privileged for the first time, and discontinued older fairs being re-established. The existing network of fairs not only grew in terms of numbers of markets, but also expanded geographically and became more specialised. Through the rulers’ granting of privileges, it also developed a more or less persistent spatiotemporal structure. The focus here is on the role of privileges in coordinating the annual sequence of fairs, especially with regard to the competition of towns over fair dates that became more intense due to the increased number of fairs. By means of an explorative analysis using a game-theoretical approach and cases of imperial privileging of ‘new’ fairs, the following can be shown: privileges were effective for managing the towns’ competition concerning the organisation of fairs, as the ruler’s granting of privileges proved to be necessary to create a coordinated network of markets with a legitimised spatiotemporal structure, which would not have emerged without third-party enforcement; different market terms like *meß*, *jarmarckt*, or *marckt* were used as synonyms and thus played only a minor role in privileging. On the other hand, the coordination of fairs by means of privileges was inefficient for three reasons: due to privileges, the spatiotemporal structure of fairs had become quasi-irreversible, which in turn narrowed the margin to find an appropriate date for a new fair and thus restricted further growth; due to the imperial chancellery’s limited overview of granted privileges, disputes over dates could not be settled properly; economic interests of the grantors of privileges in particular fairs enabled certain towns to influence the emperor—who was the most important grantor at the time—to their own benefit, but to the detriment of other fairs.

Note: This analysis was undertaken within the German-French research project CoMOR—Configurations of European Fairs: Merchants, Objects, Routes (1350–1600), funded by the Deutsche Forschungsgemeinschaft (DFG-Projektnummer 430627254) and the Agence nationale de la recherche (ANR-19-FRAL-0001).

https://doi.org/10.1515/9783111621296-002

1 Introduction: the late medieval trade fair boom

Quite obviously, trade fairs and annual markets were a pivotal element of the medieval economy in Europe. All across the continent, such periodic markets emerged in great numbers in towns, villages, and monasteries. A particular boom of market expansion can be observed throughout the thirteenth, fourteenth, and fifteenth centuries, at first in parallel to the rise of the famous Champagne Fairs, but also continuing after their decline.[1] Periodic markets were held once or twice, rarely more than four times a year, and were commonly privileged by rulers—that is, counts, dukes, and kings. Such markets then flourished particularly well into the sixteenth century.[2] The economic development in many regions of the Holy Roman Empire was completely in line with this general upward continental European trend. In the late fourteenth and fifteenth centuries,[3] the German-speaking lands of the Holy Roman Empire experienced a veritable increase in 'new' fairs, and a complex hierarchical network of supra-regional trade fairs and

1 See Stephan R. Epstein. Regional Fairs, Institutional Innovation, and Economic Growth in Late Medieval Europe. *Economic History Review* 47:3 (1994): 459–482, 459–462; Michel Pauly. Les marchés annuels en Europe aux XIVe–XVIe siècles. Études régionales et essai de classification. In *Fiere e mercati nella integrazione delle economie europee, secc. XIII–XVIII. Atti della "Trentaduesima Settimana di Studi" 8–12 maggio 2000*, Simonetta Cavaciocchi (ed.). Florence: Le Monnier Università, 2001, 669–683; Michael Rothmann. Überall ist Jahrmarkt. Entwicklungstendenzen der Institution des periodischen Marktes in Zentraleuropa vom 14. bis zum 17. Jahrhundert. In *Fiere e mercati*, Cavaciocchi (ed.), 91–108; Erik Aerts. Fairs: European Fairs. In *The Oxford Encyclopedia of Economic History*, vol. 2, Joel Mokyr (ed.). Oxford: Oxford University Press, 2003, 253–256; Michel Pauly. Jahrmärkte in Europa vom 14. bis zum 16. Jahrhundert. Regionale Untersuchungen und der Versuch einer Typologie. In *Messen, Jahrmärkte und Stadtentwicklung in Europa*, Franz Irsigler, Michel Pauly (eds.). Trier: Porta Alba, 2007, 25–40; Michel Pauly. Vom regionalen Messesystem zum internationalen Netz von Messestädten. In *Netzwerke im europäischen Handel des Mittelalters*, Gerhard Fouquet, Hans-Jörg Gilomen (eds.). Ostfildern: Jan Thorbecke, 2010, 49–100.

2 With reference to the tremendous increase in the number of fairs in the Late Middle Ages, only England was an exception. Before the Black Death, fairs had been more numerous in relative terms in England than on the continent, but thereafter their numbers actually declined, contrary to the continental European trend. This was because only few new fairs were granted and many of the older ones simply disappeared after 1350. See Epstein, Regional Fairs, 467. For an overview of the development of English fairs in the Middle Ages and in the early modern period, see Philipp Robinson Rössner. Messen und Jahrmärkte in England im Spiegel der gesamtwirtschaftlichen Entwicklung und der beginnenden europäischen Wirtschaft, ca. 1000–1800 n. Chr. In *Europäische Messegeschichte 9.–19. Jahrhundert*, Markus A. Denzel (ed.). Cologne: Böhlau, 2018, 83–114.

3 These were the reigns of Emperor Charles VI (1347–78), King Wenceslaus (1376–1400), King Rupert (1400–10), King Sigismund (1411–37), Emperor Frederick III (1440–93), and Emperor Maximilian I (1486–1519).

regional and local annual markets took shape.[4] These 'new' fairs naturally comprised the ones that were newly established or at least re-established at the time, but also those with a long-standing tradition for which privileges were only being granted for the first time by either the king or the emperor. Among the newly established fairs were also those that were held in towns that had been granted a fair before, for instance, the Trinity Sunday Fair of Erfurt or the Winter Fair of Nördlingen. Finally, even prosperous free imperial cities which had not previously organised trade fairs inside their walls, such as Nuremberg or Ulm, tried to establish their own fairs at the time.[5]

For the Holy Roman Empire, there is indication of over 5,000 periodic markets in roughly 1,500 places in the period up to around 1500, with geographical density and frequency of such markets having been the highest in southern Germany.[6] As annual markets and fairs in southern Germany were embedded into a wide-ranging network of towns,[7] this area was already highly integrated in economic terms at the time. Such an economic boom, however, cannot only be observed in southern Germany. In northern Germany, where trade was dominated by the merchants from the Hanseatic towns with their partly informal, network-based trading pattern,[8] both geographical density and frequency of periodic markets were presumably lower than in southern Germany. Large supra-regional

---

4 See Hans Conrad Peyer. Die Märkte der Schweiz in Mittelalter und Neuzeit. In *Gewässer, Grenzen und Märkte in der Schweizergeschichte*, Hans-Conrad Peyer (ed.). Zurich: Schulthess, 1979, 19–38; Franz Irsigler. Jahrmärkte und Messesysteme im westlichen Reichsgebiet bis ca. 1250. In *Europäische Messen und Märktesysteme in Mittelalter und Neuzeit*, Peter Johanek, Heinz Stoob (eds.). Cologne, Weimar, Vienna: Böhlau, 1996, 1–33; Michael Rothmann. Marktkonzepte im mittelalterlichen Europa unter besonderer Berücksichtigung des Heiligen Römischen Reiches. In *Europäische Messegeschichte*, Denzel (ed.), 181–202.

5 See Michael Rothmann. Marktnetze und Netzwerke im spätmittelalterlichen oberdeutschen Wirtschaftsraum. In *Netzwerke im europäischen Handel*, Fouquet, Gilomen (eds.), 135–188, 151.

6 See Rothmann, Marktnetze, 149.

7 See Rothmann, Marktnetze, 151–155; Michael Rothmann. Messezeit: Handelsrhythmen und Jahreszeit. In *Taktungen und Rhythmen. Raumzeitliche Perspektiven interdisziplinär*, Sabine Schmolinsky, Diana Hitzke, Heiner Stahl (eds.). Berlin, Boston: De Gruyter Oldenbourg, 2019, 25–39, 27–30.

8 See Stephan Selzer, Ulf Christian Ewert. Verhandeln und Verkaufen, Vernetzen und Vertrauen. Über die Netzwerkstruktur des hansischen Handels. *Hansische Geschichtsblätter* 119 (2001): 135–161; Ulf Christian Ewert, Stephan Selzer. Social Networks. In *A Companion to the Hanseatic League*, Donald J. Harreld (ed.). Leiden, Boston: Brill, 2015, 162–193; Ulf Christian Ewert, Stephan Selzer. *Institutions of Hanseatic Trade: Studies on the Political Economy of a Medieval Network Organisation*. Frankfurt am Main: Peter Lang, 2016, 29–98; Ulf Christian Ewert. Limited Use of Money in Late-medieval Commerce: Economic Considerations on the Viability of Hanseatic Reciprocal Trade. In *Monetisation and Commercialisation in the Baltic Sea, 1050–1450*, Dariusz Adamczyk, Beata Możejko (eds.). London, New York: Routledge, 2021, 77–97; Stephan Selzer, Ulf Christian Ewert. Nord- und Ostseeraum, 500–1600. In *Handbuch globale Handelsräume und Handelsrouten.*

fairs had not emerged in the north either.[9] Nevertheless, trade there was neither less intensive, nor was economic development belated.[10] Of course, there has also been commercial exchange at fairs on a regular basis between the northern regions and Upper Germany. This came about through the export of northern goods such as dried cod, herring, wood, ash, pitch, tar, wax, beer, and linen to southern Germany, and the import of southern commodities like wine or cloth to northern Germany and the Baltic Sea area via the fairs of Leipzig and Frankfurt.[11] Prominent Hanseatic merchants, such as Hildebrand Veckinchusen (of Bruges), his brother Sivert (of Cologne), or Hinrik Slyper (also of Cologne) who were visiting the Frankfurt fairs, operated this trade.[12]

Von der Antike bis zur Gegenwart, Mark Häberlein, Markus A. Denzel (eds.). Berlin: De Gruyter Oldenbourg, 2024, 261–303, 276–284.

9 The only fair with a supra-regional scope that emerged in the Baltic rim in the Middle Ages—indeed, outside the Holy Roman Empire—was the Scania market in the neighbouring small towns of Skanör and Falsterbo at the southern mouth of Öresund, the south-westernmost tip of what today is Sweden. This fair was usually held from late August until early October and was the centre of exchange for herring and west-European goods bound for Scandinavia. See Carsten Jahnke. Die schonischen Messen. Eine freie Marktwirtschaft in einem angeblich rigiden System. In *Märkte, Messen und Waren im hansischen Handel*, Rudolf Holbach, Jürgen Sarnowsky (eds.). Wismar: callidus. Verlag wissenschaftlicher Publikationen, 2021, 33–66.

10 See Volker Henn. Über Jahrmärkte in den östlichen Niederlanden im späten Mittelalter. In *Märkte, Messen und Waren*, Holbach, Sarnowsky (eds.), 67–96; Niels Petersen. Raum und Zeit im Landverkehr um 1500. Die Viabundus-Karte des vormodernen Verkehrs in Norddeutschland. In *Märkte, Messen und Waren*, Holbach, Sarnowsky (eds.), 229–252; Niels Petersen, Bart Holtermann, Angela Huang. Digitale Werkzeuge zur Analyse von Straßen und Wasserwegen als Rückgrat eines vormodernen Märktenetzwerks in Zentral- und Ostmitteleuropa. *Zeitschrift für Ostmitteleuropaforschung/Journal of East Central European Studies* 70:3 (2021): 325–356, 347–350; Bart Holtermann, Angela Huang. Geospatial Methods and the Premodern Economy: Mapping the Institutional Landscapes of Northern Europe, 1350–1650. *Jahrbuch für Wirtschaftsgeschichte* 64:1 (2023): 179–212, 196–203.

11 See Franz Irsigler. Messehandel—Hansehandel. *Hansische Geschichtsblätter* 120 (2002): 33–50; Rudolf Holbach. Märkte, Messen und Waren als Thema der hansischen Geschichte. In *Märkte, Messen und Waren*, Holbach, Sarnowsky (eds.), 1–32; Stephan Selzer. Als Hansehistoriker an sächsischen Geleitstellen: Wagen, Waren und Fuhrleute im Landverkehr zwischen Nord und Süd um 1500. In *Märkte, Messen und Waren*, Holbach, Sarnowsky (eds.), 129–156; Angela Huang. Von Grautuch und Leinwand: Die Stellung der Produktionslandschaften des Hanseraums im spätmittelalterlichen und frühneuzeitlichen Textilhandel. In *Märkte, Messen und Waren*, Holbach, Sarnowsky (eds.), 157–186; Cezary Kardasz. Der Export von Holz und Waldwaren aus dem südlichen Ostseeraum im Spätmittelalter. In *Märkte, Messen und Waren*, Holbach, Sarnowsky (eds.), 203–228; Jürgen Sarnowsky. Südwaren auf den Märkten im südlichen Ostseeraum. In *Märkte, Messen und Waren*, Holbach, Sarnowsky (eds.), 187–202.

12 See Michael Rothmann. "Gab gott gnad und gros gluk, gwin." Ein Beitrag über den deutschen Kaufmann im Spätmittelalter. In *Brücke zwischen den Völkern—Zur Geschichte der Frankfurter*

However, the European-wide establishment of a large number of local and regional periodic markets has long been largely overlooked by economic history because research focused on long-distance trade and large international trade fairs.[13] However, it was Stephan R. Epstein who, in his 1994 article on "Regional Fairs, Institutional Innovation, and Economic Growth in Late Medieval Europe," refocused economic history on this late medieval boom of periodic markets.[14] Epstein pointed to the fact that geographical density and frequency of such markets allow conclusions to be drawn about the level of economic development as well as about the degree of economic integration of a certain region. Michel Pauly has shown that periodic markets have made a significant contribution to supra-regional economic integration.[15] The topic of trade fairs and annual markets is therefore—directly, or at least indirectly—linked to other important topics in economic history, such as the premodern urban economy,[16] the emergence of a market

Messe, vol. 2: Beiträge zur Geschichte der Frankfurter Messe, Patricia Stahl (ed.). Frankfurt am Main: Union-Druckerei- und Verlagsanstalt, 1991, 253–262; Otfried Krafft. Eine Fehde, ein Reichsachtverfahren und das Ende zweier Grafschaften. Die Kaufleute Veckinchusen im Streit mit den letzten Grafen von Ziegenhain. *Zeitschrift des Vereins für hessische Geschichte* 111 (2006): 31–62.

13 A misinterpretation of the term 'eternal fair', coined by Max Weber, contributed to this nonobservance of smaller periodic markets. In contrast to Weber, who only wanted to conceptualise the increasing importance of stock exchanges, many economic historians understood 'eternal fair' to mean urban markets in general. Based on this misunderstanding, a thesis was therefore able to prevail according to which, due to economic modernisation in the Late Middle Ages, supra-regional fairs (such as the Champagne Fairs) had been replaced by permanent urban markets and commercial exchange had concentrated on towns. See Epstein, Regional Fairs, 459–460. In contrast, Weber saw this sort of 'eternal fair' primarily as being realised in the stock exchanges that emerged at large trading centres such as Antwerp, Amsterdam, London, and Leipzig between the sixteenth and eighteenth centuries. See Max Weber. *Wirtschaftsgeschichte: Abriss der universalen Sozial- und Wirtschafts-Geschichte*, Sigmund Hellmann, Melchior Palyi (eds.). Munich, Leipzig: Duncker & Humblot, 1923, 252–253. However, a generalisation of the argument that economic modernisation in the Late Middle Ages determined the decline of periodic fairs can be found, for instance, in the very influential work of Robert S. Lopez. *The Commercial Revolution of the Middle Ages, 950–1350*. Englewood Cliffs (NJ): Prentice Hall, 1971, 87–89.

14 See Epstein, Regional Fairs, 459–482. See also Stephan R. Epstein. Fairs, Towns, and States in Renaissance Europe. In *Fiere e mercati*, Cavaciocchi (ed.), 71–90.

15 See Michel Pauly. Der Beitrag der Messen und Märkte zur mittelalterlichen Integration Europas. In *Messen, Jahrmärkte und Stadtentwicklung*, Irsigler, Pauly (eds.), 285–314.

16 See Michael Mitterauer. Jahrmarktkontinuität und Stadtentstehung. In *Markt und Stadt im Mittelalter. Beiträge zur historischen Zentralitätsforschung*, Michael Mitterauer (ed.). Stuttgart: Anton Hiersemann, 1980, 154–191; Edith Ennen. *Die europäische Stadt des Mittelalters*. 4th ed. Göttingen: Vandenhoeck & Ruprecht, 1987, 80–84; Hartmut Boockmann. *Die Stadt im späten Mittelalter*. 3rd ed. Munich: Verlag C.H. Beck, 1994, 94–124; Franz Irsigler. Messen, Jahrmärkte und Stadtentwicklung in Europa. Mittelalter und Frühe Neuzeit. In *Messen, Jahrmärkte und Stadtentwicklung*, Irsigler, Pauly (eds.), 1–24.

society[17] (not only in towns, but also in rural areas), or the so-called Consumer Revolution.[18] Hence, by using the case of the granting of privileges for 'new' fairs in the late medieval Holy Roman Empire, this paper focuses on the contribution of institutions to economic development and growth. In particular, the effect of the growing number of periodic markets will be examined, which was an increasing competition among towns that organised or planned to organise supra-regional fairs for market dates. This competition needed to be managed in order to foster continuing economic growth. More precisely, coordination of the network of fairs was an issue at the time. Were privileges functional in managing this competition and were they also an efficient means to coordinate supra-regional fairs? Could privileges be used to shape the spatiotemporal structure of fairs? These aspects, that have received little attention in research so far, shall be examined in more detail by means of an explorative analysis and by using a game-theoretical approach.

The paper is structured as follows: in section 2, the meaning of the various terms for periodic markets that were used in privileges will be shortly described. In section 3, a brief sketch of the economic effects of trade fair privileges will be given, together with an overview of the hypotheses discussed in economic history research about possible reasons for the granting of fairs. A game theoretical model is also presented, which is subsequently used (in sections 4, 5, and 6) as the framework for an exploratory analysis of various effects of privileges on the shape of the spatiotemporal structure of late medieval trade fairs. This analysis is based on cases of the emperor's privileging of 'new' fairs in the fifteenth and early sixteenth centuries. Finally, the effectiveness and efficiency of the coordination of fairs by means of privileges will be discussed in section 7.

17 See Epstein, Regional Fairs, 461–462.

18 It would, of course, be a rather promising attempt to systematically apply the concept of the 'Consumer Revolution' that has been developed to explain the specific economic development of England in the eighteenth century to the consumption patterns that can be observed in late medieval towns. For the Consumer Revolution, see Neil McKendrick. The Consumer Revolution of Eighteenth-Century England. In *The Birth of a Consumer Society: The Commercialization of Eighteenth-Century England*, Neil McKendrick, John Brewer, John Harold Plumb (eds.). London: Europa Publications, 1982, 9–33; for its potential application to medieval urban consumption, see Thomas Ertl. *Bauern und Banker. Wirtschaft im Mittelalter*. Darmstadt: WBG Theiss, 2021, 199–226.

2 *Meß*, *Jarmarckt*, *Marckt*: terms in German for periodic markets

In Early New High German—the written language in the central and southern regions of Germany between c. 1350 and c. 1650—periodic markets were referred to differently in written sources. Commonly, the terms *meß*/*messe* (*Messe*, 'fair'), *jarmarckt* (*Jahrmarkt*, 'annual market') and *marckt* (*Markt*, 'market') were in use. *Markt* (in modern German) goes back to the Latin *mercatus*, which refers to places where goods are exchanged.[19] Whereas in other European languages the designation for trade fairs has its origins in the Latin *feriae* (French: *foire*; Italian: *fiera*; English: *fair*), in German, *Messe* became the established form. It derives from the Latin *missa*, the Mass as a religious service.[20] This recalls that trade fairs and annual markets originally took place either on Sundays, on the occasion of a church feast, or on saints' days, always after the Mass.[21]

These terms give the impression that they precisely capture the difference between trade fairs—as being far-reaching supra-regional periodic markets with a longer duration—, annual markets—as being smaller, only regional periodic markets with a shorter duration—, and the more or less permanent urban daily or weekly markets. However, such connotations are recent, having arisen from historical research in Germany since the late nineteenth century. Moreover, unlike the various French, Italian, and English terms for trade fairs, the modern German terminology of annual and weekly markets—that has also been adopted by historians of other languages since the early 1950s for their definitions of medieval and early modern periodic markets[22]—implies a hierarchy of the different market forms with respect to a market's economic importance and spatial scope. In line with this earlier research, Franz Irsigler, Michel Pauly, and Michael Rothmann distinguish between different types of periodic markets—namely, those which were only of regional importance and are thus termed as 'markets' or 'an-

---

19 See Anne-Marie Dubler. Märkte. *Historisches Lexikon der Schweiz*. 27 October 2009. https://hls-dhs-dss.ch/de/articles/013739/2009-10-27/ (29 May 2024).

20 See Jan Albert van Houtte. Messe (Handelsmesse), I. Westlicher Bereich. *Lexikon des Mittelalters*, vol. 6. Munich, Zurich: Artemis & Winkler, 1993, cols. 558–560; Anne Radeff. Foires. *Dictionnaire historique de la Suisse*. 9 June 2008. https://hls-dhs-dss.ch/fr/articles/013740/2008-06-09/ (29 May 2024).

21 See Rothmann, Marktnetze, 153.

22 See Radeff, Foires. The collected volume entitled "La Foire" that appeared in 1953 and especially its concluding article were highly influential in this regard. See John Gilissen. La notion de la foire à la lumière comparative. In *La foire*, John Gilissen (ed.). Brussels: Librairie Encyclopédique, 1953, 323–333.

nual markets' in historical research nowadays, and those which were part of a wide network of periodic markets, therefore considered highly important for supra-regional trade and termed as 'fair' ('Messe').[23] In contrast, in other languages, the distinction that different terms originally captured is based solely on the periodicity of the market. In French, for instance, periodic markets with only a few repetitions per year were already called *foire* in the Middle Ages and in the early modern period, no matter how big they were and how long they lasted. In contrast to this, the rural and urban markets, which took place weekly or even daily, were known as *marché*.[24] Large fairs such as those in Frankfurt or Leipzig,[25] which were termed *jarmarckt* or simply *marckt* in German, were called *foire* in French—for example, in French-language fair calendars of the late sixteenth century.[26]

In contrast to this clear-cut system of terms for periodic markets used in modern historical research, in written German sources of the Late Middle Ages, the wording was not that clear at all. In many cases, the wording implied no differences, neither with respect to periodicity and duration, nor with respect to the geographical scope of a market. The terms *meß* and *jahrmarckt* were often used as equivalents. This may be due to the fact that until the end of the eleventh century, the term *mercatum* was used almost exclusively for (periodic) markets in charters written in Latin, and since then the term *forum* as well as the ancient term *nundinae* only gradually found their way into the texts.[27] From this, older

23 See Franz Irsigler. Zur Hierarchie der Jahrmärkte. In *Ausstellungskatalog "Spätmittelalter am Oberrhein. Große Landesausstellung Baden-Württemberg", Staatliche Kunsthalle Karlsruhe, 29. September 2001–3. Februar 2002*, vol. 2, Sönke Lorenz, Markus Dekiert (eds.). Stuttgart: Jan Thorbecke, 2001, 89–99; Pauly, Jahrmärkte in Europa, 25–40; Holger Kruse. Pariser Messen des Mittelalters. In *Netzwerke im europäischen Handel*, Fouquet, Gilomen (eds.), 101–134, 102–103; Rothmann, Marktnetze, 150–157.

24 See Radeff, Foires.

25 See Nils Brübach. *Die Reichsmessen von Frankfurt am Main, Leipzig und Braunschweig (14.–18. Jahrhundert).* Stuttgart: Franz Steiner, 1994; Michael Rothmann. *Die Frankfurter Messen im Mittelalter.* Stuttgart: Franz Steiner, 1998.

26 See Olivier Fordrin. *Almanach pour l'an M.D.LXXIII. Avec la pronostication vraye infallible à jamais. A Geneve. Par Olivier Fordrin. M. D. LXXIII.* In Bibliothèque de Genève, Su 4165. https://dx.doi.org/10.3931/e-rara-6259 (29 May 2024). The entries of this fair calendar are available online. See Ulf Christian Ewert. Bibliothèque de Genève, Su 4165 (Olivier Fordrin—Almanach pour l'an M. D. LXXIII) (COL0026). In *Configurations of European Fairs: Merchants, Objects, Routes (ca. 1350–1600)*, Jean-Louis Gaulin, Susanne Rau (eds.). https://fairs-in-history.huma-num.fr/collection/COL0026. (29 May 2024).

27 See Jürgen Sarnowsky, Meike Möller. Märkte, Marktprivilegien und Marktrecht. Unpublished manuscript, Hamburg. https://www.spaetmittelalter.uni-hamburg.de/spaetmittelalter/Lehre/Ergebnisse/Hamburg/themen/MaerkteMarktprivilegienUndMarktrecht.html (29 May 2024).

historical research has already attempted to construct a conceptual difference between ordinary fairs with a short duration and a regionally limited circle of visitors (*forum annuale*), and privileged trade fairs with a longer duration which attracted merchants from far away (*nundinae*).[28] Although this difference in meaning between the terms seems straightforward, it can often not be proved in historical practice. For example, in the 1356 privilege of Emperor Charles IV permitting a fair in Hamburg, to be commenced two weeks before Pentecost and lasting until eight days after Pentecost, the two terms are given equal rights in the text which reads as follows: "[. . .] an annual fair that also is called annual market [. . .]."[29] To cope with this problem of terminology, Manfred Straube and Markus A. Denzel propose to call the trade-fair-like annual markets with a supra-regional scope in the Holy Roman Empire 'Große Jahrmärkte' ('great annual markets').[30]

The equivalent use of the two terms continued even after the late fourteenth century when trade fair privileges were no longer written exclusively in Latin but also in German. In the text of such charters, the pair of terms *meß* and *marckt* can still be found again and again—as, for instance, in the privilege of 1429 for the fair of Ulm.[31] Such practice also had repercussions for the usage of market terms in other texts well into the sixteenth century. Fair calendars written in German—like the one printed in the arithmetic book of Adam Ries in 1586, for instance—use both *Messe* and *Markt*, but the latter term is also attributed to the large supra-regional fairs in Antwerp and Bolzano. On the other hand, the Whitsun Fair of Nördlingen was still termed *Messe*,[32] even though in the middle of the

---

28 See Heinrich Reincke. Die Hamburger Messe und die Weltverkehrspläne Karls IV. *Zeitschrift des Vereins für Hamburgische Geschichte* 23 (1912): 85–88, 85.

29 "[. . .] nundinae annuales, quae alias annuale forum vocantur [. . .]." Werner Spieß. *Das Marktprivileg. Die Entwicklung von Marktprivileg und Marktrecht insbesondere auf Grund der Kaiserurkunden*. Heidelberg: Winter, 1916, 343, cited from Sarnowsky, Möller, Märkte, Marktprivilegien und Marktrecht.

30 See Manfred Straube. Die Leipziger Messen zur Zeit der Privilegierungen als Mittler nach Ostmitteleuropa. In *Leipzigs Messen 1497–1997. Gestaltwandel—Umbrüche—Neubeginn*, vol. 1: 1497–1914, Hartmut Zwahr, Thomas Topfstedt, Günter Bentele (eds.). Cologne: Böhlau, 1999, 121–132; Markus A. Denzel. Das System der Messen in Europa—Rückgrat des Handels, des Zahlungsverkehrs und der Kommunikation (9. bis 19. Jahrhundert). In *Europäische Messegeschichte*, Denzel (ed.), 369–431.

31 See Privileg König Sigismunds für Ulm zur Einrichtung eines Jahrmarkts, Preßburg, 9. August 1429 ('Privilege of King Sigismund granted to Ulm to set up an annual market, Bratislava, 9 August 1429'). In Haus der Stadtgeschichte—Stadtarchiv Ulm, A Urk. 1406; CoMOR online exposition 'Foires, villes et marchands (1350–1600)/Messen, Städte und Kaufleute (1350–1600).' https://fairs-in-history.huma-num.fr/expo/online/theme_lyon_1?object=privilege_ulm (29 May 2024).

32 See Adam Ries. *Rechenbüchlein auff der Linien vnd Federn/den angehen=den Rechnern/vnd allen Kaufha^{e}nd=lern zu gut vnd nutz mit vielen scho^{e}nen Exempeln/auff allerley Handthie=rung*

sixteenth century it had already lost its once far-reaching supra-regional importance and had become a regional annual market only. Finally, the term *marckt* can be found even in private documents, which probably shows the contemporary use of the various terms for periodic markets most clearly. In a tavern invoice issued by an unknown Frankfurt innkeeper for the Erfurt merchant David Nacke about his stay at the Frankfurt fair in Lent (c. 1590), the fair is referred to as the *Ostermarckt* ('Easter market') and not as *Messe*.[33] Hence, even if the modern distinction between *Messe* ('fair') and *Jahrmarkt* ('annual market') is extremely fruitful for historical research as it enables the classification of periodic markets and also the distinction of the degree of importance of such markets in quantitative terms, it is quite obvious that modern terminology only partially reflects the meaning of those market terms that were used by contemporaries.[34]

---

gemacht durch Adam Riesen. [. . .] M. D. LXXXVI. Frankfurt am Main: Bassae, 1586. In Staats- und Universitätsbibliothek—Sächsische Landesbibliothek Dresden, 1.A.5915, fols. 93 r–94 r. https://digital.slub-dresden.de/id276477103 (29 May 2024). The entries of this fair calendar are stored in the FAIRS-IN-HISTORY database and are available online. See Ulf Christian Ewert. Staats- und Universitätsbibliothek—Sächsische Landesbibliothek, Adam Ries, Rechenbüchlein auff der Linien und Federn (COL0020). In *Configurations of European Fairs*, Gaulin, Rau (eds.). https://fairs-in-history.huma-num.fr/collection/COL020 (29 May 2024). In the headline of the famous 'Allegory of trade and merchants' of Jost Amman, printed in 1585, both terms—*Märckt* and *Messen*—can be found together as well, again without any distinction in meaning. See Jost Amman. *Eigentliche Abbildung deß ganzen Gewerks der löblichen Kaufmannschaft/Samt etlich der nahmhafft und fürnehmsten Handelstädt Signatur und Wappen zum Theil fürnehmlich die Märckt und Messen begriffen seyn/so deß Jahr über in jedem Monath einfallen/auch hin und wider in Europa zu unterschidlichen Zeiten gehalten [. . .]* ('Allegory of trade and merchants'), woodcut, printed on paper. Nuremberg: Jost Amman (draft), Augsburg: Hans Schultes (print), Wilhelm Peter Zimmermann (publisher), 1585. In Museum Plantin-Moretus, Antwerp, PK.OP.21317. https://museumplantinmoretus.be/de/seite/allegorie-des-handels (29 May 2024). The entries of the fair calendar included in this print are available online. See Ulf Christian Ewert, Noémie Lacroix. Museum Plantin-Moretus, PK.OP.21317 (Jost Amman's allegory/fair calendar) (COL0104). In *Configurations of European Fairs*, Gaulin, Rau (eds.). https://fairs-in-history.huma-num.fr/collection/COL0104 (29 May 2024).

33 See Wirtshausrechnung des Erfurter Kaufmanns David Nacke auf der Frankfurter Fastenmesse, um 1590 ('Tavern invoice of the Erfurt merchant David Nacke at the Frankfurt fair in Lent, c. 1590'). In Stadtarchiv Erfurt, 0–1/8- 208 (7). CoMOR online exposition 'Foires, villes et marchands.' https://fairs-in-history.huma-num.fr/expo/online/theme_lyon_4?object=facture_taverne (29 May 2024).

34 See Kruse, Pariser Messen, 102–103.

3 The economic effect of privileges: different hypotheses and a game-theoretical model

What are privileges for and why were rulers probably necessary for the coordination of fairs? In his seminal paper of 1994, Epstein, taking an economic viewpoint, discusses two hypotheses that can be used to explain the new rise of fairs in many European regions since the second half of the fourteenth century. Thereby, Epstein distinguishes between two sorts of explanation: an economic explanation on the one hand and an institutional explanation on the other hand. The economic explanation of the proliferation of periodic markets emphasises the effect of a growing demand of both producers and consumers for such markets (what he terms the 'demand-driven rise of fairs').[35] This is plausible, because the largely evolved regional specialisation in the economic boom of the High Middle Ages called for a denser and more sophisticated market infrastructure for commercial exchange. But why did this expansion of periodic markets continue and even gain momentum in the Late Middle Ages, after the Black Death? Interestingly enough, the sharp demographic and economic downturn in the wake of the Black Death in the middle of the fourteenth century inhibited trade only for a rather short time, having little impact on the development of a dense European-wide market infrastructure in the long run.[36] Moreover, since wages rose tremendously in many regions of Europe in the decades after the Black Death and inequality of both wealth and income declined significantly,[37] causing increasing demand for non-essential foodstuffs and craft goods, there is good reason to believe that the Black Death indirectly contributed to the continued flourishing of trade fairs and annual markets in the Late Middle Ages. So, following this economic explanation, the late medieval boom of fairs was due to the fact that periodic markets, by reducing transaction costs, were a very efficacious and also effi-

35 See Epstein, Regional Fairs, 462–467.

36 See Lars Börner, Battista Severgnini. Epidemic Trade. *Diskussionsbeiträge, No. 2011/12, Freie Universität Berlin, Fachbereich Wirtschaftswissenschaft*. Berlin 2011; Lars Börner, Battista Severgnini. Measuring and Comparing Economic Interaction Based on the Paths and Speed of Infections: The Case Study of the Spread of the Justinianic Plague and Black Death. In *Complexity Economics: Building a New Approach to Ancient Economic History*, Koenraad Verboven (ed.). London: Palgrave Macmillan, 2021, 327–356.

37 For a general overview, see Guido Alfani, Thomas E. Murphy. Plague and Lethal Epidemics in the Pre-industrial World. *Journal of Economic History* 77:1 (2017): 314–343; Guido Alfani. Epidemics, Inequality, and Poverty in Preindustrial and Early Industrial Times. *Journal of Economic Literature* 60:1 (2022): 3–40, 5–16. For Germany, in particular, see Guido Alfani, Victoria Gierok, Felix Schaff. Economic Inequality in Preindustrial Germany, ca. 1300–1850. *Journal of Economic History* 82:1 (2022): 88–125.

cient way of meeting the increased consumer demand within a growing economy, which at the same time became further specialised, including geographically.[38]

In addition to that, the institutional explanation underlines the importance of privileges in this process (what Epstein describes as the 'supply-driven rise of fairs').[39] Both explanations are therefore not mutually exclusive.

Privileges granted for trade fairs defined the rights and regulatory measures deployed by towns while holding a fair. Usually, such institutional arrangements were supplied by rulers, that is, by counts, dukes, and kings. In economic terms, trade fair privileges are monopolies, limited in space and time. They are limited in space because a particular town is granted the right to hold a periodic market within its walls, and they are limited in time in terms of the date or duration of this market. To derive the economic incentives of both the rulers (as the agents who granted privileges for fairs) and towns (as the agents who obtained such privileges) more clearly, it seems useful to distinguish within the institutional explanation between a supply-side argument and a demand-side argument. On the one hand, the supply-side argument emphasises the rulers' vested interests in granting privileges, mainly to create revenues from the fees that towns had to pay to be granted a fair, to attract trade to their own realm, and to gain access to financial capital provided by the merchants visiting a fair. Thus, rulers granted fairs because they were paid for them and because they hoped to take advantage of the medium- and long-term financial opportunities fairs typically provided in the Late Middle Ages. The demand-side argument, on the other hand, would explain the fact that rulers granted privileges to towns as a reaction of the towns' aim of obtaining for themselves a 'fair' share of the aggregated trade volume. However, this common interpretation seems too simple because it would only make sense in a stable, non-growing economy. Economic growth, as can be observed in terms of a growing and even more specialising commerce in the Late Middle Ages, was not a zero-sum game—that is, the rise of a particular trade fair would not automatically imply the decline of others.[40]

There is also a second reason why the demand-side argument of the institutional explanation for the late medieval rise of periodic markets seems too simple. With such an interpretation, privileges are solely understood as being the

38 See Epstein, Regional Fairs, 460–462; John H. Munro. The 'New Institutional Economics' and the Changing Fortunes of Fairs in Medieval and Early Modern Europe: The Textile Trades, Warfare, and Transaction Costs. *Vierteljahrschrift für Sozial und Wirtschaftsgeschichte* 88:1 (2001): 1–47; Jeremy Edwards, Sheilagh C. Ogilvie. What Lessons for Economic Development Can We Draw from the Champagne Fairs? *Explorations in Economic History* 49:2 (2012): 131–148.

39 See Epstein, Regional Fairs, 467–470.

40 See Epstein, Regional Fairs, 460–461.

cause of economic development and boom, not as a reaction to it. Receiving a monopoly was a strong economic incentive for towns to aim for trade fair privileges, and towns aimed at being granted a fair because by organising one, they wanted to participate in this economic growth. This, in turn, was an investment for towns and this investment could be hedged by paying a fee for a privilege. Such an investment yielded higher returns, of course, if it could be capitalised as a monopoly. Hence, it would be straightforward to conclude that the number of granted periodic markets rose in the Late Middle Ages because it was profitable for towns to organise such markets and because the supply of an appropriate institution—that is, the privileges for these markets—provided strong economic incentives for rulers.

The proliferation of fairs in the Late Middle Ages was thus characterised by the interaction between rulers and towns as well as by the interaction between the many towns that organised or aimed at organising a fair. In particular, the towns competed for organising a fair and for economically attractive trade fair dates. In this context, privileges were not only an institutional solution supplied by the rulers to cope with the rapid economic growth at the time, but also instruments used to control the competition among towns. This latter argument, however, gives rise to a discussion of the overall economic impact of granting fairs. A well-coordinated network of fairs produced positive externalities for both merchants and rulers. In such a network, merchants could rely on the fact that fairs took place on specific dates and, even more importantly, that the dates of important fairs did not overlap so that they were able to visit several fairs in a year. However, if merchants could trade at several fairs within a year, the overall trade volume also grew and, as a consequence, those who granted privileges also benefited from this, for example, through the revenue of taxes on goods and for escort.

However, creating and maintaining such a well-coordinated system of trade fairs was not self-evident. In principle, towns should have had a strong interest in both the formation and maintenance of a well-coordinated network of fairs because of the economic benefits such a network provided to them. They would especially benefit from a coordination of market dates because merchants wouldn't have to choose between fairs and would be able to visit several within a year, which in turn would increase the likelihood of one's own fair being attended for all towns. Therefore, the towns' willingness to contribute actively to the coordination of trade fair dates is a necessary but non-sufficient condition for effective cooperation. However, due to the positive externalities coming from coordination, a free-riding of towns was very likely—that is, towns were taking the economic benefits provided by a well-coordinated network of fairs for free and did not pay for the coordination of such a network.[41]

This can be shown with a non-cooperative game: the so-called n-player prisoner's dilemma game.[42] All n players (towns) choose, simultaneously and independently of each other, whether they would like to cooperate with the other towns with respect to trade fair dates or whether they want to defect—that is, trying to put through the most favourable date for one's own economic interests. Depending upon the outcome, each player will receive different payoffs: the full return r can be realised by insisting on the preferred date vis-à-vis the other players who choose cooperation; $r-r_c$ if all players compromise about fair dates, with r_c representing the individual costs of compromising; $r-r_d$ if all players insist on their preferred date, where r_d are the individual losses due to failure of coordination; and finally, $r-r_c-r'_d$ by compromising while other players insist on their preferred dates. Here, r'_d refers to the losses due to failure of coordination produced by defecting players. Concerning the magnitude of payoffs the following applies: $r > r-r_c > r-r_d > r-r_c-r'_d \geq 0$. According to this condition, the incentive for non-cooperative behaviour is higher than that for cooperative behaviour, and all players together receive a lower total payoff if all defect rather than if all cooperate. This model is a non-cooperative game because it is assumed that players cannot communicate and thereby agree upfront on strategy choice. Players thus behave strategically—that is, they choose their own strategy according to what they expect the other players to choose.[43]

In a one-shot game (a game played for only a single round) and under common behavioural assumptions, players seek to maximise personal utility and want to avoid any risk. Indeed, without third-party enforcement available, rational players will always choose defection. The outcome will be an equilibrium solution to the game (the so-called Nash-equilibrium[44]) that is sub-optimal in both

41 Due to the positive externalities provided to users (both merchants and towns), problems in establishing and maintaining a coordinated network of fairs are very similar to those of public goods. On this point in general, see Ulf Christian Ewert. Collective Goods in the Middle Ages. In *Methods in Premodern Economic History: Case Studies from the Holy Roman Empire, c. 1300–c. 1600*, Ulla Kypta, Julia Bruch, Tanja Skambraks (eds.). London: Palgrave Macmillan, 2019, 64–67.

42 See Miklos N. Szilagyi. An Investigation of N-person Prisoners' Dilemmas. *Complex Systems* 14:2 (2003): 155–174.

43 For non-cooperative games in general, see David M. Kreps. *Game Theory and Economic Modelling*. Oxford: Clarendon Press, 1990, 9–36.

44 By definition, a Nash-equilibrium is characterised by mutual best answers of all players to the strategy choices of all other players—that is, there is no incentive for anyone to change one's own choice. See Kreps, Game Theory, 28–36.

individual and common returns. Despite the fact that for each of them, the individual net benefit of cooperation is greater than zero and also the fact that the aggregate return of all players would be greater in case of cooperation than in case of defection, from an individual perspective, such a decision is nonetheless rational. Players try to avoid the risk of bearing the due costs of coordination alone—that is, forgoing parts of the possible benefit on account of compromising with regard to fair dates—whereas all others enjoy the positive externalities from a coordinated network of fairs without bearing any share of the coordination costs.

However, since economic incentives for towns to organise a fair were high, a network of fairs, even though uncoordinated, will emerge anyway. But if each town would organise its fair on the date preferred, fairs would not be coordinated, and the extra benefit provided by such a network could not be realised. Thus, the difficulty here is obviously to enhance the towns' cooperation in terms of coordination of fairs. In this respect, third-party enforcement is a potential solution, by which free-riding becomes unattractive so that its detrimental effects could be avoided. In the Middle Ages, such enforcement was commonly provided by rulers by means of privileges in which dates and duration of fairs were defined bindingly. However, only if the privileges granted were exactly aligned to each other, the resulting network of fairs would finally be a Pareto-efficient equilibrium.[45] This equilibrium not only provides a higher aggregated benefit to all towns involved as compared to an uncoordinated network, but also makes it impossible for any town to improve individual returns without cutting other towns' returns.

Even though the assumptions made in this simple model about the towns' rationale are very strict and, in a sense, unrealistic, it nevertheless provides a possible explanation for why the emperor—or even regional rulers—were increasingly petitioned by towns to grant trade fair privileges. The patently unrealistic assumption of a lacking coordinating authority makes it possible to show that rulers were apparently necessary for the coordination of fairs. Implications of further assumptions of the model like the one-shot character of the game or the simultaneity of strategy choices, will be elaborated in more detail in the subsequent sections of the article by using cases of the emperor's privileging of 'new' fairs.

45 In a Pareto-efficient equilibrium, no player can improve on his own return without reducing the returns of other players. This concept was originally developed in welfare economics by Vilfredo Pareto (1848–1923). See Hugh Gravelle, Ray Rees. *Microeconomics*, 3rd ed. Harlow: Pearson Education, 2004, 289–299.

4 'New' privileges for 'old' fairs: the towns' effort for the legitimacy of their fairs

As mentioned above, the growing network of fairs in the Holy Roman Empire also became more structured in the Late Middle Ages. To be among those towns at the top level, organising a fair with a supra-regional scope was, of course, most profitable. One of these supra-regional fairs was the Whitsun Fair of Nördlingen which had a long-standing tradition.[46] Until the beginning of the sixteenth century, it was the most important fair in southern Germany. Many traders came there every year, including merchants from Geneva, the Rhineland, Flanders, and Italy. For merchants from the leading cities in Upper Germany such as Nuremberg, Augsburg, and Ulm, the fair had established itself as an important date for payments.[47] Nevertheless, this fair was newly privileged at the time. Even though it was first mentioned in a charter of Emperor Frederick II (1212–50) in 1219, King Wenceslaus (in 1398) and Emperor Sigismund (in 1434) were the first to officially grant privileges to the free imperial city (*urbs imperialis libera*) of Nördlingen. In both privileges, escort rights and the sovereignty of the fair court were either granted or confirmed, and in 1418, Sigismund also established an imperial mint in Nördlingen that existed until 1571. In the latter privilege, in particular, the long tradition of the Whitsun Fair is stressed, and the terms *Jahrmarkt* and *Messe* are

46 On the Nördlingen Whitsun Fair, see Josef Spieß. Die Nördlinger Messen im Mittelalter. PhD diss., University of Munich, 1923; Heinrich Steinmeyer. *Die Entstehung und Entwicklung der Nördlinger Pfingstmesse im Spätmittelalter mit einem Ausblick ins 19. Jahrhundert*. Nördlingen: Georg Wagner, 1960; Dietmar-Henning Voges. Werden und Wirken der Pfingstmesse. In *Die Reichsstadt Nördlingen. 12 Kapitel aus ihrer Geschichte*, Dietmar-Henning Voges (ed.). Munich: C. H. Beck, 1988, 47–69; Rolf Kießling. Die Nördlinger Pfingstmesse im 15./16. Jahrhundert. Aufstieg und Strukturwandel eines süddeutschen Wirtschaftszentrums. *Jahrbuch des Historischen Vereins für Nördlingen und das Ries* 29 (1999): 69–95; Marco Veronesi. Wessen Freiheit. Messeprivileg, Freihandel und städtische Gerichtsbarkeit im späten Mittelalter am Beispiel Nördlingens. *Annales Mercaturae* 3 (2017): 23–49; Marco Veronesi. "Bös gelt und liderlich volck": die Stadt, der Rat und die lieben Gäste. In *800 Jahre Nördlinger Mess. Von der internationalen Fernhandelsmesse zum größten Volksfest Nordschwabens*, Stadtarchiv Nördlingen (ed.). Olching: WIKOMmedia Verlag für kommunale- und Wirtschaftsmedien, 2019, 12–25.

47 For example, Thomas Dost, citizen of Nuremberg, confirms with a handwritten certificate of indebtedness to the Nuremberg merchant Konrad Imhoff and his company a debt to the amount of 315 (Rhenish) guilders, 7 shillings, and 9 hellers for 4 sacks of pepper and 1 sack of cloves, payable at the next Whitsun Fair in Nördlingen. See Schuldverschreibung des Thomas Dost an Konrad Imhoff, 20. Januar 1482 ('Certificate of indebtedness of Thomas Dost vis-à-vis Konrad Imhoff, 20 January 1482'). In Germanisches Nationalmuseum Nürnberg, IA 19, Nr. 22b. CoMOR online exposition 'Foires, villes et marchands.' https://fairs-in-history.huma-num.fr/expo/online/theme_lyon_4?object=titre_creance (29 May 2024).

mentioned two times together, on one occasion connected by 'and' and on the other occasion connected by 'or.'[48] However, neighbouring towns like Augsburg, for instance, commonly used the words *Jahrmarkt* or simply *Markt* to denote the Whitsun Fair in their letters to the council of Nördlingen.[49]

Why were the Whitsun Fair privileges only granted to Nördlingen in 1398 and 1434, respectively, although it had existed for a very long time without such a privilege? Variation of the one-shot character of the model helps to answer this question. First of all, the fact that towns refrained from participating in the coordination of fairs and instead tried to enforce their preferred date would also occur if their cooperation with regard to fair dates was modelled in a more realistic setting—that is, with an infinite game in which towns repeatedly cooperate with each other without knowing in each round of the game when this cooperation would end. Yet, in this sort of game, a Pareto-efficient equilibrium can not only be reached by third-party enforcement, but also through mutual trust of players. This is possible because players would have the opportunity to acquire reputation and to build up mutual trust over time. Reputation and trust are both instrumental to enhance cooperation, especially given that in the long run, the cooperation strategy can be successful, even if it might lead to short-term losses of utility.[50] A decisive factor here is the number of players. In a game with many players, it is not only difficult to build up mutual trust, but players might also think that their personal contribution to cooperation is more or less dispensable (in the sense that cooperation will be effective to a sufficient degree even without their participation), and therefore might decide to defect.[51]

In principle, this reflects the historical situation of the coordination of fairs quite accurately. Especially towns of the rather densely populated and highly developed regions in the south and the south-west of Germany cooperated with regard to political and economic issues within different networks of towns.[52] Coordination of fairs could thus certainly be achieved without being enhanced by

48 See Veronesi, "Bös gelt und liderlich volck", 13.

49 See Hektor Ammann. Die Nördlinger Messe im Mittelalter. In *Aus Verfassungs- und Landesgeschichte. Festschrift zum 70. Geburtstag von Theodor Mayer, dargebracht von seinen Schülern und Freunden*, vol. 2, Heinrich Büttner, Otto Feger, Bruno Meyer (eds.). Lindau, Constance: Jan Thorbecke, 1955, 283–315.

50 See Ewert, Selzer, Institutions of Hanseatic Trade, 51–53; Ulf Christian Ewert. Zusammenfassung: Vertrauen in vormodernen ökonomischen Tauschbeziehungen—eine Zwischenbilanz. In *Ökonomisch bestimmtes Handeln in der Vormoderne—eine Frage des Vertrauens?*, Jan Hirschbiegel, Stefanie von Welser, Angelika Westermann (eds.). Husum: Matthiesen, 2021, 299–311, 304–307.

51 See Rothmann Marktnetze, 141.

52 See Rothmann, Marktnetze, 141–143.

rulers. Due to the increase in the number of fairs, however, competition among towns for the most favourable fair dates became more intense, which is probably why cooperation based on mutual trust was no longer possible. For towns that had long been organising supra-regional fairs, it was now evidently necessary to protect themselves legally within the increasing rivalry for trade fair dates. Thus, it was certainly a consistent strategy that the free imperial city of Nördlingen sought legitimacy to strengthen its traditional fair. With the imperial privileges, Nördlingen was able to assure the ancestral position of the Whitsun Fair within the network of supra-regional fairs.

In this case, to request such a privilege from the emperor was consistent because the emperor was the official sovereign of the free imperial city of Nördlingen. For other towns like Erfurt, Halle, and Leipzig, that were not free imperial cities, but also successfully requested trade fair privileges from the emperor, this was not at all straightforward. There were actually several agents available at the time who could enhance the coordination of fairs through privileges. These not only included the king or the emperor, but also regional sovereigns, such as the Prince-Electors. In the course of the ongoing territorialisation within the Holy Roman Empire, regional sovereigns, in particular, had a great interest in promoting trade in their territory by granting privileges because this helped strengthen their sovereign rights vis-à-vis the emperor. As a result, towns already holding a fair were eager to obtain the best possible privileges in order to formally secure their customary rights. However, in the end, only the king or emperor could grant such privileges with the highest legal validity.

This notwithstanding, imperial privileges were not always entirely advantageous for the towns. Sigismund had granted far-reaching rights to Nördlingen, similar to those granted to Frankfurt and Nuremberg. In particular, in this type of privilege, the escort right (*conductus*) lacked the right to also allow banished merchants or merchants from towns under an imperial ban from trading at the fair, the reason being that the emperor wanted to oblige the free imperial cities to legally prosecute banished persons. Even though this particular sort of escort right —together with the fact that the fair was termed *Messe*—underlined both the prestigious status of a free imperial city and the supra-regional scope of the Whitsun Fair, it was in fact a very costly duty for Nördlingen, just as it was for Frankfurt and Nuremberg. Both Frankfurt and Nuremberg repeatedly tried to convince the emperor to change their privileges in such a way that they would be released from the burdensome obligation of suing banished merchants. Whereas Frankfurt was partly successful with its request, the failure of Nuremberg's request contributed to the fair never really developing into a supra-regional fair. Likewise, this special form of privilege may also have partly accounted for the decline of the Whitsun Fair of Nördlingen since the early sixteenth century.[53]

5 Privileges for newly established fairs: path-dependence and sequential choice of dates

With the number of granted privileges increasing, the network of fairs developed a fixed spatiotemporal structure.[54] Any further change in the temporal sequence of fairs was path-dependent, though. The spatiotemporal structure of fairs showed all characteristics typical of path dependency:[55] first, the structure was determined by decisions that had been made in the past, since the origin of some fairs dated back to the High Middle Ages, like for instance, the date of the Nördlingen Whitsun Fair; second, as dates of the established trade fairs had become more coordinated over time, there was a network effect from which all organising towns benefited, for example, through mutual visits by merchants or through the common practice of having the dates of their own fairs announced at other fairs; third, because of the network effect, any change of dates would have caused high costs and considerable economic damage, not only for the organising town,

53 See Veronesi, "Bös gelt und liderlich volck", 20–23.

54 Written evidence of the perception of this spatiotemporal structure can be found in the initially handwritten fair calendars which, from the middle of the sixteenth century, were printed in merchant manuals, postal route directories, travel books, and almanacs. See Ulf Christian Ewert, Susanne Rau, Leif Scheuermann. Räumliche Konfigurationen des Messehandels im frühneuzeitlichen Europa: Gedruckte Messekalender des 16. und 17. Jahrhunderts und ihre computergestützte Analyse. *Vierteljahrschrift für Sozial- und Wirtschaftsgeschichte* 110:4 (2023): 494–541.

55 The concept of path dependence was developed in economics to explain why technical standards prevail and under what conditions they are often not replaced after having turned inefficient. This idea can be applied to the institutional change as well. On path dependence in general see Paul A. David. Clio and the Economics of QWERTY. *American Economic Review* 75:2 (1985): 332–337; W. Brian Arthur. Competing Technologies, Increasing Returns, and Lock-in by Historical Events. *Economic Journal* 99 (1989): 116–131; Paul A. David. Why are Institutions the 'Carriers of History'? Path Dependence and the Evolution of Conventions, Organizations and Institutions. *Structural Change and Economic Dynamics* 5:2 (1994): 205–220; Jörg Sydow, Georg Schreyögg, Jochen Koch. Organizational Path Dependence: Opening the Black Box. *Academy of Management Review* 34:4 (2009): 689–709.

but also for the other towns. Thus, the existing spatiotemporal structure of the trade fair network, now secured by privileges, had become quasi-irreversible.[56]

Within the already tight annual calendar of fairs, towns that wanted to set up a new fair had to find a suitable date. This makes it particularly clear that assuming simultaneous choice of dates by all towns is, of course, unrealistic. Instead, a sequential model in which actors take their decisions one after the other would be more appropriate. Newcomers had to base their own choices on the dates of the established and already privileged fairs with which they wanted to avoid an overlap. Therefore, they were limited in their choice by the quasi-irreversibility of the temporal structure of fairs. What impact this had in practice will be shown using the following cases.

In the Holy Roman Empire, several types of new fairs with an intended supra-regional scope can be observed in the late fourteenth and early fifteenth centuries. First, there were those fairs organised by towns that already held another fair. Erfurt is a typical case, as in 1473 Emperor Frederick III had granted the town a second three-week fair, to be commenced on Trinity Sunday in 1473, in addition to the Misericordia Sunday Fair that had been granted by Emperor Louis IV of Bavaria (1328–1347) in 1331.[57] In the privilege for this new fair, it is explicitly mentioned that the grant is made to help the town to recover from the devastating fire of 1472.[58] Second, there were existing annual markets which were sought to be upgraded to genuine supra-regional fairs on the same scale as Frankfurt, Nördlingen, or Zurzach. Strasbourg, Zurich, Basle, and Nuremberg aimed at widening the scope of their annual markets, but none of these initiatives

---

56 The long-lasting legacy of this quasi-irreversible spatiotemporal structure of fairs can be seen in the printed fair calendars of the sixteenth and seventeenth centuries in which fairs are listed that had been abandoned in the meantime, for example the Winter Fair in Nördlingen that was only held from 1522 until 1541, initially in autumn and, since 1529, in January. See Voges, Werden und Wirken, 66. In the fair calendar published in the 1586 edition of Ries' famous arithmetic book, this fair is still listed with its date in January. See Ries, *Rechenbüchlein*, fols. 93 v–94 r.

57 See Kaiser Ludwigs IV. Messeprivileg für die Stadt Erfurt, Frankfurt am Main, 13. Dezember 1331 ('Privilege of Emperor Louis IV of Bavaria granted to the city of Erfurt, Frankfurt am Main, 13 December 1331'). In Stadtarchiv Erfurt, 0–0/A 36- 2. The fair was to last from Misericordia Sunday up to and including Ascension Day, a duration of nearly a month. Misericordia Sunday is the third Sunday of Easter—that is, the second Sunday after Easter—and is also known as Good Shepherd Sunday.

58 See Kaiser Friedrichs III. Privileg für die Stadt Erfurt, wegen eines neuen, nach Trinitatis zu haltenden Jahrmarktes, Augsburg, 14. Mai 1473 ('Privilege of Emperor Frederick III granted to Erfurt to set up a new annual market that was to be held after Trinity Sunday, Augsburg, 14 May 1473'). In Stadtarchiv Erfurt, 0–0/A 36–8. CoMOR online exposition 'Foires, villes et marchands.' https://fairs-in-history.huma-num.fr/expo/online/theme_lyon_1?object=privilege_erfurt (29 May 2024).

really succeeded.[59] In the case of Strasbourg, an old annual market was re-established, transferred from late October to mid-June and restricted in tenure from a whole month to a fortnight.[60] Finally, there were also attempts to set up new supra-regional fairs, as was the case in Ulm.

In contrast to Nördlingen with its traditional Whitsun Fair, Ulm, another free imperial city, only tried to establish its own trade fair in the early fifteenth century.[61] One of the reasons was to facilitate the marketing of crafted goods produced in Ulm and thereby to sponsor the city's craftsmen. In 1429, King Sigismund (he was crowned Holy Roman Emperor only in 1433) authorised the city of Ulm to hold an annual market in the city by means of a charter issued in Bratislava on 9 August. Sigismund first referred in detail to the manifold services that Ulm had provided to him, the king and to the empire in the past—a common wording in such documents. He then stated that Ulm would always be loyal to him in the future and therefore was granted the imperial 'grace' to hold a fair: "[. . .] and graciously allow for all times an annual market and a fair each year [. . .]."[62] Again, the text mentions both *Messe* and *Jahrmarkt*, connected with 'and.'

Establishment as well as the success or failure of the Ulm fair in its early days can be traced with the help of various surviving documents. This tradition is remarkable because even though numerous trade fairs were granted in the Holy Roman Empire throughout the fifteenth century, the process of granting of privileges can be reconstructed in detail for only a few cases. How one received such a privilege is very clear here: although King Sigismund granted his permission to the Ulm fair, this was not on his own initiative. Rather, a few weeks earlier, the mayor and burghers of Ulm had sent an envoy to the imperial court in Bratislava with a letter in which Ulm requested imperial permission to establish a fair that would have all rights, freedoms and 'graces.' This was asked against payment of a

59 See Hektor Ammann. Die deutschen und die schweizerischen Messen des Mittelalters. In *La foire*, Gilissen (ed.), 149–173, 171; Friedrich Lütge. Der Untergang der Nürnberger Heiltumsmesse. *Jahrbücher für Nationalökonomie und Statistik* 178 (1965): 133–157; Friedrich Lütge. Die Nürnberger Heiltumsmesse (erw. Fassung). In *Friedrich Lütge. Beiträge zur Sozial- und Wirtschaftsgeschichte. Gesammelte Abhandlungen*, Eckhart Schremmer (ed.). Stuttgart: Gustav Fischer, 1970, 193–215.

60 See Tom Scott. *Regional Identity and Economic Change: The Upper Rhine, 1450–1600*. Oxford: Clarendon Press, 1997, 83.

61 See Heinrich Steinmeyer. Die Entwicklung der Ulmer Sommermesse (des späteren Veitsmarktes) und ihre Einordnung in das süddeutsche Handelssystem bis zum Ende der Reichsstadtzeit. *Vierteljahrschrift für Sozial- und Wirtschaftsgeschichte* 77:3 (1990): 323–349.

62 The Early New High German text reads as follows: "[. . .] vnd gnediclich erloubet ewiclich alle Jahre eynen Jarmerckt vnd messe in derselben stat [. . .]." See Privileg König Sigismunds für Ulm.

sum of money of between 300 and 1,000 guilders in return, staggered according to the extent of the privileges actually granted.[63] Since Ulm was a free imperial city, it was straightforward to make this request to its sovereign, the king (and designated emperor).

The choice of date for the fifteen-day trade fair, which was to begin eight days before Ascension Day and end eight days after this feast, was also proposed by Ulm in this letter. Exactly this period was then prescribed in the privilege. Nonetheless, a different date was also expressly permitted by the emperor, provided that Ulm ensured that date and duration once chosen would not overlap with the dates of other imperially privileged fairs in the wider area surrounding Ulm.[64] This sort of restrictive clause provides insight into both the effectiveness and efficiency of the coordination of fairs by means of privileges. As stated above, a coordinated network of fairs would only be a Pareto-efficient equilibrium if the privileges granted were aligned to each other, at least to a sufficient degree. However, in the fifteenth century, the granting and renewal of numerous trade fair privileges by the emperor must have overwhelmed the imperial chancellery, especially because privileges were granted on the request of the organising towns and the charters issued usually remained with them. Thus, given its administrative capacities and procedures, it can be doubted whether the imperial chancellery really had an overview of the privileges that had been granted. In addition, the king's or emperor's proper economic interests in a certain respect often precluded a precise coordination of individual privileges. Since he was always eager to grant privileges for fairs, mainly because of the fees that towns had to pay in return for a grant, the imperial chancellery could not guarantee that the dates of fairs set in these privileges were inter-operable. By including such a restrictive clause, the risk of an eventual dispute resulting from an actual overlap in dates with another fair was passed on to the town that had made the request. Even if the granting of privileges was, in principle, useful to ensure the coordination of fairs, its practical handling was therefore inappropriate and inefficient because it could lead to disputes between the towns over dates. This, to a certain degree, inhibited further growth of fairs, as new fairs could not be integrated into the existing network and would likely fail in the long run, simply because it was impossible to find an appropriate date for them that was economically attractive for the organising town as well as it was undisputed by other towns.

Exactly this happened in Ulm's initiative of establishing a new supra-regional fair. Despite the city's geographical location being favourable to transport and de-

63 See Steinmeyer, Ulmer Sommermesse, 324.

64 See Steinmeyer, Ulmer Sommermesse, 325–326.

spite its integration into a large and dense network of towns in southern Germany, the fair never developed the originally intended supra-regional significance alongside the fairs of Frankfurt, Nördlingen, and Zurzach. Ulm's aspirations with regard to the economic success and geographical reach of the new fair were high. This can be seen from a surviving letter of invitation to the fair of 1441, dated 29 December 1440, that was sent out to other towns to announce the fair[65] and from a surviving list of towns that had been the recipients of a similar letter the year before.[66] The planned supporting programme of the fair included a highly remunerated horse race, similar to the famous *Scharlach* race which was held during the Whitsun Fair in Nördlingen.[67] The list of recipients of the letter of invitation to the fair of 1440, dated 23 December 1439, reveals Ulm's fairly clear idea of how far the economic impact of the new fair would extend into the late medieval Holy Roman Empire. Hektor Ammann has mapped the towns addressed, of which the majority are located in the late medieval Upper German economic area, which included Franconia, Swabia, the Swiss Confederation, the Upper Rhine area, and Alsace, as well as towns along the trade routes down the Danube and the Rhine. Further down the Rhine, important places in Flanders and Brabant are mentioned, such as Bruges, Antwerp, and Bergen-op-Zoom. Numerous places are also mentioned along the trade route—the *Via Regia*[68]—from Frankfurt to Bohemia and Silesia as far as

---

65 See Brief des Rates der Stadt Ulm an die Städte über die Errichtung einer Messe und eines vierzehntägigen Marktes in Ulm ab dem dritten Sonntag nach Fronleichnam 1441, 29. Dezember 1440 ('Letter of the council of Ulm to other cities to announce a fair and a two-week-market in Ulm which will begin on the third Sunday after Corpus Christi 1441, 29 December 1440'). In Haus der Stadtgeschichte—Stadtarchiv Ulm, A Urk. 1587. CoMOR online exposition 'Foires, villes et marchands.' https://fairs-in-history.huma-num.fr/expo/online/theme_lyon_3?object=lettre_ulm (29 May 2024)

66 See Steinmeyer, Ulmer Sommermesse, 328; Rothmann, Marktnetze, 142–144.

67 See Steinmeyer, Ulmer Sommermesse, 327. On the *Scharlach* races in Upper Germany, see Christian Jaser. Urban Palio and Scharlach Races in Fifteenth- and Early Sixteenth-Century Italy and Germany. *International Journal of the History of Sport* 37:3–4 (2020): 272–287.

68 For the *Via Regia*, see Gustav Hildebrand, Ludwig Kramarczyk. *Des Reiches Straße. Alte Frankfurt-Leipziger Handelsstraße*. Würzburg: Weidlich Flechsig, 1990; Ludwig Steinfeld. *Chronik einer Straße. Die alte Straße von Frankfurt nach Leipzig: Geschichte, Ereignisse, Reiseberichte*. Horb am Neckar: Geiger, 1994; Kamen Pawlow. *Via Regia, Königsstrasse oder Hohe Strasse. Thüringer Impressionen. Begleitheft zur Wanderausstellung Erfurt—Bonn—Eisenach—Gotha*. Erfurt: Europäisches Kultur- und Informationszentrum, 1998; Winfried Müller, Swen Steinberg (eds.). *Menschen unterwegs. Die via regia und ihre Akteure. Essayband zur 3. Sächsischen Landesausstellung "via regia—800 Jahre Bewegung und Begegnung", Görlitz, 21. Mai bis 31. Oktober 2011*. Dresden: Sandstein, 2011; Pierre Fütterer. Die Via regia—Kritische Bemerkungen zu einem "Mythos" oder: Auf der Suche nach der "Königlichen Straße." In *WegBegleiter. Interdisziplinäre Beiträge zur Altwege- und Burgenforschung. Festschrift für Bernd W. Bahn zu seinem 80. Geburtstag*, Martin Freudenreich, Pierre Fütterer, Anna Schwieder (eds.). Langenweißbach: Beier & Beran—

Wroczław, including Erfurt, Leipzig, and Halle, and then of course Geneva, Bolzano, Trento, and Venice as links to northern Italy and the Mediterranean.[69] Finally, some of the places mentioned belonged to the Hanseatic area—for example, Dortmund, Münster, Soest, Brunswick, Magdeburg, and Lübeck.[70] Following Ammann, this is strong evidence of the knowledge that people in Ulm had about trade and trading centres in the Holy Roman Empire.[71] In this respect, the area spanned by the addressed cities could also be understood as a kind of imagined trading area, demonstrating the supra-regional significance that Ulm had hoped its newly established fair would have. In fact, the free imperial city of Ulm was part of a large and dense network of towns, and Ulm merchants were therefore integrated into a widespread trading network that extended primarily across southern and southwest Germany, present-day Switzerland, and the eastern Alpine region. Rothmann, on the other hand, emphasises Ulm's political networking with other towns and the economic networking of its merchants and craftsmen with with those of other towns which, in his opinion, can be seen in the compilation of this list of places.[72]

However, the new fair had only moderate success and developed regional importance at best. This was not only because the fair was controversial due to fact that various groups in the city of Ulm had different interest in relation to it. In 1445, for example, the craftsmen complained in a letter of the guilds of Ulm to the city council above all that out-of-town traders were given preferential treatment, and that the economic benefits provided to them by the fair were therefore very limited.[73] Also the period requested by Ulm for the fair around Ascension Day, which King Sigismund had approved, turned out to be ultimately unfavourable.

Archäologische Fachliteratur, 2019, 169–195. On the great importance of trading routes in premodern Europe to link markets, see Petersen, Holtermann, Huang, Digitale Werkzeuge, 326–329.

69 See Markus A. Denzel. Märkte und Messen im vorindustriellen Alpenraum. Ihre Bedeutung für den trans- und inneralpinen Handelsverkehr. In *Transits—Transit. Infrastructures et sociétié de l'Antiquité à nos jours/Infrastrukturen und Gesellschaft von der Antike bis heute*, Anne-Lise Head-König, Luigi Lorenzetti, Andrea Bonoldi (eds.). Zurich: Chronos, 2016, 43–62.

70 See Hektor Ammann. Einladungen zur Ulmer Messe, 1439, Karte 1955 (Map of 1955: 'Invitations to the Ulm fair, 1439'). In Institut für vergleichende Städtegeschichte Münster, Nachlass Hektor Ammann, Rolle/Mappe 1, Nr. 166. CoMOR online exposition 'Foires, villes et marchands', https://fairs-in-history.huma-num.fr/expo/online/theme_lyon_3?object=carte_lettre_ulm (29 May 2024). This map is printed in Rothmann, Marktnetze, 143. A brief overview of the late medieval Upper German economic area can also be found in this article (141–144).

71 See Hektor Ammann. Vom geographischen Wissen einer deutschen Handelsstadt des Spätmittelalters. *Ulm und Oberschwaben* 34 (1955): 39–65.

72 See Rothmann, Marktnetze, 142.

73 See Steinmeyer, Ulmer Sommermesse, 329.

Even if the first eight days before Ascension Day did not directly overlap with the two important Whitsun Fairs in Nördlingen and Zurzach, the Ulm fair nevertheless clashed with them in the sense that the two Whitsun Fairs had become accepted payment dates (such as for bills of exchange) for merchants in Upper Germany. A visit to both the Ulm fair and after that the fairs in either Nördlingen or Zurzach therefore was hardly possible because the time gap between them was too short.[74] This also interfered with Ulm merchants' business, many of whom traditionally visited the Nördlingen Whitsun Fair on a regular basis.[75] Consequently, Ulm set a later date—the third Sunday after Corpus Christi—after a few years, which was allowed by the imperial privilege of 1429.[76] Thus, even if an imperial privilege was necessary to give the new fair the greatest possible legitimacy right from the start, it did not help much in finding a proper date for the fair. Thus, the practice of granting privileges was not suitable for bindingly coordinating fair dates in every case because the emperor's actual coordinating impact was fairly restricted. In addition, the path-dependent character of the already established spatiotemporal structure of the network of fairs made the choice of date and integration into this network difficult. Even Ulm's willingness to compromise regarding the date finally did not succeed. On the contrary, the city's cooperative behaviour on this point contributed to the fact that due to the rescheduling in its early days, the new fair could not find the right time slot to prosper and to achieve the intended supra-regional significance.

6 Privileges prohibiting 'new' fairs: prospects of non-cooperative behaviour

The increase in the number of trade fair privileges granted by the emperor not only narrowed the scope for cities wishing to set up a new or additional trade fair, but also led to an increasing number of overlaps between existing fairs. This was due to the fact that the ability of the imperial chancellery to control the com-

74 See Steinmeyer, Ulmer Sommermesse, 326–327.

75 See Rothmann, Marktnetze, 173–177; Ulf Christian Ewert. Handelsräume der vormodernen Stadt: Raumzeitliche Aspekte des Messehandels am Beispiel der Nördlinger Pfingstmesse. *Moderne Stadtgeschichte* 54:2 (2023): 147–172, 165–170.

76 This is proven by the previously mentioned letter of invitation to the fair of 1441. However, the date was subsequently rearranged several times—on Saint Ulrich's Day (4 July), on Roodmas (Finding of the True Cross, 3 May), and finally, on Saint Vitus Day (15 June). See Steinmeyer, Ulmer Sommermesse, 329.

patibility of the granted privileges was rather limited. In addition, some towns had privileges for their fairs granted by grantors other than the emperor, for example regional sovereigns. Of course, the imperial chancellery had no overview of these privileges either. Due to conflicting privileges for different cities, the very thing that the granting of privileges by the king, the emperor, or any other sovereign was supposed to prevent occurred. Conflicting privileges stimulated the competition among towns even more instead of guaranteeing their cooperation with respect to dates. Hence, disputes between cities over trade fair dates were inevitable, and if all parties to the dispute insisted on their desired dates, an amicable and therefore efficient solution—that is, a well-coordinated network of fairs—could not be achieved. This follows from the mechanism of the game theoretical model described above. Using the example of the rise of the Leipzig fairs in the fifteenth and early sixteenth centuries, this section will show that under certain conditions, non-cooperative behaviour on the part of the towns involved in a dispute over dates succeeded and thus would change the temporal structure of the trade fair network.

In 1497, Maximilian I, Roman-German king and, since 1508, also Holy Roman Emperor, granted a privilege for all three Leipzig fairs—the New Year's Market, Easter Market, and Michaelmas Market.[77] This was a vital step in raising the Leipzig fairs to the same level as those of the free imperial cities privileged by the emperor, like the Frankfurt fairs. In this way, the Leipzig fairs were elevated in a sense to imperial fairs, whose prestige was now greater than it has been with only privileges granted by the Saxon Prince-Elector. The far-reaching privilege for the Leipzig fairs was accompanied by the imperial ban on the institution of any new fair in the bishoprics of Magdeburg, Halberstadt, Meißen, Merseburg, and Naumburg. This was certainly a reaction to Magdeburg's initiative to establish another fair, but above all it shows that Leipzig's strategy was to use its proper sovereign—the Prince-Elector of Saxony—to influence the emperor in such a way that other regional sovereigns were delegitimised as grantors of trade fair privileges.[78]

---

77 See *Keyserlich Privilegium Der Stadt Leipzig Jahrmärkte*, Worms, 20. Juli 1497 ('Privilege of Maximilian I for the fairs of Leipzig, Worms, 20 July 1497'), single-sheet print, Leipzig. In Stadtgeschichtliches Museum Leipzig, I D 590. https://www.stadtmuseum.leipzig.de/document/literatur/00023724 (29 May 2024). CoMOR online exposition 'Foires, villes et marchands.' https://fairs-in-history.huma-num.fr/expo/online/theme_lyon_1?object=privilege_leipzig (29 May 2024).

78 See Pauly, Messesystem, 78–79. On the Leipzig fairs in the Middle Ages, see Markus A. Denzel. Die Leipziger Märkte vom 12. Jahrhundert bis zu den Privilegierungen von 1497, 1507 und 1514. In *Geschichte der Stadt Leipzig, vol. 1: Von den Anfängen bis zur Reformation*, Enno Bünz (ed.). Leipzig: Leipziger Universitätsverlag, 2015, 322–340.

However, before this happened, Leipzig had already taken very strict action against trade fair dates in other cities on several occasions in the previous decades. When in 1448 Magdeburg aimed at organising an additional fair shortly before the Leipzig Michaelmas Market, the Council of Leipzig was able to obtain a charter from Prince-Elector Frederick II, the Gentle (1428–64) in which he forbade the residents of the Electorate of Saxony from visiting the Magdeburg fair. In 1458, the Leipzig New Year's Market was privileged by Frederick II and thus overlapped with the older New Year's Market in Halle. Both Halle (1464) and Leipzig (1466) received privileges from Emperor Frederick III for their New Year's Markets. The dispute between the two cities arose because Leipzig then banned merchants from attending the New Year's Market in Halle. Halle successfully complained about this to the emperor, who immediately revoked his privilege for the Leipzig New Year's Market. The emperor justified this by saying that Leipzig had not informed him about the New Year's Market in Halle when it requested the privilege,[79] a statement which clearly proves how little overview the imperial chancellery had over the granting of imperial trade fair privileges. However, Leipzig did not give in and again sought help from its sovereign, Prince-Elector Ernest of Saxony (1464–86) who, being a relative of the emperor,[80] was in fact able to persuade the emperor not only to grant a new privilege for the Leipzig New Year's Market, but at the same time also revoke his privilege for the New Year's Market in Halle, thereby banning this much older fair. Neither the Magdeburg fair nor the New Year's Market in Halle gained supra-regional importance, even though both of them continued to be held.[81]

The next improvement of rights granted to Leipzig for its fairs came with an imperial privilege in 1507.[82] This was again the result of a dispute over dates of fairs in a quite distant, but nonetheless rivalling town—Erfurt in this case. Erfurt

---

79 See Pauly, Messesystem, 78; Elfie-Marita Eibl. Kaiser Friedrich III. (1440–1493) und die Wettiner. Aspekte des Verhältnisses Zentralgewalt—Fürsten in einer königsfernen Landschaft. *Neues Archiv für Sächsische Geschichte* 71 (2000): 27–51, 42–45.

80 Ernest of Saxony was the nephew of Emperor Frederick III, as his mother Margret of Austria (c. 1416–86), was the sister of Emperor Fredrick III.

81 For the New Year's Market in Halle, the start date was rearranged to a date after the New Year's Market in Leipzig had closed. See Pauly, Messesystem, 78–79.

82 See *Keyserlich Privilegium Der Stadt Leipzig Jahrmärkte Stapell vnd Niederlage*, Konstanz, 23. Juni 1507 ('Privilege of Maximilian I for the fairs of Leipzig, Constance, 23 June 1507'), single-sheet print, Leipzig. In Stadtgeschichtliches Museum Leipzig, I D 561. https://www.stadtmuseum.leipzig.de/document/literatur/00007614 (29 May 2024). CoMOR online exposition 'Foires, villes et marchands.' https://fairs-in-history.huma-num.fr/expo/online/theme_lyon_3?object=conflit_naumburg_leipzig (29 May 2024).

was also on the *Via Regia* and, like Leipzig,[83] it benefited from the west-east trade that was carried out along this road[84]—a fact certainly contributing to the rivalry between the two cities. In response to Erfurt's aim of advancing its Misericordia Sunday Fair to Easter, which would have overlapped with the Leipzig Easter Market, the emperor not only confirmed the rights granted to Leipzig in 1497, but also extended the privilege to the extent that towns within a radius of 15 German miles (approximately 136 km) were henceforth prohibited from instituting new trade fairs. Furthermore, commodities transported within this radius were now subject to the Leipzig staple law—that is, they had to be brought to Leipzig and weighed, cleared through customs, and offered for sale there for three days. The emperor had a particular interest in the Leipzig trade fairs because Leipzig had developed into a hub for the west-east trade and an important financial centre.[85] Once again, Leipzig had behaved uncooperatively and was able to assert its own economic interests with the backing of the Saxon Prince-Elector, and by influencing the grantor of privileges.[86]

After Emperor Maximilian I had granted his second privilege for the Leipzig fairs in 1507, Naumburg, whose fairs were much older than those of Leipzig, endeavoured to move its fair from Maundy Thursday to the Sunday before Estomihi[87] so that it did not coincide with the Easter Market in Leipzig. In return for the payment of 70 guilders, Naumburg received the requested imperial permission. Even though Naumburg was very cooperative in avoiding any overlap with the Leipzig fairs, Leipzig continued to hold on to its uncooperative strategy. Because the privilege granted to Leipzig stipulated that no 'new' fair was allowed to be set up within a radius of 15 miles around the city, Leipzig regarded the change of date of the

---

83 See Susanne Schötz. Leipzig im Schnittpunkt von via regia und via imperia. Über Bedeutung und Akteure des Messehandels. In *via regia—800 Jahre Bewegung und Begegnung. Katalog zur 3. Sächsischen Landesausstellung, Görlitz, 21. Mai bis 31. Oktober 2011*, Roland Enke, Bettina Probst (eds.). Dresden: Sandstein, 2011, 86–90.

84 See Manfred Straube. *Geleitswesen und Warenverkehr im thüringisch-sächsischen Raum zu Beginn der Frühen Neuzeit*. Cologne, Weimar, Vienna: Böhlau, 2014.

85 See Herbert Eiden. The Fairs of Leipzig and the Eastern European Economies, 15th–18th centuries. In *Fiere e mercati*, Cavaciocchi (ed.), 723–739; Manfred Straube. *Wirtschaftliche Frequenzen der Leipziger Großen Märkte/Messen. Statistische Zeugnisse aus den Leipziger Stadtrechnungen 1471/72 bis 1814/15*. Leipzig: Leipziger Universitätsverlag, 2015; Uwe Schirmer. *Der Finanz- und Messeplatz Leipzig vom 13. bis zur Mitte des 17. Jahrhunderts. Geldwesen—Waren- und Zahlungsverkehr—Rentengeschäfte*. Stuttgart, Leipzig: S. Hirzel, 2021.

86 See Pauly, Messesystem, 79–80.

87 Estomihi is the last Sunday in the pre-Passion period, the Sunday before Ash Wednesday. Since the duration from Estomihi up to and including Easter is fifty days, another name for it is Quinquagesima.

Naumburg fair as a new foundation and protested against it to the emperor. With the tried and tested approach of exerting influence on the emperor through the Saxon Prince-Elector, Leipzig at first was again able to persuade the emperor to revoke the privilege granted to Naumburg, which he did in autumn of the same year. However, Leipzig's resistance to the shift of the Naumburg fair provoked a long and bitter dispute between the two towns.[88] This is evidenced by a letter, for instance, which the Naumburg town council sent to the town's sovereign, Bishop Philip of Freising, asking him for help in the dispute with George the Bearded, Duke of Saxony, and Leipzig, which was sustained by the duke.[89]

After the death of Maximilian I in January 1519, Naumburg tried again—once more without success—to obtain permission from the new emperor, Charles V to advance the date of the Maundy Thursday Market. Simon Duringe, treasurer of the town, and Johan Hochen travelled to Worms, where the emperor was holding the imperial diet, to discuss the matter. The expenses for their mission were recorded in the town's account of 1520 on "Friday after Saint Dorothea" (9 February).[90] In a charter issued on 25 May 1521, Emperor Charles V (1519–56) finally granted the citizens of Naumburg permission to hold a market on the day of Saints Peter and Paul (29 June).[91] This meant that there was no longer any overlap with one of the Leipzig fairs. The charter itself has not survived, but the text can be found in Naumburg's municipal register of documents and letters.[92] Again, there are no differences in the meaning of the words *Messe* and *Jahrmarkt*. Even

---

88 See Pauly, Messesystem, 80; Wieland Held. Der Messeplatz Naumburg und sein Verhältnis zur Leipziger Messe am Anfang des 16. Jahrhunderts. In *Leipzigs Messen 1497–1997*, Zwahr, Topfstedt, Bentele (eds.), 75–86.

89 See Brief an den Stadtherren Naumburgs, Bischof Philipp von Freising, 23. Januar 1521 ('Letter to the sovereign of the city of Naumburg, Bishop Philip of Freising, 23 January 1521'). In Stadtarchiv Naumburg (Saale), MS 57, fol. 395r. CoMOR online exposition 'Foires, villes et marchands.' https://fairs-in-history.huma-num.fr/expo/online/theme_lyon_3?object=conflit_naumburg_leipzig (29 May 2024); For the support provided by the dukes of Saxony (of the Albertine Branch of the House of Wettin) for the Leipzig fairs, see Karlheinz Blaschke. Die Kurfürsten von Sachsen als Förderer der Leipziger Messe. Von der landesgeschichtlichen Grundlegung zur kontinentalen Wirkung. In *Leipzigs Messen 1497–1997*, Zwahr, Topfstedt, Bentele (eds.), 61–73.

90 See Naumburger Ratsrechnung 1520 ('Account of the council of Naumburg, 1520'). In Stadtarchiv Naumburg (Saale), MS 138, fol. 79v. CoMOR online exposition 'Foires, villes et marchands.' https://fairs-in-history.huma-num.fr/expo/online/theme_lyon_3?object=conflit_naumburg_leipzig (29 May 2024).

91 See Fritz Heydenreich. *Die Geschichte der Naumburger Peter-Pauls-Messe*. PhD diss., University of Halle (Saale), 1927.

92 See *Keiser Karls Bestetigunge voer denn Jarmargkt [. . .]*, 25. Mai 1521 (Kopie im Kopialbuch Naumburgs) ('Confirmation of the fair privilege by Emperor Charles IV, 25 May 1521', extract from the copy book of Naumburg, Saale). In Stadtarchiv Naumburg (Saale), MS 40, fols. 148r–151v.

though the Naumburg fair, which was of far-reaching economic significance at the time, had a long tradition, it was called *Jahrmarkt*. Likewise, although Leipzig sought to gain such a far-reaching economic significance for its three annual markets, they were still referred to as *Jahrmarkt* in the two imperial privileges of 1497 and 1507.

The rise of the Leipzig fairs shows clearly that it was possible to assert one's own interests with regard to trade fair dates against the resistance of other towns and to overcome the quasi-irreversibility of the trade fair network, provided that one succeeded in influencing the grantor of privileges to grant one a spatial and temporal fair monopoly that excluded competitors. By repeatedly playing a non-cooperative strategy, Leipzig demonstrated its lack of willingness to compromise to rivals, which in turn prompted them to either change their own strategy or withdraw. For Leipzig, this meant economic success, but this regional sustained change of the spatiotemporal structure of the network of fairs came at the expense of the rivalling towns, which had been forced to compromise on this issue.

7 Concluding remarks: effectiveness and efficiency of granting privileges

The analysis so far can be summarised with a few concluding remarks: during the trade fair boom of the Late Middle Ages, the rulers of the Holy Roman Empire granted numerous privileges for either the institution of new fairs or the confirmation of established fairs. Since the determination of date and duration of a fair was an essential part of such privileges, they may have made it possible to coordinate the timing of the rapidly growing and increasingly differentiating trade fair network, at least at its highest level—the supra-regional fairs. Game-theoretical analysis cannot fully falsify this hypothesis. Trade fair privileges were certainly useful for the coordination of fairs, as it can be shown that the rulers' enhancement of cooperation of towns with regard to dates of fairs was necessary. In this respect, privileges were certainly an effective means to enable coordination.

As far as the intended geographic reach and economic significance of fairs are concerned, wording and the various market terms apparently only played a secondary role. It is all too obvious that although in German different words for a trade fair were in use at the time (such as *Messe*, *Jahrmarkt*, and *Markt*), in privileges they were mostly used as synonyms. Without further clarification, these

---

CoMOR online exposition 'Foires, villes et marchands.' https://fairs-in-history.huma-num.fr/expo/online/theme_lyon_3?object=conflit_naumburg_leipzig (29 May 2024).

terms *per se* did not imply any hierarchy with respect to the degree of regulation of a privilege or the economic impact of a fair. Even around 1500, the term *Messe* was not deliberately used to give certain towns an advantage over others, as the cases of the imperial privileges for the Leipzig fairs in 1497 and 1507 show, in which the fairs are still named as annual markets (*Jahrmärkte*).

If trade fair privileges were an effective means to enable the coordination of fairs, have they also been efficient? Given the way privileges were granted, their efficiency must be doubted. The emperor had his own economic interest in the granting of privileges because of the revenues generated through the fees paid by the towns for their requests. Hence, this was an important incentive for the ruler to assume the role of a third party to enhance cooperation of towns. But this had a rather negative effect on the efficiency of coordination of fairs by privileges because the ruler's objectives did not always concur with those of towns that requested privileges and confirmation of favourable dates. In addition, by granting legally binding privileges, he fostered the quasi-irreversibility of the spatiotemporal structure of the trade fair network. The further development of the network became path-dependent because this imperial legitimisation of fair dates narrowed the margin for new fairs to be established. Meanwhile, the imperial chancellery had only limited opportunities to keep track of the exact 'fair calendar' that had evolved from all the privileges, issued either by the emperor or regional sovereigns. Therefore, the emperor was only too happy to grant a desired date to the town making the request. At the same time, by including a restrictive clause concerning the date, he passed on to this town the responsibility to avoid any overlap with other fairs and eventual conflict over dates, as can be seen in the case of Ulm. Strictly speaking, the ruler's interest in avoiding a dispute between towns was rather low, since in such an event both parties involved would again incur fees for the re-issuance of charters, which once again generated revenues. Finally, in the event of a dispute between towns, the emperor also did not prove to be independent. His economic interest (as was the case in the dispute between Leipzig and Naumburg) or his dynastic interest (as can be seen in the dispute between Leipzig and Halle) in a particular fair could well tip the balance in favour of the town that played a non-cooperative strategy and credibly insisted upon the desired fair date. Thus, in the long run, privileges proved not to be a viable solution to handle the increasing competition among towns to organise fairs and for attractive trade fair dates, as the way in which they were granted restricted the further growth of fairs. However, the extent to which the granting of privileges was inefficient and what impact this had on economic growth in the German-speaking lands of the Holy Roman Empire in the fifteenth and sixteenth centuries will be the subject of further research.

Bibliography

Primary Sources

Amman, Jost. *Eigentliche Abbildung deß ganzen Gewerks der löblichen Kaufmannschaft/Samt etlich der nahmhafft und fürnehmsten Handelstädt Signatur und Wappen zum Theil fürnehmlich die Märckt und Messen begriffen seyn/so deß Jahr über in jedem Monath einfallen/auch hin und wider in Europa zu unterschidlichen Zeiten gehalten [. . .]* ('Allegory of trade and merchants'). Woodcut, printed on paper. Nuremberg: Jost Amman (draft), Augsburg: Hans Schultes (print), Wilhelm Peter Zimmermann (publisher), 1585. In Museum Plantin-Moretus, Antwerp, PK.OP.21317. https://museumplantinmoretus.be/de/seite/allegorie-des-handels (29 May 2024). The entries of the fair calendar included in this print are available online: Ewert, Ulf Christian, Noémie Lacroix. 'Museum Plantin-Moretus, PK.OP.21317 (Jost Amman's allegory/fair calendar) (COL0104)'. In *Configurations of European Fairs: Merchants, Objects, Routes (ca. 1350–1600)*, Jean-Louis Gaulin, Susanne Rau (eds.). https://fairs-in-history.huma-num.fr/collection/COL0104 (29 May 2024).

Ammann, Hektor. Einladungen zur Ulmer Messe, 1439, Karte 1955 (Map of 1955: 'Invitations to the Ulm fair, 1439'). In Institut für vergleichende Städtegeschichte Münster, Nachlass Hektor Ammann, Rolle/Mappe 1, Nr. 166. CoMOR online exposition 'Foires, villes et marchands (1350–1600)/Messen, Städte und Kaufleute (1350–1600)', https://fairs-in-history.huma-num.fr/expo/online/theme_lyon_3?object=carte_lettre_ulm (29 May 2024).

Brief des Rates der Stadt Ulm an die Städte über die Errichtung einer Messe und eines vierzehntägigen Marktes in Ulm ab dem dritten Sonntag nach Fronleichnam 1441, 29. Dezember 1440 ('Letter of the council of Ulm to other cities to announce a fair and a two-week-market in Ulm which will begin on the third Sunday after Corpus Christi 1441, 29 December 1440'). In Haus der Stadtgeschichte—Stadtarchiv Ulm, A Urk. 1587. CoMOR online exposition 'Foires, villes et marchands (1350–1600)/Messen, Städte und Kaufleute (1350–1600)', https://fairs-in-history.huma-num.fr/expo/online/theme_lyon_3?object=lettre_ulm (29 May 2024).

Brief an den Stadtherren Naumburgs, Bischof Philipp von Freising, 23. Januar 1521 ('Letter to the sovereign of the city of Naumburg, Bishop Philip of Freising, 23 January 1521'). In Stadtarchiv Naumburg (Saale), MS 57, fol. 395r. CoMOR online exposition 'Foires, villes et marchands (1350–1600)/Messen, Städte und Kaufleute (1350–1600)', https://fairs-in-history.huma-num.fr/expo/online/theme_lyon_3?object=conflit_naumburg_leipzig (29 May 2024).

Fordrin, Olivier. *Almanach pour l'an M.D.LXXIII. Avec la pronostication vraye infallible à jamais. A Geneve. Par Olivier Fordrin. M. D. LXXIII.* In Bibliothèque de Genève, Su 4165. https://dx.doi.org/10.3931/e-rara-6259 (29 May 2024). The entries of this fair calendar are available online: Ewert, Ulf Christian. 'Bibliothèque de Genève, Su 4165 (Olivier Fordrin—Almanach pour l'an M. D. LXXIII) (COL0026)'. In *Configurations of European Fairs: Merchants, Objects, Routes (ca. 1350–1600)*, Jean-Louis Gaulin, Susanne Rau (eds.). https://fairs-in-history.huma-num.fr/collection/COL0026. (29 May 2024).

Kaiser Friedrichs III. Privileg für die Stadt Erfurt, wegen eines neuen, nach Trinitatis zu haltenden Jahrmarktes, Augsburg, 14. Mai 1473 ('Privilege of Emperor Frederick III granted to Erfurt to set up a new annual market that was to be held after Trinity Day, Augsburg, 14 May 1473'). In Stadtarchiv Erfurt, 0–0/A 36–8. CoMOR online exposition 'Foires, villes et marchands (1350–1600)/Messen, Städte und Kaufleute (1350–1600)', https://fairs-in-history.huma-num.fr/expo/online/theme_lyon_1?object=privilege_erfurt (29 May 2024).

Kaiser Ludwigs IV. Messeprivileg für die Stadt Erfurt, Frankfurt am Main, 13. Dezember 1331 ('Privilege of Emperor Louis IV of Bavaria granted to the city of Erfurt, Frankfurt am Main, 13 December 1331'). In Stadtarchiv Erfurt, 0–0/A 36–2.

Keiser Karls Bestetigunge voer denn Jarmargkt [...], 25. Mai 1521 (Kopie im Kopialbuch Naumburgs) ('Confirmation of the fair privilege by Emperor Charles IV, 25 May 1521, extract from the copy book of Naumburg, Saale). In Stadtarchiv Naumburg (Saale), MS 40, fols. 148r–151v. CoMOR online exposition 'Foires, villes et marchands (1350–1600)/Messen, Städte und Kaufleute (1350–1600)', https://fairs-in-history.huma-num.fr/expo/online/theme_lyon_3?object=conflit_naumburg_leipzig (29 May 2024).

Keyserlich Privilegium Der Stadt Leipzig Jahrmärkte, Worms, 20. Juli 1497 ('Privilege of Maximilian I for the fairs of Leipzig, Worms, 20 July 1497'). Single-sheet print. In Stadtgeschichtliches Museum Leipzig, I D 590. https://www.stadtmuseum.leipzig.de/document/literatur/00023724 (29 May 2024) and CoMOR online exposition 'Foires, villes et marchands (1350–1600)/Messen, Städte und Kaufleute (1350–1600)', https://fairs-in-history.huma-num.fr/expo/online/theme_lyon_1?object=privilege_leipzig (29 May 2024).

Keyserlich Privilegium Der Stadt Leipzig Jahrmärkte Stapell vnd Niederlage, Konstanz, 23. Juni 1507 ('Privilege of Maximilian I for the fairs of Leipzig, Constance, 23 June1507>'). Single-sheet print. In Stadtgeschichtliches Museum Leipzig, I D 561. https://www.stadtmuseum.leipzig.de/document/literatur/00007614 (29 May 2024) and CoMOR online exposition 'Foires, villes et marchands (1350–1600)/Messen, Städte und Kaufleute (1350–1600)', https://fairs-in-history.huma-num.fr/expo/online/theme_lyon_3?object=conflit_naumburg_leipzig (29 May 2024).

Naumburger Ratsrechnung 1520 ('Account of the council of Naumburg, 1520'). In Stadtarchiv Naumburg (Saale), MS 138, fol. 79v. CoMOR online exposition 'Foires, villes et marchands (1350–1600)/Messen, Städte und Kaufleute (1350–1600)', https://fairs-in-history.huma-num.fr/expo/online/theme_lyon_3?object=conflit_naumburg_leipzig (29 May 2024).

Privileg König Sigismunds für Ulm zur Einrichtung eines Jahrmarkts, Preßburg, 9. August 1429 ('Privilege of King Sigismund granted to Ulm to set up an annual market, Bratislava, 9 August 1429'). In Haus der Stadtgeschichte—Stadtarchiv Ulm, A Urk. 1406. CoMOR online exposition 'Foires, villes et marchands (1350–1600)/Messen, Städte und Kaufleute (1350–1600)', https://fairs-in-history.huma-num.fr/expo/online/theme_lyon_1?object=privilege_ulm (29 May 2024).

Ries, Adam. *Rechenbüchlein auff der Linien vnd Federn/den angehen=den Rechnern/vnd allen Kaufhaͤnd=lern zu gut vnd nutz mit vielen schoͤnen Exempeln/auff allerley Handthie=rung gemacht durch Adam Riesen. [. . .] M. D. LXXXVI.* Frankfurt am Main: Bassae, 1586. In Staats- und Universitätsbibliothek—Sächsische Landesbibliothek Dresden, 1.A.5915. https://digital.slub-dresden.de/id276477103 (29 May 2024). The entries of this fair calendar are available online: Ewert, Ulf Christian. 'Staats- und Universitätsbibliothek—Sächsische Landesbibliothek, Adam Ries, Rechenbüchlein auff der Linien und Federn (COL0020)'. In *Configurations of European Fairs: Merchants, Objects, Routes (ca. 1350–1600)*, Jean-Louis Gaulin, Susanne Rau (eds.). https://fairs-in-history.huma-num.fr/collection/COL020 (29 May 2024).

Schuldverschreibung des Thomas Dost an Konrad Imhoff, 20. Januar 1482 ('Certificate of indebtedness of Thomas Dost vis-à-vis Konrad Imhoff, 20 January 1482'). In Germanisches Nationalmuseum Nürnberg, IA 19, Nr. 22b. CoMOR online exposition 'Foires, villes et marchands (1350–1600)/Messen, Städte und Kaufleute (1350–1600)', https://fairs-in-history.huma-num.fr/expo/online/theme_lyon_4?object=titre_creance (29 May 2024).

Wirtshausrechnung des Erfurter Kaufmanns David Nacke auf der Frankfurter Fastenmesse, um 1590 ('Tavern invoice of the Erfurt merchant David Nacke at the Frankfurt fair in Lent, c. 1590').

In Stadtarchiv Erfurt, 0–1/8–208 (7). CoMOR online exposition 'Foires, villes et marchands (1350–1600)/Messen, Städte und Kaufleute (1350–1600)', https://fairs-in-history.huma-num.fr/expo/online/theme_lyon_4?object=facture_taverne (29 May 2024).

Literature

Aerts, Erik. Fairs: European Fairs. In *The Oxford Encyclopedia of Economic History*, vol. 2, Joel Mokyr (ed.). Oxford: Oxford University Press, 2003, 253–256.

Alfani, Guido. Epidemics, Inequality, and Poverty in Preindustrial and Early Industrial Times. *Journal of Economic Literature* 60:1 (2022): 3–40.

Alfani, Guido, Thomas E. Murphy. Plague and Lethal Epidemics in the Pre-industrial World. *Journal of Economic History* 77:1 (2017): 314–343.

Alfani, Guido, Victoria Gierok, Felix Schaff. Economic Inequality in Preindustrial Germany, ca. 1300–1850. *Journal of Economic History* 82:1 (2022): 88–125.

Ammann, Hektor. Die deutschen und die schweizerischen Messen des Mittelalters. In *La foire*, John Gilissen (ed.). Brussels: Librairie Encyclopédique, 1953. 149–173.

Ammann, Hektor. Die Nördlinger Messe im Mittelalter. In *Aus Verfassungs- und Landesgeschichte. Festschrift zum 70. Geburtstag von Theodor Mayer, dargebracht von seinen Schülern und Freunden*, vol. 1–2, Heinrich Büttner, Otto Feger, Bruno Meyer (eds.). Lindau, Constance: Jan Thorbecke, 1955, 283–315.

Ammann, Hektor. Vom geographischen Wissen einer deutschen Handelsstadt des Spätmittelalters. *Ulm und Oberschwaben* 34 (1955): 39–65.

Arthur, W. Brian. Competing Technologies, Increasing Returns, and Lock-in by Historical Events. *Economic Journal* 99 (1989): 116–131.

Börner, Lars, Battista Severgnini. Epidemic Trade. *Diskussionsbeiträge, No. 2011/12, Freie Universität Berlin, Fachbereich Wirtschaftswissenschaft.* Berlin 2011.

Börner, Lars, Battista Severgnini. Measuring and Comparing Economic Interaction Based on the Paths and Speed of Infections: The Case Study of the Spread of the Justinianic Plague and Black Death. In *Complexity Economics: Building a New Approach to Ancient Economic History*, Koenraad Verboven (ed.). London: Palgrave Macmillan, 2021, 327–356.

Boockmann, Hartmut. *Die Stadt im späten Mittelalter*. 3rd ed. Munich: C.H. Beck, 1994.

Blaschke, Karlheinz. Die Kurfürsten von Sachsen als Förderer der Leipziger Messe. Von der landesgeschichtlichen Grundlegung zur kontinentalen Wirkung. In *Leipzigs Messen, 1497–1997*, 61–73.

Brübach, Nils. *Die Reichsmessen von Frankfurt am Main, Leipzig und Braunschweig (14.–18. Jahrhundert)*. Stuttgart: Franz Steiner, 1994.

Cavaciocchi, Simonetta (ed.). *Fiere e mercati nella integrazione delle economie europee, secc. XIII–XVIII. Atti della "Trentaduesima Settimana di Studi" 8–12 maggio 2000.* Florence: Le Monnier Università, 2001.

David, Paul A. Clio and the Economics of QWERTY. *American Economic Review* 75:2 (1985): 332–337.

David, Paul A. Why are Institutions the 'Carriers of History'? Path Dependence and the Evolution of Conventions, Organizations and Institutions. *Structural Change and Economic Dynamics* 5:2 (1994): 205–220.

Denzel, Markus A. Die Leipziger Märkte vom 12. Jahrhundert bis zu den Privilegierungen von 1497, 1507 und 1514. In *Geschichte der Stadt Leipzig*, vol. 1: Von den Anfängen bis zur Reformation, Enno Bünz (ed.). Leipzig: Leipziger Universitätsverlag, 2015, 322–340.

Denzel, Markus A. Märkte und Messen im vorindustriellen Alpenraum. Ihre Bedeutung für den trans- und inneralpinen Handelsverkehr. In *Transits—Transit. Infrastructures et sociétié de l'Antiquité à nos jours/Infrastrukturen und Gesellschaft von der Antike bis heute*, Anne-Lise Head-König, Luigi Lorenzetti, Andrea Bonoldi (eds.). Zurich: Chronos, 2016, 43–62.

Denzel, Markus A. Das System der Messen in Europa—Rückgrat des Handels, des Zahlungsverkehrs und der Kommunikation (9. bis 19. Jahrhundert). In *Europäische Messegeschichte.* Denzel (ed.). Cologne et al.: Böhlau, 2018, 369–431.

Denzel, Markus A. (ed.). *Europäische Messegeschichte 9.–19. Jahrhundert.* Cologne et al.: Böhlau, 2018.

Dubler, Anne-Marie. Märkte. *Historisches Lexikon der Schweiz.* 27 October 2009. https://hls-dhs-dss.ch/de/articles/013739/2009-10-27/ (29 May 2024).

Edwards, Jeremy, Sheilagh C. Ogilvie. What Lessons for Economic Development Can We Draw from the Champagne Fairs? *Explorations in Economic History* 49:2 (2012): 131–148.

Eibl, Elfie-Marita. Kaiser Friedrich III. (1440–1493) und die Wettiner. Aspekte des Verhältnisses Zentralgewalt—Fürsten in einer königsfernen Landschaft. *Neues Archiv für Sächsische Geschichte* 71 (2000): 27–51.

Eiden, Herbert. The Fairs of Leipzig and the Eastern European Economies, 15th–18th centuries. In *Fiere e mercati*, Cavaciocchi (ed.). 723–739.

Ennen, Edith. *Die europäische Stadt des Mittelalters.* 4th ed. Göttingen: Vandenhoeck & Ruprecht, 1987.

Epstein, Stephan R. Regional Fairs, Institutional Innovation, and Economic Growth in Late Medieval Europe. *Economic History Review* 47:3 (1994): 459–482.

Epstein, Stephan R. Fairs, Towns, and States in Renaissance Europe. In *Fiere e mercati*, Cavaciocchi (ed.). 71–90.

Ertl, Thomas. *Bauern und Banker. Wirtschaft im Mittelalter.* Darmstadt: WBG Theiss, 2021.

Ewert, Ulf Christian. Collective Goods in the Middle Ages, In *Methods in Premodern Economic History: Case Studies from the Holy Roman Empire, c. 1300–c. 1600*, Ulla Kypta, Julia Bruch, Tanja Skambraks (eds.). London: Palgrave Macmillan, 2019: 64–67.

Ewert, Ulf Christian. Limited Use of Money in Late-medieval Commerce: Economic Considerations on the Viability of Hanseatic Reciprocal Trade. In *Monetisation and Commercialisation in the Baltic Sea, 1050–1450*, Dariusz Adamczyk, Beata Możejko (eds.). London, New York: Routledge 2021, 77–97.

Ewert, Ulf Christian. Zusammenfassung: Vertrauen in vormodernen ökonomischen Tauschbeziehungen—eine Zwischenbilanz. In *Ökonomisch bestimmtes Handeln in der Vormoderne—eine Frage des Vertrauens?*, Jan Hirschbiegel, Stefanie von Welser, Angelika Westermann (eds.). Husum: Matthiesen, 2021, 299–311.

Ewert, Ulf Christian. Handelsräume der vormodernen Stadt: Raumzeitliche Aspekte des Messehandels am Beispiel der Nördlinger Pfingstmesse. *Moderne Stadtgeschichte* 54:2 (2023): 147–172.

Ewert, Ulf Christian, Stephan Selzer. Social Networks. In *A Companion to the Hanseatic League*, Donald J. Harreld (ed.). Leiden, Boston: Brill, 2015, 162–193.

Ewert, Ulf Christian, Stephan Selzer. *Institutions of Hanseatic Trade: Studies on the Political Economy of a Medieval Network Organisation.* Frankfurt am Main: Peter Lang, 2016.

Ewert, Ulf Christian, Susanne Rau, Leif Scheuermann. Räumliche Konfigurationen des Messehandels im frühneuzeitlichen Europa: Gedruckte Messekalender des 16. und 17. Jahrhunderts und ihre computergestützte Analyse. *Vierteljahrschrift für Sozial- und Wirtschaftsgeschichte* 110:4 (2023): 494–541.

Fouquet, Gerhard, Hans-Jörg Gilomen (eds.). *Netzwerke im europäischen Handel des Mittelalters.* Ostfildern: Jan Thorbecke, 2010.

Fütterer, Pierre. Die Via regia—Kritische Bemerkungen zu einem “Mythos” oder: Auf der Suche nach der “Königlichen Straße”. In *WegBegleiter. Interdisziplinäre Beiträge zur Altwege- und Burgenforschung. Festschrift für Bernd W. Bahn zu seinem 80. Geburtstag*, Martin Freudenreich, Pierre Fütterer, Anna Schwieder (eds.). Langenweißbach: Beier & Beran—Archäologische Fachliteratur, 2019, 169–195.

Gilissen, John. La notion de la foire à la lumière comparative. In *La foire*, Gilissen (ed.), 323–333.

Gravelle, Hugh, Ray Rees. *Microeconomics*. 3rd ed. Harlow: Pearson Education, 2004.

Henn, Volker. Über Jahrmärkte in den östlichen Niederlanden im späten Mittelalter. In *Märkte, Messen und Waren*, Holbach, Sarnowsky (eds.), 67–96.

Heydenreich, Fritz. *Die Geschichte der Naumburger Peter-Pauls-Messe*. PhD diss., University of Halle (Saale), 1927.

Held, Wieland. Der Messeplatz Naumburg und sein Verhältnis zur Leipziger Messe am Anfang des 16. Jahrhunderts. In *Leipzigs Messen, 1497–1997*, 75–86.

Hildebrand, Gustav, Ludwig Kramarczyk. *Des Reiches Straße. Alte Frankfurt-Leipziger Handelsstraße*. Würzburg: Weidlich Flechsig, 1990.

Holbach, Rudolf. Märkte, Messen und Waren als Thema der hansischen Geschichte. In *Märkte, Messen und Waren*, Holbach, Sarnowsky (eds.)., 1–32.

Holbach, Rudolf, Jürgen Sarnowsky (eds.). *Märkte, Messen und Waren im hansischen Handel*. Wismar: callidus. Verlag wissenschaftlicher Publikationen, 2021.

Holtermann, Bart, Angela Huang. Geospatial Methods and the Premodern Economy: Mapping the Institutional Landscapes of Northern Europe, 1350–1650. *Jahrbuch für Wirtschaftsgeschichte* 64:1 (2023): 179–212.

Houtte, Jan Albert van. Messe (Handelsmesse), I. Westlicher Bereich. *Lexikon des Mittelalters*, vol. 6, Munich, Zurich: Artemis & Winkler, 1993, cols. 558–560.

Huang, Angela. Von Grautuch und Leinwand: Die Stellung der Produktionslandschaften des Hanseraums im spätmittelalterlichen und frühneuzeitlichen Textilhandel. In *Märkte, Messen und Waren*, Holbach, Sarnowsky (eds.), 157–186.

Irsigler, Franz. Jahrmärkte und Messesysteme im westlichen Reichsgebiet bis ca. 1250. In *Europäische Messen und Märktesysteme in Mittelalter und Neuzeit*, Peter Johanek, Heinz Stoob (eds.). Cologne, Weimar, Vienna: Böhlau, 1996, 1–33.

Irsigler, Franz. Zur Hierarchie der Jahrmärkte. In *Ausstellungskatalog “Spätmittelalter am Oberrhein. Große Landesausstellung Baden-Württemberg”, Staatliche Kunsthalle Karlsruhe, 29. September 2001–3. Februar 2002*, vol. 1–2, Sönke Lorenz, Markus Dekiert (eds.). Stuttgart: Jan Thorbecke, 2001, 89–99.

Irsigler, Franz. Messehandel—Hansehandel. *Hansische Geschichtsblätter* 120 (2002): 33–50.

Irsigler, Franz. Messen, Jahrmärkte und Stadtentwicklung in Europa. Mittelalter und Frühe Neuzeit. In *Messen, Jahrmärkte und Stadtentwicklung*, Irsigler, Pauly (eds.), 1–24.

Irsigler, Franz, Michel Pauly (eds.). *Messen, Jahrmärkte und Stadtentwicklung in Europa*. Trier: Porta Alba, 2007.

Jahnke, Carsten. Die schonischen Messen. Eine freie Marktwirtschaft in einem angeblich rigiden System. In *Märkte, Messen und Waren*, Holbach, Sarnowsky, 33–66.

Jaser, Christian. Urban Palio and Scharlach Races in Fifteenth- and Early Sixteenth-Century Italy and Germany. *International Journal of the History of Sport* 37:3–4 (2020): 272–287.

Kardasz, Cezary. Der Export von Holz und Waldwaren aus dem südlichen Ostseeraum im Spätmittelalter. In *Märkte, Messen und Waren*, Holbach, Sarnowsky (eds.), 203–228.

Kießling, Rolf. Die Nördlinger Pfingstmesse im 15./16. Jahrhundert. Aufstieg und Strukturwandel eines süddeutschen Wirtschaftszentrums. *Jahrbuch des Historischen Vereins für Nördlingen und das Ries* 29 (1999): 69–95.

Krafft, Otfried. Eine Fehde, ein Reichsachtverfahren und das Ende zweier Grafschaften. Die Kaufleute Veckinchusen im Streit mit den letzten Grafen von Ziegenhain. *Zeitschrift des Vereins für hessische Geschichte* 111 (2006): 31–62.

Kreps, David M. *Game Theory and Economic Modelling*. Oxford: Clarendon Press, 1990.

Kruse, Holger. Pariser Messen des Mittelalters. In *Netzwerke im europäischen Handel*, Fouquet, Gilomen (eds.). 101–134.

Lopez, Robert S. *The Commercial Revolution of the Middle Ages, 950–1350*. Englewood Cliffs (NJ): Prentice Hall, 1971.

Lütge, Friedrich. Der Untergang der Nürnberger Heiltumsmesse. *Jahrbücher für Nationalökonomie und Statistik* 178 (1965): 133–157.

Lütge, Friedrich. Die Nürnberger Heiltumsmesse (erw. Fassung). In *Friedrich Lütge. Beiträge zur Sozial- und Wirtschaftsgeschichte. Gesammelte Abhandlungen*, Eckhart Schremmer (ed.). Stuttgart: Gustav Fischer, 1970, 193–215.

McKendrick, Neil. The Consumer Revolution of Eighteenth-Century England. In *The Birth of a Consumer Society: The Commercialization of Eighteenth-Century England*, Neil McKendrick, John Brewer, John Harold Plumb (eds.). London: Europa Publications, 1982, 9–33.

Mitterauer, Michael. Jahrmarktkontinuität und Stadtentstehung. In *Markt und Stadt im Mittelalter. Beiträge zur historischen Zentralitätsforschung*, Michael Mitterauer (ed.). Stuttgart: Anton Hiersemann, 1980, 154–191.

Müller, Winfried, Swen Steinberg (eds.). *Menschen unterwegs. Die via regia und ihre Akteure. Essayband zur 3. Sächsischen Landesausstellung "via regia—800 Jahre Bewegung und Begegnung", Görlitz, 21. Mai bis 31. Oktober 2011*. Dresden: Sandstein, 2011.

Munro, John H. The 'New Institutional Economics' and the Changing Fortunes of Fairs in Medieval and Early Modern Europe: The Textile Trades, Warfare, and Transaction Costs. *Vierteljahrschrift für Sozial und Wirtschaftsgeschichte* 88:1 (2001): 1–47.

Pauly, Michel. Les marchés annuels en Europe aux XIVᵉ–XVIᵉ siècles. Études régionales et essai de classification. In *Fiere e mercati*, Cavaciocchi, 669–683.

Pauly, Michel. Der Beitrag der Messen und Märkte zur mittelalterlichen Integration Europas. In *Messen, Jahrmärkte*, Irsigler, Pauly (eds.) 285–314.

Pauly, Michel. Jahrmärkte in Europa vom 14. bis zum 16. Jahrhundert. Regionale Untersuchungen und der Versuch einer Typologie. In *Messen, Jahrmärkte und Stadtentwicklung*, Irsigler, Pauly (eds.)., 25–40.

Pauly, Michel. Vom regionalen Messesystem zum internationalen Netz von Messestädten. In *Netzwerke im europäischen Handel*, Fouquet, Gilomen, 49–100.

Pawlow, Kamen. *Via Regia, Königsstrasse oder Hohe Strasse. Thüringer Impressionen. Begleitheft zur Wanderausstellung Erfurt—Bonn—Eisenach—Gotha*. Erfurt: Europäisches Kultur- und Informationszentrum, 1998.

Petersen, Niels. Raum und Zeit im Landverkehr um 1500. Die Viabundus-Karte des vormodernen Verkehrs in Norddeutschland. In *Märkte, Messen und Waren*, Holbach, Sarnowsky (eds.), 229–252.

Petersen, Niels, Bart Holtermann, Angela Huang. Digitale Werkzeuge zur Analyse von Straßen und Wasserwegen als Rückgrat eines vormodernen Märktenetzwerks in Zentral- und Ostmitteleuropa. *Zeitschrift für Ostmitteleuropaforschung/Journal of East Central European Studies* 70:3 (2021): 325–356.

Peyer, Hans Conrad. Die Märkte der Schweiz in Mittelalter und Neuzeit. In *Gewässer, Grenzen und Märkte in der Schweizergeschichte*, Hans-Conrad Peyer (ed.). Zurich: Schulthess, 1979, 19–38.

Radeff, Anne. Foires. *Dictionnaire historique de la Suisse*. 9 June 2008. https://hls-dhs-dss.ch/fr/articles/013740/2008-06-09/. (29 May 2024).

Reincke, Heinrich. Die Hamburger Messe und die Weltverkehrspläne Karls IV. *Zeitschrift des Vereins für Hamburgische Geschichte* 23 (1912): 85–88.

Rössner, Philipp Robinson. Messen und Jahrmärkte in England im Spiegel der gesamtwirtschaftlichen Entwicklung und der beginnenden europäischen Wirtschaft, ca. 1000–1800 n. Chr. In *Europäische Messegeschichte*, Denzel (ed.), 83–114.

Rothmann, Michael. "Gab gott gnad und gros gluk, gwin". Ein Beitrag über den deutschen Kaufmann im Spätmittelalter. In *Brücke zwischen den Völkern—Zur Geschichte der Frankfurter Messe*, vol. 2: Beiträge zur Geschichte der Frankfurter Messe, Patricia Stahl (ed.). Frankfurt am Main: Union-Druckerei- und Verlagsanstalt, 1991, 253–262.

Rothmann, Michael. *Die Frankfurter Messen im Mittelalter*. Stuttgart: Franz Steiner, 1998.

Rothmann, Michael. Überall ist Jahrmarkt. Entwicklungstendenzen der Institution des periodischen Marktes in Zentraleuropa vom 14. bis zum 17. Jahrhundert. In *Fiere e mercati*, Cavaciocchi (ed.), 91–108.

Rothmann, Michael. Marktnetze und Netzwerke im spätmittelalterlichen oberdeutschen Wirtschaftsraum, In *Netzwerke im europäischen Handel*, Fouquet, Gilomen (eds.), 135–188.

Rothmann, Michael. Marktkonzepte im mittelalterlichen Europa unter besonderer Berücksichtigung des Heiligen Römischen Reiches. In *Europäische Messegeschichte*, Denzel, 181–202.

Rothmann, Michael. Messezeit: Handelsrhythmen und Jahreszeit. In *Taktungen und Rhythmen. Raumzeitliche Perspektiven interdisziplinär*, Sabine Schmolinsky, Diana Hitzke, Heiner Stahl (eds.). Berlin, Boston: De Gruyter Oldenbourg, 2019, 25–39.

Sarnowsky, Jürgen, Meike Möller. Märkte, Marktprivilegien und Marktrecht. https://www.spaetmittelalter.uni-hamburg.de/spaetmittelalter/Lehre/Ergebnisse/Hamburg/themen/MaerkteMarktprivilegienUndMarktrecht.html (29 May 2024). Unpublished manuscript, Hamburg. (29 May 2024).

Sarnowsky, Jürgen. Südwaren auf den Märkten im südlichen Ostseeraum. In *Märkte, Messen und Waren*, Holbach, Sarnowsky (eds.), 187–202.

Schirmer, Uwe. *Der Finanz- und Messeplatz Leipzig vom 13. bis zur Mitte des 17. Jahrhunderts. Geldwesen—Waren- und Zahlungsverkehr—Rentengeschäfte*. Stuttgart, Leipzig: S. Hirzel, 2021.

Schötz, Susanne. Leipzig im Schnittpunkt von via regia und via imperia. Über Bedeutung und Akteure des Messehandels. In *via regia—800 Jahre Bewegung und Begegnung. Katalog zur 3. Sächsischen Landesausstellung, Görlitz, 21. Mai bis 31. Oktober 2011*, Roland Enke, Bettina Probst (eds.). Dresden: Sandstein, 2011, 86–90.

Scott, Tom. *Regional Identity and Economic Change: The Upper Rhine, 1450–1600*. Oxford: Clarendon Press, 1997.

Selzer, Stephan. Als Hansehistoriker an sächsischen Geleitstellen: Wagen, Waren und Fuhrleute im Landverkehr zwischen Nord und Süd um 1500. In *Märkte, Messen und Waren*, Holbach, Sarnowsky (eds.), 129–156.

Selzer, Stephan, Ulf Christian Ewert. Verhandeln und Verkaufen, Vernetzen und Vertrauen. Über die Netzwerkstruktur des hansischen Handels. *Hansische Geschichtsblätter* 119 (2001): 135–161.

Selzer, Stephan, Ulf Christian Ewert. Nord- und Ostseeraum, 500–1600. In *Handbuch globale Handelsräume und Handelsrouten. Von der Antike bis zur Gegenwart*, Mark Häberlein, Markus A. Denzel (eds.). Berlin: De Gruyter Oldenbourg, 2024, 261–303.

Spieß, Josef. *Die Nördlinger Messen im Mittelalter*. PhD diss., University of Munich, 1923.

Spieß, Werner. *Das Marktprivileg. Die Entwicklung von Marktprivileg und Marktrecht insbesondere auf Grund der Kaiserurkunden*. Heidelberg: Winter, 1916.

Steinfeld, Ludwig. *Chronik einer Straße. Die alte Straße von Frankfurt nach Leipzig: Geschichte, Ereignisse, Reiseberichte*. Horb am Neckar: Geiger, 1994.

Steinmeyer, Heinrich. *Die Entstehung und Entwicklung der Nördlinger Pfingstmesse im Spätmittelalter mit einem Ausblick ins 19. Jahrhundert*. Nördlingen: Georg Wagner, 1960.

Steinmeyer, Heinrich. Die Entwicklung der Ulmer Sommermesse (des späteren Veitsmarktes) und ihre Einordnung in das süddeutsche Handelssystem bis zum Ende der Reichsstadtzeit. *Vierteljahrschrift für Sozial- und Wirtschaftsgeschichte* 77:3 (1990): 323–349.

Straube, Manfred. Die Leipziger Messen zur Zeit der Privilegierungen als Mittler nach Ostmitteleuropa. In *Leipzigs Messen 1497–1997*, 121–132.

Straube, Manfred. *Geleitswesen und Warenverkehr im thüringisch-sächsischen Raum zu Beginn der Frühen Neuzeit*. Cologne, Weimar, Vienna: Böhlau, 2014.

Straube, Manfred. *Wirtschaftliche Frequenzen der Leipziger Großen Märkte/Messen. Statistische Zeugnisse aus den Leipziger Stadtrechnungen 1471/72 bis 1814/15*. Leipzig: Leipziger Universitätsverlag, 2015.

Sydow, Jörg, Georg Schreyögg, Jochen Koch. Organizational Path Dependence: Opening the Black Box. *Academy of Management Review* 34:4 (2009): 689–709.

Szilagyi, Miklos N. An Investigation of N-person Prisoners' Dilemmas. *Complex Systems* 14:2 (2003), 155–174.

Veronesi, Marco. Wessen Freiheit. Messeprivileg, Freihandel und städtische Gerichtsbarkeit im späten Mittelalter am Beispiel Nördlingens. *Annales Mercaturae* 3 (2017): 23–49.

Veronesi, Marco. "Bös gelt und liderlich volck": die Stadt, der Rat und die lieben Gäste. In *800 Jahre Nördlinger Mess. Von der internationalen Fernhandelsmesse zum größten Volksfest Nordschwabens*, Stadtarchiv Nördlingen (ed.). Olching: WIKOMmedia Verlag für kommunale- und Wirtschaftsmedien 2019, 12–25.

Voges, Dietmar-Henning. Werden und Wirken der Pfingstmesse. In *Die Reichsstadt Nördlingen. 12 Kapitel aus ihrer Geschichte*, Dietmar-Henning Voges (ed.). Munich: C.H. Beck, 1988, 47–69.

Weber, Max. *Wirtschaftsgeschichte: Abriss der universalen Sozial- und Wirtschafts-Geschichte*, Sigmund Hellmann, Melchior Palyi (eds.). Munich, Leipzig: Duncker & Humblot, 1923.

Zwahr, Hartmut, Thomas Topfstedt, Günter Bentele (eds.). *Leipzigs Messen 1497–1997. Gestaltwandel—Umbrüche—Neubeginn*, vol. I: 1497–1914, Cologne et al.: Böhlau, 1999.

Nicolas Sarzeaud

Festa and *Feria*: on the exhibitions of Christ relics during fairs and the coordination of sanctuary and merchant calendars in the Middle Ages

Among the many avenues opened up by Jacques Le Goff for an anthropology of the Middle Ages is the dialectical opposition between two conceptions of time that could be summed up in these two irreconcilable propositions: "time belongs only to God" (the time of the Church) and "time is money" (the time of the merchant).[1] According to this logic, the rise of commerce would have been accompanied by a gradual secularisation of time, which would have become more measured and controlled, gradually freed from the hold of the Church.

Recent historiography has nuanced this opposition. Firstly, it has reassessed the relationship between the Church and money. Giacomo Todeschini has shown that we must abandon the naïve picture of a medieval Church reluctant to the idea of wealth. At the very least, the clergy participated in the emergence of a new conception of wealth, valued by Christian discourses as well as new techniques and practices for the administration of goods and capital.[2] On the very question of time management, Jean-Claude Schmitt underlines the nuances to be brought to a supposed rationalisation of time and shows that these new market rhythms did not make the "old rhythms" disappear.[3]

Fairs, often named after the saint of the day, are a good example of the ever-present synchrony between professional and religious time. Moreover, the Church was far from turning its back on these commercial events. On the one hand, the bishops and abbeys were responsible for founding numerous fairs and

1 Jacques Le Goff. Au Moyen Âge: temps de l'Église et temps du marchand. *Annales E.S.C.* 15:3 (1960): 417–433.

2 Giacomo Todeschini. *I mercanti e il tempio. La società cristiana e il circolo virtuoso della ricchezza fra medioevo ed età moderna.* Bologna: Il Mulino, 2002. See also Clément Lenoble. Avant l'ascèse intramondaine. Comptabilités ecclésiastiques, gouvernement et rationalité économique (XIIIe–XVe siècles). *Archives de Sciences Sociales des Religions, 66e année*, 195 (2021): 51–81; Susanne Rau. Rhythmusanalyse nach Lefebvre. In *Taktungen und Rhythmen. Raumzeitliche Perspektiven interdisziplinär*, Sabine Schmolinsky, Diana Hitzke, Heiner Stahl (eds.). Berlin, Boston: De Gruyter, 2018, 9–24. I would like to thank both Jean-Louis Gaulin and Suzanne Amy Foxley very much for their help and comments.

3 Jean-Claude Schmitt. *Les rythmes au Moyen Âge.* Paris: Gallimard, 2016, 556–563.

https://doi.org/10.1515/9783111621296-003

markets from which they reaped substantial profits.[4] On the other, they accompanied them with rituals—for example, by blessing the fair ground, as happened at the Lendit fair in Saint-Denis which has been documented since the early twelfth century.[5] Étienne de Givry's Pontifical, dating from around 1405–1410, includes among its additions the text of this blessing of the field, performed by the bishop of Paris, and an image of this ritual.[6]

This case is not unique: many markets and fairs in the Middle Ages saw their calendar coincide with that of specific religious events and particularly with that of the *ostensions*, the ceremonies at which the relics were displayed. In these cases, did the merchants align their calendar with that of the relics or did the relics follow the merchants' rhythm? Our aim here is to study a series of synchronies between the ostensions of relics and fairs. We will confine ourselves to the relics of Christ, especially to the Holy Shrouds which were regularly the subject of this type of event.[7]

The invention of a pious origin: the cases of Saint-Denis and Saint-Corneille of Compiègne fairs

An important document narrated the origins of both the cult of the relics of Saint-Denis and the Lendit fair—the *Descriptio qualiter Karolus Magnus clavum et coronam Domini [. . .] ad Sanctum Dionysium retulerit*,[8] written by a monk of the abbey during the second half of the eleventh century. According to this legend,

4 Michel Bur. Les autres foires de Champagne. In *Städtelandschaft—Städtenetz—zentralörtliches Gefüge. Ansätze und Befunde zur Geschichte der Städte im hohen und späten Mittelalter*, Monika Escher, Alfred Haverkamp, Frank G. Hirschman (eds.). Mainz: Philipp von Zabern, 2000, 349–365.
5 Rolf Große. Reliques du Christ et foires de Saint-Denis au XIe siècle. A propos de la *Descriptio clavi et corone domini. Revue d'histoire de l'Église de France* 87 (2001): 357–375.
6 "Ordo in die benedictionis indicti," Pontifical d'Étienne de Givry, Paris, Bibliothèque nationale de France (hereafter BnF), ms. lat. 962, 264r°–268v°.
7 For this inquiry, I used several documents transcribed from my doctoral thesis. See Nicolas Sarzeaud. Copie et culte. Le Suaire du Christ, une relique reproductible (XIVe–XVIe s.). PhD diss., EHESS, 2021 and *Les Suaires du Christ en Occident du Moyen Âge à nos jours*. Paris: Cerf, 2024.
8 Anne Lombard-Jourdan. Les foires de l'abbaye de Saint-Denis: revue des données et révision des opinions admises. *Bibliothèque de l'École des chartes* 145 (1987): 274–338. On this text, see also Matthew Gabriele. The Provenance of the *Descriptio qualiter Karolus Magnus*: Remembering the Carolingians in the Entourage of King Philip I (1060–1108) before the First Crusade. *Viator* 39:2 (2008): 93–117; Carla Rossi. Le Voyage de Charlemagne: le parcours vers Jérusalem et les reliques. *Critica del testo* 2:2 (1999): 619–653; Große, Reliques du Christ.

Charlemagne was called to the rescue by the Byzantine emperor and regained Jerusalem. He was then rewarded with the gift of a collection of the relics of Christ, the Virgin, and saints, brought them back to Aachen, and made the announcement (*indictum*) of their display to the faithful. The *Descriptio* narrated the unfolding of this ritual and the order given to repeat this *indictum* every year on the Wednesday of the second week of June: this is the Lendit.[9]

This document is very early in the history of the rituals of ostensions. While procession-type celebrations existed earlier, during the early Middle Ages, the term *ostensio* referred only to a specific stage of the *translatio*: when a relic was moved from one place to another, it was briefly exhibited to the crowd of worshippers. Here, Charlemagne was placed in the position of creating a certain mode of organising the ritual, a regular *ostensio*, which gave rise to the Lendit trade fair.[10] This association between the sovereign and the ostension serves as a model, and from the thirteenth century onwards, kings used it in the Sainte-Chapelle.[11]

Of course, Charlemagne never went to Jerusalem, but there's more to the story. At the very time that this text was written, during the second half of the eleventh century, no sources described annual ostensions of relics at Saint-Denis. The only known ritual to which this text may refer was a one-off event—the opening of the reliquaries at Saint-Denis Abbey in 1053–1054, in connection with the appearance of other Saint-Denis relics at Saint-Emmeran Abbey in Regensburg. According to Rolf Große, this event may have given rise to the idea of developing this narrative.[12]

9 *Postea vero rex ipse cum clero dei laudibus vacante in promunctorium quoddam foris iuxta castrum venit secum sancta deferens; deinde circumstanti populo omnique clero que apportaverat prememorata sancta satagebat denudare; preterea qui aderant sancti viri fecerunt sermonem ad populum atque quotannis fieri indixerunt indictum spinee corone domini, clavi et ligni crucis sudariique ac plurimarum sanctarum reliquiarum et hoc semper in Iunio mense et in ebdomada secunda, in ieiunio scilicet quatuor temporum quarta feria.* In *Die Legende Karls des Grossen im 11. und 12. Jahrhundert*, Gerhard Rauschen (ed.). Leipzig: Duncker & Humblot, 1890, 98–125, esp. 120–121. The original can be found at BnF, ms. lat. 12710.

10 Hartmut Kühne. *Ostensio Reliquiarum. Untersuchungen über Entstehung, Ausbreitung, Gestalt und Funktion der Heiltumsweisungen im Römisch-Deutschen Regnum.* Berlin, New York: De Gruyter, 2000. See also Christof L. Diedrichs. *Vom Glauben zum Sehen. Die Sichtbarkeit der Reliquie im Reliquiar. Ein Beitrag zur Geschichte des Sehens.* Berlin: Weissensee, 2001; Gia Toussaint. *Kreuz und Knochen. Reliquien zur Zeit der Kreuzzüge.* Berlin: Reimer, 2011.

11 Murielle Gaude-Ferragu. *Le trésor des rois. Sacré et royauté, des rois maudits aux princes de la Renaissance.* Paris: Perrin, 2022, 167–177, esp. 174–175 for the Carolingian model.

12 Große, Reliques du Christ, 371.

For its part, the Fair of June was already well under way when this text was written. The existence of this fair can be documented since the early Middle Ages, initially in the form of a market, probably spontaneous, institutionalised as the Lendit in connection with the writing of the *Descriptio* and the setting up of an ostension ritual. It experienced significant success in the twelfth and thirteenth centuries. The date on which the *Descriptio* was written is debated, but this narrative of an old and holy foundation was clearly an attempt to provide a Christian origin to an existing economic event in which the abbey was financially interested.[13] The ritual of blessing the fair ground, which appeared in the documentation at the beginning of the twelfth century, was part of this logic: it is described by Abbot Suger around 1140, who also mentioned the presence of pilgrims during fairs.[14]

At the beginning of the fifteenth century, Étienne de Givry's Pontifical described the benediction of the fair ground, after a Mass said on the morning of June 11.[15] The clergy carried a piece of the True Cross in procession through the cemetery, where they sang for the dead, "to the place of the Lendit (*usque ad locum indicti*)" where the bishop began the hymn *O Crux* "holding the relics in his hands (*tenens inter suas manus reliquias*)." On the highest spot (*in altiori loco*), the archdeacon initiated the Kyrie, then the bishop, "holding the relics, turn[ed] towards the East signing the people with the sign of the holy cross," then repeated the motion to the south, west, and north, before singing the *Humilitate nos*.[16]

In addition to this call to humility, the liturgy included psalms—notably Psalm 44, *Deus auribus nostris*—praising the work done by the Lord during his own days, emphasising for the actors of the fair the theme of the working week. Interestingly, this ritual is called *benediction* and not ostension, even though it is the term chosen in the *Descriptio*. It does, however, give the festivity its full religious dimension, placing the places and times of commerce under the *signum* of the Church.

This case is not isolated. In 1092, a charter from the Capetian king, Philip I instituted a fair in honour of the Shroud of Christ at Compiègne. It recounted the

13 Lombard-Jourdan, Les foires, 286–294.

14 Suger, De consecratione ecclesiae sancti Dionysii. In *Œuvres complètes de Suger*, Albert Lecoy de la Marche (ed.). Paris: Renouard, 1867, 216, 230. See also „Vita Ludovici regis", *op. cit.*, 120.

15 Paris, BnF, ms. lat. 962, 264r°–268v°.

16 *Cum vero pontifex primam pertulerit orationem sanctas tenens reliquias vertat se ad orientem signando populum ex eis signo sancte crucis. Cum secundam dixerit se dirigat ad meridiem. Cum tertiam respiciat ad occidentem. Quartam pernunciet versis vultibus ad aquilonem. Eodem modo, ut prius signans populum, ut sit populus dei sancte crucis signo salubri munitus ex omni parte climatis tueatur ab hostibus.* Paris, BnF, ms. lat. 962, f. 266v°.

translation of the relic in the Abbey of Saint-Corneille, which would have taken place a few years earlier, probably on 3 March 1079, in a gold shrine offered by Matilda of Flanders, Queen of England.[17] The Shroud of Compiègne is part of the collection of Charlemagne's relics, and the *Descriptio* tells us that the object was deposited at Saint-Corneille by Charles the Bald before he brought the rest of the collection to Saint-Denis. As Matthew Gabriele has shown, both the *Descriptio* of Saint-Denis and the Charter of Compiègne demonstrated a growing interest within the networks of the Capetian royalty in the figure of Charlemagne, particularly glorified through the narrative of his mythical pilgrimage to Jerusalem.[18]

To commemorate this translation, Philip instituted a fair on Lætare Sunday, at the half of Lent, "*Mi-Karesme*" in Middle French. It was initially the fair of the Abbey of Saint-Corneille, but a disjunction occurred in the twelfth century between a three-day fair benefiting the abbey and a two-week fair benefiting the city of Compiègne and the king. The fair was at its peak during the thirteenth and early fourteenth centuries but declined after the raids of the Hundred Years' War in northern France.[19]

Although Mi-Karesme was placed under the patronage of the Shroud, the documentation does not mention any regular ostensions. The only ritual known to us, at a late date, is the placing of a candle by the town in front of the relic on the day of Lætare.[20] Moreover, as in Saint-Denis, a market was already active in the Carolingian era: after the *translatio*, Philipp just added some special rights to the abbey. In both cases, then, the cult of the relic appeared after the economic event, used as a means of endowing it with a Christian founding narrative, situating their *raison d'être* around the relics of Christ that these shrines claim to have possessed for a long time. In these two cases, it was not the merchants who secularised the Christian calendar but, on the contrary, sanctuaries who gave religious meaning to secular events.

17 Philip I of France. Charter on the Shroud's *translatio* (1092). In *Cartulaire de l'abbaye de Saint-Corneille de Compiègne I*, Émile Morel (ed.). Montdidier: Bellin, 1904, 52–53.

18 Gabriele, Provenance; Matthew Gabriele. *An Empire of Memory. The Legend of Charlemagne, the Franks, and Jerusalem Before the First Crusade*. Oxford: Oxford University Press, 2011, 58–60.

19 Louis Carolus-Barré. Le mi-Karesme, foire de Compiègne au Moyen Âge et sa survie jusqu'en 1792. *Bulletin de la Société historique de Compiègne* 26 (1979): 19–72.

20 "Item jour le fraict du cierge du sainct Suaire renouvellé le jour du dimanche Letare pour ce: X sous parisis." Municipal Deliberations of Compiègne, 30 August 1530, Compiègne, Archives municipales, BB18, f. 65r°. See also Sarzeaud, Copie et culte, 32.

The rise of ostensions and their connection with fairs

Local festivities in honour of the relics—known as *festa reliquiarum*—first appeared in the eleventh century and became more common by the thirteenth century. They were celebrated through dedicated liturgical services but could also be the subject of processions or ostensions.[21] These displays tended to become regular occurrences, with fixed dates on which pilgrims converged to see the relics.

The precise chronology of this change is difficult to establish due to the scarcity of prescriptive documents. One exception, however, has been much debated. In 1215, the sixty-second canon of the Fourth Lateran Council observed:

> Because some people exhibit the relics of the Saints for money (*reliquias exponunt venales*) and show them indiscriminately (*ostendunt passim*), the Christian religion has often been diminished. In order to prevent this from happening any further, we decree that ancient relics shall no longer be displayed outside their reliquaries or exhibited for money.[22]

An ambiguity remains here: at what point should an ostension of relics be considered venal? If any kind of collection of offerings is targeted, then would this be tantamount to banning ostensions altogether? Most of the canonists of the thirteenth and fourteenth centuries perceived it as a more limited ban—the prohibition of the trade of relics, which was flourishing under the reign of Innocent III, just after the sacking of Constantinople in 1204.[23]

The synodal assemblies of the thirteenth and fourteenth centuries proposed various interpretations of this canon, some of which, by slavishly repeating the formula of Lateran IV, seemed to forbid in general the removal of relics from their shrines.[24] Others treated the adverb *passim*—"here and there"—as the key

---

21 Kühne, *Ostensio Reliquiarum*, 522–580; François Dolbeau. La prédication pour les fêtes de reliques. In *Ad libros! Mélanges d'études médiévales offerts à Denise Angers et Joseph-Claude Poulin*, Jean-François Cottier, Martin Gravel, Sébastien Rossignol (eds.). Montréal: Presses de l'Université de Montréal, 2010, 139–161.

22 *Cum ex eo, quod quidam Sanctorum reliquias exponunt venales et eas passim ostendunt, christianae religioni detractum sit saepius: ne posterum detrahatur, praesenti decreto statuimus, ut antiquae reliquiae amodo extra capsam nullatenus ostendantur nec exponantur venales.* In *Les décrets: Nicée I à Latran V. Les Conciles œcuméniques*, vol. II, Giuseppe Alberigo (ed.). Paris: Cerf, 1994, 560–561.

23 Kühne, *Ostensio Reliquiarum*, 556–558.

24 The Synod of Bordeaux in 1255 prescribed "quod amodo reliquiae extra capsam nullatenus extrahantur, nec exponantur venales." See *Sacrorum conciliorum nova et amplissima collection*, Giovanni Domenico Mansi (ed.). Venice: Zatta, 1758–1798, t. 23, col. 85. The Synod of Bayeux in 1300 prescribed: "quod antiquae reliquiae amodo extra capsam nullatenus ostendatur, nec ve-

to reading this prohibition. For example, the Synod of Budapest in 1259 forbade "the relics to be shown outside the shrines except on special feasts and, for this purpose, to pilgrims arriving out of devotion, as prescribed by the praiseworthy custom of certain Churches."[25]

Fixed ostensions would therefore be authorised, but less regulated practices would be in sight of the Church. For example, around 1200, Philip Augustus granted a "*sauf-conduit*" to the religious of Saint-Corneille of Compiègne who were transporting the relic within the royal domain during an itinerant quest.[26] We can imagine that ostensions were made "*passim*" on this occasion. Whatever the correct interpretation of the sixty-second canon of Lateran IV, the situation observed from the end of the thirteenth century onwards was indeed the same as that described in Budapest—in an increasing number of places, regular rituals of ostension on fixed dates were documented.

One of them is none other than Rome. Boniface VIII instituted a jubilee year in 1300, following the same principle of concentrating the flow of pilgrims over a specific period of time, during which the clergy performed an ostension of the relics, in particular of Saint Veronica in the Vatican. For Hartmut Kühne, the success of the jubilees may have served as a model, explaining the marked expansion of relic ostension liturgies in the fourteenth and fifteenth centuries.[27]

The period saw the emergence of numerous events combining fairs and ostensions of relics. In some cases, it is possible to document the intention of associating a fair with an existing liturgy, taking advantage of the influx of the faithful. This is the case for the Shroud of Cadouin, transferred to Toulouse in September 1392. A letter from Charles VI, dated January 1393 and sent to his seneschal, mentioned the following request from the '*capitouls*':

> [They] told us that, since the Holy Shroud [. . .] has recently been brought to Toulouse, they hope that many people will come out of devotion to see and adore it. For this reason, it would be profitable for the public institution of the city if two fairs were held [. . .] during

nales exponantur." See *Sacrorum conciliorum*, Mansi (ed.), t. 25, col. 68. The Synod of Marsac in 1326 and Lavaur in 1368 prescribed: "ut antiquae reliquiae amodo extra capsas vel vasa nullatenus ostendatur, nec exponantur venales." See *Sacrorum conciliorum*, Mansi (ed.), t. 25, col. 793, t. 26, col. 522.

25 "ut amodo reliquiae extra capsam nullatenus ostendatur, nisi in praecipuis festivitatibus velad hoc ex devotione concurrentibus peregrinis, sicut quarumdam ecclesiarum laudabilis consuetudo exposcit." See *Sacrorum conciliorum*, Mansi (ed.), t. 24, col. 283.

26 Philippe Auguste. Safe-conduct letters for Shroud carriers. In *Cartulaire*, Morel (ed.), vol. I, 257–258.

27 Kühne, *Ostensio Reliquiarum*, 579–580.

> which the Holy Shroud would be shown [. . .] that is to say one at Easter and the other on the feast of the Assumption, and that each of them last eight days.[28]

The king commanded additional information to the seneschal: there is no trace of such fairs, which the administration may not have seen fit to organise. The argument put forward by the city councillors nevertheless remains interesting. They argued that these fairs should be established in honour of God and the Holy Shroud and associated with the days of displays. The idea here is to promote a synergistic effect between fairs and ostensions, bringing together merchants and pilgrims.

Without necessarily turning into fairs, other cases show that the influx of pilgrims to relics tended to generate significant markets on the days of display. We can take, for example, another Shroud, the one of Turin: during its presence in Chambéry, it was celebrated by public ostensions on Good Friday and on 4 May (called "Holy Shroud Day"), becoming stronger and stronger in the first three decades of the sixteenth century.[29]

The influx of pilgrims compelled the syndics—elected governors of the city—to issue "*ordonnances*" for the days of display. These included security measures as well as controls on commerce to prevent merchants from taking advantage of the situation and oversell goods, and to ensure that the increased commercial activity did not clutter and dirty the streets. For example, in 1518:

> [A]ll, hoteliers, tavern-keepers, confectioners, bakers and all retailers [should] stock up on bread, wine, flesh, hay, straw, oats and all other foodstuffs, made up by weight, measure and at reasonable prices in the town and according to the current rate, and [. . .] no one [should deign] to oversell them, on pain of losing the goods and 25 pounds.

---

28 "Nos bien amez les capitolz de notre ville de Thoulouse nous ont exposé que pour ce que de nouvel le saint suere en quoy nostre Seigneur Jhesu Christ fu miz ou saint sépulcre a esté apporté en la dite ville de Thoulouse, ils espèrent que plusieurs personnes par devocion y vendront de cy en avant pour le voir et adourer. Et par ce, seroit expédient à la chose publique de la dite ville qu'il eust en icelle encores deux foires, avec celles qui y sont a certains jour en l'an, aux quelz le dit saint Suere seroit monstré. Et pour ce nous ont supplié que pour honneur de Dieu et du dit saint Suere, et pour le bien de la ville, nous leur voulsissions octroyer les dites deux foires chacun an dorenavant en la dite ville, avec celles qui y sont, c'est assavoir une à Pasques et l'autre à la feste de l'Assumption Notre-Dame, et que chacune d'icelles dure huit jours." Charles VI of France. Letters to the seneschal of Toulouse about the Shroud's fair, January 1393, Toulouse, Archives municipales, AA36/107; Sarzeaud, Copie et culte, 76–77. About this devotion, see Michelle Fournié. Une municipalité en quête de reliques. Le saint suaire de Cadouin et son dépôt à Toulouse à la fin du Moyen Âge. *Mémoires de la Société Archéologique du Midi de la France* 71 (2011): 127–162.

29 Andrea Nicolotti. *The Holy Shroud of Turin: The History and Legends of the World's Most Famous Relic.* Waco, TX: Baylor University Press, 2020, 153–165.

Retailers were also forbidden from buying goods until two o'clock in the afternoon to prevent obstructions in the streets and to regulate the slaughter of sheep and calves in homes.[30] This success of the Shroud had a knock-on effect on other cities, such as Geneva, where a measure to provide the city with bread was taken while several pilgrims were "going to the Shroud of Chambéry."[31]

Coordinating ostension relics and fairs at Besançon in the first half of the sixteenth century

Besançon is known to be a significant venue for fairs, especially exchange fairs in the sixteenth century, studied by Domenico Gioffré.[32] From the eleventh century, an important fair was held on 3 October, the day of the dedication of St. Stephen's Cathedral. As early as 1268, Lombards appeared, especially as money changers, and in 1384 the town added four new annual fairs to the four old ones that remained. One of these fairs lasted for a week from the day before Ascension Day. Merchants from Besançon were forbidden to open their shops during these events.[33]

30 "Item que l'on nectoie les chymynees et que l'on garde le feu, que Dieu le garde. Item que tous, hostelliers, tavernyez, patissie, bolongiez et tous revendeurs, fassent provision dez payn, vin, chers, feyn, palliez, avoyne et de tous autres vivres, faiet a pois, mesure et pris reysonable de laz ville et selon le taulx qui est apresent et quel nul nez soiet, si ose nez si ardi dez les survendre sus la poyne de perdre laz dicte marchandise des vivres et de XXV livres. [. . .] Item que l'on deffend a tous hostelliers, tavernyers, patissiers, et toctes autres gens, qu'ils nez soient, si ose nez si ardi de tue moton nez veaulx en leur meyson nez autre par sans apoynte avecque l'ovre, sus la poyne de perdre la marchandise et de XXV livres. Item que lon deffend a tous revendeurs et revenderesses quel soient, si ose nez si ardi dez achete riens en laz placez jusques a deulx hores apres mydi, sur la poyne de perdre laz marchandise et de XXV livres [. . .]. Item que lon deffend a tous revendeurs et revenderesse qu'el nez tiegnent poent de banc nez autres choses quelconques empachemens devant leur tavernes, sus laz poyne de perdre la marchandise et de XXV livres." Deliberation of the Chambery's syndic, 25 April 1518, Archives départementales de Savoie (AD Savoie), 189E, dépôt 80, f. 294r°–295v°, also f. 314r°–315v°. Ed. in Sarzeaud, Copie et culte, 50–51.

31 *Registres du conseil de Genève*, 30 April 1518 and 6 May 1522. Geneva: Société d'histoire et d'archéologie, 1906-, t. 8, p. 230 and t. 9, p. 168. A similar case occurred in 1487, when the elected officials of Bergerac took emergency measures to replenish their wine stocks, which had been emptied by pilgrims on their way to the Shroud of Cadouin and Notre-Dame de Rocamadour. See Sarzeaud, *Les Suaires du Christ*, 59, 225, note 54.

32 Gioffrè Domenico. *Gênes et les foires de change. De Lyon à Besançon*. Paris: S.E.V.P.E.N., 1960.

33 See Michel Vernus and Daniel Greusard. *Foires et marchés en Franche-Comté*. Saint-Avertin: Allan Sutton, 2012.

During the 1530s, the city significantly strengthened this activity with, on the one hand, the arrival of Genoese merchants and, on the other, the appearance in the documentation of a "*foire du Suaire*." The arrival of the Genoese reveals the proactive strategy of the citizens of Besançon in the matter of fairs. At this time, the merchants established in Lyon faced significant challenges, particularly relating to tensions between the Duchy of Savoy, the French Crown, and Charles V. The Genoese turned to Montluel and then Chambéry, from where they were expelled by the Duke of Savoy in 1534.

After passing through Lons-le-Saunier and Lucerne, the Genoese held fairs in Besançon in 1535. Indeed, the city was very keen to host the Genoese and took numerous steps in this direction.[34] Thus, on 2 February 1535, the governors wrote to the Genoese in Lons-le-Saunier. One Genoese person in particular—Colonel Gianbattista de Insula, a resident of Lucerne—had come to plead their cause. He can also be found in the decade as an ambassador of the cities of Lucerne, Ury, Suitz, Underwalle, and Zug, to Clement VII and Charles V. The governors expressed

> [. . .] the desire of the people and ourselves to honour and gratify you with a good treatment as much as ourselves, well assured that it will be the honour, profit and convenience of all parties [. . .]. Very ready to do you all pleasures, honours and services, depending on our powers.[35]

After this kind welcome, the Genoese stayed in Besançon, playing a role in the affirmation of the economic power of the city. The Genoese presence, however, was not without its challenges, and several documents indicate that while the civic government treated the Genoese relatively well, their presence in the city was not well-received by the people of Besançon.[36]

---

34 Letters from the Gouverneurs of Besançon to the genoese merchants, being at Lons-le-Saunier, 10 February 1535 (n.st.), Bibliothèque municipale de Besançon (hereafter BMB), BB 17, f. 34v°–35v°.

35 "pour vous remercier en premier lieu la bonne volunte et reputacion que pourtes aladite cité et vous asseurer que, ledit cas advenant le traictement, que recepvres pourtera par effect tesmoignaiges du desir que le peuple d'icelle a nous avons vous y veoir honorer et gratifier en bon traictement austant que a nous mesmes, bien asseurez que ce sera l'honneur, proufit et commodite de toutes parties aussi chose tres agreable à l'impériale maiesté, selon que par iceulx nos commis le pourrez plus amplement entendre lesquelz, surce il vous plaira croire que nous mesmes et estre certains que en toutes choses ou vous nous vouldrez emploier, servir, sans aulcune retardacion, tres prestz a vous faire tous plaisirs, honneurs et services deppendens de noz povoirs." BMB, BB 17, f. 35r°–v°.

36 To keep the thread of our argument, I summarise here the findings of my investigation on the Genoese in Besançon. According to the Municipal Deliberations, in July 1552, safe-conduct was granted to Baptiste Impérial Balien, a Genoese merchant who settled in Besançon where his

In March 1523, the canons of Saint-Etienne de Besançon announced in their registers a "mystery of the Resurrection" on Easter Sunday, showing a shroud. It was, in fact, a completely new object, a cloth copying the Shroud of Chambéry, which was to be exhibited by clerics re-enacting the role of the holy women who found the empty tomb. Two months later, it was described as the Holy Shroud, to be shown on Easter Day and Ascension Day.[37] The following years were marked by the growing of these annual public ostensions of a new holy relic.

In 1529, the town intervened to take measures comparable to those of Chambéry because of the "great influx of people to see the Holy Shroud." In addition to measures to make the city safer and cleaner, many concerned the control of trade, limiting the prices and profits taken by hoteliers and innkeepers on bread, wine, and meat, and furthermore, taking steps to ensure that retailers were adequately supplied with bread and meat. As for wine, "there's no need to issue a policy, because citizens will sell enough."[38]

---

brother was already living (BMB, BB 26, f. 125). On 7 July 1557, the city took advantage of a correspondence with the Bernese to transmit the protestation of his compatriots of good reputation residing in Besançon, concerning a Genoese imprisoned in Lausanne for debts made in Lyon and whose life had been threatened, following which governors asked for clemency (BMB, BB 28, f. 19v°). On 5 May 1560, following the murder of one Milanese person by another, the governors decided to forbid all Genoese, Lucquois, Milanese, and Italians from carrying weapons in the city without a license (f. 357v°). On 15 July 1561, justice was rendered to a Genoese, Flore de Torrente, who brought a lawsuit against Jean Gauthiot d'Ancier, a member of a prominent family from Besançon. D'Ancier had caused Flore de Torrente to be injured by his servants and had to pay reparations to both the city and the victim (f. 529).

37 Andrea Nicolotti. *Le Saint Suaire de Besançon et le chevalier Othon de la Roche*. Vy-lès-Filain: Franche-Bourgogne, 2015; Sarzeaud, *Les Suaires du Christ*, 113–116.

38 "Item lesdits quatres [gouverneurs, Jacques Bonvallot, Charles Prévost, Symon Gaulthyot, Adryen Jouffroy] ordonneront a tous hostelliers et cabarettiers prendre seullement ung nicquet de prouffit par pinte sur le vin et vendre le pain blant deux engroignes et non plus à peinne l'emender arbbitrairement. [. . .] Du pain: La charge du pain est commise au tresourier et aultres officiers du grenier a bled, lesquels mesmes ledit tresourier feront touttes ordonnances et commandemens aux bolangiers estre bien pourveuz en facon que necessité ne survienne. Du vin: Il n'est ja besoing y donner police pour ce que les citiens d'eux mesmes en vendront assez. Des bouchiers: L'on ordonne esdits bouchiers estre bien pourveuz de touttes chars selon la presente sayson et la vendre seullement au pris qu'ilz font au jour d'huy a penne d'en estre pugny arbitrairement. Et pour ad ce avoir regard depputons Pierre Charmel en la grand boucherie et Jehan Bietrux en la boucherie Sainct-Quantin dont ilz feront serment aux saincts evangilles de dieu touchez fayre executer ceste presente ordonnance et rappourter par escript les defaillans et transgresseurs. Publiees en l'hostel consistorial de la cité de Besançon en presence des quatres des sept bannières et bouchiers et de ladite cité le jeudy XXIX jour d'avril l'an mil cinq cens vingtz et neufs. [Signé Lambelin]." Ordinance for the ostension of the Shroud of Besançon, BMB, ms. 719, f. 30r°–31v°.

The display during the Ascension period quickly became very crowded. In 1533, the town announced 33,000 foreign worshippers; in 1534, 16,000, which would have been a massive influx, the town having 8–10,000 inhabitants.[39] Moreover, in May 1533, the town sent a letter to the Archbishop of Besançon, Antoine de Vergy, asking him to hold the ostension of the Shroud not on Thursday, but on the Sunday after Ascension Day:

> [F]or the honour and great convenience of both your church and the inhabitants of the city, it has seemed best from now on to show the most precious jewel of the Holy Shroud of our Benedict Redeemer, which it is customary to show, on the Sunday following Ascension Day, for several good reasons, advantages and prudence may fairly be considered [. . .].[40]

Three days later, the canons announced in their register that they had agreed to move the date. They added a *caveatur*: "Warning from the churchwarden of Saint Etienne that no merchant may set up his bench or stall on the day the Shroud is to be shown in the churchyard of Saint Etienne."[41]

---

39 Besançon municipal deliberations, 23 May 1533: "Le jour feste ascension notre seigneur XXIIIe jour de may, le Sainct Suaire a esté monstré et y avoit plus de trente mil parsonnes estrangières. La veille, le jour et lendemain de ladite feste ascension, fut vendu et distribué du pain a vendre de ladite cité, cinquante cinq mil pains blancs d'ung lyard piece, sans le pain bis." 15 May 1534: "Dymenche de Exaudi, XVII de may 1534, le saint suaire a esté monstré en la place près l'église saint Estienne de ceste cité de Besancon et y estoient gens estrangiers, plus de seize mil personnes." BMB, BB15, f. 491v° and BB17, f. 86r°; Sarzeaud, Copie et culte, 183.

40 "par l'advis des commung et peuple de ceste cité hier assemblez pour l'honneur et très grande commodité tant de votre église que des habitans en icelle, a semblé pour le myeulx doresenavant debvoir monstrer le très précieux joyaul ou sainct suaire de nostre benoist rédempteur au dymenche suyvant le jour de l'ascencion, que l'on a accoustumé de monstrer, pour plusieurs bonnes considéracions que votre vertu et prudence de votre conseil peult assez considerer, dont monseigneur suyvant noz debvoirs n'avons voulsu failly vous en adverty, par et pourteur que pource envoyons expressément et supplier très humblement en vouloir par icelluy escripre et mander deans demain votre bon plaisir et advis à messieurs du vénérable chappitre de votre église, afin monseigneur selon qui vous plaira y adviser a l'honneur d'icelle votre église, commodité et contentement dudit peuple et commung de ceste cité, en faire publicacion à jeudi prouchain quant il se monstrera, laquelle monseigneur et tous vous nous treuverez tousiours prestz vous faire le service qui vous plaira nous commande." Municipal deliberations, 17 May 1523, BMB, BB15, f. 460; Sarzeaud, Copie et culte, 184.

41 *Caveatur per matricularium sancti Stephani ne aliqui mercatores sua banna et stellagia apponent, eadem die qua ostendetur predictum sanctum sudarium, in cimiterio ecclesie sancti Stephani,* Besançon municipal deliberations, 17 May 1533. *Stellagium* designate an "*étallage,*" stalls for merchants. *Bannum* is probably here equivalent to *bancum*, the bench. Deliberations of the Besançon chapter, 23 May 1533, Archives départementales du Doubs (hereafter AD Doubs), G193, f. 317; Sarzeaud, Copie et culte, 124.

If the city's "good reasons" to transfer the ostension are not specified, the most convincing one is precisely to associate the ostension, which welcomes a large number of faithful, and the fair, which traditionally began on Monday. The two are particularly linked in the records—as, for example, in 1537, when the city announced that, because of the plague, the ostension of the Shroud and the fair beginning on the Monday after the Ascension would be cancelled.[42] This case illustrates the adjustments made to the liturgical calendar, with the ritual originally designed for Ascension being shifted to facilitate the synergy with a commercial event.

Nothing indicates that the Genoese played any role in this Shroud Fair, which appears to be much more eclectic than the exchange fairs. However, it seems clear that the governors were particularly involved in promoting different types of fairs in the decade of the 1530s and after. In particular, they took ordinances for the influx of pilgrims and merchants in Ascension, particularly in 1551 and 1555, reminiscent of those taken in Chambéry.[43] They prescribed an obligation for butchers and bakers to be well provided and not to oversell, but also for hoteliers not to receive people carrying weapons. Travellers were to be "treated honestly, without taking excessive payments" ("*qu'ilz les traictent honnestement sans prendre payement excessifz*"). Butchers were forbidden to blow into carcasses to give the impression that they were bigger, and female butchers were specifically asked to put the food on the benches and to clean the square around the stand.

In addition to measures on trade, fines were imposed on merchants who had violated the ordinances. Thus, in 1548, Roland Briselorz, a baker at the oven of François Thiébaut, with the appealing nickname "Malcuyt," received 60 sous of fines for having cooked bread without having paid for his entry in the trade. On 10 June 1550, the parchment-maker Adrien Chay, a citizen of the town, was fined "for having bought, killed and sold meat in his house on the day of the ostension

---

42 "pour raison et crainte tant de la peste que aultres diverses et contagieuses maladies présentement régnantes, l'on remect la monstre du très précieux et sainct suaire de nostre saulveur et redempteur Jhesucrist pour la presente année, tans en feste de pasques que dymenche après l'ascencion monseigneur prouchain venant, pour ceste foys seullement, et jusques a ce que lesdits dangiers de peste et maladie seront cessez. Dont lors et du jour que se pourra estre mesmes publications en sera faite, item au semblable l'on fait savoir que sur la foyre accoustumé tenus en ceste cité le lundy après le dymenche de la feste ascension monseigneur prouchain venant ne se tiendra pour ceste foys, pour les causes et considéracions susdictes." Besançon municipal deliberations, 22 March 1537, BMB, BB 18, f. 509r°; Sarzeaud, Copie et culte, 185.

43 Municipal deliberations, 30 April 1551 and 22–25 May 1555, BMB, BB 25, 369–370 and BB 27, f. 129v°–130v°; Sarzeaud, Copie et culte, 197–199, 203–204.

of the Holy Shroud."[44] Similar to Chambéry, where slaughtering livestock was prohibited, this could be a health directive aiming to avoid odours and organic waste during the peak of the crowd. Alternatively, it might have been the punishment of a deviation from the regulations of the "*métiers*," with a vendor attempting to capitalise on the influx by improperly selling meat.

Security measures prevented the entry of people who came from places experiencing epidemics and those with warlike intentions, but also, more generally, the poor and people without jobs were debarred. They were given a charity donation at the gates so that they did not enter. The gates and bridges were secured, as was the loop of the Doubs, a natural barrier protecting the city. The shuttles were suspended, and all the boats were asked to be taken out of the water to prevent intrusions.[45] In 1564, strangers were described as going into the town with armour and pistols and refusing to lay them down despite two requests from a city officer. The guard was sent to confiscate the weapons of these eighteen strangers. They were returned on Monday with a reprimand.[46]

Among other measures, in 1555, the porters were asked to inform the merchants entering the city with carts to sell wood and coal that next year these carts would be forbidden. They also had to direct the cattle towards Chamars[47] to avoid too much congestion in the town, giving us a view of the type of goods sold in this Ascension Fair as well as of the topography of this fair. Among the expenses of the city, those for the guard were numerous, but others were related to musical instruments. The salary of François Aubriot, ordinary trumpeter of the city, was mentioned "for having sounded the trumpet on the Sunday that the Holy Shroud is shown."[48] The trumpet was usually used to introduce the publication of the edicts of the city in the squares and crossroads.

---

44 "pour avoir acheté, tué et vendu en sa maison le jour de la monstre du sainct suaire char, contrevenant aux ordonnances des dits sieurs sur ce faictes aux bouchers d'icelle." Municipal accounts of Besançon, BMB, CC 109, f. 119r°; Sarzeaud, Copie et culte, 242.

45 Municipal deliberations, 11 May 1556, BMB, BB 27, f. 246v°–247r°; Sarzeaud, Copie et culte, 205.

46 Municipal deliberations, 1 and 3 April 1564, BMB, BB 29, f. 291r°–v°; Sarzeaud, Copie et culte, 218–219.

47 "Les pourtiers diront a tous charretiers estrangiers amenans boys et charbon à vendre, quant ilz partiront ce jourd'huy de la cité, qu'ils n'amènent leurs chariotz le jour de la prouchaine foire, affin ne donner empeschement en icelle cite pour ladite foire. L'on fera aller le bestial à vendre en Champmars, a scavoir les chevaulx en l'hospital de Champmars, les beufs et vaches en La Mortie, esquelx iceux se tiendra la foire dudit bestial." Municipal deliberations, 25 May 1555, BMB, BB 27, f. 130v°; Sarzeaud, Copie et culte, 204.

48 "Plus a payé le dit tresorier cinq groz viez monnoie à Francois Aubryot, trompette, pour ses peinnes d'avoir sonné la trompette au dimenche que l'on monstra le sainct suayre." Municipal account, May 1535, BMB, CC96, f. 197v°.

The governors also paid musicians, particularly flute and tambourine players, to play on the Shroud's Day.[49] These instruments, generally of a military nature, must be understood as being intended for the city's guard companies. At the Ascension Day of 1559, the governors gathered to "see several beautiful breastplates *(hallecretz)*"[50] distributed to soldiers of the guard (which were, in fact, citizens in duty) who had been chosen by the captain. The manifestation of Ascension provided the opportunity for a military parade, the guard representing the city as an institution to its visitors. Generally, with the measures of guarding, cleaning, orders to the merchants, and so on, we can observe that the governors wanted to take advantage of the fair to show the city in its best light.

The extent of this celebration was probably mainly regional, as the few origins of people mentioned are mainly from Franche-Comté, and news such as the cancellation of the fair for one year was specifically spread in the diocese of Besançon. In 1579, however, the chapter reports that people coming from afar had not been warned of the cancellation and were therefore put on the spot. They asked whether or not the Shroud should be shown, which the governors refused, but canons decided to do so anyway.[51]

The relics, objects of fair

Around 1369, a document listed the relics of St. Vitus of Prague, including a shroud, which was to be displayed on the second Friday after Easter.[52] This document stated that these relics should be displayed on the cattle marketplace. There were probably some practical reasons for this: this very large square (the current Place Charles IV) was perfect for accommodating the crowd. Simultaneously, this

49 See, for example, municipal accounts, September 1535 and 1 June 1547, BMB, CC 96, f. 226v° and CC106, f. 155v°; Sarzeaud, Copie et culte, 236 and 239.

50 "Le présent conseil a esté assemblé pour veoir plusieurs beaux hallecretz appartenans à Claude Monnet et a esté ordonné à messieurs Bonvalot et de Nobilers capitaines de la bende que doibt aller par la ville aujourd'huy et demain, à la monstre du sainct suayre, qu'ilz choisissent telz personnaiges que bon leur semblera pour pourter lesdits hallecretz, leur donnant quand à ce tout pouvoir nécessaire." Municipal deliberations, 6 May 1559, BMB, BB28, f. 239r°; Sarzeaud, Copie et culte, 208.

51 Municipal deliberations, 19, 22, and 30 May 1579, BMB, BB 37, f. 172r°, 173r°, and 176v°; Sarzeaud, Copie et culte, 230–231.

52 List of the relics of St. Vitus of Prague to be displayed on the second Friday after Easter, c. 1369, Munich, Bayerische Staatsbibliothek, Clm. 6686, f. 324v°. In *Karl IV: 1316–2016*, Jiří Fajt, Markus Hörsch (eds.). Prague: Národní galerie v Praze, 2016, 157. On Charles IV and the relics, see also Pierre Monnet. *Charles IV: Un empereur en Europe*. Paris: Fayard, 2020, 223–234.

choice reflects the resonances between the grand celebrations associated with relics and markets—the gathering of numerous individuals, coming from afar, assembled in a unique location. The visual dimension is also common: the term "*monstre*," used to describe the exhibition of items at the beginning of the fair before the transactions, also refers in Middle French to the display of relics, particularly in Besançon. These comparable conditions sometimes prompted the organisers of these two types of events to combine them, strengthening the attendance of both and facilitating event management by concentrating the organisational tasks over a shorter period. We can note that the cases studied tend to show that ostension fairs were generally large markets or general fairs, which had everything to gain by diversifying their audience, rather than professional fairs, such as those of the Genoese money changers.

If we address the question in terms of a chicken-and-egg problem, it is not always clear in the records whether it was the relic that adjusted its calendar to coincide with the fair or vice versa, but at the very least, the picture does not correspond to the narrative of the secularisation of a liturgical calendar. Various situations are observed—commercial events created in connection with an ostension, as in Toulouse, or conversely, an adjustment of the liturgical calendar in Besançon to align the display with the fair. In some cases, such as in Saint-Denis and Compiègne, there was even the outright creation of a ritual to impart a Christian dimension to an existing market. Here, it was the Church that saw all the economic and pastoral benefits of aligning itself with the rhythm of the merchants.

Bibliography

Primary Sources

Abbot Suger. *Œuvres complètes*, Albert Lecoy de la Marche (ed.). Paris: Renouard, 1867.

Alberigo, Giuseppe (ed.). *Les décrets: Nicée I à Latran V. Les Conciles œcuméniques*. Vol. II. Paris: Cerf, 1994.

Charles VI of France. Letters to the seneschal of Toulouse about the Shroud's fair, January 1393. Toulouse, Archives municipales, AA36/107.

Deliberations of the Besançon chapter. Archives départementales du Doubs, G193.

List of the relics of St. Vitus of Prague to be displayed on the second Friday after Easter. Munich, Bayerische Staatsbibliothek, Clm. 6686, f. 324v.

Mansi, Giovanni Domenico (ed.). *Sacrorum conciliorum nova et amplissima collectio*. Venice: Zatta, 1758–1798, t. 23–25.

Morel, Émile (ed.). *Cartulaire de l'abbaye de Saint-Corneille de Compiègne I*. Montdidier: Bellin, 1904.

Municipal accounts of Besançon. Bibliothèque municipale de Besançon, CC 96, 106, 109.

Municipal deliberations of Besançon. Bibliothèque municipale de Besançon, BB 15, 17, 18, 25–29, 37.
Municipal deliberations of Compiègne. Compiègne, Archives municipales, BB18.
Municipal deliberation of Chambery. Archives départementales de Savoie, 189E, dépôt 80.
Ordo in die benedictionis indicti, Pontifical d'Étienne de Givry. Paris, Bibliothèque nationale de France, ms. lat. 962, 264r°–268v°.
Ordinance for the ostension of the Shroud of Besançon. Bibliothèque municipal de Besançon, ms. 719, f. 27–31.
Rauschen, Gerhard (ed.). *Die Legende Karls des Grossen im 11. und 12. Jahrhundert*. Leipzig: Duncker & Humblot, 1890.
Registres du conseil de Genève. Geneva: Société d'histoire et d'archéologie, 1906-, t. 8–9.

Literature

Bur, Michel. Les autres foires de Champagne. In *Städtelandschaft—Städtenetz—zentralörtliches Gefüge. Ansätze und Befunde zur Geschichte der Städte im hohen und späten Mittelalter*, Monika Escher, Alfred Haverkamp, Frank G. Hirschman (eds.). Mainz: Philipp von Zabern, 2000, 349–365.
Carolus-Barré, Louis. Le mi-Karesme, foire de Compiègne au Moyen Âge et sa survie jusqu'en 1792. *Bulletin de la Société historique de Compiègne* 26 (1979): 19–72.
Diedrichs, Christof L. *Vom Glauben zum Sehen. Die Sichtbarkeit der Reliquie im Reliquiar. Ein Beitrag zur Geschichte des Sehens*. Berlin: Weissensee, 2001.
Dolbeau, François. La prédication pour les fêtes de reliques. In *Ad libros! Mélanges d'études médiévales offerts à Denise Angers et Joseph-Claude Poulin*, Jean-François Cottier, Martin Gravel, Sébastien Rossignol (eds.). Montréal: Presses de l'Université de Montréal, 2010, 139–161.
Fajt, Jiří, Markus Hörsch (eds.). *Karl IV : 1316–2016*. Prague: Národní galerie v Praze, 2016.
Fournié, Michelle. Une municipalité en quête de reliques. Le saint suaire de Cadouin et son dépôt à Toulouse à la fin du Moyen Âge. *Mémoires de la Société Archéologique du Midi de la France* 71 (2011): 127–162.
Gabriele, Matthew. *An Empire of Memory: The Legend of Charlemagne, the Franks, and Jerusalem Before the First Crusade*. Oxford: Oxford University Press, 2011.
Gabriele, Matthew. The Provenance of the *Descriptio qualiter Karolus Magnus*: Remembering the Carolingians in the Entourage of King Philip I (1060–1108) before the First Crusade. *Viator* 39:2 (2008): 93–117.
Gaude-Ferragu, Murielle. *Le trésor des rois. Sacré et royauté, des rois maudits aux princes de la Renaissance*. Paris: Perrin, 2022.
Gioffrè, Domenico. *Gênes et les foires de change. De Lyon à Besançon*. Paris: S.E.V.P.E.N., 1960.
Große, Rolf. Reliques du Christ et foires de Saint-Denis au XIe siècle. A propos de la *Descriptio clavi et corone domini*. *Revue d'histoire de l'Église de France* 87 (2001): 357–375.
Kühne, Hartmut. *Ostensio Reliquiarum. Untersuchungen über Entstehung, Ausbreitung, Gestalt und Funktion der Heiltumsweisungen im Römisch-Deutschen Regnum*. Berlin, New York: De Gruyter, 2000.
Le Goff, Jacques. Au Moyen Âge: temps de l'Église et temps du marchand. *Annales E.S.C.* 15:3 (1960): 417–433.
Lenoble, Clément. Avant l'ascèse intramondaine. Comptabilités ecclésiastiques, gouvernement et rationalité économique (XIIIe–XVe siècles). *Archives de Sciences Sociales des Religions, 66e année*, 195 (2021): 51–81.

Lombard-Jourdan, Anne. Les foires de l'abbaye de Saint-Denis: revue des données et révision des opinions admises. *Bibliothèque de l'École des chartes* 145 (1987): 274–338.
Monnet, Pierre. *Charles IV: Un empereur en Europe*. Paris: Fayard, 2020.
Nicolotti, Andrea. *Le Saint Suaire de Besançon et le chevalier Othon de la Roche*. Vy-lès-Filain: Franche-Bourgogne, 2015.
Nicolotti, Andrea. *The Holy Shroud of Turin: The History and Legends of the World's Most Famous Relic*. Waco, TX: Baylor University Press, 2020.
Rau, Susanne. Rhythmusanalyse nach Lefebvre. In *Taktungen und Rhythmen. Raumzeitliche Perspektiven interdisziplinär*, Sabine Schmolinsky, Diana Hitzke, Heiner Stahl (eds.). Berlin, Boston: De Gruyter, 2018, 9–24.
Rossi, Carla. Le Voyage de Charlemagne: le parcours vers Jérusalem et les reliques. *Critica del testo* 2:2 (1999): 619–653.
Sarzeaud, Nicolas. Copie et culte. Le Suaire du Christ, une relique reproductible (XIVe–XVIe s.). PhD diss., EHESS, 2021.
Sarzeaud, Nicolas. *Les Suaires du Christ en Occident du Moyen Âge à nos jours*. Paris: Cerf, 2024.
Schmitt, Jean-Claude. *Les rythmes au Moyen Âge*. Paris: Gallimard, 2016.
Todeschini, Giacomo. *I mercanti e il tempio. La società cristiana e il circolo virtuoso della ricchezza fra medioevo ed età moderna*. Bologna: Il Mulino, 2002.
Toussaint, Gia. *Kreuz und Knochen. Reliquien zur Zeit der Kreuzzüge*. Berlin: Reimer, 2011.
Vernus, Michel, Daniel Greusard. *Foires et marchés en Franche-Comté*. Saint-Avertin: Allan Sutton, 2012.

Jean-Louis Gaulin

Shopping at the Geneva fairs: the contribution of Savoyard accounting records in the time of Duke Amadeus VIII

With the decline of the Champagne Fairs and the transformations of large-scale commerce during the fourteenth century, the question of the connection between the principality of Savoy and distant markets arose in new terms. On the one hand, the major companies of northern Italy and Tuscany organised their own networks by establishing permanent agents in major consumption centres like Paris, London, Bruges, and Avignon. On the other hand, a long-term trend, evident after 1350, pushed sovereigns to create numerous regional fairs across the continent.[1]

None succeeded in capturing the legacy of the Champagne Fairs, and none replaced them. Several regional fair systems coexisted—in Flanders (Bruges), along the Middle Rhine (Frankfurt), in central Germany (Leipzig, Erfurt), in Castile (Medina del Campo), not to mention the fairs of Chalon-sur-Saône, Geneva, and, in the fifteenth century, those of Lyon.[2] Before Lyon's rise, Geneva became an international hub during the fourteenth century, and its fairs reached their peak during the first half of the following century. A "quasi-Savoyard" city, it was ideally positioned to connect the Alpine principality to large-scale commerce, as the Champagne Fairs had done in the thirteenth century.[3] The need to access goods

1 Peter Spufford. Trade in fourteenth-century Europe. In *The New Cambridge Medieval History, VI, c. 1300–c. 1415*, Michael C.E. Jones (ed.). Cambridge: Cambridge University Press, 2000, 155–208; Stephan R. Epstein. Fairs, Towns, and States in Renaissance Europe. In *Fiere e mercati nella integrazione delle economie europee secc. XIII–XVIII*, Simonetta Cavaciocchi (ed.). Florence: Le Monnier, 2001, 71–90.

2 Michel Pauly. Les foires de Champagne—et après? In *Relations, échanges, transferts en Occident au cours des derniers siècles du Moyen Âge*, Bernard Guenée, Jean-Marie Moeglin (eds.). Paris: Académie des Inscriptions et Belles-Lettres, 2010, 235–261.

3 Frédéric Borel. *Les Foires de Genève au XVe siècle*. Geneva: H. Georg, 1892; Antony Babel. *Histoire économique de Genève: des origines au début du XVIe siècle*, vol. II. Geneva: Alexandre Jullien, 1963, 345–436; Jean-François Bergier. *Genève et l'économie européenne de la Renaissance*. Paris: S.E.V.P.E.N., 1963. About the city, its political history, and its ties with the House of Savoy, see Mathieu Caesar. *Le pouvoir en ville. Gestion urbaine et pratiques politiques à Genève (fin XIIIe–début XVIe siècles)*. Turnhout: Brepols, 2011.

Note: Translation by Jonathan Fruoco.

https://doi.org/10.1515/9783111621296-004

that Savoy did not produce—or produced in insufficient quantity or quality—was heightened during the fourteenth and fifteenth centuries by the emergence of a court that became a significant centre of consumption, requiring housing, supplies, and satisfying luxury tastes.[4] Although difficult to quantify, the purchases made by the Prince of Savoy in Geneva are undeniable.[5] Did the fairs themselves still play a role in supplying the court and, more generally, how were these periodic gatherings useful to the Prince of Savoy? This is the question I attempt to answer from the perspective of the research program CoMOR (Configurations of European Fairs: Merchants, Objects, Routes) by relying on a sample of accounting sources produced by the principality.[6] After presenting the corpus, I will broadly outline the markets from which the court sourced its supplies before examining the role and function (or functions) of the fairs.

Savoyard accounting as a source for the history of fairs

Starting in the mid-thirteenth century, the County of Savoy established a solid administration whose abundant documentary production has been the subject of extensive study over the past thirty years.[7] However, as highlighted more gener-

4 About the court of Savoy, see Paola Bianchi, Luisa Gentile (eds.). *L'affermarsi della corte sabauda: dinastie, poteri, élites in Piemonte e Savoia fra tardo Medioevo e prima età moderna.* Turin: Silvio Zamorani, 2006. Under Amadeus VIII, around a hundred servants received wages, and the court as a whole must have numbered up to three hundred people, according to the data gathered by Guido Castelnuovo. See Guido Castelnuovo. A la court et au service de nostre prince: l'hôtel de Savoie et ses métiers à la fin du Moyen Âge. In *L'affermarsi della corte sabauda*, Bianchi, Gentile (eds.), 23–53.

5 Mathieu Caesar. Économie urbaine et dépenses princières. La cour de Savoie au XVe siècle. In *La cour et la ville dans l'Europe du Moyen Âge et des Temps Modernes*, Denis Menjot, Léonard Courbon (eds.). Turnhout: Brepols, 2015, 197–212.

6 The CoMOR project [Configurations of European Fairs. Merchants, Objects, Routes (ca. 1350–1600)] was supported by the ANR (2019-FRAL-0001) and the DFG (Project number 430627254) from March 2020 to October 2023. I benefited from a one-year secondment to the CNRS (CIHAM-UMR 5648 laboratory) during this period.

7 Guido Castelnuovo. Les officiers princiers et le pouvoir de l'écrit. Pour une histoire documentaire de la principauté savoyarde (XIIIe–XVe siècle). In *Offices, Écrit et Papauté (XIIIe–XVIIe siècle)*, Armand Jamme, Olivier Poncet (eds.). Rome: École française de Rome, 2007, 17–46; Bernard Andenmatten, Guido Castelnuovo. Produzione documentaria e conservazione archivistica nel principato sabaudo, XIII–XV secolo. *Bullettino dell'Istituto Italiano per Il Medio Evo* 110:1 (2008): 279–348.

ally in the introduction of this volume, one would search in vain for a specific collection dedicated to markets and fairs in the archives left by the former States of Savoy. Dispersion is the rule, whether one is interested in charters of franchise, through which the counts granted communities the right to hold a market or fair, tolls which could be managed directly, enfeoffed or leased, court decisions involving merchants, or purchases made by officers at the prince's request.[8]

Savoyard accounting undoubtedly provides the most directly useful data for our inquiry into the fairs. It is a complex accounting system that juxtaposes rather than hierarchises various series of accounts produced by different administrative entities.[9] With markets and fairs, three accounting series primarily draw attention.

The castellany accounts provide information about possessions and domain rights at the local level.[10] The officer (called castellan), who locally represents the count, is responsible for collecting seigneurial revenues which, where applicable, include income from the rights on markets (*mercati*) and fairs (*nundinae*). Thus, in the small town of Montluel, located at the western edge of the States of Savoy on the border with Dauphiné and the Kingdom of France, a fair was held twice a year. The revenues derived from it appear in the annual account rendered by the castellan in a section entitled "*Lingua boum.*" It was only through this specific seigneurial right to claim the tongue of each ox or cow slaughtered during the fair that the central administration was aware of the commercial activity.[11] Although other sources indicate that long-distance merchants sometimes passed through Montluel—which was on the route between Chambéry and Lyon—the

8 For an overview of the existing collections, see the still-indispensable directory by Robert-Henri Bautier, Janine Sornay. *Les sources de l'histoire économique et sociale du Moyen Age*, vol. 1: *Provence, Comtat Venaissin, Dauphiné, États de la Maison de Savoie*. Paris: CNRS, 1968.

9 For an extensive bibliographic review, see Guido Castelnuovo. The Rolls, the Prince, and their Depositories: The Archiving of Late Medieval Financial Accounts Reconsidered (Savoy, Mid-Fourteenth to Mid-Fifteenth Century). In *Accounts and accountability in late medieval Europe: records, procedures, and social-political impact*, Ionuț Epurescu-Pascovici (ed.). Turnhout: Brepols, 2020, 183–202.

10 Mario Chiaudano. *La finanza sabauda nel sec. XIII, I. I rendiconti del Dominio dal 1257 al 1285*. Turin: Società Storica Subalpina, 1933; Guido Castelnuovo, Christian Guilleré. Les finances et l'administration de l'État savoyard au XIIIe siècle. In *Pierre II 'Le petit Charlemagne'*, Bernard Andenmatten, Eva Pibiri, Agostino Paravicini Bagliani (eds.). Lausanne: Université de Lausanne, 2000, 33–125. Transcriptions of thirteenth-century castellany accounts are published on the website: http://castellanie.net/.

11 Archives départementales de la Côte d'Or, B 8546 (1/04/1355-12/02/1356), membrane 2: "Idem reddit computum quod recepit ibidem in nundinis dicti loci que fiunt bis in anno videlicet die dominica ante festum Penthecoste et die dominica ante festum beati Andree ubi levatur de quolibet bove occiso ab idem lingua pro domino [. . .]."

castellany accounts usually make no mention of this since they primarily document the exploitation of the estate's resources.[12]

The toll accounts, whose importance in the history of the principality is well known, constitute another series that has long been used to study routes, stops, merchandise flows, and tariffs. However, researchers have rarely noted that these toll accounts sometimes mention, for tax reasons, the fairs that certain merchants declared they were heading to. This is evident from the edition of the toll accounts of Villeneuve, located where the Upper Rhône flows into Lake Geneva, produced by F. Morenzoni. Typically, toll collectors usually recorded the names, goods, amount of tax collected, date of passage, and, sometimes, the direction of the passersby. They made an exception for Milanese merchants, who were listed separately because they were privileged to be exempt from unpacking their goods, provided they had been bought or sold at the Geneva fairs. This exception allows us to link these merchants' movements to the Geneva fair calendar.[13]

To determine which of these merchants came into contact with the Savoyard administration, not only as toll passers but also as vendors, one must turn to the series of accounts from the General Treasury.[14] This body, which can be described as the main "treasury," managed major financial flows—revenues from the castellanies and tolls, income from the exercise of justice involving the prince, subsidies (exceptional taxes), more or less forced loans, the sale of franchise charters to rural communities. However, one cannot confuse the amount of the Treasury's revenues with the total resources available to the prince. Many expenses were made directly by the castellans or other officers without being integrated into central accounting, and transfers of funds between accounts were frequent. Similarly, the expenses recorded in the General Treasury accounts do not represent the totality of outgoing funds. At the local level, castellany resources could occasionally be called upon. Generally, however, the sums disbursed by the castellans at their lord's request were primarily for the maintenance of castles and domain

12 Christian Guilleré, Jean-Louis Gaulin. Des rouleaux et des hommes. Premières recherches sur les comptes de châtellenies savoyards. *Études Savoisiennes* 1 (1992): 51–108.

13 Franco Morenzoni. *Marchands et marchandises au péage de Villeneuve de Chillon (première moitié du XVe siècle).* Lausanne: Université de Lausanne, 2016, 123–141, with bibliography. We thank Franco Morenzoni for granting us permission to enter the data from the Villeneuve toll, mentioning the Geneva fairs, into the Fairs-in-History database: https://fairs-in-history.huma-num.fr/ (collections 95 to100).

14 For information on the central accounts during the time of Amadeus V, see Christian Guilleré, Sylvain Macherat. Introduction. In *Les finances d'Amédée V de Savoie (1285–1308).* Chambéry: Université Savoie Mont-Blanc, 2021, 21–129. For the fifteenth century, see the references cited below in footnote 22.

buildings by local artisans and, secondarily, for merchants. At the central level, specific accounts were kept separate from the general accounts to fund military expeditions (military accounts[15]) and to finance the princely household's expenses (household accounts).[16]

The complexity suggested by this brief overview should not diminish the importance of the treasurers' accounts. Although they do not aggregate all the principality's revenues and expenses, they remain the cornerstone of the Savoyard financial system. Close to the prince, the treasurer manages substantial sums and, in terms of expenses, is responsible for paying the many suppliers of goods and services benefiting the court.

The series of General Treasurers' accounts (a title that replaced "receiver" in the mid-fourteenth century) begins in 1297 and has few gaps. However, accounting techniques underwent significant changes under count Amadeus VI (1343–1383), which play to our advantage. Firstly, the recording of expense data expanded, which benefits us. Short entries listing the recipient's name, reason for payment, and amount were replaced by detailed accounting narratives. Scribes transcribe the expense receipts sent to them, which support the claims of the prince's creditors. These supporting documents (known as *particula*) are briefly described using the scribes' familiar vocabulary: they are referred to as a schedule (*cedula*), sheet (*folium*), roll (*rotulus*), memorandum (*memorialis*), or notarial act (*instrumentum*). Their content is then copied into the main register, respecting the original language (Latin or vernacular) in which they were written. Following this, the treasurer notes the letter by which the prince authorised the reimbursement of the expense made in his name, a letter that is sometimes transcribed in full as well. Secondly, in the late 1350s, vernacular documents began to appear in accounting records, which had previously been written exclusively in Latin. This vernacularisation is strictly limited to certain justificatory documents (*particula*) that the scribes start to include in the accounts. That is why this linguistic shift introduced clarifications and details previously unknown in Savoyard accounting. Written in Middle French with Franco-Provençal features, these documents inserted into the treasurers' accounts provide us with more market-specific infor-

15 Clarification in Roberto Biolzi. Military recruitment and funding in Savoy: Piedmond and Chablais, late-thirteenth to mid-fourteenth century. In *Accounts and accountability*, Epurescu-Pascovici (ed.), 47–72.

16 See, for example, the study of the hotel accounts by Fanny Abbott. *Des comptes d'apothicaires: les épices dans la comptabilité de la Maison de Savoie (XIVe et XVe s.)*. Lausanne: Université de Lausanne, 2012.

mation on goods and merchants, prices, and currencies.[17] Finally, although it does not impact our research beyond improved readability, the shift from parchment rolls to paper registers occurred in the early 1380s.

This valuable series remains largely unpublished, and in the absence of research tools, only selective sampling is possible due to the scale of the task.[18] Our efforts have so far focused on two periods related to the CoMOR programme: the first half of the fourteenth century, corresponding to the decline of the Champagne Fairs and the rise of the Geneva fairs, and the first half of the fifteenth century, which marks the beginning of the history of the Lyon fairs. The results are mixed. For the first half of the fourteenth century, fair mentions are sporadic, and the highly concise nature of the accounts limits their contribution to our inquiry.[19] However, the findings for the early fifteenth century are more promising.

The court of Savoy and its supply chain under Amadeus VIII: an overview

Under Amadeus VIII (1383–1451), who was elevated to the rank of Duke by Emperor Sigismund in 1416, the States of Savoy reached their maximum territorial extent for the medieval period. To the possessions inherited from his ancestors—Savoy, Bugey, Bresse, Valbonne, Chablais, Faucigny, Vaud, the Aosta Valley, and the Susa Valley, along with the New Lands of Provence, including Nice—Amadeus VIII added the County of Geneva, the former apanage of Piedmont-Achaea, and several Lombard cities, including Ivrea, Biella, and Vercelli.

The expanded principality was also more heterogeneous. Factors contributing to its diversification included the varying degrees of antiquity in the relationships between the communities and their lord, the ability of some lands to retain institutional and social singularity (Bresse, Piedmont-Achaea), and linguistic diversity. These were counterbalanced by two main forces of cohesion: the prince's

17 Jean-Louis Gaulin. Latin et vernaculaire dans les écritures administratives de la principauté de Savoie. L'exemple des comptes généraux du XIVe siècle. *Médiévales* 75 (2018): 11–26. https://journals.openedition.org/medievales/8979.

18 The accounts are kept at the Archivio di Stato di Torino, Sezioni Riunite, Camera dei conti Savoia, Inv. 16 (now cited as Inv. 16, followed by the number in the series). The earliest accounts of the receivers (1297–1308) have been recently published in *Les finances d'Amédée V*, Guilleré, Macherat (eds.), 131–281. The account of the treasurer André Belletruche for the years 1377 to 1382 (Inv. 16, 34) has been published by Jean Jaccod (Abbé). *La comptabilité d'Amédée VI dit le "Comte Vert", 1377–1382. Sa vie, ses monnaies.* Turin: La Pallatina, 1939.

19 As the data is being processed, it will be entered into the Fairs-in-History database.

service and court on the one hand, and a central administration that sought to unify this aggregation of "countries" through pragmatic writing on the other.[20]

In terms of financial organisation, Amadeus VIII inherited a system whose central hub was the Chamber of Accounts, created in 1351. Strengthened in its duties in 1390, the Chamber audited the accounts produced by various administrative entities and oversaw the process that led to the payment of the prince's creditors. As mentioned earlier, among the abundant accounting documentation produced under Amadeus VIII, it is the records of the General Treasury that provide us with the most data on the fairs. Analysing these thick registers, structured into "items," is complex because the accounting emphasises the recipients of payments rather than the reasons for them. Moreover, although documentary sequences are discernible, the items sometimes gather very diverse matters. According to Christian Guilleré, these "items" can be grouped into five major categories: war, diplomacy (very active under Amadeus VIII[21]), administration, construction work, and court expenses. The latter are of two types. Some large payments were made to the steward of the prince's and princess' households. These were fund transfers without specific justification, moving from one treasury to another under the general treasurer's supervision. Other payments, however, correspond to specific and routine expenses for the court, particularly in textiles for liveries and food products.[22]

However, our perspective differs. We are interested in all expenditures related to the purchase of material goods, regardless of their destination. For example, a horse acquired at Amadeus VIII's request could be used for military or administrative purposes (if it serves an officer on a mission), given to a member of

---

20 Bernard Andenmatten, Agostino Paravicini Bagliani (eds.). *Amédée VIII–Félix V, premier duc de Savoie et pape, 1383–1451*. Lausanne: Université de Lausanne, 1992; Alessandro Barbero. *Il ducato di Savoia. Amministrazione e corte di uno stato franco-italiano (1416–1536)*. Rome, Bari: Laterza, 2002; Laurent Ripart, Christian Guilleré, Pascal Vuillemin (eds.). *La naissance du duché de Savoie (1416)*. Chambéry: Université Savoie Mont-Blanc, 2020.

21 See the fundamental work by Eva Pibiri. *En voyage pour Monseigneur. Ambassadeurs, officiers et messagers à la cour de Savoie au XIVe–XVe siècles*. Lausanne: Société d'Histoire de la Suisse Romande, 2011.

22 Christian Guilleré. Le financement de la cour savoyarde du milieu du XIIIe siècle au début du XVe siècle: essai de typologie des dépenses de cour. In *L'affermarsi della corte sabauda*, 145–161; Christian Guilleré. Quelques réflexions sur l'organisation des comptes de trésorerie savoyarde. L'exemple du premier compte de Martin Deschaux sous le règne d'Amédée VIII (1391–1392). In *L'honnête homme, l'or blanc et le duc d'Albe: mélanges offerts à Alain Becchia*, Andreas Nijenhuis-Bescher, Émilie-Anne Pépy, Jean-Yves Champeley (eds). Chambéry: Université Savoie Mont-Blanc, 2016, 223–246; Christian Guilleré. Les finances d'Amédée VIII (1391–1416). In *La naissance du duché*, 237–276.

the court, or offered as a diplomatic gift. Two clarifications should be made: first, the intended use of a good is sometimes unclear; second, the definition of an item purchased from merchants and artisans varies. The recorded price sometimes distinguishes between the raw material (woollens, silk, etc.) and the craftsmanship, but sometimes aggregates them, providing the total price of the "finished product."

Let us take as an example the register kept by the treasurer Antoine du Pont, which covers part of the year 1417. Since it does not explicitly mention purchases made at fairs, it allows us to glimpse the markets where the newly appointed Duke of Savoy made purchases for his family, his officers, and various court members.

The analysis of this register shows that out of 143 expense categories, 46 (one-third) involve identifiable purchases, with a total expenditure of 5,567 florins out of 34,005 florins spent overall.[23] While some categories concern only a single expense, others include multiple items. In total, the account comprises 405 items, each of which is identified as an expense by the Savoyard administration.

The table should be seen as a snapshot of a changing reality, where significant expenditures are closely linked to the life of the court (see Tab. 1). In the category of fabrics and clothing, for instance, a significant expense of over a thousand florins was made that year to clothe the ambassadors and their entourage sent by the duke to the Council of Constance.[24] Similarly, the 1417 payment of several old debts presented by Lyon merchants raises Lyon's importance relative to Geneva. This register provides a minimal picture of the court's supply relations, whereas other accounts document purchases at markets in Provence, Piedmont, and also in Paris.

From a geographic perspective, it remains significant that expenditures primarily benefit the duchy's capital, followed by Lyon and Geneva. Most of the pur-

23 The amounts received or spent by the treasurer are expressed in several currencies—mainly small-weight florins, francs, and gold crowns. The accounting currency used for calculating the balance is the small-weight florin. The conversion between the various currencies was done based on information provided by the treasurer himself (Inv. 16, reg. 63, allegato). The accounting system is based on the florin—a small-weight *gros*, or common *gros*, which was in use in the southeast of France in the fourteenth and fifteenth centuries, with a ratio of 12 *gros* to 1 florin and 24 small *deniers* to 1 gros. The treasurer also uses the *franc-gros* system (as seen in the document published in Appendix 2) with 1 *franc*=16 *gros*. See the classic work by Étienne Fournial. *Les villes et l'économie d'échange en Forez aux XIIIe et XIVe siècles*. Paris: Les Presses du Palais Royal, 1967, 571–614. See also Marc Bompaire, Françoise Dumas. *Numismatique médiévale: monnaies et documents d'origine française*. Turnhout: Brepols, 2000, 318–336.

24 Nadège Gauffre-Fayolle. Vêtir une ambassade en partance pour le concile de Constance (Savoie, 1417). In *Le vêtement au Moyen âge: de l'atelier à la garde-robe*, Danièle Alexandre-Bidon, Nadège Gauffre-Fayolle, Perrine Mane, Mickaël Wilmart (eds.). Turnhout: Brepols, 2021, 109–130.

chases were made in Chambéry, where the variety of goods was the greatest—fabrics, clothing, weapons, but also paper and goldsmith items. Many of the merchants and artisans identified as being from Chambéry had only recently settled there, as suggested by the name of Janin (Gianni?) from Milan, referred to as a resident of Chambéry and a seller of crossbow bolts.[25] Other artisans occasionally came to work at the court and were reimbursed for their travel from Geneva, Lyon, or even Grenoble.[26] The court attracted these specialists to the point that it became difficult to assign them a specific geographic "home." Such is the case with the Michelet and Jaquemet brothers from Ges (or Getz), embroiderers who worked for years for the court of Savoy. Though they were Lyon citizens (and taxpayers in the Rhône city), the treasurer considered them in the service of the lord of Savoy, without needing to assign them any other identity.[27]

Tab. 1: Typology, geography, and rounded amount (in small-weight florins) of purchases in the register of treasurer Antoine du Pont (1417).[28]

Types of purchases (number)	Amount in florins	Chambéry	Geneva	Lyon	Other (Valais, Mâcon)	Not specified
Fabric and clothing (19)	3907	1261	177	600	–	1869
Horses (11)	460	–	–	–	–	460
Debts to merchants (5)	596	25	–	466	–	105
Weapons (3)	246	119	–	–	–	127
Others (8)	358	100			258	–
Total	5567	1505	177	1066	258	2561

In Geneva, two purchases were made at dates close to the holding of a fair. However, since no travel or transport expenses between Chambéry and Geneva are

25 Inv. 16, reg. 63, f. 111–111v.: "Libravit Janino de Milan habitatori Chamberiaci [. . .] pro precio trium millium fustarum virotonorum."

26 Thus, this anonymous master embroiderer from Grenoble who comes occasionally as reinforcement: "Item pour les despens dou maistre brodiour de Greynoble pour venir a Chamb[ery] querre des robes pour deux fois qu'il est venus et retornés et pour le loier d'un cheval qu'il a mené: xxii gros." (Inv. 16, reg. 63, f. 66).

27 "Libravit [. . .] Micheleto et Jaquemeto de Ges brodeatoribus domini [. . .] dictis fratribus per dominum debitorum [. . .]," Inv. 16, 63, f. 140v. In Lyon, among other mentions: "Michelet le brodour et Jaquemet." See Édouard Philippon, Charles Perrat (eds.). *Le livre du Vaillant des habitants de Lyon en 1388. Estimation des biens meubles et immeubles pour servir à l'assiette de la taille.* Lyon: M. Audin, 1927, 165. The spelling of the name varies (*de Gez, de Ges, de Gayo*).

28 In the first column, the numbers in parentheses indicate the number of categories that include purchases and expenses related to purchases (workmanship, transport).

mentioned, one is inclined to conclude—though we will revisit this point—that these purchases were made without direct connection to the Geneva fairs.

Overall, this global analysis of this register might lead to the conclusion that the Duke of Savoy's court attracts the products and skilled artisans it needs and that merchants' networks converge towards Chambéry—or, if not, pass through Geneva and Lyon—regardless of the fair calendar.

Buying, borrowing, and administering at the Geneva fairs

The next two registers, successively kept by the treasurers Guigonet Maréchal and Barthélemy du Razet, cover more than two years—from August 1417 to October 1419. They mention the Geneva fairs (*nundinae Gebennarum*) nine times.[29] Although only four of these occurrences detail expenses—which may seem marginal in a collection of over 500 folios (see Table in Appendix 1)—they allow us to outline the relationships between the court of Savoy and the fairs, which served multiple functions.

The 1387 Geneva charters enumerate seven fairs—a very high number—on the significance of which historians remain divided. During these two years, the Duke of Savoy's envoys attended four of these fairs, three of which are easily identifiable: the Epiphany Fair, the Easter Fairs (1418 and 1419), and the Saints Simon and Jude Fair (October 28, in 1418 and 1419). From the mid-fifteenth century, this latter fair became known as the All-Saints Fair, but this term is not used in our registers.[30]

The mention of a Saint Peter's fair on two occasions might refer to one of three fairs documented in the fifteenth century: the Chair of Saint Peter (February 22), Saints Peter and Paul (June 29), or Saint Peter in Chains (August 1).[31] This lack of specificity is due to the fact that, contrary to established accounting practices, the treasurers, when recording an expense related to a fair, omit the usual date details (day, month, and year) they usually employ. In the early fifteenth-century registers I consulted, the Savoyard administration rarely used liturgical calendar dates, which makes the identification of the fairs even more pronounced. Referring to the "foyre de Genève de la saint Symond et Jude de l'an m

29 Account of Guigonet Maréchal, from 3 August 1417 to 21 October 1418, Inv. 16, reg. 64, and of Barthélemy de Razet, from 22 October 1418 to 21 October 1419, Inv. 16, reg. 65. See Table in Appendix 1.

30 Borel, *Les foires de Genève*, 57–58.

31 Regarding the number and dates of the Geneva fairs, a subject addressed by all the authors cited in note 3, see most recently Morenzoni, *Marchands et marchandises*, 124–127.

cccc xvii" was sufficient to date the purchases made without the need to specify the day and the month.

The importance of these commercial gatherings, integrated into the calendar of the court and the Savoyard administration, is confirmed by the quality of the emissaries the duke sent to Geneva. The appointed representative of Amadeus VIII at the Geneva fairs in the studied registers is Pierre de Menthon. Described as a "stable squire" (*scutiffer scutifferie*), he was attached to the stables—one of the three major court services, alongside the household and the chamber.[32] A loyal servant of the duke, he was authorised to handle purchases, the costs of which were later reimbursed to him by the general treasurer. While responsible for managing purchases himself ("*par sa meyn*"), he was accompanied by experts during his travels. When purchasing cloth, Pierre de Chignin, also known as Pierre le chambrier, the duke's tailor, was present.[33] When buying horses at the Easter Fair of 1419, Jean Maréchal, another stable squire, and a groom were dispatched to Geneva.[34] All of them stayed for several days in the Lemanic city, as evidenced by the per diem allowance allocated to them, which also covered the round trip from Chambéry (or another location) to Geneva.[35] Pierre de Menthon's regular attendance is noteworthy: present for six days at Easter 1418 and nine days the following year, he stayed

32 On the stables, see Castelnuovo, *L'hôtel de Savoie*, 34–44. Regarding Pierre de Menthon a member of an important family in the county of Geneva, future advisor and bailiff, see scattered information in Borel, *Foires de Genève*, 148, note 1; Max Bruchet. *Le château de Ripaille*. Paris: Delagrave, 1907, 459–461; Guido Castelnuovo. *Ufficiali e gentiluomini. La società politica sabauda nel tardo medioevo*. Milan: Franco Angeli, 1994, *ad indicem*; Elisa Mongiano. Da Ripaille a Losanna: papa del concilio o duca di Savoia. In *Amédée VIII*, 363–373: 371, n. 40; Pibiri, *En voyage*, 597–599. In 1423, he is referred to as an advisor in Inv. 16, reg. 69, f. 168v: "Libravit Petro de Menthone consiliario et scutiffero scutifferie domini [. . .]."

33 In my corpus: Inv. 16, reg. 64, f. 337v: "Item a Pierre chambrier pour ses despens [. . .]"; f. 341: "Item a Pierre le chambrier pour les despens [. . .]"; Inv. 16, reg. 65, f. 163v: "Item a Pierre le chambrier [. . .]." See also reg. 66, f. 231v–232: "Libravit Petro de Chignino chambrerio domini [. . .]. Ce sunt les despens que Piere le chambre a fait a Geneve [. . .]." On Pierre de Chignin, see Nadège Gauffre-Fayolle. Pierre de Chignin (1396–1425 ?), un tailleur au service d'Amédée VIII de Savoie. In *La fabrique de l'habit: artisans, techniques et production du vêtement (XVe–XVIIIe siècle)*, Astrid Castres, Tiphaine Gaumy (eds.). Paris: École nationale des chartes, 2020, 21–37.

34 Inv. 16, reg. 65, f. 164–164v: "Item pour les despens de Johan le marescal et Belloys pallafrenier qui se sont audies achiter lesdicts chivaulx en viii jours que chascun y a demoure a v gros par jour pour chascun: vi flor. viii gr." Other mentions: Inv. 16, reg. 63, f. 115: "Libravit [. . .] pro una veste pro Johanne Marescalli scuttifero domini [. . .]." He receives 60 florins "pro una veste status fienda eundo Constanciam ad ambassiatores." See Inv. 16, reg. 63, f. 77v. Also Pibiri, *En voyage*, 593. For Belloy, see "Belloy le palafrenier," Inv. 16, reg. 64, f. 335.

35 See Appendix 2: "Item pour les despens de moy Pierre de Menthon qui a fait a Geneve pour l'espace de IIII jours qu'il a demouré a la foyre de Geneve et pour II jours pour aller et pour venir a ung florin par jour [. . .]."

for the entire duration of the fair and even beyond.[36] Although we do not know where the Savoyard emissaries lodged—it should be remembered that the House of Savoy did not have an official residence in Geneva until 1446[37]—it is clear that they had sufficient time to conduct various commercial, financial, and—more broadly—political affairs.

The Duke of Savoy's large purchases were made during the two fairs reputed to be the best—those of Saints Simon and Jude and, even more so, Easter.[38] The duke spent 1,262 florins in 1418 and more than double that in 1419. These are considerable sums—among the highest recorded for those two years. These purchases met specific needs, which gives the supporting documents, fully transcribed in the registers, the appearance of "shopping lists" given by the prince to his servants. Their content is specific yet unsurprising. The 1418–1419 registers highlight high-quality cloths, mostly from Brabant (Malines), Normandy (Rouen, Montivilliers—cloths called "*de vicomté*"), or Champagne (Saint-Loup).[39] The acquisition of skins, linens, horses, and weapons completed the list for the Easter fairs. While it is unnecessary to revisit these expected goods, the information provided by the accounts and especially by the detailed supporting documents allows us to underscore two aspects directly related to the theme of the fair.

First, our source emphasizes the importance of logistics necessary for purchasing goods at fairs. The expense report does not merely list the acquired goods, but also includes the cost of their packaging and transport to their destination. Pierre de Menthon purchased canvas, ropes, and heavy thread to make bales. The packaging was done by hired helpers ("*enfardelleurs*") paid for this work. The bales were then entrusted to a mule driver, or alternatively transported by cart ("*veyture*"), and sent to Chambéry or another princely residence. The meticulous recording of these logistical expenses underscores the importance of these purchases during the fairs.

Another contribution of the supporting documents is that they scrupulously record the names of suppliers. Anonymity is the exception.[40] Initially noted by Pierre de Menthon on a small roll made of sheets of paper ("*in particulis scriptis in quodam rotulo papireo duo folia simul suta continente*") that the squire submitted to the treasury at the end of his mission, these names were then transcribed

36 At the beginning of the fifteenth century, the maximum duration of the Geneva fairs was six days. See Morenzoni, *Marchands et marchandises*, 127.

37 Caesar, Économie urbaine, 199–200.

38 Borel, *Les foires de Genève*, 56–58; Babel, *Histoire économique de Genève*, 360.

39 Agnès Page. *Vêtir le Prince. Tissus et couleurs à la Cour de Savoie (1427–1447)*. Lausanne: Université de Lausanne, 1993.

40 The anonymity concerns humble service providers, such as attendants and muleteers (see Appendix 2).

into the central accounting register after verification. One might question the need for this long copying process. As the transactions were completed and the accounts were not intended to legally certify the purchases (unlike a notarial deed), this effort was likely related to control by the treasury and thus by the Chamber of Accounts over the expenses made by servants. However, since it would have been possible to conduct such verification without copying the content of the supporting documents word for word, one might hypothesise that the central administration also wanted to preserve the memory of the suppliers' names. Some of them, whose presence in the registers is recurrent, are even highlighted in the left margin, making them easily recognisable. Among the Geneva cloth merchants, Pierre and Jean Tingeron, Jean Hengleys (or Lengloys, Lenglois), and Jean Ciclat[41] were clearly trusted partners in the eyes of Pierre de Menthon, who relied on them not only for purchasing raw materials but also for custom work. Another important cloth merchant is Termon Luc, from Romans-sur-Isère in Dauphiné, with whom the representatives of the Duke of Savoy frequently do business.[42] The horse market involved merchants from Bern and two merchants named Jehan and Griquet "of Bavaria." The weapons mainly came from Lombardy. One of the Milanese merchants met by Pierre le chambrier, a certain Bertino Busca, entered the service of Amédée VIII as Master of the Mints of Ivrea and Nyon in 1427.[43] Without overlooking the fact that occasional vendors are mentioned in the accounts, the overall impression is of two categories of privileged commercial contacts for the duke's emissaries: "notable" merchants with established reputations in Geneva and merchants from afar, primarily Milanese or "*alemans*," encountered at the fairs.

---

41 On the (de) Tingerons, see Caesar, *Le pouvoir en ville*, *ad indicem*. On Jean Ciclat, see Mathieu Caesar. Économie urbaine et dépenses princières. In *La cour et la ville dans l'Europe du Moyen Âge et des Temps Modernes*, Denis Menjot, Léonard Courbon (eds.). Turnhout: Brepols, 2015, 202–203, 210.

42 Termon Luc, mentioned several times in my corpus (see Appendix 2), is explicitly referred to as "marchian de Romans" (Inv. 16, reg. 63, f. 65v). The Luc family was among the most notable in the town of Romans in the fourteenth and fifteenth centuries due to their wealth from trade, their role in the consulate, and their connections with the collegiate church of Saint-Barnard. See Ludovic Viallet. *Bourgeois, prêtres et cordeliers à Romans (c. 1280–c. 1530). Une société en équilibre*. Saint-Étienne: Publications de l'université de Saint-Étienne, 2001, *ad indicem*.

43 "Item a Berthin de Vosca marchiand de Millan pour VII coctes d'acier, ung gorgerin, ungs bracelles, ungs gantelles et une celade: CLX escus." Inv. 16, reg. 65, f. 164. This is to be compared with the "Bertino Buscaz" from Milan who, along with several compatriots, received a license from the duke in 1423 to refine any metal, as mentioned in Morenzoni, *Marchands*, 130, n. 25. See also Giorgio Di Gangi. L'attività estrattiva e metallurgica nel Piemonte medievale: spostamenti di maestranze e trasmissione di tecnologie, «imprenditori minerari» ed insediamenti specializzati. In *La sidérurgie alpine en Italie (XIIe-XVIIe siècle)*, Philippe Braunstein (ed.). Rome: École française de Rome, 2001, 327–392, 348.

In addition to these detailed purchases, the duke also used the Geneva fairs for their financial function.[44] This explains the presence of Barthélemy Chabod, a senior officer who would later become president of the chamber of accounts, at the Epiphany Fair of 1418. He was tasked by Amadeus VIII with repaying 500 *écus* to a money changer from Fribourg—a certain Foguilly, who had advanced the funds to the Savoyard ambassadors sent to the Council of Constance. The banker delayed his arrival, and Chabod had to wait five days, increasing his mission expenses.[45]

Financial matters occupy a more prominent place in other registers than those covering the years 1417–1419. Although the principality's revenues had been stabilised,[46] the duchy faced extraordinary expenses that made borrowing unavoidable. The incorporation of the County of Geneva into Savoy, following a complex succession, cost Amadeus VIII "many efforts and a lot of money."[47] The settlement with the last heir, Matilda of Savoy-Achaea, wife of the Duke of Bavaria, for the sum of 70,000 florins, was paid in several instalments, documented in the treasurers' accounts until 1423. The account register kept by Guigonet Maréchal from 15 July 1423 to 14 July 1424, shows that to pay this sum, Amadeus VIII had to borrow from a consortium of international bankers based in Nuremberg, Basel, Fribourg, Geneva, and Florence.[48] However, what is significant in this matter is that the repayment schedule was aligned with the Geneva fairs' calendar ("*solvere promiserat tercio termino tunc proximo apud Gebennas in nundinis ibidem existentibus*"), whose rhythm set the temporal framework for the relationship between debtor and creditors.

44 Bergier, *Les foires*, 269–278.

45 Inv. 16, reg. 64, f. 377v–378: "Libravit Bartholomeo Chabodi [. . .]"; Pibiri, *En voyage*, 143.

46 Guilleré, Les finances d'Amédée VIII.

47 Pierre Duparc. *Le comté de Genève, IXe–XVe siècle*. Geneva: Société d'histoire et d'archéologie, 1955, 328–347.

48 Inv. 16, reg. 69, f. 243v–244: "Allocantur sibi de mandato domini quos dictus thesaurarius de eodem mandato soluit et libravit honorabilibus amicis dicti domini nostri et dilectis Vincencio Mater, Symondo Eburguer de Berno, Thome Vischer de Nurlinguent, Henrico Arbisen de Basilia, Henrico Bonivicini de Friburgo, Michaeli de Ferro de Gebennis, Anthonio de Laxaio de Florentia et Iacobo de Rotulo civi Gebennarum, quibus prefatus dominus noster ipsas seu ipsos confessus fuit se debere et legitime tenere videlicet centum quatuorviginti decem marchas unam onciam et tresdecim denarios ad pondus Troyes et boni auri scutorum cugni et stampe serenissimi principis regis Franchorum. Et hoc pro et mediantibus quindecim millibus quingentis nonaginta sex florinis Alamagnie per ipsos pro domino solutis serenissimo principi domino nostro Romanorum regi seu allibi de eius mandato ad causam comitatus gebennensis quamquid auri summam prefatus dominus noster eisdem solvere promiserat tercio termino tunc proximo apud Gebennas in nundinis ibidem existentibus cum submissione hostagiorum tenendorum apud Salodorum per dominos consilarios et fideles dicti domini nostri inferius nominatos per licteram dicti domini nostri de dicto debito et de testimonio premissorum cuius tenor talis est [. . .]." I thank Ulf Christian Ewert for bringing Wolfgang von Stromer's article to my attention. See Wolfgang von Stromer.

In addition to being a supply point for the court and a financial centre, the Geneva fairs played another role in the life of the Duchy of Savoy. Somewhat unexpectedly, the treasurers' registers attest that the fairs also served as a time and place for meetings between central authorities and officials in charge of the northern territories of the duchy. To cite one example: Barthélemy Chabod, already mentioned, did not only go to Geneva to deliver 500 *écus* to the money changer Foguilly. At the same Epiphany Fair of 1418, he was also tasked with collecting money owed to their lord by the castellans and officers of the bailiwicks of Vaud, Chablais, Faucigny, and Genevois.[49] This perfectly illustrates the overlapping of financial, political, and administrative activities at the fairs.

The sample studied seems to support the decision to analyse the extensive accounting records of the former States of Savoy. Firstly, there is confirmation that purchases made at the Geneva fairs are identified as such by the Savoyard administration. Although purchases were also made in the lakeside city outside of fair periods, the "fair season," with its own calendar, is clearly noticeable in the General Treasury registers of Savoy. Secondly, the inclusion of receipts for expenses made at the Geneva fairs provides the reader with valuable information on goods, prices, merchants, and their networks through multiple detailed entries. Although it may be unrealistic to quantify the proportion of princely purchases made at the fairs compared to other marketplaces, the awareness of the fairs' unique nature and the importance of attending them is clear. This required careful organisation on the part of buyers, travel arrangements, and logistics, which the records allow us to reconstruct in detail.

More fundamentally, the role of the fairs is reinforced by the analysis of this princely accounting. The Geneva fairs were multifunctional: they not only provided goods and served as a financial hub, but they also intersected with the practices of the Savoyard administration, which had many reasons to frequent these periodic markets.

Further research should reveal how long the Geneva fairs remained a key point of reference for the Duchy of Savoy during the fifteenth century, as well as the timeline and extent to which the Lyon fairs eventually altered this system, which flourished under the rule of Amadeus VIII.

Landmacht gegen Seemacht: Kaiser Sigismunds Kontinentalsperre gegen Venedig, 1412–1433. *Zeitschrift für Historische Forschung* 22 (1995): 145–189 who mentions this case. See also Wolfgang von Stromer. *Oberdeutsche Hochfinanz 1350–1450*. Wiesbaden: Franz Steiner, 1970, *ad indicem* for Michael de Ferro, Conrad Vischer, and Jacobus de Rotulo.

49 Inv. 16, reg. 64, f. 377v–378: "pro recuperando ibidem in nundinis epiphanie Domini anno Domini (1418) pecunias a castellanis et officiariis domini bailliviatuum Vuaudi, Chablaysii, Foncigniaci et Gebennensis nec non ab omnibus aliis officiariis domini."

Appendix 1:
Main attestations of Geneva fairs in Inv. 16, reg. 64 and 65

Location and Date (liturgical date)	Representatives of the Duke Amédée VIII	Receipt	Motifs	Amount of expenditure in *denarius*/denier (d.), *florinus*/florin (fl.), *franchus*/franc (fr.) and *grossus*/gros (gr.)	Reference
Geneva, 1417 "a la foyre de Geneve de la saint Pierre" (1 August 1417)	Pierre de Menthon stays for three days	1 Item among 19 "in particulis scriptis in quodam rotullo papireo duo folia simul suta continente"	Subsistence expenses	3 fl. among 37 fl. 7 gr.	Inv. 16, reg. 64, f. 335
Geneva, 1417 "a la foyre de Geneve de la saint Symond et Jude de l'an mil CCCC XVII" (28 October 1417)	Pierre de Menthon stays for four days, plus two days of travel	27 Items "in particulis scriptis in quodam rotulo papireo duo folia simul suta continente"	Purchase of fabrics and transportation expenses included	118 fl. 9 d. ob. gr. and 785 fr. ½ "ad 16"	Inv. 16, reg. 64, f. 336v–338
Geneva, 1418 "in nundinis epiphanie Domini anno Domini millesimo quatercentesimo decimo octavo" (6 January 1418)	Barthélemy Chabod, "commissarius domini" stays twelve days, from 4 to 15 January 1418, including five days waiting for the banker Foguilly	1 Item "pro suis et sui equi salario et expensis"	Meeting with officers and with "Foguilly de Friburgo"	6 fl.	Inv. 16, reg. 64, f. 377v–378

Geneva, 1418 “a la foyre de pasques de l’an courant mil CCCC et XVIII” (27 March 1418)	Pierre de Menthon stays for eight days and round trip	49 Items “in particulis scriptis in quodam rotulo papireo quatuor folia integra simul suta continente”	Purchase of fabrics and furs; services, transportation expenses	1262 fl. 6 d. gr.	Inv. 16, reg. 64, f. 339–341v
Geneva, 1418 “apud Gebennas ad nundinas festi pasche” (27 March 1418)	Barthélemy Chabod, clerk of the treasurer stays for twelve days and round trip	1 Item “pro suis et sui equi salario et expensis”	Meeting with officers “pro recuperando pecunias”	6 fl.	Inv. 16, reg. 64, f. 380v
Geneva, 1419 “a la foyre de pasques de Geneve comenczant le XXIIIIe jour d’avril l’an M IIIIC et XIX” (16 April 1419)	Pierre de Menthon stays for nine days and has assistants on site to select the fabrics and the horses	58 Items “in particulis seriose descriptis in quodam rotulo papireo quatuor folia simul suta continente”	Purchase of fabrics, cloths, weapons, horses *et alia*; services and expenses	2449 fl. 677 gold ecus and 850 king’s fr.	Inv. 16, reg. 65, f. 163–165v
Geneva, 1419 “in nundenis pasche” (16 April 1419)	Barthélemy Chabod clerk of the treasurer; his twelve-day mission took him from Chambéry to Thonon and then on to Geneva	1 Item among 17 “in particulis scriptis in quodam rotulo papirei duo folia papirea simul suta continente . . .”	Administrative reason “pro fieri faciendo memoriale de hiis que erant necessaria in nundenis pasche”	6 fl.	Inv. 16, reg. 65, f. 322v

(continued)

(continued)

Location and Date (liturgical date)	**Representatives of the Duke Amédée VIII**	**Receipt**	**Motifs**	**Amount of expenditure in *denarius*/denier (d.), *florinus*/florin (fl.), *franchus*/franc (fr.) and *grossus*/gros (gr.)**	**Reference**
Geneva, 1419 “a la foere de la saint Pierre l’an de grace mil cccc xix a Genève” (1 August 1419)	Jean de Compeys « escuyer d’escuyrie » stays for three days together with François de Compeys	12 Items “in particulis scriptis in quodam folio papiri”	Purchase of fabrics, cloths; services and expenses	124 fl. 6 d. and 9 king’s gold écus	Inv. 16, reg. 65, f. 176v–178
Geneva, 1419 “*in proximis nundinis Gebennarum*” (not specified, but between april and october 1419)	François de Menthon, knight and advisor to the duke	1 Item	Payment for his services (“laudabilibus serviciis”), to be paid at the next Geneva fair	200 fl.	Inv. 16, reg. 65, f. 275–v

Appendix 2: Purchases made for the Duke of Savoy at the Fair of Saints Simon and Jude in Geneva in 1417

This excerpt from the register of the general treasurer Guigonet Maréchal presents the text of the expenses incurred at the fair of Saints Simon and Jude in Geneva in 1417. The presentation of the expense is in Latin, as is the letter from Amadeus VIII, which is copied at the end. This letter, dated Chambéry, 9 November 1417, instructs the treasurer to reimburse Pierre de Menthon for the expenses he incurred on behalf of his master.

These expenses were recorded in French by the buyer on a small roll of paper consisting of two sheets, which is transcribed in the treasurer's register as supporting documentation. The list details the purchases made in Geneva, labour costs, and expenses incurred for travel, lodging, and the transport of the acquired goods. It offers a glimpse, in vernacular, into the Geneva fair of autumn 1417, its participants, the available goods, their origins, and their prices.[50]

Libravit eidem Petro de Menthone scutiffero domini quos pro domino eiusque vice nomine mandato soluit realiter et libravit personis et racionibus modoque et forma contentis et descriptis in particulis scriptis in quodam rotulo papireo duo folia simul suta continente quarum particularum tenores sequuntur prout infra.

Si appres s'en sieguent les dras achectés pour monseigneur à la foyre de Geneve de la Saint Symond et Jude l'an mil CCCCXVII par la meyn de Pierre de Menthon.

Et premierement pour la livrée des servitours de mondit segn(our) pour IX pieces de gris de Saint-Loup a XXII frans la piece achettées de Johan Lengloys qui montent en somme: IX^{xx} XVIII frans.

Item pour une piece de gris de Saint-Loup achect(ée) de Girard Ribol: XXII frans.

Item de Johan Hudel III pieces de gris de Saint-Loup a XXII frans la piece achect(ée) de luy, valent: LXVI frans.

Item de Johan Lengloys une piece de gris de Saint-Loup: XXIII frans.

Item dudit Johan II pieces de gris de Feugieres a XII frans et dimi la piece: XXV frans.

50 Inv. 16, reg. 64, f. 336v–338. I have generally followed the *Conseils pour l'édition des textes médiévaux*. Paris: Comité des travaux historiques et scientifiques, École nationale des chartes, vols. I and II, 2001. Developments made uncertain by the hybrid nature of the language are indicated in parentheses.

Item de Termon Luc pour II pieces de blanc d'Evreux pour fere la devise de la livrée: XXIX frans.

Item dou dist Termon une piece de rouge pour la dicte devise dou pont de Laeche achect(ée) de ly pour tant: XXIIII frans.

Item a Johan Lengloys pour une piece de brunete de Saint-Loup pour la dicte devise achectée de ly: XXIIII frans.

Item dudit Termon Luc XII aunes de gris de Ruant pour les deulx chappellans de mons(eigneur) a I franc et dimi l'aune achect(ée) de ly: XVIII frans.

Item pour les V pages de mons(eigneur) et pour Loys de Myolans et Ypprant de la Rongnie, de Johan Lenglois, pour une piece de gris de Saint-Loup: XXIII frans.

Item pour lesditz pages et lesdits Loys et Ypprant pour fere chauces et chappirons et pour fere raube, chauces et chapirons a Challes et a Monfalcon, pages, pour une piece et V aunes de brunete de Saint-Loup a XXIIII frans la piece achectée dudit Johan Lenglois, qui montent en somme: XXX frans.

Item dudit Johan Lengloys pour VI aunes et I quart de brunete de Bernay pour fourrer les II robes de Challes et Montfalcon, pages, a XVIII gros l'aune: VII frans et obole gros.

Item pour la Guilliemete de Geneve pour VII aunes achectées de Johan Lengloys de vert de Ruans a XXX gros l'aune: XIII frans II gros.

Item de Termon Luc II pieces de vert de Loviers pour les femes [sic] et escuiers de la dicte Guilliemete et pour forrer la robe de ladicte Guilliemete a XXII frans: XLIIII frans.

Item dudit Termon pour dimy piece de vert de Loviers pour forrer les robes de lesdites femes achect(ées) d'audit Termon: X frans.

Item de Johan de Tingeyron VI aunes pour le bastard de Bussi de brunete de la Vicomté a XXVIII gros l'aune: X frans et dimy.

Item pour XXIIII aunes de toille pour enfardeller les draps a XVI deniers l'aune pour tant: II florins VIII deniers gros.

Item pour VI cordes pour fere VI balles des draps dessus dictz: III gros.

Item pour de gros fil pour coudre les dictes balles: I denier gros.

Item a deux enfardelleurs pour fere les dictes VI balles: III deniers gros.

Item a ung mulatier pour porter lesdictes VI balles qui sont III charges de Geneve à Chambry [sic]: XXVIII deniers obole gros.

Item pour les despens de moy Pierre de Menthon qui a fait a Geneve pour l'espace de IIII jours qu'il a demouré a la foyre de Geneve et pour II jour pour aller et pour venir a ung florin par jour pour achecter les chosses dessus escriptes: VI florins petit poids.

Item a Pierre chambrier pour ses despens de IIII jour qu'il a demouré a la dicte foyre et pour III jours pour aller et pour venir, chascun jour IIII deniers gros, qu'il a vacqué pour les chouses dessus dictes: XXVIII deniers gros.

Item pour les robes de mestre Luquyn Pascal, pour Guigonet Mareschal tresourier et Pierre de Menthon escuyer de escuerie a XX escus par robe: IIII^{xx} X florins.

Item a Johan Escoffra brodieur pour une uncze et dimy de perlies desquelles la demy uncze est des grosses et l'autre demy des menues qui faillient pour la raube grise de mons(eigneur) lesquelles il a achecté pour tant: XIIII florins VIII deniers gros petit poids.

Item achecté a Chamb(ery) dudit Termon Luc le VIIIe jour dou moys d'octobre VIII pieces de blanc de Segans desquelx les deux pieces sont pour forrer les robes des pages de Loys de Miolan et Ypprant de la Rognie et celle du bastard de Buxi et pour les deulx escuiers de la Guilliemete de Gruere. Et les six pieces sont pour la livrée mons(eigneur) pour forrer les robes des plus honorables, la piece XIII frans et demy valent: CVIII frans.

Item pour XII pieces de blanc de Gigniat pour la dicte livrée a IX frans et quart la piece montent en somme: CXI frans achectés dudit Termon.

Summe des particules dessus escriptes: VII^{c} IIII^{xx} V frans et dimy de roy et CXVIII florins IX deniers obole gros petit poids.

Quem rotulum in quo predicte particule sunt descripte reddit annexum lictere domini de testimonio premissorum et mandato solvendi ac eciam sine difficultate qualibet allocandi habita cum dictis rotulo et lictera domini de confessione et recepta sigillo consilii domini Chamberiaci residentis, cancellario absente, sigillate et manu Guidonis Columbi eius secretarii signate, cuiusque lictere domini tenor sequitur in hiis verbis:

"Amedeus dux Sabaudie dilecto fideli Guigoneto Marescali thesaurario nostro Sabaudie generali salutem. Mandamus tibi quantus visis presentibus, libres, solvas et realiter vice nostra expedias dilecto fideli scutiffero nostro Petro de Menthone, videlicet centum decem octo florinos novem denarios et obolum grossorum parvi ponderis. Item et septies centum quaterviginti quinque franchos cum dimidio auri regis ad XVI quolibet quos pro nobis de mandatoque nostro soluit et libravit causis et racionibus modoque et forma in rotullo presentibus annexo descriptis, recipiendo ab eodem Petro cum presentibus et dictis annexis licteram de confessione et recepta opportunam. Et nos ipsos centum decem octo florinos novem denarios obolum grossorum parvi ponderis et septies centum quaterviginti quinque franchos cum dimidio auri regis quos sic eidem solueris tibi in tuo primo computo per magistros et receptores computorum nostrorum precipimus et mandamus sine difficultate qualibet allocari. Datum Chamberiaci die nona mensis novembris anno Domini millesimo quatercentesimo decimo septimo sub sigillo con-

silii nostri ibidem residentis, cancellario nostro absente, per dominum Guido Columbi. Vigore cusiuquidam lictere domini, soluit dictus thesaurarius prefato Petro de Menthone quantitates supra et infrascriptas ut per notam instrumenti de confessione et recepta facta per dominum Petrum de Menthone de predictis et subscriptis quantitatibus per ipsum habitis a prefato thausaurario [sic], causis superius insertis et declaratis, receptam sub anno predicto Domini millesimo quatercentesimo decimo septimo die nona mensis novembris manu Bartholomey Chabodi notam et signatam: CXVIII florinos IX denarios obolum grossorum parvi ponderis et VII^c IIII^xx V frans et dimidium regis ad XVI."

Bibliography

Primary Sources

Compte de la châtellenie de Montluel (1355–1356). Archives départementales de la Côte d'Or, B 8546.

Comptes des receveurs d'Amédée V, comte de Savoie, 1297–1308. Archivio di Stato di Torino, Sezioni Riunite, Camera dei conti Savoia, Inv. 16, rot. 1 and 2. Guilleré, Christian, Sylvain Macherat (eds.). *Les finances d'Amédée V de Savoie (1285–1308)*. Chambéry: Université Savoie Mont-Blanc, 2021, 131–281.

Compte du trésorier général de Savoie Antoine du Pont (1417). Archivio di Stato di Torino, Sezioni Riunite, Camera dei conti Savoia, Inv. 16, reg. 63.

Compte du trésorier général de Savoie Guigonnet Maréchal (1417–1418). Archivio di Stato di Torino, Sezioni Riunite, Camera dei conti Savoia, Inv. 16, reg. 64.

Compte du trésorier général de Savoie Barthélemy de Razet (1418–1419). Archivio di Stato di Torino, Sezioni Riunite, Camera dei conti Savoia, Inv. 16, reg. 65.

Compte du trésorier général de Savoie Guigonnet Maréchal (1423–1424). Archivio di Stato di Torino, Sezioni Riunite, Camera dei conti Savoia, Inv. 16, reg. 69.

Jaccod, Jean (Abbé). *La comptabilité d'Amédée VI dit le "Comte Vert", 1377–1382. Sa vie, ses monnaies.* Turin: La Pallatina, 1939.

Philippon, Édouard, Charles Perrat (eds.). *Le livre du Vaillant des habitants de Lyon en 1388. Estimation des biens meubles et immeubles pour servir à l'assiette de la taille*. Lyon: M. Audin, 1927.

Literature

Abbott, Fanny. *Des comptes d'apothicaires: les épices dans la comptabilité de la Maison de Savoie (XIVe et XVe s.)*. Lausanne: Université de Lausanne, 2012.

Andenmatten, Bernard, Agostino Paravicini Bagliani (eds.). *Amédée VIII–Félix V, premier duc de Savoie et pape, 1383–1451*. Lausanne: Université de Lausanne, 1992.

Andenmatten, Bernard, Guido Castelnuovo. Produzione documentaria e conservazione archivistica nel principato sabaudo, XIII–XV secolo. *Bullettino dell'Istituto Italiano per Il Medio Evo* 110:1 (2008): 279–348.

Babel, Antony. *Histoire économique de Genève: des origines au début du XVIe siècle*. Geneva: Alexandre Jullien, 1963.

Barbero, Alessandro. *Il ducato di Savoia. Amministrazione e corte di uno stato franco-italiano (1416–1536)*. Rome, Bari: Laterza, 2002.

Bautier, Robert-Henri, Janine Sornay. *Les sources de l'histoire économique et sociale du Moyen Age*, vol. 1: *Provence, Comtat Venaissin, Dauphiné, États de la Maison de Savoie*. Paris: CNRS, 1968.

Bergier, Jean-François. *Genève et l'économie européenne de la Renaissance*. Paris: S.E.V.P.E.N., 1963.

Bianchi, Paola, Paola, Gentile (eds.). *L'affermarsi della corte sabauda: dinastie, poteri, élites in Piemonte e Savoia fra tardo Medioevo e prima età moderna*. Turin: Silvio Zamorani, 2006.

Biolzi, Roberto. Military recruitment and funding in Savoy: Piedmond and Chablais, late-thirteenth to mid-fourteenth century. In *Accounts and accountability in late medieval Europe: records, procedures, and social-political impact*, Ionuț Epurescu-Pascovici (ed.). Turnhout: Brepols, 2020, 47–72.

Bompaire, Marc, Françoise Dumas. *Numismatique médiévale: monnaies et documents d'origine française*. Turnhout: Brepols, 2000.

Borel, Frédéric. *Les Foires de Genève au XVe siècle*. Geneva: H. Georg, 1892.

Bruchet, Max. *Le château de Ripaille*. Paris: Delagrave, 1907.

Caesar, Mathieu. *Le pouvoir en ville. Gestion urbaine et pratiques politiques à Genève (fin XIIIe–début XVIe siècles)*. Turnhout: Brepols, 2011.

Caesar, Mathieu. Économie urbaine et dépenses princières. La cour de Savoie au XVe siècle. In *La cour et la ville dans l'Europe du Moyen Âge et des Temps Modernes*, Denis Menjot, Léonard Courbon (eds.). Turnhout: Brepols, 2015, 197–212.

Castelnuovo, Guido. *Ufficiali e gentiluomini. La società politica sabauda nel tardo medioevo*. Milan: Franco Angeli, 1994.

Castelnuovo, Guido, Christian Guilleré. Les finances et l'administration de l'État savoyard au XIIIe siècle. In *Pierre II 'Le petit Charlemagne'*, Bernard Andenmatten, Eva Pibiri, Agostino Paravicini Bagliani (eds.). Lausanne: Université de Lausanne, 2000, 33–125.

Castelnuovo, Guido. A la court et au service de nostre prince: l'hôtel de Savoie et ses métiers à la fin du Moyen Âge. In *L'affermarsi della corte*, Bianchi, Gentile (eds.), 23–53.

Castelnuovo, Guido. Les officiers princiers et le pouvoir de l'écrit. Pour une histoire documentaire de la principauté savoyarde (XIIIe–XVe siècle). In *Offices, Écrit et Papauté (XIIIe–XVIIe siècle)*, Armand Jamme, Olivier Poncet (eds.). Rome: École française de Rome, 2007, 17–46.

Castelnuovo, Guido. The Rolls, the Prince, and their Depositories: The Archiving of Late Medieval Financial Accounts Reconsidered (Savoy, Mid-Fourteenth to Mid-Fifteenth Century). In *Accounts and accountability*, Epurescu-Pascovici (ed.), 183–202.

Chiaudano, Mario. *La finanza sabauda nel sec. XIII, I. I rendiconti del Dominio dal 1257 al 1285*. Turin: Società Storica Subalpina, 1933.

Conseils pour l'édition des textes médiévaux, vols. I and II. Paris: Comité des travaux historiques et scientifiques, École nationale des chartes, 2001.

Di Gangi, Giorgio. L'attività estrattiva e metallurgica nel Piemonte medievale: spostamenti di maestranze e trasmissione di tecnologie, «imprenditori minerari» ed insediamenti specializzati. In *La sidérurgie alpine en Italie (XIIe-XVIIe siècle)*, Philippe Braunstein (ed.). Rome: École française de Rome, 2001, 327–392.

Duparc, Pierre. *Le comté de Genève, IXe–XVe siècle*. Geneva: Société d'histoire et d'archéologie, 1955.

Epstein, Stephan R. Fairs, Towns, and States in Renaissance Europe. In *Fiere e mercati nella integrazione delle economie europee secc. XIII–XVIII*, Simonetta Cavaciocchi (ed.). Florence: Le Monnier, 2001, 71–90.

Fournial, Étienne. *Histoire monétaire de l'Occident médiéval.* Paris: Fernand Nathan, 1970.

Gauffre-Fayolle, Nadège. Pierre de Chignin (1396–1425?), un tailleur au service d'Amédée VIII de Savoie. In *La fabrique de l'habit: artisans, techniques et production du vêtement (XVe–XVIIIe*, Astrid Castres, Tiphaine Gaumy (eds.). Paris: École nationale des chartes, 2020, 21–37.

Gauffre-Fayolle, Nadège. Vêtir une ambassade en partance pour le concile de Constance (Savoie, 1417). In *Le vêtement au Moyen âge: de l'atelier à la garde-robe*, Danièle Alexandre-Bidon, Nadège Gauffre-Fayolle, Perrine Mane, Mickaël Wilmart (eds.). Turnhout: Brepols, 2021, 109–130.

Gaulin, Jean-Louis. Latin et vernaculaire dans les écritures administratives de la principauté de Savoie. L'exemple des comptes généraux du XIVe siècle. *Médiévales* 75 (2018): 11–26. https://journals.openedition.org/medievales/8979.

Guilleré, Christian, Jean-Louis Gaulin. Des rouleaux et des hommes. Premières recherches sur les comptes de châtellenies savoyards. *Études Savoisiennes* 1 (1992): 51–108.

Guilleré, Christian, Sylvain Macherat (eds.). *Les finances d'Amédée V de Savoie (1285–1308).* Chambéry: Université Savoie Mont-Blanc, 2021.

Guilleré, Christian. Le financement de la cour savoyarde du milieu du XIIIe siècle au début du XVe siècle: essai de typologie des dépenses de cour. In *L'affermarsi della corte*, Bianchi, Gentile (eds.), 145–161.

Guilleré, Christian. Les finances d'Amédée VIII (1391–1416). In *La naissance du duché de Savoie (1416)*, Laurent Ripart, Christian Guilleré, Pascal Vuillemin (eds.). Chambéry: Université Savoie Mont-Blanc, 2020, 237–276.

Guilleré, Christian. Quelques réflexions sur l'organisation des comptes de trésorerie savoyarde. L'exemple du premier compte de Martin Deschaux sous le règne d'Amédée VIII (1391–1392). In *L'honnête homme, l'or blanc et le duc d'Albe: mélanges offerts à Alain Becchia*, Andreas Nijenhuis-Bescher, Émilie-Anne Pépy, Jean-Yves Champeley (eds). Chambéry: Université Savoie Mont-Blanc, 2016, 223–246.

Mongiano, Elisa. Da Ripaille a Losanna: papa del concilio o duca di Savoia. In *Amédée VIII–Félix V, premier duc de Savoie et pape, 1383–1451*, Bernard Andenmatten, Agostino Paravicini Bagliani (eds.). Lausanne: Université de Lausanne, 1992, 363–373.

Morenzoni, Franco. *Marchands et marchandises au péage de Villeneuve de Chillon (première moitié du XVe siècle).* Lausanne: Université de Lausanne, 2016.

Page, Agnès. *Vêtir le Prince. Tissus et couleurs à la Cour de Savoie (1427–1447).* Lausanne: Université de Lausanne, 1993.

Pauly, Michel. Les foires de Champagne—et après? In *Relations, échanges, transferts en Occident au cours des derniers siècles du Moyen Âge*, Bernard Guenée, Jean-Marie Moeglin (eds.). Paris: Académie des Inscriptions et Belles-Lettres, 2010, 235–261.

Pibiri, Eva. *En voyage pour Monseigneur. Ambassadeurs, officiers et messagers à la cour de Savoie au XIVe–XVe siècles.* Lausanne: Société d'Histoire de la Suisse Romande, 2011.

Ripart, Laurent, Christian Guilleré, Pascal Vuillemin (eds.). *La naissance du duché de Savoie (1416).* Chambéry: Université Savoie Mont-Blanc, 2020.

Spufford, Peter. Trade in fourteenth-century Europe. In *The New Cambridge Medieval History, VI, c. 1300–c. 1415*, Michael C.E. Jones (ed.). Cambridge: Cambridge University Press, 2000, 155–208.

Viallet, Ludovic. *Bourgeois, prêtres et cordeliers à Romans (v. 1280–v. 1530). Une société en équilibre*. Saint-Étienne: Publications de l'université de Saint-Étienne, 2001.

Von Stromer, Wolfgang. Landmacht gegen Seemacht: Kaiser Sigismunds Kontinentalsperre gegen Venedig, 1412–1433. *Zeitschrift für Historische Forschung* 22 (1995): 145–189.

Von Stromer, Wolfgang. *Oberdeutsche Hochfinanz 1350–1450*. Wiesbaden: Franz Steiner, 1970.

Chapter II: **Credit and financial techniques**

Armand Jamme

Papacy and fairs: an elusive link?

The main purpose of this research is to examine how fairs, as a social and economic phenomenon, were illustrated, analysed, understood, and eventually used by a power with no equivalent in the Middle Ages—one that combined spiritual and temporal authority and legally decided on various matters.[1] For one of the earliest historians of pontifical finance, the Austrian Clemens Bauer, who published his works at the beginning of the last century, the "most universal" period for pontifical finance would have been the fourteenth century, since the Church and the bankers would have completely relied on one another.[2] In more recent times, Peter Partner, who shared these interpretations, even believed that this had been, "an essential precondition for the growth of early European capitalism."[3] Such stereotyped interpretations still influence the economic analysis offered by Anglo-Saxon historiography on the papacy today. Following the collapse of the system of the collectories developed by the Avignon popes, the Roman popes would have been condemned to rely on the limited resources of the Papal State, thus withdrawing into themselves the huge tax network that their predecessors had been able to develop in Europe. In reality, the resources coming from the ecclesiastical institution did not even play a marginal role during the Renaissance, as the 'budgets' kept for 1480 and 1525 prove.[4] And in the sixteenth century, the sums collected in the periphery increased again with the conflicts between the Papacy and the Turks as well as against the Protestants, and especially through a reevaluation of taxation in the Iberian and Italian peninsulas.[5] It is therefore impossible to subscribe to the Anglo-Saxon thesis that absolutely wants

1 This research has been financially supported by the ANR-DFG CoMOR programme.

2 Clemens Bauer. Die Epochen der Papstfinanz. Ein Versuch. *Historische Zeitschrift* 138 (1928): 457–503, republished in *Gesammelte Aufsätze zur Wirtschafts- und Sozialgeschichte*, Freiburg: Herder, 1965, 112–147.

3 Peter Partner. Financial Papal Policy in the Renaissance and Counter-Reformation. *Past and Present* 88 (1980): 19.

4 On that point, see Armand Jamme. Taxation and State in the Church Lands: a long Term Overhaul (1200–1550). In *The Routledge Handbook of Public Taxation in Medieval Europe*, Mathieu Caesar, Florent Garnier, Denis Menjot, Pere Verdés Pijuan (eds.). Abingdon: Routledge, 2023, 214. What was no longer paid in the peripheries was paid again (as in the eleventh and twelfth centuries) in the curia, with the development of the revenue coming from the central administration, mostly the Dataria.

5 Massimo Carlo Giannini. *L'oro e la tiara: la costruzione dello spazio fiscale italiano della Santa Sede (1560–1620)*. Rome: Il Mulino, 2003.

https://doi.org/10.1515/9783111621296-005

to transform the Pope, from the fifteenth century onwards, into a single territorial prince. Nevertheless, between the Middle Ages and the Renaissance, the financial networks used by the Church of Rome underwent a series of reconfigurations, which meant that they no longer covered the whole of Christendom.

To better define the relationship between the 'system' of fairs and the Roman Church, considered both in its institutional and social dimensions—that is, as a jurisdictional power and as a court—it is essential to test first a lexical question, given the polysemy of the concept 'fair' in the Middle Ages. Indeed, one must verify if the writers of the letters (notaries, abbreviators, secretaries, etc., as the titles of apostolic writers have changed during these centuries[6]) had a clear idea of what a fair was in relation to a market. The pontifical correspondence, fairly well-preserved for the thirteenth and fourteenth centuries and moreover largely accessible through the database, gives some answers on that point and reveals what the main problematic features in the organisation or management of fairs traced back to the Apostolic See were as well. Subsequently, it is necessary to question the role of fairs in the circulation of money generated by the ecclesiastical taxation within a burgeoning Christendom—the sources illustrate a space stretching north from Greenland to Poland—and the ways in which the calendar of the fair system could be integrated into these mechanisms. This development is important, even if the management of money transfers evidently changed between the thirteenth and sixteenth centuries, as much from the residence of the curia as from the evolution of taxation itself. Finally, it will be possible to test the real impact of fairs on the volume of businesses developed around the Pope, thus using both the Apostolic Chamber documentation and the accounts of the merchants and bankers employed by the Papacy.

Words for a fair—topics for a Pope

The *Ut per litteras apostolicas* database offers the contents of 80 volumes of papal letters published by the *École française de Rome* over more than one hundred years, between the nineteenth and twentieth century. Currently, this comprises a total of roughly 257,000 documents analysed and compiled by a multitude of his-

6 Armand Jamme. Écrire pour le pape du XIe au XIVe siècle. Formes et problèmes. *Mélanges de l'École française de Rome—Moyen-Âge* 128:1 (2016). https://journals.openedition.org/mefrm/3121 (14 October 2024).

torians for the years 1216 to 1378[7]—a sufficient ground for a lexical analysis. The search terms employed were *feria, mercatum, forum,* and *nundinae*. It appears that, out of 163 results, *feria* has 0 instances of use with the meaning of fair. The term always referred to a public feast or anything related to a feast or event. *Mercatum* was similarly always used in the sense of market. *Forum* had many meanings in medieval times, especially legal, but in the thirteenth and first half of the fourteenth century at least, was often associated by the conjunctions '*aut*' or '*sive*' to *mercatum* and then never designated a fair. For the last decades of the fourteenth century, on the other hand, we can have some doubts as to this clear classification. However, this could be the sign of the lowering standard of Latin of the apostolic writers already noted by some historians:[8] indeed, in 1371, Pope Gregory XI ordered the bishop of Cambrai to solicit the people in the churches under his rule to help in the recovery of 600 florins fraudulently taken in Brabant from Guillaume Ade, out of a sum of 4,000 entrusted to him by his patron, Henri de Vos, a merchant from Cambrai who in that time was on his way from the "*forum civitatis Gebennensis*" to the "*forum civitatis Cabilonensis.*"[9] The already known fairs of Chalon and Geneva are probably behind these two forums. The term preferred by the writers in the service of the pope in both the thirteenth and fourteenth centuries to indicate a fair is '*nundinae,*' even though in Roman times this word properly designated the market days. All the database hits of this term—a total of 58, of which 40 pertain to the thirteenth century alone—refer only to fairs.

The oldest preserved letter is a confirmation from 1230, at the request of the abbot of Lagny, corroborating a prior confirmation of the Lagny fairs in Champagne by Hadrian IV in 1158.[10] The second is a 1279 confirmation of a privilege issued by Celestine III in 1194 to the church of Saint-Peter of York, which obviously refers to those fairs.[11] However, the papal confirmations of letters establishing fairs are not particularly numerous in these registers. The arbitration, concerning the said fairs of Lendit, stipulated by the King of France between the bishop of Paris and the abbot of Saint-Denis in 1213 and confirmed by him as

7 These volumes contain either analyses of these letters, or analyses and editions of letters, since the registers themselves sometimes do not contain all the text of letters, but very brief analyses. On that database, see https://www.brepols.net/products/IS-9782503609188-1. The references below give the information to access the texts both on the database and in the paper volumes.

8 Anne-Marie Hayez. D'Urbain V à Grégoire XI. Un dangereux retour au passé? In *L'écrit dans la société médiévale. Divers aspects de sa pratique du XIe au XVe siècle. Textes en hommage à Lucie Fossier*, Caroline Bourlet, Annie Dufour (eds.). Paris: CNRS, 1991, 151–164.

9 Gregory (Fr. Grégoire) XI, Lettres communes, 11253.

10 Gregory IX, 483.

11 Nicholas (Fr. Nicolas) III, 673.

early as 1217, are registered,[12] but perhaps because one of the two or both the ecclesiastical parties asked for this as part of the conclusion of a long procedure. It means as well that for the thirteenth century, there are few privileges of establishing fairs. In 1250, from Lyons, Innocent IV granted the Order of Saint-James the right to establish fairs in its Spanish lands where this order was mainly present.[13] In 1255, Alexander IV, responding to the plea of the inhabitants who had proved their loyalty to the Church and as well to recall the control of the Church on the kingdom of Naples while the bastard son of Frederick II was considered a usurper by the curia, granted Capua the right to organise fairs in the first fifteen days of July.[14] This is the entire extent of thirteenth-century privilege confirmations in the database—not exactly impressive. The absence in these registers is relevant and a bit suggestive of privileges granted to lords and communities of the provinces under the official sovereignty of the Church in central Italy: it was often other levels of the political hierarchy that were asked to grant this type of privilege, as demonstrated by the later documentation produced in Avignon.[15]

These registers provide better information on the use of fairs by the papacy in the activation of the Apostolic See procedures. The fairs of Champagne, for example, were considered a specific theatre where the supreme authority of the Church was to be manifested. In 1225, the Pope ordered to republish the sentence of excommunication against the provosts, jurors, and *scabins* of Cambrai, which had already been formulated by their bishop in that city.[16] Ten years later, the Pope ordered that the sentence of excommunication issued by the archbishop against his city of Reims be republished at the fairs.[17] It is clear therefore that the Church, in its policy of forcibly normalising and punishing behaviours in contradiction with its doctrine, used the most busy fairs as a means of communicating

12 Honorius III, 655.

13 Innocent IV, 4830.

14 Alexander (Fr. Alexandre) IV, 822.

15 It can be noted that for the fourteenth century, it was the vicar general of the bishop of Avignon who, on 30 July 1335, granted the inhabitants of Châteauneuf the establishment of two three-day fairs: one beginning on the first of May and the other on Saint-Martin's Day (Archives Départementales de Vaucluse, Archives communales de Châteauneuf-du-pape, AA1). Another case is offered by the concession of fairs at Noves in Provence, but under the jurisdiction of the bishop of Avignon, then under pontifical administration, granted by Emperor Charles IV during his visit to Avignon and published by the bishop's vicar for temporal affairs on 25 June 1365 (see Armand Jamme. 'Garsabal.' Voyages, carrière et fortune d'un officier pontifical. In *Identités juives et chrétiennes. France méridionale (XIV*[e]*–XIX*[e] *siècle), Études offertes à René Moulinas*. Aix-en-Provence: Presses universitaires de Provence, 2003, 7–28, esp. 13).

16 Honorius III, 5676.

17 Gregory IX, 2811.

and propagating its own sentences. Some even became a tool in the hands of the Papacy to blackmail communities that challenged its authority into submission. In 1237, for example, Gregory IX threatened Vercelli, which had enacted statutes contrary to ecclesiastical freedom, with an excommunication, so that *"nullus ad nundinas Vercellenses accedat"*![18] Given the partial recording of papal correspondence in the thirteenth century, it remains difficult to measure the frequency of these forms of instrumentalisation of fairs by certain Popes, who considered them as propaganda tools and arguments for obedience.

Evidently, as places and dates to settle payments, fairs appear frequently in their correspondence. Numerous letters for Roman merchants who had to recover all or part of the sums owed to various prelates are recorded. Some were even establishing the repayment schedule according to the calendar of the fairs, especially in this area where north and south met and then structured the money market over a larger space.[19] The most curious letter is undoubtedly that of Gregory IX addressed to the archbishop of Trier in 1233. The Pope asked him to publish in all the fairs and other appropriate places the prohibition of granting loans to the indebted archbishop of Cologne and, at the same time, to inform the latter that if he ever came to sign one in that fair, he would be withdrawn from the government of his diocese.[20] As a first-rate financial center, the Champagne Fairs played a major role in the political programmes promoted by the papacy, particularly in the Crusades and the replacement of the Staufen in southern Italy by the Capetians: the conventions negotiated by Innocent IV with the French court for the conquest of Sicily in 1253 provided for the payment of 200,000 pounds *in nundinis Campanie.*[21]

---

18 Gregory IX, 3539, 4084. These fairs, known as All Saints' Fair and St. Eusebius' Fair, were confirmed to the commune by Innocent IV in 1245, since Frederick II had tried to move them to Turin (Innocent IV, 1291).

19 See Marco Vendittelli. Testimonianze sui rapporti tra 'mercatores' romani ed i vescovati di Metz e Verdun nel secolo XIII. *Archivio della Società romana di storia patria* 118 (1995): 69–99; Marco Vendittelli. Un inedita lettera di Gregorio IX a favore del romano Giovenale Mannetti. In *Sit liber gratus, quem servulus est operatus. Studi in onore di Alessandro Pratesi per il suo compleanno*, Paolo Cherubini, Giovanni Nicolaj (eds.). Citta del Vaticano: Scuola vaticana di paleografia, diplomaticae archivistica, 2012, 447–462; Marco Vendittelli. *Mercanti-banchieri romani tra XII e XIII secolo: una storia negata*. Rome: Viella, 2018.

20 Gregory IX, 1214.

21 Urban (Fr. Urbain) IV, 183; Innocent IV, 6819b. On the last question, see the work of Mathias Thumser. Kredite für den Krieg. Clemens IV., Karl von Anjou und die Finanzierung des negotium regni Sicilie. In *Die römische Kurie und das Geld. Von der Mitte des 12. Jahrhunderts bis zum frühen 14. Jahrhundert*, Werner Maleczek (ed.). Ostfildern: Jan Thorbecke, 2018, 373–402.

Some papal letters—but only a few—are related to religious cases. Of course, the letters, generally speaking, confirm the strong link between feasts in honour of a saint and the organisation of fairs, which they recall even if the purpose of the letter isn't religious. However, some already denounce that during the fairs, on Sundays, religious feasts, and holidays, no one was going to the churches to pray. In 1221, Honorius III intervened at the archbishop's request to separate the Magdeburg fairs from the feasts in honour of St. Mary's Day.[22] *Cessent in ecclesiis earumque cimeteriis negotiationes, et precipue nundinarum ac fori cujusque tumultus* specify the constitutions proclaimed at the end of the Council of Lyons by Gregory X,[23] which didn't seem to have any lasting effect on people's behaviour, since a century later, Gregory XI wrote to the archbishop of Lund that "ad nostrum pervenit auditum quod in regno Dacie malus inoluit abusus quod gentes dicti regni, etiam ecclesiastice [!], diebus dominicis et festivis nundinas atque fora tenent et ad ecclesias prout tenentur accedere non curant, sed per vicos et plateas discurrere pernicia et alia enormia committendo non verentur."[24] The fairs were somehow devouring spirituality, even if there was sanctity at their beginning—but this is perhaps one of the paradoxes of any form of feast!

During the residence of the Papacy in Avignon, the letters related to fairs, even if the registration increased enormously at that time (as we know), are less numerous. Moreover, they reveal a clear change in scale. Of course, the Pope still intervened in favour of Italian merchants to resolve legal and economic issues.[25] However, the great majority of registered letters were now referring to small and little-known fairs, related to an area which was the real hinterland of the Avignon papacy for a century—namely, the countries of *langue d'oc.*[26] The last letters referring to the fairs of Champagne are from 1334–5, but they only concern the beneficial career of the French Chancellor of the fairs.[27] The pope's interventions now consisted of settling disputes about the fairs of Saint-Bertrand de Comminges in 1309, or of Saint-Sulpice, near Toulouse, in 1352, and obtaining the confirmation of those of Saint-Ambroix in the diocese of Uzès in 1363–1365.[28] Evidently, the

---

22 Honorius III, 3289.

23 Gregory X, 576.

24 Gregory XI, Lettres secrètes et curiales Etranger 34448.

25 John (Fr. Jean) XXII, Lettres secrètes et curiales France 1182.

26 On that question, see Armand Jamme. Avignone tra mobilità e conservatismo sociale: riconsiderazioni intorno al nepotismo di curia. In *La mobilità sociale nel Medioevo italiano. 3. Il mondo ecclesiastico (secoli XII–XV secolo)*, Sandro Carocci, Amedeo de Vincentiis (eds.). Rome: Viella, 2017, 125–155.

27 John XXII, Lettres communes 62497, 63116; Benedict (Fr. Benoît) XII, 377.

28 Clement (Fr. Clément) V, 3949; Clement VI, Lettres secrètes et curiales France 5305; Urban V, Lettres secrètes et curiales 492, 1786.

communities and lords of the Venaissin asked more often for his sanction. Even if the Pope sometimes postponed the processing of their supplication until the rector of the province had given him an informed opinion—as in the case of Mormoiron in 1336[29]—Urban V granted Isle-sur-Sorgues the creation of fairs on Saint-Pancras Day directly in 1366[30] and approved a privilege for Elzéar de Puyloubier, lord of part of Saint-Saturnin d'Apt, that was comparable to the one granted by Queen Jeanne of Naples to the other lord of this *castrum*.[31] However, the number of cases dealt with in pontifical correspondence remains very small, if we compare it with what we know about the "fairs" phenomenon informed by other sources and which, at the time, had an impact on the existence of many urban and village communities.

For the fifteenth century, we can no longer interrogate such a representative corpus. Only the German area can be queried through the *Repertorium Germanicum* databases.[32] Nevertheless, this documentation shows a new and strong tendency towards social concerns, approached frequently through confessional themes, to the detriment of legal and economic aspects that previously structured the interventions of the Apostolic See. For example, the Pope intervened because some people at fairs were taking advantage of the immunity enjoyed by sacred spaces to take refuge there after committing petty theft. After a man was killed and a canon wounded during the fairs which attracted people "from all parts of the world," John of Glymes, lord of Berghen-op-Zoom, asked Eugene IV in June 1442 for the privilege of seizing the criminals after 24 hours.[33] These registers—and particularly, of course,

29 The Pope ordered the rector to inquire about a petition from Mormoiron, ready to cede half the entrance fees, requesting to hold an annual fair on Saint Lawrence's Day. The papal sanction took place on October 14 of the following year (Benedict XII, Lettres communes 3810, 4963).

30 Urban V, Suppliques 334; Lettres communes 17563.

31 We have also kept the petition of the lord Elzéar, who asked to hold fairs and a market in Saint-Saturnin d'Apt, whose lordship was half under the authority of the Pope and half under the authority of the Queen of Naples, because Foulque d'Agout, who held the other half of the lordship in the name of Queen Joan, had asked her for a privilege of holding two fairs on two days—the first on the Sunday after Saint-Andrew and the following Monday, the second eight days after Saint-Andrew and the following day—in addition to the weekly market day fixed for Wednesday. Because of this, the jealousy of the men under the other rule increased, because these fairs were only held in the part of the territory under the queen's jurisdiction, and accordingly the jurisdiction over the persons who came to the fairs was only brought to Foulque d'Agout. The supplicant concluded that all this could be detrimental to the part of the lordship held in the name of the Church. He therefore obtained a privilege comparable to that of Foulque on 18 June 1366 (Urban V, Suppliques 226; Lettres communes 17214).

32 See http://rg-online.dhi-roma.it/denqRG/index.htm.

33 Hermann Diener, Brigide Schwarz (eds.). Eugen IV. 1431–1447. In *Repertorium Germanicum*, 3 vols. Tübingen: Niemeyer, 2004, 4648.

those of the Penitentiary—are therefore full of more or less amazing anecdotes, which are not necessarily located and dated. In 1441, for example, the case of a priest who went to the fairs was penalised, but it was not said where and when in Denmark. He met another priest there, a great drinker and blasphemer, from whom he decided to keep distance in order to find peace. However, the latter, furious about his sudden indifference, rushed and hit him on the head several times with a lead pint to such an extent that he felt threatened. Having pulled out the knife he had at his side to defend himself, he mortally wounded the drunkard, and therefore asked for absolution.[34] These anecdotes ultimately illustrate not so much the sequence of fairs, which were sometimes not even mentioned—the texts speak about fairs in a generic way, considering them as a characteristic social phenomenon and not as a particular event linked to an institution or a festival, as in the correspondence of previous centuries, which obviously marks the extreme dispersal of the phenomenon—as the cases of conscience that these accidents created. To give another example (this one sanctioned in 1450), we can speak about a priest who bought a horse at a fair. He then sat on its back, but the animal was nervous. On the road he lost control and fell off the horse, which escaped, knocking down and killing a passer-by. Feeling responsible for this death, the priest asked the pope for indulgency.[35] This does not mean, of course, that the needs of the faith disappeared entirely from the horizon of apostolic letters. In June 1481, for example, the Dominicans of Cologne obtained the right to hear confessions and administer penances from Sixtus IV, because the fairs attracted large numbers of people of both sexes seeking confession and eucharist. In the same year, such a license was also granted to other convents, including Frankfurt.[36]

In a certain sense, the papal correspondence is a good testimony of the evolution of the fair system between the twelfth and the sixteenth centuries. However, it only illustrates an evolution that must be studied with other sources. The letters show various aspects of the fair system, their creation and organisation, the problems of jurisdiction, the security for merchants, the settlement of debts and loans, and even the financing of major political projects, right up to the cases of conscience raised by homicides committed during the fairs. But all these matters appear as the results of petitions which, for various reasons correlated to the development of the curia's *dicasteries* (court of justice) and the recording of administrative

34 Hans Braun, Paolo Ostinelli, Ludwig Schmugge (eds.). Eugen IV. 1431–1447. In *Repertorium Poenitenciariae Germanicum*, vol. I. Tübingen: Niemeyer, 1998, 648.

35 Krystyna Bukowska, Alessandra Mosciatti, Ludwig Schmugge (eds.). Nikolaus V. 1447–1455. In *Repertorium Poenitenciariae Germanicum*, vol. II. Tübingen: Niemeyer, 1999, 406.

36 Michael Marsch, Alessandra Mosciatti, Ludwig Schmugge (eds.). Sixtus IV. 1471–1484. In *Repertorium Poenitenciariae Germanicum*, vol. VI. Tübingen: Niemeyer, 2005, 3177–3179.

data, could reach the level of an official papal sanction. These letters then cannot reveal one specific policy of the Apostolic See regarding fairs.

Fairs in transfers

The circulation of money issued from ecclesiastical taxation and perceived outside the Roman curia developed strongly in Europe between the thirteenth and fourteenth centuries, then retracted without subsequently dying out. Italian merchant-bankers potentially played a major role in the transfer and exchange of these funds[37] from the very beginning of this expansion, even if this role was repeatedly redefined by economic issues (for instance, the bankruptcy of companies), political matters (such as a family or a commune falling into Ghibellinism or opposition to the See[38]), social affinities (such as the Popes' tendencies to promote people who had previously been in their service), not to mention moral decisions of the Apostolic See itself (since the first Avignon Popes considered the inclusion of bankers in the organisation of the Apostolic Chamber anomalous and denounced the contracts signed with several companies to develop their own management system[39]). Despite these factors, the predominance of Italian merchants in the Church's finances spanned the centuries.

However, it may be worth clarifying their real function. Even before the ecclesiastical taxation in the periphery began to develop, the Pope or rather his *camerarius* (papal attendant) sent commissioners with a specific mission to various territories to collect taxes.[40] With the development of pontifical taxation in the thirteenth century, the documentation highlights now well-known figures of specialised officers who travelled throughout Europe, such as Alberto da Parma

37 About the question of the geographical coincidence between Christianity and the Italian business network in the end of the thirteenth century, see Armand Jamme. De Rome à Florence: les banquiers et la curie (XIIe–XIIIe siècles). In Maleczek (ed.), *Die römische Kurie*, 167–205.

38 Giuliano Milani. Uno Snodo nella storia dell'escluzione. Urbano IV, la crociata contro Manfredi e l'avvio di nuove diseguaglianze nell'Italia bassomedievale. *Mélanges de l'École française de Rome* 125:2 (2013). https://journals.openedition.org/mefrm/1278 (14 October 2024).

39 Yves Renouard, *Les relations des papes d'Avignon et des compagnies commerciales et bancaires de 1316 à 1378*. Paris: De Boccard, 1941, 94–97.

40 For Spain, see the activities of the hospitaller Gonzalo Garcia in Peter Linehan. *The Spanish Church and the Papacy in the Thirteenth Century*. Cambridge: Cambridge University Press, 1971, 18–19, 190f.

and Jacobo di Sinizzo.[41] These commissioners demanded payments or promises to pay the sums owed from the beneficiaries and deposited what they had collected in the hands of various bankers. The account of the sexennial tithe of 1274 collected in northern Italy, written in the name of Ventura, archpriest of Chiusi, who succeeded a certain Ardizzone as collector of Lombardy, is very suggestive. The register lists a total number of over 60 deposits made by the collectors, more than 15 being ecclesiastical institutions (bishoprics and convents) and 45 merchants or bankers, some from well-known companies (Bonsignori, Ammanati, Chiarenti), but for the most part, they were small moneylenders, often coming from Lucca, whose presence appears very dense in the western part of Lombardy.[42]

This register therefore sheds light on the necessary distinction between accountancy and the movement of money. This case, of course, is not unique, as this sort of organisation prevailed in the kingdom of Sicily after the Angevin conquest as well.[43] The dispersal of officially collected money implied a series of transfers for concentrating cash, so that the fruits of taxation became available to be spent by the Papacy through one of the three or four "Merchants of the Camera" that, one week after the other, had the task in the curia to do the payments decided by the Apostolic See.[44] Indeed, the banking network used by the collectors of Lombardy is in total contrast to the list of companies activated in the curia at the time, specifically the Pulci, Rimbertini, Spiliati, Spini, and Bonsignori. In such an organisation, it was clear that the papal collector—often a cleric entitled to use the ecclesiastical sentences—was only a verifier of the payments. In other words, the real collectors of the money were the banking companies under contract with the Camera.

Some then presided over huge sums on the current account of the Church administered by them, which perhaps led them to cover immodestly the loans of some kings—especially if we consider, for example, the cases of the Frescobaldi

---

41 See the suggestive study of Stefan Reinke. *Kurie—Kammer—Kollektoren. Die Magister Albertus de Parma und Sinitius als päpstliche Kuriale und Nuntien im 13. Jahrhundert*. Vienna, Cologne, Weimar: Böhlau, 2012.

42 Jamme, De Rome à Florence, 195–197.

43 Renouard, *Les relations des papes*, 68, 149–54. Also see the more recent works of Antonio Antonetti. 'Cupientes subiectos fecliciter gubernari.' Diocesan administration in southern Italy under the Angevin rule: structural limits and reforming initiatives. *Revue d'histoire ecclésiastique* 118 (2023): 65–116.

44 See the description of the system in Tilmann Schmidt. *Libri rationum Camerae Bonifatii papae VIII (Archivum Secretum Vaticanum, Collect. 446 necnon Intr. et Ex. 5)*. Città del Vaticano: Scuola Vaticana di Paleografia, Diplomatica e Archivistica, 1984, XLI–XLVIII.

and Ricciardi bankruptcies in England.[45] To show the importance of the Church deposits on various accounts handled by these companies, there is nothing better than to consider the backgrounds of the first dispute between Boniface VIII and Philip the Fair.[46] Of course, the sums kept by Italian bankers in England and France did not all come from ecclesiastical taxation, as these bankers developed other businesses in parallel, but it is clear that it was the importance of the sums they managed for the Pope that led the kings of England and France to get their hands on them.

By deduction, it is therefore clear that ecclesiastical taxation, with its specific organisation, contributed to the general functioning of the thirteenth-century European economy and to the success of the Champagne Fairs, where products from the north and south were sold, but which also acted as a banking centre where currencies of all kinds were exchanged and debts settled. The repeated interventions of the Apostolic See to settle the excessive debts of some prelates at these fairs in the thirteenth century reveal their importance. It is known—but to what extent remains difficult to say—that the product of ecclesiastical taxation in England was able to help Italian merchants buy wool there, to then be sold at fairs or elsewhere in Flanders, as well as to buy various products—including sheets, of course—finally sold in southern markets. The money transfer system set up by the major Tuscan companies enabled them to multiply their revenues—on the resale of wool, on the resale of sheets, and other goods, and ultimately on change and money transfers. However, if we are able to understand the economic mechanisms, the problem is that papal documents preserved for the thirteenth and fourteenth centuries do not allow us to go beyond these deductions.

By the fourteenth century, the diversification of the ecclesiastical tax system increased the gross income of taxation, implying both the growth and the stabilisation of the collectors, but also modifying the methodologies deployed by the Apostolic Chamber. On the one hand, the collectors could henceforth act as dele-

---

45 Armando Sapori. *La compagnia dei Frescobaldi in Inghilterra*. Florence: Leo S. Olschki, 1947; Richard W. Kaeuper. The Frescobaldi of Florence and the English Crown. *Studies in Medieval Renaissance history* 10 (1973): 41–95; Christopher Guyol (ed.). *Kings, Knights and Bankers: The Collected Articles of Richard W. Kaeuper*. Leiden, Boston: Brill, 2015, 43–93; Ignazio Del Punta. Il fallimento della compagnia Ricciardi del secolo XIII: un caso esemplare? *Archivio storico italiano* 160 (2002): 221–268; Sergio Tognetti. Nuovi documenti sull fallimento della compagnia Frescobaldi in Inghilterra. In *Città e campagne del basso Medioevo: studi sulla società italiana offerti dagli allievi a Giuliano Pinto*. Florence: Olschki, 2014, 135–158.

46 Agostino Paravicini Bagliani. *Boniface VIII. Un pape hérétique?* Paris: Payot, 2003, 140f.; Armand Jamme. Le pape et les princes. Deux cas d'espèces: Clericis laïcos—Guînes. In *Gouverner par les lettres, de l'Antiquité à l'époque contemporaine*, Agnès Bérenger, Olivier Dard (eds.). Metz: Centre de Recherche Universitaire Lorrain d'Histoire, 2015, 117–145, esp. 126–128.

gated treasurers. Indeed, not all the fruits of ecclesiastical taxation reached the Roman curia, as they made various payments in the name of the Pope far in the periphery—for example, in Paris for the construction of the church of Saint-Bernard, in Italy to finance the wars of the Papacy, in Spain for Crusades, etc. On the other hand, most of these collectors could take the remaining money directly to Avignon which, thanks to its geographical location, was easy to reach. And they could do this more or less regularly, especially for the delivery and revision of their accounts.[47] It was then above all the sums collected far away from the curia that went through the intermediation of banking and mercantile companies.

Nonetheless, in Avignon, the Tuscan companies remained preponderant, and this for three main reasons: first of all, because they were already rooted in Languedoc and Provence—and thus in Avignon—long before the installation of the papacy;[48] secondly, because they could take advantage of the economic growth of the city (with a demographic multiplication by three or four in a few decades); thirdly, because of their unique expertise in providing all kinds of services and goods both to private individuals and to curial powers. But it's clear that their opportunities in the management of ecclesiastical funds were no longer the same as a century before, even if their knowledge on transferring funds from regions far from the curia remained quite unchallenged.

In England, for instance, they maintained their prerogatives throughout the fourteenth century. Even a thrifty Pope like John XXII ordered successive collectors to give half of their money to the Bardi and Peruzzi! Unfortunately, the sources we have do not all cover the interval between the deposit of the funds in England and their delivery to Avignon. We have two documents suggesting that the transfer was not always very quick: a payment order, written in Avignon on 13 May 1332 to the Bonaccorsi in England, and the receipt for the amount required, written in Avignon as well on 26 August of the same year—that is, a little more than three months later. However, the interest rates were so important that several companies competed. The Bonaccorsi went so far as to propose so advantageous an exchange rate from the English mark to the florin that the Bardi and

47 Charles Samaran, Guillaume Mollat. *La fiscalité pontificale en France au XIVe siècle, période d'Avignon et du Grand Schisme d'Occident*. Paris: Fontemoing, 1905, 142–158; Jean Favier. *Les Finances pontificales à l'époque du Grand Schisme d'Occident (1378-1409)*. Paris: De Boccard, 1966, 399–523.

48 See the relations in 1282 between the Chiarenti of Avignon and Cardinal Gudiel in Francisco J. Hernández, Peter Linehan. *The Mozarabic Cardinal: The life and times of Gonzalo Pérez Gudiel*. Florence: Sismel, 2004, 215f.

Peruzzi reduced their profit margins in order to keep their position.[49] These societies must have had real capital in the most important financial centres of Christendom to successfully tackle the problems of transfer, as it seems difficult to make money by working as described above in three months. However, it is true that documents of this type make it impossible to know whether the Bonaccorsi used a bill of exchange or actually transported cash in 1332.

In order to transfer the funds collected in Poland, where Italians were very rare at the beginning of the fourteenth century, the apostolic collector used the services of merchants from Krakow and Wroclaw who travelled to Bruges to sell timber, hides, and other products. Transferring money in this case was very slow as Polish merchants required a minimum of one year between the date of delivery of the funds and the deposit of cash in Bruges. This tends to show that the sums entrusted to them by the collector were used to buy goods in Poland to be sold in Bruges. In this perspective, the taxation of Polish beneficiaries really served the economic dynamism of the kingdom. However, this obvious slowness was evidently a problem, and in his correspondence with the Pope, the collector gave the advice to encourage the Bardi, Peruzzi, and Acciaiuoli to establish themselves in Krakow and Wroclaw.[50] The non-integration of some of Christianity's margins in the credit market driven by the most important Italian companies also concerned Scandinavia at that time. However, here the papal collector chose a different solution. Rather than going through local merchants, he forced the bishops to directly deposit the sums they owed in Bruges, including what might have been walrus teeth sent by the bishop of Greenland where the monetisation of the economy was reduced![51]

It seems from this perspective that the development of ecclesiastical taxation played a certain role in the decline of the Champagne Fairs and the development of Bruges as financial centre, as this city became *the* meeting point between north and south precisely in the time of John XXII. Draining the resources of the pontifical tax system from the fringes of Christianity required the settling in Bruges of Tuscan companies, at least if they wanted to maintain their good relations with the curia. Given the large sums of money coming to Bruges—sums which moreover increased in the second half of the century by the union of the kingdoms of Poland and Hungary under Louis of Anjou,[52] which drew a large part of Hun-

---

49 Renouard, *Les relations des papes*, 136.

50 This, however, did not happen, and the transfer of Polish money remained particularly slow throughout the century. See Renouard, *Les relations des papes*, 143–144.

51 Janus Møller Jensen. *Denmark and the crusades (1400–1650).* Leiden: Brill, 2007, 162–163.

52 For Hungary, see Fedeles Tamás. Petrus Stephani collector apostolicus. In *Magyarország és a római szentszék II. Vatikáni magyar kutatások a 21. Században*, Kornel Svozak, Fedeles Tamás,

gary's resources towards Bruges—these companies clearly must have at least had representatives here. And after the collapse of the Bardi and the Peruzzi companies, the Spifami, Malabayla, Salucci, and Alberti Antichi families were conveniently installed in the city.[53]

If, during the first half of the century, two types of money transfer had been developed—one by the collectors themselves and the other by merchant companies, especially although not exclusively by Italian ones—the reversal of the political situation by mid-century pushed the collectors, now facing increasing risks, to use mercantile companies more and more often. The disorganisation of the ancient system is evident in the case of the *Hispania*: money seems to have been systematically assigned to merchants who frequented the main ports. In the Crown of Aragon, the collectors used the skills of merchants settled in Barcelona, Valencia, and Montpellier, and in the case of Sardinia, of merchants from Marseilles. In Castile, after the collapse and closing of the Bardi's agency in Seville, the injunctions of Innocent VI to his collector to use *mercatores fide ac facultatibus ydoneos per modum secreti et tuti cambii* found a full echo. For the collector of Portugal, the problem was even more complicated. He turned to merchants from Genoa, Barcelona, and Narbonne, who delivered the sums he gave to them, not in Avignon, but in Valencia or La Rochelle. Afterwards, the money entered the Italian or the French system of concentrating ecclesiastical revenues, using the intermediation of merchants such as Raymond Garrigue.[54] The case of [the] *Hispania* is interesting because the adopted solutions did not involve real banking transfers: the collectors tried to avoid land routes, sending money on galleys instead, perhaps considering piracy at that time a lesser threat than brigandage.[55]

The massive return of bankers in money transfers in the second half of the fourteenth century due to the insecurity of both the roads and the economy in general also resulted in the atomisation of transfers and subsequently the disappearance of the Tuscan monopoly built in the last century. After the bankruptcy

---

Peter Tusor (eds.). Budapest: Gondolat, 2017, 31–88; Fedeles Tamás, Ecclesiastical Career of the Apostolic Collector Petrus de Monasterio. In *Incorrupta monumenta Ecclesiam defendunt. Studi offerti a mons. S. Pagano, prefetto dell'ASV*, vol. 1, Andreas Gottsmann, Pierantonio Piatti, Andreas Rehberg (eds.). Rome: Archivio Segreto Vaticano, 2018, 575–588.

53 See Andrew Brown, Jan Dumolyn (eds.). *Medieval Bruges (c. 850–1550).* Cambridge: Cambridge University Press, 2018; Bart Lambert. Making size matter less: Italian firms and merchant guilds in late medieval Bruges. In *The company in law and practice: did size matter?*, Albrecht Cordes, Serge Dauchy, Dave De Ruysscher, Heikki Pihlajamäki (eds.). Leiden: Brill, 2017, 34–48.

54 Renouard, *Les relations des papes*, 234–243.

55 However, this was not true. See Daniel Williman, Karen Corsano (eds.). *The Spoils of the Pope and the pirates, 1357: the complete legal dossier from the Vatican Archives.* Cambridge, MA: Ames Foundation, 2014.

of the Malabayla of Asti in 1362, the Apostolic Chamber had to change its policy and use merchants from Languedoc, who nonetheless had relations or associates in Bruges, Paris, and elsewhere. The reasons for this are unclear, but the skills of these merchants from Languedoc were undoubted. In 1362, for example, some of them coming from Montpellier took 5,168 florins in Bergen, now Norway, which they turned back two-and-a-half months later in Avignon. At the same time, the Alberti Antichi couldn't do better on precisely the same route.[56] The war initiated by Florence against the Papacy in 1376 further nullified all contracts with Florentine merchants.[57] However, this new opportunity was not a lasting one, as the See returned to Italy in the same time, and all merchants from Languedoc, Marseilles, and elsewhere were then eliminated from the circle of merchants working with the curia. In Rome, the Apostolic Chamber used the Interminelli of Lucca and some Pistoiese merchants such as Andrea di Tici. In any case, ecclesiastical taxation cannot be considered a driving force anymore by the second half of the fourteenth century, even less a contributor to economic development, as the Papacy became increasingly indebted for various reasons.[58] Significantly, no trace of the huge deposits of money that slept on the current accounts managed by various bankers a century earlier remains in the extant documentation.

The documentation available for the fifteenth century, as shown by Kurt Weissen's recent work, is scarce. In almost every chapter, his investigations lead him to turn to the fourteenth century, and even to describe phenomena such as the performativity of Bruges, which was already slowing down by the middle of the fifteenth.[59] The sources he really can call upon are a few bankers' account books and the 500 *lettere di cambio* and receipts from the years 1463 to 1469 referring to *Lionardo Spinelli e compagni di corte*, which reveal the business networks of these companies operating between *Germania* and Italy, rather than the transfer of ecclesiastical money from the Germanic area to the curia. Anyway, this theme is not very visible in Scandinavian, Scottish, and Polish documentation either.[60] Even Pietro

56 Renouard, *Les relations des papes*, 146, 309.
57 Richard Trexler. *The Spiritual Power: Republican Florence under Interdict.* Leiden: Brill, 1974.
58 On the cost of political power in Italy, see Armand Jamme. Lo Stato della Chiesa del secondo Trecento: un ignoto 'Fiscal-Military State'? Le lezioni degli archivi. In *Documenta. Rivista internazionale di studi storicofilologici sulle fonti* 5 (2022): 17–33.
59 Kurt Weissen. *Marktstrategien der Kurienbanken. Die Geschäfte der Alberti, Medici und Spinelli in Deutschland (1400–1475).* Heidelberg: Heidelberg University Publishing, 2021, 93f.
60 Ludvig Magnus Baath. *Diplomatarium Suecanum. Appendix. Acta pontificum Suecica. I. Acta Cameralia*, vol. 1. Stockholm: P.A. Norstedt & filii, 1936–42; see the accounts of the collector Pierre Gervais in *Dacia, Suetia, Gotia* and *Norvegia* in 1330–34 published under no. 311, p. 305–348. For Scotland, see Andrew Barrell. William de Grenlaw, papal collector in Scotland. *The Innes Review* 42 (1991): 3–18; for Poland, see Marek Daniel Kowalski. *Proventus Camerae Apostolicae debiti:*

Griffi's *De officio collectoris Angliae,* written around 1510,[61] makes no mention of what this collector did with the funds collected.

The techniques for transferring money from the Germanic area, reputed to be the least secure in Europe (as Y. Renouard put it), to Italy were no different from those of the previous centuries.[62] In other words, it was still transported to the curia by merchants—a solution documented by A. Esch through the analysis of the Roman customs registers, though he found very few, infrequent cases of payments to the Apostolic Chamber[63]—or transported to Bruges, Ghent, Venice, and then Lyon, where the money was deposited to Italian bankers. In fact, the documentation of the fifteenth century above all sheds light on the new geography of financial centres and on the transformation of the financial hubs of the European economy. Bruges gradually lost its function as a payment junction between north and south for the benefit of Geneva and Lyon; moreover, more and more merchants shifted their activities from Bruges to the fairs of Bergen op Zoom and Antwerp, which increasingly took over the leading role after Maximilian of Habsburg, in his fight against the rebellious Flanders, ordered all foreign merchants to move from Bruges to Antwerp.[64]

A set of Chamber papers in the Vatican Archives entitled *Carte varie di banchieri di Camera,* covering the years 1484–91 and related to seven banking compa-

opłaty duchowieństwa polskiego na rzecz papiestwa w latach (1417–1484). Krakow: Miejsce, 2010 (with English summary). Once the costs were deducted, there was, in fact, little profit for the Pope. See also Marek Daniel Kowalski. Rationes Iacobini de Rubeis, collectoris in regno Poloniae. Rachunki Giacomina Rossiego, papieskiego kolektora generalnego w Polsee z lat (1426–34). *Studia zrodloznawcze* 49 (2011): 61–96; Marek Daniel Kowalski. The Papal Collectorate in the 15th century Poland. *Quaestiones Medii Aevi Novae* 19 (2014): 447–460; Andrzej de Palatio, papieski kolektor generalny w Polsee w latach (1442–45). In *Ecclesia, Regnum, Fontes. Studia z dziejow sredniowiccza. Prace ofiarowane prof. Marii Koczerkiej,* Bartosz Dzialoszynski (ed.). Warsaw: Wydany przez, 2014, 119–127.

61 Michele Monaco. *Il De officio collectoris in regno Angliae di Pietro Griffi da Pisa (1469–1516).* Roma: Ed. di Storia e Letteratura, 1973.

62 Weissen summarises them in *Marktstrategien der Kurienbanken,* 67.

63 Arnold Esch. Mercanti tedeschi a Roma nella seconda metà del Quattrocento. In *Archivi e cultura. Rassegna dell'Associazione nazionale archivistica italiana* 37(2004): 47–56.

64 Nonetheless, the Bruges banker Konrad Pangortiner still played the role that some Italian companies had played in the previous century under Pius II under the title of *depositarius.* See Benjamin Weber, *Lutter contre les Turcs: les formes nouvelles de la croisade pontificale au XVe siècle.* Rome: École française de Rome, 2013, 336; Arnold Esch. Bruges come piazza di cambio nei pagamenti dal Nord'Europa alla curia romana nel Quattrocento e l'importazione di merci a Roma dal Nord. In *Economia, cultura materiale ed arte nella Roma del Rinascimento: studi sui registri doganali romani (1445–1485).* Rome: Roma nel Rinascimento, 2007, 369–412.

nies,[65] bears witness to what could be considered an involution in the organisation of papal finances in the fifteenth century, which became merely a copy of thirteenth-century practices. In these papers, the *computo partiti magni*—an expression used a century later in Lyon as well to designate a group of bankers lending large sums to the king of France[66]—shows how papal finances worked at the end of the fifteenth century. A grouping of bankers, fictitiously created by the Chamber or really existing before the contract they signed with it, termed *appaltatori*, made a loan of 30,000 ducats to the Pope. This sum was pledged against ecclesiastical revenues widely dispersed across Europe. This means that the resources of the collectories of Ireland, England, Spain, and Italy were granted to them, just as in the times of Boniface VIII. This re- or neo-inclusion of private banks into the papal financial system, correlating with the proliferation of cash registers and treasurers (even in the church lands in central Italy) and with the fractioning of fund transfers,[67] helps to explain the abandonment of the production of real general accounts by the Apostolic Chamber, which evidently would have been useful to understand the financial circuits and their evolution.

It is clear, then, that during the thirteenth and fourteenth centuries, the collection of ecclesiastical taxes contributed to the functioning of a certain number of fairs related to the channels of large-scale trade. For the fifteenth and sixteenth centuries, on the other hand, the documentation we have does not provide any indicative evidence.

Supplying at fairs

To test the real impact of fairs on the volume of business developed around the Pope, we shall examine the surviving accounts of the Apostolic Chamber and of the merchants and bankers employed by the papacy, even if perceiving the effective role of fairs, in the light of what has just been said, is a somewhat problematic perspective. The various accounts drawn up by the clerks under the command of the apostolic treasurer rarely make it possible to know where the enormous quantities of goods consumed by the papal household were purchased—perhaps at

65 Archivum Apostolicum Vaticanum, Instrumenta Miscellanea 7310.

66 Angela Orlandi. *Le Grand Parti. Fiorentini a Lione e il debito pubblico francese nel XVI secolo.* Firenze: Olschki, 2002.

67 In 1463, for example, Antonio de Veneriis sent 17,000 *livres* from Spain to Rome, using the services of nine different companies, all of them Florentine. See Weber, *Lutter contre les Turcs*, 335.

fairs, but surely from merchants who had various sources of supply. In the general accounts, the particulars obviously indicate the type of goods, their cost, and the dates of the official purchase, but they do not always give the name of the seller, the origin of the product, and the place where they had been bought. Obtaining precise and reliable information on the boosting of fairs, because of the supplying of the Pope or his donation policy or the needs of the court, is therefore not (so) easy.

In the Avignonese accountancy, where very few accounting records have been preserved for the thirteenth century,[68] the first mention of a purchase expressly made at fairs dates from 1326. On 6 July, Bertrand Faraud/Féraud, a merchant from Avignon, was paid for the sheets he had bought on the orders of the Chamber at the fairs of Villemagne, not far from Béziers. He had purchased large quantities of *burel, bruneta,* and *blanquet* for a sum which, including the transport to Avignon, was close to a hundred pounds of *deniers tournois.*[69] Two years later, the same merchant went there again to make the same purchases, also for the Mendicants of Avignon. However, before 24 December of that year, he had also gone to the fairs of Pézenas and to Clermont-l'Hérault,[70] once more to give alms of clothing to the friars, but this time in Montpellier, Toulouse, and Cahors. Faraud was accompanied by a cleric from the Almonry, Arnal Jordan, who no doubt chose the sheets according to the number of brothers to be clothed, while the merchant negotiated the prices and took care of the transportation and the distribution for a sum of more than 300 pounds. In June 1329, he was sent to the Villemagne fairs, again for the same reasons, at a cost of 251 pounds.[71] Later, another Avignon merchant, Raimbaud Clément, replaced him at the Pézenas fairs in September, still in the company of Arnal Jordan, to buy the same types of cloth for the Mendicants of Montpellier, Toulouse, and Cahors, which *eundo, morando in nundinis, eundo et distribuendo religiosis dictorum locorum,* now exceeded 375 pounds. And so on. On 8 July 1330, Raimbaud returned from the Villemagne fairs and presented an invoice for the same sheets, the *serpelheriis, cordis, carratagio,*

68 On that point, see Schmidt, *Libri rationum.* The following references all refer to the expenditures of Popes John XXII and Benedict XII, published in their entirety on the website: http://ressourcescomptables.huma-num.fr/corpus/index.php?q=Avignon. The development of the editing programme will later enable more precise lexical researches for the pontificates following these two. Karl Heinrich Schäfer's analytical editions are generally very good, but lexically incomplete and sometimes erroneous.

69 Archivum Apostolicum Vaticanum, Introitus et Exitus 73, fol. 92v.

70 The text doesn't specify whether or not it was at fairs that were also held there at the time. For a list, see Jean Combes. Les foires en Languedoc au Moyen Âge. *Annales E.S.C.* 13 (1958): 231–259.

71 Respectively, Archivum Apostolicum Vaticanum, Introitus et Exitus 92, fols. 92 and 94v.

loquerio hospitii in dictis nundinis, expensis factis et portatura to Avignon.[72] In the autumn, he returned to the Pézenas fairs to buy the same sheets for the convents of Montpellier, Toulouse, and Cahors. The details of the account reveal that the renting of a *hospicium* at fairs was used to store the sheets purchased—which in counterpart indicates the presence of large stocks under the sellers' 'tents' during the fairs—before their moving to Montpellier and Béziers,[73] where the friars from Toulouse and Cahors would no doubt have come to collect them.

With the election of Benedict XII in 1334, a few changes were made to the supply system put in place to run the Almonry, but they seem minor. The institution sometimes had one of the clerics in its service buying the sheets at fairs directly, and evidently, with the development of the Pignotta,[74] the horizon of the purchased goods expanded. However, the annual rhythm of purchases based on the Villemagne and Pézenas fairs remained unchanged.[75] All these sheets, apparently made in Languedoc, could have been bought directly from the manufacturers in Carcassonne, Béziers, Narbonne, and elsewhere.[76] We must therefore conclude that the large quantities required the possibility for the Apostolic Chamber to concentrate the supplies, and the low prices negotiated at fairs justified sending commissioners—especially for reputedly thrifty popes like John XXII and Benedict XII—for their almsgiving and the running of the Pignotta. Incidentally, other types of acquisitions appear in the accounts. In September 1335, for example, Raimbaud Clément bought a mule in Pézenas for the papal stables. The following year, in November, the Pope sent his marshal to the Pamiers fairs—Benedict XII was from Saverdun—to buy two other mules, evidently from his country![77]

However, most of the time, the account particulars did not mention where the purchases were made. We can also suspect that the writing underrepresents a phenomenon much more important than what it appears in the supplying of the papal household and the procedures of the Apostolic Chamber. The following case will demonstrate this. In February 1341, Jean Courtois, canon of Amiens, was paid for his purchases of sheets from Lagny (worth 510 pounds), Aumale and Hesdin (560 pounds), and Saint-Denis (228 pounds), made *in partibus Flandrie*, in

72 Archivum Apostolicum Vaticanum, Introitus et Exitus 29, fols. 87 and 91.

73 Archivum Apostolicum Vaticanum, Introitus et Exitus 108, fol. 96v.

74 As stated from the number of tunics and loaves distributed by Daniel Le Blévec. *La part du pauvre. L'assistance dans les pays du Bas-Rhône du XIIe siècle au milieu du XVe siècle*, 2 vols. Rome: École française de Rome, 2000, 514–543.

75 Archivum Apostolicum Vaticanum, Introitus et Exitus 146, fols. 110–112; 150, fol. 116.

76 See Dominique Cardon. *La draperie au Moyen Age. Essor d'une grande industrie européenne.* Paris: CNRS, 1999.

77 Archivum Apostolicum Vaticanum, Introitus et Exitus 146, fol. 72; 150, fol. 66v.

order to clothe the Pope's officers and to give alms to poor young girls wishing to marry, as well as *burel*, black *brunet* from Pontoise, and *blanquet* from Béziers, to be distributed to the Mendicants of Avignon. Including travel and transport to the curia, all this represented more than 1,500 florins, of which two-thirds were previously given to Jean Courtois in Bruges by the Acciaiuoli's factor.[78] These account details clearly prove that the proceeds of the ecclesiastical taxation concentrated in Bruges were used to buy supplies needed for the functioning of the curia. Even if the text does not mention them, must we conjecture that all these were bought at fairs—in Malines, Ypres, or another place—because of the diversity of origins of the sheets selected?

This specific case claims a revision of the interpretation created by the writing of the general accounts. Regarding the fairs, the drafting of the accounts under John XXII and Benedict XII seem to state a true 'Languedoc tropism.' However, in reality, pieces of cloth already bought in Flanders under John XXII were not uncommon.[79] Further, if we consider the supply procedures, the parallel is obvious: it was another Avignon merchant, Ricaud de Gordes, who was regularly sent to Flanders and Brabant almost every year from 1321 to 1336 to buy sheets to clothe the Pope's family and officers.[80] Even if the accounts do not mention the fairs, how can we fail to see in his missions an undertaking similar to those entrusted to Bertrand Faraud and Raimbaud Clément? If the Chamber knew where to get supplies in Flanders, why would it employ the services of a merchant, whose profession was to properly compare qualities and prices, especially at fairs?

In any case, it seems clear that attendance at Languedoc fairs became uncertain after 1340, even if the accounts do mention purchases such as black *brunetta* in 1359.[81]

---

78 Archivum Apostolicum Vaticanum, Introitus et Exitus 190, fol. 139v.

79 On that point, see Robert Delort. Notes sur les achats de draps et d'étoffes effectués par la Chambre apostolique des papes d'Avignon (1316–1417). *Mélanges d'archéologie et d'histoire* 74:1 (1962): 215–288. However, Delort is often confused about the places in which purchases were effectively made.

80 Archivum Apostolicum Vaticanum, Introitus et Exitus 41, fol. 146; 54, fol. 55; 73, fols. 49–50; 81, fol. 44v, 45, and 47; 86, fols. 62 and 64; 29, fols. 53v and 55v; 108, fols. 59v and 60v; 146, fol. 79.

81 Karl Heinrich Schäfer. *Die Ausgaben der apostolischen Kammer unter Benedikt XII., Klemens VI. und Innocenz VI.* Paderborn: F. Schöningh, 1914, 738. However, the sergeant provider, Dominique de Lucarel, went as far as Bordeaux and Auch to find enough to give to young girls to be married off to orphans and widows!

While Pézenas is still mentioned,[82] Villemagne disappears completely,[83] apparently in favour of Montanhac. In August 1363, 1,146 florins were paid for sheets still purchased at these fairs for the Almonry to the merchants Guilhem Quot from Darbain, Pere Ragas from Narbonne, Ramun Rocanat from Narbonne, Ramun Formic from Roses, and Pere Galiserie from Béziers[84]—all coming from the Mediterranean Languedoc region, which doesn't seem to make the case for the attractiveness of these fairs in that time.

After 1340, the main fair purchases commissioned by the Apostolic Chamber concerned events in Burgundy and beyond.[85] The sudden importance of the Chalon fairs for the papal household must be related to the ease with which heavy goods could be transported to Avignon (sailing on the Saone and then the Rhône), to the connections of the Chalon fairs with the economic areas of northern Europe, as well as to the wide variety of products that could be traded there —sometimes in very large quantities—in exchange for cloth, wheat, wine, fish,[86] and so on. In a few years, the organisation of purchases in Chalon seems to have moved in a real Cameral way, indicating the curia's attachment to the facilities offered by this business centre. In autumn 1352, the Avignon draper, Jean de Saint-Basile and the clerk, Jean Rosset once again attended the Chalon fairs. This time, the account is given in its entirety, which makes it possible to understand the extent of the reductions in terms of information made by the Chamber's notaries when they prepared the general accounts, so as the fragmentation of purchases carried out with a large number of sellers coming from Normandy above all, Picardy, and the current Paris region.[87] Although the two men regularly attended these fairs,[88] this didn't mean that all the cloth needed by the papal court

82 Karl Heinrich Schäfer. *Die Ausgaben der apostolischen Kammer unter den Päpsten Urban V. und Gregor XI.* Paderborn: F. Schöningh, 1937, 426. A factor from Alberti Antichi had already been sent to Pézenas before May 1373 to buy sheets for the Almonry.

83 Jean Combes asserts that the Villemagne fairs "disappear from the texts after 1346." See Combes, Les foires en Languedoc, 243.

84 Schäfer, *Die Ausgaben . . . unter den Päpsten Urban V. und Gregor XI.*, 44–45.

85 Before 13 October 1340, Raimbaud Clément bought cloth of Reims at the Chalon fairs. See Schäfer, *Die Ausgaben . . . unter Benedikt XII.*, 128.

86 Henri Dubois. *Les foires de Chalon et le commerce dans la vallée de la Saône à la fin du Moyen Âge (1280–1430).* Paris: Imprimerie Nationale, 1976. For the wine and fish, see Stefan Weiss. *Die Versorgung des päpstlichen Hofes in Avignon mit Lebensmitteln (1316–1378). Studien zur Sozial- und Wirtschaftsgeschichte eines mittelalterlichen Hofes.* Berlin: Akademie, 2002, 373–374, 379, 397–398, 400.

87 See the document in the appendix (Apostolicum Vaticanum, Introitus et Exitus 265, fols. 125v–126v). On the diversity of merchants' attendance at fairs, see Dubois, *Les foires de Chalon*, 160f.

88 Schäfer, *Die Ausgaben . . . unter Benedikt XII.*, 552, 580, 624.

was now purchased there, as the same Jean de Saint-Basile also regularly visited Anduze to supply the Pignotta[89] and probably other fairs, as large quantities were still purchased in Flanders.[90] However, Chalon did become a major supply centre for the curia, as shown by the career of the man who appears to have been a key provider during these years—Jean Rosset. Born in Martigny (some 60 kilometres southwest of Chalon), he first appeared as a familiar of the apostolic collector of Lyon, and then opportunely became a canon of Chalon around 1356.[91] The purchases he was then able to make for the Chamber went far beyond the fairs, as he also procured large quantities of cloth *in foro communi*[92] and was commissioned to send beans and oats to the Pignotta, and fish and wine to the curia. And since all these goods had to be transported to Avignon, why not take advantage of this opportunity to entrust him with the balance of the revenues of the apostolic collector of Lyon?[93] As we can see, the system set up by the Apostolic Chamber in Chalon was very efficiently thought out. From the fairs, a veritable supply system was built up by the court.

We can't discard the hypothesis as well that the Chalon fairs acted as relays, bringing together the needs of the Roman curia and the sellers from the north of the kingdom of France, as in 1352, sheets purchased by the Chamber directly in Paris were properly passing through Chalon before reaching Avignon.[94] The merchants settled in Avignon were also in the habit of frequenting these fairs for their own business, as revealed by some papal letters when they were robbed by men-at-arms. In 1361, when insecurity was at its height, merchants from Avignon, probably wanting to make purchases at the Chalon fairs, signed a contract with the Chamber which stipulated that the collector in Lyon would give 2,000 florins to their agent in charge of making their purchases in Chalon in exchange for the prior payment they made in the curia.[95] There is no doubt, therefore, that at the

89 However, the word 'fair' is never mentioned. See Schäfer, *Die Ausgaben . . . unter Benedikt XII.*, 438, 497, 533, 552, 561, 588, 623, 668, 738.

90 In 1360, for example, without saying where precisely. See Schäfer, *Die Ausgaben . . . unter Benedikt XII.*, 771–773.

91 Gregory XI, Lettres communes 32552; Schäfer, *Die Ausgaben . . . unter Benedikt XII.*, 588, 616. The 50's correspond to the boom period for the Chalon fairs, according to Dubois.

92 Schäfer, *Die Ausgaben . . . unter Benedikt XII*, 624.

93 Schäfer, *Die Ausgaben . . . unter Benedikt XII*, 761. Jean Rosset subsequently became fully involved in the service of the Chamber, following the court to Italy twice; he died as the notary of the Chamber before April 1389, according to the *Liber Officiariorum* of Clement VII, which he had helped to keep.

94 Schäfer, *Die Ausgaben . . . unter Benedikt XII*, 445–446.

95 Renouard, *Les relations des papes*, 205.

end of Benedict XII's pontificate, the papal supply and the Avignon business community shifted their focus.

Other fairs are nonetheless mentioned in the accounts, but only incidentally. At the Montferrand fairs of mid-Lent in 1352, the apostolic sub-collector also bought cloth for the Pignotta.[96] At the Barjols fairs, in the diocese of Fréjus, pigs were purchased before December 1354.[97] Either way, references remain rare. In the selection of fairs, the role played by the merchants themselves should not be underestimated. Precisely because their expertise was sought, they probably advised or decided to carry out the order they had been given in a place they knew or had already frequented. In this perspective, with the exception of the Chalon fairs (as we have seen), the accountancy of the Apostolic Chamber somehow illustrates the evolution of the economic structure much more than an economic policy of the Camera, inclined to consider only the costs and the quality of products. It is suggestive that none of the recorded letters of the papal camerary between 1361 and 1378 analysed by D. Williman mentioned a fair.[98]

These references to fairs, which were already random, seem (since the edition of the general account by K.H. Schäfer is incomplete) to become rarer from the 1360s onwards, although this phenomenon cannot be linked to a drop in the attendance of papal agents due to the insecurity in the kingdom of France,[99] for example, or to a structural reduction in the use of fairs, the Apostolic Chamber being able to draw on a large address book of suppliers since the curia was installed in Avignon for so many decades. Moreover, the relative silence about fairs as an economic phenomenon is not only a feature of the general accounts. This can also be found in the lower levels of the accounting pyramid. For example, on 23 April 1365, the account of the collector in Lyon, stated that the administrator of the Pignotta bought "XXXII pecias tele magnas, XVI mapas, III longerias, IIII saumatas pisorum et I saumatam fabarum in Cabilone" that he had to pay.[100] It is quite obvious that this officer coming from Avignon went to the renowned fairs of Chalon-sur-Saône, but it is not explicitly written in the account. In turn, this makes it difficult to measure the impact of the fairs on the volume of goods paid

96 Schäfer, *Die Ausgaben . . . unter Benedikt XII*, 497

97 And probably also in December 1341. See Schäfer, *Die Ausgaben . . . unter Benedikt XII*, 142, 561.

98 Daniel Williman (ed.). *Calendar of the letters of Arnaud Aubert, camerarius apostolicus (1361–1371)*. Toronto: Pontifical Institute of Mediaeval Studies, 1972; Daniel Williman. *The letters of Pierre de Cros, chamberlain to pope Gregory XI (1371–1378)*. Tempe: ACMRS, 2009.

99 The collapse of these fairs between 1361 and 1365 has been noted by H. Dubois.

100 "[. . .] que omnia decostaverunt in Cabilone, tam in prima emptione quam in portu per aquam et fardellis et pedagiis et aliis expensis usque ad Avinionem, 339 flor. 10 gros." Archivum Apostolicum Vaticanum, Collectoriae 67, fol. 78.

by the Apostolic Chamber, while on the other hand, the said impact clearly must have been much higher than mentioned in the written record.

The worst is that, if we consider the few accounts preserved for Italian companies providing their services to the Papacy and the population of the city, they curiously seem to be the same. A statement of a current account opened for Clement VI by Antonio Malabayla, which ran from 25 December 1347 (perhaps a surprising date to open an account for a Pope) to 6 December 1352 (the Pope's death), certainly didn't emphasise the phenomenon. Clement VI sometimes ordered precious tableware and other goods from him, though Antonio was to receive the proceeds of various taxes from the collectors of Tuscany, Scotland, or Poland. In December 1352, he was still to receive 41,000 florins—a clue that the transfers were not as automatic as administrative sources suggest. Nevertheless, among the orders of the pope were also woollen sheets for the Pignotta, for which the camerary paid him 2,000 florins. Antonio bought them *in nundinis Cabilonensis* and undertook the transport to the curia, proving that the total cost was higher than this sum.[101] A single indication of a fair in five years of accounts does not amount to much!

If we look at the accounts of the Italian companies, the impact of fairs on their activities was not great. In the *Libro vermiglio di chorte di Roma e di Vignione* of the Corbizzi, which covers the years 1332–37, many loans of money to clerics and nobles, not always from the surrounding area, are mentioned as well as expenditures for various cardinals, notably Colonna and La Motte, and transfers of funds carried out for by private individuals—for example, in favour of a son of a lord of Nîmes, who was in Bologna probably in the service of Cardinal Bertrand du Pouget. The three associates established in Avignon, Nîmes, and Montélimar could obviously circulate the available sums among themselves and were in contact with other moneylenders and companies.[102] In short, the Corbizzi developed a certain turnover. However, this book does not contain the slightest mention of a fair, in Languedoc or elsewhere, for the years 1332 to 1337.

The two *libri mastri* of the Alberti—one of the major Italian companies established in Avignon, especially in the years 1348–1358 covered by these books—are full of details of their numerous activities around the curia. However, they do not mention the interventions of their factors at fairs. The writing refers only—though frequently—to goods, like clothes from Provins and Bar, from Malines

101 Account edited by Renouard, *Les relations des papes*, 649.

102 Mario Chiaudano. *Il libro vermiglio di corte di Roma e di Avignone del segnale del C. della compagnia fiorentina di Iacopo Girolami, Filippo e Tommaso Corbizzi (1332–37).* Turin: Vincenzo Bona Tipografo, 1963, 16, 29, 171 for the details mentioned above.

and Bruges,[103] at the time necessarily negotiated in the fairs of Champagne and Flanders, but the specific costs of their factors at fairs and even their mission there remain under wraps. It is clear that keeping track of diversified purchases in accounts mainly requires the designation, the origin, and the price of the goods acquired and sold by the company, rather than the place and circumstances of their purchase.

The same lack of interest in fairs as an economic opportunity can be seen in the letters written by merchants at the court of Rome at the turn of the century.[104] In the fifteenth century, the accounts of the Apostolic Chamber were much more laconic than in the previous century. There is therefore no need to dwell on Roman *Introitus* and *Exitus* of that time. However, if we look at the administrative sources relating to the city's economic activity—that is, the customs registers of Ripa and Ripetta—it's the same story. The official tariffs mention the entry into Rome of cloth from Flanders, Champagne, and Languedoc, without ever mentioning a fair of any kind.[105]

Some accounts and statements of account with companies based in Rome have also been preserved, particularly for the second half of the century, marked by a greater stability of the curia in the Eternal City. These attest, of course, to changes in the European economic map, and in particular to the development of Lyon as a financial centre, following the founding of the fairs. However, it's still quite difficult to go beyond. For example, the receipts delivered by the Apostolic Chamber on the 14 and 16 February 1469 to the Pazzi and to the Medicis installed in Rome for the 14,000 and 16,000 florins deposited by the papal *nuncius* in France in the agencies of the Pazzi and Medicis in Lyon, say nothing about the fairs.[106] It was clearly in Lyon that the resources of ecclesiastical taxation in France were concentrated—Lyon having supplanted Avignon at this time—but it is difficult to link this financial power of the city to the fairs, because no account books of the collectors of Lyon have been preserved for that time and for the sixteenth century in the cameral collection of the Archivio di Stato in Rome.

103 Richard Goldthwaite, Enzo Settesoldi, Marco Spallanzani (eds.). *Due Libri Mastri degli Alberti, una grande compagnia di Calimala*. Florence: Cassa di Risparmio di Firenze, 1995.
104 Luciano Palermo. *Il mercato romano nel carteggio di Francesco Datini (1377–1409). Appendice documentaria: lettere da Roma a Barcellona, Valenza e Maiorca (1397–1407).* Rome: Roma nel Rinascimento, 2020.
105 See the regulations of 1416 in Maria Luisa Lombardo. *La dogana di Ripa e Ripetta nel sistema dell'ordinamento tributario a Roma dal Medioevo al secolo XV*. Rome: Centro di Ricerca, 1978; Maria Luisa Lombardo. *Camera urbis. Dohana Ripe et Ripecte. Liber introitus 1428*. Rome: Istituto di studi romani, 1978; Maria Luisa Lombardo. *Dohana minuta Urbis: liber introitus 1422*. Rome: Centro di Ricerca Medievali e Protocolli Notarili, 1983.
106 Archivum Apostolicum Vaticanum, Diversa Cameralia 34, fols. 213v-4.

The *Liber obligationum* of the Spinelli bank covering the years 1472–77 contains various commitments to repay sums borrowed in Rome, in Milan, Naples, Ferrara, Viterbo, Venice, Bruges, Montpellier, Geneva, and Lyon, but without any mention of fairs. A ledger kept by Francesco di Pescia, still for the Spinelli company, proves that in 1478, some merchants from Lyon came as far as Rome to buy some goods, but the mention of the Lyon fairs appears only as one of the possible places of repayment, and only as a payment term (*in proximis nundinis omnium Sanctorum*). And in that transaction, the receiver had to be not a passing merchant who frequented the Lyon fairs, but the stable agency of Lorenzo de Medicis.[107]

Conclusion

The silence surrounding fairs in the processes of writing and memorising financial data, both of the Apostolic Chamber and of the leading banking and commercial companies, obviously raises questions. In the last two well-documented centuries of the Middle Ages, the phenomenon of fairs was potentially so widespread as part of everyday economic life that it rarely needed to be specified in writing, except when dates and places were essential for administrative purposes.

The papal documentation as a whole (epistolary and accountancy) highlights certain phenomena impossible to perceive for the medieval times elsewhere. While the founding of fairs was clearly abandoned to the lower echelons of the political hierarchy, the impact they had on economic activity in the thirteenth century above all was clearly displayed when the Apostolic See took a decision to be obeyed by people who challenged its primacy. This is no longer the case thereafter, perhaps due to the extreme spread of the fair phenomenon and therefore the lesser extent of economic impact of each one. In the fifteenth century, the epistolary documentation seems to emphasise other aspects of fair time, which was conducive to all forms of expansiveness and excess—and subsequently, of course, called for penance! However, we have seen that the social use of the economic fair—in other words, its funfair side—was already denounced by the Council of Lyon in 1274.

---

107 On 15 October 1482, Jean Balestier, dean of Sion, in the name of Jodon de Siluon, *primicier* of the bishop of Grenoble and Sion, Antoine de Saint-Priest, lord of *Vallibus*, and Pierre Carron, secretary of the *Dauphin*, were taking 5,294 ducats which were to be deposited either in Milan at the company of Ambrosio de Rosinis and nephews, or that of Francesco Dominici of Florence and sons, or in Lyon *in proximis nundinis omnium Sanctorum* with Lorenzo de Medicis and Francesco de *Suxcitis*. See Archivio di Stato di Roma, Camerale I, Appendice 22, fol. 4.

On the other hand, the development of ecclesiastical taxation in the fourteenth century and, above all, the stabilisation of collectors throughout Europe in that time, placed part of the Church's finances close to areas where fairs were concentrated. As each collector was, in fact, at the head of a particular fund, he was able to make payments on the spot by order of the Chamber or to organise money transfers to the curia. The Avignon documentation reveals the plasticity with which the Apostolic Chamber dealt with the question of the use of its resources, sometimes putting the so-called Tuscan hegemony on financial transfers to the test, often preferring the actual transport of cash, which tends to show that the use of the fairs in financial ecclesiastical transfers in the fourteenth century probably had a marginal role, or at any rate was left to the discretion of the banking and trading companies.

When it comes to supplying goods of all kinds in great quantities—both for the poor, for beggars, for officers, and for the Pope himself and those close to him—the role of fairs on the contrary seems unmistakeable, particularly in the fourteenth century, even if the recording of expenditures does not always reflect this. The contrast with the Papacy of the previous century is striking. The Popes of the thirteenth century, who did not always reside in the Eternal City, found enough to meet all their needs in Rome itself, among the Roman and Tuscan merchants who had settled there,[108] whereas the Popes of Avignon—admittedly much more generous in terms of almsgiving—never ceased to send their emissaries to take care of their supplies of low and high quality products from afar. Despite the installation of numerous Italian companies in Avignon and despite the economic impetus necessarily created by the city's demographic and political development, the historian can only observe the lasting contraction of Avignon's skills—in complete contradiction to the legendary leitmotif of Anglo-Saxon historiography on the abundance and luxury of the Avignon court—as local merchants were unable to supply all the products required by the curia. However, no comparable phenomenon can be seen, much less easily accessible, in Roman documentation from the fifteenth century, which once again seems to show a great detachment from fairs and to privilege local expenditures. With regards to differences in administrative supplying systems or differences in the economic structures on either side of the Alps, the historian is sometimes condemned to glimpse rather than see.

108 See Schmidt, *Libri rationum Camerae Bonifatii papae VIII*; Armand Jamme. Festività, mercanti e contabilità. Il resoconto delle celebrazioni matrimoniali e del cavalierato di un pronipote di Bonifacio VIII. *Bullettino dell'Istituto Storico Italiano per il Medio Evo* 125 (2003): 185–222.

Appendix

Report of Jean de Saint-Basile and Jean Rosset about their mission for supplying the papal almonry at the Chalon fairs, prior to 17 December 1352
(Archivum Apostolicum Vaticanum, Introitus et Exitus 265, fols. 125v–126v).

Die XVII mensis decembris Sede vacante. Sequitur computum Johannis de Sancto Basilio, draperio Avinion., et Johannis Rosseti, clerici, de pannis per ipsos emptos in nundinis Cabilonen. a personis infrascriptis pro provisione elemosine facienda prout sequitur:

Et primo dixerunt se emisse a Johannis de Montorvet XXIII pecias panni, qualibet pretio X flor., II^{c}XXX flor.; item, a dicto Bossinel de Sancto Lupo XIIII pecias, qualibet pretio X flor. VI gross., CXLVII flor.; item a Guillelmo lo Viel de Bernay VII pecias nigras minoris forme, videlicet III peciis computatis pro duobus, qualibet pretio X flor., LXX flor.; item a Rotberto Cont de Sancto Lupo IIII pecias brunete maioris forme, qualibet pretio XIIII flor. cum dimidio, LVIII flor.; item a Nicolao de Mentil I pecia brunete, XI flor.; item a Nicolao Petit Dauboton XIX pecias maioris forme, qualibet precio XII flor. I quart., II^{c}XXXII flor., IX gross.; item a Bauduno de Beumont I pecia, X flor. VI gross.; item a Balduino Vassellin de Saint Omer II pecias, qualibet precio XXI flor., XLII flor.; item a Johanne de Fornollo Rothomagen.,[109] qualibet pretio IX flor. cum dimidio, XIX flor.; item a Giraudo de Dignant VIII pecias, qualibet pretio XI flor., LXXXVIII flor.; item a Guillelmo de Vauh de Sancto Jacobo,[110] qualibet pretio V flor., XXV flor.; item a Johanne Chalon. de Branmont II pecias, qualibet pretio XI flor., XXII flor.; item a Nicolao Lo Viel de Bernay I pecia maioris forme pretio IX flor.; item a Balduino de Belmont I pecia X flor.; item a Johanne et Wellmi de Grantmont XXVIII pecias maioris forme, qualibet pretio XV flor., IIII^{c}XX flor.; item a Rotgerio Lupi de Nanteau V pecias de verguat, qualibet pretio VII flor., XXXV flor.; item a Thoma de Meres de Sancto Lupo VII pecias maioris forme, qualibet XVI flor., CXII flor.; item a dicto Rae de Belme de Sancto Lupo XIII pecias, qualibet pretio XII flor. cum dimidio, XXV flor.; item a Guillaudo Mallart de Sancto Lupo VIII pecias burels et eschaquat, qualibet precio IX flor. cum dimidio, LXXVI flor.; item a Guillelmo de Bernay XXI pecias maioris forme, qualibet precio IX flor., CLXXXIX flor.; item ab Odone Picart, lo Boleguer de Bernay, VI pecias minoris forme, pretio qualibet IX flor., LIIII flor.; item a Guillelmo de Pistol de Malaval VI pecias minoris forme, qualibet pretio VI flor., XXXVI flor.; item a Johanne Daviers Deurens (sic) XXXIIII

109 The copyist has obviously omitted a few words here, so it's not clear whether Rouen indicates the origin of the merchant or the product.
110 Same remark.

pecias minoris forme, qualibet precio IX flor., III^{c}VI flor.; item a Petro de Chalon de Sancto Lupo dimidiam peciam V flor VI gross.

[126] Summa totalis pannorum II^{c}XX pecias cum dimidio, tam maioris forme quam minoris, videlicet CXLV maioris forme et LXXVI (sic) minoris forme, tam de Bernay quam Deurens (sic).

Summa totius pecunie emptionis: II^{m}III^{c}XLIII flor. III gross.

Sequntur expense facte per dictos J. de Sancto Basilio et J. Rosseti in emendo dictos pannos:

Et primo pro expensis ipsius J. de Sancto Basilio in veniendo de Avinion. usque Cabilon. et pro dicto J. Rosseti in eundo de Lugdun. Cabilon. et stando in Cabilon. et in reveniendo Lugdun. pro se equis suis famulis et fuerunt per spatium XXXVIII dierum pro omnibus, XL flor.; item pro II^{c} ulnis tele ad mensuram Cabilon., qualibet alna pretio II s. VI d. tur., val. XXV lbr. tur., flor. boni ponderis pro XXII s. tur. computato, val. XXII flor. XVI s.; item pro conductu cuiusdam botique in qua fuerunt reponiti dicti panni, XL s. tur., flor. ut supra; item pro quodam penoncello et pro signando gibas seu fardellos, IX s. tur.; item pro aromcando (lecture incertaine) et broissando dictos pannos, II flor.; item in fardelando seu faciendo IIII flor.; item pro cordis necessariis pro dictis gibis, II flor. VI gross.; item pro quodam nuncio qui portavit pannos de botiqua ad locum ubi fiebant gibe, VI s.; item pro portando gibas seu fardellos de dicto loco usque ad Sagonam, XXII s. VIII d.; item pro vino dato et potato in faciendo gibas et pluribus aliis, X s. tur.; item pro telo unus spelerie que deficiebant II flor. II s. tur.; item pro faciendo tendutas, IX s. tur.; item pro vino dato castellano Cabilon. qui promisit dictos pannos extrahi a Burgundia, I flor.; item pro portando dictos pannos de aulis seul loco ubi emebantur, I flor.; item pro denariis datis in faciendo forum, V s. tur; item pro conductu camere nostre et stabuli in Cabilon., III flor.; item pro II peciis tele albe pro usu domini nostri, qualibet pecia continente XIX aln. ad mensuram Cabilon., qualibet pretio VIII s. VI d. tur., flor. pro XXII s. tur. valent. VIIII lbr. V s. tur. que val. VII flor. unus [s.] XII d.; item pro expensis duorum nuntiorum qui continue fuerunt in navigio cum dictis pannis de Cabilon. usque Lugdunum, et fuerunt pro octo dies in veniendo propter tenuitatem aquarum et destin [ationis], pro omnibus, IIII flor.; item pro vino dato pedagiariis de Cabilon. usque Lugdunum et de Lugdun. usque Avinion. VII flor.; item pro expensis J. Rosseti et nuncii quas fecit in ducendo dictos pannos et in reveniendo de curia usque Lugd. et pro quodam alio nuncio qui custodiebat pannos, et fuerunt per [126v] XXI dies et ultra super aquam propter tenuitatem aquarum XI flor. et M po. et III gross.; item pro portu dictorum pannorum de Cabilon. usque Avinion. et dictos pannos dux[it] dictus Ramos Prelli nauta, pro omnibus, XLV flor.; item pro portando dictos pannos de portu Avinion. usque ad palacium et pro expensis dicti Johannis qui ivit obvium pannis predictis II flor.

Summa universalis omnium expensarum predictarum pecunie reducte ad flor., scilicet flor. pro XXII s. computato ut superius continetur, CLXIII flor. XI gross. VIII d.

Summa universalis omnium summarum, tam emptionis pannorum omnium quam expensis eorumdem, et fuit eisdem solutum in II^{m}V^{c}VIII flor. II gross. VIII d.

De quibus confitentur se habuisse a domino thesaurario II^{m}V^{c} flor. de Florencia et reducuntur pro maiori valore dictorum flor. pro quolibet II d., que ascendant VII flor. VIII s. VIII d.

Bibliography

Primary Sources

Archivum Apostolicum Vaticanum, Introitus et Exitus 29, 41, 54, 73, 81, 86, 92, 108, 146, 190, 265; Collectoriae 67; Diversa Cameralia 34; Instrumenta Miscellanea 7310.Archivio di Stato di Roma, Camerale I.

Archives Départementales de Vaucluse, Archives communales de Châteauneuf-du-pape, A 1.

Archives Départementales de Vaucluse, Archives communales de Châteauneuf-du-pape, A 1.

Bååth, Ludvig Magnus. *Diplomatarium Svecanum. Appendix. Acta pontificum Svecica. I. Acta Cameralia.* Vol 1. Stockholm: P.A. Norstedt & filii, 1936–42.

Braun, Hans, Paolo Ostinelli, Ludwig Schmugge (eds.). *Repertorium Poenitenciariae Germanicum I. Eugen IV. 1431–1447.* Tübingen: Niemeyer, 1998.

Bukowska, Krystyna, Alessandra Mosciatti, Ludwig Schmugge (eds.). *Repertorium Poenitenciariae Germanicum II. Nikolaus V. 1447–1455.* Tübingen: Niemeyer, 1999.

Chiaudano, Mario. *Il libro vermiglio di corte di Roma e di Avignone del segnale del C. della compagnia fiorentina di Iacopo Girolami, Filippo e Tommaso Corbizzi (1332–37).* Turin: Vincenzo Bona Tipografo, 1963.

Diener, Hermann, Brigide Schwarz (eds.). *Repertorium Germanicum. Eugen IV. 1431–1447.* 3 vols. Tübingen: Niemeyer, 2004.

Goldthwaite, Richard, Enzo Settesoldi, Marco Spallanzani (eds.). *Due Libri Mastri degli Alberti, una grande compagnia di Calimala.* Florence: Cassa di Risparmio di Firenze, 1995.

Hayez, Anne-Marie, Armand Jamme, Laurent Vallière (eds.). *Grands Livres de la Chambre apostolique.* http://ressourcescomptables.huma-num.fr/corpus/index.php?q=Avignon (28 October 2024).

Jamme, Armand. Festività, mercanti e contabilità. Il resoconto delle celebrazioni matrimoniali e del cavalierato di un pronipote di Bonifacio VIII. *Bullettino dell'Istituto Storico Italiano per il Medio Evo* 125 (2003): 185–222.

Lombardo, Maria Luisa. *Camera Urbis. Dohana Ripe et Ripecte. Liber introitus 1428.* Rome: Istituto di studi romani, 1978.

Lombardo, Maria Luisa. *Dohana minuta Urbis: liber introitus 1422.* Rome: Centro di Ricerca Medievali e Protocolli Notarili, 1983.

Marsch, Michael, Alessandra Mosciatti, Ludwig Schmugge (eds.). *Repertorium Poenitenciariae Germanicum VI. Sixtus IV. 1471–1484.* Tübingen: Niemeyer, 2005.

Monaco, Michele. *Il De officio collectoris in regno Angliae di Pietro Griffi da Pisa (1469–1516)*. Rome: Ed. di Storia e Letteratura, 1973.

Schäfer, Karl Heinrich. *Die Ausgaben der apostolischen Kammer unter Benedikt XII., Klemens VI. und Innocenz VI.* Paderborn: F. Schöningh, 1914.

Schäfer, Karl Heinrich. *Die Ausgaben der apostolischen Kammer unter den Päpsten Urban V. und Gregor XI.* Paderborn: F. Schöningh, 1937.

Schmidt, Tilmann. *Libri rationum Camerae Bonifatii papae VIII (Archivum Secretum Vaticanum, Collect. 446 necnon Intr. et Ex. 5)*. Città del Vaticano: Scuola Vaticana di Paleografia, Diplomatica e Archivistica, 1984.

Ut per litteras apostolicas. https://www.brepols.net/series/litpa-o.

Williman, Daniel (ed.). *Calendar of the letters of Arnaud Aubert, camerarius apostolicus (1361–1371)*. Toronto: Pontifical Institute of Mediaeval Studies, 1972.

Williman, Daniel (ed.). *The letters of Pierre de Cros, chamberlain to pope Gregory XI (1371–1378)*. Tempe: ACMRS, 2009.

Williman, Daniel, Karen Corsano (eds.). *The Spoils of the Pope and the pirates 1357: the complete legal dossier from the Vatican Archives*. Cambridge, MA: Ames Foundation, 2014.

Literature

Antonetti, Antonio. 'Cupientes subiectos fecliciter gubernari.' Diocesan administration in southern Italy under the Angevin rule: structural limits and reforming initiatives. *Revue d'histoire ecclésiastique* 118 (2023): 65–116.

Barrell, Andrew. William de Grenlaw, papal collector in Scotland. *The Innes Review* 42 (1991): 3–18.

Bauer, Clemens. Die Epochen der Papstfinanz. Ein Versuch. *Historische Zeitschrift* 138 (1928): 457–503.

Bauer, Clemens. *Gesammelte Aufsätze zur Wirtschafts- und Sozialgeschichte*. Freiburg: Herder, 1965.

Brown, Andrew, Jan Dumolyn (eds.). *Medieval Bruges (c.850–1550)*. Cambridge: Cambridge University Press, 2018.

Cardon, Dominique. *La draperie au Moyen Age. Essor d'une grande industrie européenne*. Paris: CNRS, 1999.

Combes, Jean. Les foires en Languedoc au Moyen Âge. *Annales E.S.C.* 13 (1958): 231–259.

Del Punta, Ignazio. Il fallimento della compagnia Ricciardi del secolo XIII: un caso esemplare? *Archivio storico italiano* 160 (2002): 221–268.

Delort, Robert. Notes sur les achats de draps et d'étoffes effectués par la Chambre apostolique des papes d'Avignon (1316–1417). *Mélanges d'archéologie et d'histoire* 74:1 (1962): 215–288.

Dubois, Henri. *Les foires de Chalon et le commerce dans la vallée de la Saône à la fin du Moyen Âge (1280–1430)*. Paris: Imprimerie Nationale, 1976.

Esch, Arnold. Bruges come piazza di cambio nei pagamenti dal Nord'Europa alla curia romana nel Quattrocento e l'importazione di merci a Roma dal Nord. In *Economia, cultura materiale ed arte nella Roma del Rinascimento: studi sui registri doganali romani (1445–1485)*. Rome: Roma nel Rinascimento, 2007, 369–412.

Esch, Arnold. Mercanti tedeschi a Roma nella seconda metà del Quattrocento. *Archivi e cultura. Rassegna dell'Associazione nazionale archivistica italiana* 37 (2004): 47–56.

Favier, Jean. *Les Finances pontificales à l'époque du Grand Schisme d'Occident (1378–1409)*. Paris: De Boccard, 1966.

Giannini, Massimo Carlo. *L'oro e la tiara: la costruzione dello spazio fiscale italiano della Santa Sede (1560–1620).* Bologna: Il Mulino, 2003.
Guyol, Christopher (ed.). *Kings, Knights and Bankers: The Collected Articles of Richard W. Kaeuper.* Leiden, Boston: Brill, 2015.
Hayez, Anne-Marie. D'Urbain V à Grégoire XI. Un dangereux retour au passé? In *L'écrit dans la société médiévale. Divers aspects de sa pratique du XIe au XVe siècle. Textes en hommage à Lucie Fossier*, Caroline Bourlet, Annie Dufour (eds.). Paris: CNRS, 1991, 151–164.
Hernández, Francisco J., Peter Linehan. *The Mozarabic Cardinal. The life and times of Gonzalo Pérez Gudiel.* Florence: Sismel, 2004.
Jamme, Armand. Avignone tra mobilità e conservatismo sociale: riconsiderazioni intorno al nepotismo di curia. In *La mobilità sociale nel Medioevo italiano. 3. Il mondo ecclesiastico (secoli XII–XV secolo)*, Sandro Carocci, Amedeo de Vincentiis (eds.). Rome: Viella, 2017, 125–155.
Jamme, Armand. De la Banque à la Chambre? Les mutations d'une culture comptable dans les provinces de l'Etat pontifical (1270–1430). In *Offices, Écrit et Papauté (XIIIe–XVIIe siècle)*, Armand Jamme, Olivier Poncet (eds.). Rome: École française de Rome, 2007, 97–251.
Jamme, Armand. De Rome à Florence: les banquiers et la curie (XIIe–XIIIe siècles). In *Die römische Kurie und das Geld. Von der Mitte des 12. Jahrhunderts bis zum frühen 14. Jahrhundert*, Werner Maleczek (ed.). Ostfildern: Jan Thorbecke, 2018, 167–205.
Jamme, Armand. Écrire pour le pape du XIe au XIVe siècle. Formes et problèmes. *Mélanges de l'École française de Rome—Moyen-Âge* 128:1 (2016). https://journals.openedition.org/mefrm/3121 (14 October 2024).
Jamme, Armand. 'Garsabal.' Voyages, carrière et fortune d'un officier pontifical. In *Identités juives et chrétiennes. France méridionale (XIVe–XIXe siècle), Etudes offertes à René Moulinas*, Gabriel Audisio (ed.). Aix-en-Provence: Presses universitaires de Provence, 2003, 7–28.
Jamme, Armand. Le pape et les princes. Deux cas d'espèces: Clericis laïcos–Guînes. In *Gouverner par les lettres, de l'Antiquité à l'époque contemporaine*, Agnès Bérenger, Olivier Dard (eds.). Metz: Centre de Recherche Universitaire Lorrain d'Histoire, 2015, 117–145.
Jamme, Armand. Lo Stato della Chiesa del secondo Trecento: un ignoto 'Fiscal-Military State'? Le lezioni degli archivi. *Documenta. Rivista internazionale di studi storicofilologici sulle fonti* 5 (2022): 17–33.
Jamme, Armand. Taxation and State in the Church Lands: a long Term Overhaul (1200–1550). In *The Routledge Handbook of Public Taxation in Medieval Europe*, Mathieu Caesar, Florent Garnier, Denis Menjot, Pere Verdés Pijuan (eds.). Abingdon: Routledge, 2023, 203–223.
Kaeuper, Richard W. The Frescobaldi of Florence and the English Crown. *Studies in Medieval Renaissance history* 10 (1973): 41–95.
Kowalski, Marek Daniel. Rationes Iacobini de Rubeis, collectoris in regno Poloniae. Rachunki Giacomina Rossiego, papieskiego kolektora generalnego w Polsee z lat (1426–34). *Studia zrodloznawcze* 49 (2011): 61–96.
Kowalski, Marek Daniel. Andrzej de Palatio, papieski kolektor generalny w Polsee w latach (1442–45). In *Ecclesia, Regnum, Fontes. Studia z dziejow sredniowiccza. Prace ofiarowane prof. Marii Koczerkiej*, Bartosz Dzialoszynski (ed.). Warsaw: Wydany przez, 2014, 119–127.
Kowalski, Marek Daniel. *Proventus Camerae Apostolicae debiti: opłaty duchowieństwa polskiego na rzecz papiestwa w latach (1417–1484).* Krakow: Miejsce, 2010.
Kowalski, Marek Daniel. The Papal Collectorate in the 15th century Poland. In *Quaestiones Medii Aevi Novae* 19 (2014): 447–460.

Lambert, Bart. Making size matter less: Italian firms and merchant guilds in late medieval Bruges. In *The company in law and practice: did size matter?*, Albrecht Cordes, Serge Dauchy, Dave De Ruysscher, Heikki Pihlajamäki (eds.). Leiden: Brill, 2017, 34–48.

Le Blévec, Daniel. *La part du pauvre. L'assistance dans les pays du Bas-Rhône du XIIe siècle au milieu du XVe siècle*. 2 vols. Rome: École française de Rome, 2000.

Linehan, Peter. *The Spanish Church and the Papacy in the Thirteenth Century*. Cambridge: Cambridge University Press, 1971.

Lombardo, Maria Luisa. *La dogana di Ripa e Ripetta nel sistema dell'ordinamento tributario a Roma dal Medioevo al secolo XV*. Rome: Centro di Ricerca, 1978.

Møller Jensen, Janus. *Denmark and the crusades (1400–1650)*. Leiden, Boston: Brill, 2007.

Orlandi, Angela. *Le Grand Parti. Fiorentini a Lione e il debito pubblico francese nel XVI secolo*. Florence: Olschki, 2002.

Palermo, Luciano. *Il mercato romano nel carteggio di Francesco Datini (1377–1409). Appendice documentaria: lettere da Roma a Barcellona, Valenza e Maiorca (1397–1407)*. Rome: Roma nel Rinascimento, 2020.

Milani, Giuliano. Uno Snodo nella storia dell'escluzione. Urbano IV, la crociata contro Manfredi e l'avvio di nuove diseguaglianze nell'Italia bassomedievale. *Mélanges de l'Ecole française de Rome—Moyen Âge* 125:2 (2013). https://journals.openedition.org/mefrm/1278 (14 October 2024).

Paravicini Bagliani, Agostino. *Boniface VIII. Un pape hérétique?*. Paris: Payot, 2003.

Partner, Peter. Financial Papal Policy in the Renaissance and Counter-Reformation. *Past and Present* 88 (1980): 17–62.

Reinke, Stefan. *Kurie—Kammer—Kollektoren. Die Magister Albertus de Parma und Sinitius als päpstliche Kuriale und Nuntien im 13. Jahrhundert*. Vienna, Cologne, Weimar: Böhlau, 2012.

Renouard, Yves. *Les relations des papes d'Avignon et des compagnies commerciales et bancaires de 1316 à 1378*. Paris: De Boccard, 1941.

Samaran, Charles, Guillaume Mollat. *La fiscalité pontificale en France au XIVe siècle, période d'Avignon et du Grand Schisme d'Occident*. Paris: Fontemoing, 1905.

Sapori, Armando. *La compagnia dei Frescobaldi in Inghilterra*. Florence: Olschki, 1947.

Tamás, Fedeles. Petrus Stephani collector apostolicus. In *Magyarország és a római szentszék II. Vatikáni magyar kutatások a 21. Században*, Kornel Svozak, Fedeles Tamás, Peter Tusor (eds.). Budapest: Gondolat, 2017, 31–88.

Tamás, Fedeles. Ecclesiastical Career of the Apostolic Collector Petrus de Monasterio. In *Incorrupta monumenta Ecclesiam defendunt. Studi offerti a mons. S. Pagano, prefetto dell'ASV*, vol. 1, Andreas Gottsmann, Pierantonio Piatti, Andreas Rehberg (eds.). Rome: Archivio Segreto Vaticano, 2018, 575–588.

Thumser, Mathias. Kredite für den Krieg. Clemens IV., Karl von Anjou und die Finanzierung des negotium regni Sicilie. In *Die römische Kurie und das Geld. Von der Mitte des 12. Jahrhunderts bis zum frühen 14. Jahrhundert*, Werner Maleczek (ed.). Ostfildern: Jan Thorbecke, 2018, 373–402.

Tognetti, Sergio. Nuovi documenti sull fallimento della compagnia Frescobaldi in Inghilterra. In *Città e campagne del basso Medioevo: studi sulla società italiana offerti dagli allievi a Giuliano Pinto*. Florence: Olschki, 2014, 135–158.

Trexler, Richard. *The Spiritual Power: Republican Florence under Interdict*. Leiden: Brill, 1974.

Venditelli, Marco, *Mercanti-banchieri romani tra XII e XIII secolo: una storia negata*. Rome: Viella, 2018.

Venditelli, Marco. Un inedita lettera di Gregorio IX a favore del romano Giovenale Mannetti. In *Sit liber gratus, quem servulus est operatus. Studi in onore di Alessandro Pratesi per il suo compleanno*, Paolo Cherubini, Giovanni Nicolaj (eds.). Citta del Vaticano: Scuola vaticana di paleografia, diplomaticae archivistica, 2012, 447–462.

Vendittelli, Marco. Testimonianze sui rapporti tra 'mercatores' romani ed i vescovati di Metz e Verdun nel secolo XIII. *Archivio della Società romana di storia patria* 118 (1995): 69–99.

Weber, Benjamin. *Lutter contre les Turcs: les formes nouvelles de la croisade pontificale au XV*[e] *siècle*. Rome: École française de Rome, 2013.

Weiss, Stefan. *Die Versorgung des päpstlichen Hofes in Avignon mit Lebensmitteln (1316–1378). Studien zur Sozial- und Wirtschaftsgeschichte eines mittelalterlichen Hofes*. Berlin: Akademie, 2002.

Weissen, Kurt. *Marktstrategien der Kurienbanken. Die Geschäfte der Alberti, Medici und Spinelli in Deutschland (1400–1475)*. Heidelberg: Heidelberg University Publishing, 2021.

Ezio Claudio Pia

Interactions between regional and international markets: Asti, credit, and fairs between the Middle Ages and the Early Modern Age

1 Outward: "per vias asperas et planas"

The enduring vitality of the urban settlement of Asti is rooted in its central position in an articulated system of communication routes linking the Po Valley, the Ligurian coast—and thus some of the main Mediterranean ports—and the Alpine area, a centrality dating back to the Roman times.[1] Two long-lasting features of Asti's history are linked to its peculiar position at a crossroads, with an inclination towards trade and financing on a European scale on the one hand, and pervasive political-territorial planning, which allowed Asti to gain control over a wide stretch of central-southern Piedmont from the eleventh to the twelfth century on the other. The markedly experimental political resources that established Asti's decisive role in communal Italy were thus combined with its recurrent participation in the markets of Liguria and beyond the Alps, as well as, from the late Middle Ages, with the widespread banking activities transacted by the so-called 'Lombards' on the main European markets.[2]

1 In addition to the landmark work of Renato Bordone. *Città e territorio nell'alto medioevo. La società astigiana dal dominio dei Franchi all'affermazione comunale*. Turin: Deputazione subalpina di Storia Patria, 1980, overviews of the city's history include Gian Giacomo Fissore. *Autonomia notarile e organizzazione cancelleresca del comune di Asti. I modi e le forme dell'intervento notarile nella costituzione del documento comunale*. Spoleto: Cisam, 1977; Luisa Castellani. *Gli uomini d'affari astigiani. Politica e denaro tra Piemonte ed Europa*. Turin: Paravia Scriptorium, 1998; and Ezio Claudio Pia. *Asti*. Spoleto: Cisam, 2017.

2 With regard to the enduring history of the Lombards, new and decisive historiographical perspectives have been provided by Renato Bordone (ed.). *L'uomo del banco dei pegni. "Lombardi" e mercato del denaro nell'Europa medievale*. Turin: Paravia Scriptorium, 1994; Renato Bordone. I Lombardi in Europa: uno sguardo d'insieme. In *Lombardi in Europa nel Medioevo*. Renato Bordone,

Note: Translation by Sergio Knipe. This research was carried out within the framework of the CoMOR Project (Configurations of European Fairs: Merchants, Objects, Routes—1350–1600), a collaboration between the CIHAM-UMR 5646 (Lyon) and the University of Erfurt financed by the ANR and the DFG. I would like to thank the staff of the *Archivio di Stato* in Asti and of the *Archivio storico del Comune di Asti* for their helpfulness and cooperation.

https://doi.org/10.1515/9783111621296-006

The sources provide evidence of early mercantile activities: while the *negucians* documented in the purchase and sale of a meadow taken from the Versa in 788 can only be assumed to have come from Asti, we can be sure of the local origin of the *asinarius* Theutprand, whose profession reflects this area's role as a crossroads and trading centre (and who in 812 purchased land near the city); the noun *asinarius* in fact is likely connected to the activity of transporting goods by means of donkeys.[3]

Related to more extensive mercantile relations is the 992 charter granted by Otto III to Petrus, the Bishop of Asti, which states that "negociatores [. . .] civitatis ubicumque velint habeant licentiam negociandi sine contradictione alicuius hominis."[4] This is evidence of a substantial interaction between the bishop's authority and the needs of the merchant class in Asti, a relationship confirmed in 1037 by the concession obtained by Obertus, the Bishop of Asti, from Emperor Conrad II, in which the merchants of Asti were guaranteed free passage "per vallem seuciensem [the Susa Valley] et per omnes valles et per omnia montana et per vias asperas et planas": a concession designed to ensure enduring relations with France and Burgundy.[5]

Sixty years later, in 1098, with the emergence of the commune of Asti—a political process in which urban economic forces played a leading role—a draft agreement with the Count of Moriana established the people of Asti's exemption from tolls and other charges on the road that he controlled and would continue to control in the future "et ultra montes et ex hac parte montium."[6]

The management of trade within the city also required certain measures, confirming the pervasiveness of the economic interests that underpinned community relations. In 1197, following a dispute over the ox market, the *podestà* established that this should take place for six months "a volta Gardinorum supra," and for the

---

Franco Spinelli (eds.). Milan: Franco Angeli, 2005, 9–39; and Renato Bordone. Una Lobby finanziaria internazionale?. In *Dal banco di pegno all'alta finanza. Lombardi e mercanti-banchieri fra Paesi Bassi e Inghilterra nel Trecento.* Renato Bordone (ed.). Asti: Centro studi sui lombardi, sul credito e sulla banca, 2007, 9–25. More recently, see also Ezio Claudio Pia. "Multam pecuniam, multa mala." I "Lombardi" astigiani e il mercato del credito nel Basso Medioevo. *Nuova Rivista Storica* 105: 1 (2021): 33–61.

3 Ferdinando Gabotto (ed.). *Le più antiche carte dell'Archivio capitolare di Asti.* Pinerolo: Chiantore-Mascarelli, 1904, 2–3, doc. 2; 5–6, doc. 4.

4 Monumenta Germaniae Historica. *Diplomata regum et imperatorum Germaniae*, vol. II. Hannover: Impensis Bibliopolii Hahniani, 1893, 510, doc. 99.

5 Bordone, *Città*, 237.

6 See Matilde Travaglini. La donazione sabauda del 1098 al comune di Asti. *Bollettino storico-bibliografico subalpino* 69 (1971): 544–551; Fissore, *Autonomia*, 18–20; and Bordone, *Città*, 296, n. 143.

remaining six months "a volta Gardinorum infra." The reference here is to a partition of the urban topography based on an architectural structure known as the *volta dei Gardini* (the Gardini family's vault), which stood near what is now Piazza Roma, in an area of the city still characterised by an obvious difference in height between the area surrounding the cathedral and the site of Piazza San Secondo below, which are identified respectively by the indications *supra* and *infra* in the *podestà*'s ruling.[7] Interestingly, this agreement converges with the statutory provision on fairs, which states that these are to be held "bis in anno": one eight days before and one eight days after the feast of Saint Secundus (29 or 30 March) "a volta Gardinorum infra," the other at the kalends of November for a duration of fifteen days "a volta Gardinorum super." The location corresponds to that indicated for livestock markets in 1197 and suggests an overlap between the two attestations, therefore allowing us to hypothesise an early date for the fairs.[8] Evidence of the spread of commercial activities—not necessarily fairs—comes from an insight that Renato Bordone draws from Adolf Schaube's *Handelsgeschichte der romanischen Völker des Mittelmeergebiets bis zum Ende der Kreuzzüge*, in which he recalls that a tenth century Arab source mentions a "peculiar way of organising the fixed price system in Asti, which [. . .] [the Arab narrator] calls Escht in the land of the Franks."[9] The merchants of Asti were undoubtedly present at international fairs beyond the Alps early on—at the Lendit fair from the eleventh century and in Champagne from the late twelfth century.[10] It was precisely the banking and commercial skills which they acquired through their participation in such fairs that enabled them to undertake the kind of financial ventures that would ensure the Lombards' unique position at the top of the European economy between the thirteenth and seventeenth centuries.

The sources thus highlight a dual economic vocation for Asti and the surrounding area. On the one hand, what emerges is a long-lasting expansion into external markets, as evidenced at the commercial level by the concessions granted by Otto III in 992 and Conrad II in 1037—and subsequently by the presence of Asti merchants at French fairs between the twelfth and thirteenth centuries—and at the financial level by the sustained activity of 'Lombard' financiers

7 Quintino Sella, Pietro Vayra (eds.). *Codex Astensis qui de Malabayla communiter nuncupatur.* Rome: Salviucci, 1880, II, 616, doc. 596.

8 *Rubrice Statutorum civitatis Ast per ordinem alphabeti.* Asti: Franciscum Garonum de Liburno, 1534, coll. IX, cap. 16.

9 Adolf Schaube. *Storia del commercio dei popoli latini del Mediterraneo sino alla fine delle Crociate*, Pietro Bonfante (trans.). Turin: Unione tipografico-editrice torinese, 1915, 95, cited in Bordone, *Città*, 289. My translation from the Italian.

10 Bordone, *Città*, 289, 295–296.

between the thirteenth and seventeenth centuries. No less important, however, was the city's involvement in regional and supra-regional trade networks, as shown by the early evidence of livestock markets from the late twelfth century and, a little later, of fairs with lively dynamics, which marked the area's commercial development between the Middle Ages and the Early Modern Age.

2 Within: "quolibet anno fiant nundine sive ferie"

These long-term processes reveal commercial and financial dynamics that combine trade centred on the city's markets with the wider role played by the people of Asti in European markets. From this complex chronological and spatial picture, the Piedmontese city emerges as a node in a web of commercial relations, functioning not just as a point of conversion, but also as a starting point for an international network.

The skills of Asti's businessmen are therefore not only linked to their presence in continental Europe's primary markets, but also to the dynamic trade in their home town, which is clearly revealed by the statutory chapters referring to fairs and the *Statuta revarum* concerning goods and duties.[11] The statutory rubric outlines a supra-local network, as the *podestà* is expected to "mandare litteras ad omnes civitates et loca que et quas cives et habitantes in eis verisimile est posse venire [. . .] ut [. . .] veniant salve et secure nonostantibus aliquibus cartis cambiorum [. . .] et ibi salvi sint et securi in eundo stando et redeundo," fifteen days before the two fairs. However, the local trade network continued to be the focus of attention, as during the fair favourable conditions were reserved for the citizens of Asti and the *posse*—that is, the part of the countryside that was dependent on the commune—who were authorised to display and sell their goods anywhere in the city and the surrounding villages.

Between the end of the fourteenth and the beginning of the sixteenth century, this lively context was enriched by the economic prospects offered to Asti and central-southern Piedmont by their incorporation into the polity governed by

11 See *Rubrice*, coll. IX, capp. 16–17. The *Statuta revarum* have been published in *Rubrice*. See also Elio Arleri (ed.). *Gabelle e dazi in Asti nel medioevo: versione degli Statuta Revarum Civitatis Ast*. Asti: Della Rovere, 2008; Anna Maria Nada Patrone. Glosse latine e francesi nel ms. astigiano K.K. 1415 degli Statuta revarum Ast. In *Miscellanea di studi romanzi offerta a Giuliano Gasca Queirazza per il suo 65° compleanno*, vol. II. Anna Cornagliotti, Lucia Fontanella, Marco Piccat, Alda Rossebastiano, Alessandro Vitale-Brovarone (eds.). Alessandria: Edizioni dell'Orso, 1988, 744–768.

the French House of Orléans.[12] The objectives of the people of Asti and those of the French princes converged precisely in the exploitation of the economic-productive potential of the territory, centring on the city which for over a century was a veritable French capital on Italian soil. This is demonstrated by the plan, which was shared by the city's ruling class and the Orléans, to strengthen the local economy by building a canal to supply factories and mills. This operation was financed in 1397 by a company with mixed Asti and French capital that was known as the *Società del Moleggio*, and the shares of which were veritable bonds redeemed by Asti investors in 1416.[13]

Some seventy years later, Duchess Marie of Clèves, the widow of Charles of Orléans, gave an equally significant boost to the local economy, as evidenced by the privilege for two annual fairs granted in 1468, one to be held in mid-Lent—so as to include the feast of the patron Saint Secundus—and the other to begin on 18 October, the feast of Saint Luke. This was essentially a revival of the earliest initiatives with an adjustment of the dates ("bina vice quolibet anno fiant nundine sive ferie [. . .] une fiant in media Quadragesima et alie die decimaoctava mensis octobris").[14] These events were part of the supra-regional trade networks that, in 1495, were brought together in a "fair" district near the central Troya Tower by order of Louis XII.[15]

Marie of Clèves is known for her cultural and especially literary interests, which she shared with her consort Charles, as well as for her religious sensitivity. She proved to be a far-sighted and authoritative princess for the people of Asti.[16]

---

12 Ezio Claudio Pia. Asti tra "dominazione straniera" e autonomia negoziata (secoli XIV–XVI). *Bollettino storico-bibliografico subalpino* 115:1 (2017): 125–142.

13 Franca Garesio Pelissero. La società del moleggio in Asti durante il dominio orleanese. *Bollettino storico-bibliografico subalpino* 91:2 (1993): 477–545; 92:1 (1994): 47–79. In addition to solidarity with the ruling authorities, the project highlights the newfound internal cohesion of the city's power relations, as attested in 1397 by the coexistence of the Guelph (Solaro, Ricci, Gardini, Malabaila), Ghibelline (Catena, Roero, Layolo, Buneo, Asinari, Pallidi), and popular (de Curia and Sala) families, and confirmed in 1416 by the participation in the acquisition of the former Orléans shares of the nobles de Regibus, Pelletta, Garetti, Scarampi, Cacherano, and Montafia, as well as the *popolari* Follo and Damiano.

14 See the text corresponding to note 8 above. The privilege issued by Marie of Cléves is preserved at the *Archivio Storico del Comune di Asti* (hereafter ASCA), Casa d'Orléans, perg. 10. See Renato Bordone. "La forest de longue actente". Maria di Clèves, Duchessa d'Orléans e Signora di Asti. *Il Platano* 33 (2008): 216–217. Some brief references can also be found in Gianluigi Bera. *Asti. Edifici e palazzi nel Medioevo*. Savigliano: Gribaudo, 2004, 208–217.

15 Bera, *Asti*, 212.

16 Bordone, "La forest," 201–223; Patrizio Tucci. Morire di sete vicino alla fontana. Charles d'Orléans e la polifonia poetica alla corte di Blois. In *L'autorialità plurima. Scritture collettive, testi a più mani, opere a firma multipla*. Atti del XLII Convegno Interuniversitario di Bressanone,

From 1465, after the death of Charles of Orléans, she ruled the county of Asti in the place of his youngest son, the future King of France, Louis XII.[17] The Dukes of Orléans regained control of this area of central Piedmont after a long hiatus, which lasted from the 1410s to the 1440s as a result of succession disputes that were further complicated by international tensions. Charles himself, who had been held prisoner by the English for a quarter of a century following the defeat at Agincourt, managed to assert his claim to Asti after his release and made a glorious entry into the city in 1447.[18] The long break with the years of Valentina Visconti and her husband Louis of Orléans probably led to the need to redefine relations with the political body centred on Asti. This was done on an experimental basis, by reconciling local needs with those of the princes beyond the Alps. Political power was largely shared: the governor and his lieutenants were French, while the members of the Privy Council were chosen from among the courtiers of Asti. This supreme governing body of French origin, which was also typical of the Visconti administration, included the treasurer, the ducal secretary, and the castellans of Bra and Cherasco, the lynchpins of the territorial and military organisation that made the county a valuable French base on Italian soil. Finally, the city's *podestà* could be either French or a native of Asti.[19] This political arrangement ensured the Piedmontese subjects' enduring loyalty to the French dynasty: a bond emphasised by the contemporary writer Giovanni Andrea Saluzzo di Castellar, who in his diary recalls the fact that, at the time of the Italian wars and France's darkest moments, the "gentlemen of Asti [. . .] were good Frenchmen and preferred to lose what was theirs than to disavow their king."[20] While French politi-

---

10–13 luglio 2014. Alvaro Barbieri, Elisa Gregari (eds.). Padua: Esedra, 2015, 379–403; Marco Robecchi. Le ms. 125 de la Burgerbibliothek de Berne: de Charles d'Orléans à Jacques Bongars (en passant par Marie de Clèves). *Medioevi. Rivista di letterature e culture medievali* 3 (2017): 157–192. http://www.medioevi.it/index.php/medioevi/article/view/49/66 (14 November 2023); Paola Corti. Mécénat et culture dévote chez Marie de Clèves, duchesse d'Orléans (1426–1487). In *Les femmes, la culture et les arts en Europe entre Moyen Âge et Renaissance/Women, art and culture in medieval and early Renaissance Europe*, Cyntha J. Brown, Anne-Marie Legaré (eds.). Turnhout: Brepols, 2016, 13–32.

17 Bordone, "La forest," 205–215.

18 Vanda Forghieri. Asti e la politica francese in Lombardia. *Rivista di storia, arte e archeologia per la provincia di Alessandria* 45 (1936): 5–77; Renato Bordone. La dominazione francese di Asti: istituzioni e società tra Medioevo ed età moderna. In *Gandolfino da Roreto e il Rinascimento nel Piemonte meridionale*, Giovanni Romano (ed.). Turin: Fondazione CRT, Banca CRT, 1998, 19–30.

19 Bordone, La dominazione, 27–29. See also Francesca Maria Vaglienti. "Fidelissimi servitori de Consilio suo secreto". Struttura e organizzazione del Consiglio segreto nei primi anni del ducato di Galeazzo Maria Sforza (1466–1469). *Nuova Rivista Storica* 76 (1992): 645–708.

20 Vincenzo Promis (ed.). *Memoriale di Gio. Andrea Saluzzo di Castellar dal 1482 al 1528*. Turin: Stamperia Reale, 1869, 509.

cal measures in the land of Asti proved efficient during the almost twenty years of Charles' rule, Marie's leadership was no less successful, strengthening local social and economic structures in close agreement with the local authorities. The decrees issued by Marie highlight the centrality of the local magistracies and the role of guarantor that the Duchess played towards her subjects in Asti. This role was confirmed the year after Charles' death with the restoration of the right to exercise control over the work of the *podestà*, the deputies, and their officials, a procedure which gave new importance to the city's administrative mechanisms and their proper functioning.[21] In the decade that followed, the formation of a veritable local elite was fostered, made up of members of prestigious, established families who held civil, military, and ecclesiastical offices according to the principle of direct interaction between the citizens and the House of Orléans.[22] Within this complex framework—a kind of triangulation between traditional civic autonomy, ducal authority, and bureaucracies, both French and local—measures were taken to restore the fairs. This project reflects the stabilisation of the Orléans administration as it had developed in the twenty years following Charles' arrival, according to a form of dynastic continuity readily accepted by the people of Asti. This stability was the result of an efficient negotiation between the centre and the periphery, which tended to make the most of the subalpine county's geopolitical features, located at the crossroads of various political entities and favoured by its consolidated presence along communication routes.

The compelling remarks that have been made about the "strategic" potential of another larger mercantile and agricultural city in northern Italy—Verona—also seem to apply to the Asti area. The analysis in question has noted the convergence of a series of favourable circumstances, ensured by a considerable agricultural and entrepreneurial development as well as the presence of the Adige river, described as "a gateway to Germany [. . .] through which any number of people and goods can be transported to and from in a few hours."[23] These elements can be extended to several other cities and apply to the case of Asti in terms of the robustness of its primary sector, the positive influence of the local milling industry on artisanal activities—through the agreement between local elites and the French dynasty—and, finally, the advantages offered by the course of the Tanaro

21 Bordone, "La forest," 208; *Rubrice*, coll. II, cap. 3.

22 Bordone, "La forest," 208, 211–214.

23 Edoardo Demo. "Una compagnia per attender al traffico di Bolgiano, Vienna et altre fiere solite". I Cerminati dalla Luna, mercanti veronesi nell'Europa centro-orientale del secondo Cinquecento. *Studi Storici Luigi Simeoni* 59 (2009): 38.

river which, unlike the Adige, did not lead to continental Europe in a few hours, but rather opened the city to the Po Valley and the western Alps.[24]

The presence of the Montferrat domains to the south and east and those of the Savoy to the north and west—as well as the Milanese territories bordering the Tanaro river's eastern sector—created a kind of belt around the district of Asti, which historians have called the Calais of Italy.[25] This interweaving of borders did not isolate the city, but strengthened its tendency to act as a trading hub that was able to reduce the pressure of competing forces, as is demonstrated by the compromise on the organisation of the fairs reached by the Duchess with the Marquis of Montferrat, whose domain was suffering from commercial competition with Asti.[26]

Marie of Clèves' 1468 decree on the two fairs thus seems to be the result of a strategic vision of the Asti market's potential within a wider system of relations. It should be recalled that the timing of the fair in mid-Lent reinforced the economic impact of the city's festivities dedicated to its patron saint Secundus, which took place at the same time, while the fair that began on Saint Luke's Day was linked to similar transalpine initiatives, such as the All Saints' Day Fair in Lyon.[27] Both lasted fifteen days, during which the merchants had free access to the city, where they were obliged to stay for at least three days, displaying their goods—exempt from taxation—in designated places.

The careful planning that inspired the project is demonstrated not only by the creation of the aforementioned fair district, but also by the establishment of a dedicated bureaucratic structure as early as 1468: Marie's decree provided that the city council annually elect four "conservators and judges" who were responsible for managing the fairs and settling any disputes in accordance with the most common ways of managing similar events.[28]

---

24 Pia, *Asti*, VII, 35.

25 Forghieri, Asti, 25.

26 See the text corresponding to footnote 35 below.

27 On the fairs in Lyon, see Michele Cassandro. *Le fiere di Lione e gli uomini d'affari italiani nel Cinquecento*. Florence: Baccini & Chiappi, 1979; Jean-Louis Gaulin, Susanne Rau. Rétablissement de deux foires à Lyon (mai 1487). In *Lyon, entre empire et royaume, 843–1601. Textes et documents*. Alexis Charansonnet, Jean-Louis Gaulin, Pascale Mounier, Susanne Rau (eds.). Parigi: Classiques Garnier, 2015, 523–528. A compelling overview of medieval fairs can be found in Alberto Grohmann. *Fiere e mercati nell'Europa occidentale*. Milan: Bruno Mondadori, 2011.

28 The attestation of four conservators responsible for settling any disputes suggests a link between the fairs of Asti and those of Lyon, as evidenced by the letters patent of 1463 in which Louis XI established four annual fairs for the benefit of the latter city, including the figure of the "conservateur et gardien des foires." For a documentary overview, see Romain Benoit. Tribunal de la Conservation des privilèges des foires de Lyon 8B 1-8B5269. 1438–1820, Archives du départe-

The 1468 privilege confirms Orléans' tendency to grant the Asti authorities broad powers in the political-economic field: the fair was entrusted to the local council, which was responsible for its organisation and for settling any disputes. These in turn were referred to the *podesta*—usually someone from Asti—or to the governor, if the case involved a sum exceeding 500 gold ducats.[29] Other disputes, even protracted ones, remained in the hands of the local judges, with the possible assistance of a jurist; the records would then be "received" by citizen appointees, a notary, or a clerk of the curia.[30] The privilege was intended to ensure that cases would be settled swiftly, and it is clear that entrusting them to the local government was a way of achieving this. Moreover, as Guido Castelnuovo has rightly noted,[31] it was precisely through this internal bureaucratic management that cities were able to preserve or affirm an objective degree of autonomy within the framework of the supra-local polities that emerged in the fifteenth century. This recognised autonomy constitutes a leitmotif of Orléans' rule and is reflected in the minute statutory regulation of ordinary trade during fairs in order to avoid any overlap between the two trade circuits or irregularities that would damage the city's economy. The usual rhetoric regarding the protection of their subjects' interests by the authorities confirms, in the concreteness of these relations, the attempt to reconcile the government's demands with local ones, formally framed as the Duchess' response to the "supplicationibus et requisitionibus comunitatis [. . .] civitatis Ast."[32]

The demand for fairs can be viewed within the context of a weakening of the Asti merchants' international presence, albeit to varying degrees depending on the area in which they had settled, leading to a renewed commercial commitment in their home city.[33] This causal relationship must nonetheless be traced back to a more complex political and economic framework. Firstly, the Lombards of Asti continued to operate profitably in Europe, while ceding some positions to other businessmen.[34] In all likelihood, the financial and commercial experience that the Asti merchants had acquired on the international stage led them to make the

ment du Rhône et de la métropole de Lyon. https://archives.rhone.fr/media/140adefe-857e-49b1-ba44-d966ea48139c.pdf (6 March 2024); Gaulin, Rau (eds.), *Rétablissement.*

29 *Rubrice*, f. 108v.

30 *Rubrice*, f. 108v.

31 Guido Castelnuovo. Principi e città negli stati sabaudi. In *Principi e città alla fine del medioevo*, Sergio Gensini (ed.). Rome: Ministero per i beni culturali e ambientali, Ufficio centrale per i beni archivistici, 1996, 91–93.

32 *Rubrice*, f. 107r. and v.

33 Donatella Gnetti, Giulia Scarcia. Splendore e declino dei lombardi. In *Lombardi in Europa*, 76–97.

34 Bordone, I Lombardi, 21, 22.

most of the opportunities offered by the pacification of their home region and the shared political management practices that had characterised Orléans' presence since the time of the *Società del Moleggio*. This process highlights the Asti area's centrality, not only due to its entry into European markets, but also due to the equally significant 'centripetal' attraction that it exercised on neighbouring regions in terms of medium-range trade.

The two fairs must have found a place in the 'calendar' of fairs, starting with those that involved neighbouring territories. As mentioned above, the Marquis of Montferrat immediately began negotiations to avoid competing with the Casale fair. As a result, the Asti fair was postponed to the middle of March, before being set for mid-Lent, a decision that risked jeopardising the participation of merchants from Venice, Genoa, and Florence, who were busy with the fairs in Lyon and Geneva. Negotiations continued until 1474, and it is plausible that a settlement concerning the Asti events was reached in the mid-1470s.[35]

In the following decades, however, the political uncertainty that characterised central Piedmont at the beginning of the sixteenth century, during the Italian wars, probably reduced the frequency of fairs in Asti. In the 1520s, the *referendario* Gerolamo Malabaila reported "nil actum fuit" in documents verifying the local treasury's accounts[36]—a sign of an interruption in political and fiscal operations due to the occupation by either the Duke of Milan or the imperial troops as a result of the conflict. An indirect clue to the likely slackening of fair activities may derive from the oldest notarial register kept in the Asti State Archives, which was attributed to the notary Stefano Perrone (1511–1527). Upon a cursory investigation, this volume actually appears to be a factitious collection of deeds dating back to the late fourteenth and fifteenth centuries, probably assembled as a model for the drafting of similar documents.[37] Among the deeds collected in this practical formulary, there are none relating to fairs—a peculiarity that could be attributed to the nature of the activity exercised by the notary himself (if this were an actual register of the notary, Perrone) but which, given the probable 'exemplary' nature of the collection, seems to indicate a lower incidence of fair trading in the first decades of the sixteenth century.

The situation must have changed in the following period: the fact that the Asti fair was an attractive event for commercial networks and generated a signifi-

35 On this complex negotiation, see Ferdinando Gabotto. *La vita in Asti al tempo di Giovan Giorgio Alione*. Asti: Bianchi, 1899, 22–23; Niccola Gabiani. *Notizie sulla Ferrazza o politica della città d'Asti dal XIV al XVIII secolo: ricerche storiche*. Turin: Roux & C., 1892, 220–268. See also Fondo documenti antichi, 1474. In ASCA, 13.16.

36 Conti Orleanesi. In *Archivio di Stato di Asti* (hereafter ASA), f. 53 v.

37 Notaio Stefano Perrone, 1511–1527. In ASA, Archivio notarile.

cant volume of business is demonstrated by the 'cavalier' behaviour of the Duke of Savoy, Charles Emmanuel I at the end of the sixteenth century. During the plague of 1599, he deliberately concealed the seriousness of the sanitary conditions in order to obtain tax revenues from the merchants attending the Asti fair.

On 21 April 1599, the Venetian resident Simeone Contarini stated unequivocally that the Duke had concealed the danger:

> [. . .] so that the Asti fair, which had already begun, could take place, by ordering, or rather forcing, the merchants of Turin to bring all their merchandise to the fair, so that he could obtain from them the amount of money that he is now accustomed to obtaining by various means, without leaving them the excuse of not having any because they were unable to trade.[38]

Indeed, between the late sixteenth and early seventeenth century, several dozen deeds for the sale of goods with deferred payments at successive fairs specify the origin of the merchants who were present at the Asti fairs. These documents reveal a medium-range circulation that involved the sub-Alpine area (the Canavese, Turin, the Aosta Valley, the Vercelli area, and Milan), the Alpine valleys of Provence (Draguignan and Barcelonnette), and the Tarentaise Valley (the area crossed by the Isère, in Savoy), as well as the Dauphiné and Lyon.[39] This complex trade network included representatives of the company owned by the merchants Enrico and Sebastiano Splinder and Gaspar Scherer, described as "German" by the Asti notaries, but based in Turin. A notarial deed of 1582 attests that these merchants were holding a ten-year lease, whose start date is unknown, concerning a house and warehouse belonging to the noble lords of Ferrere located on the town's main street.[40] This proof of the city's continuing economic role suggests that we should at least partly reconsider the idea of a steady decline following Asti's absorption into the Savoy domains after 1529.[41] The relevant role of the "German" merchants Splinder and Scherer—who were Swiss merchants from St. Gallen—is consistent with the long-standing and robust trade relations between central and northern Italy and the German-speaking area. In the case of

38 Fabio Mutinelli (ed.). *Storia arcana ed aneddotica d'Italia raccontata dai veneti ambasciatori*, vol. II, *sec. XVI*. Venice: Naratovich, 1856, 299–300.
39 Notaio Cesare Vinea, 1566–1591. In ASA, Archivio notarile. Deeds of 15, 20, 21 March, 2, 3, 5, 9 November 1581, 14 March 1582.
40 Notaio Cesare Vinea, 1566–1591. In ASA, Archivio notarile. Deed of 20 March 1582.
41 For an assessment, see Ezio Claudio Pia. "Riposare sotto lo scettro sabaudo"? Autonomia contrattata e rappresentazione della città in Asti nel Cinquecento. In *Francesco Panigarola. Predicazione, filosofia e teologia nel secondo Cinquecento*, Francesco Ghia, Fabrizio Meroi (eds.). Florence: Olschki, 2013, 163–174.

the Asti merchants, these relations were mainly linked to banking activities, but in the case of merchants of other origins, they were based on systematic exchanges within the German trade fair networks.[42] The Splinder & Scherer company bears witness to the stability of this trade, since members of these families —sometimes referred to as the heirs of Enrico and Sebastiano, whose company operated in Asti in the 1580s—were among the leading merchants handling letters of exchange at Milan's major market until the central decades of the seventeenth century. At that time, they were not just managing large sums of money, but also formed part of an extensive system of relations that involved, among other places, the trading centres of Frankfurt, Cologne, St. Gallen, Lyon, Nuremberg, Lille, Turin, and Genoa, to name but a few.[43]

3 "The convenient location of the site": a versatile mercantile vocation

In the following decades, the fairs did not lose their relevance despite the military conflicts and epidemics that affected the territory, especially during the reigns of Charles Emmanuel I and Victor Amadeus I. While the municipal documents of

42 Winfried Reichert. *Lombarden in der Germania-Romania. Atlas und Dokumentation*, 2. 1,2,3. Trier: Porta Alba, 2003; Kurt Weissen. I mercanti toscani alle fiere tedesche nel tardo medioevo. In *Fiere e mercati nella integrazione delle economie europee. Secc. XIII–XVIII*, Simonetta Cavaciocchi (ed.). Florence: Le Monnier, 2001, 887–908; Wilhelm Tobler-Meyer. Das Junker-Geschlecht der Scherer aus der Stadt St. Gallen, sein Erlöschen und seine Erbschaft. *Schweizer Archiv für Heraldik* 16 (1902): 13–27.

43 Giovanna Tonelli. "Mercanti che hanno negotio grosso" fra Milano e i Paesi riformati nel primo Seicento. In *Mercanti, eresia e Inquisizione nell'Italia moderna*, Germano Maifreda (ed.). *Storia economica* 17:1 (2014): 104, 123, 127, 129, 136. A useful overview of the extensive circulation of merchants—with evidence relating to Asti, its surroundings (Villafranca d'Asti, Nizza Monferrato), and neighbouring areas (Fossano, Pontestura, Revello, Casale Monferrato, Saluzzo, Alessandria, Ivrea, Valenza, Pinerolo, Bra, Vercelli, Racconigi, Fossano, Chieri, Carignano, Moncalvo, Felizzano, Poirino, Moncalieri, Torino, Mondovì, Cuneo, and Rivoli, among the main places)—is provided by Théodore Turquet de Mayerne's *Description*. See Ulf Christian Ewert. Bayerische Staatsbibliothek Münchner Digitalisierungszentrum, Théodore Turquet de Mayerne, Description de la France, Allemagne, Italie & Espagne. Avec la Guide des chemins pour aller & venir par les provinces, & et aux villes plus renommees de ces quatre régions. A quoy est adiousté en receuil des foires plus celebres presque de toute l'Europe. Et un traicté des monnoyes & leur valeur esdits pays, provinces & villes (COL0024). In *Configurations of European Fairs: Merchants, Objects, Routes (ca. 1350–1600)*. Jean-Louis Gaulin, Susanne Rau (dir.). https://fairs-in-history.huma-num.fr/collection/COL0024 (6 March 2024).

1637 complain about the damage done to the structures set up to host the fair by the troops billeted there, in the medium-term, the negotiations between the city and the Savoys focused precisely on the organisation of the fairs, with an increasing interest in lucrative "cattle fairs."[44] These long-standing events—which can be traced back to 1197, when the *podestà* decided to rotate the location of the oxen market on a six-monthly basis—are linked to the specific features of the area: high agricultural productivity, which both favoured and benefited from livestock farming, and proximity to the main road junctions of north-west Italy, which required the efficient transportation of goods using animal traction. Indeed, between the late Middle Ages and the modern age, livestock-related mercantile activities were of considerable importance and constituted a profitable investment for areas with adequate structural resources as well as technical and economic know-how, such as central-southern Piedmont. The impression we gain is that the rather uncertain political situation in the central decades of the seventeenth century led to a redefinition of the economic potential of the city and its territory. It should not be overlooked that a dynamic view open to possible changes in the market was present in Maria's charter of 1468 which stipulates that, should the concession regarding the fairs be revoked for "reasonable cause," the events must nonetheless continue for the following two years—a provision that takes account of possible market adjustments, while at the same time seeking to safeguard this kind of events benefiting the city and the State.[45] The centrality of the livestock market is also reflected in the priorities set out in the privilege of 1468, which lists a series of exceptions in favour of the local meat trade, mainly to ensure that the incentives provided for the fairs would not lead to negotiations, buying and selling, or slaughtering in opposition to the rules.[46]

The supply of livestock, which was essential for a significant part of the food chain, was a structural necessity that helped to connect distant and very different markets, resulting in quite extensive and profitable investments. While nomadic livestock farming generated a considerable volume of business until the sixteenth century, the subsequent period witnessed the beginning of sedentary animal husbandry, supplemented by large-scale purchases of animals from abroad. This is documented by recent studies of negotiations in the 1660s for the purchase of several thousand head of Moldovian cattle by the Venetians and Florentines, Venice being an especially large market.[47] Supplies in the seventeenth century, especially

44 Gabiani, *Ferrazza*, 239.

45 The expression used is "propter [. . .] iustas et rationabiles causas." See *Rubrice*, f. 109r.

46 *Rubrice*, f. 107v.

47 Giorgio Dell'Oro. Carne rossa, carne bianca: allevamenti e consumi in Italia settentrionale in età moderna. In *Le vie del cibo Italia settentrionale (secc. XVI–XX)*. Marina Cavallera, Silvia

in the central decades, became more complex due to the constant warfare in Europe, and the Savoy lands benefited from the easing of interest in the cattle sector in Lombardy. Moreover, the Savoy supported the cattle trade both by identifying dedicated routes in the Vercelli area—that is, not far from Milan—and by supporting the establishment of trading hubs, such as the fairs in Asti.[48] As early as 1545, Emmanuel Philibert granted the people of Asti the right to host, in addition to the two "general" fairs of October and March, "two livestock fairs without any toll or tax, one on the feast of the Holy Cross in the month of May, the other after that of Saint Lawrence in the month of August, each lasting six days." This must have been a rather experimental venture, as is suggested by the city's request for "permission to advertise and announce these fairs and markets: and to advertise them in all the territories of Your Excellency's jurisdiction," since "perhaps our neighbours and people from other lands may not have heard of these fairs".[49]

This experimental venture (although based on local tradition) was destined to enjoy considerable success, since livestock fairs were held constantly during the first decades of the seventeenth century, even increasing to five a year. This is evidenced by the concessions granted by Charles Emmanuel I, who between 1613 and 1621 reinforced the city's presence on this market:

> Aware of the privilege we granted to our city, Asti, on 12 August 1613 to hold four livestock fairs a year in the usual places of the city, as ratified by our Chamber of Audit on this side of the mountains [i.e. the official body with authority over the Savoy territories on the Italian side of the Alps] on 26 May 1614, it is hereby decreed that from now on there shall be five fairs a year and a weekly livestock market, in addition to the other fairs and markets usually held for other kinds of trade and merchandise. Such livestock fairs and markets are to be held not on the days set down in the said privilege, but as follows, i.e. the first will begin on the coming 9 February, the second on the following 25 March, the third on 10 June, the fourth on 15 August, and the fifth on 8 September, and the market will be held each week on Thursday, and the fairs will last three days each.[50]

This consolidation of the fairs was linked to the city's long-standing vocation for this type of trade and was a contingent response to the economic uncertainties

A. Conca Messina, Blythe Alice Raviola (eds.). Rome: Carocci 2019, 251–264; Cristian Luca. Un tentativo d'importazione dalla Moldavia di bovini destinati mercato fiorentino all'epoca di Cosimo I de' Medici. In *Italia ed Europa centro-orientale tra Medioevo ed Età moderna: economia, società, cultura*, Andrea Fara (ed.). Heidelberg: Heidelberg University Publishing, 2022, 303–322.

48 Dell'Oro, Carne rossa, 253; Gabiani, *Ferrazza*, 239. See also Andrea Fara. Il commercio di bestiame ungherese verso la Penisola italiana tra tardo Medioevo e prima Età moderna (XIV–XVI secolo). *Mélanges de l'École française de Rome—Moyen Âge* 127:2 (2015). https://journals.openedition.org/mefrm/2709 (14 November 2023).

49 Gabiani, *Ferrazza*, 239–240.

50 Gabiani, *Ferrazza*, 241–242.

caused by the military situation: the decree of 1621 was justified by the fact that the previous measures had "not been applied on account of the past wars." At the same time, a strategic vision for the area was outlined, since the concession referred not only to the "beloved peoples" of the Duchy of Savoy, but also to the fact that, thanks to "such trade and commerce, the peoples will be able to enjoy countless comforts, which, due to the convenient location of the site, will also be enjoyed by foreign states, as it seems that many desire them."[51] As mentioned, in the following decades, the Savoy projects in this sphere would prove more effective than the Lombard measures: this is shown by the limited impact of the Milanese fairs, which were negatively affected by competing initiatives—Asti being one example—and above all by the commercial incentives granted by the Savoys. A record from the Valsesia community dating back to 1656 highlights the fact that the Piedmontese fairs' success was due to the fact that "foreign merchants lead their livestock across the borders of Piedmont, France, and Savoy [. . .] with much less expense in terms of pastures and taxes, and with greater comfort and shorter journeys."[52]

The case of Asti shows once again how the Savoy measures not only integrated the specific features of the various territories, but also aimed to ensure the overall stability of the economy, which had been put to the test by the military conflicts. This is revealed by the continued support for the "general" fairs, which was reaffirmed precisely in the years of great political uncertainty between 1633 and 1634, when Victor Amadeus I not only extended the duration of the livestock fairs to eight days, but also relaunched the October and March fairs of communal and Orléans origin.[53]

Over the course of the century, the Asti area's position on the border led to two recurring situations: on the one hand, the state of war affected commercial enterprise, but on the other, the resumption of such projects was encouraged, precisely because of the area's strategic location, as shown by the patents issued by Charles Emmanuel II in 1672 which provided for exemptions or reductions in customs duties:

> [T]he goods and wares which will be brought into this fair from abroad in the future until the end of the year 1674, and which will be sold at the time of the fair (with the sole excep-

51 Gabiani, *Ferrazza*, 242. An analysis of the development of fairs between the sixteenth and seventeenth centuries is provided by Donatella Calabi, Paola Lanaro. Lo spazio delle fiere e dei mercati nella città italiana di età moderna. In *Fiere e mercati*, Cavaciocchi (ed.), 109–141.

52 Dell'Oro, Carne rossa, 253–254.

53 Gabiani, *Ferrazza*, 245.

> tion of those from France and from across the mountains, as well as all spices, drugs, waxes, and dyes) must be exempted from the usual customs duty by a full quarter.[54]

Between the twelfth and thirteenth centuries, fairs thus marked the beginning of the enduring international presence of Asti businessmen, whose participation in French fairs paved the way for the financial role they were to play in Europe for centuries to come. At the same time, fairs also brought together the networks of economic and commercial relations in Piedmont, adapting to their home area the 'Lombard' propensity for connecting local and supra-regional markets. What emerges is a dynamic system in which the credit networks of businessmen who were operating in Europe and their inclusion in trade relations on this side of the Alps paint a dynamic picture of the Asti's financiers' pervasive economic and commercial planning.

It is therefore the perspective of market integration that highlights the enduring and versatile interaction between regional and international trade axes. This long-term process can be reconstructed by examining the connections between regional and international trade axes, thus enabling us to identify the areas which served as European crossroads on both sides of the Alps.

Asti's long-standing commercial and financial vocation has thus been more clearly articulated. The international expansion of its merchants (linked to early imperial concessions made to local bishops in the tenth and eleventh centuries) and the widespread presence of 'Lombard' bankers (which have been investigated in a relatively recent historiography) outline a set of relations within which Asti played an important role, not only for its financial activity on the main European markets, but also as a centre for the organisation of trade on a supra-regional level. A survey of published documents and historical studies has made it possible to establish links between political-institutional events and fairs in the late Middle Ages and the early modern period which were promoted by the local ruling class as well as the princes of Orléans, and then further consolidated in the Savoy era. The analysis of notarial and municipal documents from the sixteenth and seventeenth centuries has instead brought to light extensive commercial relations centred on the two annual 'general' fairs and the livestock fairs granted by the Savoy dynasty on several occasions. There are certain breaks in this historical trajectory, marked by scarce documentation and possibly reflecting moments of political uncertainty, as evidenced by the frequent measures taken by the Savoy to 'compensate' for the crises affecting the city and its surrounding territory following the wars at the end of the sixteenth and the beginning of the seventeenth centuries.

54 Gabiani, *Ferrazza*, 249.

Besides, the CoMOR project has lent concreteness to the interactions between places and markets, viewing cities and larger geographical areas in relation to the financial and commercial dynamics that affected vast sectors of continental Europe.[55] Through the use of hitherto rather neglected sources, this concreteness extends to the actors within this system of relations: despite the documentation's relative discontinuity, when it comes to fairs, a link emerges not only in relation to specific possibilities in terms of road communication, production, and trade, but also in terms of the constant political fluctuations. The interactions involving the Asti area are not unrelated to the progressive settlement of the city and its surrounding area within the Orléans and later the Savoy polities. Emanuele Tesauro's "official" interpretation describes the return of Asti to the Savoy household in 1615, after the war against Monferrato, as the overcoming of "various misfortunes,"[56] foreshadowing an expected period of rest "under the shadow of the Royal House of Savoy." As far as fairs are concerned, the impression we get is that they represented a choice shared by the centre and the periphery, and that they were partly aimed at compensating Asti via financial and commercial support for its role as a military outpost during the fifteenth and seventeenth centuries. This is a sign that, far from being based on "impersonal" dynamics, the markets were rather the result of a close negotiation between the central and municipal authorities—a negotiation that the sources, however, trace back to a more articulated perspective than the authority-based relationship between the sovereign and the city, given that the territory's potential was the result of its inclusion in a tried and tested network of social and economic relations. The fairs testify to the effectiveness of a careful negotiation process in which the Savoy government's planning and local forces found a meeting point. The result was a pragmatic plan—subject to constant revision—that harmonised the territory's commercial characteristics with the wider community's needs, delineating inward and outward flows of goods and money and establishing services that were sometimes complementary and sometimes competitive with respect to other state entities. The circulation of products and the itineraries attested by notarial sources, the projects and claims of the centre and the periphery testified to in municipal documentation, as well as its participants' "point of view"—partly identifiable through the analysis carried out on a European scale by the CoMOR project[57]—help shed

55 See https://fairs-in-history.huma-num.fr/about (6 March 2024).

56 Maria Luisa Doglio. Un'inedita storia di Asti di Emanuele Tesauro. In *Civiltà del Piemonte. Studi in onore di Renzo Gandolfo nel suo settantacinquesimo compleanno*, Gianrenzo Clivio, Riccardo Massano (eds.). Turin: Centro di studi piemontesi, 1975, 165. See also Pia, "Riposare sotto lo scettro sabaudo," 163–174.

57 See footnote 43.

light on the articulation of economic relations, permanence and change, and political influences, identifying centres and networks in a medium- and long-term economic system which linked regional and wider markets.

Bibliography

Primary Sources

Casa d'Orléans. In *Archivio Storico del Comune di Asti*.
Conti Orleanesi. In *Archivio di Stato di Asti*.
Notaio Cesare Vinea, 1566–1591. In *Archivio di Stato di Asti*, Archivio notarile.
Notaio Stefano Perrone, 1511–1527. In *Archivio di Stato di Asti*, Archivio notarile.
Rubrice Statutorum civitatis Ast per ordinem alphabeti. Asti: Franciscum Garonum de Liburno, 1534.
Sella, Quintino, Pietro Vayra (eds.). *Codex Astensis qui de Malabayla communiter nuncupatur*, vol. II. Rome: Salviucci, 1880.

Literature

Arleri, Elio (ed.). *Gabelle e dazi in Asti nel medioevo: versione degli Statuta Revarum Civitatis Ast*. Asti: Della Rovere, 2008.
Benoit, Romain. *Tribunal de la Conservation des privilèges des foires de Lyon 8B 1-8B5269. 1438–1820*. Archives du département du Rhône et de la métropole de Lyon. https://fairs-in-history.huma-num.fr/collection/COL0024 (6 March 2024).
Bera, Gianluigi. *Asti. Edifici e palazzi nel Medioevo*. Savigliano: Gribaudo, 2004.
Bordone, Renato. *Città e territorio nell'alto medioevo. La società astigiana dal dominio dei Franchi all'affermazione comunale*. Turin: Deputazione subalpina di Storia Patria, 1980.
Bordone, Renato (ed.). *L'uomo del banco dei pegni. "Lombardi" e mercato del denaro nell'Europa medievale*. Turin: Paravia Scriptorium, 1994.
Bordone, Renato. La dominazione francese di Asti: istituzioni e società tra Medioevo ed età moderna. In *Gandolfino da Roreto e il Rinascimento nel Piemonte meridionale*, Romano, Giovanni (ed.). Turin: Fondazione CRT, Banca CRT, 1998, 19–30.
Bordone, Renato. I Lombardi in Europa: uno sguardo d'insieme. In *Lombardi in Europa nel Medioevo*, Renato Bordone, Franco Spinelli (eds.). Milan: Franco Angeli, 2005, 9–39.
Bordone, Renato. Una Lobby finanziaria internazionale?. In *Dal banco di pegno all'alta finanza. Lombardi e mercanti-banchieri fra Paesi Bassi e Inghilterra nel Trecento*, Renato Bordone (ed.). Asti: Centro studi sui lombardi, sul credito e sulla banca, 2007, 9–25.
Bordone, Renato. "La forest de longue actente." Maria di Clèves, Duchessa d'Orléans e Signora di Asti. *Il Platano* 33 (2008): 201–223.
Calabi, Donatella, Paola Lanaro. Lo spazio delle fiere e dei mercati nella città italiana di età moderna. In *Fiere e mercati nella integrazione delle economie europee, secoli XIII-XVIII*, Simonetta Cavaciocchi (ed.). Florence: Le Monnier, 2001, 109–141.

Cassandro, Michele. *Le fiere di Lione e gli uomini d'affari italiani nel Cinquecento*. Florence: Baccini & Chiappi, 1979.

Castellani, Luisa. *Gli uomini d'affari astigiani. Politica e denaro tra Piemonte ed Europa*. Turin: Paravia Scriptorium, 1998.

Castelnuovo, Guido. Principi e città negli stati sabaudi. In *Principi e città alla fine del medioevo*, Sergio Gensini (ed.). Rome: Ministero per i beni culturali e ambientali, Ufficio centrale per i beni archivistici, 1996, 91–93.

Corti, Paola. Mécénat et culture dévote chez Marie de Clèves, duchesse d'Orléans (1426–1487). In *Les femmes, la culture et les arts en Europe entre Moyen Âge et Renaissance/Women, art and culture in medieval and early Renaissance Europe*, Cynthia J. Brown, Anne-Marie Legaré (eds.). Turnhout: Brepols, 2016, 13–32.

Dell'Oro, Giorgio. Carne rossa, carne bianca: allevamenti e consumi in Italia settentrionale in età moderna. In *Le vie del cibo Italia settentrionale (secc. XVI–XX)*, Marina Cavallera, Silvia Antonia Conca Messina, Blythe Alice Raviola (eds.). Rome: Carocci, 2019, 251–264.

Demo, Edoardo. "Una compagnia per attender al traffico di Bolgiano, Vienna et altre fiere solite." I Cerminati dalla Luna, mercanti veronesi nell'Europa centro-orientale del secondo Cinquecento. *Studi Storici Luigi Simeoni* 59 (2009): 37–48.

Doglio, Maria Luisa. Un'inedita storia di Asti di Emanuele Tesauro. In *Civiltà del Piemonte. Studi in onore di Renzo Gandolfo nel suo settantacinquesimo compleanno*, Gianrenzo Clivio, Riccardo Massano (eds.). Turin: Centro di studi piemontesi, 1975, 165–181.

Fara, Andrea. Il commercio di bestiame ungherese verso la Penisola italiana tra tardo Medioevo e prima Età moderna (XIV–XVI secolo). *Mélanges de l'École française de Rome—Moyen Âge* 127: 2 (2015). https://journals.openedition.org/mefrm/2709 (14 November 2023).

Fissore, Gian Giacomo. *Autonomia notarile e organizzazione cancelleresca del comune di Asti. I modi e le forme dell'intervento notarile nella costituzione del documento comunale*. Spoleto: Cisam, 1977.

Forghieri, Vanda. Asti e la politica francese in Lombardia. *Rivista di storia, arte e archeologia per la provincia di Alessandria* 45 (1936): 5–77.

Gabiani, Niccola. *Notizie sulla Ferrazza o politica della città d'Asti dal XIV al XVIII secolo: ricerche storiche*. Turin: Roux & C., 1892.

Gabotto, Ferdinando. *La vita in Asti al tempo di Giovan Giorgio Alione*. Asti: Bianchi, 1899.

Gabotto, Ferdinando (ed.). *Le più antiche carte dell'Archivio capitolare di Asti*. Pinerolo: Chiantore-Mascarelli, 1904.

Garesio Pelissero, Franca. La società del moleggio in Asti durante il dominio orleanese. *Bollettino storico-bibliografico subalpino* 91:2 (1993): 477–545; 92:1 (1994): 47–79.

Gaulin, Jean-Louis, Susanne Rau. Rétablissement de deux foires à Lyon (mai 1487). In *Lyon, entre empire et royaume, 843–1601. Textes et documents*, Alexis Charansonnet, Jean-Louis Gaulin, Pascale Mounier, Susanne Rau (eds.). Parigi: Classiques Garnier, 2015, 523–528.

Gnetti, Donatella, Giulia Scarcia. Splendore e declino dei lombardi. In *Lombardi in Europa nel Medioevo*, Renato Bordone, Franco Spinelli (eds.), 76–97. Milan: Franco Angeli, 2005.

Grohmann, Alberto. *Fiere e mercati nell'Europa occidentale*. Milan: Bruno Mondadori, 2011.

Luca, Cristian. Un tentativo d'importazione dalla Moldavia di bovini destinati al mercato fiorentino all'epoca di Cosimo I de' Medici. In *Italia ed Europa centro-orientale tra Medioevo ed Età moderna: economia, società, cultura*, Andrea Fara (ed.). Heidelberg: Heidelberg University Publishing, 2022, 303–322.

Monumenta Germaniae Historica. *Diplomata regum et imperatorum Germaniae*, vol. II. Hannover: Impensis Bibliopolii Hahniani, 1893.

Mutinelli, Fabio (ed.). *Storia arcana ed aneddotica d'Italia raccontata dai veneti ambasciatori*, vol. II, *sec. XVI*. Venice: Naratovich, 1856, 299–300.

Nada Patrone, Anna Maria. Glosse latine e francesi nel ms. astigiano K.K. 1415 degli Statuta revarum Ast. In *Miscellanea di studi romanzi offerta a Giuliano Gasca Queirazza per il suo 65° compleanno*, vol. II, Anna Cornagliotti, Lucia Fontanella, Marco Piccat, Alda Rossebastiano, Alessandro Vitale-Brovarone (eds.). Alessandria: Edizioni dell'Orso, 1988, 744–768.

Pia, Ezio Claudio. "Riposare sotto lo scettro sabaudo"? Autonomia contrattata e rappresentazione della città in Asti nel Cinquecento. In *Francesco Panigarola. Predicazione, filosofia e teologia nel secondo Cinquecento*, Francesco Ghia, Fabrizio Meroi (eds.). Florence: Olschki, 2013, 163–174.

Pia, Ezio Claudio. Asti tra "dominazione straniera" e autonomia negoziata (secoli XIV–XVI). *Bollettino storico-bibliografico subalpino* 115:1 (2017): 125–142.

Pia, Ezio Claudio. *Asti*. Spoleto: Cisam, 2017.

Pia, Ezio Claudio. "Multam pecuniam, multa mala". I "Lombardi" astigiani e il mercato del credito nel Basso Medioevo. *Nuova Rivista Storica* 105:1 (2021): 33–61.

Promis, Vincenzo (ed.). *Memoriale di Gio. Andrea Saluzzo di Castellar dal 1482 al 1528*. Turin: Stamperia Reale, 1869.

Reichert, Winfried. *Lombarden in der Germania-Romania. Atlas und Dokumentation*, 2. 1,2,3. Trier: Porta Alba, 2003.

Robecchi, Marco. Le ms. 125 de la Burgerbibliothek de Berne: de Charles d'Orléans à Jacques Bongars (en passant par Marie de Clèves). *Medioevi. Rivista di letterature e culture medievali* 3 (2017): 157–192. http://www.medioevi.it/index.php/medioevi/article/view/49/66 (14 November 2023).

Schaube, Adolf. *Storia del commercio dei popoli latini del Mediterraneo sino alla fine delle Crociate*, Pietro Bonfante (trans.). Turin: Unione tipografico-editrice torinese, 1915.

Tobler-Meyer, Wilhelm. Das Junker-Geschlecht der Scherer aus der Stadt St. Gallen, sein Erlöschen und seine Erbschaft. *Schweizer Archiv für Heraldik* 16 (1902): 13–27.

Tonelli, Giovanna. "Mercanti che hanno negotio grosso" fra Milano e i Paesi riformati nel primo Seicento. In *Mercanti, eresia e Inquisizione nell'Italia moderna*, Germano Maifreda (ed.). *Storia economica* 17:1 (2014): 101–142.

Travaglini, Matilde. La donazione sabauda del 1098 al comune di Asti. *Bollettino storico-bibliografico subalpino* 69 (1971): 544–551.

Tucci, Patrizio. Morire di sete vicino alla fontana. Charles d'Orléans e la polifonia poetica alla corte di Blois. In *L'autorialità plurima. Scritture collettive, testi a più mani, opere a firma multipla*. Atti del XLII Convegno Interuniversitario di Bressanone, 10–13 luglio 2014, Alvaro Barbieri, Elisa Gregari (eds.). Padua: Esedra, 2015, 379–403.

Vaglienti, Francesca Maria. "Fidelissimi servitori de Consilio suo secreto". Struttura e organizzazione del Consiglio segreto nei primi anni del ducato di Galeazzo Maria Sforza (1466–1469). *Nuova Rivista Storica* 76 (1992): 645–708.

Weissen, Kurt. I mercanti toscani alle fiere tedesche nel tardo medioevo. In *Fiere e mercati nella integrazione delle economie europee, secoli XIII-XVIII*, Simonetta Cavaciocchi (ed.). Florence: Le Monnier, 2001, 887–908.

Related CoMOR-Collection

Ewert, Ulf Christian. Bayerische Staatsbibliothek Münchner Digitalisierungszentrum, Théodore Turquet de Mayerne, Description de la France, Allemagne, Italie & Espagne. Avec la Guide des chemins pour aller & venir par les provinces, & et aux villes plus renommees de ces quatre régions. A quoy est adiousté en receuil des foires plus celebres presque de toute l'Europe. Et un traicté des monnoyes & leur valeur esdits pays, provinces & villes (COL0024). In *Configurations of European Fairs: Merchants, Objects, Routes (ca. 1350–1600)*, Jean-Louis Gaulin, Susanne Rau (dir.). https://fairs-in-history.huma-num.fr/collection/COL0024 (6 March 2024).

Heinrich Lang

Accounting fairs: Florentine and south German merchant-bankers at the fairs in 16th-century Lyon

Introduction

The fairs in sixteenth-century Lyon belonged to the most important events of the European economy alongside the fairs in Antwerp and Castilla. They were at the beginning of the development that preceded the rise of the exchange fairs before the rise of the renowned fairs of Bisenzone and Piacenza. The Lyon fairs were early reference points for the increasing clearing processes to refinance commerce, banking, and later also government finance from the late fifteenth century.

The site of Lyon has been subject to extensive studies. In particular, the activities of business companies and merchant-bankers have been in focus in the last years. However, works examining the Lyon fairs in particular date back to the 1970s. Only very recently, some new research has been carried out around the fairs in Southern France by members of the research group 'Configurations of European Fairs: Merchants, Objects, Routes.'[1]

The framework of the research group is grounded on a critical review of the different traditions of historiography on late medieval fairs and on new ap-

1 Jointly financed by the French Agence nationale de la Recherche (ANR) and the German Research Foundation (DFG, project number 430627254). The research for this article was conducted from September 2022 to February 2023. The generous support of the University of Erfurt (Susanne Rau) permitted the archival stay in Pisa from September to November 2022. The period from December 2022 to February 2023 was financed from my own private funds. I am very grateful to the archivist, dottoressa Maddalena Taglioli for her neverending help and her incredible patience with me. I am indebted to my colleagues, Adina Eckart and Richard A. Goldthwaite (who sadly passed away on 5 March 2024) for their advice. In particular, Markus A. Denzel, eminent expert on fairs, helped me generously with his comments and productive questions. A study on the Easter fair in Lyon in 1508 from the perspective of Alamanno and Jacopo Salviati and company is part of the common database of the CoMOR [Configurations of Fairs: Merchants, Objects, Routes (1350–1600)] project and is an essential component of this study. See Heinrich Lang. Scuola Normale Superiore di Pisa (hereafter SNS), Archivio Salviati (AS), ser. I, no. 439, Libro di fiera segnato A (Fiera di Pasqua 1508) (COL0106). In *Configurations of European Fairs: Merchants, Objects, Routes (ca. 1350–1600)*, Jean-Louis Gaulin, Susanne Rau (eds.). https://fairs-in-history.huma-num.fr/collection/COL0106 (7 October 2024).

https://doi.org/10.1515/9783111621296-007

proaches in addition to research undertaken in the past. Here, the study of the accounting of a major business company present at the fairs in Lyon concentrates on the evolution of the Lyon fairs, and hence sheds new light on the emergence of the secondary markets—that is, markets of production factors like land, labour, and money that are detached from commerce—due to government finances in the course of the sixteenth century. Therein, the perspective of a Florentine company characterises the key issues of the fairs in Lyon in terms of commerce and, above all, banking and the essential pathways of being a cornerstone within the European system of fairs.

In consequence, the text is structured as follows: the first part deals with the general state of the art of the history of the Lyon fairs and the merchant-bankers operating there for a better understanding of the approach chosen in this article. Then the sources will be presented and discussed. Account books offer a very basic orientation to the proceedings of fairs and what merchant-bankers actually did there. To what extent they present proxy data for the evaluation of the goings-on at Lyon fairs will be also highlighted. Above all, a quantitative analysis of the account books shall provide an in-depth survey of the transfers due to the fairs and a comparison to understand these long lines of development. In particular, the quantitative study sheds new light on the creation of secondary markets which especially derive from government finance. Some concluding remarks will finally try to link these findings with the historiographical background described before.

There are only very few works on business companies and merchant bankers active in Lyon during the late Middle Ages and early modern Europe. Given the overwhelming situation of the Italian archives in general, and the Florentine archives in particular, it is astonishing that scholars have only turned to the business companies' perspectives on the fairs in Lyon in recent years, despite the common opinion that the site of Lyon as a place of commerce, banking, and government finance was essential for the European economy in the later fifteenth and sixteenth centuries. Moreover, the Salviati archives preserve the most interesting and coherent collection of account books brought back from the business activities in southern France. For a period of about fifty years, we are provided with perfect quantitative data which refers to the fairs held in Lyon that also permits us to characterise the proceedings in detail.

Historiographical Background

The seminal works of Richard Gascon on the economic development of the business site of Lyon in the context of the urban society, and of Roger Doucet on the financial and banking activities in Lyon and its fairs, lay the ground for any further consideration. These studies also provide us with statistical data material which could be confronted with the collection of new data.[2]

Much research has been conducted on European fairs in general. However, the works of Franz Irsigler, Michel Pauly, and, more recently, Markus A. Denzel open up the perspectives on fairs and their interrelations, their co-ordination, and their specialisation.[3]

When the French king Louis XI issued his privileges on the fairs in 1462/63, Lyon became a significant player on the international ground of the European system of fairs.[4] The interest in the European system of fairs was clearly bound to the studies on the trade in bills of exchange and then in the spatio-temporal connection of the fairs themselves.

In his *Economic History of Renaissance Florence*, Richard A. Goldthwaite points out that the Florentine merchant-banking companies sought to establish branches in Lyon because of the major opportunities offered by that business site. He explains the general lines of Florentine presence in Lyon. Three categories of business were decisive for the activities in Lyon—commerce, banking, and government finance. The export of luxury goods (like silk cloth) to sell to the solvent French nobility was one major reason for Florentine merchants to move to the rivers Rhône and Saône. Moreover, trade in spices and raw materials seemed

---

2 Richard Gascon. *Grand commerce et vie urbaine au XVIe siècle. Lyon et ses marchands (environs de 1520–environs de 1580).* Paris, La Haye: Mouton, 1971; Roger Doucet. *L'état des finances de 1523.* Paris: Imprimerie Nationale, 1923; Roger Doucet, Le grand parti de Lyon. *Revue Historique* 171 (1933): 472–513; 172 (1933): 1–41; Roger Doucet. *Finances municipales et crédit public à Lyon au XVIe siècle.* Geneva: Magariotis Reprints, 1980.

3 Franz Irsigler, Michel Pauly. Vom regionalen Messesystem zum internationalen Netz von Messestädten. In *Netzwerke im europäischen Handel des Mittelalters*, Gerhard Fouquet, Hans-Jörg Gilomen (eds.). Ostfildern: Jan Thorbecke, 2010, 49–100; Markus A. Denzel. *Das System des bargeldlosen Zahlungsverkehrs europäischer Prägung vom Mittelalter bis 1914.* Stuttgart: Franz Steiner, 2008; Markus A. Denzel (ed.). *Europäische Messegeschichte 9.–19. Jahrhundert.* Cologne, Weimar, Vienna: Böhlau, 2018.

4 For the privileges, see Alexis Charansonnet, Jean-Louis Gaulin, Pascale Mounier, Susanne Rau (eds). *Lyon, entre empire et royaume: 843–1601: textes et documents.* Paris: Classiques Garnier, 2015; Mark Häberlein, Heinrich Lang, Thomas Weller, Clé Lesger, Margrit Schulte Beerbühl, Jürgen G. Nagel, Susanne Rau. Weltwirtschaftszentren. In *Enzyklopädie der Neuzeit Online*, Friedrich Jaeger (ed.). Stuttgart: J.B. Metzler/Springer, 2017: 10. Lyon. http://dx.doi.org/10.1163/2352-0248_edn_COM_380404 (14 August 2024).

to be rather attractive for Florentine players. A key issue was financing commerce and the trade in bills of exchange. Particularly, all kinds of banking activities and financial services alike made Florentine companies appear in Lyon. In the course of the sixteenth century, the trade in bills of exchange was transformed into secondary markets of credit and money. The demand of the church and high dignities of the clergy for the transfer of monetary means and the particular needs of the nobility, but also the desperate claim of the French king for the enormous loans, became the main business of Florentine companies. When his book was published in 2009, Goldthwaite was still deploring the absence of research on the basis of the abundant evidence preserved in Tuscan archives to work on the Florentine companies that did business in Lyon.[5]

Very recently, four scholars have highlighted the fabulous opportunities offered by the Tuscan archives to researchers of individual companies present in Lyon.

Angela Orlandi has studied Giambattista Botti's struggle with the repayment of loans given to the French king, Henry II, in the period of the regulated administration of the Crown's debts and its organisation through the markets of bills of exchange on the Lyon fairs, called the 'Grand Parti' (1555–1559).[6]

Sergio Tognetti has analysed the activities of the Gondi companies with their branches in Lyon during the second and third decades of the sixteenth century and has written a history of the businesses operated by the Gondi between 1516 and 1523.[7]

Nadia Matringe has used the account books of the company of Averardo Salviati to depict a broad-ranging picture of the trade in bills of exchange in the 1540s (mainly 1545–1550) and its connections to the other cornerstones of the system of European fairs—that is, Antwerp and the fairs of Castile. In her most recent studies, she concentrates on the crediting instruments featured by the bills of exchange.[8]

On the basis of the same Salviati material, the author of this article has contributed a study on co-operative networks between southern German merchant-

5 Richard A. Goldthwaite. *The Economy of Renaissance Florence*. Cambridge: Cambridge University Press, 2009, 131–152; Richard A. Goldthwaite. Performance of the Florentine Economy, 1494–1512: the silk and wool industries. *Archivio Storico Italiano* 178 (2020): 311–373.

6 Angela Orlandi, *Le Grand Parti. Fiorentini a Lione e il debito pubblico francese nel XVI secolo*. Florence: Leo S. Olschki, 2002.

7 Sergio Tognetti. *I Gondi di Lione. Una banca d'affari fiorentina nella Francia del primo Cinquecento*. Florence: Leo S. Olschki, 2013, 12.

8 Nadia Matringe. *La Banque en Renaissance. Les Salviati et la place de Lyon au milieu du XVIe siècle*. Rennes: Presses universitaires de Rennes, 2016.

banking companies and the Florentines in Lyon (1507–1559). Moreover, he has particularly considered the secondary markets in the context of the loans to the French kings and the multilayered facets of government finance.[9]

Tommaso Brollo has written a PhD thesis which, unfortunately, has not been published yet. He concentrates on the vast material to be found in Florence for the Capponi companies operating in Lyon and Besançon between 1553 to 1584.[10] This is the period when the documents deriving from the Salviati companies are not available anymore, because they ceased their activities around 1560.[11]

Similar to this context, we have only one study at hand about the Bonvisi from Lucca, mainly referring to the later period after 1575, by Françoise Bayard[12] and an unpublished PhD thesis by Ilario Mosca on Giancarlo and Cosimo Martelli di Lione and company in the 1560s and 70s.[13]

For the sake of completeness, I should mention the book Agnès Pallini-Martin has written on the early years of the Salviati companies in Lyon. This gives a broad overview of the Salviatis operating in commerce and provides glimpses into the first years after the establishment of the Alamanno di Averardo e Jacopo di Giovanni Salviati & Co. on site.[14]

In this study, the perspective on the Lyon fairs is on the activities of the business partnership and on how an important player at the Lyon fairs shaped the practices of doing fairs. The extraordinary material taken from the archives of the Florentine Salviati companies in Lyon is subjected to a combined quantitative

9 Heinrich Lang. Herrscherfinanzen der französischen Krone unter Franz I. aus Sicht italienischer und oberdeutscher Bankiers. Die Rolle der Florentiner Salviati als Financiers der französischen Regierung. In *Das Blut des Staatskörpers. Forschungen und Perspektiven zur Finanzgeschichte der Frühen Neuzeit*, Peter Rauscher, Andrea Serles, Thomas Winkelbauer (eds.). Munich, Vienna: Oldenbourg, 2012, 457–508; Heinrich Lang. Credito e insolvenza sovrana. I prestiti alla Corona francese di mercanti-banchieri toscani e tedeschi meridionali (1550–1559). *Annali dell' Istituto Storico Italiano-Germanico in Trento* 41 (2015): 12–38; Heinrich Lang. *Wirtschaften als kulturelle Praxis. Die Florentiner Salviati und die Augsburger Welser auf den Märkten in Lyon (1507–1559).* Stuttgart: Franz Steiner, 2020, 477–537.

10 Tommaso Brollo. Money and Credit in Early Modern Europe: The 'banco' Capponi in Florence and at the fairs of Lyon and Besançon, 1533–1584. PhD diss., Florence, Pisa, Siena, 2021/2022.

11 Lang, *Wirtschaften*, 232–236.

12 Françoise Bayard. Les Bonvisi, marchands banquiers à Lyon, 1575–1629. *Annales* 26 (1971): 1234–1269.

13 Ilario Mosca. Les Martelli de Florence et de Lyon. Stratégies et relations socio-économiques à l'époque préindustrielle. PhD diss., École Pratique des Hautes Études, Paris/Università di Pisa, 2016. Michele Cassandro ha salso made use of the Martelli archives. See Michele Cassandro. *Le fiere di Lione e gli uomini d'affari italiani nel Cinquecento*. Florence: Baccini e Chiappi, 1979.

14 Agnès Pallini-Martin. *Banque, négoce et politique. Les Florentins à Lyon au moment des guerres d'Italie.* Paris: Classiques Garnier, 2018.

and qualitative approach, thus shedding new light on fairs in the first half of the sixteenth century.

The perspective of the Salviati companies

When Alamanno and Jacopo Salviati established a business company in Lyon in 1508, they sought out the opportunities offered by the markets of Lyon. This expansion was embedded in the network of the de facto heirs (successors) of the business partnership agglomerate held by the Medici. The year before, Francesco Naldini began a collaboration with the south German Hans Vöhlin: the two young merchants founded an *accomandita* in Toulouse, mainly for the trade in pastel, using the investment capital of Francesco's relative, Domenico Naldini and Hans Vöhlin's patron, Konrad Vöhlin. Francesco Naldini, who originated from Florence and left his hometown in 1497, heading to southern France, became the first director of the Salviati company in Lyon until his death in 1518. During that decade, the Salviati companies in Lyon increasingly developed into one of the key players at the Lyon fairs.[15]

The Florentine Salviati family was very prominent in the early sixteenth century. The aforementioned Jacopo Salviati was married to Lucrezia de' Medici, daughter of Lorenzo the Magnificient and sister of Pope Leo X. Amongst their children were Giovanni (a Cardinal from 1517 onwards and even *papabile* in 1549), Maria (married to Giovanni di Giovanni de' Medici, called *dalle Bande Nere*, and mother of Cosimo, later first Granduke of Tuscany), and Alamanno (see the section on him below). The Salviati family made their career with strong bonds to the early Medici regime in the middle of the fifteenth century and continued their ascendence even after their involvement in the complot against the Medici in 1478.[16]

15 Agnès Pallini-Martin. L'installation d'une famille de marchands-banquiers florentins à Lyon au début du XVIe siècle, les Salviati. In *Lyon vu/e d'ailleurs (1245–1800): Échanges, compétitons et perceptions*, Jean-Louis Gaulin, Susanne Rau (eds.). Lyon: Presses universitaires de Lyon, 2009, 71–90; Pallini-Martin, *Banque, négoce et politique*, 83–115, 145–151; Lang, *Wirtschaften*, 194–205.
16 For a general overview, see Pierre Hurtubise. *Une Famille-témoin. Les Salviati*. Rome: École française de Rome, 1985.

The Salviati account books

The Salviati archive, hosted at the Scuola Normale Superiore in Pisa, preserves an utterly unique inventory of account books for the companies operating in Lyon in the first part of the sixteenth century (1507–1554). This consists of nearly 200 registers of different types of books: ledgers, preparatory (preliminary) and specialised books, waste books, copies of letters, and even a secret book (*libro segreto*).[17] This is to say that we do not just have a fragmented series of account books or a simple series of account books (like A to Z) at hand, but the whole system of accountability—at least everything that the main shareholders, who had lent their name to the companies, thought they had to keep for their familial documentation. In many other archives, we find only fragmentary selections of account books of the businesses.[18]

In the context of this study, the analysis of the period from 1508 to 1517 touched on 31 account books. As the example of the signature *C* shows below (Fig. 2), each signature is composed of about seven books (labelled not just *A, B, C*, but also occasionally *AA, AAA, AAAA*, and *BB* books). Therein, the survey comprises 39 fairs held in Lyon, and for each fair, between 100 and 150 personal accounts can be found. Some of these accounts are rather small and are built up of only one or two entries on the debit-side and on the credit-side. However, some of these accounts are quite large and consist of 15 to 20 entries each on either side. In addition to the series of the books of fairs, the ledgers—*libri debitori e creditori*—were used for conjectures—when the *libri di fiera* were absent—and contain special features, like the cash accounts or the merchandise accounts (see section below). Moreover, in the context of the Foire des Rois in early 1550 and the *fiera di Pasqua* in the same year, we only quote all the respective accounts in the *Libro di fiera V Rosso* and the *Libro debitori e creditori V Rosso* instead of using the whole system of the books.[19]

The signatures refer to accounting periods due to the business partnership's contract. The first contract to set up a company bears the signature "A", then

17 Valeria Pinchera. L'Archivio Salviati. La storia degli affari attraverso un Archivio familiare. *Società e storia* 13 (1990): 979–986; Matringe, *La Banque*, 37–45; Heinrich Lang (ed.). *Internationale Kapital- und Warenmärkte, transalpiner Handel und Herrscherfinanzen. Die Kooperation zwischen den Handelsgesellschaften der Welser und den Florentiner Kaufmannbankiers Salviati.* Stuttgart: Franz Steiner, 2021, 29–34; Brollo, Money and Credit, 18–22.

18 Lang, *Kapital- und Warenmärkte*, 68–71. Tommaso Brollo gives a detailled account of great accuracy on the books of the Capponi companies active in Lyon during the second half of the sixteenth century. He shows that the preserved books have survived by chance rather than through a conscious selection by a person in charge. See Brollo, Money and Credit, 24–32.

19 Lang, *Kapital- und Warenmärkte*, 68–71.

comes “B” which indicates the follow-up firm. This is also the reason why we speak of Salviati companies in the plural here. The Florentines called their firms “*ragione*” (= account) and named it after the signature—like our *ragione A*, for instance.

Each signature is identified by a colour: in the case of the account books which belong to the signature letter *C*, it is *Bianco* (= white). Given that the books lay in the shelves horizontally, they had to be recognisable without tearing each one out. This is why the books were marked with a simple signature and a colour on the cover or the bands (*correggie*).[20]

In the late 1520s, within the process of separation of shares between the lineages of the Salviati family that were involved in founding the Lyon branch in 1508—the future papal banker Jacopo di Giovanni and his older cousin Alamanno di Averardo—the partition of the company was not clear and remained in suspense instead. For this reason, the whole series of the Lyon account books was kept to render the distribution among the respectable heirs legitimate.

In order to fully understand how the fairs were transposed into data processing according to the accounting from the perspective of the Salviati business partnership, we have to represent the full procedure of processing data from the preliminary accounts to the balancing operations hidden in the *libro segreto*. In simple terms, we have to evaluate the sources at hand.

Here, the reconstruction of the accounting procedure is illustrated by the example of the accounting series under the signature *C* of the years 1516 and 1517, when the firm was called *Jacopo e redi d'Alamanno Salviati & co di Lione* (Jacopo and the heirs of Alamanno Salviati). The signature *C* refers to just one accounting year and comprises four fairs: the All Saints' Fair in November 1516 (*fiera di Tutti Santi*), the Foire des Rois in January 1517 (the Kings' Fair, *fiera d'Apparizione*), the Easter Fair 1517 (that year, Easter had happened to be on 12 April: *fiera di Pasqua*), and the August Fair in 1517 (15 August, *fiera d'Agosto*).[21]

We shall bear in mind that this chosen year is not only one of the last years when Francesco Naldini was the director of the Salviati company in Lyon, but it was also an accounting year not mentioned in literature so far when the fairs of

---

20 The only textbook which gives some hints on the very basic features of account books on the material level is Federigo Melis. *Aspetti della vita economica medievale*. Siena: Leo S. Olschki, 1962. The author of this study is working on a major textbook on the material aspects and the process of accounting.

21 Please note that the Florentine legal year (*ab incarnatione*) began on 25 March each year. So, the last day of the year 1516 was on 24 March 1517. This is why the Foire des Rois (*fiera d'Apparizione*) is referred to as the fourth fair of the year 1516 here in order to imitate Florentine accounting. See Lang, *Kapital- und Warenmärkte*, 66.

Besançon were not established yet. In this sense, the evidence extracted from the Salviati archive shows something truly unknown.

However, in Tommaso Brollo, we find the most elaborate description for the use of the book of the fairs—the *libro di fiera*. In other publications, I have already explained how to read the various series of account books with respect to business relationships.[22]

While Fig. 1 shows how the book system presented here works, Fig. 2 displays the system of account books that form part of the signature *C* from the All Saints' Fair in 1516 to the August Fair in 1517 and, of course, in what direction these account books should be analysed. The book of the fairs—*Libro di fiera C*—is a book kept for the accounts open throughout the fairs (All Saints' Fair 1516, Foire des Rois 1516 *stile fiorentino* = 1517, Easter Fair 1517, August Fair 1517). Though it is a preliminary book to the ledger, the *Libro debitori e creditori C Bianco* (opened on 1 November 1516, closed on 31 October 1517), at the core of the signature *C*, was not taken by the negotiating merchant banker-in-charge along with the *libro di fiera* of the Salviati companies in Lyon. Apparently, these account books were only kept at the branch office as they do not show any signs of usage on the place (out of office) and are written most accurately. For preparing the book of fairs, a large booklet was employed which included two subdivisional books—the *Entrata e uscita* (incoming and outgoing) and the *Quaderno di cassa* (the booklet of the cashier).[23]

Within this particular kind of 'dual' bookkeeping, we find the cross-references which mark the carryover to the book of the fairs. However, there are also cross-references from the *Entrata e uscita/Quaderno di cassa* directly to the ledger. The *Libro debitori e creditori C Bianco* also reports carryovers from the book of the fairs and shows the cross-references "back" to the *Libro di fiera C* (Fig. 2).[24]

So, the accounts open during the fairs and put down in the book of the fairs are in a way an extension of the personal accounts in the ledger or might be read as personal accounts in a second degree (as a substitute account).[25] Obviously, the bookkeeper wanted to distinguish the entries in the personal account during the

22 Brollo, Money and Credit, 30–32; Lang, *Wirtschaften*, 284–298; Lang, *Kapital- und Warenmärkte*, 38–40.

23 For the categories of books within the system of account books, see Melis, *Aspetti*.

24 In fact, the *Entrata e uscita/Quaderno di cassa*, the *Libro di fiera*, and the ledger form a bookkeeping triangle 'around' the fairs. Following the accounts open during the fairs and the closing of the accounts of the fairs depends on the interpretation of the connection between these three books. The accounts of the book of the fairs were copied to the ledger, but the accounts in the ledger are not a simple representation of the previously running accounts during the fairs.

25 What hints at this interpretation is that the logic of the accounts kept during the fairs as given in the *Libro di fiera C* and the *Libro debitori e creditori C Bianco* is the same (we do not find

fairs from other aspects of the personal account as presented in the ledger. In consequence, it seems easy to count what happened during the fairs as accounted in the *Libro di fiera C*, because we simply have to sum up the numbers of the respective accounts during each fair.

Alongside, there is the *Libro di giornale C* which also cross-references the ledger. Additionally, the ledger shows the carryovers from the journal where the bookkeeper wrote only some of the incoming and outgoing merchandise. The *Libro di giornale C* was copied from notes like slips of paper or some kind of notebook which were then thrown away (Fig. 2). Apparently, the *Libro di giornale C* does not belong to the fairs' context at all. The connections to be drawn only refer to the credits and refinance during the fairs on the behalf of commerce.

The ledger reports some cross-references to the *Libro di ricordanze C* where we find some explicit reports in addition to accounts (Fig. 2). It is fairly clear that the bookkeeper decided to put down some notes which could serve in any event or represent a kind of record.

The register of outgoing letters—the *Copialettere*—does not contain a copy of every letter that was sent, and, especially under the signature *C*, we mainly find letters that were sent *di là a' Monti*—that is, across the Alps. This register contains letters which are also mentioned in the *Libro di ricordanze C* and echo some of the entries from the *Libro di giornale C*. Since letters were the medium of the accounting entity to communicate with the outside (other companies for instance), this book belongs to the accounting system as the external dimension of the account books presented here. It is not entirely clear how to describe the register of the outgoing letters as inserted in the system. The letters copied seem to have been used as the internal memory of ongoing business relationships and to outline how the internal processing data constituted the outside relationships.

The signature *C* comprises a *Quaderno di lettere e ricordi di giovani* as well. This booklet shows a register for the payment for sending the outgoing letters and the expenses for the apprentices.

In the period from 1508 to 1528, the directors of the Salviati companies in Lyon kept a *Libro Segreto Rosso*, the Red Secret Book (which is preserved). The connections to the accounting systems go through the capital accounts: the profit or loss on the capital accounts in the *Libro debitori e creditori C* was carried over to the *Libro segreto Rosso*.[26]

---

the inversion of putting down *dare* and *avere*—'receivables' and 'liabilities' respectively—as it would be if we had two levels of keeping accounts).

26 SNS, AS, ser. III, no. 8.

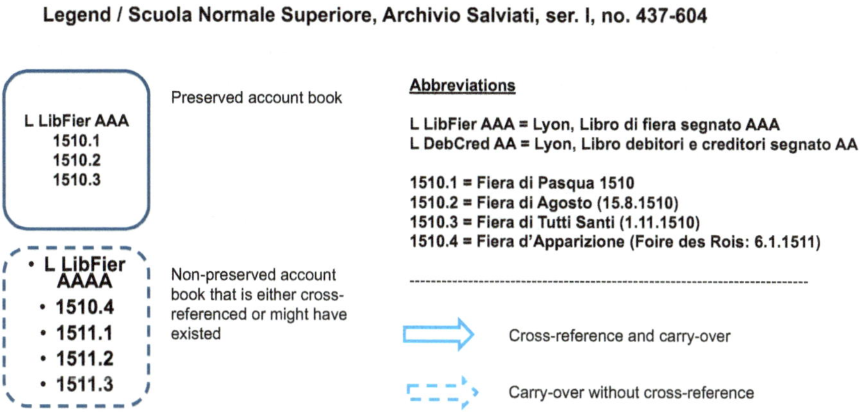

Fig. 1: Legend to Fig. 2.

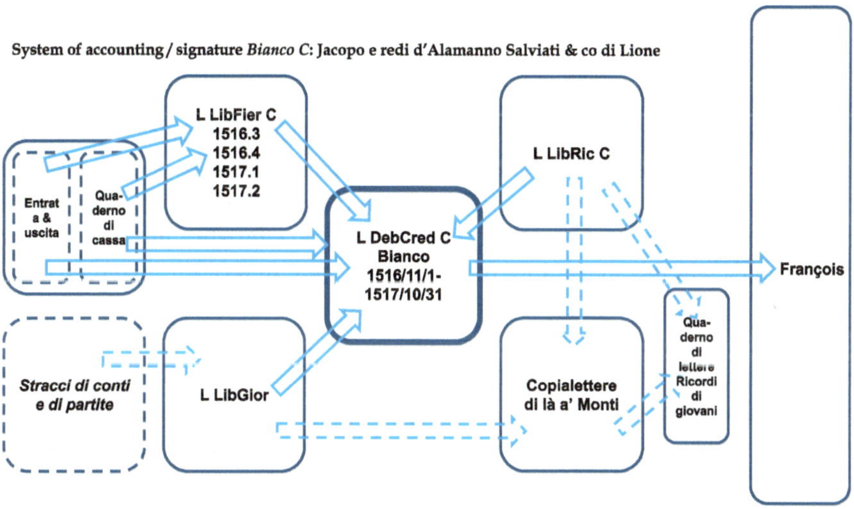

Fig. 2: System of the account books (signature C, 1516–17).

The quantitative analysis of the Salviati accountability

Before beginning the quantitative analysis, we should identify some accounts for the categories of interpretation within the accounting system as shown in the example here. Generally, the books of the fairs (*libri di fiera*) only include personal accounts. Therein, the bookkeeper put down the transfers due to the correspondents and business friends at the place during the fairs. The business relationships between the companies and individual merchant-bankers were identified on the level of payments.

In fact, this was rather complex: financial transactions were operated in bills of exchange, in payments derving from rescontre mechanisms, and cash. When a fair began, a large amount of payments was due, conducted by bills of exchange. In a later period, the merchant-bankers gathered and ran through the actual clearing processes. When the fair came to an end, some cash transfers followed. As for the accounts, each account was closed after the fair (when payments were concluded) and had to be balanced at par. We hardly ever find a carryover from one fair account to another (an account that is balanced at debt).[27]

From the accounts' perspective, we are able to observe the thousands of series of transfers within varying constellations and an ever-recurring formation of correspondents. During the fairs, commerce appeared in the payment dimension, when the transfer of merchandise was due to the settlement of credits and debts (clearing).[28] So, the turnover of a fair displays the payments operations. Consequently, we are able to see the volume of each business relationship from fair to fair, or the whole turnover from fair to fair, by totalling all individual turnovers.

For any other parameter, we have to turn to the ledger: because there are no cash accounts in the books of the fairs—apart from some rare exceptions—we have to look up the cash accounts in the *libro debitori e creditori* to show the total cash moved during the fairs. One of the basic characteristics of double entry bookkeeping was the appearance of the cash account. In fact, this is essential because the abstract bookkeeping produced book money, however money was coined from precious metals and consisted of a valuable material. At the beginning and at the end of business transactions was cash. Additionally, the respective merchandise, the profit on bills of exchange, or payments from clearing processes or any other payments, as well as the total loss or profit in a certain predefined period is only present in the ledger. In the *libro debitori e creditori*, the processed data of accounting is evaluated, and for that reason it shows every kind of accounts necessary—personal accounts, merchandise accounts, business accounts.

---

27 These mechanisms are documented in Domenico Gioffrè. *Gênes et les foires de change de Lyon à Besançon*. Paris: Éditions de l'École des hautes études en sciences sociales, 1960. For the practical issues at the Lyon fairs, see Gascon, *Grand commerce*, 242–248.

28 See Lars Börner, John William Hatfield. The Design of Debt-Clearing Markets: Clearinghouse Mechanisms in Preindustrial Europe. *Journal of Political Economy* 125:6 (2017): 1991–2037, esp. 1992, 1997–2003.

Quantitative analyses

Given the preservation of comprehensive series of account books in the case of the Salviati companies in Lyon, a merely quantitative analysis from the business' perspective is rendered possible and matches an exceptional range of research. The other archives of companies active in Lyon during the sixteenth century—like the Gondi company mentioned in the *Archivio di Stato di Firenze* or the Bartolini companies in the private archives of Bartolini Salimbeni around 1500—examine shorter periods and do not represent an entire series of the book system.[29] Moreover, the complex accounting system of the Salviati companies in Lyon opens the survey to a highly differentiated categorisation of various types of transfers, especially from one fair to another in the long term. In particular, the accounts show the distinct ways of payment, and we are able to quantify exactly which merchandise the Salviati companies traded in. The quantitative analyses here will help us understand the markets as constituted by the fairs of Lyon through the lenses of the accountability of a business partnership active here.

The proportion of paper money to cash

On the basis of the books of the fairs from the establishment of a Salviati company in Lyon until the death of the first director Francesco Naldini, the first quantitative analysis is on transfers in paper money and in cash. Paper money appears in two categories: one is bills of exchange, the other is payments due to the clearing procedure (Fig. 3). The *libri di fiera* start in early 1509 during the Foire des Rois. Between the All Saints' Fair in 1510 and the August Fair in 1514, the Salviati did not keep any books of the fairs.[30] They restart during the All Saints' Fair in late 1514 and then continue until the All Saints' Fair in 1517.

The numbers are given in *scudi di marchi*, the book money brought to Lyon by the Florentines. It was fixed at 65 *scudi di marchi* per *marco*, the *marco d'oro* being the accounting money unit. Apart from its crisis from 1550 to 1552, when gold was under pressure, the *marco d'oro* was a stronghold of the *affaires*.[31]

---

29 Tognetti, *Gondi*, 12–13; Götz-Rüdiger Tewes. *Kampf um Florenz. Die Medici im Exil 1494–1512*. Cologne, Weimar, Vienna: Böhlau, 2011.

30 The *Libro di fiera AAA* terminates after/before/with the All Saints' Fair in 1510, and the *Libro di fiera B* only restarts documentation during the All Saints' Fair in 1514 (SNS, AS, ser. I, no. 442/453). There are no *libri di fiera* in this period, because there are no cross-references to the *libro di fiera* (it is not a simple loss in the series of books of the fairs; there actually were none).

31 Gascon, *Grand commerce*, 567–572.

In fact, with the second period of the documentation in the books of the fairs, we are able to observe the recurrent pattern of the most important fair—that is, the Easter Fair—and subsequently, the turnover becomes less and less from fair to fair, to the smallest fair—the Foire des Rois. During the annual cycle, the smallest fairs are still at the size of two-thirds of the biggest fair. This reassures the "*indice d'activité*" on fairs provided by Richard Gascon.[32]

The total transfers in bills of exchange made up more than half of the total turnover in almost every fair, while the transfers in cash were negligibly small in relation to the total turnovers from fair to fair—apart from the nearly 30,000 *scudi di marchi* on the Foire des Rois in early 1516. The total turnovers oscillate between 75,280 *scudi di marchi* on the Foire des Rois in early 1509 and 354,830 *scudi di marchi* on the *fiera di Pasqua* in 1517, which seemed to be an exceptional fair. The average total turnovers of the twenty fairs shown here, excluding the first fair, would be 214,903 *scudi di marchi* (Fig. 3).[33]

The total transfers in bills of exchange varied between 40,085 *scudi di marchi* on the Foire des Rois in early 1509 and 185,880 *scudi di marchi* on the *fiera di Agosto* in 1510 by an algebraic average, with a computed value of 105,246 *scudi di marchi* if we skip the small initial fair in 1509.[34] In contrast to the small totals of the turnovers of payments in mobilised cash, the numbers differ between 3,149 *scudi di marchi* on the *fiera di Agosto* in 1509 and 22,193 *scudi di marchi* on the *fiera di Pasqua* in 1516; that is, if we leave out the exceptional fair in cash—the Foire des Rois in early 1517. The average of the turnovers in cash would be 11,841 *scudi di marchi*—which does not seem to be a verifiable number, because many fairs show mobilised cash at around 3,149 *scudi di marchi* and 4,177 *scudi di marchi* on the one hand and around 14,323 *scudi di marchi* and the aforementioned 22,193 *scudi di marchi* (Fig. 3).[35]

32 Gascon, *Grand commerce*, 242.

33 The first fair taken into consideration is a statistical outlier, which is why I have excluded it. For the more apropriate averages, the four fairs of each cycle should be distinguished: the average of the total turnover on the five Foires des Rois would be 137,292 *scudi di marchi*; on the five *fiere di Pasqua* would be 246,286 *scudi di marchi*; on the five *fiere di Agosto* would be 249,875 *scudi di marchi*; on the five *fiere di Tutti Santi* would be 198,238 *scudi di marchi*.

34 The average of the turnovers of transfers operated by bills of exchange on the five Foires des Rois would be 59,580 *scudi di marchi* (excluding the first Foire des Rois in 1509, it would be 64,545 *scudi di marchi*; on the five *fiere di Pasqua* it would be 110,222 *scudi di marchi*; on the five *fiere di Agosto* it would be 138,429 *scudi di marchi*; on the five *fiere di Tutti Santi* it would be 99,719 *scudi di marchi*).

35 A distinction should be made between the fairs during the cycle of the year. However, the comparison of the turnovers in mobilised cash on all fairs by categories seems somewhat useless. The only rule appears to be that in the second period documented here, from the *fiera di Pasqua*

The numeric gap between the transfers in bills of exchange and the ones in cash are due to the clearing procedure: a good proportion of the whole turnover from fair to fair was operated by payments deriving from rescontre mechanisms, which were also operated without cash and hence count as book money (Fig. 3). Obviously, we are talking about a considerable amount of the totals—generally about a half of the payments on the fairs.[36]

The share of business transactions in total turnover

The second dimension of our quantitative analyses refers to commerce in relation to the total turnover of all business affairs (Fig. 4). The temporal gap which derives from the limited documentation of the books of the fairs between the All Saints' Fair in 1510 and the August Fair in 1514 could be widely filled by the *libri debitori e creditori* during that period. The remaining lack of data from the All Saints' Fair in 1510 to the one in 1511 is a result of practical reasons: the absence of comparable data made it far too laborious to complete the whole set of internal differentiation at this point.[37]

The merchandise accounts generally do not appear in the *libri di fiera*, so we have to turn to the ledger where one can find all classes (types) of accounts and where the payment procedures are also spelled out. Thus, we can explain when the payments were due and show that the bulk of the transfers in commerce were paid for by bills of exchange cleared at the fairs.[38]

The general lines shown in the merchandise accounts sum up a total turnover in commerce that is between less than five percent and about twelve percent of the total turnover. There is only one exception: during the Foire des Rois in 1516, the total turnover of the Salviati company was (noted as) only 182,229 *scudi di marchi*,

in 1515, there was an average turnover in cash transactions of 19,282 *scudi di marchi* at the *Pasqua* and the *Agosto* fairs.

36 Marie-Thérèse Boyer-Xambeu, Ghislain Deleplace, Lucien Gillard. *Private Money & Public Currencies. The 16th Century Challenge*. Armonk, London: M.E. Sharpe, 1994, 190–198; Börner, Hatfield, Design of Debt-Clearing Markets, 1993–1994, esp. 1997–2003 for an in-depth description.

37 The requested data could be raised from the *Libro debitori e creditori AAA* which covers the period from 31 December 1510 to 30 December 1511. However, it would be an enormous effort to reconstruct all the business activities from banking businesses to differentiation within goods in trade. I have some data at hand, but I hesitate to insert it into the graphs because of its limited character. This would require further examination of the archival material, which would be wonderful.

38 For this procedure, see Gascon, *Grand commerce*, 242–248.

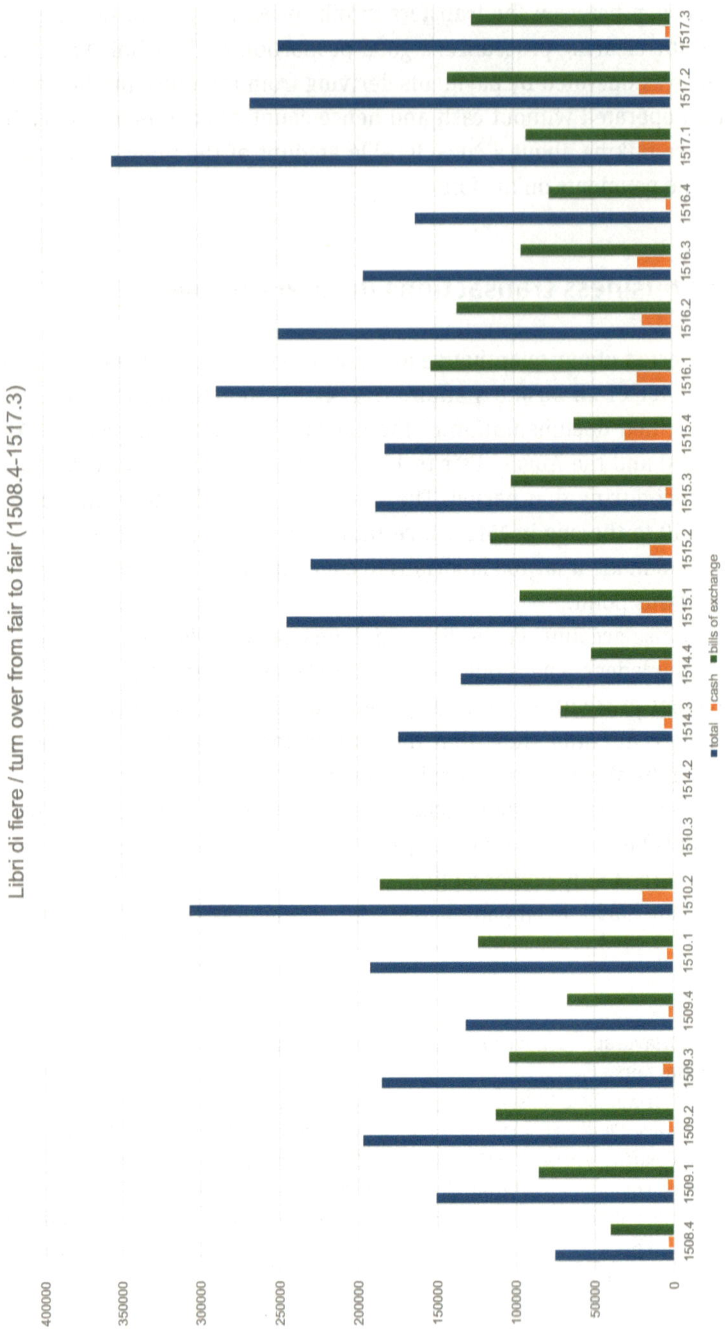

Fig. 3: Proportions of total turnover, cash, and bills of exchange.

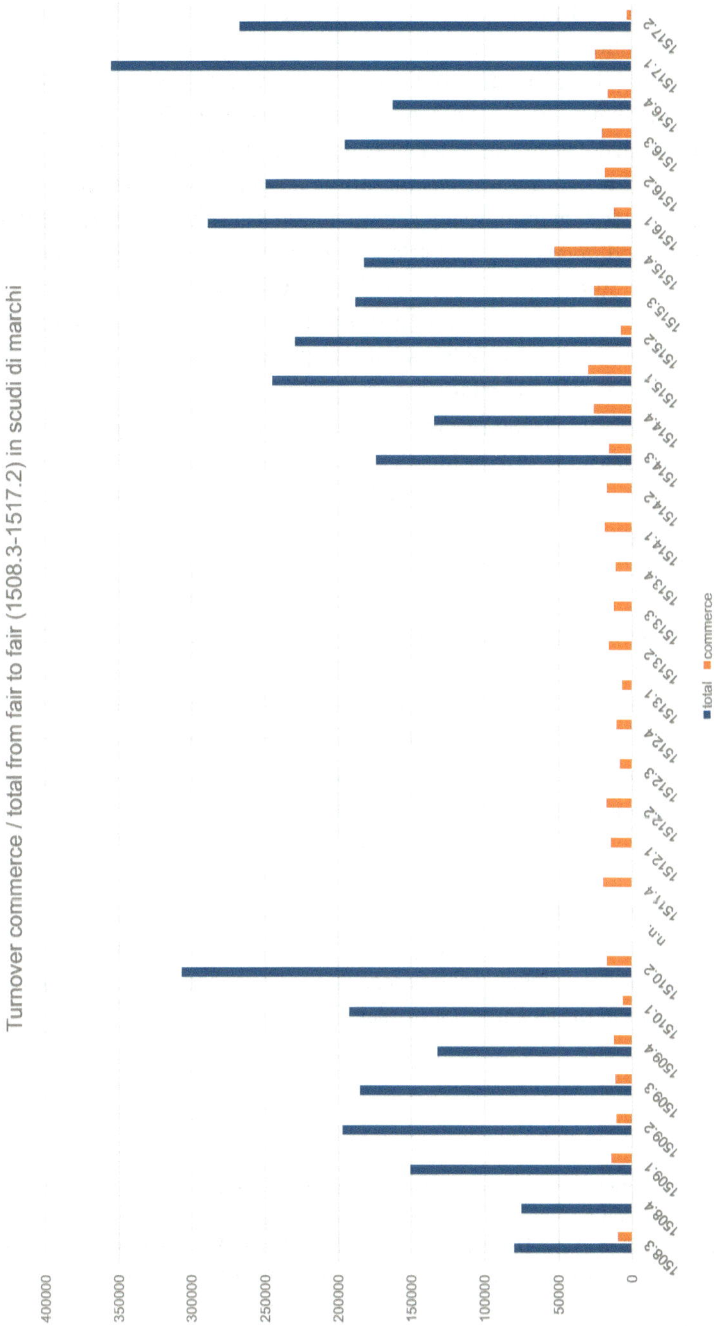

Fig. 4: Propotion of total turnover to total commerce.

while the total turnover in commerce reached a fantastic total of 52,921 *scudi di marchi*—that is, 29% (almost a third of the total turnover) (Fig. 4).

For understanding the proportion of commerce in the entire turnovers of the fairs better, we must compare the different fairs. As we have already seen, the average of the total turnover at the five Foires des Rois would be 137,292 *scudi di marchi,* whereas at the five *fiere di Pasqua,* the average total turnover would amount to 246,286 *scudi di marchi,* rising slightly to 249,875 *scudi di marchi* at the five *fiere di Agosto* and decreasing to 198,238 *scudi di marchi* at the five *fiere di Tutti Santi.*[39] The computed values of the total turnovers in commerce were related to the fairs as follows: on the seven All Saints' Fairs, commerce amounted to 7.5%, at the eight *fiere di Apparizione* it constituted 13.6% (if we leave out the two exceptional fairs in early 1509—when the turnover in commerce was extremely low—and in early 1515—when the turnover in commerce was very high—the average percentage would be 11.7%), at the eight Easter Fairs it was at 6.5%, and at the eight *fiere di Agosto* it accounted for 5.4%.[40]

In fact, this exceptional turnover in commerce was caused by a very special transfer. In late 1515, the Salviati company sold artillery and gunpowder to the French king Francis I, who was preparing the defence of the city of Milan he had just conquered. These weapons played a growing importance in the context of the Italian wars.[41]

There are only a few cases with exact numbers for a comparison. Sergio Tognetti, for instance, gives the assets and the liabilities of the opening accounts of Antonio e Pierantonio Gondi & Co. in Lyon for 1 November 1516. The assets consist of *crediti* at 58,267.12.8 *scudi di marchi* and merchandise at 4,237*scudi di marchi.* The assets in total (we have to add the value of objects in the household and the tax on silk cloth, which amounts to 514.13.10 *scudi di marchi*) stand at 62,918.9.3 *scudi di marchi.* The company's liabilities matched the total of the assets, of course.[42] The Gondi company set up the *ragione E,* the firm of Antonio e Pierantonio Gondi & Co., with the capital stock of 19,000 *scudi di marchi* in November 1516 and raised it to 20,000 *scudi di marchi* in December of the same year.[43]

39 See footnote 26.

40 We draw the exact numbers from Fig. 4, and using the average, we can compare the numbers of all the fairs in each season.

41 Michael Mallett, Christine Shaw. *The Italian Wars, 1494–1559. War, State and Society in Early Modern Europe.* Harlow: Pearson Education, 2012, 126–132 on the first campaigns brought to Italy by Francis I, 182–183 on the special "impact of gunpowder weapons."

42 Tognetti, *I Gondi,* 64 (tabella 5).

43 Tognetti, *I Gondi,* 27.

At about the same time, the Salviati founded a new firm on 17 August 1517 which bore the name of Redi di Alamanno e Battista Salviati & Co. di Lione. The opening account of the *ragione nuova* shows liabilities at 108,800 *scudi di marchi*, while the capital stock was at 22,000 *scudi di marchi*.[44] On the (synchronically ongoing) August Fair instead, the Salviati company performed a notable total turnover of 266,985 *scudi di marchi*, whereas the turnover in sold merchandise was only at 3,393 *scudi di marchi* (Fig. 4).

Silver trade and commerce

A particular issue which results from the analysis of the goods traded on the fairs in Lyon was the distinction of the silver trade from commerce in general. The acquisition of silver from the eastern parts of central Europe and from the Alpine region, and the transport of the precious metal either to the mints in Spain or to Italy, was a business affair of its own. In his seminal study on the Lyon fairs, Richard Gascon also draws this distinction between merchandise and silver.[45] The reason for this was the essential meaning of silver, it being the key ingredient in valuable coins from the late fifteenth century onwards.[46] In his work on *Money in Sixteenth-Century Florence*, Carlo M. Cipolla characterises the production of coins and the politics imposed by the Florentine Republic and the Dukedom on coining precious metals. From August 1504, the Florentine Republic minted silver coins using fine silver at 958.333/1,000 called *popolino*-silver.[47] Cipolla also claims that the raw silver came from Bohemia, Saxony, and Tyrol, before the waves of South American silver bullion arrived in Europe from the 1540s.[48] In conse-

---

44 Lang, *Wirtschaften*, 205.
45 Gascon, *Grand commerce*, 238.
46 Eddy H. H. van Cauwenberghe (ed.). *Precious Metals, Coinage and the Changes of Monetary Structures in Latin-America, Europe and Asia: Late Middle Ages–Early Modern Times*. Leuven: Leuven University Press, 1989; Peter Hammer. *Metall und Münze*. Leipzig: Deutscher Verlag für Grundstoffindustrie 1993, 77–104. See also Torsten Fried. Silbermünzen. In *Enzyklopädie der Neuzeit*, vol. 12 (Silber-Subsidien), Friedrich Jaeger (ed.). Stuttgart: Metzler, 2010, coll. 9–11.
47 Carlo M. Cipolla. *Money in Sixteenth-Century Florence*. Berkeley: University of California Press, 1989, 4–7. In other words each *libra*-silver coin contained 3.37 grams of fine silver, and its weight was fixed at 3.512 grams (the *carlino* as it was first called and later the *barile* and then the *giulio* showed a nominal value of *soldi* 12 *danari* 6 *piccioli*). Only in 1530/1531 were the silver coins devalued down to 3.3 grams of silver content per silver coin.
48 Cipolla, *Money*, 1989, 2.

quence, the trade in silver appeared to be rather delicate and was not the same as other luxury goods due to the authorities' very strict regulations.[49]

The Salviati bought mainly silver from merchant bankers from Nuremberg and, in some cases, from Augsburg and sold it to the mints in Spain and Florence. In 1508/9, Anton Welser, Konrad Vöhlin & Mitverwandte of Augsburg sold argentic bullion to their Florentine correspondent, Lanfredino Lanfredini & Co. The Salviati company in Lyon arranged the payment at the All Saints' Fair in 1508. In the case of the three *pani d'argento* of the *popolino*-quality, a total of 1,737.4.6 *scudi di marchi* was due.[50]

However, we have to underline that the silver we are talking about here is not South American silver. The argentic bullion (*pani d'arienti* = German "*Silberbrote*") received by the Salviati from the hands of south German merchant-bankers came from European silver mines. This insight confirms traditional research that in the second decade of the sixteenth century, there was still a continuously flourishing silver trade within Europe. The growing amounts of bullion in silver from South America only came into play during the second third of the century—although the numbers then were not exceptionally high.[51]

Therefore, an analysis of the total turnover in the silver trade on the one hand, and in commerce overall, is presented in Fig. 5. The quality of the data has already been explained in the foregoing section. What we can conclude from the columns that represent the turnover in commerce in general (Fig. 5: *totale commercio*) is also true for the trade in silver (Fig. 5: *arienti*): there is no subsequently recurring pattern of growth and decrease. In the later period—from the Foire des Rois in early 1512 to the Easter fair in 1517—the total turnover in commerce roughly increased, as is also the case for silver from the All Saints' Fair in 1514 onwards. The quantities of argentic bullion sold to Spanish merchant-bankers and to the Florentine mint seems to have been even less stable from one fair to

49 Silver is never mentioned regarding luxury trade as far as it appears in bullion. The quality of luxury goods in this sense depended very much on the refinement of the artisanship and, of course, on the materials used for production, like golden threads or silver. The silver which went to the mints is rather distinguished from all that. For a summary overview, see Christof Jeggle. Economies of Quality as a Concept of Research on Luxury. In *Luxury in the Low Counties: Miscellaneous Reflections on Netherlandish Material Culture, 1500 to the Present*, Rengenier C. Rittersma (ed.). Brussels: Pharo/ASP editions, 2010, 25–44.

50 Lang, *Kapital- und Warenmärkte*, doc. II.17 and doc. III.1.1.

51 Ward Barret. World Bullion Flows, 1450–1800. In *The Rise of Merchant Empires. Long-Distance Trade in the Early Modern World, 1350–1750*, James D. Tracy (ed.). Cambridge: Cambridge University Press, 1990, 224–254. See Ulrich Pfister. Silber. In *Enzyklopädie der Neuzeit*, vol. 12 (Silber-Subsidien). Stuttgart: Metzler, 2010: coll. 1–8. Here we also find a very illuminating table on the production of silver in the global trade of silver, which confirms our observations.

another than the portions of commerce overall. The remarkable turnover in the silver trade—at 25,104 *scudi di marchi* during the Easter Fair in 1515—resulted from extraordinary sales to Spanish bankers and to the Florentine mint.[52] That an unexpectedly incremental need for cash—above all, silver coins—was induced by the campaigns against the young French King Francis I, who received his crown in Reims on 25 January 1515, is just a bold speculation.[53]

Due to the comparatively small quantities of all the other categories of merchandise (like dyestuff, pepper, or saffron), they may be excluded here. In Fig. 6, silver (*arienti*) is set in relation to silk products consisting of raw silk in bolts (*seta*) on the one hand and silk fabric and drapery on the other (*drappi*). This particular comparison shows that the silk trade—be it raw silk or silk fabric—was a highly significant commercial feature. Italian merchant bankers like the Salviati exported draperies to France at remarkable prices and paid the export of raw silk from Spain to the Tuscan production places in considerable quantities at the Lyon fairs.[54]

Apparently, there are no obvious patterns of increase or decline in the course of the four fairs over the years. Generally, the volume of trade in raw silk and silk fabric seems to be quite consistent. Let us take the Easter Fair in 1514 and the All Saints' Fair in late 1515 on the raw silk side, and the August Fair in 1509, the Foire des Rois in early 1512, the Foire des Rois in early 1515, and the Easter Fair in 1517 for draperies on the other as exceptions. This supports Richard Gascon's observations on the silk trade at Lyon fairs: he refers to the Bonvisi of Lucca and states that the trade in silk fabric was the largest share in the total turnover in commerce. However, he only uses the municipal documents from Lyon and does not consider the rich archival material in Lucca.[55]

52 SNS, AS, ser. I, no. 453 (*Libro debitori e creditori BBBB*), ac 232/CCXXXII (*Arienti chomperj per chonto di Diegho di Medina di Burghus; Arienti chonperj per chonto de Salamanchi e Charion di Burghus; Arienti chonperj per chonto de' Salamanchi e Charion di Burghus per loro chonto aparte; Arienti chonperj per Francesco Santa + e Alvero di Sandoval di Burghus; Arientj chonperj per Francesco di Ghovarubies di Burghus*); ac 233/CCXXXIII (*Arienti chonperj per Martino di Pores di Burghus*); ac 234/CCXXXIIII (*Arienti e fustani in Monte; Arienti e fustani per noi*).

53 On the mechanism in a later epoch, see Niklot Klüßendorf. Edelmetallsammlungen zur Kriegsfinanzierung am Ende des Alten Reiches. *Abhandlungen der Braunschweigischen Wissenschaftlichen Gesellschaft* 53 (2003): 97–135.

54 For a contextualising overview, see Sergio Tognetti. I drappi di seta. In *Commercio e cultura mercantile*, Franco Franceschi, Richard A. Goldthwaite, Reinhold C. Mueller (eds.). Treviso: Angelo Colla, 2007, 143–170.

55 Gascon, *Grand commerce*. See also Françoise Bayard. Les Bonvisi, marchands banquiers à Lyon, 1575–1629. *Annales* 26 (1971): 1234–1269.

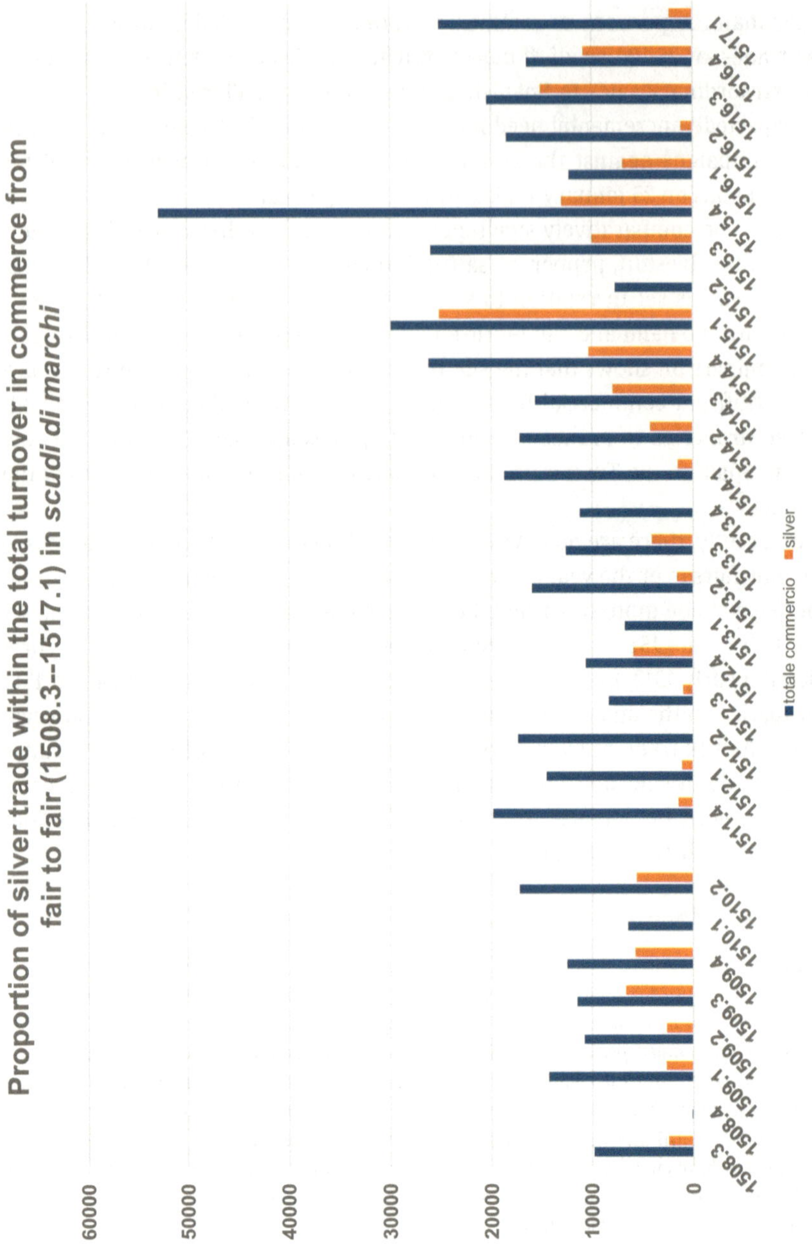

Fig. 5: Proportion of total turnover in commerce to total turnover in silver.

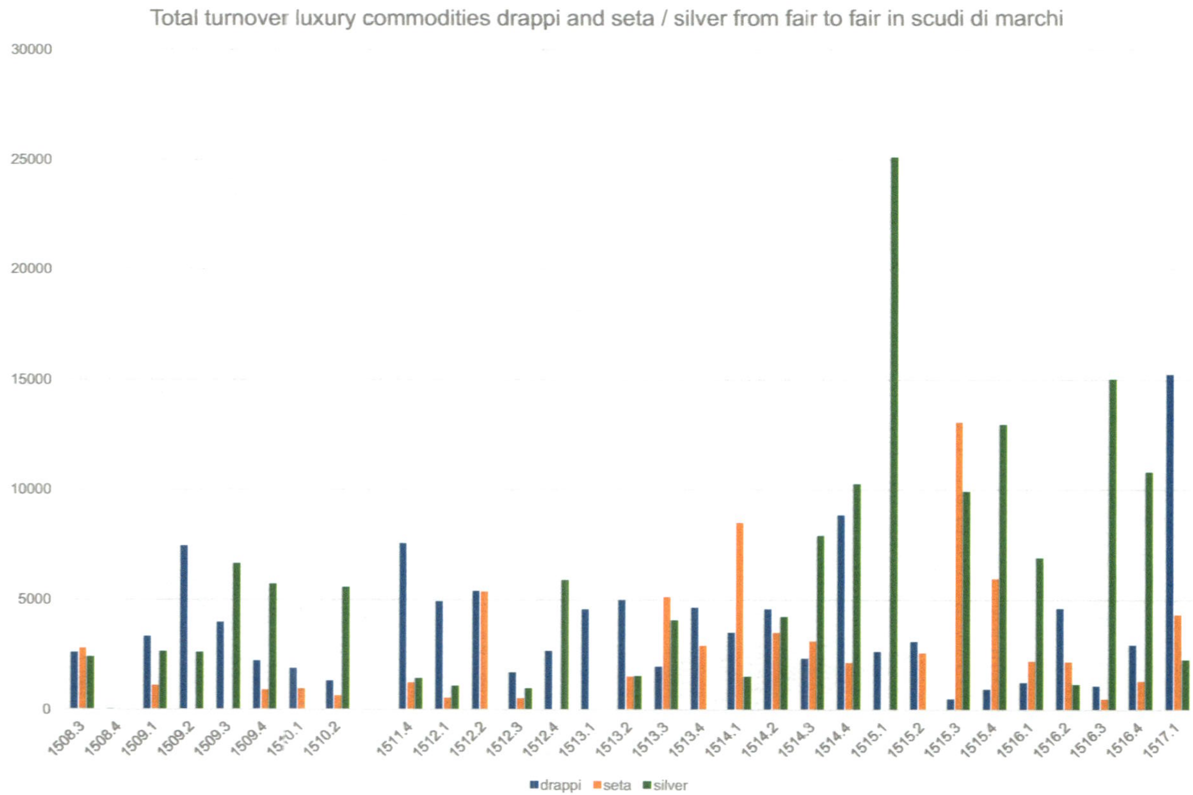

Fig. 6: Total turnover of luxury commodities (silk fabrics and raw silver) to silver.

In contrast, the trade in silver became more important from the All Saints' Fair in late 1514. Nonetheless, at the beginning of the period, the Salviati company was already selling argentic bullion in substantial quantities. This grounded the relationships the Salviati fostered from the time their Lyon branch opened: the ties with south German companies—especially with the Welser-Vöhlin of Augsburg—were one of the preconditions for the establishment of the Salviati company by Francesco Naldini in Lyon, and the Salviati company purchased silver mainly from south German merchants.[56]

This section on silver trade and commerce (Figs. 5 and 6) reveals that the Salviati companies dealt in argentic bullion as a major component of the total turnover in commerce. In many fairs, the trade in silver exceeded the trade in silk fabric and raw silk. For a rough comparison, we might simply sum up the totals from the Foire des Rois in early 1512 to the *fiera di Pasqua* in 1517. During those years (totalling 22 fairs), the Salviati traded in silver worth 123,061 *scudi di marchi* overall and 403,928 *scudi di marchi* in the entire sector of commerce. The most important single group of merchandise—the *drappi*, which were exported from Florentine production to France—accounted for 90,084 *scudi di marchi*. The total in raw silk was at 66,590 *scudi di marchi* during this time. No other group of traded goods was numerically shown to be of similar importance. Indeed, even the trade in the famous *ciambellotti*—*camellotum* (Medieval Latin), a blended fabric mainly consisting of camel or goat hair and imported from the Levant[57]—amounted only to 29,330 *scudi di marchi* at that time.[58]

This characteristic seems to be rather exceptional. For the commerce operated by the Gondi companies between 1516 and 1523, the result is different. While silver is absent from the goods the Gondi traded in, the quantity of sold spices outperformed all the other merchandise. The total return in commerce was more than 466,000 *scudi di marchi* in these years, when spices alone matched close to 232,000 *scudi di marchi*—which is nearly half of the entire return on commerce. The individual numbers (apart from the spices that do not play any role in the Salviati portfolio) are quite similar, but silver is missing from the Gondi trading.[59]

---

56 Tewes, *Kampf um Florenz*, 620–645; Pallini-Martin, L'installation d'une famille, 71–90; Lang, *Wirtschaften*, 194–211.

57 Antonina Licatese. *Stoff- und Seidenbezeichnungen im mittelalterlichen Italien*. Saarbrücken: Universität des Saarlandes, 1989; David Jacoby. Camlet Manufacture, Trade in Cyprus and the Economy of Famagusta from the Thirteenth to the Late Fifteenth Century. In *Medieval and Renaissance Famagusta. Studies in Architecture, Art and History*, Michael J. K.Walsh, Peter W. Edbury, Nicholas S. H. Coureas (eds.). London: Routledge, 2012, 15–42, esp. 16–17. I am indebted to Jean-Louis Gaulin for drawing my attention to this.

58 In proportion, the total in *drappi* was at three-quarters to the total in silver during these 22 fairs.

59 Tognetti, *I Gondi*, 40.

The spice trade only became more relevant for the Salviati in the late 1530s and 1540s, when the company sought to play a more active role in the context of the trade with the Levant.[60]

Quantitative comparison of the Salviati performance in 1550

This last quantitative analysis helps to interpret the dense analyses of the period from 1508 to 1517 from a later perspective. In fact, this is only an extract drawn from the Foire des Rois and the Easter Fair in the first half of 1550. At these two fairs, the company was called Averardo Salviati & Co. and had been just renewed in September 1549 when it held a stock capital of 20,853 *scudi di marchi*. When the ledger was opened in autumn 1549, the outside capital of the company was at 539,903 *scudi di marchi*, of which about 72,900 *scudi di marchi* belonged to the inner circle of the Salviati family and the shareholders within their group. Of course, this is only a snapshot, but it helps to understand dimensions.[61]

The director at that time was Lionardo Spina who became the director of the company after the death of Francesco Naldini in late 1517. Spina strongly drove the company towards government finance—which he was blamed for in 1528, when one of the leading figures of the Salviati family and businesses, Jacopo di Giovanni (d. 1533), wrote a letter to Averardo, son of Alamanno Salviati, the co-founder of the Lyon branch in 1508 and major shareholder in 1549/50.[62]

From the first half of the 1530s, the markets for bills of exchange—which were situated within the triangle of Lyon, Antwerp, and the fairs of Castile—expanded through book money due to the massively growing loans of the European Crowns. This development reached its first peak in the mid-1550s. In 1555, the French king set up the *Grand Parti* to stabilise his financial needs, to regulate public debt through bonds (which his ministers sold to the merchant-bankers active in Lyon), and to disguise the insolvency of the Crown.[63]

This development is reflected in the quantitative analysis presented here from an exceptional case—the Salviati company was still one of the greatest players on Europe's markets. A particular account book, the *libro di committenti*, was kept for the personal accounts that became extraordinarily large because of the

60 Matringe, *La Banque*, 196–211; Lang, *Wirtschaften*, 425–477.

61 Lang, *Wirtschaften*, 220.

62 Lang, *Wirtschaften*, 199–202.

63 Boyer-Xambeu, Deleplace, Gillard, *Private Money*; Lang, *Wirtschaften*, 477–537. For an introduction to the *Grand Parti*, see Doucet, Le grand parti; Orlandi, *Le Grand Parti*. On the activities of the Salviati companies in the 1540s, see Matringe, *La Banque*.

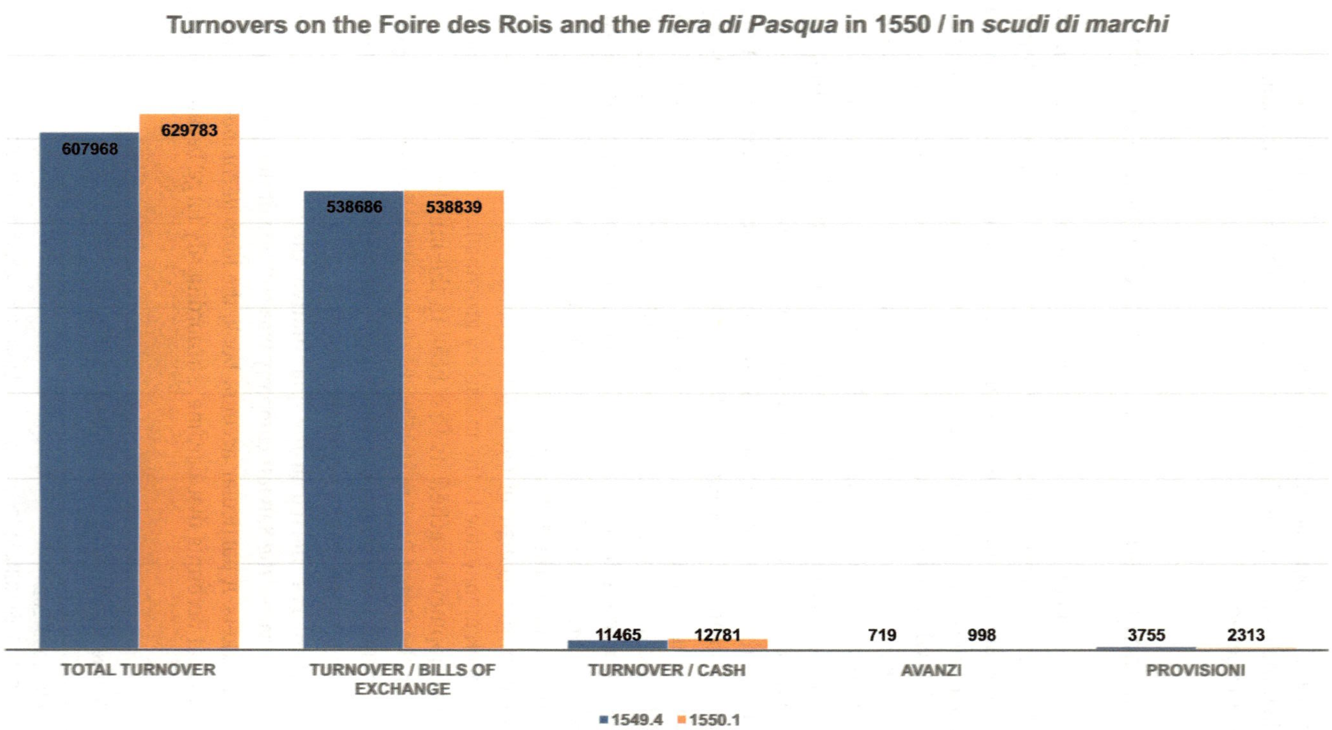

Fig. 7: The turnovers on the Foire des Rois and the Easter Fair in 1550 (total, bills of exchange, cash, profits, provisioni).

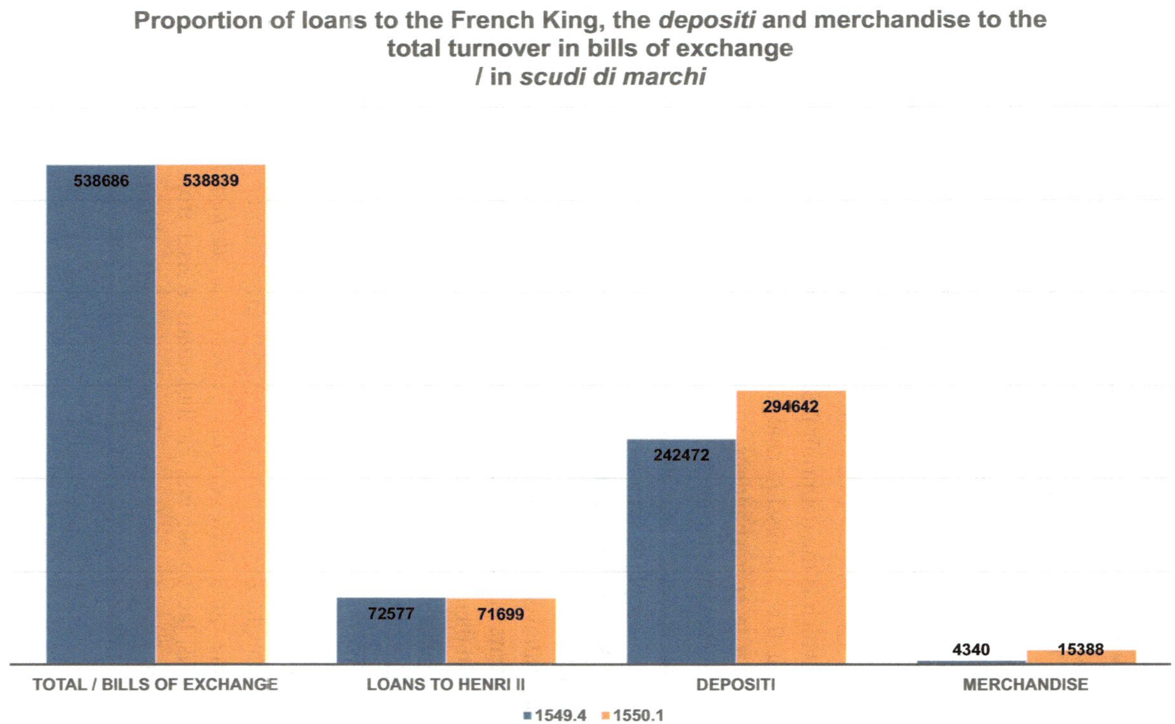

Fig. 8: Proportions of loans to the French king, the depositi, and the merchandise to the total turnover in bills of exchange.

exploding numbers of bills of exchange in use. This is a sort of clients' book in which the whole turnover of bills of exchange taken by the Salviati company is put down fair by fair.[64]

At first glance, the most significant result from the numbers of the two fairs in early 1550 is, without any doubt, the enormous expansion of the business and the overwhelming proportion of bills of exchange within it. The proportion of the payments in cash is about the same as in previous years. The payments of credits and debits deriving from the clearing processes were comparably low whereas the total turnover from fair to fair had more than doubled. The quantity of bills of exchange was extraordinary high. This is also why I inserted two more columns: the *avanzi*, which is the net profit from the businesses in general, and the *provisioni*, which is the commission charge imposed on every bill of exchange taken from a client (a correspondent, the *committente*). Although the charge stayed at two- to maximum four-tenths of a percent, Averardo Salviati & Co. still realised 3,755 *scudi di marchi* at the Foire des Rois in 1550 and 2,313 *scudi di marchi* at the Easter Fair of the same year by the *provisioni* (Fig. 7).

For a closer look at the exceptionally large total turnover in bills of exchange, we should consider the *depositi* and the loans to the French king, Henry II (reigned 1547–59). The *depositi* were formed of the bills of exchange that were not sold during the respective fairs in question. The merchant-bankers took these bills in *deposito* as loans and sold them at the next fair when they tried to get a better arbitrage on them to pay a percentage—two to five percent—to the remitting client. At the first two fairs in 1550, about half of the bills were not sold (Fig. 8). The higher proportion of bills in *deposito* after the Easter Fair also explains the lower profit rate of the *provisioni* at the same fair (Figs. 7 and 8).[65]

The loans to the Crown worked like the *depositi*, because these were short-term loans and brought good interest rates. The dimension of the loans to the Crown had become quite high—around 72,000 *scudi di marchi* at each fair (Fig. 8). In the 1520s, Jacopo Salviati, Bartholomäus Welser from Augsburg, and Claudius May from Bern gave a loan to King Francis I on the lease of the duties on the silk fabric imported to France. They provided the king with a loan of

---

64 SNS, AS, ser. I, no. 582 (*Libro di fiera segnato V Rosso*); no. 588 (*Libro debitori e creditori segnato V Rosso*); no. 586 (*Libro di committenti segnato V Rosso*). The signatory *V* begins on 13 September 1549 and covers an entire period of fairs. There is no literature on the *libri di committenti*, but see Lang, *Wirtschaften*, 285–287, 496–499.

65 Nadia Matringe. *Credit Reallocation and Trade Finance in the Early Modern Age: the Fair Deposit.* https://eprints.lse.ac.uk/69189/1/Matringe_Credit_reallocation_and_trade_finance_author_combined_2017.pdf (15 August 2020).

40,000 *scudi di marchi*. This was a long-term loan, because it was paid back through an eight-year lease of the silk duties, the *Gabella di seta*.[66]

In 1545, King Henry's father, King Francis, compelled the Italian bankers resident in Lyon and the Germans to issue him loans totalling about 107,000 *scudi di marchi* and about 54,000 *scudi di marchi* respectively.[67] During the year 1552, Averardo Salviati & Co. provided bond loans to the French Crown with a total value of about 480,000 *scudi di marchi*.[68]

The significant expansion of the trade in bills is the main issue of the development in the first half of the sixteenth century. In 1550, the loans to the French Crown alone were at the same proportion as the turnovers in bills of exchange on some of the fairs earlier in the century. Commerce obviously lost importance in comparison to the fairs of 1508 to 1517. The trade in silver had nearly vanished from the scene completely—at least according to the Salviati account books.

The emergence of secondary markets

In this last section, we will examine the development of the Lyon fairs as inferred from the account books of the Salviati, but now from the perspective of the investors in the operated businesses, to qualify our data.[69] Therefore, we start with some details drawn from the quantitative analyses in the previous sections.

The negligible proportions paid in cash during both periods studied in section 4, but particularly on the fairs in early 1550 (Figs. 3 and 7), show that bills of exchange circulated like assigned credits and were not sold on the spot. Even more, bills of exchange were increasingly put *in deposito* to be subsequently sold at the following fair.[70]

On the one hand, the strict regulation on the methods of payment in the case of the bills of exchange clearly reflect these tendencies. The rulers of a territory where fairs were held tried to keep cash money—that is, precious metals—inside their domains. So, from the 1540s, the Habsburg government of Brabant where

66 Heinrich Lang. Creating Markets: Swiss Intermediaries in the Cooperation between the Salviati of Florence and the Welsers of Augsburg, 1520–1540. *Annales Mercaturae* 4 (2018): 67–88, esp. 84–87.

67 Philippe Hamon. *L'argent du roi. Les finances sous François Ier*. Paris: Imprimerie Nationale, 1994, 175–188. The rounding in the *scudi di marchi* derives from the fact that the totals given by the evidence of the French government are nominal values, given either in *livre tournois* or in *scudi di sole* (*écu au soleil*).

68 Matringe, *La Banque*, 222.

69 Matringe, *La Banque*, 238–242: "Pourquoi prêter au roi de France?"

70 Matringe, *La Banque*, 238–242.

the Antwerp fairs took place imposed the quite high proportion of payment in cash at thirty percent on the sell-off of bills of exchange. This decree forced bankers to sell their bills of exchange at a considerable share in cash which they had to reinvest at the following Antwerp fair and which they could not transfer to another place—other than transporting it away in coffers. In fact, these deliberations caused a temporary exit of some of the bankers like the Salviati, who closed down their Antwerp branch, which only ran between 1540 and 1544.[71]

On the other hand a particular feature of the fairs held in Lyon came into play and became more and more important: the sale of bills of exchange was permitted to be postponed from one fair to another. This procedure established the *deposito* and rendered possible the growing loans to the French Crown. In consequence, bills of exchange could be treated as if they were short-term bonds.[72]

With regard to the loans to the French Crown, these were at approximately 72,000 *scudi di marchi* per fair in 1550. The king, however, did not pay any interest, but instead "donated" to his borrowers.[73] The bankers like the Salviati who raised the loans to the Crown passed on a previously fixed interest rate on the loans to their clients—the investors. So, the investors from outside the business received the *dono* on their credits, which corresponded to the interest rates—usually at four percent (although the rate also varied)—at each fair.[74]

The four percent interest rate was not subjected to usury regulations. Interest rates beyond five percent were forbidden by canon law.[75] It was the same canon law, by the way, which opened the possibility of postponing the sale of bills of exchange from one fair to another—because it paved the path for special arrangements. The decree of the Archbishop of Lyon allowed the postponement of

71 Lang, *Wirtschaften*, 224–226, 416–419.

72 Gascon, *Grand commerce*, 252–254; Boyer-Xambeu, Deleplace, Gillard, *Private Money*, 37–39; Orlandi, *Le Grand Parti*, 74.

73 This refers to the actual term used in the account books: "*dono*" (= "donation"). The usual technical term in the context of loans ("*prestiti*") is "*interesse*" or "*interesso.*" Only in the case of the king, the concept was different—probably because nobody could oblige the king to refund the loans of the pubblic debt.

74 Doucet, *Le Grand Parti*, 492–5; Felix Krämer, Heinrich Lang. Verbriefen. In *Marktgeschehen. Fragmente einer Geschichte frühneuzeitlichen Wirtschaftens*, Netzwerk "Das Versprechen der Märkte" (ed.). Frankfurt, New York: Campus, 2023, 197–208, esp. 197–201; Matringe, *La Banque*, 238–242.

75 On this in particular, see Clément Lenoble in this volume. For a broader context, see Clément Lenoble. L'économie des hérétiques. Note sur le rapprochement entre usure et hérésie. In *Aux marges de l'hérésie: inventions, formes et usages polémiques de l'accusation d'hérésie au Moyen âge*, Franck Mercier, Isabelle Rosé (eds.). Rennes: Presses universitaires de Rennes, 2017, 111–152.

the sale of bills of exchange and hence legitimised and permitted implicitly a sixteen percent interest rate per annum.[76]

The bankers who provided the loans to the French Crown refinanced their investments through circulating the bills of exchange. Meanwhile, the banker was speculating on better arbitrage rates on the amounts he changed by the bill of exchange in currencies, beyond the *provisioni* he charged for each transaction. Hence, the banker was able to pay the interest—still called *dono*—to his clients and make a profit from circulating bills of exchange, which were the fundamental means of transfer.[77]

This kind of market for trade in bills of exchange is called a *secondary market*. In fact, these markets were constituted like financial markets to back up the business of the loans to the Crowns. This is why we can see a contemporary emergence of growing *depositi* to support the secondary markets for the profit of the bankers when the turnover in trading in bills of exchange increased (Fig. 8).[78]

In practice, this explains the detachment of the trading in bills of exchange from the loans to the Crowns. Due to the special, somewhat asymmetric flow of payments between the bankers and the Crowns, this detachment lowered the risk when the king defaulted. This mechanism was already known from the credit on goods. The commercial loans worked through the refinancing of the credits provided.[79]

The technological instruments these businesses required were accounting to create book money. The amounts circulating through the bills of exchange had to be accepted as ghost money or money of account. The monies of account in the books established the secondary markets and, therefore, the loans to the Crown. This also explains why the king as a notoriously bad debtor was due to permit liquidity on the markets only by the release of the *dono* and was not to bail out the entire loans at once. Through their accounting techniques, bankers issued "giro money" (in avoidance to send issued coins).[80]

The secondary markets were created to refinance the investments in the loans of the Crown. The Dutch historian Bas van Bavel has recently argued that

---

76 On the interest rates, see Gascon, *Grand commerce*, 259–263; Orlandi, *Le Grand Parti*, 74.

77 Orlandi, *Le Grand Parti*, 77.

78 Lang, *Wirtschaften*, 477–537.

79 Boyer-Xambeu, Deleplace, Gillard, *Private Money*, 34–37, 180–184.

80 Boyer-Xambeu, Deleplace, Gillard, *Private Money*, 41–44, 169–176. For a better understanding, see Orlandi, *Le Grand Parti*, 77–82. For the basic modus operandi of bills of exchange, see Markus A. Denzel. *Das System des bargeldlosen Zahlungsverkehrs europäischer Prägung vom Mittelalter bis 1914*. Stuttgart: Franz Steiner, 2008, 51–62. On "giro money" and the basic technological mechanisms, see Denzel, *Das System*, 62–64.

the families of merchant-bankers in towns—particularly those of Flanders, Brabant, southern Germany, Tuscany, Venice, and Genoa—and the other winners of the restructuring of wealth in the fifteenth century—like princes and high clergymen—became extraordinary rich and sought for investment.[81]

An investor: the case of Alamanno di Jacopo Salviati

The case of Alamanno Salviati, son of the aforementioned papal banker Jacopo, illustrates the mechanisms that drove these secondary markets. In his letters copied into his account books, Alamanno, who was more of a capitalist rentier than a banker himself, explains his strategies and the banking operations which were at the ground of the referring economic practices.

On 8 September 1556, Alamanno Salviati received a letter from his banker in Lyon, Piero Mannelli, who also was Consul of the Florentine community,[82] wherein the Florentine correspondent refers to the *dono* of nearly 119.10.2 *scudi di sole* paid by the French king. This small amount was due on a loan of more than 2,987.15.7 *scudi di sole* that Alamanno Salviati had provided to the Crown on behalf of Giovanni Girolamo de' Rossi (1505–64), at that time titular bishop of Padova.[83] The designation of the currency as *scudi di sole*—sun shields—hints at the mobilisation of cash. The 'commodity' provided to the French king was money, implying that the Crown had to receive cash because soldiers were to be paid. The referring money of account was the *scudo* in gold (Appendix).[84]

Mannelli, however, did not directly send the *dono* to Florence, but gave a credit—consisting of the loan to the Crown and the *dono*—to his fellow banker in Lyon, Ruberto Gualterotti, who put the suitable amount, presumably on a bill of exchange, in *deposito* at the interest rate of two-and-a-half percent. What Mannelli in his note to Alamanno Salviati did not write was, of course, how he managed to generate his profit on the initially assigned loan.[85]

---

81 Bas van Bavel. *The Invisible Hand? How Market Economies Have Emerged and Declined since AD 500*. Oxford: Oxford University Press, 2016, 20–21; Matringe, *La Banque*, 226–237.

82 Orlandi, *Le Grand Parti*, 35, 47.

83 Letizia Arcangeli. Rossi (De' Rossi), Giovanni Girolamo. In *Dizionario Biografico degli Italiani* 88 (2017). https://www.treccani.it/enciclopedia/giovanni-girolamo-rossi_(Dizionario-Biografico)/ (14 August 2024).

84 Bibilioteca Apostolica Vaticana (hereafter BAV), Archivio Salviati (AS), no. 300, c. 352v (the Appendix reproduces the entire document); Orlando, *Le Grand Parti*, 5–6; Krämer, Lang, Verbriefen, 197–198.

85 BAV, AS, no. 300, c. 352v.

Nevertheless, we know how it worked (as described just before). Piero Mannelli had to create profit on book money from bills of exchange which were to be circulated. The refinance of a personal loan went to the Lyon fairs and, hence, benefited from the bills of exchange that were drawn on the bankers resident and were assigned from fair to fair on the spot. It depended on the arbitrage that arose from the exchange rates between Lyon and Florence.[86]

Alamanno Salviati was investing a loan from a clergyman, the nobleman and scholar Giovanni Girolamo de' Rossi. Therefore, he used his connections to his banker in Lyon to invest the original loan into banking affairs for a regular interest rate on a loan of 3,020.8.9 *scudi di marchi* which returned to Florence as 3,176.6.9 *scudi di marchi* (Appendix).[87]

Concluding remarks

The quantitative analyses show that we have to adapt our view of the Lyon fairs. While it is possible to describe various features that we are well aware of—for instance, the need to distinguish between the four fields of business interests in Lyon, namely commerce, banking, government finance, *and* the silver trade, instead of the traditionally described three fields of activities, namely commerce, banking, government finance, and that payments in cash played a considerably small role in general—the Salviati appeared to be a particularly avant garde business company. They were at more than 85%, only by doing banking. Their ways of operating obviously highlight the character of Lyon as a banking site and lead to more complex considerations about the role of the Lyon fairs for the emergence of secondary markets founded on the trade of bills of exchange.

In this context, the results of the analyses here underline Richard Gascon's statement that Lyon was a plattform "dans la création du système des paiements des foires qui reste unique en Europe."[88] This is especially true for its quality of being not so much an innovative hotspot for banking, but more of a centre of refinance for investors and hence a hotspot for the transmission of wealth. The numbers quoted clearly show this development and how activities were transformed and created new markets—the secondary markets. The Salviati companies shifted the organisation of the business activities from a more traditional form of bank-

86 Orlando, *Le Grand Parti*, 54–55.
87 BAV, AS, no. 300, c. 352v.
88 Gascon, *Grand commerce*, 339.

ing to trading bills of exchange, which is much more similar to 'investment banking' than commercial credit banking.[89]

Here, this enormous proportion of banking affairs illustrates the importance of bills of exchange *before* the creation of the fairs which were concentrating on the bills of exchange only—like the *Bisenzone* fairs. The detachment of finance—money markets driven by trading in bills of exchange—from commerce was a tendency that was present during the entire sixteenth century. However, we can recognise this in an early but still drastic stage. Secondary markets obviously existed before the expansion of the enormous loans to the Crowns emerged. The bills of exchange were used preemptively based on credit and hence were on their path to the evolution of money markets.

The exceptional material preserved in the Salviati archives offers the great opportunity of conducting a detailed study. Through this study, some previous research was confirmed while some hypotheses were modified. On a quantitative level, if Richard Gascon was right with his estimation that in 1522/23, the total annual turnover on the Lyon fairs was about nine to ten million *livres tournois*, in 1516 the Salviati would have contributed by more than 915,000 *scudi di marchi*—that is, about 1.8 million *livres tournois*—to the global annual turnover on the Lyon fairs. In 1517, they contributed more than one million *scudi di marchi*—that is, about two million *livres tournois*.[90] Given Gascon's numbers, the businesses of the Salviati companies would seem to constitute one of the major players at the Lyon fairs—that would be between one-tenth and a fifth!—a number which certainly seems exaggerated. Nevertheless, only the scale in relation to the annual proceedings shows that the Salviati were an avant garde business company on the spot.

On a more qualitative level, the interpretation of the archival material used here also explains why the merchant-bankers attended the Lyon fairs. Apparently, the emergence of the secondary markets attracted bankers to participate. For the scale of the Salviati performance, we shall consider that the Salviati companies belonged to the group of bankers that created the secondary markets by intention, trying to gain from the growing markets of the circulating bills of exchange. The case of Alamanno Salviati, however, hints towards another direction:

---

89 To be clear, I leave this in quotation marks, because I do not think it was like deposit banking is in our days. Moreover, I disagree with Nadia Matringe and her hypothesis of *depositi* as an innovative instrument for bankers active on the spot (see Matringe, *Credit Reallocation*). The *depositi* are a by-product when the bills of exchange could not be sold during a fair. From outside, the *depositi* attracted investors like Alamanno Salviati who was not a banker, but more of a rentier.

90 Gascon, *Grand Commerce*, 238; Orlandi, *Le Grand Parti*, 82–88.

it is very likely that investors who sought opportunities for their rich funds fuelled the development of secondary markets and provoked the Crowns to absorb ever-growing loans. The run for investments and good interest rates was due to the growing riches of the merchant-bankers' families in their hometown. The numbers taken from the Salviati archives tell this story in the most realistically possible manner, for these documents show the investor's side and the banker's activity on the Lyon fairs.

Appendix

Biblioteca Apostolica Vaticana, Archivio Salviati, no. 300, c. 352v: *Libro Giornale e Ricordi di Alamanno di Jacopo Salviati segnato C*, Ricordo on 8 September 1556.

Transliteration from Alamanno di Jacopo Salviati's Journal C.

In this Ricordo, put down on 8 September 1556, Alamanno di Jacopo Salviati refers to his letters to his banker Piero Mannelli in Lyon. Herein, he describes accurately the transactions and their conditions in the context of his loan to the French Crown.

((in margine sinistro)) di marchi	∇	3020.8.9
		140.9.-
		4.13.-
		1.18.-
		2.2.8
		6.15.4
	∇	3176.6.9

+ yhs 1556

Ricordo come questo dì 8 di settembre s'è auto aviso da Lione da Piero Manellj come in fiera paxata di Pasqua m'à fatto buono per un conto de' Bandinj di Roma aparte F.Z. vno credito che gl'avevano sotto detto loro nome sopra la Maestà del Re X(ristianissi)^{mo} ∇ 2987.15.7 di sole e più di ∇ 119. ß 10. d ij di sole per il dono e me lj ànno fattj buoni a questo conto aparte F.Z. sopra di me nel g(ra)^{do} che sono se qualj danari atenghano a Mons(igno)^{re} vescovo di Pavia M(esser) Johan G(irola)^{mo} de' Rossi per farglj buonj giornalmente quello si risquottere di detto credito e tutto sopra di luj / el quale Piero [Mannelli] disse che in su detta fiera di Pasqua avere di nuovo rjdato hovero rescritto al detto Re X(ristianissi)^{mo} sopra el Gran Partito ∇ 2954,13,5 di sole a nostro rischio con fondo di ∇ 3050 dj sole con dono dj 4 per cento sino alla fiera d'Aghosto che sono ∇ 3020. ß 8.9 di marchi e più disse per conto di quello pensava risquottere [in] detta fiera a buonconto avere dato in diposito a Ruberto Ghualterottj per averglj a paghamentj d'aghosto ∇ 140.9 di marchi a 2 ½ per cento et ∇ 4.13.– di marchi per le spese si fanno per glj donativj e altre spese per conto de' crediti del Gran Partita a 1 ½ per mille e ∇ 1.18 di marchi per il danno di quello tochava del riscosso la fiera paxata d'Ap(parizio)^{ne} che ancora non era riscosso e ∇ 2.2.8 di marchi per agjo da ∇^{di} di marchi a m(one)^{ta} ha 1 $^{2}/_{5}$ per cento per quella pensi risquottere questa fiera di Pasqua che hongnj se debono risquottere ∇ 152 ½ di sole e ∇ 6.15.4 per sua provjsione e consolato a 2 $^{0}/_{8}$ per M / che disse el conto restarà parj e in fiera d'Aghosto proxima debbe risquottere ∇ 140.9 di marchi ha 2 ½ per cento che n'à seghujre nostra hordine –

Questo dj 12 di settembre Mons(igno)^{re} R(everendissi)^{mo} di Pavja di sopra nom(ina)^{to} era com(m)esso che tutto quello si risquottere in fiera d'Aghosto si faccj dare a diposito con fare stare del credere / Et così s'è hordjnato questo dj ditto a Lione al detto Piero Manellj / e tutto s'intende sopra di detto vescovo che si tjene questo'brigha per farglj servizio e non altrjmenti –

Questo dj 19 di novembre el detto Mons(ignor)^{re} cj dette conmes(s)ione che hordjnasimo che tutto el rischosso e quello rescoterebono in fiera di Tutti Santi hordinasimo al detto Piero Manelj rjtenessj quj a me perché disse se ne voleva servjre qua –

Bibliography

Primary Sources

Biblioteca Apostolica Vaticana, Archivio Salviati, no. 300.

Pisa, Scuola Normale Superiore, Archivio Salviati, ser. I, nos. 437–604; ser. III, no. 8.

Literature

Arcangeli, Letizia. Rossi (De' Rossi), Giovanni Girolamo. In *Dizionario Biografico degli Italiani* 88 (2017). https://www.treccani.it/enciclopedia/giovanni-girolamo-rossi_(Dizionario-Biografico)/ (14 August 2024).

Barret, Ward. World Bullion Flows, 1450–1800. In *The Rise of Merchant Empires: Long-Distance Trade in the Early Modern World, 1350–1750*, James D. Tracy (ed.). Cambridge: Cambridge University Press, 1990, 224–254.

van Bavel, Bas. *The Invisible Hand? How Market Economies Have Emerged and Declined since AD 500.* Oxford: Oxford University Press, 2016.

Bayard, Françoise. Les Bonvisi, marchands banquiers à Lyon, 1575–1629. *Annales* 26 (1971): 1234–1269.
Börner, Lars, John William Hatfield. The Design of Debt-Clearing Markets: Clearinghouse Mechanisms in Preindustrial Europe. *Journal of Political Economy* 125:6 (2017): 1991–2037.
Boyer-Xambeu, Marie-Thérèse, Ghislain Deleplace, Lucien Gillard. *Private Money & Public Currencies: The 16th Century Challenge*. Armonk, London: M.E. Sharpe, 1994.
Brollo, Tommaso. Money and Credit in Early Modern Europe. The 'banco' Capponi in Florence and at the fairs of Lyon and Besançon, 1533–1584. PhD diss., Florence, Pisa, Siena, 2021/2022.
Cassandro, Michele. *Le fiere di Lione e gli uomini d'affari italiani nel Cinquecento*. Florence: Baccini e Chiappi, 1979.
van Cauwenberghe, Eddy H. H. (ed.). *Precious Metals, Coinage and the Changes of Monetary Structures in Latin-America, Europe and Asia: Late Middle Ages–Early Modern Times*. Leuven: Leuven University Press, 1989.
Charansonnet, Alexis, Jean-Louis Gaulin, Pascale Mounier, Susanne Rau (eds.). *Lyon, entre empire et royaume: 843-1601: textes et documents*. Paris: Classiques Garnier, 2015.
Cipolla, Carlo M. *Money in Sixteenth-Century Florence*. Berkeley: University of California Press, 1989.
Denzel, Markus A. *Das System des bargeldlosen Zahlungsverkehrs europäischer Prägung vom Mittelalter bis 1914*. Stuttgart: Franz Steiner, 2008.
Denzel, Markus A. (ed.). *Europäische Messegeschichte 9.-19. Jahrhundert*. Cologne, Weimar, Vienna: Böhlau, 2018.
Doucet, Roger. *L'état des finances de 1523*. Paris: Imprimerie Nationale, 1923.
Doucet, Roger. Le grand parti de Lyon. *Revue Historique* 171 (1933): 472–513; 172 (1933): 1–41.
Doucet, Roger. *Finances municipales et crédit public à Lyon au XVIe siècle*. Geneva: Magariotis Reprints, 1980.
Fried, Torsten. Silbermünzen. In *Enzyklopädie der Neuzeit*, vol. 12 (Silber-Subsidien), Friedrich Jaeger (ed.). Stuttgart: Metzler, 2010, coll. 9–11.
Gascon, Richard. *Grand commerce et vie urbaine au XVIe siècle. Lyon et ses marchands (environs de 1520–environs de 1580)*. Paris, La Haye: Mouton, 1971.
Gioffrè, Domenico. *Gênes et les foires de change de Lyon à Besançon*. Paris: Éditions de l'École des hautes études en sciences sociales, 1960.
Goldthwaite, Richard A. *The Economy of Renaissance Florence*. Cambridge: Cambridge University Press, 2009.
Goldthwaite, Richard A. Performance of the Florentine Economy, 1494–1512: the silk and wool industries. *Archivio Storico Italiano* 178 (2020): 311–373.
Häberlein, Mark, Heinrich Lang, Thomas Weller, Clé Lesger, Margrit Schulte Beerbühl, Jürgen G. Nagel, Susanne Rau. Weltwirtschaftszentren. In *Enzyklopädie der Neuzeit Online*, Friedrich Jaeger (ed.). Stuttgart: J.B. Metzler/Springer, 2017: 10. Lyon. http://dx.doi.org/10.1163/2352-0248_edn_COM_380404 (14 August 2024).
Hammer, Peter. *Metall und Münze*. Leipzig: Deutscher Verlag für Grundstoffindustrie 1993.
Hurtubise, Pierre. *Une Famille-témoin. Les Salviati*. Rome: École française de Rome, 1985.
Irsigler, Franz, Michel Pauly. Vom regionalen Messesystem zum internationalen Netz von Messestädten. In *Netzwerke im europäischen Handel des Mittelalters*, Gerhard Fouquet, Hans-Jörg Gilomen (eds.). Ostfildern: Jan Thorbecke, 2010, 49–100.
Jacoby, David. Camlet Manufacture, Trade in Cyprus and the Economy of Famagusta from the Thirteenth to the Late Fifteenth Century. In *Medieval and Renaissance Famagusta: Studies in*

Architecture, Art and History, Michael J. K. Walsh, Peter W. Edbury, Nicholas S. H. Coureas (eds.). London: Routledge, 2012, 15–42.

Jeggle, Christof. Economies of Quality as a Concept of Research on Luxury. In *Luxury in the Low Counties: Miscellaneous Reflections on Netherlandish Material Culture, 1500 to the Present*, Rengenier C. Rittersma (ed.). Brussels: Pharo/ASP editions, 2010, 25–44.

Krämer, Felix, Heinrich Lang. Verbriefen. In *Marktgeschehen. Fragmente einer Geschichte frühneuzeitlichen Wirtschaftens*, Netzwerk "Das Versprechen der Märkte" (eds). Frankfurt, New York: Campus, 2023, 197–208.

Lang, Heinrich. Herrscherfinanzen der französischen Krone unter Franz I. aus Sicht italienischer und oberdeutscher Bankiers. Die Rolle der Florentiner Salviati als Financiers der französischen Regierung. In *Das Blut des Staatskörpers. Forschungen und Perspektiven zur Finanzgeschichte der Frühen Neuzeit*, Peter Rauscher, Andrea Serles, Thomas Winkelbauer (eds.). Munich, Vienna: Oldenbourg, 2012, 457–508.

Lang, Heinrich. Credito e insolvenza sovrana. I prestiti alla Corona francese di mercanti-banchieri toscani e tedeschi meridionali (1550–1559). *Annali dell' Istituto Storico Italiano-Germanico in Trento* 41 (2015): 12–38.

Lang, Heinrich. Creating Markets: Swiss Intermediaries in the Cooperation between the Salviati of Florence and the Welsers of Augsburg, 1520–1540. *Annales Mercaturae* 4 (2018): 67–88.

Lang, Heinrich. *Wirtschaften als kulturelle Praxis. Die Florentiner Salviati und die Augsburger Welser auf den Märkten in Lyon (1507–1559)*. Stuttgart: Franz Steiner, 2020.

Lang, Heinrich (ed.). *Internationale Kapital- und Warenmärkte, transalpiner Handel und Herrscherfinanzen. Die Kooperation zwischen den Handelsgesellschaften der Welser und den Florentiner Kaufmannbankiers Salviati*. Stuttgart: Franz Steiner, 2021.

Lenoble, Clément. L'économie des hérétiques. Note sur le rapprochement entre usure et hérésie. In *Aux marges de l'hérésie: inventions, formes et usages polémiques de l'accusation d'hérésie au Moyen âge*, Mercier, Franck, Isabelle Rosé (eds.). Rennes: Presses universitaires de Rennes, 2017, 111–152.

Mallett, Michael, Christine Shaw. *The Italian Wars, 1494–1559: War, State and Society in Early Modern Europe*. Harlow: Pearson Education, 2012.

Matringe, Nadia. *Credit Reallocation and Trade Finance in the Early Modern Age: the Fair Deposit*. https://hal.archives-ouvertes.fr/hal-01152952/document: 2015 (15 August 2020).

Matringe, Nadia. *La Banque en Renaissance. Les Salviati et la place de Lyon au milieu du XVIe siècle*. Rennes: Presses universitaires de Rennes, 2016.

Melis, Federigo. *Aspetti della vita economica medievale*. Siena: Leo S. Olschki, 1962.

Mosca, Ilario. Les Martelli de Florence et de Lyon. Stratégies et relations socio-économiques à l'époque préindustrielle. PhD diss., École Pratique des Hautes Études, Paris/Università di Pisa, 2016.

Orlandi, Angela. *Le Grand Parti. Fiorentini a Lione e il debito pubblico francese nel XVI secolo*. Florence: Leo S. Olschki, 2002.

Pallini-Martin, Agnès. L'installation d'une famille de marchands-banquiers florentins à Lyon au début du XVIe siècle, les Salviati. In *Lyon vu/e d'ailleurs (1245–1800): Échanges, compétitons et perceptions*, Jean-Louis Gaulin, Susanne Rau (eds.). Lyon: Presses universitaires de Lyon, 2009, 71–90.

Pallini-Martin, Agnès. *Banque, négoce et politique. Les Florentins à Lyon au moment des guerres d'Italie*. Paris: Classiques Garnier, 2018.

Pfister, Ulrich. Silber. In *Enzyklopädie der Neuzeit*, vol. 12 (Silber-Subsidien). Stuttgart: Metzler, 2010: coll. 1–8.

Pinchera, Valeria. L'Archivio Salviati. La storia degli affari attraverso un Archivio familiare. *Società e storia* 13 (1990): 979–986.

Tewes, Götz-Rüdiger. *Kampf um Florenz. Die Medici im Exil 1494–1512*. Cologne, Weimar, Vienna: Böhlau, 2011.

Tognetti, Sergio. *I Gondi di Lione. Una banca d'affari fiorentina nella Francia del primo Cinquecento*. Florence: Leo S. Olschki, 2013.

Claudio Marsilio

'News from the South': price lists and currents from the Spanish and Italian exchange fairs between the 15th and 17th centuries

The European exchange fairs: a long journey

The origins of the international financial system have been quite extensively investigated, but the first attempt at integrating the European monetary and financial markets in the early modern period has been less comprehensively studied. Northern European financial centres—such as Amsterdam and London—have been defined as the "cradle of the modern financial market."[1] It is fair to say that this affirmation is unquestionable, but a deeper analysis of the Italian and Spanish financial markets during the 'long sixteenth century' offers us a well-focused image of the multilateral international payment system. Further, such an analysis allows us to better understand the multilateral relations among the most important European financial centres. The origins of the international financial system have been investigated quite exhaustively since the 1950s, when Raymond de Roover's crucial research sparked the beginning of a historical debate concerning the development of a well-organised foreign exchange market in early modern Europe.[2] In contrast, I would like to focus on the first attempt at integrating money markets where exchange fairs had the role of *trait d'union* between different national currencies.[3] During these meetings, the most important and influential European bankers and brokers gather in a single town—more specifically, in a single place (a private or public building like a square or a house)—to settle their business on an international level.

1 Carlos Álvarez Nogal, Luca Lo Basso, Claudio Marsilio. La rete finanziaria della famiglia Spinola. Spagna, Genova e le fiere dei cambi (1610–1656). *Quaderni Storici* 124:1 (2007): 97–110.

2 Raymond de Roover. *L'evolution de la lettre de change, XIVe–XVIIIe siècles*. Paris: Armand Colin, 1953; Raymond de Roover. Money, Banking, and Credit in Medieval Bruges. *Journal of Economic History* 2 (1942): 52–65; Raymond de Roover. *Gresham on Foreign Exchange: An Essay on Early English Mercantilism*. Cambridge, MA: Harvard University Press, 1949.

3 For a complete bibliography, see Claudio Marsilio. *Dove il denaro fa denaro. Gli operatori finanziari genovesi nelle fiere di cambio del XVII secolo*. Novi Ligure: Città del Silenzio, 2008; Claudio Marsilio. *Exchange fairs and the money market in early modern Italy (1630–1650)/Fiere di cambio e mercato monetário nell'Italia di età moderna (1630– 1650)*. Novi Ligure: Città del Silenzio, 2018.

https://doi.org/10.1515/9783111621296-008

What was the monetary geography of Europe in the sixteenth and seventeenth centuries? The core of the debate was the international integration of money markets and the degree of 'multilateralism' of the international payment system. Charles Wilson proposed a "mercantilist vision" that describes a continent upset by international liquidity problems. On the other hand, Heckscher strongly asserted that multilateralism was a common practice since the 1650s, with bills of exchange serving as a means of settlement (for example, in the case of Amsterdam and Antwerp).[4] As frequently suggested by de Roover, looking at exchange rates is an effective way to measure the degree of multilateralism in a money market.[5] The most recent contributions on the multilateralism of the European exchange markets have been offered by McCusker and Gravejstijn, Homer and Sylla, Flandreau, Gilimard, Jobst and Nogués-Marco, and Denzel.[6] These studies are deeply grounded in original archives and rare print sources (currents, exchange rates, '*listini*', and commercial print media). Neal also underlined the relevance of the study of the exchange market in order to better understand the origins of the international financial markets.[7] As suggested by Parker, among others, we should look at the period between 1550 and 1700 as the 'long seventeenth century' (better known as the century of the 'general crisis').[8] Starting from the 1960s, the major works on this ground-breaking financial institution were those published by Gioffrè, da Silva,

4 On this debate, see Raymond de Roover. What is dry exchange? A contribution to the study of English Mercantilism. *Journal of Political Economy* 52:3 (1944): 250–266.

5 De Roover, *Gresham on Foreign Exchange*.

6 John Joe McCusker, Cora Gravejstijn. *The Beginnings of Commercial and Financial Journalism: The Commodity Price Currents, Exchange Rate Currents, and Money Currents of Early Modern Europe*. Amsterdam: NEHA, 1991, 515; Sidney Homer, Richard Sylla. *A History of Interest Rates*. New Brunswick, NJ: Rutgers University Press, 2005; Marc Flandreau, Christophe Galimard, Clements Jobst, Pilar Nogues-Marco. The Bell Jar: Commercial Interest Rates between Two Revolutions, 1688–1789. In *The Origins and Development of Financial Markets and Institutions: From the Seventeenth Century to the Present*, Jeremy Atack, Larry Neal (eds.). Cambridge: Cambridge University Press, 2009, 161–208; Marc Flandreau, Christophe Galimard, Clements Jobst, Pilar Nogues-Marco. Monetary Geography before the Industrial Revolution. *Cambridge Journal of Regions, Economy and Society* 2:2 (2009): 149–171; Markus A. Denzel. *Handbook of World Exchange Rates, 1590–1914*. Farnham: Ashgate, 2010.

7 Larry Neal. How it all began: the monetary and financial architecture of Europe during the first global capital markets, 1648–1815. *Financial History Review* 7:2 (2000): 117–140.

8 Geoffrey Parker. *Global Crisis: War, Climate Change and Catastrophe in the Seventeenth Century*. New Haven, London: Yale University Press, 2013.

Mandich, Felloni, Orlandi, Cassandro, and the French research team comprising Boyer-Xambeau, Deleplace, and Gillard.[9]

The exchange fairs represent the legacy of a centuries-old institution[10] that had been able to improve itself through the successive stages from the fairs of goods of the Champagne region (thirteenth century), to Geneva (fifteenth century), and then through the exchange fairs of Lyon and Medina del Campo (fifteenth to sixteenth centuries) up to the meetings organised in Besançon (sixteenth century) and subsequently in Piacenza, Novi, Verona, and Bolzano (sixteenth–seventeenth centuries).[11] Since the first fairs of Champagne, the credit market also began

9 Domenico Gioffrè. *Gênes et les foires de changes: de Lyon à Besançon.* Paris: Armand Colin, 1960; José Gentil da Silva, *Banque et crédit e Italie au XVIIe siècle.* Paris: Armand Colin, 1969; José Gentil da Silva, Ruggiero Romano. L'histoire des changes: les foires de 'Bisenzone' de 1600 à 1650. *Annales E.S.C.* 17 (1962): 715–721; Giulio Mandich. Delle fiere genovesi di cambi particolarmente studiate come mercati periodici del credito. *Rivista di Storia Economica* 4 (1939): 257–276; Giulio Mandich. Le fiere genovesi di soli cambi culla delle borse valori. *Rivista Milanese di Economia* 17 (1986): 132–146; Giulio Mandich. Fiere cambiarie concorrenti (genovesi, fiorentine, veneziane) nel 1622–1652. In *La repubblica internazionale del denaro tra XV secolo e XVII secolo,* Aldo De Maddalena, H. Kellenbenz (eds.). Bologna: Il Mulino, 1986, 123–151; Giuseppe Felloni. *Gli investimenti finanziari genovesi in Europa tra il Seicento e la Restaurazione.* Milano: Gioffrè Editore, 1977; Giuseppe Felloni. Asientos, juros y ferias de cambio (1541–1675). In *Dinero y crédito,* Alfonso Otazu (ed.). Madrid: Moneda y Crédito, 1978, 335–359; Angela Orlandi. *Le Grand Parti. Fiorentini a Lione e il debito pubblico francese nel XVI secolo.* Florence: Leo S. Olschki, 2002; Michele Cassandro, *Le fiere di Lione e gli uomini d'affari italiani nel Cinquecento.* Florence: Tipografia Baccini & Chiappi, 1979; Michele Cassandro. Le fiere nell'economia europea medievale e della prima età moderna. *Studi Storici Luigi Simeoni* 51 (2001): 9–27; Marie-Thérèse Boyer-Xambeau, Ghislain Deleplace, Lucien Gillard. *Private Money & Public Currencies: The 16th Century Challenge.* New York: M.E. Sharpe, 1994.

10 Stephan R. Epstein. Regional Fairs, Institutional Innovation, and Economic Growth in Late-Medieval Europe. *Economic History Review* 47:3 (1994): 459–462; Stephan R. Epstein. Fairs, Towns, and States in Renaissance Europe. In *Fiere e mercati nella integrazione delle economie europee secc. XII–XVIII,* Simonetta Cavaciocchi (ed.). Florence: Le Monnier, 2001, 71–90.

11 Jean-François Bergier. *Genève et l'économie européenne de la Renaissance.* Paris: S.E.V.P.E.N., 1963; Richard Gascon. *Grand Commerce et vie urbaine. Lyon et ses marchands (environs de 1520–environs de 1580).* Paris: La Haye, 1971; Marie-Thérèse Boyer-Xambeau, Ghislain Deleplace, Lucien Gillard. La crise du système de change Lyonnais à la fin du XVI siècle. *Revue Internationale d'Histoire de la Banque* 32–33 (1986): 145–166; Hilario Casado Alonso. Medina del Campo Fairs and the Integration of Castile into 15th and 16th Century European Economy. In *Fiere e mercati,* Cavaciocchi (ed.), 495–518; José Ignacio Martínez Ruiz. The Credit Market and the Profits from the Letters of Exchange. *Ricorsa* Exchange Operations between Seville and the Besançon Fairs (1589–1621). *Journal of European Economic History* 33:2 (2004): 331–355; Luciano Pezzolo, Giuseppe Tattara. "Una fiera senza luogo?" Was Bisenzone an International Capital Market in Sixteenth-Century Italy? *Journal of Economic History* 68:4 (2008): 1098–1122; Andrea Bonoldi, Markus A. Denzel. *Bozen im Messenetz Europas (17–19 Jahrhundert)/Bolzano nel sistema fieristico europeo*

to play a pivotal role. In fact, the driving force behind these meetings appears to be, at first glance, the international trade of goods, but starting from the last decades of the fifteenth century, bills of exchange were gradually added to the commercial trade. Later, at the exchange fairs of Piacenza in Italy (1580s), most of the transactions were linked to the public debt of the Spanish crown of the Habsburgs, which generated an endless chain of payments all around Europe.[12]

The first example of trade on an international scale is provided by the Flemish fairs of the city of Bruges (in the eleventh and twelfth centuries). Another significant case is constituted by the city of Antwerp (thirteenth century) at which the first Italian merchants coming from Asti and Chieri (known as *Lombards*), Tuscany (Siena, Florence, and Lucca), Lombardy (in particularly Milan), and Genoa gathered.[13] The first relevant significant presence of Italian operators is recorded at the Champagne Fairs.[14] The archival sources confirm that during these meetings, the commercial activity was sustained by new instruments related to the credit market, such as the bills of exchange.[15]

European monetary system and the exchange fairs during the *Ancien Régime*

The monetary system can be defined as the set of rules on which the use of money is based. In Europe, these rules—which were in force from the early Middle Ages to the turn of the twentieth century—were all attributable to a single metal-based system in which each state guaranteed the content and weight of

(secc. XVII–XIX). Bolzano: Athesia, 2007; Markus A. Denzel, *Die Bozner Messen und ihr Zahlungsverkehr (1633–1850)*. Bolzano: Athesia, 2006.

12 Giorgio Doria. Conoscenza del mercato e sistema informativo: il know-how dei mercanti-finanzieri genovesi nei secoli XVI–XVII. In *La repubblica internazionale*, De Maddalena, Kellenbenz (eds.), 57–121.

13 Paola Lanaro (ed.). *La pratica dello scambio. Sistemi di fiere, mercanti e città in Europa (1400–1700)*. Venice: Marsilio, 2003. For a clear description of the medieval exchange market, see Peter Spufford. *Handbook of Medieval Exchange*. London: Royal Historical Society, 1986; Adrian R. Bell, Chris Brooks, Tony K. Moore. Cambium non est mutuum: exchange and interest rates in medieval Europe. *Economic History Review* 70:2 (2017): 373–396.

14 Andre-Emile Sayous. Les opérations des banquiers italiens en Italie et aux foires de Champagne pendant le XIIIe siècle. *Revue Historique* 57 (1932): 1–31.

15 Michele Cassandro. Credito e banca in Italia tra Medioevo e Rinascimento. In *Credito e sviluppo economico in Italia dal Medioevo all'età contemporanea*. Verona: Società Italiana degli Storici Economici, 1988, 131–145.

'discs' minted in its mint and regulated their circulation within its jurisdiction. The effigy of the king or symbols of state entities were stamped on the metal coins to prove the legality of the means of payment or exchange. Each state followed a completely self-ruling national monetary policy, since it held the monopoly of minting and circulating coins as well as the power to fix the legal tender of all the currencies used in payments. Over the years, the exchange fair transformed into a more complex and multifaceted economic institution.

To better understand the issue of international payments and foreign exchange, let us now define how monetary sovereignty works. It can be imagined as a kind of territorial 'jurisdiction' that grants the state the right to mint money and to establish its legal tender (called 'tariff').[16] Until the reform of the European monetary and weight systems after the French Revolution, it was possible to pay with different currencies and not only with those struck by the national mint. Instead, during the exchange fairs, the currency was managed and controlled by a 'private corporation' made up of the bankers gathering at the meetings. This created a network of multilateral relations and a set of debt/credit positions. The *écu de marc*—the currency of exchange fairs—was transformed into an international unit of account which was the basis of a multilateral system of deferrals, compensation, and payments. Therefore, the *écu* was not connected to any metal equivalence (value of the intrinsic metal contained in each single metal disc). It was the bill of exchange (paper) that replaced the metal coin (gold).[17] When a merchant needed to make a payment abroad, he got into debt in the currency of the place where he was buying these goods, and he was credited in the currency of the place where he was willing to sell them. In the bill of exchange, the exchange rate between two distinct units of account was fixed. At the fair, however, there was an *ad hoc* unit of account: *écu de marc*.[18]

---

16 Claudio Marsilio. *"O dinheiro morreu. Paz à sua alma danada": Gli operatori finanziari del XVII secolo tra investimenti e speculazioni*. Palermo: Mediterranea, 2012; Claudio Marsilio. Le fiere di cambio nella prima metà del XVII secolo: evoluzione di un'antica istituzione finanziaria. In *Banca, crédito y capital: la monarquía hispánica y los antiguos países bajos (1505–1700)*, Carmen Sanz Ayán, Bernardo José García García (eds.). Madrid: Fundación Carlos de Amberes, 2006, 59–82.

17 Luca Fantacci. *La moneta. Storia di un'istituzione mancata*. Venice: Marsilio, 2005.

18 Luigi Einaudi. The theory of imaginary money from Charlemagne to the French Revolution. In *Enterprise and secular change: readings in economic history*, Frederic C. Lane, Jelle C. Riemersma (eds.). Homewood, IL: University of Michigan, 1953, 229–261; Luca Fantacci. Complementary Currencies: A Prospect on Money from a Retrospect on Premodern Practices. *Financial History Review* 12 (2005): 43–61; Luca Fantacci. The dual currency system of Renaissance Europe. *Financial History Review* 15 (2008): 55–72.

In order to fully grasp the meaning of exchange fairs, it is also necessary to clarify the concept of compensation, defined by Felloni as "a means of extinguishing the obligations between two economic subjects who are linked by reciprocal debt and credit relationships."[19] Similar in its simplest forms to bartering, compensation nevertheless exploited many technical tools unknown in the first commercial exchanges. The fundamental characteristic of this instrument is that it can be concluded in a single operation—requiring notarial deed—or repeated, often at regular intervals, within a relationship of collaboration continued over time. A typical example of direct compensation is the exchange between two business correspondents. In the case of indirect compensation, the intervention of a third party can occur, as in the case of banking clearing houses.[20] The sixteenth- and seventeenth-century Italian exchange fairs represent a market in which the clearing system was improved. 'Clearing' can be defined as the settlement of exchanges based on the offsetting of credits and debits in order to avoid unnecessary reciprocal payments thanks to 'hard coins.'

In early modern Europe, bills of exchange were the most important international means of payment, and from the fifteenth to the seventeenth centuries, creditors and debtors met at prearranged towns at set times of the year to settle their positions. Since the late Middle Ages, the volume of European trade grew exponentially, making it necessary to develop new payment instruments that were more reliable, faster, shared, and universally accepted.

The bill of exchange was arguably the most innovative and revolutionary invention. The bill of exchange was a paper document that allowed to transfer money from one place to another one. Therefore, it could be used to purchase goods and services abroad. For example, in Genoa, the creditor (in Italian, *datore*) or remitter handed over a given amount of money expressed in Genoese *lire* (the Genoese currency) to the issuer or drawer (*traente*), who signed for the remitter a bill of exchange addressed to the agent of the creditor or beneficiary (the *beneficiario*) who would be attending the exchange fair. The bill of exchange contained the order to the drawee (*trattario*)—or the agent at the fair representing the debtor—to pay the sum of money agreed to the beneficiary, expressed in *scudi di marche* (*écu de marc*). After all the parts of the bill of exchange were completed, it was sent by courier to the exchange fair locations, where the exchange transaction was concluded. During the fair, the *beneficiario* delivered the bill of exchange just received to the *trattario*, who accepted it and issued a second bill of exchange

19 Giuseppe Felloni. *Profilo di storia economica dell'Europa dal medioevo all'età contemporanea.* Torino: Giappichelli Editore, 1993, 167–169.

20 Lars Börner, John William Hatfield. The Design of Debt-Clearing Markets: Clearinghouse Mechanisms in Preindustrial Europe. *Journal of Political Economy* 125:6 (2017): 1991–2037.

ordering the debtor in Genoa—who he was representing—to pay the creditor in Genoa the agreed amount expressed in Genoese *lire*. The exchange rate indicated on the bill itself was applied, plus the commission fee added at the fair (usually 0.33% of the value of the bill of exchange).

During the *Ancien Régime*, the monetary system was characterised by a clear distinction between money of account and minted money.[21] Many coins—minted by all the European states—circulated throughout the kingdom of France, all of which certainly did not favour the immediate classification of the different monetary species. Gold, silver, and copper were the main metals used for minting these 'metallic discs.' Their intrinsic value was the cause of their different diffusion: copper or bullion coins tended to remain within the territory of issue, while those of gold and, to a lesser extent, silver were exchanged in international commercial transactions.[22] Monetary sovereignty within a state consisted in the monopoly of both the circulation and the minting of its currency, the value of which was established by the king (or the state) and expressed in the national 'unit of account.' So, exchange rates and monetary tariffs remained for several centuries some of the main topics in the mercantile literature and legal discipline.

Having defined the fair as the privileged place for compensation in various national currencies, it can be deduced that the exchange fairs perfected their own monetary system, based on a unit of account—the *écu de marc*—stably anchored to the gold contained in the most popular and trusted European gold coins. In practice, if a payment had been made in Naples (the capital of a Spanish viceroyalty), it would have been possible to use both the local currency and other currencies normally accepted as legal tender (inserted in a 'tariff' published by the state). In Antwerp, on the other hand, it was possible to pay in local currencies, but an operator could also receive other coins or a bill of exchange that had been remitted, for example, by the exchange fair in Medina del Campo. This delicate mechanism assumed that the merchant-bankers were aware of the 'prices' of all the international currencies. And how could one be informed of foreign currencies? With the help and collaboration of a trusted network of correspondents who regularly sent information on the monetary market of their commercial centres.

---

21 Luigi Einaudi. Teoria della moneta immaginaria nel tempo da Carlomagno alla rivoluzione francese. *Rivista di Storia Economica* 1 (1936): 1–35; Luca Fantacci. Teoria della moneta immaginaria nel tempo da Carlomagno a Richard Nixon. *Rivista di Storia Economica* 18:3 (2002): 301–325.

22 Massimo Amato. Scudi, fiere, principi e banchieri. Il problema monetario del cambio in epoca rinascimentale. In *Lo scudo d'oro. Moneta e potere da Augusto a Carlo V*, Silvana Balbi de Caro (ed.). Rome, Brussels: FPM, 1996, VII.11–VII.18.

The exchange fair was an economic institution that constitutes a 'model' that influenced and inspired other European banking and financial institutions such as the *Wisselbank* in Amsterdam (1609).[23] These meetings concentrated an amount of credit in one place that was immediately available to the financial circuit in the form of repayable advances at the next fair. These complex financial transactions took place over a few days (usually one or two weeks) and several times a year (over the course of three or four meetings). The exchange fairs were well-established institutions that rhythmically and cyclically marked the time of the European financial calendar. But what were the main functions of the exchange fairs? The most important functions were:

- the acceptance of bills of exchange issued in the most important European commercial centres and expiring during the days of the exchange fair
- the re-negotiation of new bills expiring in commercial centres
- the mutual compensation and payment in cash of outstanding balances (unbalanced positions)
- the exchange of information (on exchange rates and market conditions of the most relevant European centres).

The exchange fairs in Medina del Campo, Lyon, and Besançon (fifteenth to sixteenth centuries)

The zenith of these meetings was reached in the fifteenth century on account of the meetings held in Lyon and Medina del Campo.[24] The first information we have about the fairs in Medina del Campo dates back to 1404 and connects them to those celebrated in two other Castilian commercial centres—Rioseco and Villalón. In 1421, the wife of D. Fernando, Leonor de Alburquerque, mistress of Medina, granted the first Ordinances, but their international relevance was sanctioned by the Catholic kings in 1491 with the declaration of the general fairs of the kingdom in Medina del campo. The four Castilian fairs were distributed as fol-

23 Claudio Marsilio. The Genoese exchange fairs and the Bank of Amsterdam: Comparing two Financial Institutions of the 17th century. *História Econômica & História de Empresas* 18:1 (2015): 39–59; Claudio Marsilio. Four times a year for so many years. The Italian Exchange Fairs during the XVIth–XVIIth centuries: Comparing Financial Institutions. *Bankhistorisches Archiv/Banking and Finance in Historical Perspective* 36:2 (2010): 151–165.

24 Hilario Casado Alonso. Les relations entre les foires de Castille et les foires de Lyon au xvie siècle. In *Lyon vu/e d'ailleurs (1245–1800)*, Jean-Louis Gaulin, Susanne Rau (eds.). Lyon: Presses universitaires de Lyon, 2009, 91–108.

lows: May and October in Medina del Campo, Lent (February–March) in Villalón, August and Easter (March–April) in Rioseco. These meetings fitted perfectly into the calendar of other European fairs, such as those in Brabant and later in Lyon and Besançon. The two annual Medina meetings (in May and October), settled towards the end of the fifteenth century, began to attract an increasing number of operators from the main European commercial centres (Antwerp, Lyon, Lisbon, Genoa, and Florence). During the days of the fair in Medina del Campo, not only did merchants with the most varied types of merchandise gather, but also money-changers and professionals of the credit and money markets at an international level. The exchange fairs of Medina del Campo in the sixteenth century were increasingly linked to the fate of the Spanish public debt and of the Spanish *Haciend Real* (Spanish royal treasury).[25] It must be remembered that, since the last decades of the sixteenth century, the Spanish treasury had been going through a very serious liquidity crisis. Not even the 'American treasures' (gold and silver) were sufficient to support public spending, and the costs of the war effort were increasing tremendously—the uprising of the United Provinces in 1568 represented only one of the many continental wars in which the Spanish Empire was engaged.

The calendar of the fairs in Lyon remained unchanged since the first meetings of the fifteenth century. The merchant-bankers met every three months: in January (Fair of the Kings or of the Apparition), in March–April (the Easter Fair which was held from 22 March to 25 April), and in August and November (Fair of the Saints). In Lyon, as early as the fifteenth century, the main operators came from three Italian cities—Florence, Lucca, and Genoa. The growing leading role of the Genoese bankers worried their Florentine colleagues to such an extent that, in 1535, after various misunderstandings and clashes, the Genoese decided to organise a parallel meeting in Besançon (Franche-Comté), not too far from Lyon. It is important to remember that in 1528, Andrea Doria, the Genoese admiral, had established a new political and military alliance with the Spanish Empire and that the commercial centre of Besançon was in Franche-Comté under the dominion of the Habsburgs.[26]

25 On the Spanish public debt, see Alvaro Castillo Pintado. Los juros de Castilla. Apogeo y fin de un instrumento de crédito. *Hispania* 23 (1963): 43–70; Pilar Toboso Sánchez. *La deuda pública castellana durante el Antiguo Régimen (juros) y su liquidación en el siglo XIX*. Madrid: Ministerio de Hacienda, 1987.

26 Claudio Marsilio. La lunga avventura delle fiere di cambio: da Lione a Novi. In *Libri italiani del Seicento nel fondo antico della Biblioteca Civica di Novi Ligure*, Andrea Sisti, M. Balbi (eds.). Novi Ligure: Città del Silenzio, 2011, 83–90; François Bayard. *Les Bonvisi, marchands banquiers à Lyon, 1575–1629*. *Annales E.S.C.* 26:6 (1971): 1234–1269; François Bayard. Après les Bonvisi, les lucquois à Lyon aux XVIIe et XVIIIe siècles. In *Lucca e l'Europa degli affari. Secoli XV–XVII*, Rita Mazzei, Tommaso Fanfani (eds.). Lucca: Pacini Fazzi, 1990, 193–208.

In Besançon, the *écu de marc* of 5 mints became the common denominator of a basket of hard coins (the gold *scudo* of Castile, Genoa, Florence, Naples, and Venice). Unlike in the Lyon exchange fairs where an intangible money of account was used (not linked to any precious metal quantities), in the Besançon meetings, the *écu* was transformed into a 'commodity money' that responded to the laws of supply/demand and that produced interest. Ultimately, we can witness the establishment of the metal standard and the pursuit of interest-bearing loans that highlight the development of 'purely' financial relationships, thereby redefining the relationship between money and credit at this time. To better understand this process, we must refer to the *écu*—money of account of the fairs since the fourteenth century—invented by the Genoese bankers as a new coin (made of gold, a precious metal) which represented both purchasing power and a store of value.

Piacenza and Novi (sixteenth to seventeenth century): the Genoese bankers' governance

In 1528, Andrea Doria had entered a new political and military alliance with Spain and the city in Franche-Comté was under the dominion of the Spanish Crown. The Genoese controlled a good portion of the international payments and became the undisputed leaders of the fairs in Franche-Comté. The fair moved to many different places from 1562 onwards until it settled in Piacenza in 1579 under the protection of the Farnese Duchy of Parma and Piacenza. The Genoese bankers controlled the exchange market and became the undisputed leaders of the exchange fairs in Franche-Comté. Finally, in 1579, the Genoese exchange fairs moved to Piacenza (Italy), under the protection of the Farnese dukes. After establishing the regulatory aspect, the Genoese bankers, backed by the Senate, had sought a suitable and stable location for the fairs after years of precariousness and uncertainty. The government of the Republic took up the invitation of Duke Ottavio Farnese, who offered several privileges and concessions concerning not only where the fairs would be held (Piacenza), but also safe conduct passes to protect the physical safety of the participants and the integrity of their property. The following years (1580–1620), as Giuseppe Felloni has reminded us on several occasions, represent the heyday of exchange fairs.[27] The Italian exchange fairs of

27 Giuseppe Felloni. Un système monétaire atypique: La monnaie de marc dans les foires de change génoises, XVIe–XVIIe siècle. In *Études d'histoire monétaire*, John Day (ed.). Lille: PU Septentrion, 1984, 249–260.

Piacenza became the main operating centre, where an ever-increasing number of bankers from all the most important European commercial and financial centres gathered while the volume of business multiplied exponentially, transforming Italian exchange fairs into the beating heart of the international credit market. The Genoese bankers used the Piacenza fairs as an essential financial tool: thanks to the purchase and sale of bills of exchange, the credit collected at the fairs made it possible to satisfy the money requests of Philip II and Philip III in an escalation that allowed Genoese operators to control, almost in a monopoly regime, the European money market. It is quite clear that the Genoese bankers had never ceased the project of moving the exchange fairs under the jurisdiction of their Republic under the excuse of ensuring the safety of these meetings during these dangerous decades. Therefore, the Senate of the Republic issued a decree on 1 December 1621 ordering the fairs to be held in Novi from the first fair in 1622.[28] This was presented to the foreign financial operators as a temporary move, although it would seem plausible that the Genoese government's main goal was to take the first step towards operational independence. During the 'Genoese phase' (1622–1780s), the fairs were controlled according to the laws issued by the Genoese Senate[29] whereby a special tribunal (representative of the Republic of Genoa) was elected—the *tribunale di fiera*—consisting of a consul and two councillors, which supervised the proper conduct of the fair and, if necessary, also exercised judicial power.[30]

Each of the fairs lasted eight days and were held at clearly specified times. On the first day of the meeting, the bankers entered a record of the credits and debits in their books—the *scartafaccio* (or 'fair ledger')—and then presented them to the Chancellor for endorsement so that trade negotiations could begin. On the second day, the bankers came to an agreement to set off their positions and prepared an initial, provisional balance sheet. The third day was the time when the traders set the prices against the *écu de marc* for each commercial centre. On the fourth day, the bills of exchange and the price lists (*listini*) were sent out. During the fifth day, the participants entered the date and place of acceptance, the exchange rates, and the marketplaces where those transactions would

28 Archivio di Stato di Genova (State Archive, Genoa—Italy), *Senato, Senarega* (folder) n. 1090.

29 For the printed collections of the laws of the Genoese exchange fairs, see *Capitoli e ordini delle fere di Besenzone, che si fanno al presente in la città di Piacenza.* Genoa, 1622; *Capitoli e ordini delle fere di Besenzone, che si fanno al presente in la città di Piacenza, ristampate di novo con le gionte fatte dal Serenissimo Senato dall'anno 1622 sin al presente.* Genoa, 1637.

30 Claudio Marsilio. Le Utopie dei Genovesi. Contabilità e skill professionale nelle fiere di cambio dei secoli XVI–XVII. *Cheiron. Materiali e strumenti di aggiornamento storiografico* 51 (2009): 47–65.

be settled into the *calcolo* or the book of calculations. The sixth day was spent drawing up the final balance. The Chancellor met with the bankers and made a note of all the protested and outstanding entries in his own book. On the seventh day, each operator audited the entries in their *scartafaccio*, entered the addresses of the various brokers, exchanged the duly signed bills of exchange, and recorded the payments received. On the eighth and final day, the agents handed over the balance sheet to the Consul, who officially closed the fair with the words "*Christi nomine invocato*."[31] After the fair was over, each banker entered the credits and debits owed to each of the other colleagues in their balance sheet of payments. After all the proceedings, the balance sheets were compared to make sure that the amounts corresponded exactly, and the ledgers were subsequently handed over to the Consul to make the transactions official. At this point, all the debits and credits entered in the books of the operators were automatically set off and the fair achieved its main purpose: to keep the movement of hard coins to a minimum.[32]

What happened to the *scartafaccio*? The fair agent (the broker working at the exchange fair) handed them over to the firm's principal once he returned to his town. These documents were often not stored by the bankers for a very long period. These original sources are filled with hundreds of entries listing exchange rates, bullion prices, currency quotations, and exchange rates. Those that do survive are scattered across private and public archives in southern Europe. The most relevant collections for Genoa can be found in the private archives of some noble families such as the Durazzo, Sauli, Pallavicini, Grimaldi, and Brignole. For the sixteenth-century exchange fairs of Besançon and Piacenza, the best examples are stored at the *Archivio Storico del Comune di Genova* (Historical Archive of the Municipality of Genoa). For the later phase of the Genoese fairs, the best preserved *scartafacci* can be consulted at private archives, including the *Archivio Sauli*[33] and *Archivio Durazzo*.[34] Also, the Florentine bankers' *scartafacci* are well

---

31 For a detailed description of the proceedings and the calendar of the exchange fair, see Giovanni Domenico Peri. *Il negotiante*. Genoa, 1638, 73–84.

32 Claudio Marsilio. Un homme avisé est capable de faire face à toutes les catastrophes. Les compétences professionnelles des opérateurs financiers génois, florentins et portugais à l'époque des foires de change du XVIIe siècle. In *Ressources publiques et construction étatique en Europe XIIIe–XVIIIe siècle*, Katia Béguin (ed.). Paris: Institut de la gestion publique et du développement économique, 2015, 227–247.

33 Giovanni Antonio Sauli *quondam* Lorenzo for the years 1622–1630: *Archivio Durazzo Giustiniani (Genoa), Archivio Sauli*, ledgers nos. 1291, 1292, 1293, 1294, 1295, 1296, 1297, 1298, 1299, 1300, 1301, 1302, 1303.

34 Giacomo Filippo and Gerolamo Durazzo for the years 1632–1657: *Archivio Durazzo Giustiniani (Genoa), Archivio Durazzo*, from ledger 752 (1632) to ledger 776 (1657).

exemplified in two private archives: the *Archivio Caccini del Vernaccia* at the Biblioteca Roncioniana in Prato, Italy, where there are roughly 150 *scartafacci* for the years 1640–1700, and the *Archivio Saminiati*, stored at the Bocconi University in Milan, Italy.

In the context of the complex financial markets of the sixteenth- to seventeenth-century exchange fairs, the Genoese brokers were helped by their agents—the '*procuratori di fiera*'—who represented them during the days of these meetings. These financial 'specialists' used to manage a lot of different types of information, and they acted as intermediaries between the international market of the fairs and a much more local one, such as the credit markets in Genoa, in Florence, or in many different European commercial centres. Studies carried out by economic historians have rarely highlighted the significance of the agents working at the fairs, even though an understanding of the ways in which agents operated could be very useful for better understanding the professional skills of a modern banker. Thanks to laborious research, conducted in private archives in Genoa and with sources that have never been studied before, I have published a collection of letters of the brothers Nicolò and Gregorio Varese, two established 'fair agents' who worked for over half a century in Novi as representatives of the most powerful Genoese trading houses, which provides a wealth of information about not only the money market, the silver bullion market, and the exchange of international currency, but also their professional skills.[35] These commercial letters were written during the exchange fairs of Novi Ligure (first half of the seventeenth century), when this small but strategic border town of the Republic of Genoa controlled and influenced the trend of the money markets throughout Europe.

It is important to remember that fair transactions were possible as the agents were given instructions on how to comply with the necessary procedures and rules. Reliability and strength of the habits acquired were further reasons for the network's long-lasting success; in fact, it was a mechanism that eased socialisation and experienced valorisation, and the benefits obtainable grew according to the number of participants. Through the years, the finance brokers learned to 'read' the market signals relating to a whole series of economic indicators, such as the trend in monetary exchange rates and interest rates linked to money. They also needed to refine their ability to perceive the solidity and solvency of the financial situation of their customers as well as—fundamentally—that of their competitors. The qualities required were empathetic towards the variations of both the financial market and the political situation: foresight, shrewdness, and, finally, a deci-

35 Claudio Marsilio, *Exchange fairs*.

sion-making ability to prevent the loss of good opportunities. All these skills improved with the professional experience acquired over time, not only by working in the exchange fairs, but also through understanding, interpreting, and anticipating several economic trends related to different situations on the international bullion and monetary markets. Differences of price for the same currency quoted on different markets were then brought to light by these relationships, which also helped to reduce risks relating to solvency and guaranteed the bills of exchange issued on foreign markets. This, moreover, had to be done in a way that was respectful of the principles shared by a professional group—very similar to a 'club'—where the operator's skills were judged most of all on the basis of the esteem and confidence with which he was regarded.

What are the *listini*? Simón Ruiz's *listini* collection

What are the 'strips of paper' that are preserved in the Simón Ruiz Archive at Medina del Campo in Spain? During the meetings described above, the exchange rates of the main European currencies were fixed. It was these 'price lists' (*listini*)—small strips of paper—that recorded the exchange rates of the main European currencies and that brokers gathered at the fair sent to their correspondents and customers.

In English and North American historiography, they are called 'currents' and are often defined as the first example of financial journalism. As outlined above, European trade depended on a very complex international payment system. In fact, there were many currencies in circulation from different countries that were legal tender, even abroad. These 'price lists' could be printed or preserved in manuscript form. In French and Italian fairs, merchant-bankers usually compiled pre-printed price lists during the days of the fair and quickly sent them to all their correspondents and customers all around Europe. It is extremely rare to find such a large collection of price lists as are held in Ruiz's collection. In fact, very few public or private archives hold this invaluable source of information.

Simón Ruiz Envito (Belorado, 1525–Medina del Campo, 1597) was a merchant who began his professional career dedicating himself to the trade of different types of cloth, above all with France (Nantes in particular).[36] Quickly transformed into a merchant-banker, around the year 1550 he settled in Medina del Campo

36 Henri Lapeyre. *Simón Ruiz et les "asientos" de Philippe II*. Paris: Armand Colin, 1953; Henri Lapeyre. *Une famille de marchands, Les Ruiz. Contribution à l'étude du commerce entre la France et l'Espagne au temps de Philippe II*. Paris: Armand Colin, 1955.

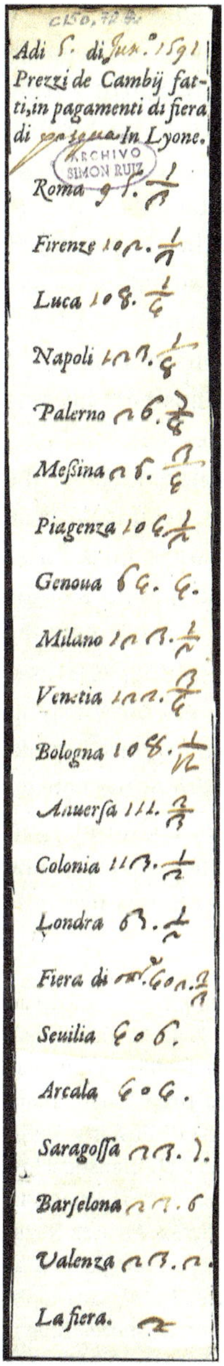
Adi 5. di Jun.o 1591
Prezzi de Cambij fatti, in pagamenti di fiera di pasqua In Lyone.

Roma
Firenze
Luca
Napoli
Palermo
Messina
Piagenza
Genoua
Milano
Venetia
Bologna
Anuersa
Colonia
Londra
Fiera di
Seuilia
Arcala
Saragossa
Barselona
Valenza
La fiera.

Fig. 1: *Listino* of the fair of *Pasqua* (Easter) celebrated in Lyon (05/06/1591) (Archivo Simón Ruiz, CC, C. 150, 72).

and, thanks to his success in international trade, in the second phase of his professional life was involved in some complex financial operations at a European level, in particular lending money to the Spanish King Philip II. Starting from 1576, we can find him as financial partner in some relevant loans to the Spanish treasury (the *asientos*).[37] Later in life, he was involved in the construction of the city hospital in Medina del Campo and supported various charitable activities in support of the weakest people of his town. Simón Ruiz traded in various goods that reached Castile from the Old Continent, and in his everyday activities, he had to use various foreign currencies. He therefore had to be able to distinguish not only between a vast type of coins, but also to use them on the international money market. At some point in his professional life, his core business became the foreign exchange market, from which he gained a lot of money.

In the Simón Ruiz Archive, we can find two types of price lists: those of the Lyon exchange fairs and those of the Piacenza fairs. Simón Ruiz lived in Medina del Campo, home to the third most important European exchange fairs (after Lyon and Piacenza), and was in contact with the most important operators of the time.[38] In order to buy or sell goods in the different markets of the continent, he needed to know the exchange rates of the coins in the different trading centres—hence the need to exchange as much information as possible (and obviously as reliably as possible) on the European money market with his colleagues. Thanks to the patient and competent work of the archivists who took care of the conservation and enhancement of the papers of the Ruiz archive, one of the most important historical business archives in the world, the 'price lists' have survived and allow us to better understand the monetary market of the sixteenth century.

---

37 Mauricio Drelichman, Hans-Joachim Voth. The Sustainable Debts of Philip II: A Reconstruction of Castile's Fiscal Position, 1566–1596. *Journal of Economic History* 70:4 (2010): 813–842; Maurício Drelichman, Hans-Joachim Voth. Lending to the borrower from hell: debt and default in the age of Philip II. *Economic Journal* 121 (2011): 1205–1227; Maurício Drelichman, Hans-Joachim Voth. Serial defaults, serial profits: Returns to sovereign lending in Habsburg Spain, 1566–1600. *Explorations in Economic History* 48 (2011): 1–19; Mauricio Drelichman, Hans-Joachim Voth. *Lending to the Borrower from Hell: Debt, Taxes, and Default in the Age of Philip II.* Princeton, CA: Princeton University Press, 2014. For a different critical approach, see Carlos Álvarez Nogal, Christophe Chamley. La crisis financiera de Castilla en 1575–1577: fiscalidad y estrategia. *Revista de la historia de la economía y de la empresa* 7 (2013): 187–211; Carlos Álvarez Nogal, Christophe Chamley. Philip II against the Cortes and the credit freeze of 1575–1577. *Revista de Historia Económica/Journal of Iberian and Latin American Economic History* 34:3 (2016): 351–382; James Conklin. The Theory of Sovereign Debt and Spain under Philip II. *Journal of Political Economy* 106:3 (1998): 483–513.

38 For a detailed description of Ruiz's *listini* collection, see Claudio Marsilio. *La colección de 'listini' del Archivo Simón Ruiz. Las ferias de cambio de Medina del Campo en el corazón del mercado del dinero europeo (1580–1600).* Valladolid: Fundación Museo de las Ferias, 2021.

By studying the books of accounts of the operators of that time, we can discover the cost of the postal service and everything related to the transmission of information, of which these price lists were one of the most relevant indicators. Without these price lists, Simón Ruiz would not have had the information necessary to make such important decisions for the business of his company. In the 'price lists' of the exchange fairs, the prices of the main international currencies as well as the price of the coins of other important exchange fairs were listed, as we will see later. In the upper part of this 'strip of paper,' the place where the fair was held (for example, Lyon) together with the date and the name of the meeting (for example, Easter Fair) were noted. Here is a list of currencies quoted at the fair of Piacenza (1580s): Lyon (another exchange fair), Rome, Genoa, Milan, Venice, Florence, Lucca, Naples, Lecce, Bari, Palermo, Messina, Antwerp, Amsterdam, Cologne, London, Valencia, Zaragoza, Barcelona, Seville, Medina del Campo (another exchange fair), Lisbon, Bologna, Ancona, Frankfurt (another exchange fair), Vienna, Nuremberg, Paris, and Hamburg. It is worth underlining that all the European exchange fairs were celebrated during almost the same week and their quotes reflected their mutual influence on very distant monetary markets. In addition, it is important to underline here that it appears—as stated in all the classical historiography—that the *listini* followed a standard physical structure (little slices of paper) for the entirety of the period covered by my research.

The exchange rates set at the Piacenza and Lyon fairs turned out to be a 'benchmark' (as we would say today)—in practice, a 'reference price' for all the merchants and bankers when the time came to buy or sell a bill of exchange in the following three months after the end of the fair. We must keep in mind that the fairs of Piacenza and Lyon, for example, were organised only four times a year. Elsewhere, on the free market, in every European commercial centre, it would have been possible to find offers of bills of exchange at slightly different prices (higher or lower). It was not uncommon, in fact, to have to accept letters at higher prices when the local market was in 'tightness' (*strettezza* in Italian) and the money supply was scarce. The evolution of the trade fair operations is linked to the improvement of the circulation of commercial information: this represents one of the most precious elements, as its rapid diffusion is a symptom of the prudent and effective management of the commercial company (*compagnia*). Often taken as a model of a successful managerial strategy, the Genoese merchant-bankers' network was perfectly aware of the importance and value of sharing information with their closest collaborators. Therefore, the bankers working at the exchange fairs quickly

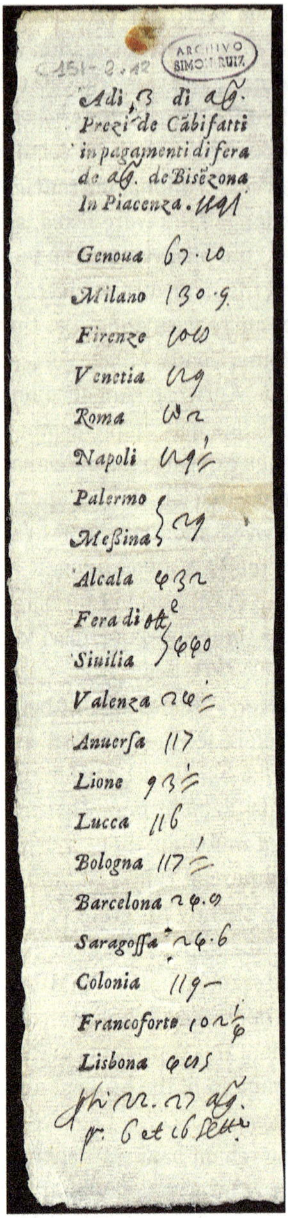
Adi 3 di ag.
Prezi de Cābi fatti
in pagamenti di fera
de ag. de Bisēzona
In Piacenza. 1591
Genoua 67.10
Milano 130.9
Firenze 1010
Venetia 129
Roma 102
Napoli 129½
Palermo
Meßina 129
Alcala 432
Fera di ott.e
Siuilia 440
Valenza 24½
Anuersa 117
Lione 93½
Lucca 116
Bologna 117½
Barcelona 24.9
Saragoßa 24.6
Colonia 119
Francoforte 102¼
Lisbona 405

Fig. 2: *Listino* of the fair of *Agosto* (August) celebrated in Piacenza (03/08/1591) (Archivo Simón Ruiz, CC, C. 151, 2.12).

developed an extremely effective coded correspondence model, much appreciated by many authors of contemporary mercantile treatises.[39]

Who sent the price lists received from the merchant Simón Ruiz? At the present stage of the research, it is not easy to answer this question. Simón's papers have been rearranged several times throughout the years, and the price lists—which were included in business letters—were extracted from correspondence and kept separately. Today, it is difficult to connect every single price list to the letter that contained it, but in the future, a meticulous reorganisation work could put them back in their original position. However, hypotheses can be made. The Lyon price lists were sent by the most trusted correspondents who, in that town, were the Bonvisi and Balbani families.[40] This hypothesis is also supported by many letters sent from Lyon which contain handwritten quotations of the fairs transcribed in the last lines of the letter.[41]

In the case of the Piacenza price lists, it is more difficult to formulate a hypothesis. Therefore, it can be hypothesised that the quotation lists of the Emilian fairs were sent to Medina by Simón's correspondents who had a company that operated on fairs and which probably also had an operational headquarters in Genoa. A sample search made it possible to verify that various companies of the Lucchese Bonvisi family operating both in Genoa and in the Piacenza fairs regularly sent letters containing the exchange rates of various European currencies. The letters sent from the fair were written during the days of the meetings, and the bankers sent their correspondents not only the price lists with the exchange rates, but also other information on the performance of the most important European credit markets and trading centres. On the other hand, more information on the trends of the Milan, Genoa, and Antwerp money markets was sent to Simón Ruiz in many letters from Genoa written by the Stefano, Antonio, and Scipione Bonvisi.[42]

---

39 Bernardo Gustiniani. *Breve trattato della continuatione de' cambi in cui si esaminano alcune moderne foggie di cambiare.* Genoa: Giuseppe Pavoni, 1619. Here we can find useful details on how to write down a commercial letter and how to compile all the books of accounts used during the exchange fairs.

40 François Bayard. *Les Bonvisi, marchands banquiers à Lyon. Annales E.S.C.* 26:6 (1971): 1234–1269; François Beynard. *Après les Bonvisi, les lucquois à Lyon aux XVIIe et XVIIIe siècles.* In *Lucca e l'Europa degli affari. Secoli XV–XVII*, Rita Mazzei, Tommaso Fanfani (eds.). Lucca: Pacini Fazzi, 1990, 193–208.

41 Archivo Simón Ruiz (Medina del Campo—Spain), *Casa de Comercio* (CC), *caja* (box) 69, nos. 200, 205.

42 Archivo Simón Ruiz (Medina del Campo—Spain), *Casa de Comercio* (CC), *cartas* (letters) nos. 168, 308.

Simón Ruiz replied to his clients and correspondents, sending them the quotations of the exchange rates fixed in the fairs of Medina as well as other commercial news related to the markets of the Iberian Peninsula. Unfortunately, among the documents of the Castilian merchant, no printed price lists—like those of the exchange fairs of Piacenza or Lyon—were found. It can be assumed that price lists were not printed in Medina to distribute the exchange rates fixed in the Castilian fairs. To date, we are not aware of any European merchant or banker who kept this type of document (the price lists fixed at Medina) in his archive. However, leafing through the letters sent by Simón Ruiz to his colleagues, we have recently discovered that in some letters sent abroad (probably to the Bonvisi company in Lyon, one of its most trusted correspondents), Simón entered the quotations of the fair held in Medina in October 1591. The fair had remained open from 4 October until Christmas Day with some delay caused by the non-arrival of the fleet from the Indies (which transported the Spanish silver from the Indies). The exchange rates he noted are for the following currencies: Piacenza exchange fair (*écu de marc*), Lyon exchange fair (*écu de marc*), Florence, Antwerp, Lisbon, and Valencia (Spain). This is just an example of how the Spanish merchant-banker shared the favour of commercial information received from his most trusted customers and correspondents.[43]

Here, it is important to underline that the only Italian exchange fairs that survived with some European relevance, at least until the beginning of the eighteenth century, were the Genoese fairs All the other fairs rapidly disappeared, relegating the Italian financial market to a subordinate level once the Dutch and British credit markets started to emerge as leaders in the first years of the eighteenth century, thanks to a series of new and more efficient financial instruments.

Conclusion

This chapter explores the monetary geography of Europe during the sixteenth and seventeenth centuries. As we have seen, European markets depended on a very complex international payment system in which many currencies from different countries were 'legally' accepted even abroad. Consequently, 'price lists' (the exchange rates' 'currents') were an extremely important work tool for carrying out the business of the Renaissance merchant-bankers. The topic of the payment system in seventeenth-century Europe may seem far removed from the con-

43 Doria, *Conoscenza del mercato*, 57–121.

temporary world, our everyday lives, and our interests, and yet exchange rates, international currencies, and the influence of the 'marketplaces' on global economies continue to monopolise public debate in the present. Therefore, to fully understand today's financial market, it is very helpful to decipher the mechanisms that regulated the exchange fairs in early modern Europe. It is important to underline that, thanks to the early modern fair, the accounting techniques used to manage exchange transactions found a new market in which the bankers were able to test and develop new procedures. Similarly, the professional skills possessed by contemporary financial brokers are the clear result of the evolution of complex computational tools and techniques. However, merchant-bankers soon discovered that printed 'price lists' attracted operators from elsewhere, so they promoted printed *listini* to boost the volume of transactions at the international fair, but shared information only with trusted counterparties and customers.

In recent years, the interest in topics such as currencies, money, and innovative payment systems has been growing at a high level. For example, during the last few years, in Sweden, the public debate about the need for the Swedish Central Bank to issue an electronic currency (the Swedish *e-Krona*) has been very animated, and I am convinced that a lot of information comes from the clearing system of the first foreign exchange fairs.[44] Accustomed as we are to a large amount of instantly available information with hidden costs, we tend to forget that, even in the past, such information used to be difficult to obtain and measure. Furthermore, if we look at the books of accounts of Renaissance companies, we discover that information was the most expensive 'service' in their everyday business.

Bibliography

Primary Sources

Archivio Durazzo Giustiniani Genova (Genoa—Italy). *Archivio Sauli*, ledgers nos. 1291, 1292, 1293, 1294, 1295, 1296, 1297, 1298, 1299, 1300, 1301, 1302, 1303.

Archivio Durazzo Giustiniani Genova (Genoa—Italy). *Archivio Durazzo*, from ledger no. 752 (1632) to ledger no. 776 (1657).

Archivio di Stato di Genova (State Archive, Genoa—Italy). *Senato, Senarega*, (folder) no. 1090.

Archivo Simón Ruiz (Medina del Campo—Spain). *Casa de Comercio* (CC), caja (box) 69, nos. 200 and 205.

Archivo Simón Ruiz (Medina del Campo—Spain). *Casa de Comercio* (CC), *cartas* (letters) nos. 168 and 308.

---

44 On this topic, see the two special issues published by the Swedish Central Bank: *Sveriges Riksbank Economic Review* 2 (2018) and *Sveriges Riksbank Economic Review* 3 (2020).

Archivo Simón Ruiz (Medina del Campo—Spain). *Casa de Comercio* (CC), *caja* (box) no. 150, 72 bis.
Archivo Simón Ruiz (Medina del Campo—Spain). *Casa de Comercio* (CC), *caja* (box) no. 151, 2.12.

Literature

Álvarez Nogal, Carlos, Christophe Chamley. Philip II against the Cortes and the credit freeze of 1575–1577. *Revista de Historia Económica/Journal of Iberian and Latin American Economic History* 34:3 (2016): 351–382.

Álvarez Nogal, Carlos, Luca Lo Basso, Claudio Marsilio. La rete finanziaria della famiglia Spinola. Spagna, Genova e le fiere dei cambi (1610–1656). *Quaderni Storici* 42:124/1 (2007): 97–110.

Álvarez Nogal, Carlos, Christophe Chamley. La crisis financiera de Castilla en 1575–1577: fiscalidad y estrategia. *Revista de la historia de la economía y de la empresa* 7 (2013): 187–211.

Amato, Massimo. Scudi, fiere, principi e banchieri. Il problema monetario del cambio in epoca rinascimentale. In *Lo scudo d'oro. Moneta e potere da Augusto a Carlo V*, S. Balbi de Caro (ed.). Rome, Brussels: FPM, 1996, VII.11–VII.18.

Bayard, François. Après les Bonvisi, les lucquois à Lyon aux XVIIe et XVIIIe siècles. In *Lucca e l'Europa degli affari. Secoli XV–XVII*, Rita Mazzei, Tommaso Fanfani (eds.). Lucca: Pacini Fazzi, 1990, 193–208.

Bayard, François. Les Bonvisi, marchands banquiers à Lyon, 1575–1629. *Annales E.S.C.* 26:6 (1971): 1234–1269.

Bell, Adrian R, Chris Brooks, Tony K. Moore. Cambium non est mutuum: exchange and interest rates in medieval Europe. *Economic History Review* 70:2 (2017): 373–396.

Bergier, Jean-François. *Genève et l'économie européenne de la Renaissance*. Paris: S.E.V.P.E.N., 1963.

Bonoldi, Andrea, Markus A. Denzel. *Bozen im Messenetz Europas (17–19 Jahrhundert)/Bolzano nel sistema fieristico europeo (secc. XVII–XIX)*. Bolzano: Athesia, 2007.

Börner, Lars, John William Hatfield. The Design of Debt-Clearing Markets: Clearinghouse Mechanisms in Preindustrial Europe. *Journal of Political Economy* 125:6 (2017): 1991–2037.

Boyer-Xambeau, Marie-Thérèse, Ghislain Deleplace, Lucien Gillard. La crise du système de change Lyonnais à la fin du XVI siècle. *Revue Internationale d'Histoire de la Banque* 32–33 (1986): 145–166.

Boyer-Xambeau, Marie-Thérèse, Ghislain Deleplace, Lucien Gillard. *Private Money & Public Currencies: The 16th Century Challenge*. New York: M.E. Sharpe, 1994.

Capitoli e ordini delle fere di Besenzone, che si fanno al presente in la città di Piacenza. Genoa, 1622.

Capitoli e ordini delle fere di Besenzone, che si fanno al presente in la città di Piacenza, ristampate di novo con le gionte fatte dal Serenissimo Senato dall'anno 1622 sin al presente. Genoa, 1637.

Casado Alonso, Hilario. Medina del Campo Fairs and the Integration of Castile into 15th and 16th Century European Economy. In *Fiere e mercati nella integrazione delle economie europee secc. XIII–XVIII*, Simonetta Cavaciocchi (ed.). Florence: Le Monnier, 2001, 495–518.

Cassandro, Michele. Le fiere nell'economia europea medievale e della prima età moderna. *Studi Storici Luigi Simeoni* 51 (2001): 9–27.

Cassandro, Michele. *Credito e banca in Italia tra Medioevo e Rinascimento*. In *Credito e sviluppo economico in Italia dal Medioevo all'età contemporânea*. Verona: Società Italiana degli Storici Economici, 1988, 131–145.

Cassandro, Michele. *Le fiere di Lione e gli uomini d'affari italiani nel Cinquecento*. Florence: Tipografia Baccini & Chiappi, 1979.

Castillo Pintado, Alonso. Los juros de Castilla. Apogeo y fin de un instrumento de crédito. *Hispania* 23 (1963): 43–70.
Conklin, James. The Theory of Sovereign Debt and Spain under Philip II. *Journal of Political Economy* 106:3 (1998): 483–513.
Da Silva, José Gentil. *Banque et crédit e Italie au XVIIe siècle*. Paris: Armand Colin, 1969.
Da Silva, José Gentil, Ruggiero Romano. L'histoire des changes: les foires de "Bisenzone" de 1600 à 1650. *Annales E.S.C.* 17 (1962): 715–721.
De Roover, Raymond. Money, Banking, and Credit in Medieval Bruges. *Journal of Economic History* 2 (1942): 52–65.
De Roover, Raymond. *Gresham on Foreign Exchange: An Essay on Early English Mercantilism*. Cambridge, MA: Harvard University Press, 1949.
De Roover, Raymond. *L'evolution de la lettre de change, XIVe–XVIIIe siècles*. Paris: Armand Colin, 1953.
De Roover, Raymond. What is dry exchange? A contribution to the study of English Mercantilism. *Journal of Political Economy* 52 (1944): 250–266.
Denzel, Markus A. *Die Bozner Messen und ihr Zahlungsverkehr (1633–1850)*. Bolzano: Athesia, 2006.
Denzel, Markus A. *Handbook of World Exchange Rates, 1590–1914*. Farnham: Ashgate, 2010.
Doria, Giorgio. Conoscenza del mercato e sistema informativo: il know-how dei mercanti-finanzieri genovesi nei secoli XVI–XVII. In *La repubblica internazionale del denaro tra XV e XVII secolo*, Aldo De Maddalena, Hermann Kellenbenz (eds.). Bologna: Il Mulino, 1986, 57–121.
Drelichman, Mauricio, Hans-Joachim Voth. Lending to the borrower from hell: debt and default in the age of Philip II. *The Economic Journal* 121 (2011): 1205–1227.
Drelichman, Mauricio, Hans-Joachim Voth. The Sustainable Debts of Philip II: A Reconstruction of Castile's Fiscal Position, 1566–1596. *The Journal of Economic History* 70:4 (2010): 813–842.
Drelichman, Mauricio, Hans-Joachim Voth. *Lending to the Borrower from Hell: Debt, Taxes, and Default in the Age of Philip II*. Princeton, CA: Princeton University Press, 2014.
Drelichman, Mauricio, Hans-Joachim Voth. Serial defaults, serial profits: Returns to sovereign lending in Habsburg Spain, 1566–1600. *Explorations in Economic History* 48 (2011): 1–19.
Einaudi, Luigi. The theory of imaginary money from Charlemagne to the French Revolution. In *Enterprise and secular change: readings in economic history*, Frederic C. Lane, Jelle C. Riemersma (eds.). Homewood, IL: University of Michigan, 1953, 229–261.
Einaudi, Luiqi. Teoria della moneta immaqinaria nel tempo da Carlomaqno alla rivoluzione francese. *Rivista di Storia Economica* 1 (1936): 1–35.
Epstein, Stephen R. Regional Fairs, Institutional Innovation, and Economic Growth in Late-Medieval Europe. *Economic History Review*, 47:3 (1994): 459–482.
Epstein, Stephen R. Fairs, Towns, and States in Renaissance Europe. In *Fiere e mercati*, Cavaciocchi (ed.), 71–90.
Fantacci, Luca. Complementary Currencies: a Prospect on Money from a Retrospect on Premodern Practices. *Financial History Review* 12:1 (2005): 43–61.
Fantacci, Luca. *La moneta. Storia di un'istituzione mancata*. Venice: Marsilio, 2005.
Fantacci, Luca. Teoria della moneta immaginaria nel tempo da Carlomagno a Richard Nixon. *Rivista di Storia Economica* 3 (2002): 301–326.
Fantacci, Luca. The dual currency system of Renaissance Europe. *Financial History Review*, 15 (2008): 55–72.
Felloni, Giuseppe. *Gli investimenti finanziari genovesi in Europa tra il Seicento e la Restaurazione*. Milano: Gioffrè Editore, 1977.
Felloni, Giuseppe. *Profilo di storia economica dell'Europa dal medioevo all'età contemporânea*. Torino: Giappichelli Editore, 1993.

Felloni, Giuseppe. Un système monétaire atypique: La monnaie de marc dans les foires de change génoises, XVIe–XVIIe siècle. In *Études d'histoire monétaire*, John Day (ed.). Lille: Presses Universitaires de Lille, 1984, 249–260.

Felloni, Giuseppe. Asientos, juros y ferias de cambio (1541–1675). In *Dinero y crédito*, Alfonso Otazu (ed.). Madrid: Moneda y Crédito, 1978, 335–359.

Flandreau, Marc, Christophe Galimard, Clemens Jobst, Pilar Nogues-Marco. The Bell Jar: Commercial Interest Rates between Two Revolutions, 1688–1789. In *The Origins and Development of Financial Markets and Institutions. From the Seventeenth Century to the Present*, J. Atack, Larry Neal (eds.). Cambridge: Cambridge University Press, 2009, 161–208.

Flandreau, Marc, Christophe Galimard, Clemens Jobst, Pilar Nogues-Marco. Monetary Geography before the Industrial Revolution. *Cambridge Journal of Regions, Economy and Society* 2:2 (2009): 149–171.

Gascon, Richard. *Grand Commerce et vie urbaine. Lyon et ses marchands (environs de 1520–environs de 1580)*. Paris: La Haye, 1971.

Gioffrè, Domenico. *Gênes et les foires de changes: de Lyon à Besançon*. Paris: Armand Colin, 1960.

Gustiniani, Bernardo. *Breve trattato della continuatione de' cambi in cui si esaminano alcune moderne foggie di cambiare*. Genoa: Giuseppe Pavoni, 1619.

Homer, Sidney, Richard Sylla. *A History of Interest Rates*. New Brunswick, NJ: Rutgers University Press, 2005.

Lanaro, Paola (ed.). *La pratica dello scambio. Sistemi di fiere, mercanti e città in Europa (1400–1700)*. Venice: Marsilio, 2003.

Lapeyre, Henri. *Simón Ruiz et les "asientos" de Philippe II*. Paris: Armand Colin, 1953.

Lapeyre, Henri. *Une famille de marchands, Les Ruiz. Contribution à l'étude du commerce entre la France et l'Espagne au temps de Philippe II*. Paris: Armand Colin, 1955.

Mandich, Giulio. Delle fiere genovesi di cambi particolarmente studiate come mercati periodici del credito. *Rivista di Storia Economica* 4 (1939): 257–276.

Mandich, Giulio. Fiere cambiarie concorrenti (genovesi, fiorentine, veneziane) nel 1622–1652. In *La repubblica internazionale del denaro tra XV e XVII secolo*, Aldo De Maddalena, Hermann Kellenbenz (eds.). Bologna: Il Mulino, 1986, 123–151.

Mandich, Giulio. Le fiere genovesi di soli cambi culla delle borse valori. *Rivista Milanese di Economia* 17 (1986): 132–146.

Marsilio, Claudio. *Dove il denaro fa denaro. Gli operatori finanziari genovesi nelle fiere di cambio del XVII secolo*. Novi Ligure: Città del Silenzio, 2008.

Marsilio, Claudio. Four times a year for so many years. The Italian Exchange Fairs during the XVIth–XVIIth centuries: Comparing Financial Institutions. *Bankhistorisches Archiv/Banking and Finance in Historical Perspective* 36:2 (2010): 151–165.

Marsilio, Claudio. La lunga avventura delle fiere di cambio: da Lione a Novi. In *Libri italiani del Seicento nel fondo antico della Biblioteca Civica di Novi Ligure*, Andrea Sisti, Mathias Balbi (eds.). Novi Ligure: Città del Silenzio, 2011, 83–90.

Marsilio, Claudio. Le fiere di cambio nella prima metà del XVII secolo: evoluzione di un'antica istituzione finanziaria. In *Banca, crédito y capital: la monarquía hispánica y los antiguos países bajos (1505–1700)*, Carmen Sanz Ayán, Bernardo José García García (eds.). Madrid: Fundación Carlos de Amberes, 2006, 59–82.

Marsilio, Claudio. *"O dinheiro morreu. Paz à sua alma danada": Gli operatori finanziari del XVII secolo tra investimenti e speculazioni*. Palermo: Mediterranea, 2012.

Marsilio, Claudio. *Exchange fairs and the money market in early modern Italy (1630–1650)/ Fiere di cambio e mercato monetário nell'Italia di età moderna (1630–1650)*. Novi Ligure: Città del Silenzio, 2018.

Marsilio, Claudio. *La colección de 'listini' del Archivo Simón Ruiz. Las ferias de cambio de Medina del Campo en el corazón del mercado del dinero europeo (1580–1600)*. Valladolid: Fundación Museo de las Ferias, 2021.

Marsilio, Claudio. Le Utopie dei Genovesi. Contabilità e skill professionale nelle fiere di cambio dei secoli XVI–XVII. *Cheiron. Materiali e strumenti di aggiornamento storiografico* 51 (2009): 47–65.

Marsilio, Claudio. Un homme avisé est capable de faire face à toutes les catastrophes. Les compétences professionnelles des opérateurs financiers génois, florentins et portugais à l'époque des foires de change du XVIIe siècle. In *Ressources publiques et construction étatique en Europe XIIIe–XVIIIe siècle*, Katia Béguin (ed.). Paris: Institut de la gestion publique et du développement économique, 2015, 227–247.

Marsilio, Claudio. The Genoese exchange fairs and the Bank of Amsterdam: Comparing two Financial Institutions of the 17th century. *História Econômica & História de Empresas* 18:1 (2015): 39–59.

Martínez Ruiz, José Ignacio. The Credit Market and the Profits from the Letters of Exchange: *Ricorsa* Exchange Operations between Seville and the Besançon Fairs (1589–1621). *Journal of European Economic History* 33:2 (2004): 331–355.

McCusker, John Joe, Cora Gravejstijn. *The Beginnings of Commercial and Financial Journalism: The Commodity Price Currents, Exchange Rate Currents, and Money Currents of Early Modern Europe*. Amsterdam: NEHA, 1991.

Neal, Larry. How it all began: the monetary and financial architecture of Europe during the first global capital markets, 1648–1815. *Financial History Review* 7:2 (2000): 117–140.

Orlandi, Angela. *Le Grand Parti. Fiorentini a Lione e il debito pubblico francese nel XVI secolo*. Florence: Le Monnier, 2002.

Parker, Geoffrey. *Global Crisis: War, Climate Change and Catastrophe in the Seventeenth Century*. New Haven, London: Yale University Press, 2013.

Peri, Giovanni Domenico. *Il negotiante*. Genoa, 1638.

Pezzolo, Luciano, Giuseppe Tattara. 'Una fiera senza luogo?' Was Bisenzone an International Capital Market in Sixteenth Century Italy?. *Journal of Economic History* 68:4 (2008): 1098–1122.

Sayous, André-Émile. Les opérations des banquiers italiens en Italie et aux foires de Champagne pendant le XIIIe siècle. *Revue Historique* 57 (1932): 1–31.

Spufford, Peter. *Handbook of Medieval Exchange*. London: Royal Historical Society, 1986.

Sveriges Riksbank Economic Review 3 (2020).

Sveriges Riksbank Economic Review 2 (2018).

Toboso Sánchez, Pilar. *La deuda pública castellana durante el Antiguo Régimen (juros) y su liquidación en el siglo XIX*. Madrid: Ministerio de Hacienda, 1987.

Markus A. Denzel

International fairs as money, credit, and exchange markets, from the 12th to 16th centuries

International fairs[1]—these "old, outstandingly adaptable tool[s] of trade," as Fernand Braudel has characterised them[2]—were always more than just places where goods and information were exchanged; these functions could also be observed by great annual markets, that is, by markets with a relatively large number of foreign participants. Furthermore, international fairs also fulfilled the function of monetary and, more importantly, credit and exchange markets. Money, credit, and exchange—these are the three financial constitutive elements of international fairs. Especially the international fairs were temporary markets for exactly these three pillars of the financial background of commerce in premodern times. Not least because of such a financial implication, fairs got an eminent importance for the preindustrial economy in Europe.

The following contribution aims to stress this central role of the great international fairs for the emergence of money, credit, and exchange markets from the twelfth to the sixteenth century, supplemented by some remarks on the fairs' development in the further centuries. That being said, I start from these three basic theses:

1. The great international fairs are almost characterised by the fact that they functioned not only as transfer hubs for goods and information but rather always as money, credit, and exchange markets. This specific financial function seems to have been a constitutive element of a fair as a wholesale market of international relevance and made the decisive difference to annual markets of only regional importance—the so-called great annual markets with their supra-regional character or the modern sample fairs. Or, vice versa, if a great international fair lost its financial function, it became altogether unimportant and obsolete or—in the nineteenth century—was transferred to a sample fair.

1 Used generally without being cited every time: Markus A. Denzel. *Handbook of World Exchange Rates, 1590 to 1914*. Farnham, Burlington: Ashgate, 2010; Markus A. Denzel. *Das System des bargeldlosen Zahlungsverkehrs europäischer Prägung vom Mittelalter bis 1914*. Stuttgart: Steiner, 2008.

2 Fernand Braudel. *Sozialgeschichte des 15.–18. Jahrhunderts. Der Handel*. Munich: C.H. Beck, 1986, 80.

https://doi.org/10.1515/9783111621296-009

2. This function of great international fairs as money, credit, and exchange markets had its closest ties to the fact that essential financial innovations were developed or emerged in connection with the transactions conducted here, and these financial innovations in turn promoted the financial function of fairs and the resulting attractiveness for internationally engaged merchant bankers.
3. Thus, great international fairs instantly and always were important, if only temporary, capital markets for a country or at least a region and in their interaction as a fair system (for example, in the sixteenth century) even for the whole of Europe, both for merchant bankers as well as for crown and state finance. This function as a capital market only fell out of use when, starting in the Netherlands, stock exchanges increasingly offered year-round, permanent financial services.

For the long-term development of trade history in Europe, the financial innovations that were developed at the great international fairs and originated there—or were accelerated by them—appear to be decisive catalysts. For this reason, my paper adopts an innovation-historical perspective from which the financial-historical significance of the great international fairs is explained. This is done in three steps: first, the development of early means of accounting and payment are examined, as it took place around the Champagne Fairs in the High Middle Ages. In this case, a more than rudimentary money and credit market had already emerged here. The next step to be taken into consideration—which evolved at the late medieval Geneva fairs—was the formation of a dedicated exchange market. In the third (and last) step, the interplay of the great western European fairs among each other in the sixteenth century is discussed which, with their close scheduling and financial coordination and with Lyon as their geographical centre, formed a year-round 'pan-European' money, credit, and exchange market for the first time. In this concert of large western European fairs, the highly specialised exchange fairs of Bisenzone-Piacenza were the peak of this development from the last decades of the sixteenth century onwards, as they functioned exclusively as money, credit, and exchange markets while there was no longer any trade in goods.

"The forcing house for the development of bill of exchange": the Champagne Fairs

Following the expansion of trade, the Mediterranean navigation, and the monetised economics in Europe during the time of the Crusades, it became more and more necessary for merchants to develop mechanisms for providing liquidity, whenever and wherever there was no or only little coined or uncoined precious metal available. This evident lack of money meant a noticeable obstruction of economic activity, especially in places where the exchange of goods was concentrated—that is, at the great markets and the emerging fairs.

However, the vast majority of fairs could not rely on such a reservoir of flows of precious metals. For most of the late Middle Ages until the take-off of precious metal supplies from Spanish America, these fairs suffered under the bullion famine—the epitome of the monetary crisis of the late Middle Ages.[3] In fact, they suffered in such a way that the lack of available precious metals would have effectively made the expansion of business impossible. Without going into other reasons, it was not least the shortage of precious metals which provoked the development of innovative means of payment transactions and credit financing at the large international fairs and made the expansion of business beyond the limitations of available precious metals possible, both for individual merchant houses and for the business of the fairs as a whole.

As the Champagne Fairs were developing into the central hubs of international trade, particularly between upper Italy and northwestern Europe in the twelfth century, on the one hand, merchants from upper Italy who travelled and did business there were urged to respond to the lack of cash and, on the other, to mitigate costs and risks of cash transport. Therefore, the Champagne Fairs became crystallisation sites for the development of new means of cashless payment from the second half of the twelfth century onwards and, in long-term perspective, to "the forcing house for the development of (the) bill of exchange," as Peter Spufford

3 Wolfgang von Stromer. Hartgeld, Kredit und Giralgeld. Zu einer monetären Konjunkturtheorie des Spätmittelalters und der Wende zur Neuzeit. In *La moneta nell'economia europea, secoli XIII–XVIII. Atti della "Settima Settimana di studio" (11–17 aprile 1975)*, Vera Barbagli Bagnoli (ed.). Florence: Le Monnier, 1981, 109. See also John Day. The Great Bullion Famine of the Fifteenth Century. *Past & Present* 79 (1978): 3–54; John H. Munro. *Wool, Cloth and Gold. The Struggle for Bullion in Anglo-Burgundian Trade, 1340–1478*. Brussels: Édition de l'Université de Bruxelles, 1972; John H. Munro. *Bullion Flows and Monetary Policies in England and the Low Countries, 1350– 1500*. Hampshire, Brookfield: Ashgate, 1992.

has aptly characterised them.[4] In this way, three steps of development can be distinguished, namely

1. the development of early forms of means of cashless payment;
2. the technique of scontration; and
3. the emergence of the bill of exchange as medium of cashless payment, money transfer, and credit.

At first, the *lettre de foire*, which was only used at the Champagne Fairs, and the *instrumentum ex causa cambii*, which was in much wider use, can be regarded the oldest instruments of cashless payment. These were developed by Italian, most likely Genoese, merchants especially for itinerant merchants who travelled to the Champagne Fairs. The *lettres de foire* simply were certificates issued by the court of the Champagne Fairs, which consisted of ecclesiastical notaries and merchants, to provide security for the sale of goods on credit. These certificates, which documented the seller's legal claim to be paid by the buyer at a later fair, were used—in the absence of cash—as a means of payment. Unlike the *lettres de foire*, the *instrumentum ex causa cambii* was a document written by a merchant—and notarially certified as well—that documented the merchant's promise to make the payment at a later date at any place, whether or not a fair took place there.

Both early means of cashless payments were combined instruments of credit and money transfer and served thus for the financing of exports as well as for transferring money without recourse to expensive and risky transfers of precious metals. In this way, they were payment obligations or promises in the form of a debt certificate written by a notary. Moreover, only two or three people were included in these cashless transactions:

1. the debtor, who raised a credit—for example, in Genoa—and had his debt certificate and promise of repayment certified by a notary, because in the eleventh and twelfth centuries not all merchants were capable of reading and writing;
2. the creditor, who lent the money and could request repayment; and possibly
3. the creditor's representative at a certain fair, who could receive the payment in place of the creditor himself.

4 Peter Spufford. *Handbook of Medieval Exchange*. London: Offices of the Royal Historical Society, 1986, xxxi.

As the merchant, who had promised repayment at a certain fair, used to travel there himself, he did not need a representative of his own who would transact the payment in his place.[5]

Secondly, as the expanding international trade at the Champagne Fairs required growing money transfers at the fairs themselves for the settlement of purchases and sales, merchants began to set off claims and liabilities on the spot in a cashless manner. The clearing mechanism of the so-called scontration—that is, the mutual settlement of liabilities between two or more business partners—had come to complete development already by 1180 and was legally guaranteed by the enforceability at the court of the fair.[6] The settlement of payments by scontration was the most sophisticated and modern technique used in high medieval international payment transactions.[7] Thus, the Champagne Fairs "assumed the function of European markets of money and credit already by the end of the twelfth century and in the thirteenth it was common practice to use the fairs in this way,"[8] both in international trade between the Mediterranean and northwestern Europe—especially Flanders as its most important economic region—to the Rhineland and also in the payment transactions of and with the Papal Curia.[9]

---

5 John H. Munro. Instrumentum Ex Causa Cambii. In *Von Aktie bis Zoll. Ein historisches Lexikon des Geldes*, Michael North (ed.). Munich: C.H. Beck, 1995, 174–175; Raymond de Roover. *L'évolution de la lettre de change, XIVe–XVIIIe siècles.* Paris: S.E.V.P.E.N., 1953, 23–42; R.D. Face. Techniques of Business in Trade between the Fairs of Champagne and the South of Europe in the 12th and 13th Centuries. *Economic History Review* 10 (1957/58): 427–438. See also Alfred Wendehorst. Wer konnte im Mittelalter lesen und schreiben? In *Schulen und Studien im sozialen Wandel des hohen und späten Mittelalters*, Johannes Fried (ed.). Sigmaringen: Thorbecke, 1986, 28.

6 Heinz Thomas. Die Champagnemessen. In *Frankfurt im Messenetz Europas—Erträge der Forschung*, Hans Pohl (ed.). Vol. 1 of *Brücke zwischen den Völkern—Zur Geschichte der Frankfurter Messe*, Rainer Koch (ed.). Frankfurt: Historisches Museum, 1991, 13–36; Heinz Thomas. Beiträge zur Geschichte der Champagne-Messen. *Vierteljahrschrift für Sozial- und Wirtschaftsgeschichte* 49 (1977): 433–467; Alexander Schönfelder, *Handelsmessen und Kreditwirtschaft im Hochmittelalter—Die Champagnemessen.* Saarbrücken-Scheidt: Dadder, 1988; Franz Irsigler, Winfried Reichert. Les foires de Champagne. In *Messen, Jahrmärkte und Stadtentwicklung in Europa. Foires, marchés annuels et développement urbain en Europe*, Franz Irsigler, Michel Pauly (eds.). Trier: Porta Alba, 2007, 89–105.

7 Jürgen Schneider. Messen, Banken und Börsen (15.–18. Jahrhundert). In *Banchi pubblici, banchi privati e monti di pietà nell'Europa preindustriale. Amministrazione, tecniche operative e ruoli economici*, vol. I. Genoa: Società Ligure di Storia Patria, 1991, 135–136. See also De Roover, *L'évolution*, 21; Face, Techniques of Business, 428; Elisabeth Bassermann. *Die Champagnermessen. Ein Beitrag zur Geschichte des Kredits.* Tübingen: Mohr, 1911, 25–33, 49–89.

8 Thomas, Die Champagnemessen, 27.

9 Markus A. Denzel. *Kurialer Zahlungsverkehr im 13. und 14. Jahrhundert. Servitien- und Annatenzahlungen aus dem Bistum Bamberg.* Stuttgart: Steiner, 1991, 95–96; Kurt Weissen. *Marktstrategien der Kurienbanken. Die Geschichte der Alberti, Medici und Spinelli in Deutschland (1400–1475).*

Finally, the Champagne Fairs expedited the diffusion of the bill of exchange which had been emerging since the late twelfth century. If merchants started to settle in a particular town, they began to stay in their offices and to instruct a trusted person—an agent or a partner—to look after their obligations at fairs or in other places.[10] With this person, they would send, along with the formal notarial contract, an informal letter of advice (*littera*) as an order of payment, which then evolved into the actual bill of exchange.[11] This development was supported by the fact that the emerging net of agents and correspondents, who knew each other personally, made notarial certification obsolete:

> A rich network of international commercial correspondents [. . .] extended to cover the entire economic and geographical area dominated by the Italian merchant bankers, and it was this that gave them the unrivalled possibilities for remitting to or drawing from any one place to any other.[12]

The 'informal' bill of exchange was much easier to handle and less expensive than the former notarially certified methods of payment. At first and in the thirteenth and fourteenth centuries, it provided only financial transactions and thus liquidity between two places, and this usually only within one trading company—for example, between the merchant and his agent. This means was called the *lettera di pagamento*. Since the fourteenth century, such bills circulated also outside a single trading company between different merchants and different companies: the bill of exchange or the so-called *lettera di cambio* in its proper sense was generated, which became the most important means of cashless payment transactions and credit instrument for providing liquidity in the centres of trade and finance of the Italian merchant bankers, taking over the position of the former

Heidelberg: Heidelberg University Press, 2021. See also R.L. Reynolds. Genoese Trade in the Late Twelfth Century, Particularly in Cloth from the Fairs of Champagne. *Journal of Economic and Business History* 3:3 (1931): 373–375.

10 Raymond de Roover. *Money, Banking and Credit in Medieval Bruges. Italian Merchant-Bankers, Lombards and Money-Changers. A Study in the Origins of Banking*. Cambridge, MA: Cambridge University Press, 1948, 51.

11 Munro, Instrumentum Ex Causa Cambii, 175. See also Raymond de Roover. Le contrat de change depuis la fin du treizième siècle jusqu'au début du dix-septième. *Revue belge de philologie et d'histoire* 25:1–2 (1946/47): 111–128; Raymond de Roover. Précisions sur l'histoire de la lettre et du contrat de change (d'après des documents inédits des Archivs Datini à Prato). *La vie économique et sociale* 23 (1952): 44–67; Georg Schaps. *Zur Geschichte des Wechselindossaments*. Stuttgart: Ferdinand Enke, 1892, 9.

12 Alfonso Leone. Some Preliminary Remarks on the Study of Foreign Currency Exchange in the Medieval Period. *Journal of European Economic History* 12 (1983): 620.

means of cashless payment transactions.[13] The most important difference between the *letters de foires* and the *instrumentum ex causa cambii* on the one hand and the bill of exchange on the other was that the first constituted a payment promise or obligation, whereas the latter was a payment order with the issuer of the bill ordering a third person at another place to settle a debt in his place.[14]

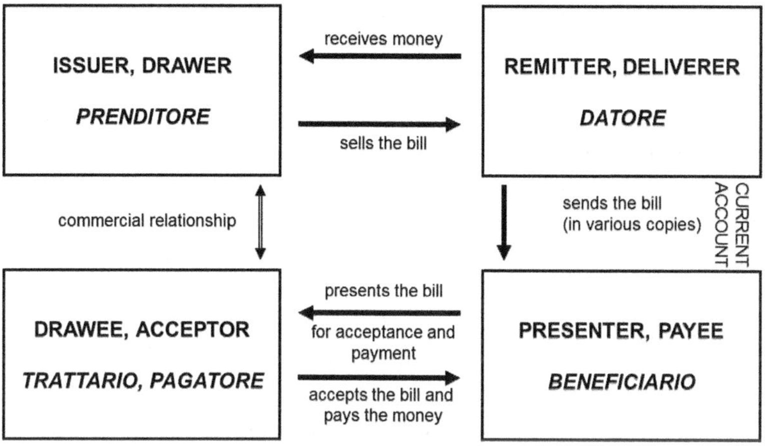

Fig. 1: The model of a 'classical' bill of exchange.[15]

Nevertheless, the 'classical' bill of exchange seems to have differed from the abovementioned early exchange contracts more formally than functionally. According to Raymond de Roover:

> [T]he *instrumentum ex causa cambii* is undoubtedly the prototype of the bill of exchange, for it fulfilled exactly the same function. True, the *instrumentum* took the form of a promise to pay, whereas the bill of exchange is an order to pay, but this distinction, being purely formal, is more superficial than real.[16]

In principle, the transfer of remaining claims and liabilities, that were not settled by the clearing to the next fair, wherever it may take place, became possible.

13 De Roover, *L'évolution*, 38–45; Markus A. Denzel. Wechsel, Wechsler, Wechselbrief. In *Lexikon des Mittelalters*, vol. VIII. Munich: LexMA, 1997, 2086–2089.

14 John H. Munro. Wechsel. In *Von Aktie bis Zoll*, North (ed.), 413.

15 Denzel, *Handbook*, xxviii.

16 Raymond de Roover. New Interpretations of the History of Banking. In *Business, Banking and Economic Thought in Late Medieval and Early Modern Europe. Selected Studies of Raymond de Roover*, Julius Kirshner (ed.). Chicago, London: University of Chicago Press, 1974, 203.

Therefore, it is possible to determine two fields where transactions with bills of exchange were of great importance, especially at fairs: the first field was the merchandise trade, where the bill of exchange was used as a means of payment and credit; the second was the pure credit transaction when only money was sent—that is, liquidity was provided, whereas no connection to any trade in goods existed.

What significance can be attributed to the exchange business conducted at the fairs? On the one hand, the great international fairs provided the opportunity to issue money and form credit, while on the other, they contributed to international clearing and the successive distribution of cashless payment methods from the thirteenth and fourteenth centuries. In other words, they pushed the process of integration towards the emergence of a European exchange market.[17] At the same time, the large international fairs often—though not always—contributed to avoiding financial and, above all, credit crises by means of their regulating impact on monetary, precious metal, and credit markets. In case of money shortages, the merchant-bankers active at these fairs put the needed liquidity at disposal, whereas in the case of available surplus money, they would divert it to different monetary markets, mostly other fairs.

This finding, worked out here by using the Champagne Fairs as a case study, is of course of a fundamental nature—that is, it applies regularly to all great international fairs of the premodern times. This is already evident in the following case study on the Geneva fairs.

"*Il primo esempio di fieri di cambi*": the Geneva fairs

In the fifteenth century, the advancing commercialisation, which was revived once more in the wake of the Black Death in the mid-fourteenth century, intensified the exchange of goods, money, and information between the Mediterranean and the northern Alpine area. In this process, the Geneva fairs, first mentioned in 1262, became evident in the first half of the fifteenth century as a commercial

17 Markus A. Denzel. Der Beitrag von Messen und Märkten zum Integrationsprozeß des internationalen bargeldlosen Zahlungsverkehrssystems in Europa (13.–18. Jahrhundert). In *Fiere e mercati nella integrazione delle economie europee, secc. XIII–XVIII*. Simonetta Cavaciocchi (ed.). Florence: Le Monnier, 2001, 819–835.

'hub' north of the Alps.[18] Without discussing the details of their ascent, it remains to be said that from the fourteenth century onwards, these were organised in a similar way to the Champagne Fairs and turned out to be the most important stop of Italian merchant-bankers north of the Alps, even more so as two of Europe's long-distance trade routes crossed at Geneva—one running from Marseilles via Lyon to Nuremberg, the other from Florence to Dijon.[19] Just as for Francesco di Marco Datini from Prato at the end of the fourteenth century, the Geneva fairs were the most important stage on the route from Bruges to Barcelona. Similarly, in 1441, the Geneva fairs were the Medici's central intermediary point—a "clearing-house," according to Jean-François Bergier—between Bruges and Venice, between their larger enterprise in Barcelona, Lombardy, Venice, Rome, and Florence on the one side, and the Netherlands and England on the other.[20]

Given the close connection with their function in transit trade, the Geneva fairs had become a market for finance and bills of exchange of international recognition since the beginning of the fifteenth century:

> [C]ette fonction financière des foires s'est assez vite distancée, pour une part tout au moins, de leur fonction proprement commerciale; une activité nouvelle est née, autour de 1420–1440, orientée essentiellement vers les opérations de change.[21]

By the middle of the fifteenth century at the latest, the Geneva fairs had gained a new quality in international payments as *"primo esempio di fieri di cambi."*[22] In this way, they partly followed in the footsteps of the Champagne Fairs and Chalon-sur-Saône and assumed a part of the intermediary function of Paris in international payments between Italy and northwest Europe at a time when the economic agency of the Seine metropolis was severely restricted due to the political turmoil of the second part of the Hundred Year's War: "Entre les centres d'Italie et ceux d'Europe du Nord, [Genève] offrait un relais aussi favorable aux opérations de

18 The following remarks, unless stated otherwise, are according to Jean-François Bergier. *Genève et l'économie européenne de la Renaissance*. Paris: S.E.V.P.E.N., 1963.

19 Wim Blockmans. Das westeuropäische Messenetz im 14. und 15. Jahrhundert. In *Frankfurt im Messenetz Europas*, Pohl (ed.), 42.

20 Bergier, *Genève*, 230, 269–271, 286–307, 311. See also Martin Körner. Kreditformen und Zahlungsverkehr im spätmittelalterlichen und frühneuzeitlichen Luzern. *Scripta Mercaturae* 21 (1987): 137.

21 Bergier, *Genève*, 269; Michele Cassandro. *Il Libro Giallo di Ginevra della compagnia fiorentina di Antonio della Casa e Simone Guadagni 1453–1454*. Prato: Istituto internazionale di storia economica "F. Datini," 1975, 55. See also Körner, Kreditformen, 137: "For Geneva, the fairs and above all their financial function were decisive for its development into a centre of exchange."

22 Cassandro, *Libro Giallo*, 54.

change qu'au trafic des marchandises."[23] Geneva was an especially vital financial hub for curial payments of *servitia*, annates, or other payments, mostly from France after the Pragmatic Sanction of Bourges (1438), to the Apostolic Camera through the mediation of Roman and Florentine bankers.[24]

The background to this remarkable expansion of cashless payment compared to the times of the Champagne Fairs was the significant increase in the economic security of such operations in the meantime: other than the exchange rates quoted in the Champagne or the Italian financial centres, those quoted at the Geneva fairs were based on a stable unit of account—the *marc d'or* at 28 Troy ounces weight, calculated at 64 or 66 *écus* respectively.[25] As silver coins—or account units based on silver, for that matter—were always subjected to high fluctuations compared to gold, which was regarded as more valuable, the reference to a universally accepted unit of gold in the merchant community (and beyond), was a decisive step in order to make payments independent from the usual silver currencies and change to the metal more precious and stable in value. Additionally, this unit of gold—the *marc d'or*—was set in a fixed relation to the *écu*, a large silver coin accepted both in Geneva and the kingdom of France, so that the greatest possible currency security existed at that time for exchange payments in or for *marc d'or* or *écu* as the sixty-fourth or sixty-sixth part of the *marc d'or*. This was a clear stabilisation of the currency relations of the money, credit, and exchange market at the Geneva fairs in an epoch in which both strong, market-induced currency fluctuations as well as officially ordered coin devaluations for the purpose of state money procurement were commonplace. The introduction of a fixed monetary reference value for payment by bills of exchange, which were decisive for the granting and repayment of credit, was an important innovation in cashless payment transactions that was to be adopted at later fairs.[26] Therefore, by the mid-fifteenth century at the latest, the Geneva fairs had become the

23 Bergier, *Genève*, 270, 433; Blockmans, Messenetz, 42–43.

24 "With the Geneva bankers one sees bankers from Avignon and also already some Lyon merchants working together; but the goal of all remained Rome" (own translation). See Michel Mollat. *Der königliche Kaufmann. Jacques Cœur oder der Geist des Unternehmertums*. Munich: Beck, 1991, 206.

25 Michael North. Von den Warenmessen zu den Wechselmessen. Grundlagen des europäischen Zahlungsverkehrs in Spätmittelalter und Früher Neuzeit. In *Europäische Messen und Märktesysteme in Mittelalter und Neuzeit*, Peter Johanek, Heinz Stoob (eds.). Cologne, Weimar, Vienna: Böhlau, 1996, 226.

26 See Markus A. Denzel. Exchange Rates and Silver Prices at European Fairs, 16th–18th Centuries. In *Mining, Money and Markets in the Early Modern Atlantic: Digital Approaches and New Perspectives*, Claudia de Lozanne Jefferies, Renate Pieper, Markus A. Denzel (eds.). London: Routledge, 2019, 349–362.

"*primo esempio di fieri di cambi*"[27] and had acquired a new quality in international payment transactions that went beyond the Fairs in Champagne.

The "*système de correspondance*": the network of the sixteenth century international fairs

However, the fifteenth century was not only the zenith of the Geneva fairs, but also the time of the rise of fairs in Castile, Brabant, and Lyon to international relevance, to which other fairs—such as those in Frankfurt am Main[28]—remained evidently subordinate. Without delving into the details of this development in Medina del Campo, Medina del Rioseco, and Villalón, in Antwerp and Bergen-op-Zoom as well as in Lyon, it should be noted that these large western European fair systems were in a "*système de correspondance*"[29] with each other in the sixteenth century—that is, the fair dates were coordinated with each other and the system was timed in such a way that the fairs as a whole formed a year-round, permanent 'pan-European' money, credit, and exchange market in which merchant-bankers could conduct their business and financial transactions almost all year round, as the following overview shows:

Tab. 1: The network of the sixteenth-century international fairs: the "système de correspondance".

Place and name of fair	Duration of fair freedom and market freedom (in Brabant)
Lyon, *Foire des Rois*	From the first Monday after Epiphany (January 6)
Villalón, *Feria de Cuaresma*	(mid-Lent)
Bergen-op-Zoom, *Paaschmarkt*	From Easter-Tuesday to Corpus Christi
Lyon, *Foire de Pâques*	From Monday after *Quasimodo geniti* (first Sunday after Easter)
Medina del Campo, *Feria de Mayo*	(4 weeks)
Antwerp, *Sinksenmarkt*	From Pentecost to Assumption (August 15)
Lyon, *Foire d'Août*	From August 4
Medina del Rioseco, *Feria de Agosto*	(4 weeks)
Antwerp, *Bamismarkt*	From St. Bavo (September 30/October 1) to mid-November
Medina del Campo, *Feria de Octubre*	In October
Lyon, *Foire de la Toussaint*	From the first Monday after All Saints'
Bergen-op-Zoom, *Kaltemarkt*	From All Saints' or end of November up to February 10

27 Cassandro, *Libro Giallo*, 54.
28 See Michael Rothmann. *Die Frankfurter Messen im Mittelalter*. Stuttgart: Steiner, 1998.
29 Henri Lapeyre. *Une famille de marchands: les Ruiz*. Paris: S.E.V.P.E.N., 1955, 285.

This systemic innovation offered the merchants of high finance the possibility of providing liquidity by switching back and forth between the different exchange markets in the *ricorsa* procedure: in this process, "the acceptor and the issuer agreed on a third party on whom they drew the bill and whom they simultaneously designated as the payment beneficiary; this third party accepted the bill, paid to himself and drew a new bill on the original issuer in favour of the acceptor."[30] At the same time, those involved in a *ricorsa* transaction could additionally realise arbitrage profits by exploiting the exchange rate differences in these places.[31] Each credit was therefore due about three to four months later, and any sum gained in the trade could be invested immediately in the financial business.[32]

The totality of exchange rate quotations reflecting this almost year-round capital market, including not only the most important financial centres in Italy, but also the Iberian and northwestern European markets, resulted—roughly speaking—in a triangle with centres in Antwerp (without the former 'partner' in the Brabant system, Bergen-op-Zoom), the Castilian fairs, and upper Italy, as well as a focal point or centre in Lyon. This geometric figure symptomatically reflects the differences in importance between the various fairs or financial centres: for large parts of the sixteenth century, Lyon, as the 'hinge' of payment transactions between south and northwestern Europe,[33] enjoyed a pre-eminence over the Brabant and Castilian fairs as well as the Italian financial markets. The significantly greater weight of the Lyon fairs in international exchange traffic was based "both

---

30 North, Von den Warenmessen, 230. See also Giulio Mandich. *Le pacte de ricorsa et le marché italien des changes au XVII*[e] *siècle.* Paris: S.E.V.P.E.N., 1953.

31 José Ignacio Martínez Ruiz. The Credit Market and Profits from Letters of Exchange. *Ricorsa* Exchange Operations between Seville and the "Besançon" International Fairs (1589–1621). *Journal of European Economic History* 33 (2004): 331–355; Claudio Marsilio. The Genoese and Portuguese Financial Operator's Control of the Spanish Silver Market (1627–1657). *Journal of European Economic History* 41:3 (2012): 69–89.

32 Valentín Vázquez de Prada. Die kastilischen Messen im 16. Jahrhundert. In *Frankfurt im Messenetz Europas*, Pohl (ed.), 117–119; Valentín Vázquez de Prada. Cambistas, mercaderes y teologos en Castilla, a mediados del siglo XVI. In *Banchi pubblici, banchi privati e monti di pietà nell'Europa preindustriale. Amministrazione, tecniche operative e ruoli economici*, vol. II. Genoa: Società Ligure di Storia Patria, 1991, 1150–1155; Emiliano Fernandez de Pinedo. Crédit et banque dans la Castille aux XVIe et XVIIe siècles. In *Banchi pubblici*, vol. II, 1035–1050; Ramon Carande. *Carlos V y sus banqueros, la vida económica de España en una fase de su hegemonía, 1516–1556*, vol. 1. Madrid: Revista de Occidente, 1943, 331–332.

33 Marie-Thérèse Boyer-Xambeu, Ghislain Deleplace, Lucien Gillard. Goldstandard, Währung und Finanz im 16. Jahrhundert. In *Geldumlauf, Währungssysteme und Zahlungsverkehr in Nordwesteuropa 1300–1800. Beiträge zur Geldgeschichte der späten Hansezeit*, Michael North (ed.). Cologne, Vienna: Böhlau, 1989, 173.

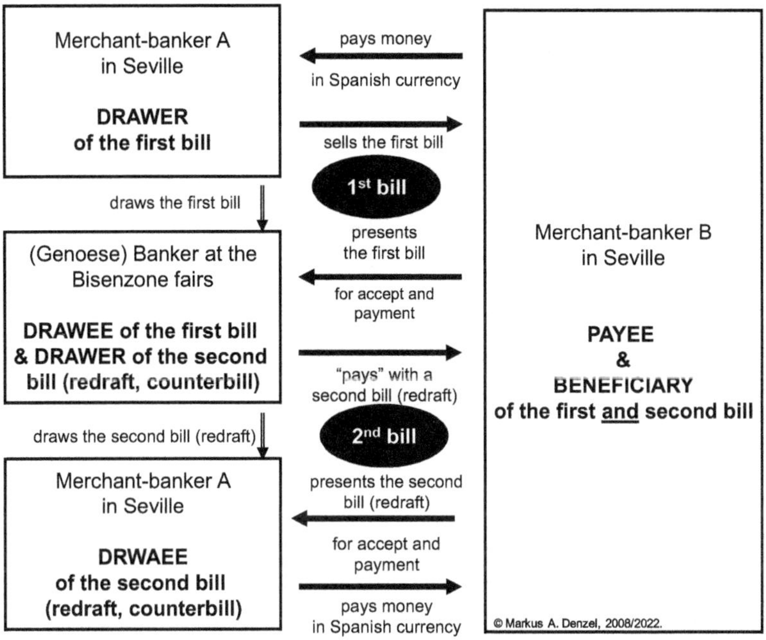

Fig. 2: A *ricorsa* transaction, sixteenth and early seventeenth centuries.

on the large number of bills of exchange scontrated here and on the European reach of this clearing centre."[34]

This monetary innovation was also important for trade fair transactions "insofar as many sales were concluded in advance at the average rate, which had not yet been fixed at all."[35] Transactions were, however, made—particularly in the case of coin deterioration—at rates deviating from this, that is, *al prezzo corrente*, even when freely negotiated.[36] However, the "reference to the official rates in private exchange legitimised the fixed exchange rates; it guaranteed tranquillity among merchants in normal times."[37] Thus, this rate corresponded to the status of *iustum pretium*, which was discussed at the same time, in the School of Salamanca in particular.[38] At the Lyon fairs, moreover, there were no longer any

34 North, Von den Warenmessen, 228.

35 Wilhelm Köpf. *Beiträge zur Geschichte der Messen von Lyon mit besonderer Berücksichtigung des Anteils der oberdeutschen Städte im 16. Jahrhundert.* Ulm: Reiser, 1910, 68.

36 Lapeyre, *Une famille*, 287–288.

37 Boyer-Xambeu, Deleplace, Gillard, Goldstandard, 173.

38 Marjorie Grice-Hutchinson. Contributions of the School of Salamanca to Monetary Theory. In *Economic Effects of the European Expansion, 1492–1824*, José Casas Pardo (ed.). Stuttgart: Steiner,

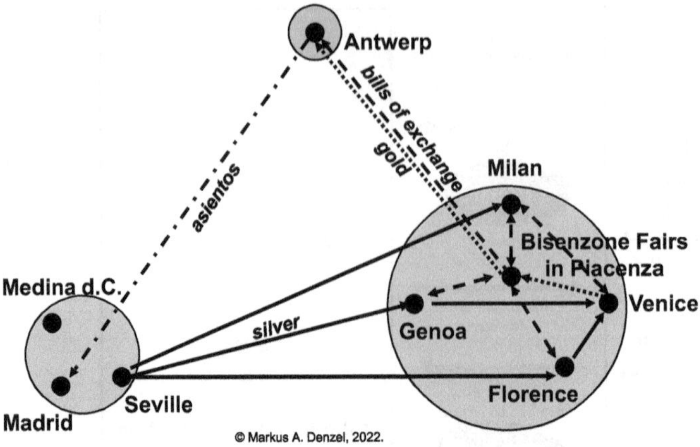

Fig. 3: The Genoese Triangle.[39]

restrictions on the exchange of money or on cashless transactions, so that money could be transferred abroad and could even be lent from fair to fair against ecclesiastical prohibition (the so-called *deposito* or *dépôt*).[40] Overall, the exchange system in Lyon was the most perfected and modern one until after the middle of the sixteenth century, while the Antwerp and Castilian fairs, each of which reverted to a *marché permanent*, embodied a much older type of exchange market that nevertheless fully satisfied the requirements of the respective money and credit markets in the Netherlands and on the Iberian Peninsula.[41] However, in the long run, the exchange and cashless payment transactions in Lyon were also more rel-

1992, 173–198. On the custom of *iustum pretium*, see *Les infortunes du juste prix: marchés, justice sociale et bien commun de l'Antiquité à nos jours*, Véronique Chankowski, Clément Lenoble, Jérôme Maucourant (eds.). Lormont: Le Bord de l'eau, 2020.

39 Source: North, Von den Warenmessen, 232 (Fig. 2).

40 North, Von den Warenmessen, 227. *Dépôts de foire en foire* were settlements of accounting balances from one fair to the next, following which de facto came up to a credit of the considered sum. Pope Pius V (1566–1572) condemned such *dépôts* as usury in 1571. Since that time, they continued to exist only on the semi-official parallel market. See Helma Houtman-de Smedt, Herman Van der Wee. Die Entstehung des modernen Geld- und Finanzwesens Europas in der Neuzeit. In *Europäische Bankengeschichte*, Hans Pohl (ed.). Frankfurt: Knapp, 1993, 106–107; Lapeyre, *Une famille*, 319.

41 Lapeyre, *Une famille*, 285–286. The discussion of this topic is, however, beyond the scope of this article.

evant than the trade in goods, which is why the amount of cash in circulation continued to be rather limited.[42]

The new fairs in Besançon were a further step on the path to exchange fairs, which had already become apparent at the Lyon fairs and at which money, credit, and exchange transactions dominated the trade fair scene. In competition with the Lyon fairs controlled by the French king from the House of Valois, Genoese bankers, who were linked to his rival for hegemony in Europe, the Habsburg Charles V, began to set up independent Italian exchange fairs in Besançon (*Bisenzone*) as early as the 1530s.[43] From the beginning, they were primarily—and later, exclusively—fairs of exchange, that is, "*foire[s] des changes par definition.*"[44] When the *dépôts de foire en foire* were banned in Lyon, the need had arisen to be able to draw bills of exchange from here to a nearby place in order to maintain the fiction of the *distantia loci* between the issuer and the acceptor of the bill. Thus, the Genoese Bisenzone fairs gained greater importance.[45] In contrast to all previous fairs, at the four Bisenzone fairs held in Piacenza since 1579, which had a similar timetable cycle to that of Lyon—albeit postponed by a few days—the money or exchange business had become the sole activity of the fairgoers. As Michael North has observed, "banking was no longer the complement of commercial activity, it became the engine of the fair business, the only centre of attraction to attract the attention of those in search of fresh money to balance their commercial transactions."[46] This "[detached] the fair exchange completely from the commodity trade [. . .]. There was only the exchange fair, and no more commodity fair."[47]

In the decades between 1580 and 1610, during the boom period of the Bisenzone fairs, a "closed club" (according to Fernand Braudel) of only 30 to about 100 *banchieri di conto*, who also set the individual rates, turned over an average of

42 Jürgen Schneider, Nils Brübach. Frankreichs Messeplätze und das europäische Messesystem in der frühen Neuzeit. In *Frankfurt im Messenetz Europas*, Pohl (ed.), 177.

43 Although the fairs did not have a fixed location from their early days and were held in various towns in Franche-Compté, Savoy, and western Italy, the Italian name 'Bisenzone' remained the characteristic name for the Genoese fairs, regardless of where they took place. See Pierre Racine. Messen in Italien im 16. Jahrhundert: Die Wechselmessen von Piacenza. In *Frankfurt im Messenetz Europas*, Pohl (ed.), 155–156; José Gentil da Silva. *Banque et crédit en Italie au XVIIe siècle*. Paris: S.E.V.P.E.N., 1969, 33–36; Giuseppe Felloni. Kredit und Banken in Italien, 15.–17. Jahrhundert. In *Kredit im spätmittelalterlichen und frühneuzeitlichen Europa*, Michael North (ed.). Cologne, Vienna: Böhlau, 1991, 19.

44 Gentil da Silva, *Banque et crédit*, 12.

45 Houtman-de Smedt, Van der Wee, Geld- und Finanzwesen, 109.

46 Racine, Messen in Italien, 169, 157.

47 North, Von den Warenmessen, 230.

about 37 million *scudi* per fair and, from 1610 to 1620, about 12 million *scudi*—and this in ever greater volume with *ricorsa* business. This made Piacenza "the centre of financial speculation in the Christian world" and the "world's banking centre [. . .] where the rates of all the great European coins are fixed." At the same time, the entire system of international financial markets was thus concentrated in the hands of a small group of bankers "who make themselves masters of the financial and money markets."[48]

At the Genoese Bisenzone fairs, all exchange rates between different currencies were defined by their relation to a basic coin—the *écu de marc* or *scudo di marche* (or *di marchi*), following the example of the Lyonnaise *écu d'or au soleil*. This was the result of a compensation process to the benefit of the Genoese—between the highest-valued coins of that year and, more precisely, between the *scudo*-coins of Spain, Antwerp, Venice, Genoa, Florence, and Naples. Unlike the fairs of Lyon, a single national currency was no longer the basis for the money of account; the merchant-bankers 'calculated,' so to speak, a common currency. Between 1552 and 1763, the proportion of this money of account to the average gold weight of the *scudo de oro in oro* (*écu d'or en or*) remained at 100:101, "which proves the strength of the moneys of account and the flexible ways and methods, by which cash payments, expressed in 'scudi di marchi', could be completed all over the world."[49] This stable money of account led to a stable *conto*, the official determination of the exchange rate, which was "always determined by taking into account the rates of the other fairs; a merchant or a banker, who drew a bill of exchange at the Genovese fairs or who lent money there, would not have to fear foreign exchange losses," which greatly enhanced the attractiveness of these exchange fairs.[50]

At the Castilian fairs, there also existed a currency of account, the *ducado de cambio* of 375 *maravedis*. In the history of the development of different moneys of account, this ducat of account should be put at the same level as the Geneva or early Lyon fairs; for the merchant-bankers trading at the Castilian fairs, it performed perfectly. It made its users independent form the rise and fall of silver prices and, consequently, from the inflationary tendencies of the Spanish price revolution. However, since it was only based on the Castilian currency, it was not

---

48 Racine, Messen in Italien, 160–161, 168, 156.

49 Houtman-de Smedt, Van der Wee, Geld- und Finanzwesen, 110. See also Giuseppe Felloni. Un système monétaire de marc dans les foires de change génoises, XVIe–XVIIIe siècles. In *Études d'histoire monétaire. Textes réunis*, John Day (ed.). Lille: Presses universitaires, 1984, 249–260; Racine, Messen in Italien, 155–156, 161; Gentil da Silva, *Banque et crédit*, 81.

50 North, Von den Warenmessen, 230.

internationally accepted like the *scudo di marche* of the Bisenzone fairs.[51] This is why quotations in *ducados de cambio* showed somewhat larger fluctuation margins than quotations in *scudi di marche.*

At the same time, the great international fairs and the entire fair system of the sixteenth century had another special function—that of financing the crown or the state, that is, the granting of credit to rulers by merchant-bankers on a scale unknown in earlier centuries. This was just as much the case at the Castilian fairs for Spain as at those in Lyon for France. The peak of this development was again the Bisenzone fairs, for the entirety of the innovations outlined above were used, in particular, by the Genoese bankers who, in the service of the Spanish Crown, played a decisive role in the redistribution of the growing influx of American silver in Europe. They made large sums available to the Spanish Crown by means of credit agreements (*asientos*), which were then repaid to them, ideally from the proceeds of the American silver as well as from the royal *juros*—that is, from the perpetual or temporary pensions that the Spanish king received. The bills of exchange that the Genoese drew in this context to trading places where the Spanish government received or expected money represented both their present and future credit. The determining elements for the fairs were thus in each case the time of the arrival of the silver in Seville, the influence of the court *camarilla* in Madrid, and the galley transport of the silver from Seville to Italy. The settlement of all these transactions took place primarily at the Bisenzone fairs. For this reason, the Bisenzone fairs lost their importance when the Genoese bankers gradually withdrew from business with the Spanish Crown after the third suspension of payment by the Spanish crown in 1607 and withdrew their funds to Italy. Held in Novi since 1641, the Bisenzone fairs were only of regional importance after 1650.[52]

Despite the innovative capacity of the great international fairs in the fields of money, credit, and exchange markets, it is important to keep in mind that as a consequence of the process of commercialisation and increasing merchant bankers' crown finance during the late fifteenth and, above all, the sixteenth century, international fairs would become the actual foci of financial crises, having developed into centres of cashless payment settlements, particularly between the state and merchant creditors.[53] Such was the case at the fairs of Brabant and Castile as

51 Claudio Marsilio. "Four times a year for so many years". The Italian Exchange Fairs during the XVIth–XVIIth Centuries. *Bankhistorisches Archiv* 36:2 (2010): 151–165.

52 Racine, Messen in Italien, 162–168; Gentil da Silva, *Banque et crédit*, 65–71.

53 Markus A. Denzel. The Role of Institutions in Financial Crises: Fairs—Public Banks—Stock Exchanges (13th to 18th Century). In *Financial Crises, 1300–1800/Le crisi financiarie, 1300–1800. Selezione di ricerche.* Florence: Firenze University Press, 2016, 427–450.

well as at the international fairs of Lyon or the Genoese Bisenzone fairs. In all cases, these exchange fairs served the settlement of payments between the crown and its creditors. When the crown was unwilling to pay off its credits with interest once or perhaps even several times in a row, a financial crisis emerged from these international fairs. Classic examples of such occurrences are the *Grand Parti* in Lyon and the Spanish financial crises of the second half of the sixteenth and the beginning of the seventeenth century, which had their origin at the Castilian fairs (even though the latter suspensions of payments have been reinterpreted recently as short-term liquidity crises rather than as a sign of unsustainable debts[54]).

Conclusion

This article attempts to show that the large international fairs played an outstanding role in European economic, trade, and financial history as money, credit, and exchange markets in three respects. On the one hand, they provided the internationally active merchants with the necessary liquidity for their expanding commercial transactions, which was necessary due to Europe's relative precious metal scarcity in order to avoid a deflationary constriction of European economic activity. On the other hand, the trade fairs were used to facilitate, settle, and secure the financing of crowns and states, especially in the sixteenth century, but also earlier in parts. Thirdly—and most importantly—the large international fairs were centres of financial innovation that contributed significantly to the development of the cashless payment and credit system typical of Europe. As places of exceptionally large gatherings of expert merchants, they accelerated the development and spread of the bill of exchange as by far the most important cashless payment and credit medium of the premodern era, enabled highly efficient settlement mechanisms among merchant bankers and, through the creation of moneys of account, contributed significantly to the monetary security of the settled payment transactions—a function that was to be taken over by the public banks from the seventeenth century onwards.

---

54 Maurico Drelichman, Hans-Joachim Voth. The Sustainable Debts of Philipp II: A Reconstruction of Castile's Fiscal Position, 1566–1596. *Journal of Economic History* 70:4 (2010): 813–842; Maurico Drelichman, Hans-Joachim Voth. *Lending to the Borrower from Hell. Debts, Taxes, and Default in the Age of Philipp II*. Princeton, Oxford: Princeton University Press, 2014. See also Maurico Drelichman, Hans-Joachim Voth. Serial Defaults, Serial Profits: Returns to Sovereign Lending in Habsburg Spain, 1566–1600. *Explorations in Economic History* 48 (2011): 1–19.

This finding, which has been developed here using the case studies of the large international fairs in Western Europe up to the sixteenth century, could be confirmed for later centuries at fairs further east:[55] the Leipzig fairs, for example, functioned in the second half of the eighteenth and in the early nineteenth century as a central financial interface between the merchant communities of western and eastern Europe, between the cashless payment system of the west and the traditional cash payments of the east. In the nineteenth century, this boundary between these two payment cultures shifted significantly further east, all the way to the fairs of Nizhny Novgorod which, not least because of their financial function, became the central fairs of the Russian Empire. Here (to put it very crudely), the merchants from large parts of Asia, with their traditional methods of payment and credit habits, met the merchants, bankers, and industrialists from Saint Petersburg and Moscow, who were now working according to western European models. These two fairs—Leipzig and Nizhny Novgorod—at the time of their respective heydays communicated the new, innovative techniques in payment transactions and credit business to ever wider commercial circles, as had already happened in the twelfth century with the financial innovations of northern Italy to the merchants of northwestern Europe via the Champagne Fairs. A similar, although not comparably sustainable, development can also be noted for the southeastern European region in the nineteenth century. Here, the fairs also developed more and more into credit markets and in some special individual cases even into exchange markets, if one thinks of the fairs in Galaţ, Jassy, and Braila in the Danubian principalities, for example, or—to a much more limited extent—Uzundžova and Serres in the Macedonian-Bulgarian area.

The outstanding function of fairs as money, credit, and exchange markets only gradually became obsolete when other financial institutions were developed that took over these tasks and did so all year round. The fact that fairs were only held at certain times of the year limited their functionality and caused them to lose their importance—a process which had begun already since the sixteenth century—when competing institutions were able to offer their services all year round. The first daily stock exchange meeting in Bruges, the extension of market freedom in Antwerp to a *marché permanent*, and the opening of public banks in Venice and Amsterdam made financial transactions possible under conditions that were secure in monetary and legal terms, as if a fair took place throughout the year. Starting in the Netherlands in the seventeenth century, the year-round

55 For a more detailed exploration, see Markus A. Denzel. Das System der Messen in Europa—Rückgrat des Handels, des Zahlungsverkehrs und der Kommunikation (9. bis 19. Jahrhundert). In *Europäische Messegeschichte, 9.–19. Jahrhundert. Forschungsstand und Forschungsperspektiven*, Markus A. Denzel (ed.). Cologne, Weimar, Vienna: Böhlau, 2018, 369–431.

trading and financial business secured and supported by stock exchanges and public banks brought about another surge in commercialisation, culminating in the Second Commercial Revolution in northwestern Europe at the turn of the seventeenth and eighteenth centuries. With their innovative techniques—such as endorsement and discounting in cashless payment and credit transactions—the new year-round institutions made the traditional fairs more and more obsolete. Since they no longer needed to function as money, credit, and exchange markets, the fairs gradually lost their function as commodity markets and thus their 'status' as international fairs. Therefore, already in the second half of the fifteenth century, the Geneva fairs as the last medieval fairs lost their financial functions to Lyon with its new, innovative institutions. The Castilian fairs lost their function as international financial markets after 1620, the Bisenzone fairs after 1650, Frankfurt am Main after 1720,[56] and the Lyon fairs only managed to survive into the eighteenth century because of their specific importance for the international silk trade. Antwerp developed further into a stock exchange-supported *marché permanent*, while Leipzig and, in its wake, Nizhny Novgorod mutated into sample fairs—a further and, for the twentieth century, decisive innovation *sui generis*.

Nevertheless, it remains to be said that the great international fairs experienced their rise not only in their function as international commodity markets and communication centres, but also and particularly because they could function as money, credit, and exchange markets since the High Middle Ages. When they lost this financial function—whether as individual fairs or as commercial institutions as a whole—their decline also set in. Although regularly flanked by a multitude of other time-related factors, the loss of the financial function was a decisive moment for the individual as well as the institutional decline of fairs. It can be said that the classical international fairs of the premodern era—not the sample fairs of the industrialised era—are always characterised by their function as money, credit, and exchange markets, and this function thus appears as a central constitutive element of the 'fair' as an institution.

---

56 See Peter Beyer. Leipzigs Auseinandersetzung mit Frankfurt am Main (1706–1726). Symptom des Aufstiegs zur führenden deutschen Messestadt. In *Leipzigs Messen 1497–1997. Gestaltwandel. Umbrüche. Neubeginn*, vol. 1, Hartmut Zwahr, Thomas Topfstedt, Günter Bentele (eds.). Cologne, Weimar, Vienna: Böhlau, 1999, 193–204.

Bibliography

Bassermann, Elisabeth. *Die Champagnermessen. Ein Beitrag zur Geschichte des Kredits*. Tübingen: Mohr, 1911.

Bergier, Jean-François. *Genève et l'économie européenne de la Renaissance*. Paris: S.E.V.P.E.N., 1963.

Beyer, Peter. Leipzigs Auseinandersetzung mit Frankfurt am Main (1706–1726). Symptom des Aufstiegs zur führenden deutschen Messestadt. In *Leipzigs Messen 1497–1997. Gestaltwandel. Umbrüche. Neubeginn*, Hartmut Zwahr, Thomas Topfstedt, Günter Bentele (eds.). Vol. 1. Cologne, Weimar, Vienna: Böhlau, 1999, 193–204.

Blockmans, Wim. Das westeuropäische Messenetz im 14. und 15. Jahrhundert. In *Frankfurt im Messenetz Europas—Erträge der Forschung*, Hans Pohl (ed.). Vol. 1 of *Brücke zwischen den Völkern—Zur Geschichte der Frankfurter Messe*, Rainer Koch (ed.). Frankfurt: Historisches Museum, 1991, 37–50.

Boyer-Xambeu, Marie-Thérèse, Ghislain Deleplace, Lucien Gillard. Goldstandard, Währung und Finanz im 16. Jahrhundert. In *Geldumlauf, Währungssysteme und Zahlungsverkehr in Nordwesteuropa 1300–1800. Beiträge zur Geldgeschichte der späten Hansezeit*, Michael North (ed.). Cologne, Vienna: Böhlau, 1989, 167–181.

Braudel, Fernand. *Sozialgeschichte des 15.–18. Jahrhunderts. Der Handel*. Munich: C.H. Beck 1986.

Carande, Ramon. *Carlos V y sus banqueros, la vida económica de España en una fase de su hegemonía, 1516–1556*. Madrid: Revista de Occidente, 1943.

Cassandro, Michele. *Il Libro Giallo di Ginevra della compagnia fiorentina di Antonio della Casa e Simone Guadagni 1453–1454*. Prato: Istituto internazionale di storia economica "F. Datini," 1975.

Chankowski, Véronique, Clément Lenoble, Jérôme Maucourant (eds.). *Les infortunes du juste prix: marchés, justice sociale et bien commun de l'Antiquité à nos jours*, Lormont: Le Bord de l'eau, 2020.

Day, John. The Great Bullion Famine of the Fifteenth Century. *Past & Present* 79 (1978): 3–54.

De Roover, Raymond. *L'évolution de la lettre de change, XIVe–XVIIIe siècles*. Paris: S.E.V.P.E.N., 1953.

De Roover, Raymond. Le contrat de change depuis la fin du treizième siècle jusqu'au début du dix-septième. *Revue belge de philologie et d'histoire* 25:1–2 (1946/47): 111–128.

De Roover, Raymond. *Money, Banking and Credit in Medieval Bruges. Italian Merchant Bankers, Lombards and Money-Changers. A Study in the Origins of Banking*. Cambridge, MA: Cambridge University Press, 1948.

De Roover, Raymond. New Interpretations of the History of Banking. In *Business, Banking and Economic Thought in Late Medieval and Early Modern Europe: Selected Studies of Raymond de Roosver*, Julius Kirshner (ed.). Chicago, London: University of Chicago Press, 1974, 200–238.

De Roover, Raymond. Précisions sur l'histoire de la lettre et du contrat de change (d'après des documents inédits des Archivs Datini à Prato). *La vie économique et sociale* 23 (1952): 44–67.

Denzel, Markus A. Das System der Messen in Europa—Rückgrat des Handels, des Zahlungsverkehrs und der Kommunikation (9. bis 19. Jahrhundert). In *Europäische Messegeschichte, 9.–19. Jahrhundert. Forschungsstand und Forschungsperspektiven*, Markus A. Denzel (ed.). Cologne, Weimar, Vienna: Böhlau, 2018, 369–431.

Denzel, Markus A. *Das System des bargeldlosen Zahlungsverkehrs europäischer Prägung vom Mittelalter bis 1914*. Stuttgart: Steiner, 2008.

Denzel, Markus A. Der Beitrag von Messen und Märkten zum Integrationsprozeß des internationalen bargeldlosen Zahlungsverkehrssystems in Europa (13.–18. Jahrhundert). In *Fiere e mercati nella integrazione delle economie europee, secc. XIII–XVIII*, Simonetta Cavaciocchi (ed.). Florence: Le Monnier, 2001, 819–835.

Denzel, Markus A. Exchange Rates and Silver Prices at European Fairs, 16th–18th Centuries. In *Mining, Money and Markets in the Early Modern Atlantic. Digital Approaches and New Perspectives*, Claudia de Lozanne Jefferies, Renate Pieper, Markus A. Denzel (eds.). London: Routledge, 2019, 349–362.

Denzel, Markus A. *Handbook of World Exchange Rates, 1590 to 1914*. Farnham, Burlington: Ashgate, 2010.

Denzel, Markus A. *Kurialer Zahlungsverkehr im 13. und 14. Jahrhundert. Servitien- und Annatenzahlungen aus dem Bistum Bamberg*. Stuttgart: Steiner, 1991.

Denzel, Markus A. The Role of Institutions in Financial Crises: Fairs—Public Banks—Stock Exchanges (13th to 18th Century). In *Financial Crises, 1300–1800/Le crisi finanziarie, 1300–1800. Selezione di ricerche*. Florence: Firenze University Press, 2016, 427–450.

Denzel, Markus A. Wechsel, Wechsler, Wechselbrief. In *Lexikon des Mittelalters*, vol. VIII. Munich: LexMA 1997, 2086–2089.

Drelichman, Maurico, Hans-Joachim Voth. *Lending to the Borrower from Hell: Debts, Taxes, and Default in the Age of Philipp II*. Princeton, Oxford: Princeton University Press, 2014.

Drelichman, Maurico, Hans-Joachim Voth. Serial Defaults, Serial Profits: Returns to Sovereign Lending in Habsburg Spain, 1566–1600. *Explorations in Economic History* 48 (2011): 1–19.

Drelichman, Maurico, Hans-Joachim Voth. The Sustainable Debts of Philipp II: A Reconstruction of Castile's Fiscal Position, 1566–1596. *Journal of Economic History* 70:4 (2010): 813–842.

Face, R.D. Techniques of Business in Trade between the Fairs of Champagne and the South of Europe in the 12th and 13th Centuries. *Economic History Review* 10 (1957/58): 427–438.

Felloni, Giuseppe. Kredit und Banken in Italien, 15.–17. Jahrhundert. In *Kredit im spätmittelalterlichen und frühneuzeitlichen Europa*, Michael North (ed.). Cologne, Vienna: Böhlau, 1991, 9–23.

Felloni, Giuseppe. Un système monétaire de marc dans les foires de change génoises, XVIe–XVIIIe siècles. In *Études d'histoire monétaire. Textes réunis*, John Day (ed.). Lille: Presses universitaires, 1984, 249–260.

Fernandez de Pinedo, Emiliano. Crédit et banque dans la Castille aux XVIe et XVIIe siècles. In *Banchi pubblici, banchi privati e monti di pietà nell'Europa preindustriale. Amministrazione, tecniche operative e ruoli economici*, vol. II. Genoa: Società Ligure di Storia Patria, 1991, 1035–1050.

Gentil da Silva, José. *Banque et crédit en Italie au XVIIe siècle*. Paris: S.E.V.P.E.N., 1969.

Grice-Hutchinson, Marjorie. Contributions of the School of Salamanca to Monetary Theory. In *Economic Effects of the European Expansion, 1492–1824*, José Casas Pardo (ed.). Stuttgart: Steiner, 1992, 173–198.

Houtman-de Smedt, Helma, Herman Van der Wee. Die Entstehung des modernen Geld- und Finanzwesens Europas in der Neuzeit. In *Europäische Bankengeschichte*, Hans Pohl (ed.). Frankfurt: Knapp, 1993, 73–173.

Irsigler, Franz, Winfried Reichert. Les foires de Champagne. *In Messen, Jahrmärkte und Stadtentwicklung in Europa/Foires, marchés annuels et développement urbain en Europe*, Franz Irsigler, Michel Pauly (eds.). Trier: Porta Alba, 2007, 89–105.

Koch, Rainer (ed.). *Brücke zwischen den Völkern—Zur Geschichte der Frankfurter Messe*, 3 Vol. Frankfurt: Historisches Museum, 1991.

Köpf, Wilhelm. *Beiträge zur Geschichte der Messen von Lyon mit besonderer Berücksichtigung des Anteils der oberdeutschen Städte im 16. Jahrhundert*. Ulm: Reiser, 1910.

Körner, Martin. Kreditformen und Zahlungsverkehr im spätmittelalterlichen und frühneuzeitlichen Luzern. *Scripta Mercaturae* 21 (1987): 116–157.

Lapeyre, Henri. *Une famille de marchands: les Ruiz*. Paris: S.E.V.P.E.N., 1955.

Leone, Alfonso. Some Preliminary Remarks on the Study of Foreign Currency Exchange in the Medieval Period. *Journal of European Economic History* 12 (1983): 619–629.

Mandich, Giulio. *Le pacte de ricorsa et le marché italien des changes au XVIIe siècle*. Paris: S.E.V.P.E.N., 1953.

Marsilio, Claudio. "Four times a year for so many years": The Italian Exchange Fairs during the XVIth–XVIIth Centuries. *Bankhistorisches Archiv* 36:2 (2010): 151–165.

Marsilio, Claudio. The Genoese and Portuguese Financial Operator's Control of the Spanish Silver Market (1627–1657). *Journal of European Economic History* 41:3 (2012): 69–89.

Martínez Ruiz, José Ignacio. The Credit Market and Profits from Letters of Exchange: *Ricorsa* Exchange Operations between Seville and the "Besançon" International Fairs (1589–1621). *Journal of European Economic History* 33 (2004): 331–355.

Mollat, Michel. *Der königliche Kaufmann. Jacques Cœur oder der Geist des Unternehmertums*. Munich: Beck, 1991.

Munro, John H. *Bullion Flows and Monetary Policies in England and the Low Countries, 1350–1500*. Hampshire, Brookfield: Ashgate, 1992.

Munro, John H. Instrumentum Ex Causa Cambii. In *Von Aktie bis Zoll. Ein historisches Lexikon des Geldes*, Michael North (ed.). Munich: C.H. Beck, 1995, 174–175.

Munro, John H. Wechsel. In *Von Aktie bis Zoll. Ein historisches Lexikon des Geldes*, Michael North (ed.). Munich: C.H. Beck, 1995, 413–416.

Munro, John H. *Wool, Cloth and Gold. The Struggle for Bullion in Anglo-Burgundian Trade, 1340–1478*. Brussels: Édition de l'Université de Bruxelles, 1972.

North, Michael. Von den Warenmessen zu den Wechselmessen. Grundlagen des europäischen Zahlungsverkehrs in Spätmittelalter und Früher Neuzeit. In *Europäische Messen und Märktesysteme in Mittelalter und Neuzeit*, Peter Johanek, Heinz Stoob (eds.). Cologne, Weimar, Vienna: Böhlau, 1996, 223–238.

Racine, Pierre. Messen in Italien im 16. Jahrhundert: Die Wechselmessen von Piacenza. In *Frankfurt im Messenetz Europas*, Pohl (ed.), 155–170.

Reynolds, R.L. Genoese Trade in the Late Twelfth Century, Particularly in Cloth from the Fairs of Champagne. *Journal of Economic and Business History* 3:3 (1931): 362–381.

Rothmann, Michael. *Die Frankfurter Messen im Mittelalter*. Stuttgart: Steiner, 1998.

Schaps, Georg. *Zur Geschichte des Wechselindossaments*. Stuttgart: Ferdinand Enke, 1892.

Schneider, Jürgen, Nils Brübach. Frankreichs Messeplätze und das europäische Messesystem in der frühen Neuzeit. In *Frankfurt im Messenetz Europas*, Pohl (ed.), 171–190.

Schneider. Jürgen. Messen, Banken und Börsen (15.–18. Jahrhundert). In *Banchi pubblici, banchi privati e monti di pietà nell'Europa preindustriale. Amministrazione, tecniche operative e ruoli economici*, vol. I. Genoa: Società Ligure di Storia Patria, 1991, 133–169.

Schönfelder, Alexander. *Handelsmessen und Kreditwirtschaft im Hochmittelalter—Die Champagnemessen*. Saarbrücken-Scheidt: Dadder, 1988.

Thomas, Heinz. Beiträge zur Geschichte der Champagne-Messen. *Vierteljahrschrift für Sozial- und Wirtschaftsgeschichte* 49 (1977): 433–467.

Thomas, Heinz. Die Champagnemessen. In *Frankfurt im Messenetz Europas*, Pohl (ed.), 13–36.

Vázquez de Prada, Valentín. Cambistas, mercaderes y teologos en Castilla, a mediados del siglo XVI. In *Banchi pubblici*, vol. II, 1135–1155.

Vázquez de Prada, Valentín. Die kastilischen Messen im 16. Jahrhundert. In *Frankfurt im Messenetz Europas*, Pohl (ed.), 113–131.

Spufford, Peter. *Handbook of Medieval Exchange*. London: Offices of the Royal Historical Society, 1986.

Von Stromer, Wolfgang. Hartgeld, Kredit und Giralgeld. Zu einer monetären Konjunkturtheorie des Spätmittelalters und der Wende zur Neuzeit. In *La moneta nell'economia europea, secoli XIII–XVIII. Atti della "Settima Settimana di studio" (11–17 aprile 1975)*, Vera Barbagli Bagnoli (ed.). Florence: Le Monnier, 1981, 105–125.

Weissen, Kurt. *Marktstrategien der Kurienbanken. Die Geschichte der Alberti, Medici und Spinelli in Deutschland (1400–1475)*. Heidelberg: Heidelberg University Press, 2021.

Wendehorst, Alfred. Wer konnte im Mittelalter lesen und schreiben? In *Schulen und Studien im sozialen Wandel des hohen und späten Mittelalters*, Johannes Fried (ed.). Sigmaringen: Thorbecke, 1986, 9–33.

Chapter III: **Merchants at fairs**

Clément Lenoble

From Florence to Lyon and Geneva fairs: the Pazzi family, the King of France, and the shifting economic geography during the late 15th century

While Avignon records suggest that the Pazzi family's business was flourishing in the Comtat Venaissin and in Provence in the fifteenth century, their deposit bank went bankrupt in 1465.[1] The head of the family, Alamano, was imprisoned for some time. This bankruptcy is not very exceptional at a time when many of Europe's largest banks, notably Florentine ones, appear to have been entangled in risky financial operations for the benefit of the French and English monarchies, and more generally in a credit system where "public" and "private" interests were intertwined.[2] These events are part of a context of "crisis" in a rapidly changing world.[3] As we shall see, the banking activities of the Pazzi family in Avignon seem to have moved to Lyon, right after the bankruptcy in Avignon. However, the conditions of this transfer need to be clarified because there are few records left. Even if this event is part of a more general process of territorial shifting in regional and European economic geography at the end of the fifteenth century, the reasons and mechanisms that led the Pazzi family to this bankruptcy and to the transfer of their activities from Avignon to Lyon in France—since Avignon

1 Deliberations of 4 September 1467, Archives municipales d'Avignon, BB (1436–1471), fol. 187.
2 Several examples of this well-known phenomenon, including the emblematic case of the Medici family, can be found in Raymond De Roover. *The Rise and Decline of the Medici Bank: 1397–1494*. Washington, DC: Beard Books, 1999; Carlo M. Cipolla. *Storia economica dell'Europa pre-industriale*. Bologna: Il Mulino, 1974; Franco Franceschi, Richard A. Goldthwaite, Reinhold C. Mueller. *Il Rinascimento italiano e l'Europa. Volume quarto. Commercio e cultura mercantile*. Treviso-Costabissara (Vicenza): Fondazione Cassamarca—Angelo Colla editore, 2007. On banking practices that mix private interests and "public finances," see the analyses of Giacomo Todeschini. *La banca e il ghetto. Una storia italiana*. Bari: Laterza, 2016. See also the recent synthesis devoted to the Florentine case by Lorenzo Tanzini. *1345. La bancarotta di Firenze. Una storia di banchieri, fallimenti e finanza*. Rome: Salerno, 2018.
3 See, in particular, Mathieu Arnoux. Croissance et crises dans le monde médiéval XIe–XVe siècle. *Cahiers du monde russe* 46:1–2 (2005). http://journals.openedition.org/monderusse/8787 (30 April 2024); Mathieu Arnoux. L'Europe de la 'grande transformation.' In *Histoire du monde au XVe siècle*, vol. 2. Paris: Pluriel, 2017, 590–617; Luciano Palermo. *Sviluppo economico e società preindustriali. Cicli, strutture e congiunture in Europa dal medioevo alla prima età moderna*. Rome: Viella, 1997.

https://doi.org/10.1515/9783111621296-010

in the fifteenth century was not part of the French Kingdom—remain obscure. I will try to shed some light on them by delving into the credit and trading activities of the Avignon branch of the Pazzis between Sicily, Marseille, Avignon, Lyon, and Geneva.

The settlement of Florentine merchant-bankers in Lyon at the end of the fifteenth century is poorly documented. However, several elements show that the Italian presence was significant at least from the years 1465–1470, when the Pazzis of Avignon transferred their activities.[4] This transfer took place at the time of the decline of the Geneva fairs and at the dawn of the rise of those in Lyon. It was precisely at this time that the kings of France tried to develop the Lyon market, its fairs under Charles VII, and the production of silk under Louis XI.[5]

The historiographical tradition inspired by economic theory tends to insist on the spontaneous, natural, or at best cyclical nature of the emergence of new markets. However, in the case study presented in this essay, we will see that there are several indications that Louis XI and his entourage may have been involved in the bankruptcy of the Pazzi's bank in Avignon. The simultaneous rise of the Lyon fairs and the success of Italian merchant-bankers on the local markets allow us to question the reasons for the emergence of new fairs and new businesses. This article is a first attempt at offering a modest contribution to the history of economic changes during the late fifteenth and early sixteenth centuries and, more particularly, to that of the transformations of European economic geography, which moved towards the north-west and of which the flourishing of the fairs in Geneva

4 Hippolyte André Suzanne de Charpin-Feugerolles. *Les Florentins à Lyon*. Lyon: Louis Brun, 1893, 160–161; Michele Cassandro. I forestieri a Lione nel'400 e '500: la nazione fiorentina. In *Dentro la città. Stranieri e realtà urbane nell'Europa dei secoli XII–XVI*, Gabriella Rossetti (ed.). Naples: Liguori, 1989, 151–162; Jacqueline Boucher. *Présence italienne à Lyon à la Renaissance du milieu du XVe à la fin du XVIe siècle*. Lyon: Éditions LUGD, 1994; Agnès Pallini-Martin. L'installation d'une famille de marchands-banquiers florentins à Lyon au début du XVIe siècle: les Salviati. In *Lyon vu/e d'ailleurs (1245–1800). Échanges, compétitions et perceptions*, Jean-Louis Gaulin, Susanne Rau (eds.). Lyon: Presses universitaires de Lyon, 2009, 71–90; Agnès Pallini-Martin. *Banque, négoce et politique. Les Florentins à Lyon au moment des guerres d'Italie*. Paris: Garnier, 2018; Heinrich Lang. *Wirtschaften als kulturelle Praxis. Die Florentiner Salviati und die Augsburger Welser auf den Märkten in Lyon (1507–1559)*. Stuttgart: Franz Steiner, 2020, 131–132.

5 André Pelletier, Jacques Rossiaud, Françoise Bayard, Pierre Cayez. *Histoire de Lyon: des origines à nos jours*. Lyon: Éditions lyonnaises d'art et d'histoire, 2007, 265; Richard Gascon. *Grand commerce et vie urbaine au XVIe siècle: Lyon et ses marchands (circa 1520–circa 1580)*. Paris, the Hague: Mouton, 1971, 308; Vital de Valous. *Étienne Turquet et les origines de la Fabrique Lyonnaise. Recherches et documents sur l'institution de la manufacture des étoffes de soie (1466–1536). Notice historique accompagnée d'une généalogie de la famille Turquet*. Lyon: Auguste Brun, 1868, 8; Joseph Vaesen, Étienne Charavay. *Lettres de Louis XI, roi de France*, vol. III: 1465–1469. Paris: Renouard, 1887, 122, no. 1.

and Lyon are tangible elements, as well as that of the history of the "economic policy" of the kingdom of France.[6]

From Florence to Avignon: the arrival of the Pazzi family

The local records do not allow, in the current state of our knowledge, to determine with precision the date of the arrival of these Florentine merchant-bankers in Avignon. Diving into the *mare magnum* of Avignon notaries' registers in search of a particular family is not easy, but local scholars and historians of Avignon have already found a good part of the information contained in this documentation.[7] These wealthy Florentine businessmen did set up a counter and a currency exchange bench in Avignon, but the date of this establishment remains unknown to this day. We can only imagine that they settled on the banks of the Rhône at the beginning of the fourteenth century, when the papal court seems to have taken up residence there permanently. This is suggested by the first known mentions of their presence in the registers of the Avignon notaries at the end of the fourteenth century. Before that, the records are too few and we cannot find any information about their businesses. It is therefore impossible to know if Aghinolfo, the first member of the family mentioned in local records, was also the first to arrive. In 1376, Aghinolfo de' Pazzi had been authorised to remain in Avignon after the court's return to Rome, and he subsequently asked the Florentine government to enter the *popolani* group.[8] This tenuous evidence seems to indicate that the arrival of the Pazzi family and their activities in the Comtat Venaissin were related to the presence of the pope up until that point. However, Yves Renouard does not seem to have found them during his investigation into the relationship between the papacy in Avignon and the Florentine companies.[9] Above

6 See (with caution) René Gandilhon. *Politique économique de Louis XI.* Paris: Presses universitaires de France, 1941; Richard Gascon. Nationalisme économique et géographie des foires. La querelle des foires de Lyon (1484–1494). *Cahiers d'histoire* 1 (1956): 253–287.

7 Léon-Honoré Labande. *Avignon au XVe siècle. Légation de Charles de Bourbon et du cardinal Julien de La Rovère.* Paris: A. Picard, 1920; Yves Renouard. *Les relations des papes d'Avignon et des compagnies commerciales et bancaires de 1316 à 1378.* Paris: E. de Boccard, 1941; Monique Cler. Un homme d'affaires avignonnais du XVe siècle: Alaman de Passis. *Provence historique* 7:30 (1957): 305–336.

8 Pompeo Litta Biumi. *Famiglie celebri di Italia. Pazzi di Firenze.* Milan: Presso l'autore (Tipografia delle famiglie italiane), 1851, table 5.

9 Renouard, *Les relations.*

all, the fact that they chose to stay in Avignon reveals that their business there was sufficiently flourishing and that the geographical situation of Avignon was favourable enough for Aghinolfo de' Pazzi to wish to remain there, probably—but not only—as an intermediary for his family's international affairs in Provence and, as we shall see in a moment, beyond. This letter also suggests that these bankers quickly integrated into local society to the point of not wanting to return to Tuscany.

We have several clues of this rapid and profound integration, starting with the use of a Provençal version of their name—Passis—from the early fifteenth century. Local archives testify to a contemporary use of the two forms for a few decades, but after the middle of the fifteenth century, only the Provençal form can be found.[10] As can be observed in other cities for similar cases of wealthy immigrants, the most tangible pieces of evidence of their integration into the highest level of local society are the positions that the men of the Pazzi family regularly occupied in urban government. Leopoldo II de' Pazzi was successively treasurer of the wine *gabelle*, one of the city's ambassadors to Pope Martin V in 1418, and a "rector of the bridge" the following year. His descendants held various positions in the service of the city's government, starting with his son, Alamano, who was elected syndic and consul of Avignon on several occasions (1452 and 1461), "master of the streets" (1454), ambassador of the city, and King René's banker and supplier of luxury items.[11] His father-in-law, Giacomo de' Pazzi, was King René's *maître-rational* and *clavaire* of Marseille.[12] Michele and Alamano lent money to the city and, in return, they obtained a monopoly on the *gabelle*, a substance that they transported from the port of Marseille and whose production they were responsible for (since they had obtained the privilege of administering the Count of Provence's *salinas* at the Vernède and Arles), thus controlling the entire salt industry in the region. The Count also granted the other branch of the

10 For instance, see the accounts of the convent of the Friars Minors in Avignon, Archives départementales de Vaucluse, 24H32 et 24H33. See also Clément Lenoble. *L'exercice de la pauvreté. Économie et religion chez les franciscains d'Avignon (XIIIe–XVe siècle).* Rennes: Presses universitaires de Rennes, 2013, 279.

11 Labande, *Avignon au XVe siècle*, 550, 552; Cler, Un homme d'affaires, 307–308.

12 Noël Coulet. La Chambre des comptes de Provence sous le règne du roi René. In *René d'Anjou (1409–1480)*, Jean-Michel Matz, Noël-Yves Tonnerre (eds.). Rennes: Presses universitaires de Rennes, 2011, 219; for "*clavaire*," see Archives départementales des Bouches du Rhône, B 1950, fol. 196 and B 1952, fol. 133. See also Jean-Luc Bonnaud. L'appareil administratif local en Provence sous le règne du roi René. In *René d'Anjou*, Matz, Tonnerre (eds.), 223–246, notes 45 and 53.

Pazzi family, established in Avignon (the Pazzi Accorri), a monopoly on coral fishing in Provence, a luxury product that they traded over Europe.[13]

Their marriages are a second symptom and tool of their integration into the upper strata of local society, starting with the second generation established there.[14] These matrimonial alliances were made with other powerful families of Florentine origin who had been settled in the region for longer than them and who already belonged to the Avignon oligarchy, such as the Tornaquincis, the Brancas, and the Panisses, another branch of the Pazzis.[15] The third generation joined forces with the Altovitis, the Peruzzis, and the Salviatis, pursuing the same strategy. A more precise investigation in the archives may make it possible to determine when they became the ones sought for matrimonial alliances by other families.

Finally, their insertion into the religious life of the city is significant to their rootedness. They joined the Italian confraternity in the Church of the Augustinian Convent and founded and built a chapel in the Church of the Friars Minor where they were buried at least from 1410.[16] They appear in the Convent's records as one of the families closest to the Friars. They also seem to be linked to the Confraternity of the Holy Spirit, established in one of the chapels of the Convent, and several members of the family acted as procurators or spiritual friends of the religious community by helping them with the administration of conventual life matters—in particular, by making purchases on their behalf and by making regular donations and loans to the Convent.[17] Accursio, one of the sons of Leopoldo II de' Pazzi, was a canon and apostolic vice-camerlengo. Again, the elements presented here are only examples taken from an overview of the local archives. Only a more in-depth investigation will make it possible to identify and reconstruct the religious life of the Pazzis in Avignon more precisely, which is, of course, not the

---

13 Cler, Un homme d'affaires, 308, 318; Archives départementales de Vaucluse, Veran et Brieude 1420, fol. 47; Gustave Arnaud d'Agnel. *Les comptes du roi René*, vol. 1. Paris: Picard et Fils, 1908, 309–310; Édouard Baratier. Production et débouchés du sel de Provence au bas Moyen Âge. In *Le rôle du sel dans l'histoire*, Michel Mollat (ed.). Paris: Puf, 1969, 133–171. Giacomo de' Pazzi obtained this monopoly from King René together with Renato de'Pazzi. He was Alamano's father-in-law.

14 Cler, Un homme d'affaires; Litta Biumi, *Famiglie*.

15 This is a well-known and well-documented strategy more recently discussed by Christiane Klapisch-Zuber. *La Maison et le nom: stratégies et rituels dans l'Italie de la Renaissance*. Paris: EHESS, 1990; Christiane Klapisch-Zuber. *Mariages à la florentine. Femmes et vie de famille à Florence (XIVe–XVe siècle)*. Paris: Éditions de l'EHESS-Gallimard-Seuil, 2020; Isabelle Chabot. *La dette des familles. Femmes, lignage et patrimoine à Florence aux XIVe et XVe siècle*. Rome: École française de Rome, 2011.

16 Lenoble, *L'exercice*, 320.

17 Lenoble, *L'exercice*, 278–283, 320.

main objective in the context of this small study. The fact remains that their closeness to the Friars Minor is certainly one of the salient features.

At the end of the fifteenth century, they acquired land and seigneury titles in the Comtat Venaissin, according to a strategy common to the families of rich merchants.[18] Somewhat paradoxically perhaps, this was precisely the moment at which their Avignon business seemed to be declining. We will focus on this moment without dwelling too much on their social and political life as well as on the constitution of their local heritage and the nature of their commercial affairs, which have already been reconstructed by Monique Cler.[19]

Commerce, deposit banking, and credit in the major European markets: the classic activities of the great merchant-bankers of the fifteenth century

No accounting records have come down to us. If we limit our investigation to local sources, the reconstruction of the Pazzi family's activities is therefore particularly difficult and depends essentially on the state of the notarial documentation which, as we know, concerns only part of the operations of the large merchant and banking companies. We are reduced to putting together the scattered pieces of a much larger puzzle that is destined to remain full of gaps and, therefore, discontinuous. Traces of the Pazzis' activities in Avignon increase in this documentation from the 1410s onwards, when Michele de' Pazzi, son of Leopoldo II, took over the management of their commercial and banking activities. These traces are, for the most part, receipts and acknowledgements of debts, occasionally contracts, and a few bills of exchange registered by the city's notaries.

The archives of Marseille notaries also bear witness to their activity in the port of Marseille, in an interregional trade ranging from Naples to Geneva and widely diversified, including salt as well as alum, sheets, corals, and various luxury items with which they supplied the count's house in Aix-en-Provence.[20] They

18 Cler, Un homme d'affaires, 325.

19 Cler, Un homme d'affaires.

20 Cler, Un homme d'affaires, 317. See the entry for 3 April 1454, Archives départementales de Vaucluse, Pierre de Blengeriès, 3E8/177.

transported cloth from Geneva, where they bought them at fairs.[21] A bill of exchange dated 1465 informs us of one of the modalities of these transactions at the Geneva fair. According to this document, the Pazzi's bank provided the necessary credits of up to 2,700 florins to Bernard Anselme who went to the fair.[22] The commodities he bought there were then shipped to Sicily by a merchant from Montpellier. An Avignon contract from 1475 mentions them, this time as intermediaries in the transport of alum and saltpetre to Lyon, for the fair sales.[23]

These commercial operations were medium-sized, if we compare them with those of the Italian companies operating directly between Byzantium, Tyre or Tunis, Venice, Bruges, and London. The Pazzis of Avignon (let us now call them Passis) must undoubtedly be considered as intermediaries in larger operations on the Naples or Florence to Geneva segment via Marseille, Aix, Avignon, and Lyon. They operated both for the commercial activities of the Florentine Pazzis and for those of other major Tuscan companies, such as the Peruzzis, the Salviatis, the Albertis, and the Baroncellis, with whom they were associated.[24]

This documentation also reveals that the Passis' involvement in long-distance trade was traditionally coupled with a deposit, credit, and exchange banking activity which probably constituted, in terms of business volume, the bulk of their income, and which was deployed from the 1410s between Italy and London via Paris, where Michele de Passis had a house.[25] In addition to credit transactions in the context of commercial transactions with their associates and customers, the sums lent varied from a few florins for small loans for consumption or for small craftsmen's professional activities in the region to thousands of florins lent to urban communities (4,000 florins in Avignon, 6,000 florins in Hyères, and 1,000 florins divided among smaller Provençal communities such as Grimaud, Borme, Cogolin, and Valletta) and to their most powerful clientele—the kings of Sicily and their court, the Duke of Calabria, the entourage of the King of France, the Duke of Berry, the entourage of the Dukes of Burgundy, bishops, and cardinals (in particular, the Cardinal Legate Pierre de Foix).[26]

This banking activity allowed them to obtain privileges and monopolies such as those already mentioned on the salt *gabelles*, the administration of the salt

21 Cler, Un homme d'affaires, 318–319; 13 April 1465, Archives départementales de Vaucluse, Pons 46. Antoine Agulhacié, fols. 43–44.

22 Cler, Un homme d'affaires.

23 Édouard Baratier, Félix Reynaud. *Histoire du commerce de Marseille*, vol. 2. Paris: Plon, 1952, 584.

24 Cler, Un homme d'affaires.

25 Jules Guiffrey. *Inventaires de Jean, Duc de Berry (1401–1416)*, vol. 1, Paris: Leroux, 1894.

26 Cler, Un homme d'affaires, 311–317.

works, or the coral fishery. With the acquisition of the farm from ecclesiastical revenues, the Passis family intertwined, again in a very classic way for Italian merchants, private interests and "public" finance, inserting their interest-bearing lending activities into a "public" circuit, whether it be that of financing cities, kingdoms and princes, the administration of saltworks, or ecclesiastical taxation.

From an ethical point of view, if we follow the texts of theologians and jurists on the subject, such as the English Franciscans John Peckham and John Duns Scotus, the Catalan friar Francesc Eiximenis, or Ramon Lull and, on the side of the jurists before them, Cardinal Henry of Susa and Sinibaldo Fieschi, Pope Innocent IV, it is precisely this articulation between private affairs, long-distance trade, and public finances that morally justifies the wealth of the great merchant-bankers.[27] This is even what made it possible to introduce the distinction between usury and investment, between interest and capital, until the use of the word "*capitale*" in contrast to "*sors*", by the Narbonne Friar Minor, Peter of John Olivi at the end of the thirteenth century, in his famous *Treatise on Contracts.*[28] As far as the extant sources allow us to judge at this stage of the investigation, there is nothing surprising or abnormal about the activities of the Passis in the fifteenth century. These activities seem to be regularly linked to the fairs of Geneva and Lyon in the years 1465–1495. The only striking fact lies, as we shall see presently,

---

27 Giacomo Todeschini. *Il Prezzo della salvezza. Lessici medievali del pensiero economico.* Rome: NIS, 1994, 204–205, 208–209; Giacomo Todeschini. *I mercanti e il tempio. La società cristiana e il circolo virtuoso della ricchezza fra Medioevo ed Età Moderna.* Bologna: Il Mulino, 2002, 311; Giacomo Todeschini. Finance and usury: The Languages of Public Economy as Rhetoric of Social Inequality. *Estados y mercados financieros en el occidente cristiano (siglos XIII–XVI).* Pamplona: Gobierno de Navarra, 2015, 83–103; Giacomo Todeschini. *La banca e il ghetto. Una storia italiana.* Bari: Laterza, 2016; Giacomo Todeschini. Gestione dei beni pubblici e amministrazione dei patrimoni privati. Il mercato cristiano come spazio di sacralizzazione della ricchezza familiare. *Mélanges de l'École française de Rome—Italie et Méditerranée modernes et contemporaines* 127:1 (2015). http://journals.openedition.org/mefrim/2028 (24 October 2024).

28 Pierre de Jean Olivi. *Traité des contrats.* Sylvain Piron (ed.). Paris: Les Belles Lettres, 2012, *Pars prima*, q. 6. 71–73, 140. See Giacomo Todeschini. *Un trattato di economia politica francescana: il De emptionibus et venditionibus, de usuris, de restitutionibus di Pietro di Giovanni Olivi.* Rome: Istituto storico italiano per il medioevo, 1980, 69; Odd I. Langholm. *Economics in the Medieval Schools: Wealth, Exchange, Value, Money and Usury According to the Paris Theological Tradition, 1200–1350.* Leiden: Brill, 1992, 345. The history of the word "capitalism" and of Olivi's use of it has been analysed by Sylvain Piron. Prêts charitables et opérations capitalistes dans l'éthique franciscaine des contrats monétaires. In *Des personnes aux institutions. Réseaux et culture du crédit du XVI*e *au XX*e *siècle en Europe,* Laurence Fontaine, Gilles Postel-Vinay, Jean-Laurent Rosenthal, Paul Servais (eds.). Louvain-la-Neuve: Bruylant-Academia, 1997, 11–27; Sylvain Piron. *L'occupation du monde.* Brussels: Zones sensibles, 2018, 173–175; Sylvain Piron. *Généalogie de la morale économique.* Brussels: Zones sensibles, 2020, 271–292.

in the conditions of their bankruptcy and the transfer of their banking activities to Lyon between 1465 and 1468—a transfer probably linked to the rise of the Lyon fairs and which explains the relative but significant increase in the documentation (only four acts known to date) of their operations between Lyon and Geneva from these years.

From Avignon to Lyon via Geneva: bankruptcy and resurrection of a bank to the rhythm of the fairs

In the current state of this investigation, traces of the presence of the Passis family in Lyon before the end of the fifteenth century are very rare and tenuous. The minutes of the consular deliberations of the city of Lyon mention, on 23 January 1425, a certain "Esnée de Passe [Aeneas of Passe], merchant of Avignion" as the holder of a debt of six hundred crowns.[29] On 4 January 1422, a claim for seven hundred and fifty *livres tournoi* in favour of "a merchant of Avignion, called Année," also recorded in the minutes of the city's deliberations, might possibly be referring to the same member of the Pazzi family, if he was indeed one of the members.[30] There is room for doubt because, for the moment, no trace of an Aeneas of Passe can be found in the archives. The name "Passe" may well correspond to the francisation of the Italian "Pace," with which the Pazzis are sometimes named in the Avignon archives.[31] He could be one of the members of the other branch of the Pazzi family that settled in Avignon, known as the Pazzi-Accorri, whose activity has left less traces but which is obviously linked to the Avignon branch—in particular, through matrimonial alliances and commercial associations.[32] Another solution would be to consider that he is one of the Lyon postmen or a clerk of the Pazzi's bank in Avignon, but the qualification of "Avignon merchant" makes this reading unlikely. If this Aeneas of Passe does indeed belong

29 Georges Guigue (ed.). *Registres consulaires de la ville de Lyon ou recueil des délibérations de la commune publiés d'après les procès-verbaux originaux*, vol. II: 1422–1450. Lyon: Archives et bibliothèques de la ville, 1926,169–170.

30 Guigue (ed.), *Registres consulaires*, 32.

31 Archives départementales de Vaucluse, 24H32 and 33.

32 Alamano de Passis's wife, Alisetta, belonged to this family. She was born from a first alliance between these two branches. Her grandfather was Piero, Alamano's uncle. She was therefore the second cousin of her husband, while already being the direct descendant of a branch of cousins in the seventh degree.

to the house of the Passis of Avignon, these references in the Lyon archives show that they were already present in the 1420s, at the time of the creation of the first fairs in Lyon.[33] However, we do not know of any archives that link them directly to the activity of the fairs from this date onwards; those that have come down to us are all contemporaneous or date from after the bankruptcy in 1465.

In 1466, Guglielmo de Passis from Avignon was associated with the Florentines Francesco Capponi and Francesco Nasi.[34] This mention of their company in a contract between the Florentine nation and the Convent of the Friars Preachers of Lyon (to which we will return in a moment) does not allow us to know how long this bank had existed. Once again, we have to deal with a Passis who does not seem to have left any traces in the Avignon archives. We therefore presently do not know the nature of his family ties with Alamano de Passis, who was at the head of the family business until that date. After 1466, he almost disappeared from the records. In 1479, two letters from the consuls to Louis XI indirectly inform us that the king had passed on to them the claims of Jean de Palence against Alamano de Passis, who owed him a debt.[35] Alamano de Passis died in 1481.[36] The Avignon business was managed in connection with this new Lyon bank by his sons, Piero and Carlo, and his sons-in-law, Piero Baroncelli, Luca Cambi, and Matteo Bongiani, all representatives of eminent Italian families well established in Avignon.[37] The association with the Capponi family of Lyon seems to have lasted for several decades, as evidenced by two recognitions of debts totalling 750 florins, dated 1457, for purchases of salt from Alamano de Passis.[38] We do not know how the Passis family encountered the Nasi, powerful Florentine merchant-bankers in Lyon.

The date of this association—1466—is synchronous both with the first boom in Lyon's fairs, the fourth of which was created by Louis XI on 8 March 1463, and with the first phase of the permanent establishment of the great families of Flor-

33 The minutes of the city's deliberations mention the request made to the Dauphin to create two free fairs in 1418. See Baratier, Reynaud. *Histoire du commerce*, 143–144. These fairs were officially created by the Dauphin in 1420. See Marc Brésard. *Les foires de Lyon aux XVe et XVIe siècles*. Paris: Picard, 1914, 1–8.

34 Archives départementales du Rhône. *Inventaire des archives du couvent de Notre-Dame de Confort par le P. Ramette*, vol. II, f. 25v; Charpin-Feugerolles, *Les Florentins*, 160–161.

35 Archives municipales d'Avignon, AA 10, fols. 153v.–155v.; CC, pièces justificatives des comptes (1479–1480), no. 185. See Labande, *Avignon au XVe siècle*, 267, footnote 5.

36 Cler, Un homme d'affaires, 330.

37 Cler, Un homme d'affaires, 334.

38 Archives départementales de Vaucluse, Jacques Girardi, 3E5/767, fol. 214.

entine merchant-bankers in 1466 as well, to the detriment of Geneva:[39] the Medicis left Geneva and settled in Lyon precisely that year.[40] The arrival of the Florentines in Lyon in the early 1460s is further attested by the drafting of the statutes of 1487 which mention those of their nation in this city in 1466 and are based on the model of the statutes of the Florentine nation in Geneva dating from 1446.[41] On 13 December 1466, Guglielmo de Passis is represented along with Francesco Nasi by their associate Francesco Capponi, among the signatories of the contract by which the Friars Preachers conceded to the Florentine nation of Lyon the main chapel in their church of Notre-Dame-de-Confort.[42] In this deed, another famous Florentine from Avignon appears, also represented by his Florentine associates from Lyon—Pierre Baroncelli, who founded a company with the Da Panzano family, and who was the husband of Leonarda de Passis, Alamano's eldest daughter. In 1469, the Passis' bank in Lyon was able to loan the town 600 gold *ecus* so that it could fulfil its free loan obligations to the king.[43] The Passis/Pazzis were therefore probably among the first active Florentines well established in Lyon, alongside the Capponi and the Nasi families who certainly arrived before them, as well as the Sacchetti, the Da Panzano, the Della Luna, the Palmieri, and the Guadagni families. By way of comparison, the Salviatis do not seem to have arrived until the beginning of the sixteenth century, after the fairs' period of crisis

---

39 Letters patent and mandates of 8 March 1462. In *Ordonnances des rois de France de la troisième race recueillies par ordre chronologique. Quinzième volume: Ordonnances rendues depuis le commencement du règne de Louis XI jusqu'au mois de juin 1463*, Emmanuel Pastoret (ed.). Paris: Imprimerie impériale, 1811, 644–648.

40 De Roover, *Medici Bank*, 74.

41 Gino Masi. *Statuti delle colonie fiorentine all'estero (secoli XV–XVI).* Milan: Giuffrè, 1941, 202: "di quelli di detta natione prima a Ginevra, ne l'anno MCCCCXLVI, a dì primo di gennaio, et di poi a Lione a dì IIII di gennaio MCCCCLXVI, fu dato forma et ordine al fine sopradetto." See also Pallini-Martin, L'installation d'une famille, 74.

42 Archives départementales du Rhône 3H40, *Inventaire manuscrit des archives du couvent des Dominicains de Lyon, rédigé par le P. Siméon André Ramette, archiviste dudit couvent*, vol. II, f. 25v; *Statuti delle colonie fiorentine all'estero (secoli XV–XVI)*, 202: "Di poi a Lione fu loro conceduta la chapelle magiore et altri membri della chiesa de' frati di Sancto Domenicho, detta di Nostra Dona di Conforto." See Jacques Gadille, René Fédou, Henri Hours, Bernard de Vergile. *Le diocèse de Lyon.* Paris: Éditions Beauchesne, 1983, 86, 109; Haude Morvan. Au Chœur des affaires. La nation florentine et les frères prêcheurs lyonnais. *Archivum Fratrum Praedicatorum* 3:2 (2018): 116–117.

43 Joseph Vaesen (ed.). *Lettres de Louis XI, roi de France.* Vol. IV: 1469–1472. Paris: Renouard, 1890, 62–63; entry for 19 December 1469, Archives municipales de Lyon, BB 15, fol. 70v. and CC 441, no. 5.

(1484–1494). And the most tangible signs of the rise of the Florentine nation in Lyon date only from the late 1480s.[44]

The transfer of the Florentines from Geneva to Lyon is well attested while that from Avignon is much harder to trace. The first occurred in the context of the competition between these two places at the end of the fifteenth century, Charles VII and especially Louis XI having actively worked on this migration of Italian financial forces to France. However, one may wonder if the people of Avignon were only attracted by the very recent dynamism of the Lyon market, given that the Passis (and with them the Baroncelli) family seem to have arrived perhaps even before the transfer of the Medicis, or at least at the same time as them. Were the people of Avignon sufficiently sensitive to what was happening in Lyon to anticipate it or move there very quickly, taking advantage of old relations with the Capponi family, for example? This cannot be ruled out, of course, together with the possibility that could have led them to turn to partners in Lyon at the right time. The conditions of the bankruptcy of the Passis in Avignon—which immediately preceded this association with the Nasis and Capponis in Lyon—may provide us with some elements of an answer.

The bankruptcy of Alamano de Passis is known, thanks to a letter from Louis XI dated 1465 in which he demanded that the Avignon banker reimburse his debt to Louis de Valperga.[45] In this letter, the king described Alamano de Passis as a "bankrupt." In addition, the ledgers of the Friars Minor of Avignon mention the bankruptcy of the Passis' bank, mentioning proceedings by their creditors against it. For its part, the convent demands that Alamano's creditors pay the pension founded by his uncle Michele.[46] This pension was based on all the property that Michele bequeathed to Alamano when he made him universal heir. This explains why the convent of the Friars Minor made this request at a time when the creditors of the Passis were recovering part of these seized goods to pay themselves. A series of archives makes it possible to hypothesise what may have happened. During the eight years preceding Louis XI's letter, the Passis bank had granted several very important loans: King René and Guillaume de Varye for the amounts of

44 Pallini-Martin, L'installation d'une famille, 71–90; Pallini-Martin, *Banque, négoce et politique*, 60–65; Nadia Matringe. *La banque en Renaissance. Les Salviati et la place de Lyon au milieu du XVIe siècle*. Rennes: Presses universitaires de Rennes, 2015; Lang, *Wirtschaften als Kulturelle Praxis*, 132.

45 This letter has not been edited by Vaesen and Charavay. See Archives municipales d'Avignon. Pintat2521; Raymond Rey. *Louis XI et les États pontificaux de France au XVe siècle d'après des documents inédits*. Grenoble: Imprimerie Allier Frères, 1899, 173; Labande, *Avignon au XVe siècle*, 152, footnote 2. See an approximate and incomplete transcription in Cler, Un homme d'affaires, 330–331.

46 Archives départementales de Vaucluse, 24H33, fol. 31; Lenoble, *L'exercice*, 359–363.

8,000 florins each. However, immediately after the loan granted to the latter, two other customers—namely, Guillaume du Chastel and Louis de Valperga—asked to recover their deposits and debts at the Passis' bank for amounts of 8,000 florins as well. Unable to satisfy their demand, Alamano de Passis went bankrupt.[47]

Several coincidences attract our attention. Firstly, the sums are the most obvious. Secondly, the actors of this bankruptcy stand out: Louis de Valperga and Guillaume de Varye were close advisors of Louis XI,[48] the former being one of his favourites, while the latter, a prior agent of Jacques Coeur, became treasurer general of finance in Languedoc. Guillaume du Chastel was "maître des ports de la sénéchaussée de Beaucaire." He was therefore also a man of the king. The closeness of these three men to Louis XI probably explains why he intervened directly in this affair, as we have mentioned, even though it took place in Avignon, and therefore outside his kingdom. Was the king really doing it to help them, thinking he could influence the local justice system? Did he see this as a pretext to intervene in Avignon's decisions; perhaps even as an opportunity to trouble or even eliminate one of the main bankers of the count, King René and the Duke of Calabria, while he was trying to claim Provence and integrate it into his own kingdom? The Passis' bankruptcy surely weakened Avignon too. Louis XI always tried to intervene in Avignon matters. He addressed letters to the consuls of the city, treating them as his subjects. However, he also acted to weaken the resources of Avignon and the Comtat Venaissin. He did so, for instance, by promoting the regional free trade fair of Briançon in 1462.[49] This had the effect of deflecting the flow of merchants and goods from the Comtat, especially cattle, coming from the Alps.[50] He also directly targeted the Florentine merchants established in the Comtat, whom he accused, in a letter to the Cardinal of Foix in 1463, of supplying his Catalan enemies.[51] In the same year, he prohibited his subjects and foreigners residing in the kingdom from importing spices through the port of Marseille. Foreign merchants not resident in the kingdom—such as the Florentine citizens of Avignon,

47 See Cler, Un hommes d'affaires, 331–333.

48 See Pierre-Roger Gaussin. Les conseillers du roi Louis XI (1461–1483). In *La France de la fin du XVe siècle.* Paris: CNRS, 1985, 105–134; Jean-François Lassalmonie. *La boîte à l'enchanteur. Politique financière de Louis XI.* Paris: Comité pour l'histoire économique et financière de la France, 2002.

49 Archives municipales de Briançon, HH 1 (1462); Emmanuel Pilot de Thorey. *Catalogue des actes du dauphin, Louis II, devenu le roi de France Louis XI, relatifs à l'administration du Dauphiné*, vol. II. Grenoble: Imprimerie de Maisonville, 1899, no. 1343, 34; Gandilhon, *Politique économique*, 218, 220; Jacques Heers. *Louis XI: le métier de roi.* Paris: Éditions Perrin, 1999, 287.

50 Thérèse Sclafert. Les routes du Dauphiné et de la Provence sous l'influence du séjour des papes à Avignon. *Annales d'histoire économique* 1 (1929): 192.

51 Joseph Vaesen and Bernard de Mandrot (eds.). *Lettres de Louis XI*, vol. X: 1482–1483. Paris: Renouard, 1908, no. 1952, 192–194.

for instance—were nevertheless allowed to travel by land to supply the Lyon fairs, and Guillaume de Varye countersigned the ordinance dated 1 November 1463.[52] There is little doubt that this measure affected the Passis' businesses in this sector, even if they were only collateral damage, with the king's decision primarily aimed at his Venetian enemies and, most likely, the Count of Provence. And finally, on 7 February 1478 or 1473 (Léon-Honoré Labande, who edited this letter, does not know if it was sent on either date), Louis XI addressed a letter to the consuls of Avignon, asking them not to lease the revenues from the salt tax to the "Passis of Florence" who had always been hostile to him, observing "qui ont toujours tenu party à nous contraire (they have always been against us)."[53] If it does date back to 1478, as Labande seems to think, this letter took place during the opposition of the salt farmer on the Empire side, whereby Francesco Capponi, an associate of the Passis in Lyon, refused to collect the toll on the salt that travelled up the Rhône.[54] We can therefore be almost certain that the sanction requested by the king was aimed at the Passis in the Comtat. Whether it dates from 1473 or early 1478, even before the outbreak of the Pazzi conspiracy in Florence which Louis XI disagreed with, this letter clearly indicates the king's hostility towards the Passis of Avignon, whom he now considered—albeit perhaps opportunistically—to be long-standing enemies.

In the light of these hypotheses and pieces of evidence of the king's hostility towards Avignon and its Florentine bankers, we can even envisage a frame-up. The fact that this misadventure had the effect of pushing the Passis to turn more towards Lyon and to associate themselves with the main Florentine bankers of the Lyon market at the precise moment when the King of France hoped to develop the fairs and attract Italian financiers, is a final troubling coincidence. In the end, all this is conjecture and speculation, but if we were to try to find out whether the bankruptcy of the Passis could have benefited anyone, then all eyes would be turned to Louis XI. If one thinks of the methods and taste for intrigue of the "universal spider" and his faithful Guillaume de Varye, one is hardly sur-

52 BNF, français, nouvelles acquisitions, 7227, fols. 87–88, edited in Gandilhon, *Politique économique*, 423, 424. On the importance of Guillaume de Varye as economic counsellor of the king, see Gandilhon, *Politique économique*, 470; Amable Sablon du Corail. *Louis XI: Le joueur inquiet*. Paris: Belin, 2015, 114.

53 Archives municipales d'Avignon, AA 38, edited as "Lettre du roi Louis XI aux consuls [. . .]," 7 February 1478 or 1473, in Labande, *Avignon au XVe siècle*, 599–600 (pièce justificative no. XXIII).

54 Labande, *Avignon au XVe siècle*, 268; also see Labande's edition of the king's letter at 599–600. On the political dimension of salt conflicts along the Rhone River as early as the mid-thirteenth century, see Simone Balossino. *La force et le droit. Enquête sur la gabelle du sel dans la vallée du Rhône au temps de Louis IX*. Paris: CNRS Éditions, 2023.

prised.[55] Guillaume de Varye often intervened and was in charge in the king's decisions regarding the trade fairs, specifically for those in Lyon.[56] The bankruptcy of the Passis family could well be one of the little-known episodes of the king's maneuvers aimed at conquering Provence, weakening Avignon and the Comtat Venaissin, and promoting the development of the fairs of Lyon.[57] This could suggest, at least, the deployment by the King of France of a conscious and aggressive economic policy towards Provence and the Comtat Venaissin, to the benefit, of course, of his kingdom.

In the end, we cannot be certain. The sources are too rare, indirect, and incomplete. The activity of the Passis family in Lyon has left too few traces. Our understanding of the conditions of their association with the Nasis and Capponis is too dependent on hypotheses that are difficult to corroborate. The fact remains that their bankruptcy in Avignon pushed them towards Lyon at a time when the king of France was trying to expand the fairs and seeking to develop them by attracting Florentine investors. They were therefore among the very first to contribute to this movement, which led, a few decades later, to the transfer of commercial and financial activities from Geneva to Lyon. Whether it was a mere coincidence, opportunism, or the king's strategy, we do not have the means to decide. Aghinolfo de' Pazzi came to Avignon to serve the papacy and do business. Economic and political developments in the fifteenth century pushed their heirs, three generations after them, towards Geneva and Lyon. This very little-known and documented history is part of the political and economic processes that led to the transfer of Tuscan bankers from Geneva to Lyon.

---

55 Paul Murray Kendall. *Louis XI: l'universelle araigne*. Paris: Pluriel, 2014; Jacques Heers. *Louis XI: le métier de roi*. Paris: Éditions Perrin, 1999; Emmanuel Le Roy Ladurie, *L'État royal: de Louis XI à Henri IV. La monarchie de la Renaissance, 1460–1610*. Paris: Hachette, 2000; Jean Favier. *Louis XI*. Paris: Fayard, 2001; Joël Blanchard. *Louis XI*. Paris: Éditions Perrin, 2015; Amable Sablon du Corail. *Louis XI*, 511–536.

56 Gandilhon, *Politique économique*, 226, footnote 7.

57 About the relationship between Louis XI and René of Anjou, see Gustave Arnaud d'Agnel. *La politique des rois de France en Provence. Louis XI et Charles VIII*. 2 vols. Marseille: Jouvène, Paris: Picard, 1914; Labande, *Avignon au XVe siècle*; Noël Coulet Alice Planche, Françoise Robin. *Le roi René. Le prince, le mécène, l'écrivain, le mythe*. Aix-en-Provence: Édisud, 1982; Henri de Forbin. L'action diplomatique de René d'Anjou. In *Le roi René. René, duc d'Anjou, de Bar et de Lorraine. Roi de Sicile et de Jérusalem. Roi d'Aragon. Comte de Provence (1409–1480)*. Actes du colloque international d'Avignon, 13–15 juin 1981. *Annales universitaires d'Avignon* 1 & 2 (1986), 63–69; Jean Favier. *Le roi René*. Paris: Fayard, 2008; Matz, Tonnerre (eds.), *René d'Anjou*; Yannick Frizet. *Louis XI, le roi René et la Provence*. Aix-en-Provence: Presses universitaires de Provence, 2015. About his relationship to Avignon and Comtat venaissin, see Labande, *Avignon au XVe siècle*; Rey, *Louis XI*.

Appendix

Letter from King Louis XI asking the consuls to urge Alamano de Passis to reimburse his chamberlain, Louis de Valperga (Orléans on 21 March 1466)

Archives municipales d'Avignon, Pintat2521. *Original on parchment.*

Les consulz et conseillers d'Avignon.
A noz tres chers et bons amys,
Les consulz et conseillers d'Avignon.

Loys par la grace de dieu Roy de France. Tres chers et bons amys, Nous avons entendu que Alemans de Pastz de la Ville d'Avignon a fait falicte au preiudice et dommage de ses crediteurs, combien qu'il ait et posside plusieurs biens et qu'il ait plusieurs crediteurs, et entre les autres notre amé et feal conseiller et chambellan, Loys de Vaulspergue sir de Roppol[58] auquel il est tenu en la somme de trois mil escuz dor comme plus a plain appert par une obligacion, de laquelle somme il ne luy veult faire paiement. Ains s'efforce le tenir en proces, comme il nous a dit. Et pour ce que nous desirons qu'il soit paié comme raison est, Nous vous prions bien acertes, que en faveur et contemplacion de nous, vous vueillez tenir la main, en bonne justice, a ce que notredit conseiller soit entierement paié de sondit debit sans figure de plait ne de proces, en luy donnant sur ce tout l'aide, conseil et confort que vous pourrez, et comme vouldriez que feissions pour luy de vous, en cas semblable envers aucuns de noz subjetz, ce que ferons quant requis en serons de par vous, en quoy faisant nous ferez ung tres agreable et singuller plaisir. Et quant ainsi ne le ferez, nous y pourverions, comme pour notre especial serviteur.

Donné a Orleans le XXIe jour de mars.
Loys.

Meurin.

Bibliography

Primary Sources

Arnaud d'Agnel, Gustave. *Les comptes du roi René*. Vol. I. Paris: Picard et Fils, 1908.

Balossino, Simone. *La force et le droit. Enquête sur la gabelle du sel dans la vallée du Rhône au temps de Louis IX*. Paris: CNRS Éditions, 2023.

Baratier, Édouard, Reynaud Félix. *Histoire du commerce de Marseille*. Vol. 2. Paris: Plon, 1952.

58 Roppolo, in Piedmont.

Guiffrey, Jules (ed.). *Inventaires de Jean, Duc de Berry (1401–1416)*. Vol. 1. Paris: E. Leroux, 1894.
Guigue, Georges (ed.). *Registres consulaires de la ville de Lyon ou recueil des délibérations de la commune publiés d'après les procès-verbaux originaux*. Vol. II: 1422–1450. Lyon: Archives et bibliothèques de la ville, 1926.
Jean Olivi, Pierre de. *Traité des contrats*, Sylvain Piron (ed.). Paris: Les Belles Lettres, 2012.
Litta Biumi, Pompeo. *Famiglie celebri di Italia. Pazzi di Firenze*. Milan: Presso l'autore (Tipografia delle famiglie italiane), 1851.
Masi, Gino. *Statuti delle colonie fiorentine all'estero (secoli XV–XVI)*. Milan: Giuffrè, 1941.
Pastoret, Emmanuel (ed.). *Ordonnances des rois de France de la troisième race recueillies par ordre chronologique. Quinzième volume: Ordonnances rendues depuis le commencement du règne de Louis XI jusqu'au mois de juin 1463*. Paris: Imprimerie impériale, 1811.
Pilot de Thorey, Emmanuel. *Catalogue des actes du dauphin, Louis II, devenu le roi de France Louis XI, relatifs à l'administration du Dauphiné*. Vol. II. Grenoble: Imprimerie de Maisonville, 1899.
Todeschini, Giacomo. *Un trattato di economia politica francescana: il De emptionibus et venditionibus, de usuris, de restitution bus di Pietro di Giovanni Olivi*. Rome: Istituto storico italiano per il medioevo, 1980.
Vaesen, Joseph, Étienne Charavay (eds.). *Lettres de Louis XI, roi de France*. Vol. III: 1465–1469. Paris: Renouard, 1887.
Vaesen Joseph (ed.). *Lettres de Louis XI, roi de France*. Vol. IV: 1469–1472. Paris: Renouard, 1890.
Vaesen, Joseph, Bernard de Mandrot (eds.). *Lettres de Louis XI, roi de France*. Vol. X: 1482–1483. Paris: Renouard, 1908.
Valous, Vital de. *Étienne Turquet et les origines de la Fabrique Lyonnaise. Recherches et documents sur l'institution de la manufacture des étoffes de soie (1466–1536): Notice historique accompagnée d'une généalogie de la famille Turquet*. Lyon: Auguste Brun, 1868.

Literature

Arnaud d'Agnel, Gustave. *La politique des rois de France en Provence. Louis XI et Charles VIII*. 2 vols. Marseille: Jouvène, Paris: Picard, 1914.
Arnoux, Mathieu. L'Europe de la 'grande transformation.' In *Histoire du monde au XVe siècle*. vol. 2, Patrick Boucheron (ed.). Paris: Pluriel, 2017, 590–617.
Arnoux, Mathieu. Croissance et crises dans le monde médiéval XIe–XVe siècle. *Cahiers du monde russe* 46:1–2 (2005). http://journals.openedition.org/monderusse/8787 (30 April 2024).
Baratier, Édouard. Production et débouchés du sel de Provence au bas Moyen Âge. In *Le rôle du sel dans l'histoire*, Michel Mollat (ed.). Paris: Puf, 1969, 133–171.
Blanchard, Joël. *Louis XI*. Paris: Éditions Perrin, 2015.
Bonnaud, Jean-Luc. L'appareil administratif local en Provence sous le règne du roi René. In *René d'Anjou (1409–1480)*, Jean-Michel Matz and Noël-Yves Tonnerre (eds.). Rennes: Presses universitaires de Rennes, 2011, 223–246.
Boucher, Jacqueline. *Présence italienne à Lyon à la Renaissance du milieu du XVe à la fin du XVIe siècle*. Lyon: Éditions LUGD, 1994.
Brésard, Marc. *Les foires de Lyon aux XVe et XVIe siècles*. Paris: Picard, 1914.
Cassandro, Michele. I forestieri a Lione nel'400 e '500: la nazione fiorentina. In *Dentro la città. Stranieri e realtà urbane nell'Europa dei secoli XII–XVI*, Gabriella Rossetti (ed.). Naples: Liguori, 1989, 151–162.

Chabot, Isabelle. *La dette des familles. Femmes, lignage et patrimoine à Florence aux XIVe et XVe siècle*. Rome: École française de Rome, 2011.
Charpin-Feugerolles, Hippolyte André Suzanne de. *Les Florentins à Lyon*. Lyon: Louis Brun, 1893.
Cipolla, Carlo Maria. *Storia economica dell'Europa pre-industriale*. Bologna: Il Mulino, 1974.
Cler, Monique. Un homme d'affaires avignonnais du XVe siècle: Alaman de Passis. *Provence historique* 7:30 (1957): 305–336.
Coulet, Noël, Planche Alice, Robin Françoise. *Le roi René. Le prince, le mécène, l'écrivain, le mythe*. Aix-en-Provence: Édisud, 1982.
Coulet, Noël. La Chambre des comptes de Provence sous le règne du roi René. In *René d'Anjou*, Matz, Tonnerre (eds.), 211–221.
De Roover, Raymond. *The Rise and Decline of the Medici Bank. 1397–1494*. Washington, DC: Beard Books, 1999.
Favier, Jean. *Louis XI*. Paris: Fayard, 2001.
Favier, Jean. *Le roi René*. Paris: Fayard, 2008.
Forbin Henri (de). L'action diplomatique de René d'Anjou. In *Le roi René. René, duc d'Anjou, de Bar et de Lorraine. Roi de Sicile et de Jérusalem. Roi d'Aragon. Comte de Provence (1409–1480)*. Actes du colloque international d'Avignon, 13–15 juin 1981. *Annales universitaires d'Avignon* 1 & 2 (1986), 63–69.
Franceschi, Franco, Goldthwaite, Richard A., Mueller, Reinhold Christopher. *Il Rinascimento italiano e l'Europa. Volume quarto. Commercio e cultura mercantile*. Treviso-Costabissara (Vicenza): Fondazione Cassamarca—Angelo Colla editore, 2007.
Frizet, Yannick. *Louis XI, le roi René et la Provence*. Aix-en-Provence: Presses universitaires de Provence, 2015.
Gadille, Jacques, René Fédou, Henri Hours, Bernard de Vergile. *Le diocèse de Lyon*. Paris: Éditions Beauchesne, 1983.
Gandilhon, René. *Politique économique de Louis XI*. Paris: Presses universitaires de France, 1941.
Gascon, Richard. *Grand commerce et vie urbaine au XVIe siècle: Lyon et ses marchands (circa 1520–circa 1580)*. Paris, the Hague: Mouton, 1971.
Gascon, Richard. Nationalisme économique et géographie des foires. La querelle des foires de Lyon (1484–1494). *Cahiers d'histoire* 1 (1956): 253–287.
Gaussin, Pierre-Roger. Les conseillers du roi Louis XI (1461–1483). In *La France de la fin du xve siècle*. Paris: CNRS, 1985, 105–134.
Heers, Jacques. *Louis XI: le métier de roi*. Paris: Éditions Perrin, 1999.
Kendall, Paul Murray. *Louis XI*. Paris: Pluriel, 2014.
Klapisch-Zuber, Christiane. *La Maison et le nom: stratégies et rituels dans l'Italie de la Renaissance*. Paris: EHESS, 1990.
Klapisch-Zuber, Christiane. *Mariages à la florentine. Femmes et vie de famille à Florence (XIVe–XVe siècle)*. Paris: Éditions de l'EHESS-Gallimard-Seuil, 2020.
Labande, Léon-Honoré. *Avignon au XVe siècle. Légation de Charles de Bourbon et du cardinal Julien de La Rovère*. Paris: A. Picard, 1920.
Lang, Heinrich. *Wirtschaften als kulturelle Praxis. Die Florentiner Salviati und die Augsburger Welser auf den Märkten in Lyon (1507–1559)*. Stuttgart: Franz Steiner, 2020.
Langholm, Odd Inge. *Economics in the Medieval Schools: Wealth, Exchange, Value, Money and Usury According to the Paris Theological Tradition, 1200–1350*. Leiden: Brill, 1992.
Lassalmonie, Jean-François. *La boîte à l'enchanteur. Politique financière de Louis XI*. Paris: Comité pour l'histoire économique et financière de la France, 2002.

Lenoble, Clément. *L'exercice de la pauvreté. Économie et religion chez les franciscains d'Avignon (XIIIe–XVe siècle)*. Rennes: Presses universitaires de Rennes, 2013.

Le Roy Ladurie, Emmanuel. *L'État royal: de Louis XI à Henri IV. La monarchie de la Renaissance, 1460–1610*. Paris: Hachette, 2000.

Matringe, Nadia. *La banque en Renaissance. Les Salviati et la place de Lyon au milieu du XVIe siècle*. Rennes: Presses universitaires de Rennes, 2015.

Morvan, Haude. Au Chœur des affaires. La nation florentine et les frères prêcheurs lyonnais. *Archivum Fratrum Praedicatorum* 3:2 (2018): 107–123.

Palermo, Luciano. *Sviluppo economico e società preindustriali. Cicli, strutture e congiunture in Europa dal medioevo alla prima età moderna*. Rome: Viella, 1997.

Pallini-Martin, Agnès. *Banque, négoce et politique. Les Florentins à Lyon au moment des guerres d'Italie*. Paris: Garnier, 2018.

Pallini-Martin, Agnès. L'installation d'une famille de marchands-banquiers florentins à Lyon au début du XVIe siècle: les Salviati. In *Lyon vu/e d'ailleurs (1245–1800). Échanges, compétitions et perceptions*, Jean-Louis Gaulin, Susanne Rau (eds.). Lyon: Presses universitaires de Lyon, 2009, 71–90.

Pelletier, André, Jacques Rossiaud, Françoise Bayard, Pierre Cayez. *Histoire de Lyon: des origines à nos jours*. Lyon: Éditions lyonnaises d'art et d'histoire, 2007.

Piron, Sylvain. *Généalogie de la morale économique*. Brussels: Zones sensibles, 2020.

Piron, Sylvain. Prêts charitables et opérations capitalistes dans l'éthique franciscaine des contrats monétaires. In *Des personnes aux institutions. Réseaux et culture du crédit du XVIe au XXe siècle en Europe*, Laurence Fontaine, Gilles Postel-Vinay, Jean-Laurent Rosenthal, Paul Servais (eds.). Louvain-la-Neuve: Bruylant Academia, 1997, 11–27.

Piron, Sylvain. *L'occupation du monde*. Brussels: Zones sensibles, 2018.

Renouard, Yves. *Les relations des papes d'Avignon et des compagnies commerciales et bancaires de 1316 à 1378*. Paris: E. de Boccard, 1941.

Rey, Raymond. *Louis XI et les États pontificaux de France au XVe siècle d'après des documents inédits*. Grenoble: Imprimerie Allier Frères, 1899.

Sablon du Corail, Amable. *Louis XI. Le joueur inquiet*. Paris: Belin, 2015.

Sclafert, Thérèse. Les routes du Dauphiné et de la Provence sous l'influence du séjour des papes à Avignon. *Annales d'histoire économique* 1 (1929): 183–192.

Tanzini, Lorenzo. *1345. La bancarotta di Firenze: una storia di banchieri, fallimenti e finanza*. Rome: Salerno, 2018.

Todeschini, Giacomo. Finance and usury. The Languages of Public Economy as Rhetoric of Social Inequality. In *Estados y mercados financieros en el occidente cristiano (siglos XIII–XVI). XLI semana de estudios medievales*. Pamplona: Gobierno de Navarra, 2015, 83–103.

Todeschini, Giacomo. Gestione dei beni pubblici e amministrazione dei patrimoni privati. Il mercato cristiano come spazio di sacralizzazione della ricchezza familiare. *Mélanges de l'École française de Rome—Italie et Méditerranée modernes et contemporaines* 127:1 (2015). http://journals.openedition.org/mefrim/2028 (24 October 2024).

Todeschini, Giacomo. *I mercanti e il tempio. La società cristiana e il circolo virtuoso della ricchezza fra Medioevo ed Età Moderna*. Bologna: Il Mulino, 2002.

Todeschini, Giacomo. *Il Prezzo della salvezza. Lessici medievali del pensiero economico*. Rome: NIS, 1994.

Todeschini, Giacomo. *La banca e il ghetto. Una storia italiana*. Bari: Laterza, 2016.

Pauline Gomes

From the markets of Chieri to the fairs of Lyon: tracing the mobility of the Pietraviva family from the 13th to 15th centuries

> Si Antoine de Gondi, sieur du Perron, n'eût été qu'un gentilhomme du commun, eût-il pris alliance avec une personne aussi relevée que l'étoit Marie de Pierrevive, et par sa naissance et par la qualité qu'elle avoit de gouvernante des enfants de France?[1]

Cardinal de Retz, victim of "slander" and "lies" depicting the Gondi family, his Florentine ancestors, as "people of nothing", was defended by his friend Pierre d'Hozier, the king's genealogist.[2] In a brief opuscule aimed at re-establishing the nobility of the cardinal's lineage, d'Hozier evoked the qualities of his grandmother, Marie-Christine de Pierrevive, married in 1516 to Antoine de Gondi, lord of Le Perron near Lyon. Nevertheless, if the genealogist insists on the functions and titles granted to the Gondi couple, it is because the reality is less flamboyant. When the Gondi family, originally from Florence, arrived in Lyon at the turn of the sixteenth century, they were merchant bankers. As for the Pierrevive family, they were originally from Piedmont and were known as spice merchants and apothecaries.[3] The reason for mentioning the Pierrevive here is not, however, to perpetuate criticism of the cardinal's commoner origins, but because their path between Piedmont, Lyon, and, later, Paris encourages reflection on the driving forces and motivations behind geographical and social mobility.

When Marie-Christine's father arrived in Lyon with his three brothers between 1470 and 1480, the Pierrevive were known only as wealthy spice merchants

1 Suggested translation: "If Antoine de Gondi, lord of Le Perron, had only been a common gentleman, would he have made an alliance with a person as distinguished as Marie de Pierrevive, both by birth and by her position as governess of the children of France?" Quote taken from Remarques sommaires sur la maison de Gondi par le sieur d'Hozier, gentilhomme ordinaire de la maison du roi, généalogiste de sa majesté et juge général des armes et blasons de France, 1652. In *Œuvres du Cardinal de Retz*, vol. 9, Régis De Chantelauze (ed.). Paris: Hachette, 1887, 420–435.

2 Although signed by Pierre d'Hozier, Régis Chantelauze attributes the authorship of this opuscule to the cardinal himself. Whether or not the cardinal's quill is hidden behind the name d'Hozier, the arguments put forward give an idea of how the cardinal could defend the nobility of his origins.

3 Amédée de Pierrevive is listed as an "espicier" in the consular deliberations of 1477, Archives Municipales de Lyon (hereafter AML), BB16, f°34v.

https://doi.org/10.1515/9783111621296-011

from Piedmont. Half a century later, they had established themselves as one of Lyon's most influential families, an achievement that was not so common among the mass of Italian merchants who frequented the city in the late Middle Ages. The Pierrevive family—or Pietraviva in Italian—was part of a wave of commercial migration that characterised the turn of the sixteenth century and which was directly linked to the resounding success of Lyon's trade fairs.[4]

This commercial mobility, particularly of Italians, has already been firmly established by a number of studies.[5] However, the Pierrevive dossier provides an opportunity to look at a number of aspects that are still not widely understood: on the one hand, while the presence of Florentines, Genoese, and Lucchese is attested and has been the subject of several studies, the settlement of Italians from other regions such as Piedmont is less well recognised, even though their presence is attested. On the other hand, while the high mobility of Italians in Lyon is already well known, a number of questions remain unanswered. Indeed, among the crowd of merchants who arrived, some decided to stay, to settle down, and put down roots in the city. What were their motivations? How did they settle? Can we talk about integration or even assimilation into their new environment? My research, which focuses on the mobility of the Pietraviva family in Lyon,[6] provides an opportunity to explore the example of a family of Piedmontese merchants who chose to settle in the region on a long-term basis, building a town house in the old town and buying estates in the surrounding countryside.

The Pietraviva family, whose earliest traces date back to the mid-thirteenth century, originated in Chieri, a medium-sized city belonging to the diocese of Turin and often cited alongside Asti for the culture of credit and usury it developed.[7] They belonged to the families of *populares* and were involved in the San

4 The attractiveness of Lyon's fairs has been highlighted by the work of Marc Brésard. *Les foires de Lyon aux XV[è] et XVI[è] siècles*. Paris: Auguste Picard, 1914. More recently, Jacques Rossiaud portrayed Lyon during its golden century (1450–1550) as the "cité *mercatrix*." See Jacques Rossiaud. *Lyon 1250–1550. Réalités et imaginaires d'une métropole*. Jean-Louis Gaulin, Susanne Rau (eds.). Lyon: Champ Vallon, 2012, 13–26.

5 Some of the earliest works on the subject include Richard Gascon. *Grand commerce et vie urbaine au XVIe siècle. Lyon et ses marchands (environs de 1520–environs de 1580)*. Paris: Mouton, 1971, 2 vols; Françoise Bayard. *Les Bonvisi, marchands banquiers à Lyon, 1575–1629*. Lyon: Annales E.C.S., 1964; Jacqueline Boucher. *Présence italienne à Lyon à la Renaissance: du milieu du XVe à la fin du XVIe siècle*. Lyon: Editions Lugd, 1994.

6 This article is based on research carried out for a Master's thesis at the École Normale Supérieure de Lyon, under the supervision of Jean-Louis Gaulin.

7 This aspect is discussed at further length in note 21.

Giorgio society, whose aim was to organise their defence against the noble families.[8] By trading and taking out loans, they became richer and increased their wealth. During the fourteenth century, they probably specialised in the spice trade and medicine, and gradually entered the service of the princes of Savoy. This was a period of significant social advancement, as they acquired new properties and new responsibilities. This favourable climate seems to have lasted throughout the fifteenth century. The mobility to Lyon, which can be dated back to the 1470s, appears to have been motivated by economic ambitions, in the context of the development of Lyon's trade fairs. In the second-largest city of the French kingdom, the four Pietraviva brothers—whose surname was simply translated to Pierrevive[9]—integrated and built a new life for themselves.

However, far from imagining their arrival in France as the necessary outcome of their career or the teleological culmination of a strategy of upward social mobility, and not wishing to add another chapter to the "*France italienne*,"[10] the interest was to retrace their itinerary from the town of Chieri in Piedmont and understand how social advancement, mobility, and professionalisation fit together. In other words, the main aim is to examine the motivations and driving forces behind the mobility of the Pietraviva family. This research is part of a historiographical renewal of the notion of mobility, spurred in particular by the work of Sandro Carocci and Sergio Tognetti.[11]

In order to retrace the Pietraviva family's history and reconstruct the main stages of their mobility, different types of sources need to be consulted. As there are no traces left of the Pietraviva family archives, it is necessary to deal with records produced by external actors and scattered across several archive depositories. In particular, these are records left by their notaries or the various municipal or princely administrations they frequented. For the thirteenth and first half

---

8 The *Societas Populi* of Chieri, dedicated to San Giorgio, was probably founded in the first quarter of the thirteenth century. Around 1250, it drew up its own statutes, which have been published in full. See Gino Borghezio, Bartolomeo Valimberti (eds.). *Statuta et capitula societatis Sancti Georgii seu populi Chariensis*. vol. 2, Turin: Regia Deputazione subalpina di storia patria, 1940. To date, there has been no study of the San Giorgio society in Chieri, or of popular societies in Piedmont in general, but I would like to mention Umberto Delmastro's ongoing thesis, "Il Popolo del Principe. Società di popolo e stato sabaudo nel secolo XIV," under the supervision of Jean-Louis Gaulin and Federica Cengarle (Pisa, Scuola Normale di Pisa).

9 There are several variants of their name: Pietraviva, Peraviva, or Petraviva on the Italian side, and Pierrevive or Pierre Vive on the French side.

10 Jean-François Dubost. *La France italienne XVIe–XVIIe siècle*. Paris: Aubier, 1997.

11 See Sandro Carocci (ed.). *La mobilità sociale nel Medioevo*. Rome: École française de Rome, 2010; Sergio Tognetti, Lorenzo Tanzini (eds). *La mobilità sociale nel Medioevo italiano*. Rome: Viella, 2016.

of the fourteenth century, the sources are mainly the work of the town of Chieri and are therefore kept at the *Archivio Storico del Comune di Chieri.*[12] For the second half of the fourteenth century, sources produced by the Savoyard administration are also included, the Piedmont part of which is held by the *Archivio di Stato di Torino.*[13] Finally, for the last quarter of the fifteenth and the beginning of the sixteenth century, sources produced by the Lyon municipality, kept at the *Archives Municipales de Lyon,*[14] are important. The same applies to notarial sources kept mainly at the *Archives Départementales et métropolitaines du Rhône.*[15]

The fate of this particular family of Piedmontese merchants highlights the attractiveness of the Lyon fairs and the role they played in their mobility—a role of polarisation, which shows the circular relationship that exists between mobility and fairs. This short dossier also echoes a number of themes at the heart of the CoMOR programme: trade routes, goods and capital, commercial operations and partners, as well as commercial immigration, methods of integration into a new environment, and family or individual strategies. As a protean historical object, this case study brings together and condenses some of the issues at stake in this research programme.[16]

Pietraviva at markets and fairs in Chieri

Let us look briefly at the context in which the Pietraviva family started out. Their hometown, Chieri, is a medium-sized commune in Piedmont, around fifteen kilometres south-east of Turin. From the point of view of networks and traffic, the

12 I have mainly consulted Chieri's *estimi* and the town's account books. See *Archivio Storico del Comune di Chieri* (hereafter ACC), art. 143, par. 1 and art. 137, par. 2, nos. 1 and 2.

13 The extensive holdings of the Savoy administration at the Archivio di Stato di Torino (hereafter AST) were analysed mainly on the basis of random samples—in particular, the archives of the Savoy Chamber of Accounts (inv. 38, f. 43: accounts of wax and spices for the hotel of the counts of Savoy; inv. 40, f. 1: accounts of the treasurers and general receivers for the prince of Achaea), the Chamber of Accounts of Piedmont (accounts of castellanies, art. 27, par. 1, Chieri), and the accounts of the general treasury (inv. 16, *camerale Savoia*). I should also mention the valuable Biscaretti fonds, which contains numerous resources relating to Chieri, and the Chieri notaries' fonds (Giovanni Visca's registers).

14 AML, mainly the *Nommées* (series CC), and consular deliberations (series BB).

15 Archives départementales et métropolitaines du Rhône (hereafter ADMR). See in particular, the archives of notary Pierre Dorlin, ADMR, 1E2241.

16 We have also been able to add a number of collections to the *Fairs in History* database: collections 30, 31, 32, 33, 34, 35, 42, 43, 44, 45, 46, 55.

town benefited from its location on the *Via Francigena*. As the work of Giuseppe Sergi[17] has shown, Chieri was located on one of the main routes taken by the famous road, which was a definite advantage when it came to capturing the flow of people and goods travelling from Italy to France via the Alpine routes. These flows fed directly into the town's two main markets, held in *platea Beccharia* and *platea Mercadillo* respectively. The link between Chieri and the Alpine routes was accentuated by the town's decision to align itself politically with the county of Savoy, which was undergoing a period of rapid territorial expansion at the time.[18] Far from hindering its economic development, this new allegiance may even have led to positive economic dynamics. From 1422, two annual fairs were granted to Chieri by the Duke of Savoy, Amadeus VIII.[19] As a result, Chieri became a small commercial centre with an influence throughout Piedmont.

With a population of around 9,000 at the end of the thirteenth century,[20] Chieri was at that time more attractive than its neighbour Turin in terms of population and trade. However, as it did not have a bishop's see, it remained dependent on Turin. Nevertheless, it became an urban municipality with its own governing bodies.[21] Despite its modest size, it has gone down in history as having developed a major credit culture, reaching into every stratum of the population. Alongside Asti, it was even one of the towns where the famous "Lombards," who specialised in lending money and were present throughout Europe from the twelfth century onwards, originated.[22] Towns such as Asti and Chieri have benefited from the revival of studies on the Lombards, thanks to the impetus

17 See the classical book by Giuseppe Sergi. *Chambéry a Torino fra X e XIII secolo*. Naples: Liguori, 1981, with map on p. 28.

18 The surrender of Chieri to Savoy took place in 1347. At that time, the town became part of the Piedmont apanage of the princes of Savoy-Achaea but maintained its autonomy and political institutions. On the territorial expansion of the county of Savoy, see Bernard Demotz. *Le comté de Savoie du XIe au XVe siècle: pouvoir, château et État au Moyen âge*. Geneva: Slatkine, 2000.

19 Massimo Raviolo. *Chieri in fiera: da San Giuliano e Santa Basilissa a San Martino*. Chieri: EDITO, 2007. The privilege granted by Amadeus VIII established two annual fairs, held for ten days on Saint Julian's Day and Saint Martin's Day.

20 Figures estimated by Mirella Montanari in her paper La popolazione di Chieri e del suo distretto alla fine del secolo XIII. In *Demografia e società nell'Italia medievale (secoli IX–XIV)*. Cuneo: Società per gli studi storici, archeologici ed artistici della provincia di Cuneo, 1994.

21 In 1168, the Bishop of Turin granted the citizens of Chieri the right to hold assemblies and appoint consuls—political institutions that testify to the birth of the Commune.

22 On the Lombards of Asti and Chieri, particular mention should be made of Renato Bordone, Franco Spinelli (eds.). *Lombardi in Europa nel Medioevo*. Milan: F. Angeli, 2005; Ezio Claudio Pia. "Multam pecuniam, multa mala": i "Lombardi" astigiani e il mercato del credito nel Basso Medioevo. *Nuova rivista storica* 105 (2021): 33–62.

given by Renato Bordone in the 1980s, but many of the sources preserved in the *Archivio Storico del Comune di Chieri* remain largely unexplored to this day.

The town of Chieri has preserved a remarkable collection of *estimi*, numbering over fifty registers, drawn up between the thirteenth and seventeenth centuries. What is even more remarkable is that Chieri has one of the oldest *estimi* in Italy, dated 1253.[23] These *estimi* are useful in order to reconstruct the Pietraviva's land holdings: family possessions were declared and recorded in these registers, which were drawn up by the municipal authorities during major surveys to establish the tax base of taxpaying citizens. These lists of possessions, known as *denunciae*, were the first stage in the tax investigation. They are declarative and written in the first person. A study of the Pietraviva family's assets reveals the family's interests and strategies.

Of all the tax declarations issued by members of the Pietraviva family that we have been able to consult,[24] I will confine myself here to mentioning two—the first dated 1289 and the second 1365—in order to effectively highlight the strategies put in place by the family and their desire to move closer to the main trading centres in Chieri.

In 1289, Gribaudo Pietraviva's tax report tells us that the family chose to settle in the Gialdo district as early as the end of the thirteenth century, as shown on the first map below.[25] The family estate was located between the city's two main shopping streets (*ruata magistra* and *ruata repentita*), making it ideally situated in the heart of the business district. What's more, as Mirella Montanari points out, the choice of the Gialdo district was significant, as it was the economic heart of the town—the entire merchant elite owned property in this district.[26]

---

23 A complete edition has been published by Maria Clotilde Daviso di Charvensod (ed.). *I più antichi catasti del comune di Chieri (1253)*. Turin: Regia deputazione subalpina di storia patria, 1939. More recently, it has been studied by Riccardo Rao. Modalités d'enregistrement des informations dans les plus anciens estimi de l'Italie nord-occidentale du Duecento (Chieri et Pavie). In *L'enquête en questions: de la réalité à la "vérité" dans les modes de gouvernement, Moyen Âge–Temps modernes*, Anne Mailloux, Laure Verdon (eds.). Paris: CNRS Éditions, 2014, 173–183.

24 In total, I found eight tax declarations between 1289 and 1579. See ACC, art. 143, par. 1, nos. 12, 16, 19, 24, 37, 44, 72, 78.

25 Map generated from the Geoportale Piemonte website: https://www.geoportale.piemonte.it/visregpigo/. I would also like to thank Vincenzo Tedesco, archivist at the ACC, for his topographical information.

26 The economic importance of the Gialdo district is recalled by Mirella Montanari. Dalla terra al denaro: un caso esemplare, I de Villa di Chieri. In *Lombardi in Europa*, Bordone, Spinelli (eds.), 196–206. Montanari also presents the distribution of activities by district in Chieri: the Albussano district was the artisan district, the Arene district was mainly occupied by small craftsmen, sala-

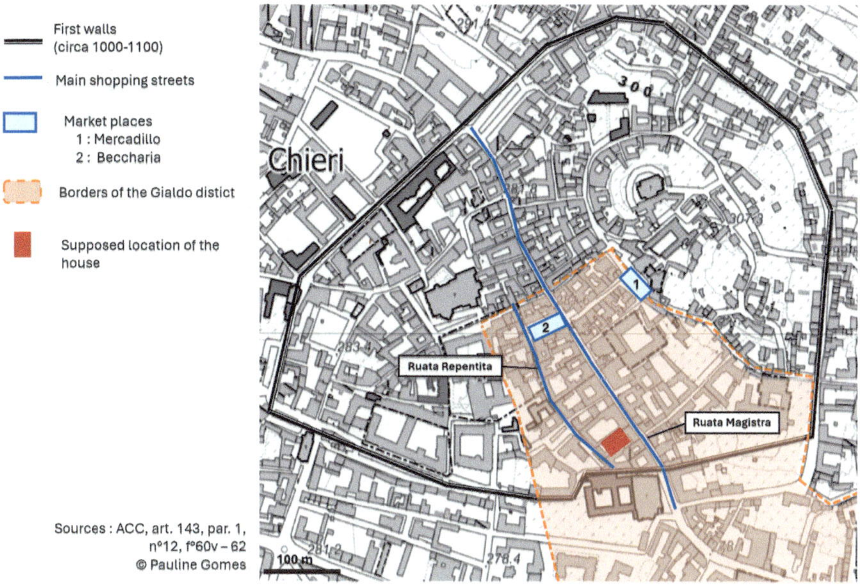

Fig. 1: Pietraviva holdings in Chieri according to the *estimo* of 1289.

However, the Pietraviva family's ambitions were not limited to a property in the Gialdo district, and the declarations made in 1365 by Amedeo, Sebastiano, and Giovanni de Pietraviva bear striking witness to this. As shown on the second map, the family experienced major economic and property growth from 1289 onwards. The possession of two shops, known as *apotheca,* testifies to the central role played by merchant activities in the rise of the Pietraviva family. The location of the properties is interesting, as in addition to the family home, which was already mentioned in the 1289 declaration, the Pietraviva family claimed to own several other houses, located in the immediate vicinity of the two market squares (*Beccharia* and *Mercadillo*) and along the Via Draparie, also known as the merchants' street. The development of their holdings in the city therefore reflects their desire to be as close to business as possible.

ried workers, seasonal workers, and farmers, while the Vairo district was mainly a residential area occupied by the town's wealthy families.

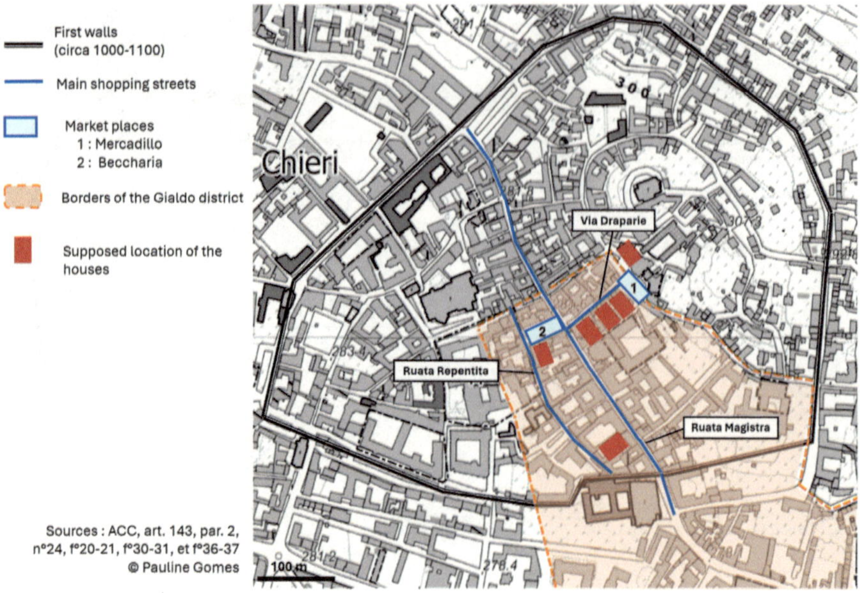

Fig. 2: Pietraviva holdings in Chieri according to the *estimo* of 1365.

It is difficult to be more precise about the nature of the Pietraviva's business in Chieri. Without family archives, account books, or correspondence, we can only speculate about the type of goods traded by the Pietraviva family at that time. The generic term *apotheca* does not in fact provide any information about the nature of the products sold. However, we do know with certainty that the family specialised in the spice trade from 1407 onwards, because one document describes the *apotheca* as a *spezieria*.[27] It is possible that the Pietraviva family had been trading in spices before then, as there were several doctors in the family as early as 1360,[28] and we know about the many interactions between medicine, the apothecary, and the spice trade. However, this hypothesis cannot yet be verified.

This specialisation in medicine and the spice trade may well have played a part in bringing the Pietraviva family closer to the princes of Savoy. Whatever the case, when the Pietraviva entered the service of the Prince of Achaea and the Count of Savoy, their activities took on a new dimension.

---

27 Filippo Noberasco. Le pergamene dell'archivio comunale di Savona. *Atti e memorie della Società Savonese di Storia Patria*, vol. 2. Savona: Tipografia Savonese, 1940, 166.

28 This aspect will be discussed in more detail in the following pages.

Merchants in the service of princes: favours and privileges

The triptych of medical practice, the spice trade, and service to princes seems to have indeed been a winning combination. We have found evidence of at least four doctors among the Pietraviva between 1360 and 1480. The first of these, Michele di Pietraviva, practised in the years 1360–1380,[29] by which time he was already occasionally hiring out his services to Amadeus of Savoy-Achaea, Lord of Piedmont, and to Amadeus VI, Count of Savoy.[30] It therefore seems plausible that the Pietraviva family supplied the courts of the lords of Piedmont and the counts of Savoy with spices and various drugs, and even with medicines that they had made themselves. Indeed, although apothecaries were long scorned by doctors, seen as mere shopkeepers authorised only to dispense the doctor's prescriptions,[31] the pairing of apothecary and medicine nevertheless appears to have been very frequent and effective, especially if we bear in mind that the medical and dietary uses of spices were often complementary.[32]

The position acquired with the princes of Savoy went hand-in-hand with rewards and privileges that enabled the Pietraviva to increase their social prestige, their connections, and their ability to take actions. In other words, their proximity to the princes served to accelerate their social success, a fate shared by several other families in the Piedmontese elite who saw it as an opportunity for social

---

29 He is mentioned by Irma Naso. *Medici e strutture sanitarie nella società tardo-medievale: il Piemonte dei secoli XIV e XV*. Milan: F. Angeli, 1982, 207.

30 Occasional traces of missions carried out by Michele di Pietraviva can be found in the accounts of the princes of Savoy. For example, on 22 September 1378, Michele came to Turin to treat the prince of Achaea, who was ill, and stayed there for two days. See AST, Sezioni riunite, Camera dei Conti di Savoia, inv. 40 accounts of the treasurers general of the princes of Achaea, roll 1, 1377–1381.

31 Jean-Pierre Bénézet. *Pharmacie et médicament en Méditerranée occidentale (XIIIe–XVIe siècles)*. Paris: H. Champion, 1999. From the thirteenth to the sixteenth century, the two professions were quite distinct. Pharmacists did not have the right to practice medicine and were mainly responsible for dispensing prescriptions.

32 In a grocer's or apothecary's shop, one would find a wide range of products, some of which were intended for food use and others for medical use. Medicines were sold alongside table spices, confectionery, sugar, oil, candles, and dispensary equipment. For more details, see Joseph Shatzmiller. Herbs and drugs in medieval Provençal medicine. In *Herbes, drogues et épices en Méditerranée: histoire, anthropologie, économie, du Moyen âge à nos jours*. Aix-en-Provence: Institut de recherches et d'études sur le monde arabe et musulman, 2014, 157–165.

advancement.[33] They rented out their services and often financed the princes, who were constantly in need of liquidity, which earned them rewards in the form of offices or fiefs and estates to manage.[34] The alliance between the princes of Savoy and this rising Piedmontese elite enabled these families to grow richer and experience a form of ennoblement, often described as *insignorimento*, which is well known to historiography.[35] The trajectory of the Pietraviva family is fully in line with this regional dynamic.

This is evidenced by a document drawn up in 1369 in the name of Count Amadeus VI.[36] This is an infeudation in favour of *magister* Michele di Pietraviva in exchange for a transfer of land. In reality, Michele appears to have been virtually expropriated from his lands, which consisted of a few *aree* and *ortorum* in Chieri, and which became the property of the Count. These areas and gardens were to be used to build a small fort next to the ramparts—the *castrum sancti Jacobi*. By way of compensation for this loss, Michele was granted usufruct of the fort, which was erected for the occasion as a *feudum franchum et nobilem*. For Michele, who was known at the time for his services as a doctor (hence the title of *magister* attached to his name), this document was the first milestone in a process of ennoblement and gradual aggregation into a class of officers and new nobles gravitating around power. He is also referred to here as *dilecto familiari et fideli nostro*, which already indicates a form of familiarity that suggests the possibility of entering the count's entourage.[37] For the Green Count, the interest was twofold: as well as securing the loyalty of a family that owed him its social standing,

---

33 This is the case, for example, of the Provana family, which was studied in an article by Giulia Scarcia. Élites del territorio piemontese e corte sabauda fra XIV e XV secolo. In *L'affermarsi della corte sabauda. Dinastie, poteri, élites in Piemonte e Savoia fra tardo Medioevo e prima età moderna*, Paola Bianchi, Luisa Clotilde Gentile (eds.). Turin: Silvio Zamorani, 2006, 163–176. The Provana, originally from Carignano, lent a great deal of money to the princes of Savoy, which enabled them to obtain the administration of fiefs and castellanies as well as public offices.

34 This gave rise to a new class of officers whose social success was directly linked to the Savoys, as Guido Castelnuovo has shown in *Ufficiali e gentiluomini: la società politica sabauda nel tardo medioevo*. Milan: Franco Angeli, 1994.

35 Renato Bordone, Guido Castelnuovo, Gian Maria Varanini. *Le aristocrazie dai signori rurali al patriziato*. Rome: Editori Laterza, 2004., esp. 106–112 on *insignorimento*, the creation of lineages, and the invention of family traditions.

36 AST, sezione corte, Fondo Biscaretti, Mazzo 1, no. 35, transcript attached.

37 On the importance of the entourage and the treatment of *familiaris*, see Bernard Demotz. Choix et représentations. L'entourage des comtes de Savoie du XIe au XVe siècle. In *À l'ombre du Pouvoir: Les entourages princiers au Moyen Âge*, Jean-Louis Kupper, Alain Marchandisse (eds). Liège: Presses universitaires de Liège, 2019, 267–276. In this type of documentation, the terms used are carefully chosen to reinforce the hierarchy between the prince and his subjects. On the subtlety of these formulas, see, for example, Florentin Briffaz. Formuler la prééminence du

it strengthened Chieri's defensive capacity. Against a tense military and political backdrop,[38] the counts sought to equip the towns of Piedmont with defensive military tools. We know for certain that the construction of the *castrum* was completed, as it appears under the name of "la Rochetta" on the engraving of an aerial view of Chieri in the *Theatrum Sabaudie* in 1682.[39]

In the light of all these factors, the rapprochement between the Pietraviva and the princes of Savoy can be seen as a springboard or accelerator in the family's mobility, both geographically and socially. The centre of gravity of their affairs shifted westwards, towards the Alps and beyond. This contact with the prince opened up new horizons for social advancement.

These strategies put in place by the Pietraviva—from practising medicine for the powerful to entering the "entourage" of princes—can be seen as "channels of mobility."[40] Subsequently (and this certainly constitutes a link or continuity in mobility), these same strategies were used in the service of the kings of France. In fact, at the end of the fifteenth century, the Pietraviva family drew closer to Charles VIII, and once again it was the practice of medicine that prompted this rapprochement. In the 1480s, Giovanni Michele di Pietraviva became the king's personal physician and adviser,[41] giving him a privileged position to supply the

prince en Savoie (XIIIe–XVe siècles). In *La formule au Moyen Âge IV*, Elise Louviot, Charles Garcia, Stephen Morrison (eds.). Turnhout: Brepols, 2021, 111–138.

38 Roberto Biolzi. Les entreprises d'Amédée VI, entre aventures étrangères et guerres intestines (1355–1383). In *"J'ay grand envie de veoir assaillir": Guerre, guerriers et finances dans les États de Savoie à la fin du Moyen Âge (XIVe–XVe siècle).* Rennes: Presses universitaires de Rennes, 2024, 73–86. The 1360s were a turbulent decade in Piedmont: firstly, because of the rebellion of the younger branch of the Savoy-Achaea family, which was finally put down by the Green Count in 1368, and secondly, because companies of mercenaries criss-crossed the region as part of the conflicts between the Viscontis of Milan and the Marquises of Montferrat and Saluces. In this context of instability, Amadeus VI reasserted his authority.

39 *Theatrum statuum Regiae Celsitudinis Sabaudiœ Ducis*, commonly abbreviated to *Theatrum Sabaudie*, is a collection of engravings depicting the States of the House of Savoy, first published in Turin in 1682. Ferruccio Ferrua identified the "*castrum Sancti Jacobi*" on the engraving of Chieri. See Ferruccio Ferrua. *La Chiesa e la confraternità di San Giacomo a Chieri.* Chieri: Chieri Edizione, 2008. The *castrum* therefore corresponds to the Rochetta fort (no. 27 on the map).

40 This expression, borrowed from sociological vocabulary, is used by Sandro Carocci, who applies it to medieval societies. See Sandro Carocci. Introduzione: la mobilità sociale e la congiuntura del 1300: ipotesi, metodi di indagine, storiografia. In *La mobilità sociale nel Medioevo*. Rome: École française de Rome, 2010, 1–37.

41 Ernest Wickersheimer, Guy Beaujouan. *Dictionnaire biographique des médecins en France au Moyen Âge*, vol. 2. Geneva: Librairie Droz, 1979, 450. Giovanni Michele's services likely earned him and his three brothers, Andrea, Nicoletto and Amedeo, ennoblement from Charles VIII in 1484: See Châtelet de Paris, Livres de couleur (1223–1604), Y//6/1, f°55 to 56v (online on francearchives.gouv.fr).

crown with drugs and other medicines, which they brought into the kingdom through their network of spice merchants.

In a way very similar to what I showed earlier with the princes of Savoy, this was an opportunity for the Pietraviva to benefit from certain privileges. King Charles VIII used his influence to intervene in a trade dispute that put the Pietraviva in a bad position. On 24 December 1486, in a letter to his "très aimé cousin le duc de Savoie," he asked to return to "notre amé et feal conseillier et medecin ordinaire maistre Jehan Michel de Pierrevive, et à noz bien amez valetz de chambre ses frères," seven bales of cloth belonging to them, having been seized by the Duke's officers in Turin[42] and which the Pietraviva "avaient entencion [de] porter à Venise et les convertir en drogues et autres singulières choses pour notre plaisir, dont nous leur avions donné charge."[43] These bales of cloth were not simply the property of the Pietraviva family; they were to be sold in Venice to buy spices with the proceeds, which were then to be imported into the kingdom via Lyon to fulfil an order placed directly by the king with his physician. This letter shows how the services provided to the king as advisor and physician were intertwined with the networks and issues involved in trade. If the services provided by the Pietraviva were appreciated by the princes, it was thanks to the complementary nature of their medical practice and the extent of their commercial network. The Pietraviva's involvement in Lyon's trade fairs helped to expand and strengthen this commercial network.

Setting up in Lyon and extending the retail network

The first member of the family to arrive in the city in the 1470s was Amedeo (Amédée or Aymé in French) de Pierrevive.[44] He then enlisted the help of his three brothers, Andrea (André), Nicoletto (Nicolet), and Giovanni-Michele (Jean-Michel),

42 The letter mentions a certain Eustace Moreau, "voyer ou conducteur" who "avait prins charge de mettre lesdictes bales sur la rivière du Pou." Moreau is explicitly named as the culprit in the case, as he allegedly failed to pay certain "gabelles" (the nature of which is not specified), leading the officers to seize his load.

43 A transcription of the letter can be found in Paul Pélicier and Bernard de Mandrot (eds.). *Lettres de Charles VIII, roi de France*, vol. 5. Paris: Renouard, 1905, 201–203.

44 The use of the particle gradually became more widespread. Infrequent in Piedmontese sources from the thirteenth century, it became systematic in Lyonnaise sources from the fifteenth century.

the same doctor we have already mentioned.[45] A whole "branch" of the Pietraviva family therefore migrated to Lyon while retaining links with their homeland.[46] This mobility therefore seems to have been chosen, and there is nothing to suggest that it was the result of family conflict or political exile. Furthermore, the Pierrevive brothers' mobility seems to have been planned from the outset for the medium to long term, as confirmed by their purchase of a "*tènement*" in the heart of the old town in the 1480s. This vast plot of land, at the corner of what is now rue Gadagne and montée du Garillon, was ideally located from a commercial point of view—in the heart of the business district, right next to the Change area and the Saône bridge. The Pierrevive family had the Maison de la Boisette—which had previously occupied the land—demolished and, within a few years, had a vast town house built. A brief description of this building can be found in Lyon's fiscal documents (the *Nommées* of 1493):

> Aymé de Pierrevive, espicier, tient une grande maison contenant plusieurs tènements et un grand jardin derrière en ladite ruelle joignant à la maison Michelet du Lard, les hoirs Germayne Gay et Martin Guillaume devers le matin, et la grande maison du Plat devers le vent et par dessus à la rue tirant de Saint-Barthelemy a Saint-Just devers soleil couchant et peult valoir par an IIIC lt.[47]

45 The latter is somewhat of an exception as he seems to have spent little time in Lyon, alternating with Paris, where he pursued a variety of activities: in addition to his work as a doctor, he was appointed councillor to the Parliament of Paris and wrote at least one play.

46 Without being able to consult their correspondence, the exact nature of the links between the Pierrevive of Lyon and the Pietraviva of Chieri is rather difficult to establish. It is known, however, that relations were maintained at least until the beginning of the sixteenth century, since Jean-Michel and Amédée stated in their respective wills (1495 and 1501) that they wished to be buried in the Pietraviva family chapel in Chieri, which is in the church of San Domenico, should they die "de là des mons," that is, on the Italian side of the Alps. Conversely, if they died on the French side of the Alps, they wanted to be buried in their adopted homeland, in the church of Saint Paul in Lyon. This dual belonging or dual identity seems characteristic of a chosen mobility. Jean-Michel's will is edited in Lorena Barale (ed.). *Testamenti chieresi del '400*. Asti: Diffusione Immagine, 2011, E39, 379–383; Amédée's will is edited by Claud Le Laboureur. *Les Masures de l'Île-Barbe, par Claude Le Laboureur, ancien prévôt de cette abbaye. Nouvelle édition, avec supplément et tables*. G. Guigue and M.-C. Guigue (eds.). Lyon: Vitte et Perrussel, 1895, 578–579.

47 AML, CC4, f°84. The *Nommées* of 1493, also known as the "great tax survey," are very dense. The municipality's aim was to carry out a major tax census in order to assess the assets of all Lyon's taxpayers, with a view to establishing their tax base. This census was then used as the basis for establishing the size. For more details, see the analyses by Jacques Rossiaud. *Lyon 1250–1550. Réalités et imaginaires d'une métropole*, Jean-Louis Gaulin and Susanne Rau (eds.). Lyon: Champ Vallon, 2012, Part Three: "Taxation," 119–189.

This extract provides not only topographical information to pinpoint the precise location of the property, but also a few descriptive elements to give an idea of the overall layout. The property consists of several buildings linked by an inner courtyard, forming a kind of urban island, similar to those described by Jacques Heers in the context of family clans or kin groups trying to protect and assert themselves in an urban environment.[48] Behind the habitable buildings is a large garden, which also represents a reserve of space for possible extensions.[49]

Over a period of fifteen years, the Pierrevive family managed not only to establish themselves in Lyon's economic, commercial, and political life,[50] but also to leave their mark on the urban landscape and topography. Indeed, their presence was so remarkable that the street in which their property is located is indicated as the "Rue Pierre Vive" on the scenographic plan of Lyon, which dates back to the 1550s.[51] In the following extract of the scenographic plan,[52] the *tènement* belonging to the Pierrevive family can be seen: located at the corner of rue du

48 Jacques Heers. *Le Clan familial au Moyen Age: Etude sur les structures politiques et sociales des milieux urbains.* Paris: Presses Universitaires de France, 1974. More recently, Marta Gravela wrote an essay about the urban roots of family groups. See Marta Gravela. Curie, fortresses and palaces: Family groups and urban space in late medieval Italy. In *La familia urbana. Matrimonio, parentesco y linaje en la Edad Media,* Jesús Á. Solórzano Telechea, Jelle Haemers, Christian Liddy (eds.). Logroño: Instituto de Estudios Riojanos, 2021, 375–400.

49 Although these gardens are sometimes mentioned in the *Nommées*, here I refer mainly to the work of the group of archaeologists who investigated the history of the building. See Christine Becker, Isabelle Parron-Kontis, Sophie Savay-Guerraz (eds.). *Le Musée Gadagne: Archéologie et histoire au coeur d'un projet patrimonial à Lyon/The Musée Gadagne: Archaeology and history at the heart of a heritage project in Lyon.* Lyon: Alpara, 2006.

50 On the political front, it is worth mentioning the involvement of Nicolet de Pierrevive who sat on the city council for at least a year in 1508. Nicolet also obtained the position of ordinary collector of the king's estates in Lyon, which he then passed on to Antoine Gondi, his son-in-law.

51 AML, 2SAT3.

52 AML, Société de topographie historique de Lyon, 2SAT 6. This is a copy restored in the nineteenth century by Joanny Séon and François Dubouchet. This extract also shows the central location of the property, just a hundred metres from the Place du Change and the Saône bridge. For information on the plots of land occupied by the Pierrevive family, see Becker, Parron-Kontis, Savay-Guerraz, *Le Musée Gadagne*, 99–120. About the scenographic plan, see Rossiaud, *Lyon 1250–1550*, 61–116. On Lyon's urban landscape and topography more generally, see Bernard Gauthiez. *The production of urban space, temporality and spatiality: Lyons, 1500–1900*. Berlin: De Gruyter, 2020.

Fig. 3: Extract of the scenographic map of Lyon around 1550: View of the right bank of the Saône, between the Saône bridge and the rue Saint Barthélémy.

Garillan and rue Pierre Vive, this is a very long plot of land, stretched out on the slopes, with a block of houses at the bottom and several terraces and gardens leading up to the imposing Belregard property at the top of the plot.

However, the marks of their presence were gradually erased by the Gadagne family, to whom they decided to sell their town house in 1545.[53] As a result, the property became known as the Hôtel Gadagne—a name it retains to this day.[54]

The mobility of the Pierrevive family in Lyon was probably guided by commercial motives,[55] possibly linked to the development of fairs which were flourishing at the time. Indeed, after several years of complaints, the Lyonnais obtained the creation of three fairs from Charles VII in 1444, followed by the addition of a fourth by Louis XI in 1463.[56] This commercial effervescence attracted merchants from all over Europe, particularly Italians, Tuscans, Genoese, Venetians, and, of course, Piedmontese. The Italian presence in Lyon has been the subject of a major bibliography—from the work of Richard Gascon[57] to more recent research by Agnès Pallini-Martin and Nadia Matringe on the major Florentine companies established in Lyon.[58] However, this historiography remains largely

53 The deed of sale, kept at the ADMR (10G847, item no. 3), is dated 6 November 1545 and bears the hand seal of notary Pierre Dorlin, who seems to have been close to the Pierrevive family. The deed was partially edited in Becker, Parron-Kontis, Savay-Guerraz, *Le Musée Gadagne*, 118.

54 The Hôtel Gadagne is now home to the Lyon History Museum and the History of Puppetry Museum.

55 It is difficult—if not impossible—for the historian to know the real motivations of the merchants. While the Pierrevives' enterprise seems to us to have been guided primarily by economic ambitions, this is probably not how they perceived their actions or how they represented themselves in society. On the figure of the merchant in the Middle Ages and his place in the medieval economy, see Marco Tangheroni. Le marchand italien: état de la question. In *Actes des congrès de la Société des historiens médiévistes de l'enseignement supérieur public*, 19e Congrès, Reims: SHMES éditions, 1992, 11–24; Peter Spufford. *Power and profit: the merchant in medieval Europe.* London: Thames & Hudson, 2002.

56 In fact, two fairs had already been established by the Dauphin Charles in 1420, before being suspended in 1425. Louis XI's act of 1463 rewarded the insistence of Lyon's municipal authorities over several decades. On the complex and eventful history of Lyon's fairs, refer to the aforementioned thesis by Brésard, *Les foires de Lyon.* See also Jean-Louis Gaulin, Susanne Rau. Rétablissement de deux foires à Lyon (mai 1487). In *Lyon, entre empire et royaume, 843–1601. Textes et documents*, Alexis Charansonnet, Jean-Louis Gaulin, Pascale Mounier, Susanne Rau (eds.). Paris: Garnier, 2015, 523–528; Gisela Naegle. Lyon se défend: délibérations, procès et foires à la fin du Moyen Âge. In *Lyon 1312. Rattacher la ville au royaume*?, Alexis Charansonnet, Jean-Louis Gaulin, Xavier Hélary (eds.). Lyon: CIHAM éditions, 2020, 269–292.

57 Gascon, *Grand commerce et vie urbaine*, 339–340. The author describes Lyon as an "Italian colony."

58 Recent studies have focused on the establishment of major families or companies in Lyon. See Agnès Pallini-Martin. L'installation d'une famille de marchands-banquiers florentins à Lyon au début du XVIe siècle, les Salviati. In *Lyon vu/e d'ailleurs (1245–1800): Échanges, compétitions, perceptions*, Jean-Louis Gaulin, Susanne Rau (eds). Lyon: PUL, 2009, 71–89; Sergio Tognetti. *I Gondi di Lione. Una banca d'affari fiorentina nella Francia del primo Cinquecento.* Florence: Leo

focused on the Tuscans, leaving aside the Piedmontese, who were nevertheless present, as the example of the Pierrevive family shows.

Like other merchant companies, the Pierrevive brothers probably arrived in Lyon with a large sum of money to invest and above all with a network of partners already established, enabling them to quickly set up an efficient and profitable goods import company. The Pierrevives imported large quantities of spices; in the case of pepper and ginger, this can be seen in the registers listing the spices entering Lyon and subject to a tax known as *grabelage*. These books, known as *garbeaux*, were preserved from 1500 onwards and list certain types of spices that entered the city to be sold at fairs.[59] For example, between the All Saints Fair in 1500 and the August Fair in 1501, the Pierrevive brothers brought 54 bales of pepper and 39 bales of ginger into Lyon.[60] These pepper and ginger imports were probably their main commercial activity in Lyon.

Apart from that, it seems difficult—if not impossible—to get an overview of what they imported, because in the absence of an account book, one can only study the spices that are subject to taxes and recorded in the *garbeau*. This information is more difficult to obtain for sugar and saffron, for instance, because these spices were not included in the *garbeau*. Nevertheless, we know from the Gondi account books in Lyon (studied by Sergio Tognetti) that the Pierrevives carried out several commercial transactions with the Gondi family involving large quantities of pepper, ginger, and saffron.[61] The Pierrevives must have also made a great deal of money from saffron, and in fact tried to grow it themselves in the Lyon countryside, as evidenced by the mention of a "*saffranière*" in the *Nommées* of 1518.[62]

S. Olschki, 2013; Nadia Matringe. *La Banque en Renaissance: les Salviati et la place de Lyon au milieu du XVIe siècle*. Rennes: Presses Universitaires de Rennes, 2016.

59 According to Gascon, this tax has existed since the 1460s, but before 1500, it was probably leased to a private individual, which is why the registers have not been preserved. See Gascon, *Grand commerce et vie urbaine*, 40–41. The spices included in the *garbeau* are very varied: aniseed, cinnamon, coriander, cumin, ginger, nutmeg, pepper, etc. On the other hand, saffron, sugar, and alum, for example, seem to have been subject to a special regime.

60 AML, CC546, no. 26, f°1 to 4. The exact provenance of these goods is unknown.

61 Tognetti, *I Gondi di Lione*, 47–48. The Pierrevives were often mentioned in the Gondi account books. In other words, a true commercial partnership was established. For example, in 1519, the Gondi family joined forces with the Florentine Giuliano Davanzati, Nicolas de Pierrevive, and Jean Camus to import a cargo of saffron from southern Italy to Lyon, worth over 7,700 ecus.

62 AML, CC50, f°65v–66: the saffron farm, located "au territoire de Pitiot," appears in Nicolet de Pierrevive's declaration in 1518's *Nommées*. According to Jacques Déniau, saffron was occasionally grown in the Lyonnais. As for the Pierrevives, they did not seem to have repeated the experiment. See Jacques Déniau. *Les Nommées des habitants de Lyon en 1446*. Lyon: A. Rey, 1930, 59

As this operation with the Gondi family shows, setting up in Lyon and taking part in the fairs enabled the Pierrevive family to enhance their network. The Lyon fairs were a meeting place for merchants from a wide range of backgrounds: the Pierrevives traded with families from Lyon,[63] but also formed alliances with major Florentine companies, such as the Salviati family[64] and the Gondi family mentioned above, with whom they set up a number of trading operations throughout the first half of the sixteenth century. In practical terms, the two families and their other associates shared investments, bought commodities from each other, lent each other money, and, above all, invested in a number of major operations to import spices. In 1517, for example, Gondi and Pierrevive shared equally a cargo of cinnamon, ginger, and smaller quantities of pepper and nutmeg. The order was placed by the Pierrevive family with a Genoese merchant, Bartolomeo Fornari.[65] The fact that several people invested in an operation not only reduced the risks in the event of failure, but also had the advantage of being a flexible and ephemeral form of association, which could be renewed or modified for each new operation.[66] Spices were mainly imported from Italy, from Genoa and Venice where the Pierrevives seemed to have representatives and partners. They could be imported by sea, entering the kingdom via the port of Marseille and then up the Rhône valley to Lyon.[67] Merchants also took the land route, crossing the Alps through the Duchy of Savoy and following the famous *Via Francigena* or *Strada di Francia*. According to

---

63 These include Jean Camus and Florimond Rubys as well as the Thomassin family, who rented a room from Nicolet de Pierrevive in 1493.

64 We refer here to the work of Heinrich Lang, who made a meticulous study of the registers of the Salviati company kept in Pisa and who confirmed the presence of the Pierrevives on several occasions in these registers. See Heinrich Lang. *Wirtschaften als kulturelle Praxis. Die Florentiner Salviati und die Augsburger Welser auf den Märkten in Lyon (1507–1559)*. Stuttgart: Steiner, 2019; Heinrich Lang. Networks and Merchant Diasporas: Florentine Merchant Bankers in Lyon and in Antwerp in the Sixteenth Century. In *Commercial Networks and European Cities, 1400–1800*, Andrea Caracausi, Christof Jeggle (eds.). London: Pickering & Chatto, 2014, 107–120.

65 Tognetti, *I Gondi di Lione*, 45–46.

66 Braudel proposed the term "participation" to term this very flexible type of association. See Fernand Braudel. *Civilisation matérielle, économie et capitalisme: XVe-XVIIIe siècle*. Vol. 2, *Les jeux de l'échange*. Paris: A. Colin, 1986, 127. Tognetti, on the other hand, speaks of a "joint venture," allowing merchants to form a sort of "ante-litteram cartel." See Tognetti, *I Gondi di Lione*, 40.

67 However, it is important to bear in mind the difficulties involved in bringing heavy goods convoys up to Lyon. According to Jacques Rossiaud, it was almost always necessary to use a traction system and the towpaths, which lay fallow and were altered by flooding. As a result, the long-distance pulls only took place during eight or nine months of the year (generally from March to November). See Jacques Rossiaud. *Le Rhône au Moyen Âge: histoire et représentation d'un fleuve européen*. Paris: Aubier, 2007, 214–220.

Sergio Tognetti, this was the case for saffron, for instance, which probably only travelled overland.[68]

The association between the Pierrevive and the Gondi family led to a true partnership with the marriage of Antoine Gondi and Marie-Christine de Pierrevive in 1516. This matrimonial alliance proved to be a success, and they even acquired a certain notoriety in Lyon in the 1420s: while Antoine de Gondi, who had become Lord of Le Perron, took on the role of representative of the Florentine nation,[69] his wife hosted a literary salon where she entertained fashionable poets.[70] The couple then moved closer to the French court through Catherine de Médicis, who struck up a lasting friendship with Marie-Christine de Pierrevive. They even went to live in Paris and remained in the entourage of the kings where they gradually acquired important functions,[71] which later enabled their descendants to rise to the highest echelons, following the example of Albert de Gondi, Marshal of Retz, and Jean-François Paul de Gondi, Cardinal of Retz. In any case, the lasting association between the Pierrevive and the Gondi families bears witness to the catalytic role that trade fairs could play: bringing together merchants from the major trading centres in the same area for specific periods of time, they encouraged contacts and associations.

Conclusion

The Pietraviva family from Lyon, now known as the Pierrevives, provided a link between the markets in Chieri and the fairs in Lyon: their mobility formed a lively and complex link between these two commercial centres. This mobility, probably motivated by commercial ambitions, was certainly voluntary and planned from the outset for the medium to long term. The Lyon fairs attracted the Pietraviva family to Lyon for around seventy years, between 1470 and 1545,

68 Tognetti, *I Gondi di Lione*, 47–48.

69 Tognetti, *I Gondi di Lione*, 27. Antonio Gondi was appointed consul of the Florentine nation in 1517.

70 See Bernadette Angleraud, Anouk Delaigue, Isabelle Doré-Rivé, Fanny Giraudier, Monica Martinat, André Pelletier, Jacques Rossiaud, André Pelletier (eds.). *Women of Lyon*. Lyon: Editions lyonnaises d'art et d'histoire, 2016, 70–71, where Marie-Christine is described as a "Lyonnaise humanist of the Renaissance."

71 Marie-Hélène Jullien de Pommerol. *Albert de Gondi maréchal de Retz*. Geneva: Droz, 1953, 13–17. To cite just two particularly eloquent examples: in 1551, Marie-Christine de Pierrevive became the governess to the fourth child of Catherine de Médicis and Henri II, and Antoine Gondi became the King's *maître d'hôtel* in 1559 (in which capacity he received 500 *livres* per year).

when most of the family left Lyon for new horizons in Paris.[72] At the same time, the influence of Lyon's fairs began to wane. But what about the Pierrevives' departure? Did they have a premonition of the impending decline of Lyon's fairs, or did they simply seize the new opportunities offered by the royal court? Or was there another reason—such as a commercial or political quarrel—that prompted them to sell their family home and leave the city? It is impossible to answer this question with any certainty at the moment, and further investigation is required.

Nevertheless, we can say that the Pierrevives' path became truly exceptional and remarkable during their time in Lyon: it was through these Lyonnaise encounters that they forged a different destiny from that of other Piedmontese families. To answer the question raised in the introduction, they managed to integrate into the Lyonnaise aristocracy through marriages and by taking part in local politics, but they remained foreigners nonetheless and it was as foreigners that they became close to the French court, through the friendship between Marie-Christine de Pierrevive and Catherine de Médicis. Up until that point, the Pietraviva/Pierrevive trajectory seemed fairly common. Indeed, as Renato Bordone's work on the Piedmontese aristocracy has shown,[73] many lineages experienced significant enrichment and a form of *insignorimento*, thanks in particular to a rapprochement with the princes of Savoy. The Pierrevive family provides the CoMOR project with a specific example of commercial mobility, whose main contribution is also its main limitation. On the one hand, the exceptionality of this trajectory shows the extent to which the actors, objects, and routes of trade can be nuanced and complex, but on the other, this exceptionality necessarily reflects a unique example that cannot be generalised. To go further, we would need to extend the research to other Piedmontese merchant families who have experienced some form of mobility in order to compare their paths and identify similarities and differences.[74]

---

72 At least one of Nicolet de Pierrevive's sons remained in Lyon: in the 1560s, Thomas de Pierrevive was receiver of the hospital on the Rhône bridge.

73 Bordone, Castelnuovo, Varanini, *Le aristocrazie dai signori rurali al patriziato*.

74 This project is at the heart of my PhD thesis currently in progress, provisionally entitled "Mobilités professionnelles et dynamiques sociales. Les marchands piémontais dans la France du sud-est du XIIIème au XVème siècle," under the supervision of Jean-Louis Gaulin (Lyon) and Marta Gravela (Turin).

Appendix

Amadeus VI of Savoy grants a fief to Michael di Pietraviva for the construction of the Sancti Jacobi castle in Chieri, 26 May 1369, AST, Fondo Biscaretti, Mazzo 1, no. 35.

> Nos Amedeus comes Sabaudie notum facimus universis quod, cum nos teneamus dilecto familiari et fideli nostro magistro Michele de Petraviva in certa pecunie quantitate occasione ejusdem sue aree et certorum ortorum acceptorum et conversorum in edificio et constructione castri nostri Querii nuper in porta Jalia incepti, volentes eidem de predictis dampnis debite compensare eidem magistro Michaeli infeudamus et in feudum franchum et nobilem damus omnia curtilia empta nostro nomine pro constructione nostri castri sancti Jacobi Querii ad habendum et tenendum et ipsis utendum et fruendum absque nostro et nostrorum impedimento. Quocumque donec quousque dictum nostrum castrum ibidem ceperimus construendum et eo tunc de dictis aree et ortis promictimus eidem satisfactione facere debite sicut decet. Datum Querii die XXVI maii anno domini millesimo CCCLXIX sub signo nostro secreto.
>
> Per dominum relatione domini Francisco de Longocomba,[75]
> Jean Ravais.[76]

Bibliography

Primary sources

Barale, Lorena (ed.). *Testamenti chieresi del '400.* Asti: Diffusione Immagine, 2011.

Borghezio, Gino, Bartolomeo Valimberti (ed.). *Statuta et capitula societatis Sancti Georgii seu populi Chariensis.* Vol. 2. Turin: Regia Deputazione subalpina di storia patria, 1940.

D'Hozier, Pierre. Remarques sommaires sur la maison de Gondi par le sieur d'Hozier, gentilhomme ordinaire de la maison du roi, généalogiste de sa majesté et juge général des armes et blasons

75 Following Octave Morel's interpretation, this *extra sigillum* note means that the lord, Amadeus VI, was not present in person and sent François de Longecombe in his place. François de Longecombe belonged to a family of Savoyard nobles, the lords of Longecombe (Ain), who were close to the power of the count. See Octave Morel. "La mention 'per regem ad relacionem . . . ' inscrite sur le repli des actes royaux au XIVe siècle." *Bibliothèque de l'École des chartes* 59:1 (1898): 73–80.

76 This is not the Count's chancellor (in office between 1353 and 1362), but his bastard brother and namesake, Lord of Cramoisy in the Chablais region, whose ducal protocols between 1362 and 1393 have been preserved, which has led to some confusion. On the Ravais brothers, see Castelnuovo, *Ufficiali e gentiluomini*, 204–205; Andrea Calzolari, Rosana Cosentino. La prima attivià contabile della cancelleria sabauda e l'organizzazione dell'ufficio a metà del secolo XIV. *Bollettino storico-bibliografico subalpino* 92 (1994): 505–553, 537.

de France, 1652. In *Œuvres du Cardinal de Retz*, Régis De Chantelauze (ed.). Vol. 9. Paris: Hachette, 1887, 420–435.

Di Charvensod, Daviso, Maria Clotilde (ed.). *I più antichi catasti del comune di Chieri (1253)*. Turin: Regia deputazione subalpina di storia patria, 1939.

Le Laboureur, Claude. *Les Masures de l'Île-Barbe, par Claude Le Laboureur, ancien prévôt de cette abbaye*, Georges Guigue et Marie-Claude Guigue (eds.). Lyon: Vitte et Perrussel, 1895.

Noberasco, Filippo. Le pergamene dell'archivio comunale di Savona. *Atti e memorie della Società Savonese di Storia Patria*. Vol. 2. Savona: Tipografia Savonese, 1940.

Pélicier, Paul, Bernard de Mandrot (eds.). *Lettres de Charles VIII, roi de France*. Vol. 5. Paris: Renouard, 1905.

Literature

Angleraud, Bernadette, Anouk Delaigue, Isabelle Doré-Rivé, Fanny Giraudier, Monica Martinat, André Pelletier, Jacques Rossiaud, André Pelletier (eds.). *Femmes de Lyon*. Lyon: Editions lyonnaises d'art et d'histoire, 2016.

Bayard, Françoise. *Les Bonvisi, marchands banquiers à Lyon, 1575–1629*. Lyon: Annales E.C.S., 1964.

Becker, Christine, Isabelle Parron-Kontis, Sophie Savay-Guerraz (eds.). *Le Musée Gadagne. Archéologie et histoire au coeur d'un projet patrimonial à Lyon*. Lyon: Alpara, 2006.

Bénézet, Jean-Pierre. *Pharmacie et médicament en Méditerranée occidentale (XIIIe–XVIe siècles)*. Paris: H. Champion, 1999.

Biolzi, Roberto. Les entreprises d'Amédée VI, entre aventures étrangères et guerres intestines (1355–1383). In *"J'ay grand envie de veoir assaillir": Guerre, guerriers et finances dans les États de Savoie à la fin du Moyen Âge (XIVe–XVe siècle)*. Rennes: Presses universitaires de Rennes, 2024, 73–86.

Bordone, Renato, Guido Castelnuovo, Gian Maria Varanini. *Le aristocrazie dai signori rurali al patriziato*. Rome: Editori Laterza, 2004.

Bordone, Renato, Franco Spinelli (eds.). *Lombardi in Europa nel Medioevo*. Milan: F. Angeli, 2005.

Boucher, Jacqueline. *Présence italienne à Lyon à la Renaissance: du milieu du XVe à la fin du XVIe siècle*. Lyon: Editions Lugd, 1994.

Braudel, Fernand. *Civilisation matérielle, économie et capitalisme: XVe–XVIIIe siècle*. Vol. 2. *Les jeux de l'échange*. Paris: A. Colin, 1986.

Brésard, Marc. *Les foires de Lyon aux XVe et XVIe siècles*. Paris: Auguste Picard, 1914.

Briffaz, Florentin. Formuler la prééminence du prince en Savoie (XIIIe–XVe siècles). In *La formule au Moyen Âge IV*, Elise Louviot, Charles Garcia, Stephen Morrison (eds.). Turnhout: Brepols, 2021, 111–138.

Calzolari, Andrea, Rosanna Cosentino. La prima attività contabile della cancelleria sabauda e l'organizzazione dell'ufficio a metà del secolo XIV. *Bollettino storico-bibliografico subalpino* 92 (1994): 505–553.

Carocci, Sandro. *La mobilità sociale nel Medioevo*. Rome: École française de Rome, 2010.

Carocci, Sandro. Introduzione: la mobilità sociale e la congiuntura del 1300: ipotesi, metodi di indagine, storiografia. In *La mobilità*, 1–37.

Castelnuovo, Guido. *Ufficiali e gentiluomini: la società politica sabauda nel tardo medioevo*. Milan: Franco Angeli, 1994.

Demotz, Bernard. Choix et représentations. L'entourage des comtes de Savoie du XIe au XVe siècle. In *À l'ombre du Pouvoir: Les entourages princiers au Moyen Âge*, Jean-Louis Kupper, Alain Marchandisse (eds.). Liège: Presses universitaires de Liège, 2019, 267–276.

Demotz, Bernard. *Le comté de Savoie du XIe au XVe siècle: pouvoir, château et État au Moyen âge*. Geneva: Éditions Slatkine, 2000.

Dubost, Jean-François. *La France italienne, XVIe–XVIIe siècle*. Paris: Aubier, 1997.

Ferrua, Ferruccio. *La Chiesa e la confraternità di San Giacomo a Chieri*. Chieri: Chieri Edizione, 2008.

Gascon, Richard. *Grand commerce et vie urbaine au XVIe siècle. Lyon et ses marchands (environs de 1520–environs de 1580)*. 2 vols. Paris: Mouton, 1971.

Gaulin, Jean-Louis, Susanne Rau. Rétablissement de deux foires à Lyon (mai 1487). In *Lyon, entre empire et royaume, 843–1601. Textes et documents*, Alexis Charansonnet, Jean-Louis Gaulin, Pascale Mounier, Susanne Rau (eds.). Paris: Garnier, 2015, 523–528.

Gauthiez, Bernard. *The production of urban space, temporality and spatiality: Lyons, 1500–1900*. Berlin: De Gruyter, 2020.

Gravela, Marta. Curie, fortresses and palaces. Family groups and urban space in late medieval Italy. In *La familia urbana. Matrimonio, parentesco y linaje en la Edad Media*, Jesús Á. Solórzano Telechea, Jelle Haemers, Christian Liddy (eds.). Logroño: Instituto de Estudios Riojanos, 2021, 375–400.

Heers, Jacques. *Le Clan familial au Moyen Age: étude sur les structures politiques et sociales des milieux urbains*. Paris: PUF, 1974.

Jullien de Pommerol, Marie-Henriette. *Albert de Gondi maréchal de Retz*. Geneva: Droz, 1953.

Lang, Heinrich. *Wirtschaften als kulturelle Praxis. Die Florentiner Salviati und die Augsburger Welser auf den Märkten in Lyon (1507–1559)*. Stuttgart: Steiner, 2019.

Lang, Heinrich. Networks and Merchant Diasporas. Florentine Merchant Bankers in Lyon and in Antwerp in the Sixteenth Century. In *Commercial Networks and European Cities, 1400–1800*, Andrea Caracausi, Christof Jeggle (eds.). London: Pickering & Chatto, 2014, 107–120.

Matringe, Nadia. *La Banque en Renaissance: les Salviati et la place de Lyon au milieu du XVIe siècle*. Rennes: Presses Universitaires de Rennes, 2016.

Montanari, Mirella. La popolazione di Chieri e del suo distretto alla fine del secolo XIII. In *Demografia e società nell'Italia medievale (secoli IX–XIV)*. Cuneo: Società per gli studi storici, archeologici ed artistici della provincia di Cuneo, 1994, 137–145.

Naegle, Gisela. Lyon se défend: délibérations, procès et foires à la fin du Moyen Âge. In *Lyon 1312. Rattacher la ville au royaume?*, Alexis Charansonnet, Jean-Louis Gaulin, Xavier Hélary (eds.). Lyon: CIHAM éditions, 2020, 269–292.

Naso, Irma. *Medici e strutture sanitarie nella società tardo-medievale: il Piemonte dei secoli XIV e XV*. Milan: F. Angeli, 1982.

Pallini-Martin, Agnès. L'installation d'une famille de marchands-banquiers florentins à Lyon au début du XVIe siècle, les Salviati. In *Lyon vu/e d'ailleurs (1245–1800). Échanges, compétitions, perceptions*, Jean-Louis Gaulin et Susanne Rau (eds.). Lyon: PUL, 2009, 71–89.

Pia, Ezio Claudio. "Multam pecuniam, multa mala": i "Lombardi" astigiani e il mercato del credito nel Basso Medioevo. *Nuova rivista storica* 105 (2021): 33–62.

Rao, Riccardo. Modalités d'enregistrement des informations dans les plus anciens estimi de l'Italie nord-occidentale du Duecento (Chieri et Pavie). In *L'enquête en questions: de la réalité à la "vérité" dans les modes de gouvernement, Moyen Âge–Temps modernes*, Anne Mailloux (ed.). Paris: CNRS Éditions, 2014, 173–183.

Raviolo, Massimo. *Chieri in fiera: da San Giuliano e Santa Basilissa a San Martino*. Chieri: EDITO, 2007.

Rossiaud, Jacques. *Lyon 1250–1550. Réalités et imaginaires d'une métropole*, Jean-Louis Gaulin, Susanne Rau (eds.). Lyon: Champ Vallon, 2012.

Rossiaud, Jacques. *Le Rhône au Moyen Âge: histoire et représentation d'un fleuve européen*. Paris: Aubier, 2007.

Scarcia, Giulia. Élites del territorio piemontese e corte sabauda fra XIV e XV secolo. In *L'affermarsi della corte sabauda. Dinastie, poteri, élites in Piemonte e Savoia fra tardo Medioevo e prima età moderna*, Paola Bianchi, Luisa Clotilde Gentile (eds.). Turin: Silvio Zamorani, 2006, 163–176.

Sergi, Giuseppe. *Potere e territorio lungo la strada di Francia: da Chambéry a Torino fra X e XIII secolo*. Naples: Liguori, 1981.

Shatzmiller, Joseph. Herbes et drogues dans la médecine provençale du Moyen Âge. In *Herbes, drogues et épices en Méditerranée: histoire, anthropologie, économie, du Moyen âge à nos jours*. Aix-en-Provence: Institut de recherches et d'études sur le monde arabe et musulman, 2014, 157–165.

Spufford, Peter. *Power and profit: the merchant in medieval Europe*. London: Thames & Hudson, 2002.

Tangheroni, Marco. Le marchand italien: état de la question. In *Actes des congrès de la Société des historiens médiévistes de l'enseignement supérieur public*, vol. 19. Reims: SHMES éditions, 1992, 11–24.

Tognetti, Sergio. *I Gondi di Lione. Una banca d'affari fiorentina nella Francia del primo Cinquecento*. Florence: Leo S. Olschki, 2013.

Tognetti, Sergio, Lorenzo Tanzini. *La mobilità sociale nel Medioevo italiano*. Rome: Viella, 2016.

Wickersheimer, Ernest, Guy Beaujouan. *Dictionnaire biographique des médecins en France au Moyen Âge*. Geneva: Librairie Droz, 1979.

Marta Gravela

Before the fairs: merchants and moneylenders in late medieval Lyon

Lyon merchants: a neglected story

Since Richard Gascon's pioneering study published in 1971, the establishment and expansion of fairs in Lyon between the late fifteenth and the mid-sixteenth century has attracted the attention of many scholars.[1] In the decades that followed, research was devoted to the success of Lyon as a commercial and financial centre as well as to the commercial specialisation of the fairs, merchants' routes and entrepreneurial activities, the development of financial instruments that radically transformed the nature of the fairs, and the economic, social, and political impact of all this on the city itself.[2] However, the vast majority of these studies focused on the activity of foreign merchants and bankers in Lyon, with special attention paid to Italians and Germans.[3] Until recently, Italian merchant-bankers, particu-

1 Richard Gascon. *Grand commerce et vie urbaine au XVIe siècle. Lyon et ses marchands (environs de 1520–environs de 1580).* Paris: S.E.V.P.E.N., 1971. Before Gascon's work, the most relevant study on these fairs dated back to 1914. See Marc Brésard. *Les foires de Lyon aux XVe et XVIe siècles.* Paris: A. Picard, 1914.

2 Richard Gascon. *Lyon et l'Europe: hommes et sociétés.* Lyon: Presses universitaires de Lyon, 1980; Henri Hours, Olivier Zeller. *Lyon, l'argent, le commerce et la soie.* Lyon: Archives du Lyonnais, la Manufacture, 1986; Giuseppe Iacono, Salvatore Ennio Furone. *Les marchands-banquiers florentins et l'architecture à Lyon au XVIe siècle.* Paris: Publisud, 1999. These topics are at the core of various essays in: Jean-Louis Gaulin, Susanne Rau (eds.). *Lyon vu/e d'ailleurs (1245–1800). Échanges, compétitions et perceptions.* Lyon: Presses universitaires de Lyon, 2009; Maria-Anne Privat-Savigny, Dorothée Gillmann, Brigitte Sanvoisin, Anne-Catherine Marin. *Lyon qui compte . . . Banques et finances lyonnaises.* Paris: EMCC, 2011.

3 Following the first analysis by Raymond de Roover, several economic historians examined the success of Italian bankers. See Raymond de Roover. *The rise and decline of the Medici Bank, 1397–1494.* Cambridge, MA: Harvard University Press, 1963, 289–311. See especially Michele Cassandro. *Le fiere di Lione e gli uomini d'affari italiani nel Cinquecento.* Florence: Baccini & Chiappi, 1979; Michele Cassandro. I forestieri a Lione nel '400 e '500: la nazione fiorentina. In *Dentro la città. Stranieri e realtà urbane nell'Europa dei secoli XII-XVI,* Gabriella Rossetti (ed.). Naples: Liguori, 1989, 151–162; Jacqueline Boucher. *Présence italienne à Lyon à la Renaissance: du milieu du XVe à la fin du XVIe siècle.* Lyon: Éditions LUGD, 1994. On German merchants and bankers, see Mark Häberlein. Commerce, formation et réseaux de compatriotes: la ville de Lyon vue par des marchands de l'Allemagne du Sud au XVIe et au début du XVIIe siècle. In *Lyon vu/e d'ailleurs,* Gaulin, Rau (eds.)., 141–159; Heinrich Lang. *Wirtschaften als kulturelle Praxis. Die Florentiner Salviati und die Augsburger Welser auf den Märkten in Lyon (1507– 1559).* Stuttgart: Steiner, 2019.

https://doi.org/10.1515/9783111621296-012

larly the Florentine, have undoubtedly dominated the historiographical landscape.[4]

Despite the fact that Gascon's work also shed light on the significant role played by Lyon merchants and French merchants more generally, in relation to the fairs, scholars have not further explored the features of this group, with the partial exception of Jacques Rossiaud, who also examined a merchant family in his studies on Lyon society, Guy de Valous, who traced the structure and characteristics of the Lyon elite, and Michèle Bonnet, who studied the Lyon changers as a group without devoting a specific analysis to any of them.[5] Despite their crucial role as intermediaries between international merchant-bankers and local buyers or investors, Lyon merchants and financial operators have thus remained in the background of historical research. Moreover, it is striking that historians have shown little interest in their activities during the fourteenth and first half of the fifteenth centuries—the period which laid the foundations for the success of the fairs.

This essay will thus focus on the group of merchants and moneylenders active in the city—and beyond—before the mid-fifteenth century, when four annual fairs were established in Lyon and the city was granted important new commercial and fiscal privileges (1464), replacing Geneva as the main fair centre of Western Europe.[6] The aim of this research is to identify the merchants and to examine their economic and political role by searching for traces of their activities and networks before the age of fairs and comparing them with the merchants' situa-

4 Angela Orlandi. *Le grand Parti, Fiorentini a Lione e il debito pubblico francese nel XVI secolo.* Florence: Leo S. Olschki, 2002; Jacques Bottin. Les foires de Lyon et les Italiens autour de 1600: déclin ou reconfiguration? In *La pratica dello scambio. Sistemi di fiere, mercanti e città in Europa (1400– 1700)*, Paola Lanaro (ed.). Venice: Marsilio, 2003, 201–218; Edoardo Demo. Sete e mercanti vicentini alle fiere di Lione nel XVI secolo. In *La pratica dello scambio*, Lanaro (ed.), 177–200; Bruno Dini. I mercanti-banchieri italiani e le fiere di Ginevra e Lione. In *L'Italia alla fine del Medioevo. I caratteri originali nel quadro europeo*, Francesco Salvestrini (ed.). Florence: Firenze University Press, 2005, 433–456; Francesco Guidi Bruscoli. Banchieri senesi nel primo cinquecento tra Roma, Lione, e la penisola iberica. In *L'ultimo secolo della Republica di Siena*, Mario Ascheri, Fabrizio Nevola (eds.). Siena: Accademia Senese degli intronati, 2007, 385–409; Sergio Tognetti. *I Gondi di Lione. Una banca d'affari fiorentina nella Francia del primo Cinquecento.* Florence: Leo S. Olschki, 2013; Nadia Matringe. *La Banque en Renaissance. Les Salviati et la Place de Lyon au milieu du XVIe siècle.* Rennes: Presses universitaires de Rennes, 2016; Agnès Pallini-Martin. *Banque, négoce et politique. Les Florentins à Lyon au moment des guerres d'Italie.* Paris: Garnier, 2018.

5 Gascon, *Grand commerce*; Jacques Rossiaud. *Lyon 1250–1550. Réalités et imaginaires d'une métropole*, Jean-Louis Gaulin, Susanne Rau (eds.). Seyssel: Champ Vallon, 2012; Guy de Valous. *Le patriciat lyonnais aux XIIIe et XIVe siècles.* Paris: Picard, 1973; Michèle Bonnet. Les changeurs Lyonnais au Moyen Age (1350–1450). *Revue Historique* 249:2 (1973): 325–52.

6 Brésard, *Les foires de Lyon.*

tion during the golden age of Lyon in order to understand the impact of the city's growth on this social group. To this end, the following sections will first consider the sources examined in the study and the methodology applied, followed by the people identified as Lyon merchants and their socio-political profile, and finally their fate when far richer foreign companies appeared on the scene.

The lack of interest in fourteenth-century Lyon merchants is not only a side-effect of the greater attention paid to Italian Renaissance merchant-bankers. What has also led scholars to focus on other research topics is the complex and fragmentary landscape of Lyon's fourteenth-century sources. The fourteenth-century records preserved in the city archives actually make it difficult to carry out research on specific socio-economic groups, since the vast majority of them are of a strictly political nature (for example, cartularies with franchises, royal and papal privileges to the city, etc.).[7] It was not until 1388 and 1416 respectively that lists of taxpayers (known as *nommées* or *Vaillant*) and registers of deliberations were kept, although in these sources citizens were not necessarily recorded as merchants.[8] Similarly, the records of consuls' elections—available with substantial gaps until the mid-fifteenth century—did not specify the consuls' professions on a regular basis.[9] Identifying merchants and financial operators in local sources thus proves problematic, and external sources have to be consulted in the search for these people.

The geographical proximity of Lyon to the Savoy territories as well as the connections between the Savoy dynasty and the city actually suggested the need to examine the presence of Lyon citizens in the Savoy records. My research therefore focused on a large body of unpublished sources preserved in the archives of the House of Savoy—namely, the registers of the notaries working for

7 Constitutional and political acts of the city, Archives Municipales de Lyon, Lyon, France (hereafter AML), series AA.

8 *Nommées* of Lyon, 1388. AML, CC 1. The first registers of *nommées* were published in *Le livre du Vaillant des habitants de Lyon en 1388. Estimation des biens meubles et immeubles par servir à l'assiette de la taille*, Edouard Philipon, Charles Perrat (eds.). Lyon: M. Audin, 1927. The deliberations can be found in Deliberations of the city of Lyon, 1416. AML, BB 1 ff. The first registers of deliberations were published in *Registres consulaires de la ville de Lyon, ou Recueil des délibérations du Conseil de la Commune de 1416 à 1423. Publiés d'après les procès verbaux originaux*, vol. I, Marie-Claude Guigue (ed.). Lyon: A. Brun, 1882; *Registres consulaires de la ville de Lyon, ou Recueil des délibérations du Conseil de la Commune de 1422 à 1450. Publiés d'après les procès verbaux originaux*, vol. II, Georges Guigue (ed.). Lyon: Archives et bibliothèque de la ville, 1926.

9 *Syndicats*, 1294–1441, AML, BB 367; *Syndicats*, 1361–1381, AML, BB 368; *Syndicats*, 1442–1499, AML, BB 369; Lists of councillors and other magistrates of Lyon, 1400–1667, AML, BB 375; Lists of councillors and other magistrates of Lyon, 1294–1673, AML, BB 376; Aldermen of Lyon, 1368–1705, AML, BB 379; Aldermen of Lyon, 1382–1593, AML, BB 380.

the lords of Savoy and Savoy-Achaea (*protocolli dei notai della corona*), which include several purchases and loans to the counts or princes, thus offering a picture of the lords' economic network.[10] As we will see shortly, the analysis revealed the participation of Lyon merchants in more than twenty loans, making it possible to identify a small group of citizens who were certainly active in trade and credit between the 1320s and the early fifteenth century. Further prosopographical research was then carried out by assessing the presence of these people in Lyon records and literature, their patrimonial assets, the activities in which they were involved, and the political and administrative tasks they performed. The outcome of this cross-check provided the basis for a better understanding of the merchants of Lyon before the age of fairs.

Cives et mercatores Lugduni

The study of notarial registers revealed a significant number of transactions between the House of Savoy and Lyon merchants throughout the fourteenth and early fifteenth centuries: twenty loans granted directly to the lords, to which we can add guarantees to Lyon merchants, suggesting a prior credit relationship.[11] Strikingly, in comparison to the reluctance of Lyon sources to mention professions, all Lyon citizens appearing in these records were defined as *cives et mercatores Lugduni*. The Savoy lords, however, did not turn to them to purchase goods,

10 On this source, see Guido Castelnuovo. Les protocoles des comtes de Savoie, moyens et enjeux du pouvoir princier sur l'écrit (première moitié du XIVe siècle). In *L'Enquête en questions. De la réalité à la "vérité" dans les modes de gouvernement (Moyen Âge–Temps modernes)*, Anne Mailloux, Laure Verdon (eds.). Paris: CNRS Editions, 2014, 185–93. On the way in which the Savoy territory was structured in the late medieval period, see Alessandro Barbero. The feudal principalities: the west (Monferrato, Saluzzo, Savoy, Savoy-Acaia). In *The Italian Renaissance State*, Andrea Gamberini, Isabella Lazzarini (eds.). Cambridge: Cambridge University Press, 2014, 177–96; Paolo Buffo. I principati piemontesi fra reti feudali, poteri pubblici e gerarchie territoriali. In *Reti italiche. Spazi e relazioni politiche da Roma alle Alpi nei tempi di Dante (1260–1330)*, Enrico Faini, Pierluigi Terenzi, Andrea Zorzi (eds.). Rome: Viella, 2023, 233–256.

11 See, for instance, the guarantee granted by Duke Louis to the merchant Jean Merlet in 1433. Ducal protocols, red series, 1447–1449, Archivio di Stato di Torino (hereafter ASTo), Corte, Materie politiche per rapporto all'interno, Protocolli dei notai della corona, Protocolli ducali (serie rossa), no. 91, f. 30r. See also Marta Gravela. Archivio di Stato di Torino Sezione Corte, Protocolli camerali 91 (COL0037). In *Configurations of European Fairs: Merchants, Objects, Routes (ca. 1350–1600)*, Jean-Louis Gaulin, Susanne Rau (eds.). https://fairs-in-history.huma-num.fr/collection/COL0037 (4 September 2024).

but rather to borrow large sums of money.[12] The frequency of loans varied over time depending on the needs of the counts and princes and on the availability of creditors from different places and social circles (Savoy officers, Lombards, subjects, Italian bankers). The analysis therefore does not provide any statistical evidence; rather, it sheds light on the existence of a group of financial operators from Lyon capable of dealing with the neighbouring principalities. Tab. 1 shows the number of loans granted by Lyon citizens to the various Savoy rulers until the mid-fifteenth century.

Given that the protocols could cover different types of transactions, such as loans, repayments, or obligations towards creditors, it should be stressed that the exact sums of money originally borrowed by the Savoy rulers were not always recorded in the sources, thus making the totals in Tab. 1 only indicative of the moneylenders' potential. For example, Léonard Caille received the repayment of a loan from Count Amédée VIII in 1398, but the contract does not specify the amount repaid or that of the original loan.[13] On the contrary, the 19,300 florins borrowed by Jacques of Savoy-Achaea corresponded to three subsequent loans granted in 1362 by the same group of creditors (Gilles de Cuysel, Henri Chevrier, and Jacques de Varey): 7,700 florins in July, another 1,600 in September, and finally, 10,000 in December.[14]

While the number of loans and financial interactions with Lyon citizens was limited in the early and late fourteenth century, it dramatically increased in the middle decades of the century under the government of Count Amédée VI in Savoy and Prince Jacques of Savoy-Achaea in Piedmont. In addition to the above-mentioned loans to Jacques, Lyon merchants lent Amédée VI huge amounts of money: nine loans in less than thirty years, for a total sum of at least 50,000 flo-

12 However, the same creditors were recorded in the protocols as selling cloth and a horse (*corserius bayus brunus*) to the nobleman Antoine de la Tour for 2,300 florins. See Ducal protocols, red series, 1367–1369, ASTo, Corte, Materie politiche per rapporto all'interno, Protocolli dei notai della corona, Protocolli ducali (serie rossa), no. 47, ff. 69r–70v; Marta Gravela. Archivio di Stato di Torino Sezione Corte, Protocolli ducali 47 (COL0017). In *Configurations*, Gaulin, Rau (eds.). https://fairs-in-history.huma-num.fr/collection/COL0017 (4 September 2024).

13 Ducal protocols, red series, 1390–1400, ASTo, Corte, Materie politiche per rapporto all'interno, Protocolli dei notai della corona, Protocolli ducali (serie rossa), no. 67, ff. 156r–157r; Marta Gravela. Archivio di Stato di Torino Sezione Corte, Protocolli ducali 67 (COL0013). In *Configurations*, Gaulin, Rau (eds.). https://fairs-in-history.huma-num.fr/collection/COL0013 (4 September 2024).

14 Ducal protocols, black series, 1362, ASTo, Corte, Materie politiche per rapporto all'interno, Protocolli dei notai della corona, Protocolli camerali (serie nera), no. 20, ff. 33v–35r, 45r–46r, 49r–51r; Marta Gravela. Archivio di Stato di Torino Sezione Corte, Protocolli camerali 20 (COL0008). In *Configurations*, Gaulin, Rau (eds.). https://fairs-in-history.huma-num.fr/collection/COL0008 (4 September 2024).

Tab. 1: Loans granted by Lyon citizens and their partners to the House of Savoy.

Savoy ruler	**Period of rule**	**No. of loans**	**Approximate total sum**	**Creditors**
Édouard	1323–1329	2	200 florins	Aymon de Durche Pierre de Chaponay
Aymon	1329–1343	1	200 florins	Aymon de Durche Pierre de Chaponay
Jacques (Savoy-Achaea)	1334–1367	3	19,300 florins	Gilles de Cuysel Henri Chevrier Jacques de Varey
Amédée VI	1343–1383	10	17,200 florins + 17,000 francs	Jehan Oddonet André Beronde Aymon Nyeurs Henri Chevrier Jacques de Varey Amblard Gerbaix* Poncet Cristin Barthelemy du Princin** Etienne Bouchon Gilles de Cuysel Mathieu de Chaponay Lantelmino Papa
Amédée VII	1383–1391	1	2,000 *scudi*	Poncet Cristin
Amédée VIII	1391–1440	3		Léonard Caille

**civis* of Belley
***de Cluny*

rins, mostly between 1358 and 1372 when Amédée was engaged in a long and costly war, first against his cousin Jacques of Savoy-Achaea and then against the Visconti, lords of Milan. The insubordination of Jacques, who was trying to free himself from the feudal control of Amédée, prompted both Savoy cousins to search for new sources of credit and thus resort to Lyon moneylenders.[15] Such a political and military conjuncture proved to be profitable for Lyon merchants

15 Buffo, I principati piemontesi; Paolo Buffo. Savoia Acaia, Giacomo di. In *Dizionario Biografico degli Italiani*, vol. 91. Roma: Istituto della Enciclopedia italiana, 2018. Further research on Amédée and Jacques' loans can be found in Marta Gravela. A 'feudalized' public debt? Loans, fiefs, and debt control in the Savoy state (fourteenth-fifteenth centuries). In *The Origins of Public Debt in Europe (13th-17th centuries)*, Armand Jamme, Pere Verdes-Pijuan (eds.). Publication forthcoming.

who could lend money to both competitors without suffering political consequences, unlike most other creditors of the House of Savoy who were the direct subjects of the count or the prince.[16]

Henri Chevrier and Jacques de Varey formed the core of the moneylenders' group. Already mentioned three times as creditors of Jacques of Savoy-Achaea, they also lent 14,000 florins to Amédée VI in 1366, receiving the income from the tithes of the Count's bishoprics for two years as repayment of the first 10,000 florins.[17] Two years later, they granted the Count another loan of 3,000 florins in association with one of the most prominent creditors of the House of Savoy, Amblard Gerbaix of Belley, and his brother Pierre, who had become the Count's treasurer.[18] Henri Chevrier appears in the sources again in 1372, granting the Count another loan (6,000 francs), this time with other financial partners from Lyon—Gilles de Cuysel (his father-in-law, as we will see in the next section), Mathieu de Chaponay, and Lantermino Papa.[19] Gilles de Cuysel was not new to these collaborations as he had contributed to the three loans to Jacques of Savoy-Achaea ten years earlier, while Mathieu de Chaponay was most likely linked to Pierre de Chaponay, a creditor of Édouard and Aymon of Savoy some decades earlier.[20]

16 See, for instance, the political overthrow of the Provana family group in Marta Gravela. Provana. In *La signoria rurale nell'Italia del tardo medioevo.* Vol. 5. *Censimento e quadri regionali*, Federico Del Tredici (ed.). Rome: Universitalia, 2021, 139–143.

17 Ducal protocols, black series, 1366, ASTo, Corte, Materie politiche per rapporto all'interno, Protocolli dei notai della corona, Protocolli camerali (serie nera), no. 70, ff. 12r–13v, 14r–14v; Marta Gravela. Archivio di Stato di Torino Sezione Corte, Protocolli camerali 70 (COL0009). In *Configurations*, Gaulin, Rau (eds.). https://fairs-in-history.huma-num.fr/collection/COL0009 (4 September 2024).

18 Ducal protocols, red series, 1368–1370, ASTo, Corte, Materie politiche per rapporto all'interno, Protocolli dei notai della corona, Protocolli ducali (serie rossa), no. 57, ff. 7r–8r; Marta Gravela. Archivio di Stato di Torino Sezione Corte, Protocolli ducali 57 (COL0012). In *Configurations*, Gaulin, Rau (eds.). https://fairs-in-history.huma-num.fr/collection/COL0012 (4 September 2024). On Pierre de Gerbaix and his brother Amblard, see Bruno Galland. Gerbaix, Pierre. In *Dizionario Biografico degli Italiani*, vol. 53. Roma: Istituto della Enciclopedia italiana, 2000.

19 Ducal protocols, black series, 1372, ASTo, Corte, Materie politiche per rapporto all'interno, Protocolli dei notai della corona, Protocolli camerali (serie nera), no. 71, f. 32v; Marta Gravela. Archivio di Stato di Torino Sezione Corte, Protocolli camerali 71 (COL0060). In *Configurations*, Gaulin, Rau (eds.). https://fairs-in-history.huma-num.fr/collection/COL0060 (4 September 2024).

20 Ducal protocols, black series, 1329, ASTo, Corte, Materie politiche per rapporto all'interno, Protocolli dei notai della corona, Protocolli camerali (serie nera), no. 128, f. 4v; no. 155, ff. 3v–3bis r; Marta Gravela. Archivio di Stato di Torino Sezione Corte, Protocolli camerali 128 (COL0047). In *Configurations*, Gaulin, Rau (eds.). https://fairs-in-history.huma-num.fr/collection/COL0047 (4 September 2024); Marta Gravela. Archivio di Stato di Torino Sezione Corte, Protocolli camerali 155 (COL0048). In *Configurations*, Gaulin, Rau (eds.). https://fairs-in-history.huma-num.fr/collection/COL0048 (4 September 2024).

Lantermino Papa, on the other hand, was a changer, textile and salt merchant of Turinese origin who had settled permanently in Lyon, although he was not formally a *civis*.[21] Lantermino was still a citizen of Turin (as evidenced by the fact that he was entered in the Turin tax lists in 1363), although he probably spent most of his time in Lyon (given that his tax declaration was written in Lyon).[22]

It is therefore possible to infer that a small group of Lyon citizens or families —such as the Chevrier, de Varey, de Cuysel, and de Chaponay—were active in trade and finance and occasionally joined forces with less prominent merchants (Papa) or financial partners well connected with the House of Savoy (Gerbaix). Other partnerships involved Lyon citizens and partners from neighbouring regions. In 1372, for instance, Poncet Cristin, Etienne Bouchon, and other Lyon citizens lent Amédée VI 10,000 francs in association with Barthelemy du Pricin from Cluny.[23] It is virtually impossible to establish whether these groups of merchants and moneylenders formed proper companies. However, it seems unlikely that they were permanent business partnerships, as the combinations of creditors in each contract seem to vary rapidly and no other evidence of joint business can be found in surviving records. As we will see shortly, other links between the moneylenders can be assumed, such as family relationships and alliances within the urban elite.

From the late fourteenth century onwards, members of the House of Savoy turned to a wider circle of creditors from elsewhere (under Amédée VIII, especially from Paris).[24] Meanwhile, the increasing presence of foreign merchants and bankers in Lyon also affected the success of local merchants. An example of this gradual replacement is provided by another transaction between the Count of Savoy and merchants residing in Lyon. In the 1390s, Amédée VIII borrowed 1,800 *scudi* from merchants in Lyon. However, these were not locals, but Lombards

21 De Valous, *Le patriciat lyonnais*, 415–17 and Bonnet, *Les changeurs Lyonnais*, 334. In the 1380s, Jean Papa must also have settled in Lyon, as suggested by the city's accounting records. See City accounting, 1380–1388, AML, CC 376.

22 On this merchant's family's origin from Turin and activity in Lyon, see Alessandro Barbero. *Un'oligarchia urbana. Politica ed economia a Torino fra Tre e Quattrocento*. Rome: Viella, 1995, 80, 154.

23 Ducal protocols, black series, 1372, ASTo, Corte, Materie politiche per rapporto all'interno, Protocolli dei notai della corona, Protocolli camerali (serie nera), no. 71, ff. 30r–32v; Marta Gravela. Archivio di Stato di Torino Sezione Corte, Protocolli camerali 71 (COL0060). In *Configurations*, Gaulin, Rau (eds.). https://fairs-in-history.huma-num.fr/collection/COL0060 (4 September 2024).

24 Christian Guilleré. Les finances d'Amédée VIII (1391–1416). In *La naissance du duché de Savoie (1416)*, Laurent Ripart, Pascal Vuillemin, Christian Guilleré (eds.). Chambery: Université de Savoie Mont Blanc, 2020, 243–98.

from Chieri in Piedmont who had settled in the city with part of their company (a *consortium* of various families from Chieri—the Dodoli, de Villa, de Cordia, and de Frassinello). The rubric "*contra Lombardos Lugduni*" in the source suggests that they were publicly identified as moneylenders and thus the primary source available to both private citizens and political authorities in need of money.[25] In the following decades, other foreign merchant-bankers moved to Lyon, and the arrival of several Florentine and Tuscan companies in Lyon after 1464 was only the final step in this process. Lyon merchants nonetheless continued to play an essential—if less evident—role. Before focusing on this stage, the next section will look into the socio-political profiles of the Lyon merchants who have been identified.

Businessmen from the urban élite

Once a group of merchants and moneylenders from Lyon had been identified, the next step in this research was to gain a better understanding of their social and political profile through the investigation of urban sources and existing literature. Although these records are late and often fragmentary, they provide valuable information on citizens of Lyon who were active in public life. If some of them—such as Jean Oddon or André Beronde—remain in the dark, others clearly emerge as the longstanding protagonists of Lyon's political administration, some of them with specific financial and accounting tasks at the service of the city, which further suggests their confidence and familiarity with the management of considerable amounts of money.

Among the first creditors to appear in the Savoy sources, Aymon de Durche does not figure prominently in the urban records, which are largely missing for the period of his life. He was a city councillor in 1336 and belonged to one of the

25 Ducal protocols, black series, 1397, ASTo, Corte, Materie politiche per rapporto all'interno, Protocolli dei notai della corona, Protocolli camerali (serie nera), no. 149, ff. 70r–71r; Marta Gravela. Archivio di Stato di Torino Sezione Corte, Protocolli camerali 149 (COL0039). In *Configurations*, Gaulin, Rau (eds.). https://fairs-in-history.huma-num.fr/collection/COL0039 (4 September 2024). On the Lombards, see Renato Bordone, Franco Spinelli (eds.). *Lombardi in Europa nel Medioevo*. Milan: FrancoAngeli, 2005; Luisa Castellani. Percorsi di affermazione di una famiglia dell'aristocrazia finanziaria astigiana: i Malabaila di Valgorrea e Carantana. *Società e Storia* 63 (1994): 19–47; Luisa Castellani. *Gli uomini d'affari astigiani. Politica e denaro tra il Piemonte e l'Europa, 1270–1312*. Turin: Paravia Scriptorium, 1998; Federico Cannelloni. *Credito e pegno, famiglie e nazioni: i Lombardi tra Piemonte e Paesi Bassi (ca. 1380–1500)*. PhD diss., Università degli Studi di Padova, KU Leuven, 2015.

oldest merchant and consular families in Lyon, whose members took part in the truce between the citizens and the archbishop in 1269, which marked a significant step towards the empowerment of the city.[26] Aymon also appears—with a relative, Jean—in the account of an archbishop residing in Avignon, whom the Durche family (or de la Dorche) supplied with wine, oats, parchment, and various types of textile for almost 3,000 florins.[27] Like Aymon and Jean, other members of the family were certainly drapers, while Anselme de Durche—Aymon's elder brother and councillor at the turn of the century—was a jurist.

The de Durche family continued to play a leading role in the local elite. In the mid-fourteenth century, two members (Jean and Antoine), most probably related to Aymon, were subsequently elected among the city consuls and held the office at the same time.[28] The lineage of Aymon, Anselme, and their brother Etienne was definitely the most influential, the most prominent member in the second half of the century being Guillaume, councillor and owner of a considerable fortune according to the *Vaillant*, the tax survey of the inhabitants' properties (4,500 francs, mostly urban buildings).[29] In the following century, which is better covered by the urban records, the de Durches were still councillors, along with another Jean in 1415 and 1419, who was also a *maître de métier* of the furriers in 1435, while his cousin Guillaume was a councillor in 1431.[30]

Alongside the de Durches, the most prominent families in the group of fourteenth-century creditors were the de Varey and de Chaponay family. The latter was one of the oldest urban families, mentioned since the late twelfth century as builders and patrons of the chapel where the city consuls met until the city acquired a proper town hall (see below).[31] Major international merchants since at least the early thirteenth century, the de Chaponays appear in the records not only as wealthy, but also as linked to the most important local religious institutions and as active participants in the citizens' struggle against the archbishop.[32] The importance of the family also emerges from a 1308 list of citizens—headed

---

26 De Valous, *Le patriciat lyonnais*, 201–209; Michel Rubellin. *Église et société chrétienne d'Agobard à Valdès*. Lyon: Presses universitaires de Lyon, 2003, 359–422.

27 Alexis Charansonnet, Jean-Louis Gaulin, Pascale Mounier, Susanne Rau (eds.). *Lyon, entre Empire et Royaume (843–1601): textes et documents*. Paris: Classiques Garnier, 2015, 457–459.

28 *Syndicats*, 1294–1441.

29 De Valous, *Le patriciat lyonnais*, 202–3.

30 Caroline Fargeix. *Les élites lyonnaises du XVe siècle au miroir de leur langage: pratiques et représentations culturelles des conseillers de Lyon, d'après les registres de délibérations consulaires*. Paris: De Boccard, 2007, 588.

31 Charansonnet, Gaulin, Mounier, Rau (eds.), *Lyon, entre Empire et Royaume*, 204; Rossiaud, *Lyon 1250–1550*, 369.

32 De Valous, *Le patriciat lyonnais*, 169–183.

precisely by Humbert de Chaponay—who acted before the royal procurators at a time when they added to their trade the profession of changers, of which André de Chaponay was also *maître de métier* in the 1350s.[33] Given the fragmentary state of early fourteenth-century records, hardly anything is known about the political career of Pierre de Chaponay, the first creditor mentioned in our sources, son of the citizen of the same name who acted as procurator of the city in 1271 and who was certainly dead by 1339. His son Jaquemet, draper and *maître de métier* in 1356, was elected councillor in 1358 and 1359,[34] but it was a different son who continued the lineage and increased its wealth—Mathieu, the second creditor on our list. A draper and changer, Mathieu de Chaponay was a member of the team that drew up the taxpayers' records (*Vaillant*). In 1388, his assets—including 34 houses in Lyon—were valued at 3,000 francs.[35] Mathieu's eldest son, Antoine, consul in 1401 and 1406, inherited the family house which was subsequently bought by the city and transformed into the first town hall; his brother Aynard, who followed in his father's footsteps, owned four houses worth a total of 400 florins and was elected councillor five times between 1417 and 1432.[36]

Other descendants of the de Chaponay family were admitted to the city council: first Jean, a draper; then his son Philibert, also a draper; and his grandson Charles, who became a Doctor of Law but did not give up the family business of trading in textiles. Another member of the family—Antoine, also a lawyer—was instead appointed general fiscal procurator of the Dauphiné.[37] By the mid-sixteenth century, the de Chaponay family had acquired a seigneurial privilege, a fate common to several Lyon elite families, which thus obtained further income. However, they did not leave the urban environment and opportunities: Nicolas de Chaponay, lord of Feyzin, remained linked to the city, where he still had a patrimony valued at 200 *livres* in 1545, and was consul and conservator of the royal privileges of the Lyon fairs.[38]

The social and political profile of the de Varey family was similar, if not higher; nonetheless, it was certainly more numerous, as several branches appear

33 Charansonnet, Gaulin, Mounier, Rau (eds.), *Lyon, entre Empire et Royaume*, 345; De Valous, *Le patriciat lyonnais*, 174.

34 De Valous, *Le patriciat lyonnais*, 175; Charansonnet, Gaulin, Mounier, Rau (eds.), *Lyon, entre Empire et Royaume*, 451.

35 *Nommées* of Lyon, 1388; *Nommées* of Lyon, 1380–1423, AML, CC 13; Rossiaud, *Lyon 1250–1550*, 148n, 150n.

36 De Valous, *Le patriciat lyonnais*, 176; Fargeix, *Les élites lyonnaises*, 585.

37 De Valous, *Le patriciat lyonnais*, 177; Fargeix, *Les élites lyonnaises*, 585; Charansonnet, Gaulin, Mounier, Rau (eds.), *Lyon, entre Empire et Royaume*, 487–8.

38 *Nommées* of Lyon, 1545, AML, CC 40; Charansonnet, Gaulin, Mounier, Rau (eds.), *Lyon, entre Empire et Royaume*, 614–5.

in the sources from the fourteenth century onwards, making it impossible to identify and link all the family members who often had the same forenames. Recorded in Lyon as early as the late twelfth century with the canon priest of Saint Paul, Pierre de Varey, the de Vareys rapidly acquired large estates in Lyon and, like the de Durches and de Chaponays, took part in the crucial deeds of the 1260s and 1270s.[39] However, according to the extant sources, they appear to have engaged in trade less than the families previously examined, with Bernard de Varey first mentioned as a draper in 1270 and elected councillor twice in the 1290s, a period in which the de Vareys began to regularly occupy the seats of the city council. In the early fourteenth century, Guillaume de Varey was actually *maître de métier* of the *terriers*, merchants who no longer practiced their trade.

Various members of the family appear as Lyon citizens in the aforementioned deed of 1308 (Bernard l'Aîné, second in line after Humbert de Chaponay, Bernard de la Porcherie, Humbert, Gui, and Jean), while others are mentioned as consuls (Bernard, Guillaume, Jeannin, Humbert, and Mathieu) or *maîtres de métier* (Bernier, Jeannin) fifty years later.[40] The merchant and moneylender Jacques, who appears in the Savoy records, must have been active in the second half of the century, although he does not appear in the local sources studied so far.[41] Humbert must have been the dominant figure: a consul, he was also in charge of the city accounts and tax collection, like several other elite members examined here.[42] The richest family member, however, seems to have been another Humbert, abbot and provost of Ainay, whose real estate was valued at 3,400 francs in 1388.[43] Several heirs of the de Varey family were elected consuls in the fifteenth century, and some also held the highest offices in the city—such as Jean, *courier* between 1416 and 1452, and Girard, provost in the 1440s and *courier* in 1458–59—while others pursued careers in the royal administration—such as Guillaume, royal procurator in 1455, and another Humbert, who climbed the social ladder to the nobility in 1473 and to the title of *maître* of the royal hotel.[44]

What is especially interesting in this case is that almost all the members of the de Varey family gradually ceased to practice their trade and the credit busi-

39 De Valous, *Le patriciat lyonnais*, 133–163.

40 *Syndicats*, 1294–1441; Charansonnet, Gaulin, Mounier, Rau (eds.), *Lyon, entre Empire et Royaume*, 345, 450–1.

41 He cannot be the *parcheminier* Jaquemin de Varey listed in the tax records. See *Nommées* of Lyon, 1388.

42 Charansonnet, Gaulin, Mounier, Rau (eds.), *Lyon, entre Empire et Royaume*, 481; *Syndicats*, 1361–1381; City accounting, 1409–1411, AML, CC 389.

43 *Nommées* of Lyon, 1388.

44 Fargeix, *Les élites lyonnaises*, 600.

ness, at least personally. Most of them are actually mentioned in the sources as drapers, but quit their profession to become landowners—and sometimes even seigneurial lords—in a short period of time, so that the various family branches were identified on the basis of their *seigneurie* (Avauges, Belmont, Rontalon). Of the many members of the family, only Bernard was still active as the *maître de métier* of drapers in the early decades of the fifteenth century, but he eventually became a *terrier* in 1423.

The other Savoy creditors belonged to a group of more recent but politically prominent families: the de Cuysel, Chevrier, and Caille families, whose sociopolitical profile reveals a greater familiarity with credit and accounting activities at the service of the city and external authorities. The de Cuysel family was part of the local elite at the turn of the fourteenth century, entering the urban council in 1320.[45] Gilles de Cuysel—who granted loans to both Jacques of Savoy-Achaea and Amédée VI of Savoy—was not only a consul in 1340 and 1364–65, but also, significantly, a creditor of the city and the local church. The available sources do not make it possible to establish the nature of the relationship existing with another influential member of the family, Guillaume de Cuysel. Guillaume was a draper and notary, but above all he was procurator and secretary of the city in the 1380s and 1390s, a period in which he also held the post of accountant and tax collector, an appointment that required considerable financial resources (to advance the money subsequently collected) and specific accounting skills.[46] Despite a considerable patrimony, his assets in the 1388 *Vaillant* (1,347 francs, most of it in movable property) were not comparable to those of the most important members of the de Chaponay or de Varey families previously examined.[47] Another Guillaume de Cuysel was mentioned in these years as draper, suggesting a large practice of trade and credit in the family.[48] The family continued to provide the city with consuls in the early fifteenth century, when Pierre de Cuysel eventually took part in the council, although he was actually a Chevrier, as we will see shortly.[49] A family member of the same name also took part in the municipal government and is mentioned in the accounts of the Savoy treasurer, but he probably died

45 De Valous, *Le patriciat lyonnais*, 243–246.

46 *Syndicats*, 1294–1441; City accounting, 1380–1388; City accounting, 1397–1408, AML, CC 385. Guillaume also worked at the book of the *Vaillant*, the tax records of the city. See Rossiaud, *Lyon 1250–1550*, 133, 147, 151n, 155, 157, 166.

47 De Valous, *Le patriciat lyonnais*, 244.

48 It is hard to tell whether Girard de Cuysel—called *Le Masson*, a mason in charge of assessing public works in the city in 1396—was a relative of the most important de Cuysels. See City accounting, 1380–1388; Charansonnet, Gaulin, Mounier, Rau (eds.), *Lyon, entre Empire et Royaume*, 481.

49 City accounting, 1409–1411.

without heirs.[50] As also proven by Pierre Chevrier/de Cuysel's will, the patrilinear line died out at the turn of the fifteenth century, his mother Catherine de Cuysel being the last descendant of the family.[51]

The Chevrier family had been active in Lyon at least since the late thirteenth century, although their origins remain uncertain. Barthélemy, a royal officer and draper, was procurator of the city and the family's first councillor, while Jean Chevrier was a canon priest of the church of Saint-Just.[52] Of Barthélemy's sons, at least two—Henri and Pierre—followed their father's footsteps as drapers. The eldest, Henri, was a leading member of the local elite: he was in charge of the city's accounts and tax collection at various times in the 1360s, he was elected to the city council at least seven times in the second half of the century, and—in addition to the loans to the House of Savoy—lent considerable amounts of money to the urban government of which he was a member while also taking on military appointments.[53] He was registered in the *Vaillant* with a total patrimony of 2,400 francs, of which one-third derived from movable property.[54] The success of the family increased following Henri's activity, when at least five Chevriers—mostly Henri's sons—were elected councillors during the fifteenth century: Jean and Pierre (since the late fourteenth century), Henri, Audry, and André, all of whom are mentioned as drapers in the sources, while Jean and André are also mentioned as *maîtres de métier*, the latter eventually becoming the *maître de métier* of merchants.[55] Pierre Chevrier was especially prominent in the lineage, as he was elected councillor fourteen times and, according to the *Vaillant*, owned a total patrimony of almost 5,000 francs.

It should be noted that Pierre was sometimes identified as Pierre de Cuysel from his mother's family name, another sign of the close links between these elite families as they often formed marriage alliances. Among the oldest consular lineages, marriage bonds were established between the jurist Anselme de Durche and Amphelise de Chaponay, who had no children, and between Mathieu de Chaponay and Marguerite de Varey. However, it was the Chevrier family in particular that forged strong links with several Lyon elite families. Not only did Henri

---

50 The deliberations mention "Pierre de Cuysel l'ainsné [. . .] et le petit Pierre de Cuysel." See *Registres consulaires de la ville de Lyon*, vol. II, 110.

51 Marguerite Gonon. *La vie quotidienne en Lyonnais d'après les testaments, XIVe–XVIe siècles.* Paris: Les Belles Lettres, 1968, 384–385.

52 De Valous, *Le patriciat lyonnais*, 247–259; Charansonnet, Gaulin, Mounier, Rau (eds.), *Lyon, entre Empire et Royaume*, 292.

53 *Syndicats*, 1361–1381; City accounting, 1364–1365, AML, CC 373.

54 *Nommées* of Lyon, 1388.

55 Fargeix, *Les élites lyonnaises*, 586.

Chevrier marry the last heiress of the de Cuysel family, Catherine (thus acquiring a large part of the family economic assets), but their daughter Huguette married Guillaume de Durche; in the next generation, Louis, Pierre Chevrier/de Cuysel's son, married Claude de Varey (Humbert's daughter). The relationship between Henri Chevrier, Gilles de Cuysel, and Jacques de Varey, who formed a rather robust business partnership lending thousands upon thousands of florins to the House of Savoy, was especially strong, as Gilles was Henri's father-in-law and the tutor of Jacques' son, Claude (see Fig. 1).

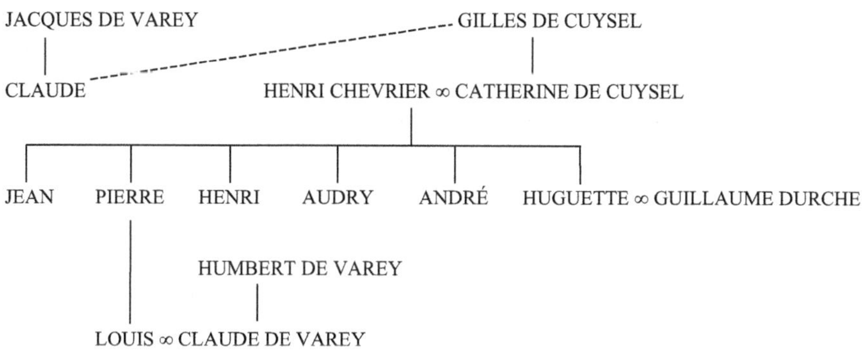

Fig. 1: Family and social relationships between Lyon merchant-moneylenders.

Such marriages and social alliances completely excluded a more recently established social group within the Lyon elite, which consisted mainly of merchants and royal officers. The last two moneylenders mentioned in the Savoy records belonged to this group. The Cailles perfectly sum up the features of these families. Resident in Lyon since the late thirteenth century, the Cailles did not rise to political office until 1358, when Andrevet Caille, a furrier and *maître de métier* in the same field, first appears as a councillor.[56] Léonard Caille, creditor of Amédée VIII of Savoy and councillor more than ten times between 1391 and 1426, was one of the sons of another furrier and councillor, Jacques, probably Andrevet's brother. Léonard continued the family business, becoming *maître de métier*, but above all he acquired a leading role in the new urban elite, becoming a councillor fourteen times and exercising various financial and accounting functions, not to mention the various diplomatic missions he undertook on behalf of the city government.[57] With a for-

56 De Valous, *Le patriciat lyonnais*, 324–330; Charansonnet, Gaulin, Mounier, Rau (eds.), *Lyon, entre Empire et Royaume*, 450.
57 Fargeix, *Les élites lyonnaises*, 585; City accounting, 1405–1423, AML, CC 392.

tune reaching 3,000 francs in the 1388 *Vaillant*, Léonard definitely placed the family at the top of the social ladder, without ceasing to practice his trade at the highest level (the Cailles' customers included the royal family and members of the high ecclesiastical institutions of Lyon).

His brother Jean pursued his profession as both a furrier and *maître de métier*, becoming a councillor in the early fifteenth century, although political fractures in the urban elite made his career less brilliant than Léonard's. Consequently, only two of Jean's sons—François and Jacques—were admitted to the local council in the 1440s–1450s and 1450s–1470s respectively, while two others entered the clergy and one had a successful career in the council of the Dauphiné and then the Parliament of Paris.[58] However, within two generations, the Caille brothers had also left the furrier trade to become first apothecaries and then professional money-changers, with François also acting as the *maître de métier* of money-changers in 1449, 1452, and 1455. Jacques and his wife also commissioned the building of a hospital for plague sufferers.[59] The social ascent was completed by Jacques' son, Jean, a Doctor of Law and councillor of the city in the 1480s and 1490s, recorded as a judge in 1501.[60]

Finally, little is known about the Cristin family, resident in Lyon since at least the early fourteenth century, but not admitted to the urban elite until the 1370s. At this time, the draper Poncet Cristin was a creditor of Amédée VII of Savoy for more than 2,000 *scudi*, showing once again how political and financial business were strongly linked.[61] The treasurer of the Archbishop of Lyon in the 1380s, Poncet was also elected councillor three times.[62] His remarkable assets (2,274 francs in the *Vaillant*) explain the social rise of a merchant and entrepreneur, but were not enough to guarantee the Cristin family a political succession.

The age of fairs

The final question of this research concerns the impact of the establishment of the Lyon fairs on this group of merchants who largely corresponded to the late medieval ruling elite of Lyon. How did these families cope with the massive settlement of foreign merchant-bankers' companies between the late fifteenth and the

58 City accounting, 1409–1411; De Valous, *Le patriciat lyonnais*, 328; Fargeix, *Les élites lyonnaises*, 585.
59 Deliberations of consuls, 1477–1478, AML, BB 350.
60 Fargeix, *Les élites lyonnaises*, 585.
61 De Valous, *Le patriciat lyonnais*, 401–2.
62 City accounting, 1382–1383, AML, CC 377.

early sixteenth centuries? Did they continue their trading and moneylending activities? Did they form new business partnerships with the newcomers? Or had they already moved their interests elsewhere? In order to address these questions, I will approach the topic from two different points of view: on the one hand, by outlining the changes in the urban elite in the fifteenth century; on the other hand, by comparing the data emerging from this research with those in Richard Gascon's study of the sixteenth century.

First, the research presented in this essay has helped to better identify the financial core of the Lyon elite while also showing that this group of families was far from unchangeable. A gradual turnover of this political and financial ruling class began as early as in the mid-fourteenth century, when new figures—such as the Chevrier or, later, the Caille—appeared on the scene. The rise of these people was directly linked to trade, credit, and royal offices, rather than to long-term membership of the urban community. Despite their rapid social rise, these lineages sometimes did not last more than a century—as was the case with the de Cuysels, who died out in the early fifteenth century. We can thus see that the Lyon elite was always open to new members capable of contributing to the management of the city and at the same time exposed to the physiological risks of lineage extinction, which led to a less dramatic but nevertheless intense turnover in the urban merchant group.

Moreover, several successful Lyon merchants gave up—or at least greatly reduced—their involvement in trade during the fifteenth century. It was precisely their remarkable achievements in trade and finance that provided them with the resources to acquire considerable amounts of land and often also feudal titles, and to retire as rentiers or, alternatively, to pursue careers in law and offices in the service of the King of France or the Dauphin. Among the families studied here, the de Vareys shifted their economic interests to land early on, acquiring various feudal estates, as did the de Chaponays, who added land to their significant careers by becoming jurists.[63] Legal professions were the main alternative to acquiring a rural estate, like the Caille family also shows.[64]

However, this did not imply a total withdrawal from trading activities. As we have seen, quite a few heirs of the families examined here stopped practising their trade personally, but continued their activity by investing in other people's companies, with a profile officially recognised as *terrier*. Consequently, their disappearance from the sources as merchants coincides with the peak of their economic success, since most of these former merchants became *terriers* and land-

63 See also Gascon, *Grand commerce*, 504–506, 813–814.
64 Gascon, *Grand commerce*, 823.

owners after they had reached this position, in a process which took place before the great success of the Lyon fairs. We can therefore infer that these families were not marginalised and excluded from trade and finance by the new foreign companies arriving after 1464; rather, they had already moved on, often diversifying their activities, leaving their place to others.

This seems to be confirmed if we look at Lyon merchants from a sixteenth-century perspective. Gascon's investigation actually uncovered quite a number of Lyon companies active during the golden age of fairs, showing that they were the second-most important group of merchants after the Italians.[65] Far from being excluded by foreign operators, the Lyon merchants played a crucial role in the import sector, with ten companies between the ninth and thirty-second in the ranking of importers, although the volume of commodities traded was unquestionably lower than that of the Italians. However, what is most significant is that none of the families of merchant-moneylenders examined in this essay appeared among those ten companies of drapers and apothecaries. Some had disappeared by then—like the Chevriers, who died out in the early sixteenth century; on the contrary, others—such as the Caille or de Varey families—were still active on the local political scene and in the royal administration. It is impossible to investigate their role as "external" investors on the basis of the surviving sources, but we can assume that they continued to finance other companies as *terriers* while no longer actively engaging in trade. The place of the late medieval Lyon merchants was thus not taken by foreigners, who occupied a completely new economic sphere; rather, a regular turnover of the local merchant elite led to the replacement of the previous merchants, who were now serving as lords and royal officers.

Bibliography

Primary Sources

Aldermen of Lyon, 1368–1705. Archives Municipales de Lyon, Lyon, France (AML), BB 379.
Aldermen of Lyon, 1382–1593. AML, BB 380.
City accounting, 1364–1365. AML, CC 373.
City accounting, 1380–1388. AML, CC 376.
City accounting, 1382–1383. AML, CC 377.
City accounting, 1397–1408. AML, CC 385.
City accounting, 1405–1423. AML, CC 392.

65 Gascon, *Grand commerce*, 203–206.

City accounting, 1409–1411. AML, CC 389.
Constitutional and political acts of the city. AML, series AA.
Deliberations of consuls, 1477–1478. AML, BB 350.
Deliberations of the city of Lyon, 1416. AML, BB 1.
Ducal protocols, black series, 1362. Archivio di Stato di Torino, Turin, Italy (ASTo), Corte, Materie politiche per rapporto all'interno, Protocolli dei notai della corona, Protocolli camerali (serie nera), no. 20.
Ducal protocols, black series, 1366. ASTo, Corte, Materie politiche per rapporto all'interno, Protocolli dei notai della corona, Protocolli camerali (serie nera), no. 70.
Ducal protocols, black series, 1372. ASTo, Corte, Materie politiche per rapporto all'interno, Protocolli dei notai della corona, Protocolli camerali (serie nera), no. 71.
Ducal protocols, black series, 1329. ASTo, Corte, Materie politiche per rapporto all'interno, Protocolli dei notai della corona, Protocolli camerali (serie nera), no. 128.
Ducal protocols, black series, 1397. ASTo, Corte, Materie politiche per rapporto all'interno, Protocolli dei notai della corona, Protocolli camerali (serie nera), no. 149.
Ducal protocols, red series, 1367–1369. ASTo, Corte, Materie politiche per rapporto all'interno, Protocolli dei notai della corona, Protocolli ducali (serie rossa), no. 47.
Ducal protocols, red series, 1368–1370. ASTo, Corte, Materie politiche per rapporto all'interno, Protocolli dei notai della corona, Protocolli ducali (serie rossa), no. 57.
Ducal protocols, red series, 1390–1400. ASTo, Corte, Materie politiche per rapporto all'interno, Protocolli dei notai della corona, Protocolli ducali (serie rossa), no. 67.
Ducal protocols, red series, 1447–1449. ASTo, Corte, Materie politiche per rapporto all'interno, Protocolli dei notai della corona, Protocolli ducali (serie rossa), no. 91.
Lists of councillors and other magistrates of Lyon, 1400–1667. AML, BB 375.
Lists of councillors and other magistrates of Lyon, 1294–1673. AML, BB 376.
Nommées of Lyon, 1388. AML, CC 1.
Nommées of Lyon, 1380–1423. AML, CC 13.
Nommées of Lyon, 1545. AML, CC 40.
Syndicats, 1294–1441. AML, BB 367.
Syndicats, 1361–1381. AML, BB 368.
Syndicats, 1442–1499. AML, BB 369.

Literature

Barbero, Alessandro. The Feudal Principalities: The West (Monferrato, Saluzzo, Savoy, Savoy-Acaia). In *The Italian Renaissance State*, Andrea Gamberini, Isabella Lazzarini (eds.). Cambridge: Cambridge University Press, 2014, 177–96.
Barbero, Alessandro. *Un'oligarchia urbana. Politica ed economia a Torino fra Tre e Quattrocento*. Rome: Viella, 1995.
Bonnet, Michèle. Les Changeurs Lyonnais Au Moyen Age (1350–1450). *Revue Historique* 249:2 (1973): 325–352.
Bordone, Renato, Franco Spinelli (eds.). *Lombardi in Europa nel Medioevo*. Milan: Franco Angeli, 2005.
Bottin, Jacques. Les foires de Lyon et les Italiens autour de 1600: déclin ou reconfiguration. In *La Pratica dello scambio. Sistemi di fiere, mercanti e città in Europa (1400–1700)*, Paolo Lanaro (ed.). Venice: Marsilio, 2003, 201–218.

Boucher, Jacqueline. *Présence italienne à Lyon à la Renaissance: du milieu du XVe à la fin du XVIe siècle.* Lyon: Éditions LUGD, 1994.

Brésard, Marc. *Les foires de Lyon aux XVe et XVIe siècles*. Paris: A. Picard, 1914.

Buffo, Paolo. I principati piemontesi fra reti feudali, poteri pubblici e gerarchie territoriali. In *Reti italiche. Spazi e relazioni politiche da Roma alle Alpi nei tempi di Dante (1260–1330)*, Enrico Faini, Pierluigi Terenzi, Andrea Zorzi (eds.). Rome: Viella, 2023, 233–256.

Buffo, Paolo. Savoia Acaia, Giacomo di. In *Dizionario Biografico degli Italiani*, vol. 91, 81–83. Roma: Istituto della Enciclopedia italiana, 2018.

Cannelloni, Federico. *Credito e pegno, famiglie e nazioni: i Lombardi tra Piemonte e Paesi Bassi (ca. 1380–1500)*. PhD diss., Università degli Studi di Padova, KU Leuven, 2015.

Cassandro, Michele. *Le fiere di Lione e gli uomini d'affari italiani nel Cinquecento*. Florence: Baccini & Chiappi, 1979.

Cassandro, Michele. I forestieri a Lione nel '400 e'500: la nazione fiorentina. In *Dentro la città. Stranieri e realtà urbane nell'Europa dei secoli XII–XVI*, Gabriella Rossetti (ed.). Naples: Liguori, 1989, 151–162.

Castellani, Luisa. Percorsi di affermazione di una famiglia dell'aristocrazia finanziaria astigiana: i Malabaila di Valgorrea e Carantana. *Società e Storia* 63 (1994): 19–47.

Castellani, Luisa. *Gli uomini d'affari astigiani. Politica e denaro tra il Piemonte e l'Europa, 1270–1312*. Turin: Paravia Scriptorium, 1998.

Castelnuovo, Guido. Les protocoles des comtes de Savoie, moyens et enjeux du pouvoir princier sur l'écrit (première moitié du XIVe siècle). In *L'Enquête en questions. De la réalité à la "vérité" dans les modes de gouvernement (Moyen Âge–Temps modernes)*, Anne Mailloux, Laure Verdon (eds.). Paris: CNRS Editions, 2014, 185–93.

Charansonnet, Alexis, Jean-Louis Gaulin, Pascale Mounier, Susanne Rau (eds.). *Lyon, entre Empire et Royaume (843–1601): textes et documents*. Paris: Classiques Garnier, 2015.

Demo, Edoardo. Sete e mercanti vicentini alle fiere di Lione nel XVI secolo. In *La pratica dello scambio*, Lanaro (ed.), 177–200.

De Roover, Raymond. *The rise and decline of the Medici Bank, 1397–1494*. Cambridge, MA: Harvard University Press, 1963.

De Valous, Guy. *Le patriciat lyonnais aux XIIIe et XIVe siècles*. Paris: Picard, 1973.

Dini, Bruno. I mercanti-banchieri italiani e le fiere di Ginevra e Lione. In *L'Italia alla fine del Medioevo. I caratteri originali nel quadro europeo*, Francesco Salvestrini (ed.), 433–456. Florence: Firenze University Press, 2005.

Fargeix, Caroline. *Les élites lyonnaises du XVe siècle au miroir de leur langage: pratiques et représentations culturelles des conseillers de Lyon, d'après les registres de délibérations consulaires*. Paris: De Boccard, 2007.

Galland, Bruno. Gerbaix, Pierre. In *Dizionario Biografico degli Italiani*, vol. 53, 375–377. Roma: Istituto della Enciclopedia italiana, 2000.

Gascon, Richard. *Grand commerce et vie urbaine au XVIe siècle. Lyon et ses marchands (environs de 1520–environs de 1580)*. Paris: S.E.V.P.E.N., 1971.

Gascon, Richard. *Lyon et l'Europe: hommes et sociétés*. Lyon: Lyon Presses universitaires de Lyon, 1980.

Gaulin, Jean-Louis, Susanne Rau (eds.). *Lyon vu/e d'ailleurs (1245–1800). Échanges, compétitions et perceptions*. Lyon: Presses universitaires de Lyon, 2009.

Gonon, Marguerite. *La vie quotidienne en Lyonnais d'après les testaments, XIVe–XVIe siècles*. Paris: Les Belles Lettres, 1968.

Gravela, Marta. A 'feudalized' public debt? Loans, fiefs, and debt control in the Savoy state (fourteenth-fifteenth centuries). In *The Origins of Public Debt in Europe (13th-17th centuries)*, Armand Jamme, Pere Verdes-Pijuan (eds.). Publication forthcoming.

Gravela, Marta. Provana. In *La signoria rurale nell'Italia del tardo medioevo.* Vol. 5, *Censimento e quadri regionali*, Federico Del Tredici (ed.). Rome: Universitalia, 2021, 139–143.

Guidi Bruscoli, Francesco. Banchieri senesi nel primo cinquecento tra Roma, Lione, e la penisola iberica. In *L'ultimo secolo della Republica di Siena*, Mario Ascheri, Fabrizio Nevola (eds.). Siena: Accademia Senese degli intronati, 2007, 385–409.

Guigue, Georges (ed.). *Registres consulaires de la ville de Lyon, ou Recueil des délibérations du Conseil de la Commune de 1422 à 1450. Publiés d'après les procès verbaux originaux.* Vol. II. Lyon: Archives et bibliothèque de la ville, 1926.

Guigue, Marie-Claude (ed.). *Registres consulaires de la ville de Lyon, ou Recueil des délibérations du Conseil de la Commune de 1416 à 1423. Publiés d'après les procès verbaux originaux.* Vol. I. Lyon: A. Brun, 1882.

Guilleré, Christian. Les finances d'Amédée VIII (1391–1416). In *La naissance du duché de Savoie (1416)*, Laurent Ripart, Pascal Vuillemin, Christian Guilleré (eds.). Chambery: Université de Savoie Mont Blanc, 2020, 243–98.

Häberlein, Mark. Commerce, formation et réseaux de compatriotes: la ville de Lyon vue par des marchands de l'Allemagne du Sud au XVIe et au début du XVIIe siècle. In *Lyon vu/e d'ailleurs*, Gaulin, Rau (eds.), 141–159.

Hours, Henri, Olivier Zeller. *Lyon, l'argent, le commerce et la soie*. Lyon: Archives du Lyonnais, la Manufacture, 1986.

Iacono, Giuseppe, Salvatore Ennio Furone. *Les marchands-banquiers florentins et l'architecture à Lyon au XVIe siècle*. Paris: Publisud, 1999.

Lang, Heinrich. *Wirtschaften als kulturelle Praxis. Die Florentiner Salviati und die Augsburger Welser auf den Märkten in Lyon (1507–1559).* Stuttgart: Steiner, 2019.

Matringe, Nadia. *La Banque en Renaissance. Les Salviati et la Place de Lyon au milieu du XVIe siècle.* Rennes: Presses Universitaires de Rennes, 2016.

Orlandi, Angela. *Le grand Parti, Fiorentini a Lione e il debito pubblico francese nel XVI secolo*. Firenze: Leo S. Olschki, 2002.

Pallini-Martin, Agnès. *Banque, négoce et politique. Les Florentins à Lyon au moment des guerres d'Italie.* Paris: Garnier, 2018.

Philipon, Edouard, Charles Perrat (eds.). *Le livre du Vaillant des habitants de Lyon en 1388. Estimation des biens meubles et immeubles par servir à l'assiette de la taille*. Lyon: M. Audin, 1927.

Privat-Savigny, Maria-Anne, Dorothée Gillmann, Brigitte Sanvoisin, Anne-Catherine Marin. *Lyon qui compte . . . Banques et finances Lyonnaises*. Paris: EMCC, 2011.

Rossiaud, Jacques. *Lyon 1250–1550. Réalités et imaginaires d'une métropole*, Jean-Louis Gaulin, Susanne Rau (eds.). Seyssel: Champ Vallon, 2012.

Rubellin, Michel. *Église et société chrétienne d'Agobard à Valdès*. Lyon: Presses universitaires de Lyon, 2003.

Tognetti, Sergio, *I Gondi di Lione. Una banca d'affare fiorentina nella Francia del primo Cinquecento.* Florence: Leo S. Olschki, 2013.

Matthias Baumgartl

Liquidity management through financial service providers and the role of fairs: the case of the Augsburg merchant David Gauger and the Bolzano merchant David Wagner

Credit and liquidity

In economics, liquidity is generally understood as "the power of disposal over commodities represented by money or other means of exchange." As a consequence, "it determines the degree of economic freedom of decision and action."[1] Liquidity is thus not only the basis of all economic activity, but also a key resource when it comes to the question of resilience, since a crucial prerequisite for the implementation of any resilience measure is the ability to act.[2] If one takes a closer look at the relationship between entrepreneurial action and liquidity, a distinction can be made on two levels. On the one hand, the current ability to act is dependent on the disposable liquidity. Without liquid funds, it is neither possible to act nor react. On the other hand, additional liquidity could expand the entrepreneur's room for manoeuvre, particularly with regard to future developments. The more capital a company had at its disposal, the greater investments could subsequently be made. While the ability to act illustrates the importance of li-

1 Liquidität. In *Gablers Wirtschaftslexikon*, vol. 4, Reinhold Sellien, Helmut Sellien (eds.). 9th ed. Wiesbaden: Gabler, 1977, 126.

2 The concept of resilience is suitable for operationalisation from a business history perspective. Understood in this way, resilience consists of a range of sub-capabilities endowing economic actors with agency and room for manoeuvre. As the final exercise of the corresponding capabilities, actions are dependent on the availability of material as well as immaterial resources. With regard to early modern merchants, liquidity, knowledge, and networks emerge as the most important resilience resources. Given the fact that even supposedly small disruptions can cause severe disruptions in the sense of tipping points and domino effects, resilience can only be determined in terms of processes and context. For a more extensive theoretical definition, see Matthias Baumgartl. *Das Resilienz-Management von Einzelunternehmern. Der Transalpenhandel des Augsburgers David Gauger und des Bozners David Wagner um 1600.* Wiesbaden: Springer Gabler, 2023, 7–31; Markus A. Denzel. Beharrungskraft und Anpassungsleistungen wirtschaftlicher Systeme angesichts schockartiger Umbrüche —oder: Von der Resilienz zum Resilienz-Management. *Vierteljahrschrift für Sozial- und Wirtschaftsgeschichte* 108:4 (2018): 528–547.

https://doi.org/10.1515/9783111621296-013

quidity in terms of the present, the room for manoeuvre primarily highlights its potential for the future.

Credit is one way of creating liquidity even when there is no direct power of disposal over the necessary funds. Credit is therefore a liquidity transfer that is created on the assumption that a granted loan would be recompensated by the debtor at some point in the future. In the premodern era, liquidity, due to lengthy cycles between procurement, production, and sales, is usually based on credit.[3] Consequently, the central challenge of early modern long-distance trade was to link the capital flows of incoming payments with outgoing ones. However, not only did the exchange of goods usually involve trade credit transactions, but credit also formed the basis of cashless payment instruments themselves. The mutual conversion of cash into book money and other monetary surrogates was dependent on the granting of credit. Not least for this reason, credit formed the basis of cashless means of payment such as the bill of exchange.[4] One crucial reason for the bill of exchange being such a secure means of payment was the constant flow of information. Regular current account transactions and the monitoring of the creditworthiness of potential business partners in commercial correspondence functioned as proactive security measures and therefore helped to prevent bills failing due to unforeseen unacceptance.[5] In order to analyse liquidity management, one needs to analyse the practices and instruments that made this management possible as well as the management of capital flows itself. All these aspects being evident in merchants' account books makes them a crucial source for examining these phenomena. The interpretation of bookkeeping as a cognitive artefact brings both its multifunctionality and its role as an instrument into the focus of research. The recording, visualisation, and modulation of information therefore not only had an effect on the perception and

3 Hans-Jörg Gilomen. Die ökonomischen Grundlagen des Kredits und die christlich-jüdische Konkurrenz im Spätmittelalter. In *Ein Thema—zwei Perspektiven. Juden und Christen in Mittelalter und Frühneuzeit*, Eveline Brugger, Birgit Wiedl (eds.). Innsbruck: Studien, 2007, 142; Giuseppe Felloni. Kredit und Banken in Italien, 15.–17. Jahrhundert. In *Kredit im spätmittelalterlichen und frühneuzeitlichen Europa*, Michael North (ed.). Cologne: Böhlau, 1991, 9.

4 Markus A. Denzel. Bargeldloser Zahlungsverkehr beim Walliser Multi-Unternehmer Kaspar von Stockalper im 17. Jahrhundert. *Blätter aus der Walliser Geschichte* 38 (2006): 101; Markus A. Denzel. *Das System des bargeldlosen Zahlungsverkehrs europäischer Prägung vom Mittelalter bis 1914*. Stuttgart: Steiner, 2008, 54–55.

5 Alexandr Osipian. Debt, Trust and Reputation in Early Modern Armenian Merchant Networks. In *Early Modern Debts: 1550–1700*, Laura Kolb, George Oppitz-Trotman (eds.). Cham: Springer International, 2020, 175–176; Ana Sofia Ribeiro. *Mechanisms and criteria of cooperation in trading networks of the first global age: The case study of Simon Ruiz network, 1557–1597*. PhD diss., University of Porto, 2011, 183.

actions of the bookkeeping subject, but also affected their actions and interactions with other individuals and networks.[6]

Two case studies from transalpine trade

In the case of the merchants David Gauger and David Wagner, such account books have survived. A journal and a ledger from the years 1588–1591, each comprising about 300 folio sheets, document the commercial activities of David Gauger from Augsburg.[7] Out of the records of David Wagner from Bolzano, the first account book covering the period from 1598 to 1603 is of particular interest.[8]

David Gauger was born to the innkeeper Hans Gauger in Augsburg in 1538. His father managed to acquire a certain amount of wealth and was accepted into the *Kaufleutestube*, the private society of non-patrician mercantile elites, and the *Großer Rat*.[9] By marrying the patrician's daughter Regina Mair in 1585, David Gauger succeeded in joining the *Mehrergesellschaft*, a social stratum that, due to its relationship to the Patricians, was allowed to join patrician sociability, but did not have patrician status.[10] Around the same time, Gauger took over the company of Kaspar Mair II and Rupert Hellthaler which was active in transalpine trade. In addition to stocks of goods, this takeover also included receivables and liabilities.[11] Gauger traded in a wide range of goods which included copper, wine, Italian textiles such as *buratto* and *taffeta*, as well as armaments such as armoured shirts and various weapons. However, David Gauger's core business consisted of exporting wool from central Germany to northern Italy, which accounted for around two thirds of his sales. The raw material purchased in cities such as Eisenach, Halberstadt, and Brunswick was primarily sold in Bolzano and Bergamo. Another central

6 Yannick Lemarchand, Cheryl Mcwatters, Laure Pineau-Defois. The Current Account as Cognitive Artefact: Stories and Accounts of la Maison Chaurand. In *Merchants and Profit in the Age of Commerce, 1680–1830*, Pierre Gervais, Yannick Lemarchand, Dominique Margairaz (eds.). London: Pickering & Chatto, 2014, 26.

7 Stadtarchiv Augsburg (StadtAA), Kaufmannschaft und Handel (KuH), 22 and 23.

8 Ledger of David Wagner, 1598–1604. In Tiroler Landesarchiv Innsbruck (TLA), Handschriften (Cod.) 4350.

9 Wolfgang Reinhard (ed.). *Augsburger Eliten des 16. Jahrhunderts. Prosopographie wirtschaftlicher und politischer Führungsgruppen 1500–1620*. Berlin: Akademie, 1996, no. 267.

10 Reinhard, *Augsburger Eliten*, no. 753. For *Mehrergesellschaft*, see Peter Geffcken. *Mehrer*. In *Stadtlexikon Augsburg*. (31 March 2024).

11 Reinhard, *Augsburger Eliten*, no. 385, 751; Mark Häberlein. Familiäre Beziehungen und geschäftliche Interessen: Die Augsburger Kaufmannsfamilie Böcklin zwischen Reformation und Dreißigjährigem Krieg. *Zeitschrift des Historischen Vereins für Schwaben* 87 (1994): 50.

component of his business model was Gauger's forwarding activities. In addition to his involvement in long-distance trade, the Augsburg native also engaged in coin production. From 1588 onwards, he organised the establishment of a mint in Mantua for Duke Vincenzo I Gonzaga. After moving there in 1593 to take up the position of Master of the Mint, Gauger died in September 1596.[12]

For the years under investigation, David Gauger operated from Augsburg. To conduct his business, he used salaried employees as well as commission agents. The employees acted as a kind of mobile agent and visited fairs and markets such as the ones in Leipzig or Bolzano. The distribution of wool in Bergamo was organised exclusively by his commission agents, Gabriele and Tommaso Zenneroni.[13]

David Wagner also originated from Augsburg, where he was born in 1560 as the son of the weaver Hans Wagner. The earliest evidence of his activity in the Bolzano area dates from the end of the 1580s. He initially seems to have worked there as a merchant's apprentice to Johann Baptist Troyla. After initially marrying a bourgeois woman from Ulm in 1581, the conclusion of his second marriage to Katharina von Fuchs zu Jaufenburg, a member of a Tyrolean noble family of knightly birth, in 1589 was already emblematic of the merchant's aspirations for social advancement. Katharina von Preysach zu Katzungen, with whom he entered into his third marriage in 1623, was also a descendant of Tyrolean nobility. The successive acquisition of real estate and landed estates also consolidated Wagner's social status. After acquiring a house in Bolzano's Laubengasse in 1598, he acquired the Rottenbuch residence in 1610. The acquisition of the Sarnthal manor ultimately laid the foundations for the rise of Wagner's descendants to the rank of count.[14]

The core areas of David Wagner's business were closely linked to his choice of location. The sale of upper German textiles to the Italian merchants, who were present in large numbers at the Bolzano markets, was his most important business area.[15] The second mainstay of his enterprise was the trade in copper and brass. Regarding the market situation, Wagner succeeded in gaining a particularly favourable position through purchase agreements for copper and brass with the Wolkenstein-Rodenegg. In view of the high demand and limited supply, the Bolzano-based company was able to generate considerable profits as a first

12 Baumgartl, *Resilienz-Management*, 61–63.
13 Baumgartl, *Resilienz-Management*, 153–174.
14 Baumgartl, *Resilienz-Management*, 63–66.
15 Baumgartl, *Resilienz-Management*, 98–104.

buyer. Due to high demand and limited supply, the Bolzano-based company was able to generate considerable profits as a first purchaser.[16]

In contrast to Gauger, there is no evidence of any employees at all for Wagner. Instead, Wagner's company is characterised by an even more extensive use of the commission system. He was a user as well as a provider of commission services in both purchasing and sales. In this respect, the location of Bolzano also played a fundamental role. With its regular trade fairs and the presence of numerous merchants, it promoted a high degree of networking, on the basis of which access to cooperation was facilitated.

Both David Gauger and David Wagner used proxy services to open up new sales markets. In return for a fee, the two merchants gained access to the expertise, networks, and infrastructure of locally integrated partners. Due to increased communication density and lower transaction costs, commission business had established itself by the end of the sixteenth century as a choice of action in large parts of Europe. Without having to rely on maintaining a subsidiary with high fixed costs, small and medium-sized merchants in particular benefited from the fact that the appointment of representatives expanded their geographical room for manoeuvre.[17]

Managing liquidity by connecting payment flows: the role of financial service providers

One of the greatest challenges in David Gauger's case was to link the incoming payment flows from the Italian market with the ones that ought to go out in Augsburg and elsewhere north of the Alps. For transalpine trade, which connected the upper German economy with the Italian economy, Venice still played a pivotal role as a financial services centre.[18] The necessary coordination of payment processing with Italian business partners required access to this financial services centre. The numerous companies specialising in banking and finance in Venice offered a wide range of different services based on the commission system. It was

16 Matthias Baumgartl. Kupfer als Handelsgut: Unternehmerische Herausforderungen und Chancen eines Rohstoffs um 1600. *Ferrum: Nachrichten aus der Eisenbibliothek, Stiftung der Georg Fischer AG* 92 (2022): 28–37.

17 Nadia Matringe. *La Banque en Renaissance. Les Salviati et la place de Lyon au milieu du XVIe siècle*. Rennes: Presses universitaires de Rennes, 2016.

18 Renate Pieper. Informationszentren im Vergleich. Die Stellung Venedigs und Antwerpens im 16. Jahrhundert. In *Kommunikationsrevolutionen. Die neuen Medien des 16. und 19. Jahrhunderts*, Michael North (ed.). Cologne: Böhlau, 1995, 57–59.

Camillo Bartoli, a merchant banker of Florentine origin, whose services Gauger used heavily. The presence of several members of the Bartoli company at the fairs of Lyon and *Bisenzone* indicates, that this enterprise offered a large geographical scope throughout various European markets. An important line of business at the end of the sixteenth century seems to have been the granting of loans to wool merchants via the *Bisenzone* fairs. Furthermore, the Bartoli were mainly involved in Florentine silk trading companies as depositors and investors.[19]

David Gauger transferred the large majority of his sales proceeds of wool in Bergamo and Bolzano to Camillo Bartoli. Of the wool sold in Bolzano, more than half (56%) was paid directly to Bartoli by the customers sending remittances to him in Venice. The remaining part (37%) of the payments was made at the Bolzano markets and recorded in the market accounts set up for this purpose.[20] In Bergamo, Gauger's commission agents, Gabriele and Tommaso Zenneroni received the outstanding sums from the customers on site and then remitted the proceeds to Camilo Bartoli by bill of exchange.

The money transferred in this way made up the majority of the credit Gauger could dispose of with Bartoli. The respective entries represented the highest figure on the debit side of Bartoli's accounts over the entire period of study—at around 42,000 Rhenish guilders. Gauger was then able to withdraw this credit by drawing bills of exchange on Bartoli from Augsburg, receiving cash in local currency in return. At the same time, this credit provided the basis for being able to act economically in other places. Entries on the credit side in the so-called *Cassa* accounts amounting to 41,331 Rhenish guilders reflect the sum that Gauger had eventually been paid in Augsburg, mainly in return for drawing bills on Bartoli. Although such financial services were already available in the fifteenth century, access to this infrastructure improved considerably in the course of the sixteenth century due to progress in communication and institutionalisation. Many small- and medium-sized entrepreneurs, like Gauger and Wagner, could finally make use of this infrastructure.[21] It was the commission system that created a generally accepted framework for exchange transactions. The possibility of using someone else's services for a fee reduced dependence on social relations and networks and thus increased flexibility. These arrangements also provided the basis for the bills drawn on Bartoli. In return for paying out the bills drawn in Augsburg, the acceptor in Venice was entitled to a commission fee. Accordingly, there are fees recorded in Bartoli's accounts for the use of these financial services. David Gauger

19 Baumgartl, *Resilienz-Management*, 245–248.

20 StadtAA, KuH, 23, fols. 36, 97, 104, 119, 227.

21 Pieper, Informationszentren, 57–59.

settled the commission fee twice a year by crediting Bartoli one-third of a percent of the sum in his *Conto Corrente* for the bills drawn on him.[22] This infrastructure allowed David Gauger to gain the liquidity necessary for his own day-to-day business in Augsburg without having to transport actual cash. Particularly the processing of the freight forwarding business in Augsburg was dependent on the access to cash, as Gauger had to make advance payments to the forwarding agents he cooperated with. This necessity is evidenced not least by the numerous entries in the *Cassa* accounts that can be traced back to the forwarding of goods.[23]

In contrast, David Gauger's payment processing on the purchase side of his core business—wool—was mainly carried out through the Leipzig and Naumburg markets. After Gauger initially had business partners and employees carry out the transactions at the fairs on site, the Nuremberg merchant Martin Adler took over the payment processing at the Leipzig and Naumburg markets in 1589. For payment at these markets, Adler received both bills drawn on Bartoli and remittances from the latter. In this way, David Gauger was able to directly reinvest a part of his credit balance with Bartoli in his core business—the export of wool. More than a third of the payments made to Adler, totalling around 10,260 Rhenish guilders, consisted of transfers from Bartoli. The Nuremberg-based Torrigiani company played a fundamental role in handling these bills of exchange. While the Torrigiani acted as payees in the event that Adler drew a bill on Camilo Bartoli, they also received the payments from the drawees for the latter in the case of incoming remittances from Venice. David Gauger managed to link the payment flows from the sales of wool in the Italian markets with capital requirements due to pending payments on the central German procurement market. This only became possible when Gauger restructured his system of payment processing regarding procurement. He began to rely on operators—like the Torrigiani and Adler—who had the capacity to smoothly link the two central financial markets of Venice and Nuremberg. The Torrigiani acted as a link for transactions between Martin Adler and Camillo Bartoli and were also involved in transfers to Adler that did not originate from Bartoli. Of the approximately 28,909 Rhenish guilders that Gauger transferred to Adler during the period of study, around 19,237 Rhenish guilders (66.5%) were paid by the Torrigiani. In addition to Bartoli's bills of exchange, these were mainly cash payments from third parties which the Torrigiani accepted on behalf of Martin Adler. Within the framework of these business relations, the Italians thus seem to have mainly carried out banking services for Adler.[24]

---

22 For the respective book entries, see StadtAA, KuH 22, fols. 36, 69, 118, 150, 248, 298.
23 Baumgartl, *Resilienz-Management*, 249–255.
24 Baumgartl, *Resilienz-Management*, 256.

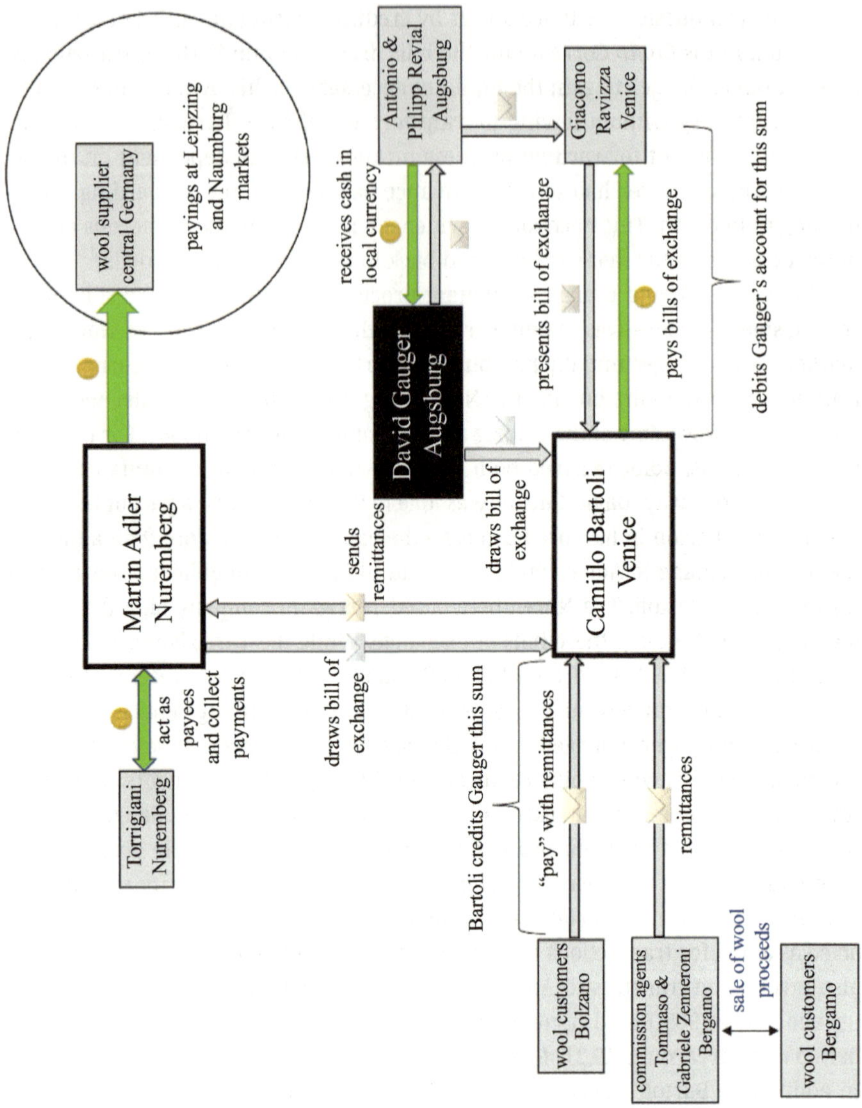

Fig. 1: Illustration of the payment transactions of David Gauger's wool trade.

Another major part of the capital received by Bartoli was transferred via Hans Forstenhäuser. This merchant settled numerous bills of exchange from Bolzano in Nuremberg. Apart from Augsburg merchants such as Leonhart Lidel, the Munich merchants Georg Karner and Sigmund Kölbl, the Nuremberg merchants Eustach and Abel Unterholzer, and the Verona company of Murari-Savioli-Fabriani appeared as remitters. These transactions were booked on accounts set up especially for the Bolzano markets. While it was mainly bills of exchange that were settled there, merchandise transactions hardly played a role in these accounts. Thus, bill of exchange transactions had a share of about 64% in the turnover of the accounts. In contrast, the share of revenues from commodity transactions—including payments for wool—was only 8%. The bills of exchange paid out by Forstenhäuser accounted for about 14% of the bill transactions made. However, at around 47%, the majority of bills drawn in Bolzano were paid in Augsburg. In addition to the Augsburg merchant houses of Paler and Fugger, it was above all members of the Geizkofler family who appeared as remitters or acceptors. Gauger used the Bolzano markets primarily as a way to transfer capital to Venice. Bartoli was paid 17,400 Rhenish guilders by Gauger through the Bolzano markets over the entire period of study. Thus, after Tommaso and Gabriele Zenneroni, the Bolzano markets were the most important payment channel for Gauger to transfer capital to Bartoli.[25]

Additionally, the Augsburg merchant also used the Bolzano markets to settle several freight forwarding services. Numerous entries in the market accounts can be traced back to the payment of carriage wages, whereby Johann Baptist Troylo from Bolzano stands out as the most important business partner of Gauger in both quantitative and qualitative terms. The Bolzano market accounts were not primarily commodity accounts, but documented how Gauger used these markets to process cashless payment transactions in the form of an accounting instrument. Although the Bolzano markets were not exchange fairs and played at best a marginal role in the international system of cashless payment transactions, they were well connected with the financial centres of Augsburg, Venice, and Nuremberg, as Gauger's capital transfers to business partners in these cities prove.[26] Due to the increasing importance of Bergamo as a sales market, declining business relations, and the final settlement of a larger loan through these accounts, the capital being transferred via the Bolzano markets strongly decreased from 1590 onwards.

---

25 Baumgartl, *Resilienz-Management*, 258–260.

26 Markus A. Denzel. *Die Bozner Messen und ihr Zahlungsverkehr (1633–1850)*. Bozen: Athesia, 2005, 50–51.

In the case of David Wagner, it was the company Titolivio Buratini which provided access to financial services in Venice and enabled him to handle his payment transactions. The Buratini also cooperated with numerous other upper German merchants from at least 1580 onwards. Evidence of this can be found in numerous powers of attorney, such as the one to the heirs of Augsburg-based merchant Hans Österreicher.[27] The Buratini fulfilled a similar function for Wagner as Bartoli did for Gauger, primarily by accepting payments from Italian business partners and transferring money to his bank accounts in the upper German financial centres of Augsburg and Nuremberg in return. Once again, the use of these financial services was also based on the commission system. In return, the company was entitled to a fee of one-third of a percent for the execution of the capital transfers. This fee was always calculated on the turnover of the *Conto Corrente* before it was balanced. After that, it was posted to the credit side of the Buratini account. In addition to the fee due, Wagner credited the Buratini expenses for correspondence in the form of *Briefgeld* (letter money) and *rapporti* (reports). This indicates a relatively high level of communication between the parties involved. The explicit mentioning of *Briefgeld* can in fact only be found in the accounts of the Buratini and Hans Christoph Fleckhammer. The posting of an item for *rapporti* was even reserved exclusively for Wagner's Venetian bank account. Accordingly, the services of the Buratini used by Wagner included not only classical financial transactions, but also the provision of information.

In the case of David Wagner, the fact that he apparently settled the majority of his exchange transactions via a separately kept—but no longer surviving—*Überweisbüchl* (transfer book) makes the analysis of payment transactions rather challenging. The items referring to this book often contain only sparse information on the parties involved and consequently elude further investigation. However, it is possible to reconstruct the functioning of this transfer book. The *Überweisbüchl* appears to be a kind of clearing instrument that preceded the actual bookkeeping. This means that the individual entries that simply referred to the *Überweisbüchl* reflect the process of offsetting numerous receivables and liabilities of various business partners during market days.

Insofar as these entries contain details of persons involved, they are mostly from textile customers. The most important customer for textiles in terms of turnover—the Neapolitan company Scipione Vespoli and Sons, for example—processed the majority of its payments via Titolivio Buratini with around 21,500 Rhenish guilders. Regarding the textile customers of David Wagner, the payment flows reveal a network of the customers among themselves. The Neapolitan company Scipione

27 Reinhard, *Augsburger Eliten*, no. 910.

Vespoli and Sons, for example, used Wagner's business partners in Venice—Angelo and Alessandro Boza as well as Antonio Maria Carminal—to make payments. Several other customers paid through Carminal, such as the Foppa-Rottigni and Pisotto-Janelli from Rome or Pantaleo Pattrini from Pesaro. The company Bernardino Borsa and brothers in Naples had their debts paid mainly by Giacomo Antonio Marino.[28] The reciprocal payments in the form of offsetting receivables and liabilities were able to significantly reduce the need for cash.

The prerequisite for such payment transactions was a high degree of compatibility between the forms of payment. Due to the spread of bills of exchange and bookkeeping, payment transactions could be carried out to a large extent with giro money. Considering that most transactions in commodities were also concluded as transactions on credit, Wagner's customers were able to settle their debts regardless of their personal presence on site. In this sense, Wagner's *Überweisbüchl* functioned as a tool for coordinating payments. Even though the entries in the *Überweisbüchl* seldom reveal whether they go back to bills of exchange or another form of payment transaction, clearing at the fairs of the sixteenth and seventeenth centuries resulted primarily from offsetting bills of exchange. The intensive use of cashless payment transactions at the Bolzano markets, which already took place before the Claudian privilege, enabled at least supra-regional clearing and accordingly formed an important financial market of transalpine trade.[29] In contrast to payments made at markets, transfers to Venice were independent of schedules.

The role of Buratini as David Wagner's central banking account is particularly evident in the payments of those merchants who were in a closer cooperative relationship with Wagner. Thus, Giovanni Battista Ficieni, Giovanni Maria Ratis, Alberto dal Passo, and Christoph and Marchantonio Güroldi's heirs, who acted as sales commission agents for Wagner, all transferred their revenues primarily to Buratini, entering their transactions in the banker's books as credit balances of Wagner. This transfer took place both through remittances sent by Wagner's respective business partners as well as through drawing bills on them. Around 86,000 Rhenish guilders of the capital received in Venice was transferred to Hans Christoph Fleckhammer in Augsburg. Fleckhammer also played a central role in Wagner's payment transactions by settling the debts with his largest supplier of upper German textiles—Peter Amann from Ulm. The approximately

---

28 For accounts of Foppa-Rottigni, see TLA, Cod. 4350, fol. 191; for Pisotto-Janelli, see TLA, Cod. 4350, fol. 94; and for Panntaleo Pattrinis, see TLA, Cod. 4350, fol. 191.

29 Markus A. Denzel. Das System der Messen in Europa—Rückgrat des Handels, des Zahlungsverkehrs und der Kommunikation (9.–19. Jahrhundert). In *Europäische Messegeschichte 9.–19. Jahrhundert*, Markus A. Denzel (ed.). Cologne: Böhlau, 2018, 428.

46,000 Rhenish guilders that were transferred to Ulm during the period of study were mainly due to bills drawn by Amann on Fleckhammer. From 1601, Wagner had another important supplier of textiles—Hans Azenholz in Constance, paid via Fleckhammer. However, with the exception of one bill of exchange transaction, these payments were made in cash. Fleckhammer used the *Lindauer Bote* to send Azenholz large quantities of *Philippstaler* and Hungarian ducats. The business partners Hieronymus Röll in Munich and Wolfgang Müller in Ulm were paid exclusively by Fleckhammer, and the transfers to Georg Mangolt in Kaufbeuren were also largely conducted by the Augsburg merchant. Finally, Fleckhammer also settled amounts for Wagner with the Kempten merchants Joseph Künig and Mathes Erdt.

Likewise, Wagner used Fleckhammer's services to transfer the proceeds from the sale of commission goods to Koch-Büttel, a company for which Wagner worked as a sales commission agent. Going by the name of *Hans Koch, Melchior Büttel und Mitverwandte*, the Memmingen- and Nuremberg-based firm was probably one of the largest textile trading companies around 1600. The turnover of goods sold on commission for the Koch-Büttel from 1599 onwards increased rapidly in the following years. At the Bolzano Pentecost market in 1603 alone, this reached a figure of around 39,000 Rhenish guilders. While the average market turnover in 1601 and 1602 was already over 20,000 Rhenish guilders, it rose to over 30,000 Rhenish guilders the following year. Fleckhammer's central role in organising the financial operations of the textile trade is reflected in his systematic involvement in the payment processing of suppliers. The fact that Fleckhammer acted in the sense of a financial service provider is evidenced by commission fee bookings that were applied on the bill of exchange transactions carried out for Wagner. After this fee had been charged for the first time at the end of the year 1599, its calculation was usually done during the balancing of accounts. The percentage of the fee was initially 2 per *mille*, which was below the usual level for such banking services but was adjusted to one-third of a percent from 1603 onwards.

Like Gauger, David Wagner made use of the financial services of the Nuremberg-based Torrigiani company too. The Bolzano merchant transferred around 67,000 ducats of the Buratini's credit balance to *Luca Torrigiani e Compagni*, which served to make payments to the Koch-Büttel (20,000 Rhenish guilders). The sales of their commission goods achieved by far the highest turnover. By drawing bills of exchange from Bolzano on the Torrigiani in Nuremberg, Wagner settled debts with numerous business partners. Although Wagner's transactions involving the Torrigiani decreased from 1601 onwards, Nuremberg continued to play a central role for him as a financial place. In place of the Torrigiani, the Bolzano resident henceforth made increasing use of Bartolomeo Castelli, who was also of Italian origin.[30]

Likewise, the majority of payments resulting from the Koch-Büttel commission trade was processed via Nuremberg. In addition to the aforementioned Torrigiani and Castelli, there were a large number of textile customers who settled their debts by issuing bills addressed to the many other Italian merchants in Nuremberg. Among them were, for example, Gerardini, Beccaria, and Maranelli (Marinelli). In this case, the customary fee of one-third of a percent was charged as well.

The transfer of the capital earned from the sale of commission goods for the Koch-Büttel was the largest capital stream within David Wagner's enterprise. A significant part of these transactions went through the account of Buratini as a joint bank account. As can be seen from one of the first entries in the *Conto Corrente* of the Koch-Büttel, the upper German company itself had an account with Tito Livio Buratini in Venice. Wagner sent remittances worth a total of 13,770 Rhenish guilders to the Buratini, who could then encash them in Venice and consequently credit the Koch-Büttel to their account. However, the Buratini could also draw bills on David Wagner, which were then offset against the Koch-Büttel credit. In fact, it was the latter variant that was used for a large part of the capital transfer to Wagner's principals. In Bolzano, Wagner paid out about 46,329 Rhenish guilders, which were due as a result of the bills drawn on him by the Buratini. In total, around 21% of the capital paid out by Wagner to his commission agents was transferred via the joint bank account in Venice. The keeping of accounts at the same banking house, which enabled the offsetting of mutual claims and liabilities, was fundamental to the relationship between principal and commission agent.

Expanding credit volume through financial techniques

Apart from expanding his financial room for manoeuvre through deposits, David Gauger used a special financial technique to increase his capital temporarily and according to need. A special form of bill of exchange loan, which was part of the range of financial services offered by Bartoli, allowed him to borrow flexibly on the capital market. These loans were the so-called *ricorsa* bills of exchange which

---

30 Baumgartl, *Resilienz-Management*, 272.

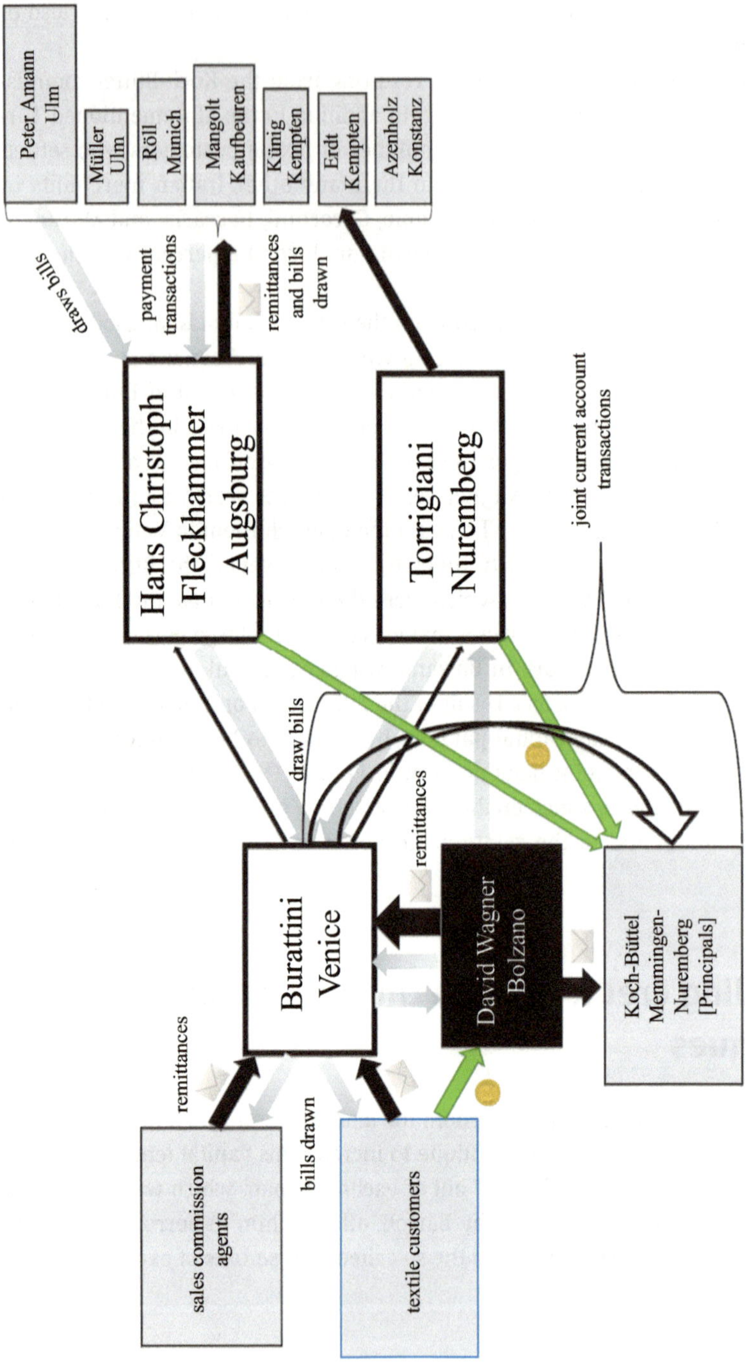

Fig. 2: Illustration of the payment transactions of David Wagner's textile trade.

were based on dry exchange operations. The dry exchange represented a pure credit operation in which no money flowed in the actual sense. Instead, an outward bill was settled by the issue of a return bill, so that the original issuer received credit for the time between them. The drawee was therefore also the beneficiary of the bill of exchange and was instructed to pay himself. The payment of the first bill of exchange was therefore limited purely to the accounting record of the transaction in the books of the drawee or beneficiary.[31] The rates at which exchange and re-change were issued usually differed in such a way that the borrower had to pay a higher price at the end of the cycle than he had received when the original bill was issued, and the lender was able to realise a profit accordingly.[32] The loan term of the dry bill was linked to the maturity of the return bill. Depending on custom, this cycle usually took between one and six months. However, the loan could be extended at will by the parties involved, repeating the bill of exchange. Multiple bills of exchange were possible as long as the creditor was prepared to grant the loan. For the creditor, the advantage of a credit transaction by means of *cambio* and *recambio* was not only the concealment of the interest rate, but above all the flexible cancellability of the loan. In contrast, those who needed liquidity in the short or medium term had the option of obtaining it by issuing bills of exchange and extending them if necessary. This process could be simplified even further by not actually sending the bill of exchange. In this case, the exchange rates were only used to calculate the interest on a loan. Eventually, the *ricorsa* was an agreement to repeat the back-and-forth of a bill of exchange transaction several times and, as a result, to grant the associated loan for longer than one cycle. In this way, medium and long-term loans could also be granted. What was specifically different about the *ricorsa* was, on the one hand, the extent to which it was used at the fairs. On the other hand, the mechanism differed in the context of its application at the *Bisenzone* fairs—above all, in its duration over several cycles—as well as in the currency used there and the corresponding exchange rate developments.[33]

The underlying improvement compared to the previous dry bills is not an innovation in the true sense of the word. Rather, the interplay of integration and centralisation of the capital markets, currency stability, and common forms of procedure ensured both better calculability for debtors and creditors and a signif-

31 Raymond De Roover. What is dry exchange? A Contribution to the Study of English Mercantilism. *Journal of Political Economy* 52:3 (1944): 262.

32 Reinhold C. Mueller. *The Venetian Money Market: Banks, Panics, and the Public Debt, 1200–1500*. Baltimore: Johns Hopkins University Press, 1997, 288–291.

33 Richard Goldthwaite. Banking in Florence at the End of the Sixteenth Century. *Journal of European Economic History* 27 (1998): 491–504.

icantly increased availability of credit. The changes that the dry bill underwent in practice thus had effects that went beyond a mere refinement of the procedure by facilitating access to liquidity. Although *ricorsa* bills are almost exclusively associated with Piacenza, such credit operations were also possible with other exchange centres even during the heyday of these fairs.[34]

The fairs held in Besançon from 1535, which were organised by the Genoese merchant-bankers originally active in Lyon, were the first to establish pure exchange fairs without any trade in goods. These fairs, which had been held in Piacenza since 1579, took place four times a year at three-month intervals. The cycle began in February with the *fiera d'apparizione*, continued in May with the *fiera di pasqua* and in August with the *fiera d'agosto*, before finally ending in November with the *fiera di santi.*[35] At the height of their importance from around 1580 to 1620, the *Bisenzone* fairs were probably the largest capital market of the time and also the central clearing centre for European payment transactions. At the turn of the century, the annual turnover was around 40,000,000 *scudi.*[36]

All *ricorsa* bills of exchange used by David Gauger were booked to an account named after the exchange fairs.[37] However, the 37 bill of exchange operations also include dry exchange transactions with Antwerp, Lyon, Milan, Naples, Cologne, Bolzano, Frankfurt, Florence, and Rome. These exchange transactions were carried out exclusively via Bartoli during the time of the period under investigation and, from Gauger's point of view, were automated to the greatest possible extent. Gauger had bills of exchange drawn on the *Bisenzone* fairs or another exchange location for his account, and received in return the corresponding amount credited to the debit balance of the Bartoli account. Subsequently, the drawee issued a bill of exchange back to the original sender to settle the claim, so that after

34 Jose Ignacio Martinez Ruiz. The Credit Market and Profits from Letters of Exchange. Ricorsa Exchange Operations between Seville and the "Besançon" International Fairs (1589–1621). *Journal of European Economic History* 33 (2004): 347, 351.

35 Markus A. Denzel. *La practica della cambiatura. Europäischer Zahlungsverkehr vom 14. bis zum 17. Jahrhundert.* Stuttgart: Steiner, 1994, 316; Hermann Kellenbenz. Karl V. und die Messen in Lyon. In *Gesammelte Aufsätze zur Kulturgeschichte Spaniens*, Johannes Vincke (ed.). Münster: Aschendorff, 1959, 194–202.

36 Luciano Pezzolo, Giuseppe Tattara. "Una fiera senza luogo": Was Bisenzone an International Capital Market in Sixteenth-Century Italy? *The Journal of Economic History* 68:4 (2008): 1102; Giuseppe Felloni. All'apogeo delle fere genovesi: banchieri ed affari di cambio a Piacenza nel 1600. In *Studi in onore di Gino Barbieri. Problemi e metodi di Storia ed Economia*, vol. II. Pisa: IPEM, 1983, 892; Claudio Marsilio. "Four times a year for so many years". The Italian Exchange Fairs during the XVIth–XVIIth Centuries. *Bankhistorisches Archiv. Banking and Finance in Historical Perspective* 36:2 (2010): 151–165; Denzel, *La practica della cambiatura*, 320–321.

37 StadtAA, KuH, fols. 23, 27, 123, 305.

a certain window of time Gauger was confronted with a 'price' for the credit he had initially received, which was now reflected in the credit balance of the Bartoli account. The average duration between exchange and re-change was 74 days, ranging from 125 to 23 days. While the median interest rate on the loans was around 11%, the annual interest rates varied widely from 1% to 24%. In general, longer-dated bill loans incurred higher costs.

Gauger's *ricorsa* operations always formed a closed credit cycle. To each exchange corresponds one re-change without any repetition of the re-changes. However, the continuous drawing of new exchanges always replacing maturing re-changes increased or decreased the volume of credit according to need. In this way, Gauger at times enjoyed considerable additional financial room for manoeuvre. While from March to June 1590 he was able to fall back on an additional credit balance of 8,000 Rhenish guilders to 12,000 Rhenish guilders, from the middle of 1590 to the end of February 1591 this ranged from 8,000 to 9,000 Rhenish guilders.

Gauger made adaptive use of this special form of financial service depending on his liquidity needs. This is particularly evident in the congruence with the cash withdrawals carried out by drafts in Augsburg which, parallel to the increased credit volume, were mainly in the years 1588 and 1590. In contrast, the volume of *ricorsa* bills of exchange fell in 1589, probably due to the payments received by Bartoli from the Zenneroni. The central advantage of *ricorsa* loans over borrowed capital in the form of deposits and cash loans thus lay in the high flexibility of their handling and the resulting adaptive capacities. Moreover, the restriction to interaction with one's own financial intermediary simplified the management process considerably.

Conclusion

The analysis of the two case studies illustrates the importance of financial services for small-and medium-sized entrepreneurs. It was thanks to these provided services that both merchants managed to coordinate the incoming payment flows from Italian markets with their pending payment obligations on markets north of the Alps. The ability to organise and secure liquidity was crucial for the degree of economic freedom of decision and action and therefore to make one's own enterprise more resilient. Cashless payment transactions allowed for netting on a giro money basis and made liquidity quickly available and accessible. This was fundamental in order to be able to act at all times, especially if one considers that the transactions were usually trade credit transactions.

While a temporary lack of liquidity could be compensated by loans, a lasting loss of solvency was considered bankruptcy. If receivables could no longer be met and investments could no longer be made, this meant the end of economic capacity to act. From the perspective of the creditors, in order to keep the impending damage as low as possible, there was the possibility of taking legal action against the bankrupt. In such proceedings, the bankrupt's assets were confiscated first. Subsequently, an attempt was made to pay off the creditors by liquidating the bankrupt's estate. The bankrupt was thus, as it were, deprived of the right to dispose of his property. Moreover, any transaction carried out after the date of insolvency was considered fraudulent.[38] Bankruptcy was therefore the manifestation of the economic failure of the entrepreneur. Severe penalties imposed on bankrupts were primarily due to their perception as individuals who harmed the common good.[39]

Particularly problematic was the fact that bankruptcy was, on the one hand, a legally relevant condition that was, on the other hand, based on a non-legally defined attribution of third parties. After all, whether proceedings were initiated by the authorities against an alleged bankrupt depended primarily on the reputation of the person concerned. If a merchant was no longer considered creditworthy, this circumstance could be sufficient to cause the authorities to take action against him.[40] There was always a critical threshold that separated the temporary liquidity bottleneck of a merchant from the threat of being condemned as a bankrupt. Exceeding this threshold was usually associated with irreversible consequences, since a lack of creditworthiness and a lack of liquidity reinforced each other. Therefore, even minor liquidity bottlenecks must already be regarded as critical disruptions. If these added up within a company, critical tipping points could be reached that fundamentally threatened the existence of the company and entrepreneur. The use of financial services enabled the internal management of capital flows, which was necessary to maintain liquidity. The commission system allowed the use of financial services under adaptive transaction costs.

Regarding transalpine trade, places like Venice, Augsburg, and Nuremberg played a central role. Although fairs and markets continued to serve as the basis for scheduling payment terms, payment processing was handled for the most part independently of these via important financial places. However, it was not

---

38 Dave De Ruyscher. Designing the limits of creditworthiness. Insolvency in Antwerp bankruptcy legislation and practice (16th–17th centuries). *The Legal History Review* 76 (2008): 307–327.
39 Paul Fischer. Bankruptcy in early modern German territories. In *The History of Bankruptcy: Economic, social and cultural implications in Early Modern Europe*, Thomas Max Safley (ed.). Abingdon: Routledge, 2013, 178.
40 De Ruyscher, Designing the limits, 319.

only payment transactions that were linked to the rhythm of fairs, but also access to capital markets, as shown by the example of the dry exchange credits used by Gauger. Apart from Gauger's use of this technique, the two upper German merchants hardly differed in the way in which they handled their payment transactions. The structural similarities between David Gauger and David Wagner in the management of liquidity are striking. The two representative case studies thus offer insights into how access to financial service providers also enabled the numerous small- and medium-sized entrepreneurs to handle complex payment flows and secure liquidity.

Bibliography

Primary Sources

Ledger of David Wagner, 1598–1604. In Tiroler Landesarchiv Innsbruck (TLA), Handschriften (Cod.) 4350.

Ledger of David Gauger, 1588–1591. In Stadtarchiv Augsburg (StadtAA), Kaufmannschaft und Handel (KuH), 22.

Journal of David Gauger, 1588–1591. In Stadtarchiv Augsburg (StadtAA), Kaufmannschaft und Handel (KuH), 23.

Literature

Baumgartl, Matthias. Kupfer als Handelsgut: Unternehmerische Herausforderungen und Chancen eines Rohstoffs um 1600. *Ferrum: Nachrichten aus der Eisenbibliothek, Stiftung der Georg Fischer AG* 92 (2022): 28–37.

Baumgartl, Matthias. *Das Resilienz-Management von Einzelunternehmern. Der Transalpenhandel des Augsburgers David Gauger und des Bozners David Wagner um 1600.* Wiesbaden: Springer Gabler, 2023.

Denzel, Markus A. *La practica della cambiatura. Europäischer Zahlungsverkehr vom 14. bis zum 17. Jahrhundert.* Stuttgart: Steiner, 1994.

Denzel, Markus A. *Die Bozner Messen und ihr Zahlungsverkehr (1633–1850).* Bozen: Athesia, 2005.

Denzel, Markus A. Bargeldloser Zahlungsverkehr beim Walliser Multi-Unternehmer Kaspar von Stockalper im 17. Jahrhundert: *Blätter aus der Walliser Geschichte* 38 (2006): 99–113.

Denzel, Markus A. *Das System des bargeldlosen Zahlungsverkehrs europäischer Prägung vom Mittelalter bis 1914.* Stuttgart: Steiner, 2008.

Denzel, Markus A. Das System der Messen in Europa—Rückgrat des Handels, des Zahlungsverkehrs und der Kommunikation (9.–19. Jahrhundert). In *Europäische Messegeschichte 9.–19. Jahrhundert*, Markus A. Denzel (ed.). Cologne: Böhlau, 2018, 369–431.

Denzel, Markus A. Beharrungskraft und Anpassungsleistungen wirtschaftlicher Systeme angesichts schockartiger Umbrüche—oder: Von der Resilienz zum Resilienz-Management. *Vierteljahrschrift für Sozial- und Wirtschaftsgeschichte* 108:4 (2018): 528–547.

De Roover, Raymond. What is dry exchange? A Contribution to the Study of English Mercantilism. *Journal of Political Economy* 52:3 (1944): 250–266.

De Ruyscher, Dave. Designing the limits of creditworthiness Insolvency in Antwerp bankruptcy legislation and practice (16th–17th centuries). *The Legal History Review* 76 (2008): 307–327.

Felloni, Giuseppe. All'apogeo delle fere genovesi: banchieri ed affari di cambio a Piacenza nel 1600. In *Studi in onore di Gino Barbieri. Problemi e metodi di Storia ed Economia*, vol. II. Pisa: IPEM, 1983, 883–901.

Felloni, Giuseppe. Kredit und Banken in Italien, 15.–17. Jahrhundert. In *Kredit im spätmittelalterlichen und frühneuzeitlichen Europa*, Michael North (ed.). Cologne: Böhlau, 1991.

Fischer, Paul. Bankruptcy in early modern German territories. In *The History of Bankruptcy. Economic, social and cultural implications in Early Modern Europe*, Thomas Max Safley (eds.). Abingdon: Routledge, 2013, 173–184.

Geffcken, Peter. Mehrer. In *Stadtlexikon Augsburg*. http://www.wissner.com/stadtlexikon-augsburg/artikel/stadtlexikon/mehrer/4757 (31 March 2024).

Gilomen, Hans-Jörg. Die ökonomischen Grundlagen des Kredits und die christlich-jüdische Konkurrenz im Spätmittelalter. In *Ein Thema—zwei Perspektiven. Juden und Christen in Mittelalter und Frühneuzeit*, Eveline Brugger, Birgit Wiedl (eds.). Innsbruck: Studien, 2007, 121–159.

Goldthwaite, Richard. Banking in Florence at the End of the Sixteenth Century. *Journal of European Economic History* 27 (1998): 471–536.

Häberlein, Mark. Familiäre Beziehungen und geschäftliche Interessen: Die Augsburger Kaufmannsfamilie Böcklin zwischen Reformation und Dreißigjährigem Krieg. *Zeitschrift des Historischen Vereins für Schwaben* 87 (1994): 39–58.

Kellenbenz, Hermann. Karl V. und die Messen in Lyon. In *Gesammelte Aufsätze zur Kulturgeschichte Spaniens*, Johannes Vincke (ed.). Münster: Aschendorff, 1959, 194–202.

Lemarchand, Yannick, Cheryl Mcwatters, Laure Pineau-Defois. The Current Account as Cognitive Artefact: Stories and Accounts of la Maison Chaurand. In *Merchants and Profit in the Age of Commerce, 1680–1830*, Pierre Gervais, Yannick Lemarchand, Dominique Margairaz (eds.). London: Pickering & Chatto, 2014, 13–32.

Marsilio, Claudio. "Four times a year for so many years". The Italian Exchange Fairs during the XVIth–XVIIth Centuries. *Bankhistorisches Archiv. Banking and Finance in Historical Perspective* 36:2 (2010): 151–165.

Martinez Ruiz, Jose Ignacio. The Credit Market and Profits from Letters of Exchange. Ricorsa Exchange Operations between Seville and the "Besançon" International Fairs (1589–1621). *Journal of European Economic History* 33 (2004): 331–355.

Matringe, Nadia. *La Banque en Renaissance. Les Salviati et la place de Lyon au milieu du XVIe siècle*. Rennes: Presses universitaires de Rennes, 2016.

Mueller, Reinhold C. *The Venetian Money Market: Banks, Panics, and the Public Debt, 1200–1500*. Baltimore: Johns Hopkins University Press, 1997.

Osipian, Alexandr. Debt, Trust and Reputation in Early Modern Armenian Merchant Networks. In *Early Modern Debts. 1550–1700*, Laura Kolb, George Oppitz-Trotman (eds.). Cham: Springer International, 2020, 153–180.

Pezzolo, Luciano, Giuseppe Tattara. "Una fiera senza luogo": Was Bisenzone an International Capital Market in Sixteenth-Century Italy? *The Journal of Economic History* 68:4 (2008): 1098–1122.

Pieper, Renate. Informationszentren im Vergleich. Die Stellung Venedigs und Antwerpens im 16. Jahrhundert. In *Kommunikationsrevolutionen. Die neuen Medien des 16. und 19. Jahrhunderts*, Michael North (ed.). Cologne: Böhlau, 1995: 45–60.

Reinhard, Wolfgang (ed.). *Augsburger Eliten des 16. Jahrhunderts. Prosopographie wirtschaftlicher und politischer Führungsgruppen 1500–1620*. Berlin: Akademie, 1996.

Ribeiro, Ana Sofia. *Mechanisms and criteria of cooperation in trading networks of the first global age. The case study of Simon Ruiz network, 1557–1597*. PhD diss., University of Porto, 2011.

Sellien, Reinhold, Helmut Sellien (eds.). *Gablers Wirtschaftslexikon*, vol. 4. 9th ed. Wiesbaden: Gabler, 1977.

Chapter IV: **Europe and beyond: time and space of fairs**

Susanne Rau

Fair rhythms: on times, spaces, and experiences of fairs

Introduction

Markets arise wherever there is a society that cannot provide for itself or that, for other reasons, develops a need for goods which are not freely available locally or could not be locally produced.[1] This gives rise to exchange, which can be spontaneous and ephemeral, but which needs to be organised once it reaches a certain level of complexity and regularity. Beyond legal and economic issues, this concerns the organisation of space and time—that is, the provision of places of exchange, the organisation of the transport of goods and people (if the presence of merchants happens to be required), the fixing of times for exchange, and sometimes the fixing of prices and payment dates.

While markets in general might be a global phenomenon, these places of economic exchange are, of course, different in many respects in terms of chronology and region. This is already signalled by the various terms—market, annual fair, (trade) fair, bazaar, souk [*sūq*]—even if the distinctions within a region can often only be made in idealised form. Although today fairs are primarily large international trade shows, if not marketing events—which, at least until the outbreak of the coronavirus pandemic, nearly always took place in large halls—pre-modern fairs were mostly held outdoors or in courtyards. Today, the term 'market' primarily suggests price formation processes that arise through supply and demand, whereas in pre-modern times, a market was primarily a place (for example, a marketplace) where products for daily needs could be purchased. Whilst markets often took place on a weekly basis, annual markets and fairs as places of wholesale and long-distance trade were held at longer intervals (one to five times a year and lasting several days). The bazaar, derived from the Persian word for 'market,' has tended to take place daily since the late Middle Ages and has a more specialised architectural structure: small and large shops lining a street or network of streets, often a separate area within a city where small- and large-scale trade intermingle. As bazaars tend to be found in cities influenced by the Islam-

1 Funded by the Deutsche Forschungsgemeinschaft (DFG, German Research Foundation)—Project number 430627254. I would like to express my thanks to my colleague Aaron French for proofreading this text.

https://doi.org/10.1515/9783111621296-014

icate world—for example in Persia or on the west coast of India[2]—they did not play a role in our research project, which focused mainly on western and central Europe. The same applies to the souk or merchants' neighbourhoods of Arabic-speaking cities.[3] However, these events, which varied in time and region, had one thing in common: they were generally not only economic places, but also places of sociability, entertainment, and (trans)cultural exchange.[4]

Our project, to which this article refers, focused on fairs in the period of about 1350 to 1600.[5] With the decline of the Champagne Fairs, fairs had already been established in many European cities, enabling merchants to conduct their business. They formed a tightly organised schedule—the so-called 'calendar of fairs'—which permitted merchants to meet in specific places on specific dates known well in advance.[6] At the same time, these fairs facilitated the interconnectivity between local and regional markets (rural as much as urban) and transregional commercial networks. It was largely this interconnectivity that made it possible for the old Champagne Fairs to be replaced by a new cycle, within which Lyon took centre stage for many years before being replaced by Besançon (as a financial fair).[7] The chronological boundaries of the project have, as such, been chosen to best account for the major transformations, such as the increasing market integration and the functional differentiation of trade.

2 Since the beginning of the twentieth century, the 'bazaar' also reached European cities in the form of large department stores. One example is the Grand Bazar in the former rue Impériale (now rue de la République) in Lyon, a renaming of a department store that had existed since 1860. The Grand Bazar was demolished in 2005 and reopened in 2007 as a glass building housing various brands or retailers.

3 To start with the classics, see Clifford Geertz. The Bazaar Economy: Information and Search in Peasant Marketing. *American Economic Review* 68:2 (1978): 28–32; Mohamed Scharabi. *Der Bazar. Das traditionelle Stadtzentrum im Nahen Osten und seine Handelseinrichtungen*. Tübingen: Wasmuth, 1985. For more analytical and comparative perspectives, see Wolfgang Kaiser (ed.). *La loge et le fondouk. Les dimensions spatiales des pratiques marchandes en Méditerranée, Moyen Âge—Époque moderne*. Paris: Karthala, 2014.

4 Frank Grüner. Microcosm bazaar. Markets as places of cultural encounters and areas of conflict. In *Engaging transculturality: Concepts, key terms, case studies*, Laila Abu-Er-Rub et al. (eds.). London: Routledge, 2019, esp. 133: "[. . .] that bazaars are not just places where economic transactions of all kinds occur and services are offered, but simultaneously places of exchange, in particular exchange of information, opinions, cultural habits and practices, and they are, above all, places of social interaction." This is meanwhile a widely shared view in culturally orientated economic history.

5 See the project website https://shs.hal.science/FAIRS-IN-HISTORY/ (29 March 2024).

6 Bur assumes that the annual cycle ("*turnus*") of the Champagne Fairs was finally fixed around 1190. See Michel Bur. Champagnemessen. In *Lexikon des Mittelalters*, vol. 2. Munich, Zurich: Artemis-Verlag, 1983, 1687.

7 Domenico Gioffrè. *Gênes et les foires de change de Lyon à Besançon*. Paris: S.E.V.P.E.N., 1960.

Organising a large market or trade fair was a major undertaking for a number of different players: emperors, kings, sometimes bishops, city councillors, trading companies, individual merchants, and, last but not least, innkeepers. Keeping an entire system of fairs in balance was an even greater accomplishment as it was controlled by several actors or stakeholders, some of whom competed with one another. How these international trade fairs operated, which functions they had (as trading hubs or as money and credit markets, etc.), and how they contributed to the development of transregional economic networks has already been researched by a generation of historians.[8] Less attention has been paid to the individual perspective, that is, that of trade fair visitors: traders who wanted to buy, sell, exchange, or pay for purchases.[9] This perspective is also fundamental for a properly functioning economy, as it could not flourish without these temporary guests of the trading cities. It therefore seems necessary to start from the perspective of the fair merchants and to investigate whether and how they took advantage of trade fair dates, how they organised appointments, how they travelled between fairs, the peculiarities they endured (such as suspensions, reinstatements, relocations, bad weather conditions, etc.), the frequency and duration of the presence of merchants and agents or factors, and the timeline of payments (whether on account, from 'fair to fair,' at another place, etc.). All this requires space and time management, which incurs costs that can influence trading for better or worse. To analyse these dynamics in more detail, a rhythmanalysis approach seems well suited. In order to provide a rhythm-analytical interpretation of the history of the fairs, this article comprises three sections: (1) interest in rhythms and rhythmanalysis; (2) trade fairs, fair rhythms, and rhythmanalysis; (3) experience: individual traders visiting fairs—the example of Andreas Ryff.

---

8 Simonetta Cavaciocchi (ed.). *Fiere e mercati nella integrazione delle economie europee, secc. XIII–XVIII*. Florence: Istituto Internazionale di Storia Economica F. Datini, 2001; Franz Irsigler, Michel Pauly (eds.). *Messen, Jahrmärkte und Stadtentwicklung in Europa/Foires, marchés annuels et développement urbain en Europe*. Trier: Porta Alba, 2007. See also Markus A. Denzel's contribution on "International Fairs" in this volume and Denzel's own list of publications.

9 The more recent studies on the larger firms or companies active at the trade fairs are an exception to this. See Hilario Casado Alonso. *Simón Ruiz y el mundo de los negocios en Europa en los siglos XVI y XVII*. Valladolid: Universidad de Valladolid, 2017; Heinrich Lang. *Wirtschaften als kulturelle Praxis. Die Florentiner Salviati und die Augsburger Welser auf den Märkten in Lyon (1507–1559)*. Stuttgart: Steiner, 2019.

Interest in rhythms and rhythmanalysis: a fresh approach

Rhythms are not typically the subject of historical scholarship, as the topic is more likely to be found in musicology, medicine, and psychology. Interestingly, two French scholars have paved the way for the observation of rhythms to be combined with the historical-critical method: the medievalist Jean-Claude Schmitt, who published "Les rythmes au Moyen Âge" in 2016,[10] and the urban thinker Henri Lefebvre (1901–1991), who initially introduced the concept.

Arranged in days of the week, Schmitt's book traces the many rhythms of life, from the heartbeat to singing to the lunar cycles and their effects on daily and nightly rhythms and our calendars. His aim is to describe the "style rythmique de l'époque" in all the impressive variety and diversity of rhythms found in the Middle Ages, including time divisions and calendars, movements in space, depictions on pictures or in chronicles, etc. However, markets and fairs are given limited attention. This is surprising in that fairs have much to do with periodicity and the church calendar, as they took place on a regular basis (usually between two and four times a year) and often began on a saint's day.[11] Schmitt does not ignore this phenomenon, yet he uses this observation to conclude that the subtle evolution of the agricultural economy and the development of markets remained inscribed within the matrix of the liturgical calendar.[12] The complex overlapping of different rhythms and the relationship between individual and social rhythms still require analysis—also for past societies, even if the key ideas in this regard owe nothing to a historian.

In the field of social sciences and cultural studies, the first analytical and systematic approach to the interplay of spatiality and temporality was introduced by the French philosopher and sociologist Henri Lefebvre (1901–1991).[13] These studies

---

10 Jean-Claude Schmitt. *Les rythmes au Moyen Âge*. Paris: Éditions Gallimard, 2016.

11 To name the most common: Pentecost, Easter, but also All Saints' Day, Michaelmas, Martinmas, and Candlemas. These are the church festivals and saints' days on which fairs and annual markets were held most frequently. See Ulf Christian Ewert, Susanne Rau, Leif Scheuermann. Räumliche Konfigurationen des Messehandels im frühneuzeitlichen Europa. Gedruckte Messekalender des 16. und 17. Jahrhunderts und ihre computergestützte Analyse. *Vierteljahrschrift für Sozial- und Wirtschaftsgeschichte* 110:4 (2023): 525 (fig. 5).

12 Schmitt, *Rythmes*, 561. See also the chapter of Nicolas Sarzeaud in this volume.

13 Henri Lefebvre. *Éléments de rythmanalyse. Introduction à la connaissance des rythmes*. Paris: Éditions Syllepse, 1992; Susanne Rau. Rhythmusanalyse nach Lefebvre. In *Taktungen und Rhythmen: raumzeitliche Perspektiven interdisziplinär*, Sabine Schmolinsky, Diana Hitzke, Heiner Stahl (eds.). Berlin, Boston: De Gruyter, 2018, 9–24.

were published posthumously in 1992 and, even though not finalised by its author, the text presents the notion of rhythm as related to urban research, while the term rhythmanalysis is implemented to explore routine movements in urban spaces. Lefebvre's method generally deduces concrete applications from concepts and categories. Two times, however, he focused on concrete applications: in the case of an observer's view from the window of a street in Paris and in a rhythmanalysis of Mediterranean cities (conducted with Catherine Régulier in the 1980s).[14]

Throughout his career, Lefebvre maintained a complicated relationship to various branches of Marxism. He was read predominantly as a Marxist theorist of urban research in the Anglo-American scientific community until his wider reception in France began in the twenty-first century.[15] It was Lefebvre's intension to establish rhythmanalysis as a new scientific discipline. His method conceptualised time in nature as cyclical, underscoring the fact that it is spatially perceived. Lefebvre notes that time in the social space of modernity is linear and artificial, conditioned by industrialisation and economic calculation based on market fluctuations. With reference to daily life rhythms, he concluded that natural rhythms based on the body are homogenised by the rationalising urban and market-oriented linear rhythms. He further claimed that remnants of non-adapted (or natural) time and rhythm react to this conditioning in the form of affectivity, energy, and creativity. The question of energy that arises in the subjects' interactions with space or time is irrelevant here, but we can state that market-orientated rhythms, particularly those in cities, influence traditional, body-based rhythms. In Lefebvre's case, this relates to modern capitalism and the market economy that resulted from industrialisation. This is not entirely unproblematic and must be addressed—not least in the context of a Marxist view of history.

The hidden distinction between nature and civilisation (or culture), as well as the blanket assumption that urbanised and market-oriented life leads to linear time rhythms (and that 'natural time' is non-linear), can be contradicted or, at least, viewed in a more nuanced way. Lefebvre is also not a historian and lumps many elements together. Yet, through his Marxist training, he at least included an important perspective on economic life and capitalism.

Rhythmanalysis thus generally examines the complex day-to-day interferences of different rhythms, cyclical or linear, particularly in urban space. In his (unfinished) book, Lefebvre emphasises repetition and difference as main catego-

14 Henri Lefebvre, Cathérine Regulier. Essai de rythmanalyse des villes méditerranéennes. In Lefebvre, *Éléments de rythmanalyse*, 97–109.

15 On his reception in France and Germany, see Susanne Rau. Preface. In *Perspectives on Henri Lefebvre: Theory, Practices and (Re)Readings*, Jenny Bauer, Robert Fischer (eds.). Berlin, Boston: De Gruyter, 2018, VII–XV.

ries brought together in the notion of rhythm.[16] In any (dichotomic) manifestation, the latter—difference—is deeply involved with measurement. For and since Lefebvre, rhythmanalysis appears to be a new field of knowledge applicable to all the diverse phenomena of individual or collective life, music, the body and its movements.

While rhythm is not a new topic in various scientific disciplines, the reception of Lefebvre's concept of rhythmanalysis has only begun to develop.[17] Expanding it to an entirely new field of knowledge would require an interdisciplinary team that is able to analyse the complexity of intertwined cosmic, physical, social, and artificial rhythms that shape groups and societies. What we set out to do in this context is a more modest approach. The central point is that fair dates, both in their setting and in their use—that is, attendance—are social constructions and practices which depend not only upon political and economic, but also cosmological and religious factors.

Since a rhythm rarely appears singularly in real life, Lefebvre also introduced terms to describe the interplay of different rhythms. These are: isorhythmy (sameness) and polyrhythmy (diversity), eurhythmy (good coordination of the rhythms) and arrhythmy (the opposite).[18]

Trade fairs, fair rhythms, and rhythmanalysis

Why should the concept of rhythm help us understand the history of trade fairs? My impression is that it is more open than the notion of fair system (*Messesystem* in German) which has been used up to this point and can include perspectives of individual fair traders who were not simply passive users but also actors that shaped the system. Up to now, trade fair research has spoken of "trade fair systems" or "market sequences" in order to consider the trade fair cities and their dates in relation to one another.[19] The starting point is correct, since hardly any

16 Lefebvre, *Éléments de rythmanalyse*, chapter 1 ("The Critique of the Thing"), 13–30.

17 On historical temporalities and rhythms/rhythmanalysis, see the recent international conference on "Urban Co-Temporalities" (Erfurt, 21–23 February 2024): https://urbrel.hypotheses.org/4709 (21 March 2024) and the conference report by Zahra Naghshband: https://www.hsozkult.de/conferencereport/id/fdkn-142949 (27 May 2024).

18 Lefebvre, *Éléments de rythmanalyse*, 91–92.

19 Franz Irsigler. Messen, Jahrmärkte und Stadtentwicklung in Europa. Mittelalter und Frühe Neuzeit. In *Messen*, Irsigler, Pauly (eds.), 3–4; Ewert, Rau, Scheuermann, Räumliche Konfigurationen, 501. See also the article of Markus A. Denzel on annual fairs in Poland and Muscovy in this volume. He continues to use the notion of 'system' for the Western European fairs, which is perfectly legiti-

fair trader visits only one fair and many places were in a competitive relationship. Certainly, there are smaller regions, especially in the late Middle Ages, for which it has been plausibly shown that the fair dates were coordinated (for example, in Champagne, Flanders, the Rhineland, or southern England). The cycle of Champagne Fairs (Troyes, Provins, Bar-sur-Aube, Lagny), which appears to have been established around 1190, was not the result of chance but the active promotion of international trade by the Counts of Champagne.[20] Lesser-known examples of such scheduling are the Vienne (Rhône Valley) and Montbrison fairs.[21] This cyclical organisation enabled individual traders, at least theoretically, to visit the fairs one after the other.

However, the disadvantage of the notion of a system is that it is quite functionalist and presumes a perspective from above. It also suggests that the system was stable, although there were always interruptions, cancellations, new privileges, postponements of dates, or declining visitor numbers. While the fairs and annual markets depended on privileges granted by the authorities, many groups of actors were ultimately involved in their establishment and change, even across national borders. First of all, there were the kings and local rulers who, by granting privileges, wanted to enable lucrative trade and generate tax revenue in their dominions; then there were groups of travelling merchants, who sought security for themselves and their goods; finally, there were municipalities that organised fairs and annual markets that had to provide the market infrastructure for them and local merchants' companies which lobbied for these contracts. Established fair rhythms could be shaken or disturbed completely when the dates for fairs were set for towns in the neighbouring region at the same time, as examples in our fair exhibition—Lyon versus Geneva, Leipzig versus Naumburg—have shown.[22] But there

mate if it is merely a matter of establishing that the fair dates took place from a certain point in time in a year-round cycle and if one is not so much interested in irregularities or disruptions.

20 Bur, Champagnemessen, 1687.

21 Jacques Rossiaud. Regards sur Vienne au temps du concile. In *Vienne au crépuscule des templiers*, Roger Lauxerois (ed.). Grenoble: PUG, 2014, 24: "Effet de cette heureuse convergence, l'existence de deux foires (l'une en juin, la seconde en novembre), attestées dès le début du XIIIe siècle, qui attirent, outre les habituels maquignons régionaux, les marchands étrangers et les denrées chères. [. . .] En outre, la foire d'hiver de Montbrison, instituée par le comte de Forez en 1308, s'achève deux jours avant que ne commence, le 11 novembre, la foire des comtes à Vienne. Les marchands étrangers avaient donc la possibilité de fréquenter l'une et l'autre."

22 The exhibition "Fairs, cities and merchants" took place from 30 March to 30 June 2023 in Lyon, and from 1 September to 15 October 2023 in Leipzig. Most of the exhibited objects and texts can also be found in the online exhibition: https://fairs-in-history.huma-num.fr/expo/home (30 May 2024). On the abovementioned disputes, see: https://fairs-in-history.huma-num.fr/expo/online/theme_lyon_3 (30 May 2024).

were also external factors such as wars or epidemics that sometimes caused the system to wobble.

Rhythmanalysis can depict these events somewhat better because it includes the irregularities (arrhythmias). Above all, it can also include the perspective of individual actors and their handling of the trade fair dates—perhaps not always the individual decisions, but nevertheless the adaptation or rejection of the trade fair calendar or its particular use, as well as the efforts that had to be made to be able to use the dates for one's own business. Thus, it is not about the perspectives of uninvolved observers, but those actors involved who have to adapt their appointments—that is, their calendars—to the general trade fair calendar (which prescribes a rhythm). Other factors included the quality of trade routes, the type of means of transport, the seasons, the weather, etc. Finally, it should be borne in mind that one needs time to travel these routes—more or less time depending on the current conditions.

Since the middle of the sixteenth century, fair calendars served as tools to organise the many dates. Yet they also do not allow for an immediate conclusion of a systematic or network character of several fairs, although all calendars would have more or less regional perspectives and could influence perceptions.

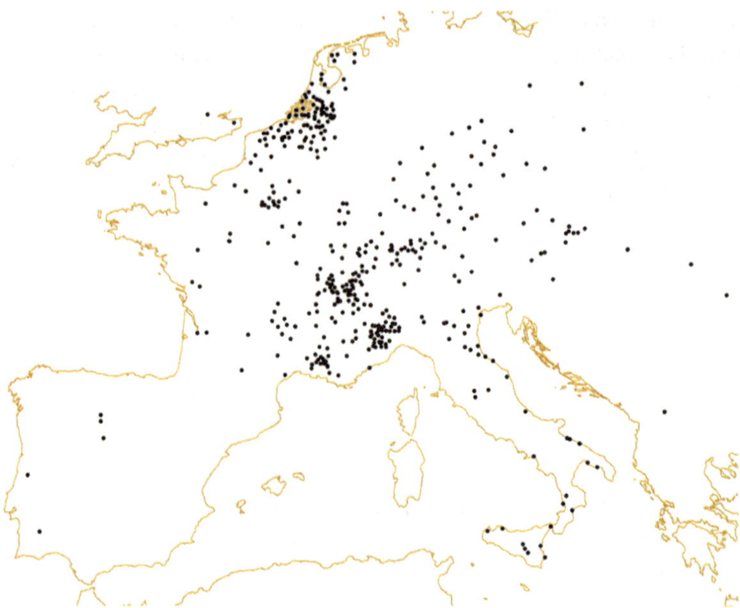

Fig. 1: Spatial distribution of trade fairs in Europe. Source: fair calendars of the sixteenth and early seventeenth century, first published in Ewert, Rau, Scheuermann, Räumliche Konfigurationen, 520. This map shows the uneven distribution of fairs in Europe based on the fair calendars.

Even when taken together—that is, when several fair calendars from a period of 80 years are superimposed—they do not convey a complete picture of the situation at that time. According to Rothmann, there were an estimated 5,000 fairs and annual markets in 1,500 places in Europe around the year 1500.[23] In contrast, the calendars only list 740 fairs with different dates at a total of 467 locations, which means 1.6 fairs on average per location, ranging from one to five per town.[24] But what does the analysis of the trade fair calendars then show? Firstly, these calendars show a certain spatial configuration (as Ewert, Rau, and Scheuermann concluded, often from the perspective of their authors or readers), and secondly, they reveal the well-known periodicity and seasonality of the fairs. Both periodicity and seasonality are undoubtedly strong characteristics for rhythms. But what this looked like from the perspective of a merchant visiting these fairs, who had to deal with these calendars and dates, has not yet been fully considered. This user perspective will be reconstructed in the following section by drawing on the records of the Basel merchant Andreas Ryff.

Experience: individual traders visiting fairs—the example of Andreas Ryff (1550–1603)

Born in Basel as the son of a cloth merchant, Ryff spent three years with a spice merchant in Geneva (1560–1563) after attending the German school and the Latin school in Basel, before completing his commercial apprenticeship (1565–1569) in Porrentruy (Pruntrut in German) and Strasbourg.[25] This was fairly typical train-

23 Michael Rothmann. Marktnetze und Netzwerke im spätmittelalterlichen oberdeutschen Wirtschaftsraum. In *Netzwerke im europäischen Handel des Mittelalters*, Gerhard Fouquet, Hans-Jörg Gilomen (eds.). Ostfildern: Thorbecke, 2010, 149.

24 The huge difference between the 740 fairs mentioned and the 5,000 estimated fairs (respectively: 467:1,500) is mainly due to the fact that the authors (or rather, 'compilers') of the fair calendars each make a specific (not at least regional) selection. This is clearly shown by the fact that only 17 fair dates (at ten sites) are mentioned in five of the seven fair calendars analysed. See Ewert, Rau, Scheuermann, Räumliche Konfigurationen, 527–528. In addition, the calendars do not include every single small annual fair.

25 Veronika Feller-Vest. Ryff, Andreas. Version from 23 February 2012. *Historisches Lexikon der Schweiz*. https://hls-dhs-dss.ch/de/articles/018704/2012-02-23/ (14 March 2024); Albert Hauser. Andreas Ryff (1550–1603). Der reisende Unternehmer aus Basel. In *Unternehmergestalten des Alpenraums im 17. Jahrhundert. Kräfte der Wirtschaft*, Louis Carlen, Gabriel Imboden (eds.). Brig: Rotten, 1992, 177–189; Friedrich Meyer. Andreas Ryff (1550–1603), Reisebüchlein: Einleitung. In *Basler Zeitschrift für Geschichte und Altertumskunde* 72 (1972): 5–15. See also Ryff's autobiography:

ing for a merchant at the time, enabling him to take over his father's business.[26] Ryff thus established himself as a successful merchant, especially as a draper and representative of an Antwerp drapery company (since 1573) as well as in the silk business, which he inherited from his wife, Margarethe Brunner, widow of Andreas Im Hof. Through his wife's dowry, Ryff also became partner and commercial manager of the silver mine in Giromagny near Belfort. As a member of the Saffron Guild and the Merchants' Guild (*Zunft zum Schlüssel*), Andreas Ryff was well integrated into Basel's civic society. He was a minor councillor (*Kleinrat*) in Basel from 1591, a deputy in charge of the churches, schools, and the university as of 1596, and from 1600 onwards, Lord of Thirteen, Lord of Buildings and Lord of Three (*Dreizehner-*, *Bau-* und *Dreierherr*), as well as holding several other offices. As the commander of Basel's expedition in the Rappen War (*Rappenkrieg*) of 1594, Ryff made a decisive contribution to resolving the conflict between the city and the subjects of the countryside.[27] He also represented the city of Basel in many legations, primarily in the conflict between Geneva and Savoy (from 1593 until the Peace of Saint-Julien in 1603).

One could argue that Ryff, who frequented the markets of his region more often than the major fairs, was not the typical fair trader, if one understands this to mean a wholesaler or long-distance trader who regularly visited fairs.[28] However,

---

Andreas Ryff, Selbstbiographie (bis 1574). *Beiträge zur vaterländischen Geschichte* 9 (1870): 37–121 (hereafter cited as Ryff, Selbstbiographie).

26 Ryff, Selbstbiographie, 48: "Dan, alß mein vatter viil jormerkt bruchte, hab ich allzith lust und liebe gehabt mitzureisen und mit kauffen und verkauffen umbzuogon, wie er mich auch uff mein trungenlichs begeren, alß ich 8 jorr alt gwesen, uff viil jormerckt angefangen mitzufieren, alß gehn Liestal, [etc.]." See Mark Häberlein. Commerce, formation et réseaux de compatriotes. La ville de Lyon vue par des marchands de l'Allemagne du Sud au XVIe et au début du XVIIe siècle. In *Lyon vu/e d'ailleurs (1245–1800). Échanges, compétitions et perceptions*, Jean-Louis Gaulin, Susanne Rau (eds.). Lyon: PUL, 2009, 141–159. In this article, Häberlein focuses on the training of Friedrich Endorfer, son of the eponymous Augsburg merchant and patrician, in the house of Daniel Herwart, another Augsburg merchant who had settled in Lyon. Business relations between southern German cities and Lyon existed between the end of the fifteenth century and the beginning of the Thirty Years' War. For further background on merchant training abroad, see Irmgard Schwanke. Briefe aus Lucca und Lyon nach Augsburg. Kaufmannsausbildung und Kulturtransfer im 17. Jahrhundert. In *Grenzüberschreitende Familienbeziehungen. Akteure und Medien des Kulturtransfers in der Frühen Neuzeit*, Dorothea Nolde, Claudia Opitz (eds.). Cologne: Böhlau, 2008, 253–271.

27 He even wrote a treatise on this war. See Friedrich Meyer (ed.). Andreas Ryff (1550–1603), Der Rappenkrieg. *Basler Zeitschrift für Geschichte und Altertumskunde* 66 (1966): 3–131.

28 Whether there was ever a typical merchant or fair merchant is questionable anyway. Pierre Jeannin once attempted to characterise the early modern merchant, emphasising, however, the different prerequisites, training paths, and the different knowledge depending on the goods traded. See Pierre Jeannin. *Marchands d'Europe. Pratiques et savoirs à l'époque moderne*, Jacques

in view of the development of trade fairs over several centuries, the increasing market integration, and the development of their training, it is by no means easy to categorise such typical traders. Furthermore, the amount of company capital, turnover, and merchandise played a role, as they required different specialisations from the traders. In other words, trade was often just one branch of their business. Fair traders in particular were often active in the credit business and acted as freight forwarders or ship owners. In the course of the early modern period, they increasingly became merchants in the putting-out system or manufacturing entrepreneurs. In the fourteenth and fifteenth centuries, it can be observed that merchants or companies, which were frequently run within a family, handed over the transport of goods to their servants or carters.[29] This increasing dissociation of trade and transport led to the development of a transport or forwarding business and generally marked a structural change in the economy. As one of the wealthier city dwellers (although not part of the European financial elite), Andreas Ryff showcases the following trade fair behaviour: throughout his active area, he visited more markets and (regional) annual fairs than (international) fairs, but he was also present at the major trade fairs in Frankfurt am Main, Strasbourg, and Zurzach, not least—as he himself wrote[30]—in order to attend payment appointments—that is, not only for buying and selling, but also for clearing.

It should be emphasised that Ryff still travelled to many fairs and markets himself while keeping his base in Basel and Porrentruy. In this respect, he did not belong to the European financial elite (in Augsburg, Florence, and Genoa), who had their agents or factors in the major trading centres.[31] The owners of these companies no longer travelled themselves but instead had themselves repre-

Bottin, Marie-Louise Pelus-Kaplan (eds.). Paris: Éditions Rue d'Ulm, 2002, esp. 289–308. For the multiple occupations of merchants, see Michael North. *Kommunikation, Handel, Geld und Banken in der Frühen Neuzeit*. Munich: Oldenbourg Verlag, 2000, 26 and 78.

29 Cornelius Neutsch, Harald Witthöft. Kaufleute zwischen Markt und Messe. In *Reisekultur. Von der Pilgerfahrt zum modernen Tourismus*, Hermann Bausinger, Klaus Beyrer (eds.). Munich: Beck, 1991, 75. The older economic history of Basel already referred to the first Basel haulage company as early as 1522 and noted that the haulage trade continued to develop over the course of the sixteenth century. See Traugott Geering. *Handel und Industrie der Stadt Basel. Zunftwesen und Wirtschaftsgeschichte bis zum Ende des XVII. Jahrhunderts, aus Archiven dargestellt*. Basel: Felix Schneider, 1886, 401.

30 Ryff, Selbstbiographie, 79: "Ich bin auch fir daß hin in alle beide Strosburger, Johanne- und wienechtmessen, auch in beide Franckforter, Herbst- und vastenmessen, gefahren; dan die handlung nam durch den segen Gottes deglich zuo und ervordert auch der handel von wegen der bezalungen, daß ich die messen brouchen muoste."

31 For the Fugger company and their resiliencing strategies, see Markus A. Denzel. *Resilienz-Management in Unternehmen im langen 16. Jahrhundert. Fallbeispiele aus oberdeutschen Familienhandelsgesellschaften*. Wiesbaden: Springer Gabler, 2023, 129–145. The Fugger family had its head-

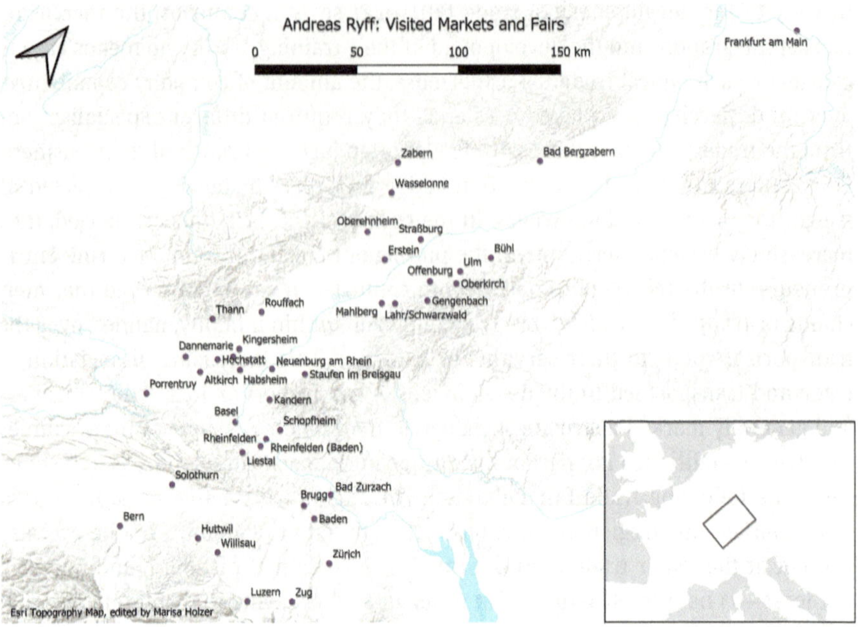

Fig. 2: Andreas Ryff: Visited markets and fairs.

sented. Ryff, on the other hand, travelled himself and covered the distances between the trading centres that he could manage by means of transport typical of the time, and thus he also experienced the geographical area.

He visited the following places with markets and fairs: Baden, Basel, (Bad) Bergzabern, Bern, Brugg, Bühl, Dannemarie, Erstein, Frankfurt am Main, Gengenbach, Habsheim, Hochstatt, Huttwil, Kandern, Kingersheim, Lahr, Liestal, Luzern, Mahlberg, Neuenburg/Rhein, Oberkirch, Obernai (Oberehnheim), Offenburg, Pruntrut, Rheinfelden, Rouffach, Saverne, Schopfheim, Solothurn, Staufen, Strasbourg, Thann, Ulm (Renchen), Wasselonne (Wasselnheim), Willisau, Zug, Zürich, and (Bad) Zurzach.

Another aspect of Ryff's life is particularly interesting for us: he travelled a great deal and wrote about it in an autobiography and a travel booklet—the *Reisbüchlein* as he called it.[32] From these, we learn that he was aware of the arduous

---

quarters in Augsburg, a main factory in Nuremberg, and an inspector who coordinated the other geographically dispersed factories.

32 According to the editor, the travel booklet was written around 1600. This means that the entire text was written after the journeys, but based on notes Ryff made during or shortly after each journey. See Meyer, Andreas Ryff, 6.

nature of travelling at the time: "Whoever wants to go away or travel, should not trust too much in luck;/but take care of yourself,/[otherwise] you will soon be brought to harm. [. . .] Andreas Ryff is my name,/I have often travelled in sweat,/ God will provide the end for us all/Blessed in Christ, our Lord."[33]

In our project, we have recorded the fair visits of Andreas Ryff in the CoMOR database as they are documented in his self-biography and travel booklet.[34] They concern the period between 1566 and 1597, which forms the basis for the argumentation of this text. From this overview, we can see that his business travels often took him to Zurzach, Solothurn, Bern, Strasbourg, and Frankfurt am Main, and that his trading activities were embedded in the timing of the fairs and markets in the region.

Tab. 1: Markets and trade fairs (underlined) visited by Andreas Ryff. Data collected by Marisa Holzer on the basis of his autobiographical texts. English translation by the author.

Markets/fairs visited by Ryff (modern name, present-day country affiliation in brackets)	Markets/fairs visited by Ryff (historic names used by Ryff)	Regular fair dates	Total number of Ryff's fair visits[35]
Altkirch (FR)	Altkilch	from Ash Wednesday to Invocavit[36]	

33 Friedrich Meyer (ed.), Andreas Ryff (1550–1603), Reisebüchlein, mit einem Beitrag v. Elisabeth Landolt. *Basler Zeitschrift für Geschichte und Altertumskunde* 72 (1972): 25–26 (hereafter cited as Ryff, Reisebüchlein): "Wer wandlen oder reisen will,/der vertrauw dem glück nitg zvyl;/sonder uff sich selbst hab acht,/du bist gar bald zuo schaden bracht./[. . .] Andreas Ryff mit nam ich heiss,/habe greiset auch oftmol im schweis,/Gott well uns allen das end beschören/Sehlig in Christo, unsrem Herrn." The translation is my own.

34 Susanne Rau, Marisa Holzer. Bayerische Staatsbibliothek Münchner Digitalisierungszentrum, Selbstbiographie des Andreas Ryff (bis 1574) (COL0091). *Configurations of European Fairs: Merchants, Objects, Routes (ca. 1350–1600)*, Jean-Louis Gaulin, Susanne Rau (eds.). https://fairs-in-history.huma-num.fr/collection/COL0091 (27 March 2024); Susanne Rau, Marisa Holzer. Universität Basel Öffentliche Bibliothek der Universität Basel, Andreas Ryff (1550–1603), Reisebüchlein (COL0093). In *Configurations of European Fairs*, Gaulin, Rau (eds.). https://fairs-in-history.huma-num.fr/collection/COL0093 (27 March 2024).

35 Martin Körner. Le système des marchés annuels et des foires en Suisse dans le cadre du marché périodique et permanent (1500–1800). In *Messen*, Irsigler, Pauly (eds.), 148.

36 Ryff, Reisebüchlein, 37.

Tab. 1 (continued)

Markets/fairs visited by Ryff (modern name, present-day country affiliation in brackets)	Markets/fairs visited by Ryff (historic names used by Ryff)	Regular fair dates	Total number of Ryff's fair visits
Baden (CH)	Baden	26 April[37]	
Basel (hometown) (CH)	Basel	Martini (11 November)[38]	
Bergzabern, Bad (DE)	Bergzaber(e)n		
Bern (CH)	Bern	Interest day after Shrove Tuesday, Easter interest day, St. Lucy (13 December), mid-Lent, Martini (11 November)[39]	29
Brugg (CH)	Bruk	14 September, 6 December[40]	
Buhl (Bühl) (Haut-Rhin, FR)	Bichel	Ascension Day[41]	
Dannemarie (Dammerkirch) (FR)	Dammerkilch, Tammerkilch	St. George's Day (23 April)[42]	
Erstein (FR)	Erstein		
Frankfurt am Main (DE)	Frankfort	Mid-Lent, 14 days after St. Bartholomew's Day (24 August)	53[43]
Gengenbach (DE)	Gengenbach		

37 Olivier Fordrin. *Almanach pour l'an M. D. LXXIII. Auec la pronostication vraye infallible à iamais*. Geneva: Fick, 1573. See also the CoMOR-Database: https://fairs-in-history.huma-num.fr/source/SRC000122 (27 March 2024)

38 Fordrin, *Almanach*.

39 Ryff, Reisebüchlein, 37.

40 Richard Rowlands. *The Post For diuers partes of the World: to trauaile from one notable citie vnto an other*. London: Thomas East, 1576. See also the CoMOR-Database: https://fairs-in-history.huma-num.fr/source/SRC000043 (31 May 2024).

41 Ryff, Reisebüchlein, 37.

42 Ryff, Reisebüchlein, 37.

43 Ryff, Reisebüchlein, 40: "Also hab ich, gönstiger läser, alle die strossen von Basel gehn Franckfort zimlicher mossen erklärt, hab dieselben alle woll geiebt und gebroucht, dan ich hab sidt anno 1569, do ich mein erste reiß dohin gethon, biß uff anno 1597 in eigner person *53 messen besuocht und do erschinen.*"

Tab. 1 (continued)

Markets/fairs visited by Ryff (modern name, present-day country affiliation in brackets)	Markets/fairs visited by Ryff (historic names used by Ryff)	Regular fair dates	Total number of Ryff's fair visits
Habsheim (FR)	Hapsen, Hapssen, Hapssenn	St. Simon and St. Jude Day (28 October)[44]	
Hochstatt (FR)	Sankt Gallenberg		
Huttwil (CH)	Hutwyl	1 or 2 weeks before Invocavit[45]	
Kandern (DE)	Kander	St. Catherine's Day (25 November)[46]	
Kingersheim (FR)	Kingerssen	Interest day after St. Bartholomew's Day (24 August)[47]	
Lahr (DE)	Loor		
Liestal (CH)	Liechstall, Liestal	Wednesday after St. Hilary's Day (13 January), Wednesday after Trinity Day (Sunday after Whitsun), Wednesday after Michaelmas day (29 September)[48]	
Luzern (CH)	Lutzern	Interest day after Shrove Tuesday, Easter interest day, interest day after Whitsun, interest day after St. Gall's Day (16 October)[49]	26[50]
Mahlberg (DE)	Molburg		

44 Ryff, Reisebüchlein, 36.
45 Ryff, Selbstbiographie, 117.
46 Ryff, Reisebüchlein, 37.
47 Ryff, Reisebüchlein, 36.
48 Ryff, Reisebüchlein, 37.
49 Ryff, Reisebüchlein, 33.
50 Ryff, Reisebüchlein, 33.

Tab. 1 (continued)

Markets/fairs visited by Ryff (modern name, present-day country affiliation in brackets)	**Markets/fairs visited by Ryff (historic names used by Ryff)**	**Regular fair dates**	**Total number of Ryff's fair visits**
Mulhouse (FR)	Milhousen, Milhusen, Mulhausen, Mulhuse	Interest day after Easter, interest day after Whitsun, interest day after Exaltation of the Holy Cross (14 September), fourth day after St. Gall's Day (16 October)[51]	
Neuenburg/Rhein (DE)	Neiwenburg	Saturday after Laetare Sunday, Monday after Assumption Day (13 November)[52]	
Oberkirch (Baden) (DE)	Oberkirch		
Obernai (Oberehnheim) (FR)	Obernähen		
Offenburg (DE)	Offenburg		
Pruntrut (CH)	Bruntrut	Reminiscere/second Sunday of Lent, "Vitae Modeste" (15 June), Exaltation of the Holy Cross, St. Andrew's Day[53]	24[54]
Rheinfelden (DE)	Reinfelden, Reinfeldn, Rinfelden, Rynfelden	Thursday after Candlemas Day (2 February), after St. Philip and James' Day (1 May), after Bartholomew's Day (24 August), after Martini (11 November)[55]	
Rouffach (FR)	Ruffach	St. Valentine's Day (14 February)[56]	

51 Ryff, Reisebüchlein, 36.

52 Ryff, Reisebüchlein, 111. This seems to be a local celebration of the Assumption of Mary (Mariä Himmelfahrt), usually dated 15 August.

53 Ryff, Reisebüchlein, 36.

54 Ryff, Reisebüchlein, 36.

55 Ryff, Reisebüchlein, 37 and 110.

56 Ryff, Reisebüchlein, 36.

Tab. 1 (continued)

Markets/fairs visited by Ryff (modern name, present-day country affiliation in brackets)	Markets/fairs visited by Ryff (historic names used by Ryff)	Regular fair dates	Total number of Ryff's fair visits
Saverne (Zabern) (FR)	Zabern, Zaberen		
Schopfheim (DE)	Schopfen, Schopffen	"der ein im meyen," Michaelmas Day (29 September)[57]	
Solothurn (CH)	Soloturn	Friday before Invocavit, Mitvasten, Monday after Whitsun, Monday before St. Gall's Day (16 October)[58]	35
Staufen im Breisgau (DE)	Stauffen	St. George's Day (23 April), Thursday after Martini (11 November)[59]	
Strasbourg (FR)	Strosburg	St. John's Day, Christmas[60]	55
Thann (FR)	Than, Thann	St. Theobald's Day (1 July)[61]	
Ulm (Renchen) (DE)	Ulm		
Wasselonne (Wasselnheim) (FR)	Waslen		
Willisau (CH)	Willesouw		
Zug (CH)	Zugg		
Zürich (CH)	Zirich	23 May, 12 September[62]	
Zurzach, Bad (CH)	Zurzach	8 days after Whitsun,[63] Saint Verena's Day (1 September)[64]	63

57 Ryff, Reisebüchlein, 37.
58 Ryff, Reisebüchlein, 32.
59 Ryff, Reisebüchlein, 37.
60 Ryff, Reisebüchlein, 40f.
61 Ryff, Reisebüchlein, 36.
62 Fordrin, *Almanach.*
63 Ryff, Reisebüchlein, 31: "8 tag nach Pfingsten."
64 Ryff, Reisebüchlein, 32.

Travelling cyclically as a merchant to markets and fairs—and the production of a region

Ryff's visits to markets and fairs in the Basel area followed the coordinated annual rhythm of the regional trade fairs.[65] We can imagine these journeys as follows:

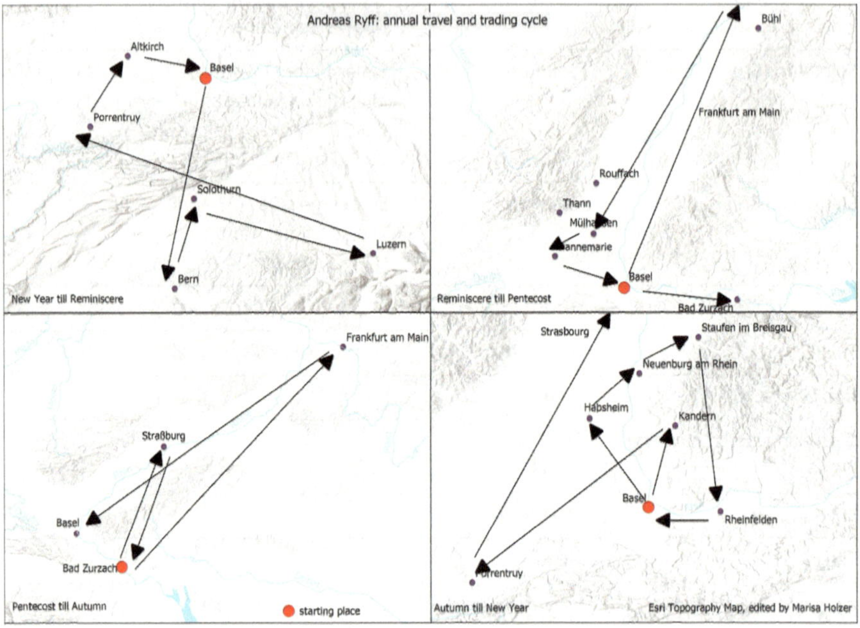

Fig. 3: Andreas Ryff: Annual cycle of travelling and trading.

At the beginning of the year, he started in Basel, went via Bern to Solothurn and Pruntrut, then he returned to Basel, stopping in Altkirch. He then travelled mostly to Frankfurt (on horseback) and sold some of the goods he had bought on his way back via Mulhouse and Dannemarie before arriving in Basel again. Once back in Basel, he cut the remaining cloth to size. He sent some of it ahead to Rouffach, Bühl, and Thann and sold another part in his boutique in Basel. Finally, he sent the remainder in advance to the Whitsun Fair in Zurzach. From there, he was able to return with a couple of bundles from his main supplier in Antwerp

65 Körner, Le système des marchés, 146. Körner has already outlined a typical itinerary, which we have specified and mapped in the project.

(Silvester-Schreiber). Shortly after the end of the fair in Zurzach, he went to Strasbourg to make further purchases. He sold these goods mainly at the St. Verena Fair in Bad Zurzach, from where he left directly for the autumn fair in Frankfurt. Around St. Martin's Fair in Basel, he travelled through the immediate surroundings of Basel with its annual markets (Habsheim, Neuenburg, Staufen, and Rheinfelden). Finally, at the end of November, he travelled from Basel to Kandern and directly to Pruntrut. Last but not least, and under great time pressure (as he complained),[66] he travelled to Strasbourg for the Christmas Fair.

Since Ryff indicated the means of transport he used—namely, by foot, on horseback, by covered wagon, a so-called "garotsche," or by ship[67]—and the places

66 Ryff, Reisebüchlein, 37: "aber die zeith ist mir am tag zuo kurtz worden" (see below, note 71).
67 Ryff, Reisebüchlein, 36: "Ich hab in suma de anno 72 biß uff anno 98 gar starck mit duochen [Tuche, cloth] in die Eidtgnoschaft gehandlet, wie meine schuld- und rechenbiecher anzeigen kennen, als daß ich gar stark im Schwitzerlandt hab über berg und thal reisen miesen, wan auch biswylen ander leuth geschloffen haben." About the boat trip from Basel to Frankfurt (twice), Ryff writes: "Erstlich, so mag man von Basel auß uff dem Rihn per schiff vahren biß gehn Mentz und von Mentz den Mein auff/biß gehn Franckfort andt statt, also daß man nienen uffs land darff. Dise schiffart hab ich 2 mol volbrocht und ist bey guottem wetter kumlich [= bequem]. Aber wan die wind entstand, das gar bald und oft under Speihr hinab beschicht, so ist eß langwylig, vertrisig und sorglich [= besorgniserregend]." See Ryff, Reisebüchlein, 37–38. See also Ryff, Reisebüchlein, 61: "*Per Venedig*: Uff mitwuchen, den 15ten augusti, a° 99, bin ich mit meinem dienner auß Meilandt uff einer garotschen oder goutschen verreist und volgende stroß und auspän genomen. [. . .] An diser statt fleist die Ade, ein schiffreich wasser. Ist ein guotter paß und die stat zimlich groß./Demnach vahrt man ebenfeld per garotschen vom wasser denen in 3 stunden gehn *Kremme; dorthin ist es 15 myllen.* [. . .] Firbaß kompt man gantz ebner stroß gehn *Suntsing; dohin ist 5 mylen.* Suntsing, die alte, zimlich woll erbouwene statt, ist Meilender gebieths. Do sind wir übernacht glägen, ist mit Spannieren besetzt. 1/4 stund wegs vor der statt gegen Pressen zuo fleust aber ein schifreich wasser, *das heist die Oy* [Oglio]. Do vahrt man/ahn einem seil über. Diß vahrt [Fähre, ferry] khert schon wider den Venedigeren zuo. Uff ein starcke stund wegs per garotschen von disem wasser, do ligt in freyem, ebnem und wythem feldt *ein gwaltige, gar überauß woll verwartte neiwe vestung; die heist Urzenove, Venediger hörschaft zuostendig; dohin ist 5 myl.*" About a bottleneck between Cleven [Chiavenna] and Splügen, Ryff writes: "Von Cleven auß tritt man gleich das gebirg, den Spligenberg, ahn, ist ein böser, sorglicher berg zuo reissen. Fir mein theil wolt ich lieber den Gothart 2 mol dan disen 1 mol reisen, nit allein von wegen der bösen, stutzigen und hochen stalden und bergen enenvohr gegen Cleven; sonderen hiedisent dem Spligenberg hat es uff dem hinderen Rihn in der enge zwischen den engen, hochen felsen gantz sorgliche, von holtz gemachte strossen, so ahn die felsen gekleibt sind, so do der lenge noch gar hoch ob dem wasser des hinderen Rihns ahn den felsen kläben wie ein schwalmennäst an einem trom [Balken, beam], und sind nit breitter, dan daß bloß ein/soumroß passieren kan. Wan dan einem die soumroß oder sonst reither entgegen koment, so hat man nit platz, ein pferd umbzuokhören oder onne gfohr uß dem weg zuo wychen. Wan man nun über den Splygenberg herab kompt, so kompt man hiedisent in das dorff Splygen. *Diser flecken Spligen hat vom berg den namen; dohin ist von Cleven über das gebirg 4*

he passed on the way in his notes, it is sometimes even possible to reconstruct the different routes he chose when he was on the move from one place to another.

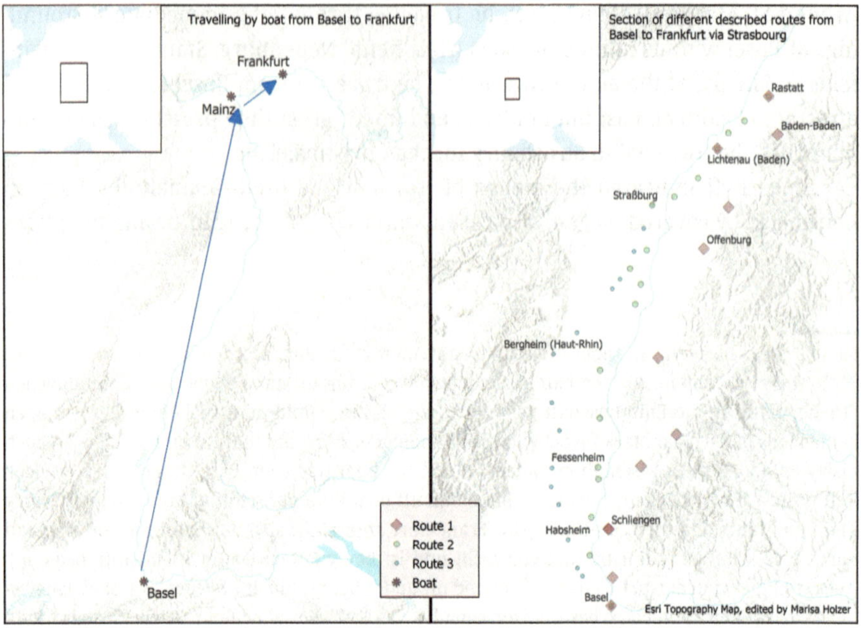

Fig. 4: Andreas Ryff: Travelling by boat from Basel to Frankfurt (and his description of different routes from Basel to Frankfurt via Strasbourg).

For the route between Basel and Frankfurt, for example, he took the shipping route twice (on the Rhine and Main), but opted more frequently for the land route. Such information cannot be gathered from merchants' manuals or account books, but only from individual testimonies.

As can be seen from the table and the maps, he travelled quite frequently in an average year. From 1570 to 1572, he visited 110 fairs and annual markets—that is, on average about 36 per year.[68] Many of his trips to trade fairs resulted in his

deitscher myl." See Ryff, Reisebüchlein, 94–95. On the means of transport that Ryff used, see also Meyer, Andreas Ryff, 8–9.

68 Körner, Le système des marchés, Annex 1, 158–159. This is consistent with our CoMOR database, which contains Ryff's trade fair visits for the years 1566 to 1597.

absence for several days, which meant that he was not often at home with his wife and her five children.[69] This only changed when he began working for the Basel Council and concentrated more on local sales.[70] But this time-consuming travel to one or several places meant that he could not be present at the roughly 100 markets and fairs that were held throughout the year in northwestern Switzerland and on the Upper Rhine around 1600. In his notes, he often complained about the arduous journeys and the associated hustle and bustle: "Now it is not a long journey, but the time was too short for me to travel from one place to the other, so I had little rest, so that the saddle did not burn my backside."[71]

Yet the fairs remained necessary, especially for the textile trade as well as for the loans he regularly used for his trading and to meet the payment dates for goods he had purchased.[72] This can be grasped clearly from the source. From a rhythmanalytical point of view, it can be said that Ryff felt a certain amount of stress from all the external rhythms and the difficulties of travelling. Unlike the presumably model Champagne Fair trader, Ryff was by no means able to attend every appointment; nevertheless, over the years, he found his own rhythm in which he could visit the fairs and markets within his region, from Bern to Frankfurt. We don't know exactly why he occasionally skipped a market, but he certainly had the fair calendar at hand, which told him where he could buy or sell his goods and where to repay a loan. In a way, this calendar was his permanent mobiliser.

There are at least two concrete indications of when his rhythm of fair visits changed: one is seasonal, the other has to do with a structural change in his business. Seasonally—that is, on an annual basis—he travelled less in the summer months of July and August. At that time, there were only the smaller markets in Thann (1 July) and in Kingersheim (end of August) as well as the shop in Basel. The commission received from the Antwerp house represented a structural and organisational change: after 1573, he reduced his visits to the smaller markets.

69 Hauser, Andreas Ryff, 177, 185; Ryff, Reisebüchlein, 113, note 48. These children were not his own but those of his wife Margareta Brunner, whom he married in 1574 after her first husband Andreas Im Hof (who was also his business friend) had died.

70 On the decision to take over his father's business, see Ryff, Selbstbiographie, 68 [anno 1568]: "dass ich entlich mir firsatzte ein feinne, lustige handlung und gwerb fürzunemen; auch gelustet mich meines vaters hauß zuom gwerb zu bouwen, daß es lustig und kumlich darzuo sein mieste." It seems that he had taken over the affairs of his father in the year 1569, when he returned to Basel from Strasbourg. See Ryff, Reisebüchlein, 31: "in meines vaters haushaltung."

71 Ryff, Reisebüchlein, 37: "Nun sind es zwor keinne withen reisen; aber die zeith ist mir am tag zuo kurtz worden, von einem orth an das ander ze reisen, hab also wenig ruow gehapt, daß mich der sattel nit ahn das hindertheil gebrent habe" (my translation).

72 Ryff, Selbstbiographie, 79 (see above, note 30).

The frequency of his visits to the fairs decreased even further as he became more involved in the services of the city of Basel.

Conclusion

The main question is, of course, if this can be generalised and whether there are other such sources from individual merchants that shed light on the everyday practices of fair trade and the rhythms of visiting fairs.

Since the survival of such records is rare, it is almost impossible to conduct a comparative study from the user's perspective. There are the huge business archives of the Italian Salviati and Martelli families, which provide insights into their trade and financial activities at European fairs, but these are business archives in the narrower sense[73]—they provide insight into accounting practices rather than into the practices of individual actors. There is also surviving correspondence from the fair merchants (with other merchants or with their customers). In the early modern period, such letters were by no means purely business-related, but instead contained further information about business practices, the circumstances of the organisation, the expected (or absent) profits, the business cycles (which were dependent on politics, weather, or epidemics), the trips made or still planned to the fairs, the supply routes of goods, as well as family matters.[74] This type of correspondence allows us to reconstruct the space and time management of a merchant to a certain extent. The disadvantage is that these letters have very different addressees and represent a less cohesive narrative than a travel diary, and this makes it less likely that all the trade fairs visited during a particular period can be recorded.

Against this background, we can draw at least some interesting if preliminary conclusions from the analysis of the unique autobiographical and entrepreneurial documents written by a Basel merchant of the late sixteenth century. As an individual trader with business contacts as far away as Antwerp, he still travelled to the markets and fairs with the goods himself during his main years as a fair trader. In this respect, he could be described as a discontinued model. On the

73 See the article by Heinrich Lang in this volume.

74 Such correspondence has already been partially analysed—for example, that of the company Specht & Gonzebat, which is held in the departmental archives in Lyon (ADRML 8B 1237/1–8), although this concerns only the early eighteenth century (1700–1721). On 4 May 2023, archivist Sophie Malavieille and I presented the inventory and some of the results of this study, a recording of which can be found on YouTube: https://www.youtube.com/watch?v=0LqxPQSUzvU. A publication of the research results is pending.

other hand, he may represent the 'middle-class' merchant who must have existed, as the fairs at the end of the sixteenth century were by no means all in the hands of European big business—that is, the financial elite. Besançon and some north Italian places developed at that time into pure financial fairs, but these cities lay in any case outside of Ryff's geographical radius. Ryff was sometimes accompanied on his travels by a servant,[75] yet he never joined a larger group. Nor did he employ any representatives or factors at the major trade fairs or financial centres in Europe, which is also reflected in the geographical radius of his activities. His trading practices—that is, his travelling patterns and logistics—changed when he was given the commission for the Antwerp Cloth House (1573). He then received the high-quality cloth (*Lindische Tuche*) directly and no longer had to buy it at a fair on his own account.[76] He paid in cash, at least in the smaller markets. When he mentions the payment function of fairs, which created a time interval (between two fairs), he paid a trade credit. In any case, he does not mention bills of exchange. Lastly, even in the heyday of his travelling, he was never just a fair trader, for he also drew income from other sources.

To conclude on a general note: While scholars of economic history tend to ask which merchants went to the fairs, what goods they traded in detail, and which prices were negotiated, the urban and spatial history approach asks about the spatiotemporal dimensions of the merchants' culture and how the micro and macro perspectives were connected. In particular, this means how individual merchants inserted themselves into the economic structures and opportunities and how they managed time and space (which was probably largely with the intention of reducing transaction costs). In this respect, such an observation is not a simple microhistory, but rather an approach that attempts to uncover the connections between the micro and the macro levels, between the individual perspective and the larger framework (in the sense of Carlo Ginzburg.)[77] Through having to adapt to the general trade fair calendar and yet not being able to be present at all trade fairs in his region, Ryff illustrates the individual link to the larger trade fair system of his time—admittedly only from the perspective of his own narrative—even as he cre-

75 Sometimes he mentions servants who supported him either in the Basel shop or when travelling to markets or fairs. See Ryff, Selbstbiographie, 85: "dienner."

76 Geering, Handel und Industrie, 402, 412–413.

77 Carlo Ginzburg. Mikro-Historie. Zwei oder drei Dinge, die ich von ihr weiß. *Historische Anthropologie* 1 (1993): esp. 190–191. Ginzburg had already conceded at the time that microhistory was not an entirely unified movement practiced by a clearly demarcated group of historians—and it probably still isn't today. Nevertheless, shared elements of microhistorians do exist: the stance against ethnocentrism, the relevance of small-scale observation, rejecting teleological assumptions, an emphasis on the perspective of the actors, and the importance of deviation from the norm.

ated his own, personal trading region. The analysis of his spatiotemporal 'fair practices' can ultimately help to explain the economic changes at the macro level.

Finally, what we can also learn from Ryff's life is the simultaneity of different spatial relationships in the economy of his time: he went to markets and to fairs and he sold (mostly cloth) in his house in Basel, while other merchants met at the exchange fairs or at the Antwerp Stock Exchange, where much higher sums were negotiated over greater geographical distances.

Bibliography

Primary Sources

Andreas Ryff. Selbstbiographie (bis 1574). *Beiträge zur vaterländischen Geschichte* 9 (1870): 37–121.

Fordrin, Olivier. *Almanach pour l'an M. D. LXXIII. Auec la pronostication vraye infallible à iamais*. Geneva: Fick, 1573.

Friedrich Meyer (ed.). Andreas Ryff (1550–1603), Der Rappenkrieg. *Basler Zeitschrift für Geschichte und Altertumskunde* 66 (1966): 3–131.

Friedrich Meyer (ed.). Andreas Ryff (1550–1603), Reisebüchlein, mit einem Beitrag v. Elisabeth Landolt. *Basler Zeitschrift für Geschichte und Altertumskunde* 72 (1972): 5–135.

Rowlands, Richard. *The Post For diuers partes of the World: to trauaile from one notable citie vnto an other*. London: Thomas East, 1576.

Literature

Bur, Michel. Champagnemessen. In *Lexikon des Mittelalters*, vol. 2. Munich, Zurich: Artemis-Verlag, 1983, 1685–1689.

Casado Alonso, Hilario. *Simón Ruiz y el mundo de los negocios en Europa en los siglos XVI y XVII*. Valladolid: Universidad de Valladolid, 2017.

Cavaciocchi, Simonetta (ed.). *Fiere e mercati nella integrazione delle economie europee, secc. XIII–XVIII*. Florence: Istituto Internazionale di Storia Economica F. Datini, 2001.

Denzel, Markus A. *Resilienz-Management in Unternehmen im langen 16. Jahrhundert. Fallbeispiele aus oberdeutschen Familienhandelsgesellschaften*. Wiesbaden: Springer Gabler, 2023.

Ewert, Ulf Christian, Susanne Rau, Leif Scheuermann. Räumliche Konfigurationen des Messehandels im frühneuzeitlichen Europa. Gedruckte Messekalender des 16. und 17. Jahrhunderts und ihre computergestützte Analyse. *Vierteljahrschrift für Sozial- und Wirtschaftsgeschichte* 110:4 (2023): 494–541. DOI: https://doi.org/10.25162/vswg-2023-0012.

Ewert, Ulf Christian, Susanne Rau, Leif Scheuermann. Räumliche Konfigurationen des Messehandels (dataset). *Vierteljahrschrift für Sozial- und Wirtschaftsgeschichte* (2023). DOI: 10.15456/VSWG.2023345.1406698497.

Feller-Vest, Veronika. Ryff, Andreas. Version from 23 February 2012. *Historisches Lexikon der Schweiz*. https://hls-dhs-dss.ch/de/articles/018704/2012-02-23/ (14 March 2024).

Geertz, Clifford. The Bazaar Economy: Information and Search in Peasant Marketing. *American Economic Review* 68:2 (1978): 28–32. http://www.jstor.org/stable/1816656.

Geering, Traugott. *Handel und Industrie der Stadt Basel. Zunftwesen und Wirtschaftsgeschichte bis zum Ende des XVII. Jahrhunderts, aus Archiven dargestellt*. Basel: Felix Schneider, 1886.

Ginzburg, Carlo. Mikro-Historie. Zwei oder drei Dinge, die ich von ihr weiß. *Historische Anthropologie* 1 (1993): 169–192.

Gioffrè, Domenico. *Gênes et les foires de change de Lyon à Besançon*. Paris: S.E.V.P.E.N., 1960.

Grüner, Frank. Microcosm bazaar: Markets as places of cultural encounters and areas of conflict. In *Engaging transculturality. Concepts, key terms, case studies*, Laila Abu-Er-Rub, Christiane Brosius, Sebastian Meurer, Diamantis Panagiotopoulos, Susan Richter (eds.). London: Routledge, 2019, 122–135.

Haasis, Lucas. *The Power of Persuasion: Becoming a Merchant in the 18th century*. Bielefeld: Transcript, 2022.

Häberlein, Mark. Commerce, formation et réseaux de compatriotes. La ville de Lyon vue par des marchands de l'Allemagne du Sud au XVIe et au début du XVIIe siècle. In *Lyon vu/e d'ailleurs (1245–1800). Échanges, compétitions et perceptions*, Jean-Louis Gaulin, Susanne Rau (eds.). Lyon: PUL, 2009, 141–159.

Hauser, Albert. Andreas Ryff (1550–1603). Der reisende Unternehmer aus Basel. In *Unternehmergestalten des Alpenraums im 17. Jahrhundert. Kräfte der Wirtschaft*, Louis Carlen, Gabriel Imboden (eds.). Brig: Rotten, 1992, 177–189.

Irsigler, Franz, Michel Pauly (eds.). *Messen, Jahrmärkte und Stadtentwicklung in Europa/Foires, marchés annuels et développement urbain en Europe*. Trier: Porta Alba, 2007.

Irsigler, Franz. Messen, Jahrmärkte und Stadtentwicklung in Europa. Mittelalter und Frühe Neuzeit. In *Messen*, Irsigler, Pauly (eds.), 1–24.

Jeannin, Pierre. *Marchands d'Europe. Pratiques et savoirs à l'époque moderne*. Jacques Bottin, Marie-Louise Pelus-Kaplan (eds.). Paris: Éditions Rue d'Ulm, 2002.

Kaiser, Wolfgang (ed.). *La loge et le fondouk. Les dimensions spatiales des pratiques marchandes en Méditerranée, Moyen Âge—Époque moderne*. Paris: Karthala, 2014.

Körner, Martin. "Berg", "Gebirg" und "Pass" bei Andreas Ryff und Heinrich Schickhart um 1600. In *Quand la montagne aussi a une histoire: mélanges offerts à Jean-François Bergier*, Martin Körner, François Walter (eds.). Bern, Stuttgart: Haupt, 1996, 265–278.

Körner, Martin. Das System der Jahrmärkte und Messen in der Schweiz im periodischen und permanenten Markt 1500–1800. *Jahrbuch für Regionalgeschichte und Landeskunde* 19 (1993/1994): 13–34.

Körner, Martin. Le système des marchés annuels et des foires en Suisse dans le cadre du marché périodique et permanent (1500–1800). In *Messen*, Irsigler, Pauly (eds.), 135–159.

Landolt, Elisabeth. Andreas Ryff (1550–1603), Reisebüchlein: Die Illustrationen. *Basler Zeitschrift für Geschichte und Altertumskunde* 72 (1972): 16–20.

Lang, Heinrich. *Wirtschaften als kulturelle Praxis. Die Florentiner Salviati und die Augsburger Welser auf den Märkten in Lyon (1507–1559)*. Stuttgart: Steiner, 2019.

Lang, Heinrich. "Li vostri che tenghono li libri non sanno tenere tanti chonnti." Useful knowledge and accounting as seen through the accountant's lenses and the logic of capitalism. In *L'economia della conoscenza: innovazione, produttività e crescita economica nei secoli XIII–XVIII*, Giampiero Nigro (ed.). Florence: Firenze University Press, 2023, 115–135. DOI: https://doi.org/10.36253/979-12-215-0092-9.08.

Lefebvre, Henri. *Éléments de rythmanalyse. Introduction à la connaissance des rythmes*. Paris: Éditions Syllepse, 1992.

Lefebvre, Henri, Catherine Régulier. Essai de rythmanalyse des villes méditerranéennes. In Lefebvre, *Éléments de rythmanalyse*, 97–109.
Meyer, Friedrich. Andreas Ryff (1550–1603), Reisebüchlein: Einleitung. *Basler Zeitschrift für Geschichte und Altertumskunde* 72 (1972): 5–15.
Neutsch, Cornelius, Harald Witthöft. Kaufleute zwischen Markt und Messe. In *Reisekultur. Von der Pilgerfahrt zum modernen Tourismus*, Hermann Bausinger, Klaus Beyrer (eds.). Munich: Beck, 1991, 75–82.
North, Michael. *Kommunikation, Handel, Geld und Banken in der Frühen Neuzeit*. Munich: Oldenbourg Verlag, 2000.
Pauly, Michel. Vom regionalen Messesystem zum internationalen Netz von Messestädten. In *Netzwerke im europäischen Handel des Mittelalters*, Gerhard Fouquet, Hans-Jörg Gilomen (eds.). Ostfildern: Thorbecke, 2010, 49–100.
Rau, Susanne. *History, space, and place*. London, New York: Routledge, 2019.
Rau, Susanne. Rhythmusanalyse nach Lefebvre. In *Taktungen und Rhythmen: raumzeitliche Perspektiven interdisziplinär*, Sabine Schmolinsky, Diana Hitzke, Heiner Stahl (eds.). Berlin, Boston: De Gruyter, 2018, 9–24.
Rau, Susanne. Preface. In *Perspectives on Henri Lefebvre: Theory, Practices and (Re)Readings*, Jenny Bauer, Robert Fischer (eds.). Berlin, Boston: De Gruyter, 2018, VII–XV.
Rossiaud, Jacques. Regards sur Vienne au temps du concile. In *Vienne au crépuscule des templiers*, Roger Lauxerois (ed.). Grenoble: PUG, 2014, 21–32.
Rothmann, Michael. Marktnetze und Netzwerke im spätmittelalterlichen oberdeutschen Wirtschaftsraum. In *Netzwerke im europäischen Handel des Mittelalters*, Gerhard Fouquet, Hans-Jörg Gilomen (eds.). Ostfildern: Thorbecke, 2010, 135–188.
Rothmann, Michael. Messezeit: Handelsrhythmen und Jahreszeit. In *Taktungen und Rhythmen: raumzeitliche Perspektiven interdisziplinär Rhythmusanalyse nach Lefebvre*, Sabine Schmolinsky, Diana Hitzke, Heiner Stahl (eds.). Berlin, Boston: De Gruyter, 2018, 25–40.
Scharabi, Mohamed. *Der Bazar. Das traditionelle Stadtzentrum im Nahen Osten und seine Handelseinrichtungen*. Tübingen: Wasmuth, 1985.
Schmitt, Jean-Claude. *Les rythmes au Moyen Âge*. Paris: Gallimard, 2016.
Schwanke, Irmgard. Briefe aus Lucca und Lyon nach Augsburg. Kaufmannsausbildung und Kulturtransfer im 17. Jahrhundert. In *Grenzüberschreitende Familienbeziehungen. Akteure und Medien des Kulturtransfers in der Frühen Neuzeit*, Dorothea Nolde, Claudia Opitz (eds.). Cologne: Böhlau, 2008, 253–271.

Related CoMOR-Collections

Ewert, Ulf Christian. The Huntington Library, Early English Books online (Richard Rowlands, The post of the world . . .) (COL0021). In *Configurations of European Fairs: Merchants, Objects, Routes (ca. 1350–1600)*, Jean-Louis Gaulin, Susanne Rau (eds.). https://fairs-in-history.huma-num.fr/collection/COL0021 (31 May 2024).
Ewert, Ulf Christian. Bibliothèque de Genève, Su 4165 (Olivier Fordrin—Almanach pour l'an M. D. LXXIII) (COL0026). *Configurations of European Fairs*, Gaulin, Rau (eds.). https://fairs-in-history.huma-num.fr/collection/COL0026 (27 March 2024).

Rau, Susanne, Marisa Holzer. Bayerische Staatsbibliothek Münchner Digitalisierungszentrum, Selbstbiographie des Andreas Ryff (bis 1574) (COL0091). *Configurations of European Fairs*, Gaulin, Rau (eds.). https://fairs-in-history.huma-num.fr/collection/COL0091 (27 March 2024).

Rau, Susanne, Marisa Holzer. Universität Basel Öffentliche Bibliothek der Universität Basel, Andreas Ryff (1550–1603), Reisebüchlein (COL0093). *Configurations of European Fairs*, Gaulin, Rau (eds.). https://fairs-in-history.huma-num.fr/collection/COL0093 (27 March 2024).

Boglárka Weisz

Foreign merchants and the new trading route in the Hungarian Kingdom in the 14th century

On 6 January 1336, King Charles I of Hungary (1301–1342) specified the route into Hungary that was to be used by merchants carrying their wares from, or to, Bohemia and the neighbouring countries. He also set the amount to be paid at toll posts that, according to the burghers of Brno and Nagyszombat, had been in existence since the reign of King Béla IV.[1] In addition to a reduction in tariffs,[2] the ordinance provided exemption from specific tariffs at other toll posts on the route, as best expressed in a phrase written on the back of the surviving copy: "*in quibus locis non datur theolonium in Ungaria.*" On 5 May 1336, Charles I extended this privilege with the order that foreign merchants were liable only for their own affairs and no one should dare to harass them for transgressions committed, or debts accumulated, by others.[3] Use of the reduced-tariff route was provided on equal terms to merchants of Bohemia and Hungary and to those from other countries.[4] Consequently, when Archbishop Csanád of Esztergom set tariffs for the tolls of Nyárhida (today Nové Zámky, Slovakia), Udvard (today Dvory nad Žitavou, Slovakia), and Esztergom—all of which lay along this route—at reduced levels, but still higher

---

1 Boglárka Weisz (ed.). *Fontes ad rem mercatoriam regni Hungariae pertinentes II. De comesciis externis (1259–1437)/Források a Magyar Királyság kereskedelemtörténetéhez II. Külkereskedelem (1259–1437).* [Sources for the Commercial History of the Kingdom of Hungary, vol. II: Foreign Trade (1259–1437)]. 2 vols. Budapest: BTK Történettudományi Intézet, 2021, 2:42–46. See also the original privilege of Charles I with its hanging seal about the reduced-tariff route, 6 January 1336, Archiv města Brna [Brno City Archives], Sbírka listin, mandátů a listů, A 1/1. no. 76.

2 On the background to the 1336 decree, see Renáta Skorka. A csökkentett vámtarifájú út kialakulása I. Károly uralkodása alatt. [The creation of the reduced-tariff route under Charles I]. *Történelmi Szemle* 55 (2013): 451–470.

3 Weisz (ed.), *Fontes*, 2:46–47. See also the original privilege of Charles I to foreign merchants, 5 May 1336, Staatsarchiv Nürnberg (hereafter StA Nürnberg), Reichsstadt Nürnberg (RN), Urkunden Münchner 510.

4 Weisz (ed.), *Fontes*, 2:45.

Note: The author is a Senior Research Fellow in the Institute of History of the Research Centre for the Humanities, and leader of the Lendület Medieval Hungarian Economic History Research Group (LP2015-3/2021). This work was supported by the Ministry of Innovation and Technology from the National Research, Development, and Innovation Fund of the Ministry of Innovation and Technology (NKFI Fund), on the basis of the TKP2021-NKTA-15 support charter (weisz.boglarka@abtk.hu).

https://doi.org/10.1515/9783111621296-015

than those of Charles I, in a diploma issued on 24 December 1337 at the request of the merchants of Mainz, Prague, Nuremberg, and Augsburg, he considered that they also applied to Bohemian, Swabian, Rhenish, and Flandrian merchants.[5] His diploma has not survived in original form, but its text is known from a sixteenth/seventeenth-century copy book held in the Prague archives,[6] and every town that requested the diploma must have had a copy of it. Subsequently, none of them ever asked for the Archbishop of Esztergom's diploma to be confirmed, no doubt because it contradicted the king's regulation and imposed higher tariffs, which were not in the merchants' interests to pay. The Archbishop's diploma is supremely informative in recording which merchants brought their wares to the kingdom of Hungary from Bohemia (*mercatores regnorum prescriptorum per viam regni Boemie mercimonia in regnum Hungarie deferentes*). We therefore know that Bohemian, Swabian, Rhenish, and Flandrian merchants came along the reduced-tariff route via Prague and Brno. Although the advantages of the reduced-tariff route were available to every Hungarian and foreign merchant, we can trace an emerging custom for every group of merchants to request a separate diploma confirming that the regulated tariffs on the route applied specifically to them. This article presents the history of this route from the perspective of the merchants (as the actors using the routes), discussing each merchant group and town separately. I will look at when and under what circumstances they applied for confirmation of their charter of privilege on this route, what routes they used to reach the kingdom of Hungary, how their road using and trading activity changed by the early fifteenth century, and what was behind this.

The study is closely linked to the "Via mercatoria" online map produced by the Medieval Hungarian Economic History Research Group.[7] With the creation of this map, we are creating and developing an open database where everyone can find information related to medieval Hungarian settlements in their relation to trade. The settlements and roads indicated on the map will be complemented with tables offering the user data on the given topographical point. In addition to the status and privileges of each settlement, the tables will also contain important pieces of trade-related information: tolls collected from travellers and merchants engaged in foreign trade, staple rights, the market(s) and market tolls collected

5 Weisz (ed.), *Fontes*, 2:47–49.

6 Copy of Archbishop Csanád of Esztergom's diploma of 24 December 1337. In *Primus Liber vetustissimus Privilegiorum, Statutorum et Decretorum Veteris Urbis Pragensis necno[n] gloriose Aureeq[ue] memorie eiusdem perpetuo dignissimus*, 34–35, Archiv hlavního města Prahy (hereafter AMP) [Prague City Archives], Kniha pamětni [The book of memory], no. 993/1.

7 *Via mercatoria*, Boglárka Weisz, István Kádas (eds.) http://viamercatoria.abtk.hu/ (26 September 2024).

there, which shops were established there, provisions connected to trading at the settlement, places of river-crossings, and whether its residents were exempt from certain customs duties. The user will also be provided with important information on the roads leading to these settlements, whether it was obligatory to use them, and what regulations were in force for the mandatory routes. The CoMOR project objective is the production of interactive historical maps ("Mapping Fairs"), but the investigation centres of the project are France, Germany, and Italy. Our map supplements the CoMOR map with medieval Hungarian data. In the long term, it will show how the Hungarian kingdom was integrated into the late medieval fair system that CoMOR is investigating and how the western road network continued into Hungary.

Merchants from Cologne, Huy, and elsewhere in the Rhineland

King Louis I of Hungary (1342–1382) made his first reference to the reduced-tariff route of 1336 in a diploma of 13 May 1344. Therein, he ordered the toll owners not to demand that merchants from Cologne, Huy, and elsewhere in the Rhineland pay higher tolls than those confirmed by the diploma (*secundum ordinationem litteris firmatam*) for the Bohemian and Moravian merchants.[8] A document issued by the royal tavernicus Lawrence on 10 March 1345 proves that the 1336 route was indeed what Louis I had in mind. Lawrence was also a castellan of Sempte (present-day Šintava, Slovakia), which lay along the reduced-tariff route,[9] and in this diploma, he ordered the toll collectors under his authority in Sempte and Farkashida (present-day Vlčkovce, Slovakia) not to collect higher tolls on the wares and horses brought for sale by merchants from Cologne, Huy, and elsewhere in the Rhineland. The order not to collect higher tolls applied only to the horses that were for sale and not to the merchants' own horses or those of their men,[10] which seems to imply that they could not collect tolls from the latter at all. According to the 1336 regulation, tolls had to be paid in Sempte and Farkashida only on large merchant coaches, commonly called '*rudas*' (*currus mercimoniale, qui*

8 Weisz (ed.), *Fontes*, 2:50–51. See also the original privilege of Louis I concerning Cologne, Huy, and Rhineland merchants, 13 May 1344, Historisches Archiv der Stadt Köln (hereafter HAStK), Urkundliche Überlieferung, Haupturkundenarchiv (HUA) U 2. 1771.

9 See 6 January 1336, in Weisz (ed.), *Fontes*, 2:45.

10 Weisz (ed.), *Fontes*, 2:51–52. See also the original writ of royal tavernicus Lawrence to the toll collectors in Sempte and Farkashida, 10 March 1345, HAStK, HUA U 1. 1803.

vulgariter rudas dicitur) and small coaches called '*ajoncás*' (*currus aynczas*), and tolls on horses are mentioned in Charles I's regulation only for bridge tolls collected in Jablonca and the lands of Korlátkő Castle,[11] but the toll collectors may have extended this, quite arbitrarily, to their own toll posts.

On 10 August 1350, the merchants of Cologne, Huy, and the Rhineland presented to King Louis I's brother, Stephen, Duke of Slavonia, Croatia, and Dalmatia, a diploma issued by Louis I that stated, *inter alia*, that the tariffs payable on their wares were the same as those paid by the merchants of Prague.[12] Stephen's diploma quotes at length from a (now unknown) privilege that Charles I granted to the citizens of Prague. This corresponds to the provisions for the reduced-toll route that Charles I defined in his diploma of 6 January 1336, but quotes only the route, the tariff items, and the remark that, according to the Brno and Nagyszombat authorities, these toll posts had existed since the reign of Béla IV. It does not include the other parts and provisions of the diploma, notably the section that lists the toll owners. Stephen also prohibited the toll owners from collecting more than the tolls specified in Charles' diploma. His grounds for doing all this were that in the absence of the king, he ruled the whole kingdom.[13] Louis I is not known to have issued a diploma conferring toll payment privileges on Prague merchants, but we have no reason to doubt the text of Stephen's diploma and so we may be reasonably sure that those from Cologne and Huy also held such a privilege. Either this predated Louis's 13 May 1344 ordinance to the toll collectors, which therefore concerned only its implementation, or the king issued it subsequently to correct his previous ordinance and redress an injury to the merchants of Cologne. Whatever its status, the Cologne merchants never had this diploma confirmed.

After Louis I's great seal was lost during the Bosnian campaign in 1363, he subsequently—sometime between 1364 and 1366—confirmed the diplomas issued

---

11 Weisz (ed.), *Fontes*, 2:44.

12 Weisz (ed.), *Fontes*, 2:56; the original diploma of Stephen, Duke of Slavonia, Croatia, and Dalmatia concerning Cologne, Huy, and Rhineland merchants, 10 August 1350, HAStK, HUA U 2. 1968.

13 Weisz (ed.), *Fontes*, 2:56–58. When Louis I departed on his second campaign April 1350, the queen mother Elizabeth and her brother Stephen, Duke of Slavonia, Croatia, and Dalmatia, deputised for him in managing the affairs of the kingdom of Hungary. See Eva B. Halász. Anjou István herceg (1332–1354) [Stephen of Anjou]. In *Hercegek és hercegségek a középkori Magyarországon* [Dukes and Duchies in Medieval Hungary], Zsoldos Attila (ed.). Székesfehérvár: Városi Levéltár és Kutatóintézet, 2016, 88; Norbert C. Tóth. *A Magyar Királyság nádora. A nádori és a helytartói intézmény története (1342–1562)* [Palatine of the kingdom of Hungary. The Institutions of Palatine and Governor (1342–1562)]. Budapest: Magyar Történelmi Társulat, 2020, 175–176.

with his own seal and with those of his father's first two seals.[14] On 5 July 1365, owing to the loss of the seal, at the request of Olf Pichman and his brother-in-law Matthias, citizens of Cologne,[15] and the citizens of Huy, the king transcribed and confirmed the diploma he had issued on 13 May 1344,[16] and the municipal authority of Cologne had an authenticated copy of it made on 23 June 1380.[17] Later, they sought confirmation only of Louis I's 1365 confirmation: at the request of the Cologne citizens Gerhard Trotzfeld and Hermann Schrempe[18] and the citizens of Huy, Queen Mary confirmed their diplomas on 30 March 1384 and 21 April 1384.[19] King Sigismund (1387–1437), at the request of the Cologne citizens Gotschalk, Cristofor, and Cristan, transcribed the latter for the Cologne merchants alone on 29 June 1393.[20]

Merchants coming to the kingdom of Hungary from Huy and Cologne mainly brought broadcloth, not exclusively the product of their hometowns. The land route from Huy first led through Aachen to Cologne, from where the merchants generally proceeded down the Rhine to Mainz, then through Nuremberg to Regensburg. From there, they sailed on the Danube to the Duchy of Austria[21] and the kingdom of Hungary.[22] On this route, however, Vienna's staple right impeded the Cologne merchants' direct trade with the kingdom of Hungary. The 1336 reduced-tariff route thus had the double benefit for Cologne merchants of freeing them from the constraints of Vienna's staple right and reducing the tolls they had to pay in the kingdom of Hungary. Upon reaching Nuremberg, they therefore

14 Albert Grünn. I. Lajos király megerősítő záradéka [Louis I's confirmation clause]. *Turul* 19 (1901): 29–33.

15 Research has revealed the possibility that the said Matthias may be Matthias von der Bach, a cloth merchant of Cologne. See Franz Irsigler. *Die wirtschaftliche Stellung der Stadt Köln im 14. und 15. Jahrhundert. Stukturanalyse einer Spätmittelalterlichen Exportgewerbe- und Fernhandelsstadt.* Wiesbaden: Franz Steiner, 1979, 56; Klaus Militzer. Tuchhandel und Tuchhändler Kölns in Österreich und Ungarn um 1400. *Blätter für deutsche Landesgeschichte* 114 (1978): 270–271; István Draskóczy. Commercial Contacts of Buda along the Danube and beyond. In *Medieval Buda in Context*, Balázs Nagy, Martyn Rady, Katalin Szende, András Vadas (eds.). Leiden, Boston: Brill, 2016, 283.

16 Weisz (ed.), *Fontes*, 2:88–89.

17 Weisz (ed.), *Fontes*, 2:142.

18 Probably the Nuremberg cloth merchant Hermann Schremp. See Militzer, Tuchhandel, 287.

19 30 March 1384: Weisz (ed.), *Fontes*, 2:164–166; 21 April 1384: Weisz (ed.), *Fontes*, 2:166–167.

20 Weisz (ed.), *Fontes*, 2:175–176.

21 The Cologne merchants may have reached Vienna from Prague via Budweis and Linz. See Militzer, Tuchhandel, 267.

22 Militzer, Tuchhandel, 266.

headed for Prague[23] and Brno,[24] a route that brought them to the Hungarian border at Újvár (present-day Holič, Slovakia). The surviving charters and some other charters mentioned in them but not known to the full extent, indicate that Cologne merchants began to take an interest in the journey to the kingdom of Hungary via Bohemian territory at the very start of Louis I's rule. In 1344, 1345, and 1350, either directly or via representatives, they submitted a relatively rapid succession of petitions to the king for charters concerning the route. In 1365, by requesting confirmation of the diploma they had previously received from Louis I, they demonstrated their knowledge in Hungarian affairs: they must have known it would be invalid otherwise, having been authenticated with king's first seal. Although the relatively low tariffs on the route and royal protection afforded to their journeys must have already been appealing for the Cologne merchants as it was, the main benefit to them was 'liberation' from the Vienna staple right. That was true even between 1340 and 1351 (and the charters are indeed concentrated in this period), when they were still able to proceed from Vienna to the kingdom of Hungary if they paid a penalty, but after 1351, they could continue only by forfeiting their goods.[25] These diplomas and confirmations, like those issued later in the century (1384 and 1393), were not transcriptions of the privilege as granted in Stephen's diploma, but only of the diplomas in which Louis I ordered the toll collectors not to demand higher tolls from them than were payable by mer-

---

23 The Prague authority specifically mentioned the Cologne merchants (and those from Regensburg and Eger) when regulating trade by foreigners on 19 May 1333 in harmony with Wenceslaus II's diploma of 23 May 1304. *Regesta diplomatica nec non epistolaria Bohemiae et Moraviae* (hereafter *RBM*). 8 vols. Lenka Blechová, Karel Jaromír Erben, Josef Emler, Helena Krmíčková, Milena Linhartová, Bendřich Mendl, Blažena Rynešová, Jirí Spěváček, Jana Zachová (eds.). Prague, 1855–2014, 3:777–779, 779–780. In 1304, Wenceslaus II granted Prague a five-day staple right, which also banned trade between foreigners. *Codex iuris municipalis regni Bohemiae* (hereafter *CIM*). 4 vols. Jaromir Celakovský, Gustav Friedrich, Antonín Haas (eds.). Prague, 1886–1961, 1:20–21. The Huy merchants acquired trading privileges in Bohemian territory from John of Bohemia in 1328. See André Joris. Documents concernant le Commerce de Huy avec la Bohême et la Haute-Meuse (XIIIe–XIVe siècles). *Bulletin de la Commission royale d'Histoire* 137 (1971): 12; Hektor Ammann. Huy an der Maas in der mittelalterlichen Wirtschaft. In *Altständisches Bürgertum*, vol. II, Heinz Stoob (ed.). Darmstadt: Wissenschaftliche Buchgesellschaft, 1978, 236.

24 On 22 March 1348, Charles IV, King of Germany and Bohemia, prohibited merchants and travellers from Austria, Hungary, Poland, and elsewhere, on pain of forfeiting their goods, from approaching the country by any route that avoided Brno. *Codex diplomaticus et epistolaris Moravie* (hereafter *CDM*). 15 vols. Berthold Bretholz, Anton Boczek, Vincenz Brandl, Peter Ritter von Chlumecky, Josef Chytil (eds.). Brünn, 1836–1903, 7:552–553.

25 Renáta Skorka. A bécsi lerakat Magyarországra vezető kiskapui [Ways to Hungary avoiding the Vienna staple right]. *Történelmi Szemle* 54 (2012): 7–8; Markus Gneiss. *Das Wiener Handwerksordnungbuch (1364–1555). Edition und Kommentar.* Vienna: Böhlau, 2017, 19.

chants from Bohemia and Moravia. As we have seen, citizens of Huy did not appear among the petitioners in 1393, possibly because by the second half of the fourteenth century, the Huy textile industry was past its peak and Huy merchants appear significantly less often in the sources.[26] After 1393, there is not even a trace of Cologne citizens attempting to exercise their rights on the route or routes out of Bohemian lands. It is possible that for a long period after obtaining Sigismund's transcription of their diploma, they did not experience any harassment that necessitated further confirmation from the same king, and after the 1420s, their relations with Hungarian partners were not sufficiently intensive[27] to warrant such a petition. In the Sigismund era, the trading activities of Cologne merchants in Hungary was mainly—if not exclusively—confined to the western borders.[28] Their Viennese factors took some part in this.[29] Aiding this process was an ordinance made in Vienna on 30 August 1408 that if a foreigner swore that he wished to pass through the city and travel beyond the Duchy with the sole intention of collecting the debts owed to him, he may do so, and if he bought a horse for his return, he may return with it, but upon payment of the *hansgraf*[30]—a

---

26 See Amman, Huy an der Maas, 247–248.

27 See Klaus Militzer. Kölner Kaufleute im Preßburg und im Donauraum im 14. und 15. Jahrhundert. In *Städte im Donauraum. Sammelband der Beiträge aus dem Symposion in Smolenice 30.9.–3.10. 1991, Bratislava–Pressburg 1291–1991*, Richard Marsina (ed.). Bratislava: Slovenská historická spolocnost, 1993, 132–134; Katalin G. Szende. Kölni kereskedők a középkori Sopronban [Cologne merchants in Medieval Sopron]. In *Tanulmányok Csatkai Endre emlékére*, Attila Környei, Katalin G. Szende (eds.). Sopron: Soproni Múzeum Alapítvány, 1996, 66–67; Irsigler, Wirtschaftliche Stellung, 57.

28 See Franz Kováts. Handelsverbindungen zwischen Köln und Pressburg (Pozsony) im Spätmittelalter. *Mitteilungen aus dem Stadtarchiv von Köln* 35 (1914): 11–18; Szende, Kölni kereskedők, 60–64.

29 23 April 1418: Weisz (ed.), *Fontes*, 2:237–241. The Köllnerhof in Vienna, where the Cologne and Rhineland merchants had their accommodation, stores, and trading houses, is first mentioned in the sources in 1394 (*Coloniensium curia*), although it was already in the possession of a merchant of undetermined origins in 1289. The building was taken on by Nuremberg and Regensburg merchants in the fifteenth century. See the entry for 29 October 1420 in *Quellen zur Geschichte der Stadt Wien. II. Regesten aus dem Archive der Stadt Wien*, vols. II/1–5, Karl Uhlirz (ed.). Vienna: Verlag und Eigenthum des Alterthums-Vereines zu Wien, 1898–1936, II/2., no. 2146; Josef Giesen. Die Kölner Hof in Wien. Jahrbuch des Kölnischen Geschichtsvereins 34–35 (1959/1960): 195–197; Richard Perger. *Strassen, Türme und Basteien: das Strassennetz der Wiener City in seiner Entwicklung und seinen Namen. Ein Handbuch*. Vienna: Franz Deuticke, 1991, 80.

30 In Vienna, the duties of the *Hansgraf* were to supervise foreign merchants and the staple right, and he was also responsible for enforcing the rules of foreign trade. He was thus also required to prevent the importation of wine from the Kingdom of Hungary. See Gneiss, *Wiener Handwerksordnungsbuch*, 160; Felix Czeike. Hansgraf. In *Historisches Lexikon Wien III*, Felix Czeike (ed.). Vienna: Kremayr and Scheriau, 1994, 52.

specified amount for each horse, namely one *groschen*.[31] A detailed examination of the activities of Cologne citizens with Hungarian merchants permits the conclusion that, as Ferenc Kováts has stressed, the actual exchange of goods took place in Vienna[32] and the surviving sources record only commercial credit. These factors combined to render unnecessary the expensive recurring confirmation of the privilege of the land route, which had effectively fallen out of use. The vanishing of Cologne citizens from Brno following their lively presence in the town in the second half of the fourteenth century[33] similarly indicates the declining significance of the route through Bohemian lands. After the 1420s, there are increasingly rare mentions of Cologne merchants' dealing with Hungarian partners (although Cologne goods did not disappear from the Hungarian market). Katalin Szende has identified the increasing domination of trade along the Danube valley by south German cities—above all, Nuremberg—as the main factor in this process,[34] while Renáta Skorka emphasises the rise of cities along the Danube (of which Nuremberg was also one) and their role as intermediaries.[35] The decreasing intensity of contacts with Cologne was no doubt due to the displacement of its merchants from Vienna, where contact actually took place. The Cologne traders did not completely disappear, however, and the sources occasionally mention their appearance in Vienna and trade with Hungarian merchants, especially from Pressburg (present-day Bratislava, Slovakia).[36] Looking at the overall commercial activity of Cologne citizens after the 1420s, we see a significant decrease of activ-

---

31 Gneiss, *Wiener Handwerksordnungsbuch*, 378.

32 Ferenc Kováts. A magyar arany világtörténeti jelentősége és kereskedelmi összeköttetéseink a nyugattal [Hungarian gold in world history and its trade connections with the West]. *Történelmi Szemle* 11 (1922): 141. Katalin Szende reached a similar conclusion from the Sopron documents (Szende, Kölni kereskedők, 66), while Emma Lederer expressed doubts that the transactions were made in Vienna. See Emma Lederer. *A középkori pénzüzletek története Magyarországon, 1000–1458* [History of Medieval Financial Transactions in Hungary]. Budapest, 1932, 91–92.

33 Günther Hirschfelder. *Die Kölner Handelsbeziehungen im Spätmittelalter*. Cologne: Kölnisches Stadt Museum, 1994, 164.

34 For a review of previous explanations of the phenomenon, see Szende, Kölni kereskedők, 66–67.

35 Renáta Skorka. Pozsony gazdasági szerepe a 15. század első felében a zálogszerződések tükrében [The economic role of Pressburg in the first half of the 15th century through lien contracts]. *Századok* 138 (2004): 445. Günther Hirschfelder reached the conclusion that Regensburg and Nuremberg merchants dominated the Vienna market in the second third of the fifteenth century. Factors in the eclipse of the Cologne merchants were the Hussite wars, the Ottoman advances in the Balkans, and the flourishing of precious ore mining in Saxony and Tyrol (which reduced the demand for Hungarian gold), and, in general, Cologne goods usually finding buyers at the Frankfurt market. See Hirschfelder, *Kölner Handelsbeziehungen*, 131.

36 Militzer, Kölner Kaufleute, 132–133; Hirschfelder, *Kölner Handelsbeziehungen*, 131–135.

ity in the east (Vienna, Prague, and Breslau) and the central areas of Germany. There was an initial surge in north Germany, but after the middle of the fifteenth century, Cologne merchants did not venture across the Main, and although Cologne wares did not disappear from these regions, they came via the Frankfurt market in later times. By contrast, contacts with Italy and lands to the west became stronger and more intense.[37] All this indicates that Cologne merchants gradually switched their attention away from the regions that had been the focus of their interest during the fourteenth and early fifteenth centuries towards places where they had previously been less active. The role of the Frankfurt fairs in transmitting Cologne wares to the eastern markets, that clearly emerges in the fifteenth century, could have started in the fourteenth century if the Cologne merchants had not been going east themselves at that time. One result of this change in destinations is that we only have sporadic records of Cologne merchants with interests in Vienna or Hungary in the late fifteenth century.

The Prague and Nuremberg merchants

In the diploma for the merchants of Cologne and Huy he issued on 10 August 1350, Stephen, Duke of Slavonia, Croatia, and Dalmatia, stated that they paid tolls in the same way as citizens of Prague. He then transcribed the ordinance for the reduced-tariff route from the diploma that Charles I had issued in 1336.[38] We do not know of any charter in which Charles I transcribed his 1336 diploma for the Prague merchants, although we have no reason to doubt its existence at the time. It may even have been the diploma Louis I was referring to when, on 13 May 1344, he permitted merchants from Cologne and Huy to pay tolls in the same way as the Bohemian and Moravian merchants.[39] The Prague merchants do not seem to have attached any subsequent importance to their own reduced-tariff-route diploma and chose another way of securing its advantages. On 6 July 1357, the Brno municipal leaders—the judge Jakob de Ror, the jurors, and the citizens[40]—transcribed Charles I's diploma of 6 January 1336.[41] The request for the transcription, however, almost certainly came from the Prague and Nuremberg merchants, because the original document (now

37 Hirschfelder, *Kölner Handelsbeziehungen*, 541–542.

38 Weisz (ed.), *Fontes*, 2:56.

39 Weisz (ed.), *Fontes*, 2:49–51.

40 Jakob de Ror was a judge in Brno between 1341 and 1364. See Berthold Bretholz. *Geschichte der Stadt Brünn*, vol. I. Brünn: Verlag des Vereins, 1911, 129.

41 Weisz (ed.), *Fontes*, 2:64–65.

lost) was held in the Nuremberg archives,[42] and at the end of the same month—July 1337—the merchants Nicolaus Scherf of Prague and Wolfram Stromer[43] of Nuremberg presented the transcript to Louis I with the request to confirm it for them. Louis I transcribed the document on 29 July and confirmed its provisions for the merchants of Prague and Nuremberg. Louis I noted in the diploma that it was not the custom to confirm diplomas of a foreign town, but he was doing so to retain these merchants in the privilege granted by his father; in addition, his mother Elizabeth had a precise memory of Charles I's ordinance and, by this, attested to the authenticity of his father's diploma. Louis I therefore confirmed with his duplex seal the diploma of Charles I that was incorporated into the document produced by the municipal authority of Brno, and the confirmation was to be regarded as equivalent to his father's original diploma. The diploma allowed the toll collectors to collect no more than the specified tolls from these merchants and prohibited them from demanding gifts (*munera aut honores aliquos*). The Prague and Nuremberg merchants were obliged to pay the same old, rightful thirtieth (*tricesima*),[44] as were the merchants of the kingdom.[45] There was no contradiction between the latter two provisions, and neither did they add anything to Charles I's diploma of 1336, which also prohibited demands on merchants beyond the specified tariffs and mentioned the obligation to pay the thirtieth.[46] Nonetheless, the provision concerning the demand for gifts—or, rather, their prohibition—is a reference to the era of Louis I, who gave several commands prohibiting the practice.[47] The diploma was issued in (at least) two copies—one for Nuremberg and the other for Prague. We can be sure of this, because after Louis I's seal was lost in 1363, the authorities of both Nuremberg and Prague had clauses of confirmation added to their own copies. The confirmation

---

42 Today, all that remains is its archive number. See StA Nürnberg, RN, Päpstliche und fürstliche Privilegien, Urkunden 48.

43 Wolfram Stromer (brother of Ulrich Stromer), a merchant of Nuremberg. See Wolfgang Stromer. Eine gesellige Versammlung der Nürnberger Rates in Ulrich Stromers Haus und der Aufenthalt Kaiser Karls IV. in Nürnberg im Jahre 1358. *Mitteilungen des Vereins für Geschichte der Stadt Nürnberg* 52 (1963/1964): 59; Peter Fleischmann. *Rat und Patriziat in Nürnberg. Die Herrschaft der Ratsgeschlechter vom 13. bis zum 18. Jahrhundert*, 3 vols. Nuremberg: Verein für Geschichte der Stadt Nürnberg, 1967, 2:947.

44 The foreign customs duty—the thirtieth, which was set at one-thirtieth of the value of the imported and, from the second part of the fourteenth century, of exported goods too—was collected in the interior of the country. This type of the duty had to be paid only once, even if a merchant passed through several thirtieth-stations on his journey.

45 Weisz (ed.), *Fontes*, 2:65–68. See Wolfgang Stromer. *Oberdeutsche Hochfinanz, 1350–1450*. 3 vols. Wiesbaden: Steiner, 1970, 1:93–94.

46 Weisz (ed.), *Fontes*, 2:48–49.

47 For example, 5 October 1364: Weisz (ed.), *Fontes*, 2:87; 22 March 1366: Weisz (ed.), *Fontes*, 2:95; 4 April 1378: Weisz (ed.), *Fontes*, 2:133; 28 April 1380: Weisz (ed.), *Fontes*, 2:141.

clause was added to the Nuremberg copy on 5 July 1364 at the request of Bertold Holzschuher[48] and Hans Ebner,[49] citizens and jurymen of Nuremberg.[50] It is not known who requested the Prague copy, which was added on 18 July and referred to Nuremberg and Prague citizens in general. This diploma with its confirmation clause has not survived, but the text is preserved in the seventeenth-century copy book *Primus Liber vetustissimus Privilegiorum, Statutorum et Decretorum Veteris Urbis Pragensis necno[n] gloriose Aureeq[ue] memorie eiusdem perpetuo dignissimus.*[51]

Despite the confirmation clauses, Lajos I transcribed the diploma of 29 July 1357 into a new diploma for the citizens of Nuremberg and Prague at the request of Bertold Holzschuher and Hans Ebner on 6 July 1364.[52] On 29 July 1357, two

---

48 Bertold Holzschuher was a Nuremberg merchant and member of the Nuremberg council in 1354, 1356, and from 1357–1358 and 1360–1365 (Fleischmann, *Rat und Patriziat*, 3:1683). According to Wolfgang Stromer, Holzschuher was already engaged in trade in Buda in the period 1358–1360 (Stromer, *Oberdeutsche Hochfinanz*, 1:98). The Nuremberg municipal ordinance on which Stromer bases his claim, however, does not clearly prove that Holzschuher traded in Buda in any of these years, because it concerns credit that he extended to two German merchants in 1358, which they should have repaid in Mainz the same year, and since they did not do so, the oxen and other goods they had purchased in Buda were seized for Holzschuher (See 7 March 1360: Weisz (ed.), *Fontes*, 2:75–76). Our first certain source on his trading in Buda is thus the above diploma of 1364, and we also know that he proceeded similarly on behalf of the Nuremberg merchants before Louis I at Damásd in Hungary in 1370 (1 July 1370: Weisz (ed.), *Fontes*, 2:113–114), and so we may conclude that he was still actively trading in the country, but he died before 18 February 1371. On Holzschuher himself, see Johann Christoph Gatterer. *Historia Genealogica Dominorum Holzschuherorum Ab Aspach Et Harlach In Thalheim Cet. Patriciae Gentis Tum Apud Norimbergenses Tum In Exteris Etiam Regionibus Toga Sagoque Illustris Ex Incorruptis Rerum Gestarum Monimentis Conquisita*. Nuremberg, 1755, 121–127; Fleischmann, *Rat und Patriziat*, 2:571.

49 Hans Ebner, merchant and member of Nuremberg Council (1367, 1369–1370, 1372–1377) traded Tournai broadcloth in Buda in the late fourteenth century. See Fleischmann, *Rat und Patriziat*, 3:1659; Stromer, *Oberdeutsche Hochfinanz*, 1:104–105.

50 Weisz (ed.), *Fontes*, 2:65–66. Sebald, abbot of Saint Giles monastery in Nuremberg, transcribed Louis I's diploma on 7 November 1469 (StA Nürnberg, RN, Ratskanzlei, A-Laden, Urkunden 60 a). In turn, his transcription was later transcribed by Matthias I on 22 February 1470 (StA Nürnberg, RN, Päpstliche und fürstliche Privilegien, Urkunden 323) and by Wladislaus II on 27 June 1497 (StA Nürnberg, RN, Päpstliche und fürstliche Privilegien, Urkunden 404). At the same time, Wladisaus II also transcribed two diplomas of Louis I, both dated 29 July 1357, for the Prague merchants. One of these was the abovementioned privilege charter transcribing the document of 1336 (AMP, Pergamenové listiny [PGL] I. 26).

51 Confirmation clause of Louis I concerning Prague merchants, 18 July 1364. In *Primus Liber vetustissimus*, 23–26. Excerpts from the text of the confirmation clause relating to the transcription are published in Weisz (ed.), *Fontes*, 2:66–67.

52 Weisz (ed.), *Fontes*, 2:81–82.

more merchants, Nicolaus Scherf of Prague and Wolfram Stromer of Nuremberg, asked for confirmation of another ordinance granted to merchants arriving from neighbouring lands, particularly Bohemia, by Louis I's father, Charles I. These were the provisions of the 5 May 1336 diploma prohibiting the arrest of merchants from these lands for the debts or offences of other merchants; all bore liability solely for themselves. Lajos I fulfilled this request, and although he noted that it was Charles I's ordinance and indeed quoted from his father's diploma almost word for word, it was not an actual transcription that he confirmed.[53] This diploma, too, was produced in two copies, one for Nuremberg[54] and the other for Prague,[55] and both survive today. The Nuremberg copy has a confirmation clause included at the request of the Nuremberg citizens and jurymen, Bertold Holzschuher and Hans Ebner, dated 5 July 1364, the same day as the diploma mentioned above, and bears Louis I's second hanging seal (although only a fragment survives), but there is no confirmation clause on the Prague copy.[56] Bertold Holzschuher and Hans Ebner wanted something more than a confirmation of the 1357 diploma, and the next day they had Louis I issue a new diploma for Nuremberg and Prague incorporating and confirming the old one.[57]

On 1 July 1370, Nuremberg received another diploma unrelated to the reduced-tariff route or the other privileges granted by Charles I. The city was again represented by Bertold Holzschuher, who on this occasion did not undertake representation for Prague. The royal ordinance laid down the rules for trade between Nuremberg citizens and inhabitants of the kingdom. It effectively denied the option of commercial credit by ordering that payment be made upon sale, and it assigned jurisdiction over the merchants to the judge competent for the place where a sale was made. The ordinance also included a promise that six or seven weeks before going to war with a neighbouring country, he would warn the Nuremberg merchants and have them escorted, together with their wares, to

53 Weisz (ed.), *Fontes*, 2:69–71. Louis I's diploma was transcribed by George, abbot of Saint Giles' monastery in Nuremberg, on 15 July 1460 (StA Nürnberg, Reichsstadt Nürnberg, Losungamt, 7-farbiges Alphabet, Urkunden 2352), and by Sebald, abbot of Saint Giles' monastery in Nuremberg on 7 November 1469 (StA Nürnberg, Reichsstadt Nürnberg, Ratskanzlei, A-Laden, Urkunden 60). Wladislaus II transcribed and confirmed this privilege charter at the request of the Prague merchants on 27 June 1497 (*Primus Liber vetustissimus*, 26).

54 The 27 June 1497 (*Primus Liber vetustissimus*, 26). The original privilege of King Louis I concerning Nuremberg merchants, 29 July 1357, StA Nürnberg, RN, Päpstliche und fürstliche Privilegien, Urkunden 50.

55 The original privilege of King Louis I concerning Prague merchants, 29 July 1357, AMP, PGL I. 10.

56 Weisz (ed.), *Fontes*, 2:69.

57 Weisz (ed.), *Fontes*, 2:83–84.

the border of the kingdom. The same Nuremberg merchants could leave the country with one servant and two horses of any value if they had paid the *tricesima* on the goods they had brought in (and could certify having done so). They had to pay tolls, where necessary, on the two horses.[58]

Soon afterwards, Louis I wished to provide Nuremberg merchants with an escort when they came into the country as well as when they left. On 15 July 1371, he reassured merchants from Nuremberg and other imperial towns that despite his wars with the dukes of Bavaria and the Holy Roman Emperor Charles IV, they may come to the country unharmed, because at his command, the castellans of Újvár and Berencs (present-day Branč, Slovakia) would provide them with an escort to the middle of the country.[59] The mention of these two Nyitra-county castellans, particularly in the case of Újvár, indicates that Louis I was guaranteeing the journeys of merchants from Nuremberg, and indeed from other imperial towns, along the 1336 reduced-tariff route. Louis I presumably found it important to communicate the provision of an escort, because in the conflict over Brandenburg that had broken out between Charles IV and Stephen the Younger of Bavaria and his sons, he was supporting the latter, and in July he made preparations for a possible outbreak of armed hostilities. There was probably no major battle, and the opposing sides signed a truce on 16 October 1371.[60] Considering that fighting was in progress in Moravia, it is astonishing that Louis I was expecting the Nuremberg merchants to arrive from these same northern regions, as we may be quite sure was the case. What Louis I most probably had in mind was that the hostilities gave the Austrian dukes an additional reason alongside the Viennese staple right for preventing the Nuremberg merchants' entry into the kingdom of Hungary from any direction other than the northern route. The escort may have been a preparation for the spread of hostilities into Hungarian territory, but another factor may have been the merchants' fear of the Hungarian armies.

On 26 June 1383, the Nuremberg cloth merchant Ulrich Eisvogel,[61] representing the Nuremberg and Prague merchants, went before Queen Mary to request a transcription of both the abovementioned diplomas of 6 July 1364 concerning the

---

58 Weisz (ed.), *Fontes*, 2:113–114.

59 Weisz (ed.), *Fontes*, 2:118–119.

60 Truce of 1371, between King Louis I, Otto V, Duke of Bavaria, Pilgrim II, Prince-Archbishop of Salzburg and Charles IV, Magyar Nemzeti Levéltár Országos Levéltára (hereafter MNL OL) [Hungarian National Archives, State Archive], Diplomatikai Fényképgyűjtemény (DF) [Collection of Diplomatic Photographs] 258468.

61 Ulrich Eisvogel, cloth merchant of Nuremberg, Hans Stromer's son-in-law and his factor in Milan. See Stromer, Eine gesellige Versammlung, 59, footnote 29; Stromer, *Oberdeutsche Hochfinanz*, 1:103; Philippe Braunstein. Wirtschaftliche Beziehungen zwischen Nürnberg und Italien im Spätmittelalter. In *Beiträge zur Wirtschaftsgeschichte Nürnberg*, vol. I, Stadtarchiv Nürnberg

1336 route[62] and the arrest of travellers,[63] as well as Louis I's diploma of 1 July 1370 regulating trade between merchants of Nuremberg and Hungary. The latter transcription, like the original, applied only to Nuremberg.[64] Three days later, on 29 June 1383, Mary duly issued a command to Hungarian collectors of thirtieths and tolls permitting them to demand only the customary tolls and taxes from the merchants of Nuremberg and Prague.[65] An entry into the Nuremberg municipal accounts book dated 8 July 1383 records the expenses of Ulrich Eisvogel's embassy and states that the purpose of his journey was to secure the freedom of the route, a privilege that did indeed feature in all three of the diplomas confirmed at his request. In addition to Eisvogel's travel and accommodation expenses, the city covered the costs relating to the diploma issued by the queen.[66] The same year, Eisvogel went to Prague to obtain trading concessions from King Wenceslaus and to negotiate the matter of a loan concerning the route to the kingdom of Hungary.[67] The latter probably arose because Eisvogel had been representing the merchants of both Prague and Nuremberg when he petitioned Mary to confirm the 1336 reduced-tariff route. No doubt the copy produced for Prague was paid for by Nuremberg, and this was the money he was attempting to recover when he visited Prague.

Another Nuremberg merchant, Leopold Schürstab the Younger,[68] was also paid by the city on 8 July 1383 for an attempt to obtain a privilege related to the route to the kingdom of Hungary.[69] Hungarian sources are silent about this embassy, and it is possible his mission to seek these privileges did not take him to the kingdom of Hungary at all, because one of the town's expenses entered in the accounts book on 23 September 1383 concerned the acquisition of a diploma from the Duke of Austria to enable Nuremberg merchants to reach the kingdom of Hungary.[70] The diploma issued by Leopold III of Austria is unknown, but a letter he sent on 16 October 1383 to his *Obersthofmeister*, Reinhard von Wehingen,

(ed.). Nuremberg: Selbstverlag des Stadtrats zu Nürnberg, 1967, 390, footnote 43; Fleischmann, *Rat und Patriziat*, 2:1101.

62 Weisz (ed.), *Fontes*, 2:152–155.

63 Weisz (ed.), *Fontes*, 2:155–157.

64 Weisz (ed.), *Fontes*, 2:157–159. The diploma was transcribed by George, abbot of Saint Giles' monastery in Nuremberg, on 15 July 1460 (StA Nürnberg, RN, Losungamt, 7-farbiges Alphabet, Urkunden 2844).

65 Weisz (ed.), *Fontes*, 2:159–160.

66 Weisz (ed.), *Fontes*, 2:160. See Stromer, *Oberdeutsche Hochfinanz*, 1:99.

67 Weisz (ed.), *Fontes*, 2:163.

68 See Fleischmann, *Rat und Patriziat*, 2:914.

69 Weisz (ed.), *Fontes*, 2:161.

70 Weisz (ed.), *Fontes*, 2:161.

states that citizens of Nuremberg had come to him with a complaint about landowners at the Hungarian border demanding payment of extraordinary tolls when they were on their way to Hungary via Styria. The Duke asked Wehingen to mediate in the affair.[71] This information clearly shows that the Nuremberg merchants in 1383 were seeking more than one route to Hungary that avoided Vienna's staple right. One of these was the reduced-tariff route, and another was a route through Styria.

There are no indications from the reign of King Sigismund (1387–1437) that Nuremberg merchants sought confirmation of their privilege concerning the reduced-tariff route, although when the privileges regarding payment of tolls and thirtieths enjoyed by the merchants of Prague and Nuremberg were conferred on the citizens and merchants of Eger (present-day Cheb, Poland) on 5 April 1396, Sigismund stated that he himself had granted these privileges.[72] Sigismund provided similarly for the merchants of Breslau on 21 March 1420, although in that case he was confirming a privilege granted by Louis I.[73] The privilege granted by Louis I unambiguously applied to the reduced-tariff route, adding to evidence from other sources that it was indeed used by the Nuremberg merchants. The same cannot be said with certainty about Sigismund's charters. Although the Nuremberg merchants seem to have abandoned the northern reduced-tariff route in the late fourteenth and early fifteenth centuries, their commercial activity in Hungary, far from decreasing, became much more intense,[74] but increasingly involved a different route and different commercial techniques. For Prague merchants, such a change may be ruled out on purely geographical grounds. Given their weaker presence in the kingdom of Hungary and the loss of support from Nuremberg, they probably did not even try to obtain confirmation of their privilege to use the route, and there are certainly no signs that they did.

The Nuremberg merchants using the reduced-tariff route, like those from Cologne, journeyed via Prague and Brno and reached the Hungarian border at Újvár. The route was important to them and to merchants from Prague as soon as it opened, as indicated by a diploma relating to the reduced-tariff route issued by

71 Weisz (ed.), *Fontes*, 2:162–163.

72 Weisz (ed.), *Fontes*, 2:185–186.

73 Weisz (ed.), *Fontes*, 2:247–248. See 29 November 1365: Weisz (ed.), *Fontes*, 2:89–91.

74 See, for example, András Kubinyi. Die Nürnberger Haller in Ofen. Ein Beitrag zur Geschichte des Südosthandels im Spätmittealter. *Mitteilungen des Vereins für Geschichte der Stadt Nürnberg* 52 (1963/1964), passim; Hans Schenk. *Nürnberg und Prag. Ein Beitrag zur Geschichte der Handelsbeziehungen im 14. und 15. Jahrhundert.* Wiesbaden: Otto Harrassowitz, 1969, 168–172; Ute Monika Schwob. *Kulturelle Beziehungen zwischen Nürnberg und den Deutschen im Südosten im 14. bis 16. Jahrhundert.* Munich: Oldenbourg, 1969, 4–16.

the Archbishop of Csanád on 24 December 1337. This document, by which the archbishop raised tolls at his own toll stations above the level set in the royal diploma, mentions by name one merchant each from Prague and Nuremberg.[75] The importance of the reduced-tariff route for the Nuremberg merchants must have stemmed in part from their increasing presence in Prague in the early fourteenth century,[76] which the Bohemian monarchs did their best to encourage by providing various privileges. On 10 July 1321, King John of Bohemia warned the citizens of Prague that citizens and merchants of Nuremberg enjoyed the same rights in Prague as citizens and merchants of Prague did in Nuremberg.[77] On 15 December 1326, he assured the Nuremberg merchants that they could travel without restriction in his kingdom on land and water for payment of the customary tolls, and if he was to withdraw this provision, he would inform them one month in advance.[78] Margrave Charles of Moravia confirmed this diploma on 14 June 1338 and, considering one month to be insufficient notice, he set the period at two months.[79] On 23 August 1339, King John prohibited the Prague authorities from demanding *Ungeld* (*nullum ungeltum*) from merchants who brought broadcloth and other goods to Prague and did not open their bales but wished to proceed further.[80] On 2 November 1347, Charles IV ordered that Nuremberg citizens should have the same rights and freedoms as the citizens of Prague and other cities in Bohemia, Moravia, Poland, or the Duchy of Luxembourg, the cities where they and Prague citizens might freely trade with foreigners, and they were exempt from tolls, as Prague citizens were in Nuremberg.[81] Although the ordinance does not specifically mention Nuremberg citizens, its provisions clearly applied to them, a view confirmed by the fact that the original of the diploma is still held in Nuremberg. The privileges granted to Nuremberg citizens by these various ordi-

75 Weisz (ed.), *Fontes*, 2:47.

76 On the commercial links between Nuremberg and Prague, see Schenk, *Nürnberg und Prag*, 21–153.

77 Gerhard Hirschmann. Nürnbergs Handelsprivilegien, Zollfreiheiten und Zollverträge bis 1399. In *Beiträge zur Wirtschaftsgeschichte Nürnbergs*, Stadtarchiv Nürnberg (ed.), no. 28.

78 *RBM*, 3:485.

79 Margrave Charles of Moravia's diploma confirmation, 14 June 1338, StA Nürnberg, RN, Päpstliche und fürstliche Privilegien, Urkunden 24a.

80 King John of Bohemia's Ungeld prohibition, 23 August 1339, StA Nürnberg, RN, Päpstliche und fürstliche Privilegien, Urkunden 24b. On 28 January 1341 in Prague, John of Bohemia exempted the Nuremberg merchants from the payment of *Ungeld* for five years. See Hirschmann, Nürnbergs Handelsprivilegien, no. 52.

81 Proclamation of Charles IV concerning Nuremberg merchants, 2 November 1347, StA Nürnberg, RN, Kaiserl. Privilegien, Urkunden 58. The diploma was confirmed by Wenceslaus of Bohemia on 30 January 1379. See Hirschmann, Nürnbergs Handelsprivilegien, no. 121.

nances surpassed those applying to other foreign merchants, who—unlike those from Bohemian and Moravian towns—were not permitted to make purchases in Prague and could spend only five days in the city after they had offered their wares for sale. Since Nuremberg citizens enjoyed the same rights and privileges as those from Prague and other Bohemian and Moravian towns, they were exempt from these restrictions.[82] These rights of Nuremberg citizens also allowed them to carry on trading beyond Prague after Charles IV had prohibited travel beyond Prague on 25 January 1359. He had done so because the kings had done something similar in Buda, Krakow, and Vienna, and he advised the Frankfurt authority to write to the rulers of these cities and ask them to lift the ban.[83] We may also reasonably infer that the ordinance was in effect for a limited time, but we cannot say how long it lasted. Charles IV, as King of Bohemia, certainly provided freedom of travel for Nuremberg merchants on 27 December 1360, promising to inform them six months in advance if he intended to make any change.[84]

Like the Cologne merchants, those from Nuremberg certainly used the route to Regensburg, and from there took their wares down the Danube into the Duchy of Austria and the kingdom of Hungary, at least until Vienna's staple right was tightened in 1351.[85] From then on, they took up the opportunity of trading with Hungarian merchants who had access to commercial credit for the purchase of goods. This mainly meant trading with the citizens of Pressburg, Sopron, and their surroundings, just as the Cologne merchants did. Although sources on commercial credit surviving in the Pressburg *Protocollum Actionale* do not provide information on the exact location of sale,[86] all of the charters in the Sopron documents concerning commercial credit were written in Vienna,[87] as were several

82 On 23 May 1304, Wenceslaus II granted Prague a five-day staple right which also banned trade among foreigners (*CIM*, 1:20–21). In 1328 (*RBM*, 3:551–552) and on 19 May 1333 (*RBM*, 3:777–779, 779–780), the city of Prague also issued regulations for trading by foreigners in line with Wenceslaus II's diploma. A detailed study of the trading between Nuremberg and Prague merchants is Schenk, *Nürnberg und Prag*, passim.

83 Johann Friedrich Boehmer (ed.). *Codex diplomaticus Moenofrancofurtanus. Urkundenbuch der Reichstadt Frankfurt.* Frankfurt am Main, 1836, 661–662.

84 Hirschmann, Nürnbergs Handelsprivilegien, no. 87.

85 On 12 May 1366, Albert III of Austria granted Prague merchants the right to travel between the Kingdom of Bohemia and Venice via Vienna without being subject to that city's staple right for a period of four years. See Christian Lackner, Claudia Feller (eds.). *Regesta Habsburgica V. Die Regesten der Herzoge von Österreich aus dem Hause Habsburg V. Abteilung: Die Regesten der Herzoge von Österreich 1365–1395. 1. Teilband (1365–1370).* Vienna, Munich: Böhlau, 2007, 115. There is no record of Nuremberg merchants receiving an exemption from Vienna's staple right.

86 For a detailed discussion, see Skorka, Pozsony gazdasági szerepe, 450–451, 453–454.

87 5 March 1426: *Sopron szabad királyi város története, I/1–II/6* [History of the Royal Free Town of Sopron]. Közli Házi Jenő. Sopron, 1921–1943. (*Sopr. tört.*), I/2:301; 1 March 1428: *Sopr. tört.*,

other surviving original documents recording Nuremberg merchants' trade with Pressburg citizens,[88] pointing to the conclusion that, like the Cologne merchants, they did most of their business in Vienna. As we have seen, a third option was the route through Styria, bringing merchants to the kingdom of Hungary via Regensburg, Passau, and Wiener Neustadt. The Bavarian dukes Stephen the Elder, Stephen the Younger, and Frederick facilitated the use of the Styrian route through a guarantee of safe travel against payment of tolls, granted on 8 June 1359.[89]

A feature of trade between Nuremberg and the Hungarian lands is that every year from 1396 onwards, an *aufdinger* (*aufdinger gen Ungern*) was elected to inspect, in the Nuremberg customs house, the loading and unloading of goods intended for Hungary. Such municipal officials were first appointed to oversee trade with Hungary, Saxony, Swabia, and Frankia, and others were appointed for Bavarian lands in the early fifteenth century (although *aufdinger* were not elected for every destination in every year).[90] On 21 April 1400, four *aufdinger*s were elected for trade with Hungarian lands and two for Swabia. They were appointed for a period of approximately one year.[91]

The Regensburg merchants

On 27 March 1359, the Regensburg merchant Albert Taucher[92] went before Louis I on behalf of his fellow merchants, requesting him to confirm to their benefit the

I/2:358–359; 25 December 1431: *Sopr. tört.*, I/3:37; 6 January 1432: *Sopr. tört.*, I/3:41; 2 April 1432: *Sopr. tört.*, I/3:45–46.

88 Pozsony council acknowledged their debt to Nuremberg's merchants on 3 March 1413, MNL OL DF 239333; Pozsony council acknowledged their debt to Nuremberg's merchants, 6 June 1414, MNL OL DF 239353; Letter of Purkhart Seebach, citizen of Nuremberg, to Pozsony council, 29 February 1416, MNL OL DF 243930; Leonard Horndl and Ludwig Königsfelder, citizens of Pozsony, acknowledged their debt to Nuremberg's citizens, MNL OL Diplomatikai Levéltár (DL) [Collection of Diplomatic] 44257.

89 Hirschmann, Nürnbergs Handelsprivilegien, no. 85.

90 Walter Bauernfeind. Güterbestätter. In *Stadtlexikon Nürnberg*. Michael Diefenbacher, Rudolf Endres (eds.). Nuremberg: Tümmel, 1999, 391. See also Alfred Bauch. Ein vergessener Schüler Albrecht Dürer's. In *Mitteilungen aus dem germanischen Nationalmuseum* (1896): 8.

91 Wilhelm Biebinger, Wilhelm Neukam (eds.). *Quellen zur Handelsgeschichte der Stadt Nürnberg seit 1400*. vol. I/1. Erlangen: Palm and Enke, 1934, 48.

92 Several members of the Taucher merchant family of Regensburg had interests in east-west trade. Their trading links in the kingdom of Hungary were mainly confined to Pressburg. See Klaus Fischer. *Regensburger Hochfinanz. Die Krise einer europäischen Metropole an der Wende zur Neuzeit*. Regensburg: Universitätsverlag, 2003, 251–252.

diploma that Charles I issued on 6 January 1336 and the Brno city authority transcribed on 6 July 1357. Louis I confirmed the ordinance, repeating the text he used to confirm the diplomas of the Nuremberg and Prague merchants the same year. This covered the confirmation of the diplomas for foreign towns, the memory of his mother Elizabeth, the demand of gifts supplementary to toll collection, and the payment of the thirtieth. One new element was the requirement to pay a toll at the gate of Buda in accordance with the privilege of the Dominican nuns of Margaret Island.[93] This stipulation represented a substantial addition to the tolls paid by Regensburg merchants on the reduced-tariff route, because what the nuns collected at the castle gate were the Buda market tolls.[94] Louis I's ordinance was in fact a return to the state of affairs in the Árpádian age: upon granting the tolls to the nuns on 25 July 1255, Béla IV ordered that everyone, even those otherwise exempted, must pay them.[95] Rather than this precedent, however, Louis I's decision most likely stemmed from an ordinance he made himself six years previously. On 1 April 1351, he required everyone, native or foreigner, to pay the full customary tolls at the toll stations of the Dominican nuns of Margaret Island, even if they had previously been granted exemption from payment.[96] This was the first confirmation of the reduced-tariff route to include a stipulation suspending the toll exemption in the case of the Buda gate toll held by the Dominican nuns of Margaret Island, although the ordinance it refers to predates the diploma Louis I issued to the Prague and Nuremberg merchants on 29 July 1357. Since Louis I first transcribed the diploma for the nuns on 27 February 1365,[97] the mention in 1359 cannot be based on Louis I having recently confirmed the nuns' privilege. The surviving sources offer no explanation as to why the stipulation concerning the Buda gate toll was applied to the Regensburg merchants but did not appear in the diploma for the merchants from Nuremberg and Prague, and neither do we know how—or indeed if—Regensburg obtained the transcription of the 1336 diploma for the reduced-tariff route made by the municipal authority of Brno 6 July 1357 (more on this below). After the loss of the royal seal in 1363, Louis I,

93 Weisz (ed.), *Fontes*, 2:72–74. See also Stromer, *Oberdeutsche Hochfinanz*, 1:106.
94 Boglárka Weisz. *A királyketteje és az ispán harmada. Vámok és vámszedés Magyarországon a középkor első felében* [The King's Second Part and the Ispán's Third: Tolls and Toll Collection in Hungary in the First Half of the Middle Ages]. Budapest: BTK Történettudományi Intézet, 2013, 11.
95 Weisz, *A királyketteje*, 98.
96 Weisz (ed.), *Fontes*, 2:74–76.
97 Confirmation of King Louis I's diploma of 1 April 1351, 27 February1365, MNL OL DL 5369.

at the request of the Regensburg merchants Nicolaus Spitzer[98] and Ulrich Kankaphar, transcribed and confirmed this diploma on 26 June 1369.[99]

On 29 March 1371, Louis I issued a charter of privilege to the Regensburg merchants of almost the same content as the 1 July 1370 diploma for Nuremberg citizens discussed above, with the exception that he would inform the Regensburg merchants not six or seven weeks prior, but three months before an armed conflict.[100]

Regensburg merchants reached the reduced-tariff route to Hungary via Prague[101] and Brno. Another option was to make contact with Hungarian merchants along the Danube route through Vienna. After 1370, the Regensburg merchants made no effort to obtain privileges in the kingdom of Hungary or to have them confirmed. Although the city declined in economic significance in the second half of the fourteenth century, its wealthy merchants moved to Nuremberg and Augsburg,[102] and at the turn of the fourteenth and fifteenth centuries, like those from Cologne and Nuremberg, they maintained active commercial relations with places in Hungary, primarily Pressburg,[103] but in such a way that the actual exchange of goods took place in Vienna.[104] After the 1440s, however, Regensburg merchants' trade with Hungary effectively ceased.[105]

98 The commercial activity of the Spitzer family of Regensburg extended to the kingdom of Hungary, Venice, Bohemia, and Austria. See Fischer, *Regensburger Hochfinanz*, 272.

99 Weisz (ed.), *Fontes*, 2:108–110. For the sixteenth-century copy and German translation of the diploma, see Bayerisches Hauptstaatsarchiv, München (hereafter BayHStA), Reichsstadt Regensburg, Reichsstadt Regensburg Amtsbücher und Akten 6. (Rotes Privilegienbuch), 78v–78r.

100 Louis I's charter concerning Regensburg merchants, 29 March 1371, BayHStA, Rotes Privilegienbuch, fol. 76r.

101 The Prague authority specifically mentioned the Regensburg merchants (and those from Cologne and Eger) when regulating trade by foreigners on 19 May 1333 in harmony with Wenceslaus II's diploma of 23 May 1304 (*RBM*, 3:777–779, 779–780). In 1304, Wenceslaus II granted Prague a five-day staple right, which also banned trade between foreigners (*CIM*, 1:20–21).

102 Skorka, Pozsony gazdasági szerepe, 445.

103 Skorka, Pozsony gazdasági szerepe, 447–448, 452–453; Fischer, *Regensburger Hochfinanz*, 248–252.

104 See Fischer, *Regensburger Hochfinanz*, 251. For the Regensburg merchants' trade in Vienna, see Fischer, *Regensburger Hochfinanz*, 242–247. The Regensburg merchants' Vienna warehouse—the Regensburger Hof—appears in the sources in 1410. See Felix Czeike. Regensburger Hof. In *Historisches Lexikon Wien IV*, Felix Czeike (ed.). Vienna: Kremayr and Scheriau, 1995, 646.

105 Fischer, *Regensburger Hochfinanz*, 248.

Merchants of Breslau, Eger (Cheb), and Aachen

On 29 November 1365, Louis I, at the request of Charles IV, Holy Roman Emperor and King of Bohemia, permitted the citizens and merchants of Breslau and Eger, in separate diplomas, to bring their wares into the country along any route and enjoy the same freedoms as the merchants of Prague and Nuremberg—namely, that after payment of the rightful tolls and thirtieths, they could not be harassed by collectors of tolls and thirtieths on either their inward or outward journeys and could not be burdened with excessive tolls and thirtieths, but travelled under royal protection. The king called on the toll and thirtieth collectors to observe this ordinance.[106] For Breslau citizens, he made the same provision in the form of a patent on 30 November 1365,[107] and there is a high degree of congruence in the text of the two documents. The latter also records its place of issue—Pressburg—implying that the charters of privilege of the previous day were issued there too. Their issue was probably connected to the visit of Charles IV in autumn 1365. Charles IV was certainly in Buda between 20 and 23 November 1365,[108] but Louis I's itinerary does not tell us when he—or they—left Buda, or by which route the emperor left the kingdom. Louis I was in Pressburg on 29 November and issued a diploma there on 1 December,[109] but on 5 December he was in Győr,[110] and a diploma he issued there suggests that he and Charles IV had discussed the possibility of Charles' son Wenceslaus marrying Elizabeth, daughter of Louis I's brother, Stephen.[111] The meeting was also a suitable occasion for the emperor to request charters of privilege for the merchants of the two cities, a request that Louis I, wishing to please him, readily fulfilled. Charles IV was in Kuttenberg on 17 December and in Prague on 23 December.[112] This suggests that Louis I might have escorted the emperor to Pressburg, and Charles IV was probably still there when the Hungarian king issued the diploma for the merchants. Their ways then

106 Weisz (ed.), *Fontes*, 2:89–91 (Breslau); Weisz (ed.), *Fontes*, 2:91–93 (Eger). Matthias I transcribed and confirmed the Breslau merchants' diploma on 25 November 1484. See Archiwum Państwowe we Wrocławiu (APW) [State Archive in Wrocław], Akta miasta Wrocławia (AMW), 3893. fols. 7r–10r.

107 Weisz (ed.), *Fontes*, 2:93–94.

108 20 November 1365: *Regesta Imperii VIII. Die Regesten des Kaisereichs unter Kaiser Karl IV. 1346–1378* (hereafter *RI VIII*), Johann Friedrich Böhmer (ed.). Innsbruck: Wagner, 1877, no. 4227; 22 November 1365: *RI VIII*, no. 4228; 23 November 1365: *RI VIII*, no. 4229.

109 *Sopr. tört.*, I/1:134.

110 Diploma issued in Győr by King Louis I in a succession case, 5 December 1365, MNL OL DL 62720.

111 *RI VIII*, no. 350. See 20 December 1365: *RI VIII*, no. 575; 24 December 1365: *RI VIII*, no. 4232.

112 *RI VIII*, no. 4230–4231.

parted, as the emperor went to Kuttenberg via Brno, possibly leaving the country through Stompfa and Malacka.

Louis I granted freedom of travel along any route in the diplomas for the Breslau and Eger merchants, but by referring to the privileges of the Prague and Nuremberg merchants, he directed attention to the reduced-tariff route, since all the diplomas we know of concerning both the towns mention the use of that route and the collection of tolls along it. The same route was also the best and easiest way for merchants from Breslau and Eger to come, via Brno, to Buda. We should bear in mind, however, that on 5 October 1365, Louis I opened a new route towards Breslau and the lands of Bohemia, along which Hungarian merchants, those from Kassa (present-day Košice, Slovakia) and Szepes (present-day Spišská Kapitula, Slovakia), and others who took part in setting up the route were obliged to pay tolls only in Liptó (present-day Liptovský Hrádok, Slovakia), Turóc (present-day Turiec, Slovakia), and Zsolna (present-day Žilina, Slovakia), namely four *garas* (*grossus*) for each heavy and large wagon, commonly called *mázsaszekér*, and were not exempt from payment of the thirtieth.[113] Since this route was probably not passable in November and the associated toll concession applied only to certain Hungarian merchants, Louis I's diploma is much more likely to have concerned the reduced-tariff route. Sigismund confirmed Louis I's diploma for the Breslau merchants on 21 March 1420. He did not simply transcribe the original, however, although he did mention that it was Louis I who had granted them this privilege.[114] Sigismund issued the diploma in Breslau, no doubt in return for generous hospitality. In this period, however, the Breslau merchants preferred to travel along a route for merchants from Bohemia that Louis I opened on 1 May 1373, starting in Újvár and going via Őr (present-day Šaštín-Stráže, Slovakia), Kukló (present-day Kuklov, Slovakia), Malacka (present-day Malacky, Slovakia), and Stomfa (present-day Stupava, Slovakia) to Pressburg. The customary tolls had to be paid along the way.[115] The Breslau merchants maintained this route principally as a way to reach Venice,[116] from which they

---

113 Weisz (ed.), *Fontes*, 2:86–87.

114 Weisz (ed.), *Fontes*, 2:247–248. On the Breslau merchants' trade in Hungary and Buda, see 14 March 1425: Weisz (ed.), *Fontes*, 2:259–260; Letter of John Lorzak to Breslau council, 8 May 1425, APW, AMW 1623.

115 Weisz (ed.), *Fontes*, 2:123.

116 See 21 June 1430: Weisz (ed.), *Fontes*, 2:275–276; Bence Péterfi. Széllel szemben. Boroszlói kísérletek Buda lerakatjogának kikerülésére a 15–16. század fordulóján [Against the Wind. Attempts by Breslau to avoid the Buda staple right at the turn of the 15th and 15th centuries]. In *Márvány, tárház, adomány. Gazdaságtörténeti tanulmányok a magyar középkorról*, Kádas István, Skorka Renáta, Weisz Boglárka (eds.). Budapest: BTK Történettudományi Intézet, 2019, 388.

had been prohibited since 1412, and it was only on 25 April 1421 that Sigismund lifted the prohibition.[117]

On 5 April 1396, at the request of his brother Wenceslaus IV, Holy Roman Emperor and King of Bohemia, Sigismund granted the privileges defined in Louis I's diploma to the town of Eger. As well as making the same provisions, Sigismund made a similar reference to a charter for the citizens of Nuremberg and Prague, although it was one he had himself granted.[118] No such charter has survived, but Queen Mary's diploma of 29 June 1383 ordered the collectors of tolls and thirtieths not to harass the citizens of Nuremberg or Prague or to collect from them anything except the lawful tolls and the thirtieth.[119] This diploma was issued the same day as the confirmation of the 1336 reduced-tariff route and so may be connected to it, which again confirms that the generally worded diploma for Breslau and Eger was primarily based on the rules for travel along the reduced-tariff route. Sigismund issued the 1396 diploma while he was in Prague on a visit where he and Wenceslaus, among other things, made a mutual inheritance agreement in the case of death without issue, and Wenceslaus appointed Sigismund vicar-general of the Holy Roman Empire. When Sigismund confirmed the rights and privileges of the city of Eger as Holy Roman Emperor on 25 January 1437, he also, as King of Hungary, confirmed the privileges that his predecessors, particularly Louis I, had granted to Eger, and those he had granted himself in respect of tolls, thirtieths, and anything else.[120] Buda was probably the chief destination for merchants of Breslau during our period, and probably also for those of Eger,[121] although the charter of privilege discussed here is the only known record of Eger citizens' commercial activity in the kingdom of Hungary.

As he had done for the merchants of Breslau and Eger, Louis I, on 2 March 1369, granted Aachen merchants the same freedoms from harassment by toll collectors as those enjoyed by the merchants of Nuremberg and Prague on their journeys to and from the kingdom of Hungary. This was a gesture of gratitude to Aachen, the city

117 Wilhelm Stieda. *Hansisch–Venetianische Handelsbeziehungen im 15. Jahrhundert*. Rostock: Universtäts-Buchdruckerei, 1894, 139–142; 1412: *Regesta Imperii XI. Urkunden Kaiser Sigmunds (1410–1437)* (hereafter *RI XI*), Wilhelm Altmann (ed.). Innsbruck, 1896–1900, XI/1, no. 3244a; 25 April 1421: *RI XI*/1, no. 4520.

118 Weisz (ed.), *Fontes*, 2:185–186.

119 Weisz (ed.), *Fontes*, 2:159–160.

120 Weisz (ed.), *Fontes*, 2:308.

121 For the routes from Breslau to the Kingdom of Hungary, see Grzegorz Myśliwski. A Silesian Town and the Hungarian Monarchy: Economic Contacts between Wrocław and Hungary, ca. 1250–1500. In *The Medieval Networks in East Central Europe: Commerce, Contacts, Communication*. Balázs Nagy, Felicitas Schmieder, András Vadas (eds.). London, New York: Routledge, 2019, 238–239.

that had helped him to build a chapel in its basilica and to acquire lands in the city and its hinterland so that he could donate them to the chapel.[122] The chapel was certainly completed in 1367, when Louis I and Abbot Henry of Pilis donated to it relics of the Hungarian Saints, Saint Stephen, Saint Ladislaus, and Saint Emeric.[123] On 2 January 1370, Louis transferred maintenance of the chapel to the city, reserving the right to appoint two Hungarian chaplains.[124] The privilege granted to the citizens of Aachen was one of a series of charters related to the chapel, and whether it was indeed important to them or was no more than a gesture by the king cannot now be established.

The Bamberg merchants

On 21 July 1366, Konrad von Geisenheim, provost of Bamberg, approached Louis I to request that he confirm to the benefit of the merchants of Bamberg Charles I's diploma relating to the 1336 reduced-tariff route, as the king had already done for the merchants of Cologne, Nuremberg, and some other merchants. Louis I fulfilled the request with the stipulation that tolls were also to be paid to the Dominican nuns of Margaret Island at the Buda city gate and river tolls to the Poor Clares nunnery on the Danube at Óbuda, as his predecessors had ordered and as he had ordered merchants and others to pay, but the merchants could not be required to pay any further tolls or make any gifts. The Bamberg merchants also had to pay the thirtieth, as other merchants had.[125] According to the king's charter, Geisenheim presented a patent sealed with Charles I's third and last seal. Charles I used his third great seal between 1331 and 1342, and although no copy of the 1336 diploma in patent form is known of, the king's third seal is preserved in the Brno archives in the form of an intact hanging seal on a charter of privilege. The Brno municipal authority also stated that Charles I's charter was a patent, and Louis I noted the same when transcribing the document transcribed by the Brno authority, and so it seems certain that Charles I's diploma also had a patent copy. The remark about Charles I's seal is conclusive evidence that what

122 Rudolf Arthur Peltzer. Ein Handelsprivileg des Königs Ludwig I. von Ungarn für Aachen, 1369. März 2. *Zeitschrift des Aachener Geschichtsvereins* 28 (1906): 452–454.

123 Copy of donation of King Louis I and Abbot Henry of Pilis to the Hungarian chapel in Aachen, 27 October 1367, MNL OL DL 36460.

124 Copy of diploma in which King Louis I transferred the maintenance of the Hungarian chapel to Aachen, 2 January 1370, MNL OL DL 36460. See Edith Tömöry. *Az aacheni magyar kápolna története* [The History of the Hungarian Chapel in Aachen]. Budapest: Németh József, 1931, 7–9.

125 Weisz (ed.), *Fontes*, 2:100–102.

Geisenheim presented to Louis I was not the diploma transcribed by the Brno municipal authority. How the Bamberg provost obtained the diploma cannot now be ascertained. Louis was in Lippa (present-day Lipova, Romania) when he issued it,[126] and Geisenheim may have visited him when he was in Transylvania, most likely when the king was in Gyulafehérvár (present-day Alba Iulia, Romania).[127] In this case, Louis I gave Geisenheim something similar to the document he gave János Szentgyörgyi in Görgény (present-day Gurghiu, Romania) on 16 June 1366, asking his chancellor, Archbishop Nicholas of Esztergom, to transcribe with royal approval the charter which Szentgyörgyi presented for confirmation and to transcribe and confirm it in the customary form with his new great seal.[128] That is, if Geisenheim visited Louis I at all.

Geisenheim appears in the sources after 1360 as Charles IV's *secretarius*,[129] and we know that on 15 June 1366, Charles IV wrote a letter from Vienna informing the city of Augsburg that he was preparing to go to Pressburg, where he would meet with the Hungarian queen.[130] There, he may have held talks on the marriage between Charles IV's son Wenceslaus and Elizabeth, daughter of Louis I's brother Stephen. We may suspect that Queen Elizabeth was indeed in Pressburg at the time, because on 24 June 1366, the river tolls payable by those arriving by ship from Vienna were regulated in Pressburg on behalf of Louis I,[131] essentially repeating the provisions of Louis I's order of 22 March 1366,[132] and Louis I transcribed the latter in Pressburg on 27 June at the request of the Pressburg judge Jakab.[133] By this time, Louis I was, as we have seen, in Transylvania. He was in Görgény on 16 June and still there on 20 June,[134] but on 24 and 26 June, he issued

126 See Donation of King Louis I issued in Lippa, 19 July 1366, MNL OL DL 34108; Wit of King Louis I to towns and villages issued in Lippa, 20 July 1366, MNL OL DF 285833. For 24 July 1366, see *Monumenta spectantia historiam Slavorum meridionalium. Listine o odnošajih između južnoga Slavenstva i mletačke republike* (hereafter *MSHS*). 9 vols. Sime Ljubić (ed.). Zagreb: Academia Scientiarum et Artium Slavorum Meridionalium, 1868–1891, 4:87.

127 Arrest prohibition of King Louis I, issued in Gyulafehérvár, 6 July 1366, MNL OL DF 277368; Writ of King Louis I to chapter of Transylvania issued in Gyulafehérvár, 14 July 1366, MNL OL DL 30393.

128 Writ of King Louis I to Archbishop Nicholas of Esztergom, 16 June 1366, MNL OL DL 61219.

129 *Hamburgs Gedächtnis—die Threse des Hamburger Rates: Die Regesten der Urkunden im Staatsarchiv der Freien und Hansestadt Hamburg.* 2 vols. Jeanine Marquard, Nico Nolden, Jürgen Sarnowsky (eds.). Hamburg: Hamburg University Press, 2014–2021, 1:182, footnote 92.

130 *RI VIII*, no. 7208.

131 Weisz (ed.), *Fontes*, 2:96–98.

132 Weisz (ed.), *Fontes*, 2:94–96.

133 Weisz (ed.), *Fontes*, 2:99.

134 *MSHS*, 4:86–87.

charters in Székelyvásárhely (present-day Târgu Mureș, Romania).[135] Although the *relator* of the diploma issued in Pressburg on 24 June was the palatine, Miklós Kont, we may reasonably surmise that Queen Elizabeth gave permission for its issuance. It is quite possible, if not verifiable, that Konrad von Geisenheim came to the kingdom of Hungary with Charles IV and stayed after the emperor departed and held talks in Hungary on the emperor's behalf, giving him the chance to proceed in the interests of the merchants of the city of the bishop of Bamberg.

Bamberg merchants went to Prague via Nuremberg, and from there through Brno to the Hungarian border, thus arriving in Buda along the reduced-tariff route. It was therefore important for them to obtain this privilege. The Bamberg merchants learned of the commercial opportunities in the kingdom of Hungary through their active contacts with Nuremberg, and since they knew of the privilege enjoyed by the Nuremberg merchants, they made some effort to obtain it for themselves. What is missing is any evidence that they exercised their privilege or ever actually went to Hungary.[136]

One of the two stipulations in the diploma issued to the Bamberg merchants for the use of the reduced-tariff route in 1366—payment of the Buda gate toll to the Dominican nuns of Margaret Island—has already been discussed in detail in connection with the Regensburg merchants. The document also ordered payment of another toll on the route—the water toll collected at Óbuda by the Poor Clares nunnery of Óbuda. On 29 March 1366, Louis I gave his consent for his mother Elizabeth to give the Poor Clares of Óbuda the queen's water toll in Óbuda in return for the nuns' toll in Szentjakabfalva, which was thus transferred to the queen's possession and attached to Óbuda Castle.[137] Since the provision that anyone was exempt from paying the tolls due to the nuns of the Poor Clares nunnery of Óbuda had been withdrawn from all of Louis I's toll-exemption diplomas on 20 May 1365, from which time everyone was obliged to pay these tolls,[138] the appearance of the stipulation in the Bamberg merchants' diploma is hardly surprising. Shortly after the Dominican nuns' privilege of 1351 was confirmed on 27 February 1365, the same privilege was granted to the Óbuda nuns.[139] The obligation to pay the Óbuda nuns' toll very strongly arouses the suspicion that it was Queen

135 *Urkundenbuch zur Geschichte der Deutschen in Siebenbürgen.* 7 vols. Gustav Gündisch, Herta Gündisch, Konrad G. Gündisch, Georg Müller, Gernot Nussbächer, Carl Werner, Franz Zimmermann (eds.). Hermannstadt, Bucharest, 1892–1991, 2:254–256, 380–381.

136 See Wilhelm Georg Neukam. Wege und Organisation des Bamberger Handels vor 1400. *Jahrbuch für fränkische Landesforschung* 14 (1954): 121, 124.

137 Permission of King Louis I to his mother Elizabeth, 29 March 1366, MNL OL DL 5445.

138 Weisz (ed.), *Fontes*, 1:142–144.

139 Confirmation of King Louis I's privilege of 1 April 1351, 27 February 1365, MNL OL DL 5369.

Elizabeth, the main sponsor of the Poor Clares nunnery, rather than Louis I, who was behind the issue of the diploma (and it is thus possible that the Bamberg provost did not visit the king, but stayed close to the queen). This is because the provision made little sense. The reduced-tariff route had no bearing on the Óbuda water toll, but it did affect the Szentjakabfalva toll recently withdrawn from the Óbuda nuns. When the 1336 diploma was issued, the latter toll still belonged to Óbuda Castle,[140] but on 9 January 1351, Louis I gave Queen Elizabeth his consent to donate it to the Poor Clares nunnery of Óbuda.[141] This means that if the exchange of tolls had not taken place, then the nuns would, in accordance with their royal diploma of 1365, have been due the full tolls from Szentjakabfalva on the reduced-tariff route. That explains the appearance of a toll that did not affect the Bamberg merchants in the diploma issued to them. Not surprisingly, this stipulation did not subsequently appear in the diploma for the Amberg merchants, as we will see.

The Amberg merchants

Louis I transcribed and confirmed the 1336 reduced-tariff route privilege charter for the Amberg merchants at the request of Rupert, Count Palatine of the Rhine, on 14 September 1369. Rupert asked the king of Hungary to permit the citizens of Amberg to exercise the rights and freedoms in respect of toll and thirtieth payment already enjoyed by the merchants of Regensburg and Nuremberg. Charles I had granted this privilege to the citizens of Brno,[142] and Louis I transcribed it for them and for the merchants of Regensburg and Nuremberg, taking the text word for word from the register of royal transcripts (*de registro nostro transsumptarum*). The diploma that Louis I subsequently issued to the Amberg merchants was also a word-for-word transcription of Charles I's 1336 charter but was based on the Brno municipal authority's transcript of 26 July 1357.[143]

Another interesting aspect of the procedure employed for the Amberg merchants' diploma is that the transcription was made in Pressburg, even though there is good reason to believe that the registers were held in the chancellery in

140 Weisz (ed.), *Fontes*, 2:44.

141 Permission of King Louis I to his mother Elizabeth, 9 January 1351, MNL OL DL 4168. See also donation of Queen Elizabeth to the Poor Clares nunnery of Óbuda, 20 January 1351, MNL OL DL 4170; 27 November 1352: Weisz (ed.), *Fontes*, 1:81–83.

142 In the most recent publication of the diploma, *Brunna* was mistakenly identified as Breslau. See Weisz (ed.), *Fontes*, 2:111, footnote 5.

143 Weisz (ed.), *Fontes*, 2:111–112.

Visegrád. Louis I was in Pressburg between 13 and 15 September 1369, and on the former date, he entered into an alliance with Philip, titular emperor of Constantinople, Charles, Duke of Durazzo, Albert, Count Palatine of the Rhine, and Rupert, Count Palatine of the Rhine and his sons.[144] This explains why the King of Hungary was willing to fulfil the request of the Count Palatine for confirmation of Charles I's 1336 privilege charter for the Amberg merchants. It is also conceivable that if the Chancellor and the keeper of the register—the Vice-Chancellor—was escorting him, they took the registers with them in case they were needed during the talks, and we have seen that there was such a need. For the Amberg merchants who made their way to Prague via Pilsen, it may have been important to obtain such a privilege, although there is no trace of them ever having it confirmed, and their commercial activity in Hungary remains obscure.

Conclusion

The privilege for the reduced-tariff route granted to Hungarian and foreign merchants by Charles I in 1336 was the subject of foreign towns' requests for transcription and confirmation even before the end of Charles' reign. The first such town was Prague (1336–1342). Most confirmations, however, were granted during the reign of Louis I, who fulfilled requests for confirmation of merchants from Cologne and Huy (around 1344), Prague and Nuremberg (1357), Regensburg (1359), Bamberg (1366), Amberg (1369), and, at an unknown date, Brno. Louis I based the confirmations of the diploma for Prague, Nuremberg, Regensburg, and Amberg on a transcription of Charles I's diploma made by the Brno municipal authority in 1357. The town of Amberg was demonstrably not in possession of the Brno transcription, and the diploma issued for its merchants was based on a copy of the Regensburg merchants' transcription in the royal register of transcriptions. The transcription by the Brno authority was almost certainly produced at the request of the Nuremberg and Prague merchants, and the high degree of congruence between the Regensburg and Nuremberg diplomas suggests that it was not presented to Louis I by the Regensburg merchants either. Instead, their diploma was also based on the text entered into Louis I's register. Although the diplomas issued to the merchants of Breslau (1365), Eger (1365), and Aachen (1369) do not contain the text of Charles I's 1336 diploma, the inclusion of a privilege identical to that received by the Prague and Nuremberg merchants implies that they had the same meaning. The merchants of Cologne and Huy, and those of Nuremberg and

144 *RI VIII*, no. 500.

Prague, asked Mary to confirm Louis I's diploma, and the Cologne merchants and those of Breslau and Eger asked Sigismund for the same. The main reason that merchants from beyond the kingdom of Bohemia attached importance to the reduced-tariff route—a longer and more expensive alternative to routes involving the Danube waterway—was that it avoided the obstacle of Vienna's staple right. Trade between Hungarian and foreign merchants in Vienna, which had long been a significant activity, grew considerably after 1408, when the authorities gave foreigners permission to travel beyond the city for the purpose of collecting debts. Foreign merchants also began to disregard the rule that they were not allowed to do business with each other except for the period of the annual fair,[145] frequently arousing the ire of Viennese merchants.[146] This was one of the reasons why little effort was put into confirming the privilege for use of the northern route under Sigismund's successor Albert, although the Hussite-related conflicts were also a factor. The following period of chaos did not favour trade, and the reduced-tariff route reappeared only under Matthias I and Wladislaus II. By then, however, only the Nuremberg and Prague merchants were interested in having it confirmed. Many foreign merchants acquired citizenship in one of the cities of the kingdom of Hungary (primarily Buda), considerably extending their rights to carry on commercial activity in the country. Several of them, indeed, built careers in the management of royal finances.

145 Ferdinand Opll. Jahrmarkt oder Messe? Überlegungen zur spätmittelalterlichen Handelsgeschichte Wiens. In *Europäische Messen und Märktesysteme in Mittelalter und Neuzeit*, Peter Johanek, Heinz Stoob (eds.). Cologne, Weimar, Vienna: Böhlau, 1996, 195–198.

146 Theodor Mayer. *Der auswärtige Handel des Herzogtums Österreich im Mittelalter*. Innsbruck: Verlag der Wagner'schen Universitäts-Buchhandlung, 1909, 74–78. Archduke Maximilian I of Austria suspended Vienna's staple right in 1506, providing free trade for foreign merchants, and although the Viennese authority reasserted their old privilege for a while, pressure from the South German trading houses finally led to its abolition in 1515. See Peter Csendes. Vom späten 14. Jahrhundert bis zur Ersten Wiener Türkenbelagerung (1529). In *Wien. Geschichte einer Stadt*, vol. I. Peter Csendes, Ferdinand Opll (eds.). Vienna: Böhlau, 2001, 179; Richard Perger. Wandlungen Wiens am Ende des Mittelalters. In *Wien*, Csendes, Opll (eds.), 241.

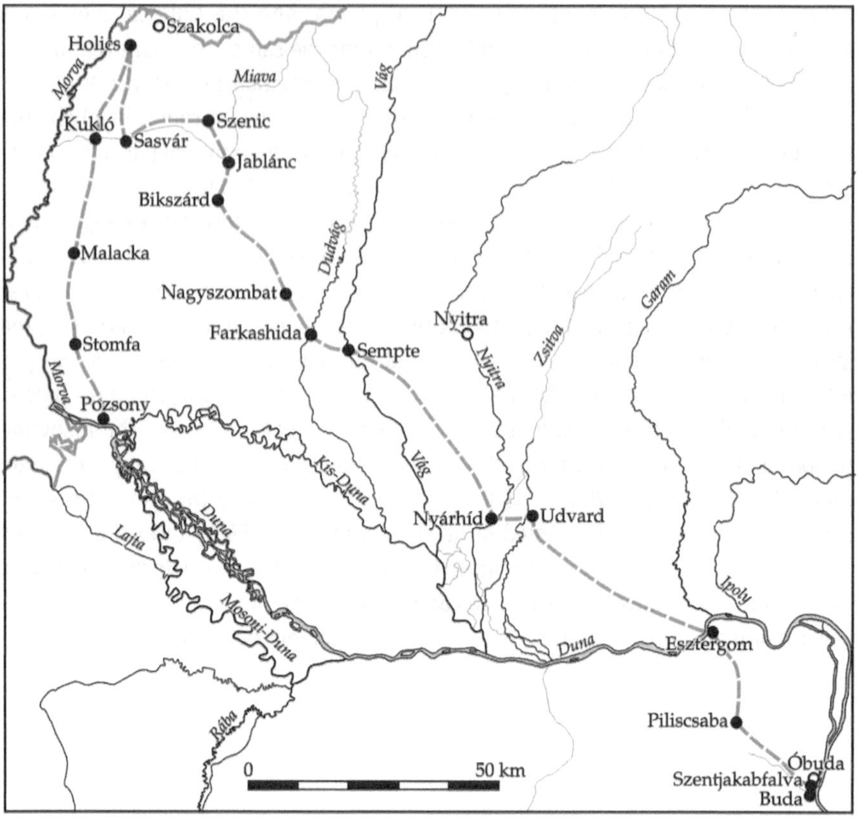

Fig. 1: Route between Újvár (Holics) and Buda/Újvár (Holics) and Pozsony. (map prepared by the author and Béla Nagy).

Bibliography

Primary Sources

Arrest prohibition of King Louis I, issued in Gyulafehérvár. 6 July 1366. Magyar Nemzeti Levéltár Országos Levéltára (MNL OL), Diplomatikai Fényképgyűjtemény (DF), 277368.

Confirmation of King Louis I's privilege of 1 April 1351. 27 February 1365. MNL OL Diplomatikai Levéltár (DL) 5369.

Confirmation of King Louis I's privilege of 29 November 1365. 25 November 1484. Archiwum Państwowe we Wrocławiu (APW), Akta miasta Wrocławia (AMW), 3893. fols. 7r–10r.

Copy of Archbishop Csanád of Esztergom's diploma of 24 December 1337. In *Primus Liber vetustissimus Privilegiorum, Statutorum et Decretorum Veteris Urbis Pragensis necno[n] gloriose*

Aureeq[ue] memorie eiusdem perpetuo dignissimus, 34–35, Archiv hlavního města Prahy (AMP), Kniha pamětni, no. 993/1.
Copy of donation of King Louis I and Abbot Henry of Pilis to the Hungarian chapel in Aachen. 27 October 1367. MNL OL DL 36460.
Copy of diploma in which King Louis I transferred the maintenance of the Hungarian chapel to Aachen. 2 January 1370. MNL OL DL 36460.
Copy of King Louis I's diploma of 26 June 1369. Bayerisches Hauptstaatsarchiv, München (BayHStA), Reichsstadt Regensburg, Reichsstadt Regensburg Amtsbücher und Akten 6. (Rotes Privilegienbuch), 78v–73r.
Confirmation clause of King Louis I concerning Prague merchants. 18 July 1364. In *Primus Liber vetustissimus*, 23–26.
Confirmation of King Louis I's diploma of 1 April 1351. 27 February 1365. MNL OL DL 5369.
Diploma of Stephen, Duke of Slavonia, Croatia, and Dalmatia concerning Cologne, Huy, and Rhineland merchants. 10 August 1350. Historisches Archiv der Stadt Köln (HAStK), Urkundliche Überlieferung, Haupturkundenarchiv (HUA) U 2. 1968.
Diploma issued in Győr by King Louis I in a succession case. 5 December 1365. MNL OL DL 62720.
Donation of Queen Elizabeth to the Poor Clares nunnery of Óbuda. 20 January 1351. MNL OL DL 4170.
Gatterer, Johann Cristoph. *Historia Genealogica Dominorum Holzschuherorum Ab Aspach Et Harlach In Thalheim Cet. Patriciae Gentis Tum Apud Norimbergenses Tum In Exteris Etiam Regionibus Toga Sagoque Illustris Ex Incorruptis Rerum Gestarum Monimentis Conquisita*. Nuremberg: Fleischmannus, 1755.
King Louis I's charter concerning Regensburg merchants. 29 March 1371. BayHStA, Rotes Privilegienbuch, fol. 76r.
Leonard Horndl and Ludwig Königsfelder, citizens of Pozsony, acknowledged their debt to Nuremberg's citizens. MNL OL DL 44257.
Letter of John Lorzak to Breslau council. 8 May 1425. APW, AMW 1623.
Letter of Purkhart Seebach, citizen of Nuremberg, to Pozsony council. 29 February 1416. MNL OL DF 243930.
Margrave Charles of Moravia's diploma confirmation. 14 June 1338. Staatsarchiv Nürnberg (StA Nürnberg), Reichsstadt Nürnberg (RN), Päpstliche und fürstliche Privilegien, Urkunden 24a.
Permission of King Louis I to his mother Elizabeth. 9 January 1351. MNL OL DL 4168.
Permission of King Louis I to his mother Elizabeth. 29 March 1366. MNL OL DL 5445.
Pozsony council acknowledged their debt to Nuremberg's merchants. 3 March 1413. MNL OL DF 239333.
Pozsony council acknowledged their debt to Nuremberg's merchants. 6 June 1414. MNL OL DF 239353.
Privilege of King Charles I about reduced-tariff route. 6 January 1336. Archiv města Brna, Sbírka listin, mandátů a listů, A 1/1. no. 76.
Privilege of King Charles I to foreign merchants. 5 May 1336. StA Nürnberg, RN, Urkunden Münchner 510.
Privilege of King Louis I concerning Cologne, Huy, and Rhineland merchants. 13 May 1344. In HAStK, HUA U 2. 1771.
Privilege of King Louis I, concerning Nuremberg merchants. 29 July 1357. StA Nürnberg, RN, Päpstliche und fürstliche Privilegien, Urkunden 50.
Privilege of King Louis I, concerning Prague merchants. 29 July 1357. AMP, Pergamenové listiny (PGL) I. 10.

Proclamation of Charles IV concerning Nuremberg merchants. 2 November 1347. StA Nürnberg, RN, Kaiserl. Privilegien, Urkunden 58.
Transcript of King Louis I's diploma of 29 July 1357. November 1469. StA Nürnberg, RN, Ratskanzlei, A-Laden, Urkunden 60 a.
Transcript of King Louis I's diplomas of 29 July 1357. 27 June 1497. AMP, PGL I. 26.
Transcript of king Louis I's diploma of 29 July 1357. 15 July 1460. StA Nürnberg, Reichsstadt Nürnberg, Losungamt, 7-farbiges Alphabet, Urkunden 2352.
Transcript of King Louis I's diploma of 29 July 1357. 7 November 1469. StA Nürnberg, Reichsstadt Nürnberg, Ratskanzlei, A-Laden, Urkunden 60.
Transcript of Queen Mary of 26 June 1383. 15 July 1460. StA Nürnberg, RN, Losungamt, 7-farbiges Alphabet, Urkunden 2844.
Transcript of Sebald, abbot of Saint Giles' monastery's diploma of 7 November 1469. 22 February 1469. StA Nürnberg, RN, Päpstliche und fürstliche Privilegien, Urkunden 323.
Transcript of Sebald, abbot of Saint Giles' monastery's diploma of 7 November 1469. 27 June 1497. StA Nürnberg, RN, Päpstliche und fürstliche Privilegien, Urkunden 404.
Truce of 1371, between King Louis I, Otto V, Duke of Bavaria, Pilgrim II, Prince-Archbishop of Salzburg and Charles IV. MNL OL DF 258468.
Ungeld prohibition of King John of Bohemia. 23 August 1339. StA Nürnberg, RN, Päpstliche und fürstliche Privilegien, Urkunden 24b.
Writ of royal tavernicus Lawrence to the toll collectors in Sempte and Farkashida. 10 March 1345. HAStK, HUA U 1. 1803.
Writ of King Louis I to Archbishop Nicholas of Esztergom. 16 June 1366. MNL OL DL 61219.
Writ of King Louis I to chapter of Transylvanian issued in Gyulafehérvár. 14 July 1366. MNL OL DL 30393.
Wit of King Louis I to towns and villages issued in Lippa. 20 July 1366. MNL OL DF 285833.

Edited Sources and Literature

Altmann, Wilhelm (ed.). *Regesta Imperii XI/1–2. Urkunden Kaiser Sigmunds (1410–1437)*. Innsbruck, 1896–1900.
Ammann, Hektor. Huy an der Maas in der mittelalterlichen Wirtschaft. In *Altständisches Bürgertum*, vol. II, Heinz Stoob (ed.). Darmstadt: Wissenschaftliche Buchgesellschaft, 1978, 210–248.
Bauch, Alfred. Ein vergessener Schüler Albrecht Dürer's. *Mitteilungen aus dem germanischen Nationalmuseum* (1896): 3–15.
Bauernfeind, Walter. Güterbestätter. In *Stadtlexikon Nürnberg*, Michael Diefenbacher, Rudolf Endres (eds.). Nuremberg: Tümmel, 1999, 391.
Biebinger, Wilhelm, Wilhelm, Neukam (eds.). *Quellen zur Handelsgeschichte der Stadt Nürnberg seit 1400*. vol. I/1. Erlangen: Palm and Enke, 1934.
Blechová, Lenka, Karel Jaromír Erben, Josef Emler, Helena Krmíčková, Milena Linhartová, Bendřich Mendl, Blažena Rynešová, Jirí Spěváček, Jana Zachová (eds.). *Regesta diplomatica nec non epistolaria Bohemiae et Moraviae*. 8 vols. Prague, 1855–2014.
Böhmer, Johann Friedrich (ed.). *Regesta Imperii VIII. Die Regesten des Kaisereichs unter Kaiser Karl IV. 1346–1378*. Innsbruck: Wagner, 1877.
Boehmer, Johann Friedrich (ed.). *Codex diplomaticus Moenofrancofurtanus. Urkundenbuch der Reichstadt Frankfurt*. Frankfurt am Main: Franz Varrentrapp, 1836.

Braunstein, Philippe. Wirtschaftliche Beziehungen zwischen Nürnberg und Italien im Spätmittelalter. In *Beiträge zur Wirtschaftsgeschichte Nürnberg*, vol. I, Stadtarchiv Nürnberg (ed.). Nuremberg: Selbstverlag des Stadtrats zu Nürnberg, 1967, 377–406.

Bretholz, Berthold. *Geschichte der Stadt Brünn*, vol. I. Brünn: Verlag des Vereins, 1911.

Bretholz, Berthold, Anton Boczek, Vincenz Brandl, Peter Ritter von Chlumecky, Josef Chytil (eds.). *Codex diplomaticus et epistolaris Moravie*. 15 vols. Brünn, 1836–1903.

Celakovský, Jaromir, Gustav Friedrich, Antonín Haas (eds.). *Codex iuris municipalis regni Bohemiae*. 4 vols. Prague, 1886–1961.

Csendes, Peter. Vom späten 14. Jahrhundert bis zur Ersten Wiener Türkenbelagerung (1529). In *Wien. Geschichte einer Stadt*, vol. I, Peter Csendes, Ferdinand Opll (eds.). Vienna: Böhlau, 2001, 145–198.

Czeike, Felix. Hansgraf. In *Historisches Lexikon Wien III*, Felix Czeike (ed.). Vienna: Kremayr and Scheriau, 1994, 52.

Czeike, Felix. Regensburger Hof. In *Historisches Lexikon Wien IV*, Felix Czeike (ed.). Vienna: Kremayr and Scheriau, 1995, 646.

Draskóczy, István. Commercial Contacts of Buda along the Danube and beyond. In *Medieval Buda in Context*, Balázs Nagy, Martyn Rady, Katalin Szende, András Vadas (eds.). Leiden, Boston: Brill, 2016, 278–299.

Fischer, Klaus. *Regensburger Hochfinanz. Die Krise einer europäischen Metropole an der Wende zur Neuzeit*. Regensburg: Universitätsverlag, 2003.

Fleischmann, Peter. *Rat und Patriziat in Nürnberg. Die Herrschaft der Ratsgeschlechter vom 13. bis zum 18. Jahrhundert*. 3 vols. Nuremberg: Verein für Geschichte der Stadt Nürnberg, 1967.

Giesen, Josef. Die Kölner Hof in Wien. *Jahrbuch des Kölnischen Geschichtsvereins* 34–35 (1959/1960): 195–198.

Gneiss, Markus. *Das Wiener Handwerksordnungsbuch (1364–1555). Edition und Kommentar*. Vienna: Böhlau, 2017.

Grünn, Albert. I. Lajos király megerősítő záradéka. *Turul* 19 (1901): 29–33.

Gündisch, Gustav, Herta Gündisch, Konrad G. Gündisch, Georg Müller, Gernot Nussbächer, Carl Werner, Franz Zimmermann (eds.). *Urkundenbuch zur Geschichte der Deutschen in Siebenbürgen*. 7 vols. Hermannstadt, Bucharest, 1892–1991.

Halász, Éva B. Anjou István herceg (1332–1354). In *Hercegek és hercegségek a középkori Magyarországon*, Zsoldos Attila (ed.). Székesfehérvár: Városi Levéltár és Kutatóintézet, 2016, 81–94.

Hirschfelder, Günther. *Die Kölner Handelsbeziehungen im Spätmittelalter*. Cologne: Kölnisches Stadt Museum, 1994.

Hirschmann, Gerhard. Nürnbergs Handelsprivilegien, Zollfreiheiten und Zollverträge bis 1399. In *Beiträge zur Wirtschaftsgeschichte Nürnbergs*, Stadtarchiv Nürnberg (ed.), 1–48.

Irsigler, Franz. *Die wirtschaftliche Stellung der Stadt Köln im 14. und 15. Jahrhundert. Stukturanalyse einer Spätmittelalterlichen Exportgewerbe- und Fernhandelsstadt*. Wiesbaden: Franz Steiner, 1979.

Joris, André. Documents concernant le Commerce de Huy avec la Bohême et la Haute-Meuse (XIIIe–XIVe siècles). *Bulletin de la Commission royale d'Histoire* 137 (1971): 1–37.

Kováts, Ferenc. A magyar arany világtörténeti jelentősége és kereskedelmi összeköttetéseink a nyugattal. *Történelmi Szemle* 11 (1922): 104–143.

Kováts, Franz. Handelsverbindungen zwischen Köln und Pressburg (Pozsony) im Spätmittelalter. *Mitteilungen aus dem Stadtarchiv von Köln* 35 (1914): 1–32.

Kubinyi, András. Die Nürnberger Haller in Ofen. Ein Beitrag zur Geschichte des Südosthandels im Spätmittealter. *Mitteilungen des Vereins für Geschichte der Stadt Nürnberg* 52 (1963/1964): 89–97.

Lackner, Christian, Claudia Feller (eds.). *Regesta Habsburgica V. Die Regesten der Herzoge von Österreich aus dem Hause Habsburg V. Abteilung: Die Regesten der Herzoge von Österreich 1365–1395. 1. Teilband (1365–1370).* Vienna, Munich: Böhlau, 2007.

Lederer, Emma. *A középkori pénzüzletek története Magyarországon, 1000–1458.* Budapest: Kovács J. ny., 1932.

Ljubić, Sime (ed.). *Monumenta spectantia historiam Slavorum meridionalium. Listine o odnošajih između južnoga Slavenstva i mletačke republike.* 9 vols. Zagreb: Academia Scientiarum et Artium Slavorum Meridionalium, 1868–1891.

Marquard, Jeanine, Nico Nolden, Jürgen Sarnowsky (eds.). *Hamburgs Gedächtnis—die Threse des Hamburger Rates: Die Regesten der Urkunden im Staatsarchiv der Freien und Hansestadt Hamburg.* 2 vols. Hamburg: Hamburg University Press, 2014–2021.

Mayer, Theodor. *Der auswärtige Handel des Herzogtums Österreich im Mittelalter.* Innsbruck: Verlag der Wagner'schen Universitäts-Buchhandlung, 1909.

Militzer, Klaus. Kölner Kaufleute im Preßburg und im Donauraum im 14. und 15. Jahrhundert. In *Städte im Donauraum. Sammelband der Beiträge aus dem Symposion in Smolenice 30.9.–3.10. 1991, Bratislava–Pressburg 1291–1991*, Richard Marsina (ed.). Bratislava: Slovenská historická spolocnost, 1993, 121–134.

Militzer, Klaus. Tuchhandel und Tuchhändler Kölns in Österreich und Ungarn um 1400. *Blätter für deutsche Landesgeschichte* 114 (1978): 265–288.

Myśliwski, Grzegorz. A Silesian Town and the Hungarian Monarchy: Economic Contacts between Wrocław and Hungary, ca. 1250–1500. In *The Medieval Networks in East Central Europe: Commerce, Contacts, Communication.* Balázs Nagy, Felicitas Schmieder, András Vadas (eds.). London, New York: Routledge, 236–262.

Neukam, Wilhelm Georg. Wege und Organisation des Bamberger Handels vor 1400. *Jahrbuch für fränkische Landesforschung* 14 (1954): 97–139.

Opll, Ferdinand. Jahrmarkt oder Messe? Überlegungen zur spätmittelalterlichen Handelsgeschichte Wiens. In *Europäische Messen und Märktesysteme in Mittelalter und Neuzeit*, Peter Johanek, Heinz Stoob (eds.). Cologne, Weimar, Vienna: Böhlau, 1996, 189–204.

Perger, Richard. Wandlungen Wiens am Ende des Mittelalters. In *Wien. Geschichte einer Stadt*, vol. I, Peter Csendes, Ferdinand Opll (eds.). Vienna: Böhlau, 2001, 241–246.

Perger, Richard. *Strassen, Türme und Basteien: das Strassennetz der Wiener City in seiner Entwicklung und seinen Namen: ein Handbuch.* Vienna: Franz Deuticke, 1991.

Péterfi, Bence. Széllel szemben. Boroszlói kísérletek Buda lerakatjogának kikerülésére a 15–16. század fordulóján. In *Márvány, tárház, adomány. Gazdaságtörténeti tanulmányok a magyar középkorról*, Kádas István, Skorka Renáta, Weisz Boglárka (eds.). Budapest: BTK Történettudományi Intézet, 2019, 385–406.

Peltzer, Rudolf Arthur. Ein Handelsprivileg des Königs Ludwig I. von Ungarn für Aachen, 1369. März 2. *Zeitschrift des Aachener Geschichtsvereins* 28 (1906): 450–453.

Schenk, Hans. *Nürnberg und Prag. Ein Beitrag zur Geschichte der Handelsbeziehungen im 14. und 15. Jahrhundert.* Wiesbaden: Otto Harrassowitz, 1969.

Schwob, Ute Monika. *Kulturelle Beziehungen zwischen Nürnberg und den Deutschen im Südosten im 14. bis 16. Jahrhundert.* Munich: Oldenbourg, 1969.

Skorka, Renáta. A bécsi lerakat Magyarországra vezető kiskapui. *Történelmi Szemle* 54 (2012): 1–16.

Skorka, Renáta. A csökkentett vámtarifájú út kialakulása I. Károly uralkodása alatt. *Történelmi Szemle* 55 (2013): 451–470.

Skorka, Renáta. Pozsony gazdasági szerepe a 15. század első felében a zálogszerződések tükrében. *Századok* 138 (2004): 433–464.

Sopron szabad királyi város története, vol. I/1–II/6. Közli Házi Jenő. Sopron, 1921–1943. (*Sopr. tört.*)

Stieda, Wilhelm. *Hansisch-Venetianische Handelsbeziehungen im 15. Jahrhundert*. Rostock: Universtäts-Buchdruckerei, 1894.

Stromer, Wolfgang. Eine gesellige Versammlung der Nürnberger Rates in Ulrich Stromers Haus und der Aufenthalt Kaiser Karls IV. in Nürnberg im Jahre 1358. *Mitteilungen des Vereins für Geschichte der Stadt Nürnberg* 52 (1963/1964): 54–64.

Stromer, Wolfgang. *Oberdeutsche Hochfinanz, 1350–1450*. 3 vols. Wiesbaden: Steiner, 1970.

Szende, Katalin G. Kölni kereskedők a középkori Sopronban. In *Tanulmányok Csatkai Endre emlékére*, Attila Környei, Katalin G. Szende (eds.). Sopron: Soproni Múzeum Alapítvány, 1996, 57–70.

Tóth, Norbert C. *A Magyar Királyság nádora. A nádori és a helytartói intézmény története (1342–1562)*. Budapest: Magyar Történelmi Társulat, 2020.

Tömöry, Edith. *Az aacheni magyar kápolna története*. Budapest: Németh József, 1931.

Uhlirz, Karl (ed.). *Quellen zur Geschichte der Stadt Wien. Regesten aus dem Archive der Stadt Wien*, vols. II/1–5. Vienna: Verlag und Eigenthum des Alterthums-Vereines zu Wien, 1898–1936.

Weisz, Boglárka. *A királyketteje és az ispán harmada. Vámok és vámszedés Magyarországon a középkor első felében*. Budapest: BTK Történettudományi Intézet, 2013.

Weisz, Boglárka (ed.). *Fontes ad rem mercatoriam regni Hungariae pertinentes II. De comesciis externis (1259–1437)/Források a Magyar Királyság kereskedelemtörténetéhez II. Külkereskedelem (1259–1437)*. 2 vols. Budapest: BTK Történettudományi Intézet, 2021.

François Gipouloux

The network of temple fairs and their actors: religious communities, brokers, and merchants in late Imperial China

Introduction

A second commercial revolution[1] took place in China in the mid-sixteenth century with the opening up of new trade routes, the formation of trans-regional networks of merchants, and changes in the perception of the role of the merchant, all of which reshaped the economic fabric of the empire.[2] Within a myriad of more or less connected, nested, or disjointed small markets, three structuring forces stood out: specialised market towns, periodic markets in rural areas, and temple fairs.

Studies of the countryside have focused on the organisation of agricultural production and consumption patterns without giving full importance to markets—their radius of activity, their limits, and their periodic nature. Temple fairs (*miaohui*, 廟會), also known as "incense-burning fairs" (*xianghuohui*, 香火會) or "temple markets" (*miaoshi*, 廟市), have been an essential component of traditional Chinese markets. Temple fairs were ceremonial gatherings during which a group of buyers and sellers met at regular intervals, determined by a religious festival. One important feature to keep in mind is that during the Ming dynasty, the territorial unit was formed around the earth god (*she*, 社) who represented the entity around whom tax collection was arranged. Ming statutes required members of a territorial community to abide by the laws and maintain the moral standards of the community. In this way, the sense of belonging to a given community, conferred by territorial sacrifice, was integrated into the administrative require-

1 A preliminary version of this chapter was presented at the international conference *Configuration of European Fairs: Merchants, Objects, Routes, 1350–1600 (CoMOR)* in Turin on 30 June 2023. I would like to thank the members of the CoMOR programme, in particular Jean-Louis Gaulin and Susanne Rau for their comments. I am also grateful to Alain Arrault (École française d'Extrême Orient), Paola Calanca (École française d'Extrême Orient), David Faure (Hong Kong Chinese University), and Vincent Goossaert (École Pratique des Hautes Etudes).

2 The first commercial revolution took place under the Song in the eleventh and twelfth centuries.

https://doi.org/10.1515/9783111621296-016

ments formulated by the State. Similarly, in the city, the parade of the city gods was a replica of the magistrates' inspection tours.[3]

Temple fairs appeared very early on. Under the Northern Wei dynasty (386–534), Buddhist monastery fairs in Luoyang (in Henan province, northern China) brought together tens of thousands of people and were already playing a major economic role. Each temple held an ostension of Buddha statues, and people travelled from far and wide to witness the spectacle.[4] It was around the middle of the Ming dynasty (1368–1644) that fairs developed on a large scale. Wars and natural disasters at the end of the dynasty and the beginning of the Qing dynasty (1644–1911) led to massive losses of people and goods. Rural markets were also dislocated, before being gradually restored during the reigns of Kangxi (1661–1722) and Yongzheng (1722–1735).

Punctuated by the liturgical calendar, temple fairs were events based on the principle of offering sacrifices to various divinities. After the religious ceremony came all sorts of cultural events—traditional opera, acrobatic performances—and, of course, commercial transactions. Temple fairs were generally held before the spring ploughing season (second to fourth months of the lunisolar calendar) and after the autumn harvest (ninth to eleventh months of the lunisolar calendar).[5] Sometimes, arrangements were made to coincide a deity's birthday with a period when work in the fields was not too intense. The temple fairs were intended to satisfy farmers' needs in terms of farming implements or grain purchases during the lean season, but they also covered a much wider spectrum, as we shall see.

A number of issues here resonate with European market fairs and with the concerns of the CoMOR research programme:

1. The vitality of the fairs and their proliferation invite us to revisit the much-debated question of the city-countryside continuum and the proto-industrial impasse of late imperial China. In what way were temple fairs a relevant indicator of the intensity of commercial activities in the countryside from the middle of the Ming dynasty (1368–1644) onwards?

---

3 Zhao Shiyu. Town and Country Representation as Seen in Temple Fairs. In *Town and Country in China Identity and Perception*, David Faure, Tao Tao Liu (eds.). Basingstoke: Palgrave, 2002, 41–57.

4 Wang Xingya 王兴亚, Ma Huaiyun 马怀云. MingQing Henan miaohui yanjiu (yi) 明清河南庙会研究 (一) [Study on temple fairs during the Ming and Qing period]. *Tianzhong xuekan* 天中学刊 10:1 (1995): 23.

5 These are the months of the lunisolar calendar traditionally used in imperial China. The Chinese calendar is a combination of two calendars: a solar (agricultural) calendar and a lunisolar (civil) calendar. The first day of each month (of 29 or 30 days) coincides with the new moon and the fifteenth day with the full moon.

2. How do rural markets, specialist market towns, and temple fairs fit together in the structuring of an empire-wide market?
3. Do the temple fairs reflect the separation of commercial and financial functions that characterised the growth of trade in Europe at the end of the Middle Ages?
4. What kind of relationship did local authorities have with these events which had religious, social, and commercial implications?

This article focuses on the place of temple fairs in a highly differentiated economic structure, where proto-industrial activities in the countryside were well developed. It then analyses the links between rural markets, market towns, and temple fairs, and finally seeks to elucidate the relationship between temple fair organisers and the local administration.

Fig. 1: Map of Chinese provinces, highlighting Henan province (Shutterstock, Image-ID: 323312816).

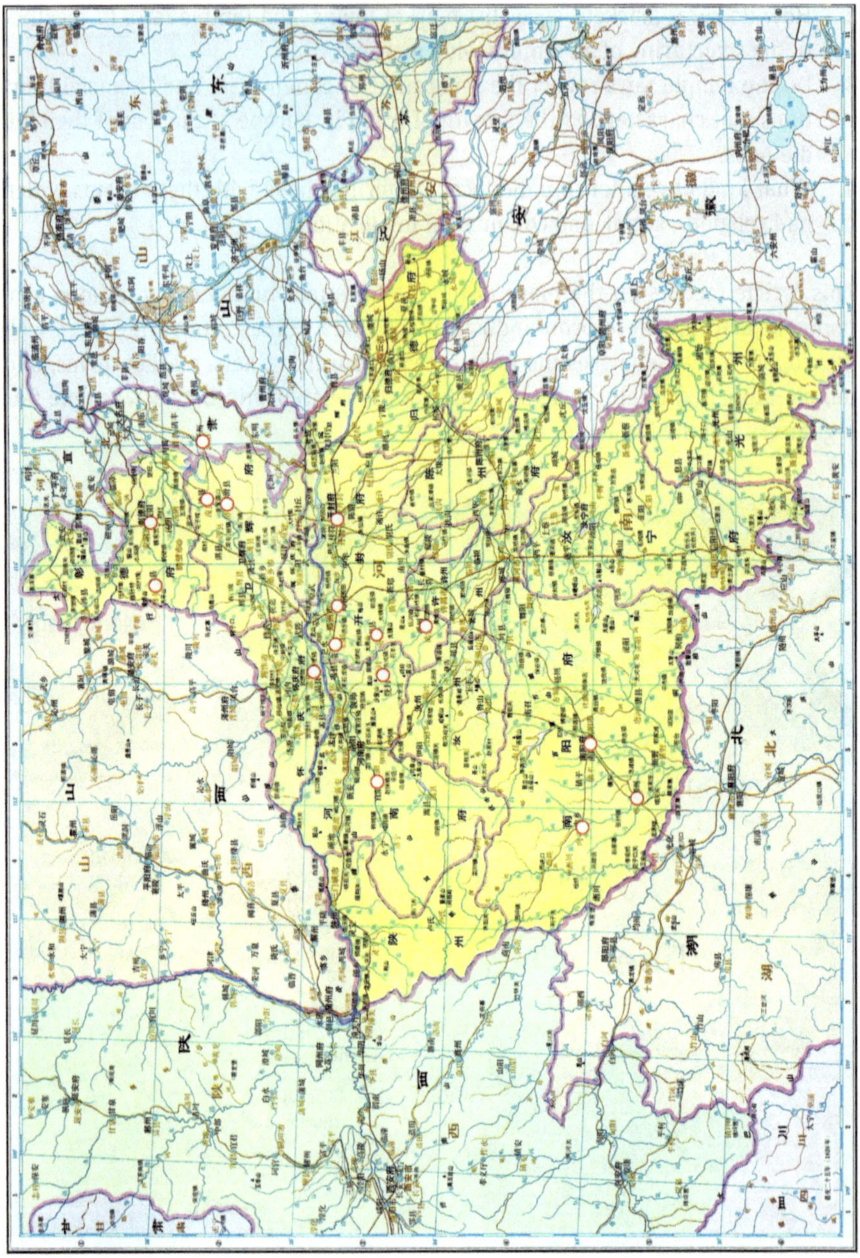

Fig. 2: Tan Qixiang, 谭其骧 *Zhongguo lishi ditu ji*, 中国历史地图集, *The Historical Atlas of China* Beijing, China Cartographic Publishing House, 1982–1988, Vol. 7 (Yuan & Ming dynasties). Henan province, p. 57–58.

The development of proto-industrial activities in the countryside: the case of Henan province

Temple fairs were held in towns, villages, or places that were neither, such as pilgrimage sites. During the Ming and Qing dynasties, Henan temple fairs were held throughout the province, in both towns and rural areas. They lasted from one day to one month. Temple fairs were located at the junction of two networks of authority: the *yamen* (local government) and the temple, whether it was a territorial temple centred on the community of inhabitants of a district or village, or other religious institutions managed by guilds of merchants or craftsmen.[6] These fairs contributed to the circulation and exchange of material goods between town and countryside as well as opening up the local economy.

Frequency of temple fairs

No exhaustive statistics have been compiled on the number of fairs held in Henan province during the Ming dynasty, but these gatherings left their mark on local chronicles (*difangzhi*) and popular literature. For example, the fair at the Temple of the City God (*chenghuang miao* 城隍廟) in the city of Dengzhou was first recorded in 1372, at the very beginning of the Ming dynasty. In Yongcheng district, local records indicate that during the Jiajing era (1521–1567), the Prince's Fair (*wang hui*, 王會) was held on the thirteenth day of the fifth month.[7]

Buddhist temples (*si* 寺), temples of the ancestors (*ci* 祠), or Taoist temples (*gong* 宫, *guan* 觀 or *miao* 廟)—these various establishments were all eligible to hold fairs throughout the year. The temple fairs were, in fact, as we have seen, directly associated with the local gods and goddesses. Thousands of deities were venerated in Chinese temples: they belonged to the Buddhist or Taoist pantheon, to popular or community religions, but also represented the patrons of commerce, medicine, fire, and many more. The most influential deities in Henan province included the Dragon King, the God of Soil, the God of Wealth, the God of Fire, Maitreya, etc. There was a clear link between the proliferation of temples and fairs.[8] Each district of Henan organised several hundred temple fairs every year. There were 231 temple fairs in the Lin district, 243 in the Wen district,

6 Vincent Goossaert. La gestion des temples chinois au XIXe siècle: droit coutumier ou laisser-faire?. La coutume et la norme en Chine et au Japon. *Extrême-Orient, Extrême-Occident* 23 (2001): 10.
7 Wang, Ma, MingQing Henan miaohui yanjiu (yi), 23.
8 Wang, Ma, MingQing Henan miaohui yanjiu (yi), 21.

247 in the Rongyang district, 269 in the Shi district, 283 in the Huaiyang district, 450 in the Mi district, and 600 in the Yu district.[9]

Kaifeng, the capital of Henan province, had a population of over a million under the Ming and Qing dynasties, and fairs were held in every street where there was a temple. A book from the early Qing dynasty, recording accounts handed down from ancient times, reported that in Kaifeng there were, among the temples and sanctuaries, some dedicated to the Boddhisattva Kṣitigarbha (*dizangwang* 地藏王), who comes to the rescue of the dead in the underworld, and some dedicated to the god and judge of the dead, the ruler of the underworld (Yanwang 閻 王). To these were added temples dedicated to the King of Medicine (Yaowang 藥王), Guandi (關帝), the holy warrior who personifies righteousness and courage, Caishen (財神), the god of Wealth, and Maitreya (Mile 弥 勒).[10]

Proliferation of fairs in the countryside

Whether they took place on a regular or irregular basis, not all temple fairs were necessarily held in a district capital or even in densely populated villages. What is more, their size varied considerably from one place to another: some were attended by just a few hundred people, while others brought together thousands or even tens of thousands. The decision to hold a fair did not depend on government initiatives, nor was it linked to the economic situation of the locality where the temple was located. A determining factor seems to have been the prestige enjoyed by the deities of the temples in which they were held, as demonstrated by the fame of the Lingshan fair in the Yiyang district, the fair at the Dushan zushi temple in Nanyang, and the fair at the Taishan temple on Fuchu mountain in Jun district. Their implicit aim, from the point of view of the religious community, was to attract worshippers and increase donations.

During the reign of Qianlong (1735–1796), there were no less than a thousand temple fairs in the Lin district, both in market towns and in rural areas. But fairs were also held in ordinary towns. Under the Ming and Qing dynasties, temple fairs were spread throughout the province in a denser network than the marketplaces in Skinner's typology.[11] In fact, temple fairs filled gaps in the market and continued to grow and prosper throughout these two dynasties.

9 Wang, Ma, MingQing Henan miaohui yanjiu (yi), 22.

10 Wang, Ma, MingQing Henan miaohui yanjiu (yi), 22.

11 William G. Skinner. Marketing and Social Structure in Rural China: Part I. *Journal of Asian Studies* 24:1 (1964): 3–43.

Date setting and duration of temple fairs

The date of a fair was generally set according to the day on which sacrifices had to be made (*jiri* 祭日) or on the birthday (*dan* 誕) of the temple's tutelary deities. The seventh day of the first lunar month was celebrated as the birthday of the Fire God while the ninth day of the first month was celebrated the birthday of the God of Jade, the God of Wealth was celebrated on the 21st day of the seventh month, and so on. But fairs were also held according to the needs of agricultural activity.

The duration of the fairs varied considerably from one temple to another: ranging from one to five days or from nine to eighteen days in most cases, they could last over a month or even longer, as was the case with the Temple of the City God in Zhengzhou.[12] The duration of the fairs was determined by a number of factors: the prosperity of the local economy, the prestige of the temple in the eyes of the local population, as well as its geographical location and ease of access. However, it should also be noted that the duration of the fairs depended on two other factors: the scale of the festivities (opera, acrobatic shows, and suchlike) organised to thank the deities, and the progress of the commercial negotiations, which took longer than the sale of products at the regular markets, given that temple fairs typically involved high-quality—and therefore expensive—items.

Organisation and management

As fairs were associated with temples, organising them required the involvement of temple association officials (*huishou*, 會首). Yet there were no institutions or officials specifically designated to take charge of the preparation and management of fairs under the Ming and Qing dynasties. Instead, the head of the local assembly, also known as the head of the religious community,[13] was in charge. This was usually a well-known and respected figure who was appointed by the residents (by drawing lots or by rotation between the heads of different families) for a term of one to three years. Various trades also formed communities.[14] In the *Lu Book of Customs (Lushi minsu zhi,* 卢氏民俗志), it is noted that "the head of

12 See details in Wang, Ma, MingQing Henan miaohui yanjiu, 23–24.

13 Called *huishou*, 會首, head of religious association, or "head of the gods"*(sheshou*, 社首, *huizhang* 會長, *huitou* 會頭, *shentou* 神頭).

14 For example, the Xiao Cao Association for civil servants, the Wen Chang Association for scholars, the Wu Sheng Guild for merchants, and Lu Ban Zao Jun 鲁班灶君 for carpenters and the God of the Home (*gongren*). See Wang, Ma, Ming Qing Henan miaohui yanjiu, 25.

the community (*huitou*, 會頭) was responsible for all matters relating to the organisation and management of the temple fair."[15] In practical terms, this meant that in winter and spring, the peasant community collected funds and formed a group to go and buy incense in the neighbouring town.

One of the functions of the temple fairs was to forge lasting and extensive commercial links. The event lent itself to this because it combined the performance of religious rites (burning incense), almsgiving to beggar monks, and trade—the purchase of incense sticks, food for pilgrims, and various utensils for everyday use. Yang Shida, magistrate of Tangying district during the reign of Qianglong (1735–1796), put it bluntly: "To institute a temple fair is to attract merchants."[16]

To ensure that transactions ran smoothly, some of the major fairs planned the location and layout of the various stalls in advance, depending on the goods on sale. During the reign of Kangxi (1661–1722), the temple fair at Dengfeng in Henan province was organised into a large number of stalls, each with a specific function. There were stalls for farm implements, bazaar items, metal goods, needles, umbrellas, fabrics, powders, hats, fans, Beijing goods, books, medicines, copper goods, silk, second-hand clothes, fabrics, black and white goods (*heibai huo*), hard goods, soft goods, hanging goods, and foreign goods. Each stall had a manager responsible for ensuring that exhibitors set up their stands in accordance with the designated locations.[17]

The organisation of a fair involved considerable expenditure, for which the entire local community was called upon. The financial resources allocated to the preparation and organisation of a temple fair came from the remaining funds raised for the construction or repair of the temple, donations made by the faithful, and income from the land owned by the temples (*miaotian* 廟田). But these three sources of income were far from sufficient to cover the expenses incurred by most of the fairs: the manufacture and installation of decorations, the processions, the performance of the various rituals, the erection of altars, and the organisation of recreational activities all proved very costly. Whether Buddhist or Taoist, the members of a community retained their religious beliefs but were nonetheless obliged to contribute financially to the fairs at the temple irrespective of its religious affiliation, because it was the symbol of the common good. Buddhism and Taoism were very much at home with this type of communal religion.[18]

15 Cao Jincai 曹金财. Lushi minsu zhi 卢氏民俗志 [Folklore record of Lushi]. Zhengzhou: zhongzhou gujichubanshe, 1991, quoted by Wang, Ma, Ming Qing Henan miaohui yanjiu, 25.

16 Wang, Ma, Ming Qing Henan miaohui yanjiu, 26.

17 Wang, Ma, MingQing Henan miaohui yanjiu (yi), 26.

18 Wu Cheng-han. *The temple fairs in late imperial China*. Princeton: Princeton University Press, 1988, 125.

Fees had to be levied on local merchants and taxes collected on stalls and transactions carried out during the fair. This was not a general rule, but Wang and Ma report that in Henan province, half of the sums collected went to the administration, with the remainder going to the temple to cover its maintenance and repair costs. However, mutual distrust must have been the order of the day, as the sources provide abundant documentation of stormy meetings of the tax collection committee.[19] Last but not least, voluntary contributions (*juanzhu* 捐助) were solicited, which were often more or less forced donations.[20] There were, however, some compensations: the day after the end of the festivities was a day of great drinking, as certain literary accounts in the vernacular language testify:

> When the shows and ceremonies were over and the crowds had left, only the elders who ran the fair remained to share the god's blessings by eating what was left of the offerings. The festivities continued to the point of intoxication. This is a custom that has been established for many years.[21]

Typology of temple fairs

An initial typology of temple fairs can thus be sketched out here, based on their field of activity and location:

- Fairs, the main purpose of which was to sell basic necessities such as firewood, oil, salt, dried fruit, garlic noodles, tea, and groceries but also manufactured goods such as tables, chairs, stools, clothes boxes, make-up boxes, shelves, bookcases, mirrors, brocade clothes, tinware, soap, crockery, silk coupons, scarves, combs, felt blankets, shoes, velvet, oiled boots, mud clogs, umbrellas, satin boots for men and women, ink, ink stones, straw shoes.
- Fairs specialising in the sale of agricultural equipment such as ploughs, spades, hoes, hoe and spade handles, whip handles, scythes, sickles, knives, spades, brooms, netting, ropes, traction equipment, axles, bamboo items, rain hats, straw hats, etc. This type of fair was held in the spring and summer.
- Fairs specialising in the sale of livestock. The temple fair in Anyang district to the north of Henan province was a fair for mules and horses and also sold all the items needed to harness them. In the district of Neixiang to the southwest of the province, the Neihu temple fair was devoted to cattle and horses, although pigs and sheep were also sold.

19 Wang, Ma, MingQing Henan miaohui yanjiu (yi), 26.
20 Wang, Ma, MingQing Henan miaohui yanjiu (yi), 26. See also Wu, *Temple fairs*, 122.
21 Ling, Mengchu 凌濛初. *Erke pai'an jingqi* 二刻拍案驚奇. Taipei: Zhengzhong shuju 正中書局, 1977, ch. 2: 16, cited by Wu, *Temple fairs*, 123.

- Fairs specialising in the trade of medicinal herbs (Henan province was a renowned producer of medicinal plants).
- Fairs specialising in the sale of stationery and theatrical utensils, such as the scholar's "Four Treasures" (paper, ink, inkstone, brushes), flutes, trumpets, gongs, swords, arrows, knives, masks of the Monkey King and other famous characters from Chinese operas, paper roosters, embroidered handkerchiefs, bibs, bracelets, necklaces, padlocks, and more.

In Jiangnan, there were temple fairs specialising in silk around Lake Tai, a major centre of sericulture in the lower reaches of the Yangzi River:

> Whenever there was a new silk market, customers gathered. In the town of Linghu, many silk merchants from all directions came to Ling'ao, and in the 4th and 5th months, boats laden with silk lined the creek and moored up to 50 kms upstream and downstream of Linghu.[22]

The links between rural market networks, specialised market towns, and temple fairs

Moving on from Henan province, we shall now examine the situation in other provinces of the empire to understand the difference between periodic markets and fairs, a local chronicle describing the economic situation in a poor district of Shanxi province in 1765 provides the following information:

> The city market, which opens every morning, is located on Mingyuan Street (明遠街). There are also three temple fairs held from 1st to 6th day of the fourth month, from 24th to 28th day of the seventh month, and from 1st to 6th day of the tenth month. The small market and around a hundred shops are located in Mingyuan street, but only supply items such as fabrics, cereals, vegetables and firewood. Other goods are sold at the fairs.[23]

Temple fairs therefore differed from both periodic markets and the sedentary trade offered by shops in that they offered items that the latter could not supply. With regard to the relationship between periodic markets and temple fairs, there are two points to be made here: 1) Compared with rural markets, temple fairs covered a wider range of goods, but the nature of the two events was different. Their relationship is more complementary than competitive. 2) The temple fairs

22 Quoted in Chen, Xuewen, 陈学文. MingQing shiqi Huzhoufu shizhen jingji de fazhan, 明清时期湖州府市镇经济的发展 [Development of Town Economy in Huzhou Prefecture during Ming and Qing Periods]. *Journal of Zhejiang*, 浙江学刊 4 (1989): 88–94.

23 *Tongguan xianzhi*, 同官縣志 [Shansi] (1765), ch. 2: 3, quoted in Wu, *Temple Fairs*, 105.

were essential support points in the formation of long-distance trade networks, which in turn contributed to the relative economic integration of an immense empire.

The function of rural markets

At the most basic level, it was obviously the rural markets that met the needs of small farmers in terms of production and subsistence. Although rural markets have a long history, they only really expanded under the Ming and Qing dynasties. The function of rural fairs was to satisfy peasant needs in terms of agricultural equipment and to facilitate the distribution of resources (surplus grain, in particular). From this point of view, they consolidated, as it were, a system of self-sufficiency in the countryside.

Each individual market compensated for surpluses and shortages between smallholders to meet their respective needs. However, the function of the network of rural markets went beyond this, providing the basis for the distribution of goods on a large scale and over long distances. For a long time, goods traded in China's commercial system passed through the cities, while the countryside was kept out of the way. Under the Ming and Qing dynasties, this pattern of trade changed radically: basic necessities were combined with luxury goods in long-distance trade, and small farmers became both producers and consumers of these different items. The rural and the urban, the small farmer and the market, – as well as the national circulation of goods – were now linked.

Rural markets had to be reachable in less than half a day's walk and, in mountainous areas, in a day's walk; in regions crisscrossed by rivers, the journey was much shorter as there were waterways. The network of rural markets was a decisive link in an economy dominated by smallholders. It was formed as a result of the marketing of basic products and made it possible to optimise the distribution of resources through the movement of goods between regions. This regular, large-scale movement linked regions with different natural environments and degrees of development. In other words, the movement of goods made it possible to redistribute work between regions and optimise the allocation of resources.

The network of rural markets was fully established in most Chinese regions during the reigns of Qianlong (1735–1796) and Daoguang (1820–1850). This network, made up of market towns and cities, enabled fluid communication between rural and urban markets and became the vehicle for a national system for the movement of goods. As a place of sociability and a point of contact with the outside world, the market functioned as an irreplaceable forum for the exchange of information, spreading news from one village to another on such matters as safety in the countryside, banditry, epidemics, etc.[24] Ultimately, however, rural markets ensured the perpetuation of a peasant economy made up of a myriad of small producers.

Temple fairs: merchant terminals in a distant trade network

Finally, temple fairs were crucial nodes in long-distance trade networks. The example of the temple fair held every year from the fifteenth to the twentieth day of the third month in Dali, a prefecture of Yunnan province in south-west China, is illuminating. In the sixteenth century, it attracted merchants from the rest of the empire.[25] This is a measure of the efficiency of the long-distance trade network without which itinerant merchants from distant provinces would not have been able to arrive in time to attend a fair that lasted just five days. The fairs therefore functioned as trading terminals for everyday consumer goods transported over medium and long distances by peddlers.

Market towns and specialisation

The third component of this empire-wide trading system was the market towns. These played a key role in structuring rural markets. However, just like the larger towns, they could also have their own fairs. Opening at midday and closing at dusk, these fairs enabled peasants to sell their fresh produce (fruit, vegetables, and fish) and city dwellers to buy supplies. The town of Wangjiangjing in Zhejiang province had various fairs specialising in salt, rice, fish, and seafood.[26] The participants in these urban fairs were essentially peasants, merchants, and city dwellers. However, it is fair to say that these fairs had lost their original function and had become integrated into the general landscape of the urban economy.

Using the methodology developed by the German geographer Walter Christaller, William G. Skinner established an equivalence between market towns and rural markets.[27] But China's economic fabric was far from homogeneous. Dense and prosperous in the lower reaches of the Yangzi river, it was much less so in the central and western regions of the empire. As a number of recent studies have shown, many reg-

24 See C.K. Yang. *A North China Market Economy*. New York: Institute of Pacific Relations, 1944, 13.

25 *Dalifu zhi* 大理府志 [Gazetteer of the Dali Prefecture, Yunnan] (1563), vol. II: 62, quoted in Wu, *Temple Fairs*, 109.

26 Ren Fang. The rural market in late imperial China. *Asian Social Science* 6 (2010): 43.

27 Skinner, Marketing and Social Structure, 3–43.

ular, uniform markets appeared in the countryside rather than in towns.[28] In regions with ethnic minorities or in frontier areas, trade was difficult and the economy was underdeveloped. Rural fairs provided a remedy for the absence of medium-sized towns and the atrophy of market mechanisms. It is therefore unfounded to imagine periodic markets with a uniform distribution across the whole of China.

Moreover, Fu Yiling, one of the pioneers of the economic and social history of China, considerably renewed the paradigm of urban studies of the Jiangnan region by developing the concept of the specialised town (*zhuanyezhen* 專業鎮).[29] The first factor to be taken into account here is the high degree of specialisation in rural society. This varies greatly from one region to another. In Jiangnan, for example, far from producing everything they needed, peasants concentrated on producing certain goods and relied on the market to acquire others. Although there were also markets for rice, most of the commercial activity in the towns along the lower reaches of the Yangzi river concerned the purchase of textiles made by rural producers. The buyers—itinerant merchants—had plenty of cash at their disposal and used brokers to buy the produce made by farmers during the off-season.[30]

When broadening the scope of the analysis, one can observe that during the Ming and Qing dynasties, in certain regions such as Jiangnan, cash crops accounted for 60% to 70% of the value of all agricultural production.[31] As agricul-

28 Fang Xing 方行. Qingdai qianqi nongcun shichang de fazhan 清代前期农村市场的发展, [Development of Rural Markets in Early Qing], lishi yanjiu 历史研究. *Historical Research* 6 (1987): 78–93; Huang Qichen 黄启臣. MingQing zhujiang sanjiaozhou shangye yi shangren ziben de fazhan 明清珠江三角洲商业与商人资本的发展 [Development in Business and Merchant Capital of Pearl River Delta in Ming and Qing Dynasties] Zhongguo shehui jingji yanjiu 中国社会经济史研究 . *Studies on History of Society and Economy in China* 3 (1984): 37–50; Li Longqian. 李龙潜, MingQing Guangdong shehui jingji yanjiu 明清广东社会经济研究. *Research on Society and Economy of Guangdong in Ming and Qing Dynasties*. Shanghai: Shanghai Ancient Books Publishing Company, 2006, 120–169; Xu Tan, 許檀 MingQing shiqi chengxiang shichang wangluo tixi de xingchengji yiyi 明清时期城乡市场网络体系的形成及意义 [The Formation and Significance of the Urban and Rural Market Network System in the Ming and Qing Dynasties]. Beijing: Social Science Press, 1998, 298–302; 305–306.

29 Fu, Yiling 傅衣凌. MingQing shidai Jiangnan shizhen jingji de fenxi 明清时代江南市镇经济的分析 [Analysis of Town Economy in the Lower Reaches of the Yangze River during Ming and Qing Ages], lishi jiaoxue 历史教学. *History Teaching* 5 (1964): 9–13.

30 The phenomenon has been well studied by Li Bozhong. 李伯重. Jiangnan de zaoqi gongyehua (1550–1850) 江南的早期工业化 (1550–1850) [Early Industrialization in the Lower Reaches of the Yangze River (1550–1850)]. *Asian Social Science* 6 (2010): 42–49.

31 Liu Shiji, 劉石吉. MingQing shidai Jiangnan diqu de zhuanye shizhen 明清時代江南地區的專業市鎮 [Professional Towns in the Lower Reaches of the Yangze River during Ming and Qing Ages]. *Shihuo yuekan* 食貨月刊 *Economy Taipei* 6 (1978): 26–43, 7, 30–41, 8, 15–30.

ture became more diversified, demand in rural areas increased and trading centres multiplied. Becoming the focal point of a rural area, the specialised market town gained a more complete economic structure fulfilling a dual function: first, as a concentration point for the distribution and processing of the region's agricultural produce, and second, as a retail centre for the livelihoods of the region's farmers. In the lower reaches of the Yangzi river, the market towns specialised in products such as cotton yarns and fabrics, mulberry trees, silkworm rearing, woven silk, and rice. There were also more than a dozen market towns specialising in salt, oil, paintbrushes, mining and metal products, pottery,[32] fish farming, mountain products,[33] embroidery, tobacco, cart making, shipbuilding, and services such as freight transport.[34]

In the coastal regions, there were also a number of districts where merchants converged and markets were held day after day. Markets were held daily in the districts of Haiyang (Shandong) and Chenghai (Guangdong). In the middle reaches of the Gan river in Jiangxi province, there were four or five market periods every ten days. Under the Qing dynasty, there were one, two, three, or five markets opening three or four times a month, and so on. By the reign of Qianlong (1735–1796), most of the country's provinces and regions had formed a network of rural markets covering a vast area and operating freely. This network of basic markets was linked to the commercial towns located on the main distribution routes, bridging the gap between urban and rural markets and forming a national commodities distribution network. Thanks to this network, virtually every district and even every village had economic links with other provinces and regions.

Trade fairs and local government

The establishment or cancellation of a rural fair was generally decided by the district magistrate, the smallest and last administrative unit in the empire where a representative of imperial authority still sat.[35] As a general rule, the local authorities viewed the fairs favourably because this festive occasion helped to calm tensions and perpetuate or restore social harmony. Most of the time, the local govern-

32 Shushanzhen, Qianjiayaozhen, Lutouzhen, Pinyaozhen.

33 Shanmaizhen.

34 Chen Zhongping 陈忠平. MingQing shiqi Jiangnan diqu shichang kaocha 明清时期江南地区市场考察 [An Examination of the Market in Jiangnan area during the Ming and Qing Dynasties], *Zhongguo jingjishi yanjiu* 中国经济史研究 2 (1990): 24–40.

35 Ren, The rural market, 42–49.

ment did not interfere in the running of the fairs and let the trade take its course. According to the neo-Confucian orthodoxy in force, the vocation of virtuous government was to act with humanity and concern for the living conditions of the population.

From this point of view, facilitating the establishment of a market and the movement of goods through fairs could only be seen as a positive contribution to maintaining social peace. The magistrate did not act alone in this endeavour—his actions were relayed by powerful clans and influential notables who formed the backbone of local society, such as retired civil servants, scholars, landowners, and wealthy merchants.

By contrast, the management of temple fairs under the Ming and Qing was, as we have seen, the responsibility of the local communities and enjoyed the benevolent attention of the administrative authority. However, the heads of the various local communities were not chosen from among the officials in place, were not appointed by the government, and did not receive subsidies or preferential treatment. Although the benevolence of the administration was also perceptible, it was tempered by numerous difficulties—such as chronic understaffing, inadequacy, and corruption—in the system of taxation imposed on the fairs.

The tax system applicable to trade fairs

Due to insufficient manpower, most local administrations preferred to require an annual quota set in the form of a licence imposed on brokerage firms (*yatieshui* 牙貼稅). According to an early seventeenth-century source:

> In addition to the four social categories—scholars, farmers, craftsmen and merchants—brokers make up the largest group. They are commonly known as "agents" (*jingji* 經紀) and are all licensed by the local authorities. Without their intervention, any attempt to hire carts, boats or pack animals to transport fish, salt, beans or grain is doomed to failure. In addition to the usual fees, they must be paid an extra commission.[36]

At the fairs of certain well-known temples that attracted large numbers of worshippers, the local authorities tried to levy a tax on the donations of worshippers rather than on the goods traded. The high cost of collecting trade taxes at the many small fairs scattered across the countryside made regular taxation of these fairs virtually impossible. To tax medium-sized fairs, the local administration

36 *Yangzhoufu zhi*, 揚州府志 [Gazetteer of Yangzhou Prefecture], 20 (1601): 5, quoted from Wu, *Temple Fairs*, 127.

adopted an easy-to-implement but inefficient method, imposing fees on local brokers rather than itinerant merchants. When temple fairs attracted more worshippers than merchants, the taxes were levied not on the goods, but on the charitable donations of the worshippers who, in the opinion of the tax collectors themselves, were more easily identifiable.[37]

Finally, the local authorities felt that it was easier to tax large fairs where the huge volume of goods traded prevented any sudden shifts in the dates and places of trade. The issue became a technical one, but the method of levy had to be devised by a chronically understaffed local administration.

Conclusion

Temple fairs were a central part of the marketing system in late imperial China. Widely distributed throughout the empire, their sheer number formed the basis for the development of the merchant economy in the countryside. How can we situate the temple fairs in this subtle organisation of markets which link the traditional economy with a complex urban economy? Temple fairs were a particular form of market, allowing an extension of the marketing area, a diversification of the products sold, a specialisation of the markets, a relative standardisation of measures, and means of exchange. However, there are still many points on which the local chronicles provide us with no information: credit mechanisms, the circulation of capital, and the spread of financial innovations. Nevertheless, two tentative conclusions can be drawn from the above development:

1. The dissociation between goods fairs and meeting places for financiers, observed in European fairs from the late sixteenth century (Besançon, Plaisance, Novi),[38] does not seem to have occurred in China. Financing agencies (pawnbrokers, local credit institutions) remained rudimentary and modest in size. What is more, there was no evidence of the emergence of instruments guaranteed by private commercial law which would take into account the interests of merchants, secure their transactions, and encourage them to expand their businesses and start manufacturing.
2. Rural fairs and markets were a vehicle for the reproduction of the family economy in the countryside during a period (16th–18th century) when market production (cereals, cash crops) and family industry were fully developed. But the growth of rural markets meant that proto-industrial activities and

37 Wu, *Temple Fairs*, 127.
38 On this aspect, see the contributions of Markus A. Denzel and Claudio Marsilio in this volume.

textiles in particular were confined to the family. Farmers needed little investment, used rudimentary equipment, and exploited family labour during the off-season. The profitability of their production was assured if the cost of equipment and raw materials (silk or cotton) was amortised. At the other end of the chain, merchants and brokers played off the competition between peasant households and had no interest in investing to create more efficient workshops or in getting involved in the production process themselves, as demonstrated by the limited role played by merchant manufacturers.[39]

Despite the blossoming of the mercantile economy, the "high equilibrium trap" (that particular equilibrium between supply and demand formalised by Mark Elvin[40]) closed—the combination of a large population and flourishing markets broke the link that had been forged between the market and technological innovation, between the market and the spread of manufacturing techniques or financial innovations. What attracted the attention of merchants were the conditions under which the market operated, not technological improvements in the production process.

Bibliography

Literature

Chen, Xuewen. 陈学文, MingQing shiqi Huzhoufu shi zhen jingji de fazhan 明清时期湖州府市镇经济的发展 [Development of Town Economy in Huzhou Prefecture during Ming and Qing Periods]. Zhejiang xuekan 浙江学刊. *Journal of Zhejiang* 4 (1989): 88–94.

Chen, Zhongping 陈忠平. MingQing shiqi jiangnan diqu shichang kaocha 明清时期江南地区市场考察 [Inspection on Market in the Lower Reaches of the Yangze River]. Zhongguo jingjishi yanjiu 中国经济史研究. *Studies on Economic History of China* 2 (1990): 24–40.

Cooper, Gene. *The Market and Temple Fairs of Rural China: Red Fire*. London: Routledge, 2013.

Elvin, Mark. The High-Level Equilibrium Trap: The Causes of the Decline of Invention in Traditional Chinese Textile Industries. In *Economic Organization in Chinese Society*, William E. Willmott (ed.). Stanford: Stanford University Press, 1972, 137–172.

39 François Gipouloux. *Commerce, argent, pouvoir: l'impossible avènement d'un capitalisme en Chine, XVI*[e]*-XIX*[e] *siècle*. Paris: CNRS Édition, 2022, 104–105.

40 Mark Elvin. The High-Level Equilibrium Trap: the Causes of the Decline of Invention in the Traditional Chinese Textile Industries. In *Economic Organization in Chinese Society*, W.E. Willmott (ed.). Stanford: Stanford University Press, 1972, 137–172. See also Mark Elvin. *The Pattern of the Chinese Past*. Stanford: Stanford University Press, 1973, 298–315.

Fan, Jinmin 范金民. MingQing Jiangnan shangye de fazhan 明清江南商业的发展. *Commercial Development of the Lower Reaches of the Yangze River in Ming and Qing Dynasties*. Nanjing: Nanjing University Press, 1998, 134–139.

Fang, Xing 方行. Qingdai shiqi nongcun shichang de fazhan 清代前期农村市场的发展 [Development of Rural Markets in Early Qing]. Lishi yanjiu 历史研究. *Historical Research* 6 (1987): 78–93.

Fu, Yiling 傅衣凌. MingQing shidai jiangnan shizhen jingji de fenxi 明清时代江南市镇经济的分析 [Analysis of Town Economy in the Lower Reaches of the Yangze River during Ming and Qing Ages]. Lishi jiaoxue 历史教学. *History Teaching* 5 (1964): 9–13.

Fu, Yiling 傅衣凌. MingQing shehui jingji bianqian lun, 明清社会经济变迁论. *On Social and Economic Changes in Ming and Qing Dynasties*. Beijing: People's Press, 1989, 37–39.

Gipouloux, François. *Commerce, argent, pouvoir: l'impossible avènement d'un capitalisme en Chine, XVI*[e]*-XIX*[e] *siècle*. Paris: CNRS Éditions, 2022.

Goossaert, Vincent. La gestion des temples chinois au XIXe siècle: droit coutumier ou laisser-faire? *Extrême-Orient Extrême-Occident* 23 (2001): 9–25.

Goossaert, Vincent. *Dans les temples de la Chine. Histoire des cultes, vie des communautés*. Paris: Albin Michel, 2000.

Goossaert, Vincent. Resident Specialists and Temple Managers in Late Imperial China. *Min-su ch'ü-yi* 153 (2006): 25–68.

Han, Dacheng 韩大成. MingQing chengshi yanjiu 明代城市研究. *Research on City in the Ming Dynasty*. Beijing: Press of Renmin University of China, 1991.

Hua, Zhiya. Renao (Heat-noise), Deities' Efficacy, and Temple Festivals in Central and Southern Hebei Province. *Journal of Cambridge Studies* 8:3–4 (2013): 1–18.

Huang, Qichen 黄启臣. MingQing zhujiang sanjiaozhou shangye yu shangren ziben de fazhan 明清珠江三角洲商业与商人资本的发展 [Development in Business and Merchant Capital of Pearl River Delta in Ming and Qing Dynasties]. *Studies on History of Society and Economy in China* 3 (1984): 37–50.

Li, Bozhong 李伯重. Jiangnan de zaoqi gongyehua 江南的早期工业化 (1550–1850) *Early Industrialization in the Lower Reaches of the Yangze River (1550–1850)*. Beijing: Social Sciences Academic Press, 2000: 57–77.

Li, Longqian 李龙潜. MingQing shehui jingji yanjiu 明清广东社会经济研究 *Research on Society and Economy of Guangdong in Ming and Qing Dynasties*. Shanghai: Shanghai Ancient Books Publishing Company, 2006, 120–169.

Ling, Mengchu 凌濛初. *Erke pai'an jingqi* 二刻拍案驚奇正中書局. Taipei: 1977.

Liu, Shiji 劉石吉. MingQing shidai Jiangnan diqude zhuanye shizhen 明清時代江南地區的專業市鎮 [Professional Towns in the Lower Reaches of the Yangze River during Ming and Qing Ages]. shihuo yuekan 食貨月刊 *Economy* 6 (1978): 26–43; 7 (1978): 30–41; 8 (1978): 15–30.

Mosca, Matthew W. Indian Mendicants in Ming and Qing China: A Preliminary Study. Paris: Collège de France, 2017. https://books.openedition.org/cdf/7531?lang=fr (28 December 2023).

Naquin, Susan. *Peking: Temples and City Life, 1400–1900*. Berkeley: University of California Press, 2000.

Ren, Fang. The rural market in late imperial China. *Asian Social Science* 6 (2010): 42–49.

Schipper, Kristofer. Liturgical Structures and Civil Society in Beijing. *Materials for the Study of Chinese Religion—Sanjiao wenxian* 1 (1997): 9–23.

Skinner, William G. Marketing and Social Structure in Rural China: Part I. *The Journal of Asian Studies* 24:1 (1964): 3–43.

Wu, Cheng-han. *The Temple Fairs in Late Imperial China*, PhD diss., Princeton University, 1989.

Xu, Tan 許檀. MingQingshiqi chengxiang shichang wangluo tixi de xingchengji yiyi 明清时期城乡市场网络体系的形成及意义 [The Formation and Significance of the Urban and Rural Market Network System in the Ming and Qing Dynasties]. Beijing: Social Science Press, 1998.

Yang, C.K. *A North China Market Economy*. New York: Institute of Pacific Relations, 1944.

Yang, Lien-sheng. Government Control of Urban Merchants in Traditional China. *Journal of Tsinghua University* 8:1 (1970): 186–209.

Yue, Yongyi. 岳永逸. Miaohui de shengchan: Dangdai Hebei Zhao xian Li qu miaohuì de tianye kaocha 庙会的生产:当代河北赵县梨区庙会的田野考察 [The production of temple fairs: a field study of contemporary temple fairs in Li District, Zhao County, Hebei Province]. Unpublished dissertation, Beijing Normal University, 2004.

Yue, Yongyi. 岳永逸. Xiangcun miaohui de zhengzhi xue 乡村庙会的政治学 Zhongguo xiangcun yanjiu (di wu ji) 中国乡村研究(第五辑) The Politics of Rural Temple Fairs. Chinese Rural Studies (vol. 5) in Huang Zongzhi (ed.) 黄宗智主编. Fuzhou: Fujian jiaoyu chubanshe, 2007.

Zhao, Shiyu. Town and Country Representation as Seen In Temple Fairs. In *Town and Country in China: Identity and Perception*, David Faure, Tao Tao Liu (eds.). Basingstoke: Palgrave Macmillan, 2002, 41–57.

Zhao, Shiyu. 赵世瑜. *Kuanghuan yu richang: Ming qing yilai de miaohui yu minjian shehui* 狂欢与日常:明清以来的庙会与民间社会 [Carnival and Everyday Life: Temple Fairs and Civil Society since the Ming and Qing Dynasties]. Beijing: Sanlian shudian, 2002.

Markus A. Denzel

East of Leipzig: great annual markets and fairs in Poland and Muscovy up to the 17th century

Introduction

In international trade fair research, the focus is mostly on western Europe and its innovative developments.[1] This begins with the Fairs in Champagne, which are seen as the nucleus of an almost year-round fair system, and ends with the Bisenzone fairs which, highly specialised in cashless payments and the credit transactions of European high finance, can be characterised as the culmination of the development of innovative and elaborate financial techniques. The western European fair system essentially comprises France, Italy, Castile, and the Netherlands, whose fairs in their heyday were timed to coincide in a "*système de correspondance*"[2] and represented an almost year-round cycle. According to this perception, the fairs at Frankfurt am Main were initially—at least until the fifteenth century—the easternmost outpost of this system,[3] and the Frankfurt fairs were then gradually replaced by those in Leipzig in this function from the sixteenth century onwards.[4] And further east? What about the fairs east of Leipzig, in eastern-central Europe—in Poland, Bohemia, and Hungary—and beyond that in eastern Europe—in Muscovy—and in the Ottoman Empire?

To put it in a nutshell: in all these countries of eastern Europe, there were more or less large, supra-regionally important markets. Whether these can be described as 'fairs' in a sense comparable to those in western Europe, however, is an open question that requires further discussion. In the Ottoman Empire, for example, the 'fair tradition,' so to say, was based on the continuation of the great

1 In particular, *La foire*. Brussels: Édition de la Librairie Encyclopédique, 1953; Peter Johanek, Heinz Stoob (eds.). *Europäische Messen und Märktesysteme in Mittelalter und Neuzeit*. Cologne, Weimar, Vienna: Böhlau, 1996.

2 Henri Lapeyre. *Une famille de marchands: les Ruiz*. Paris: S.E.V.P.E.N, 1955, 285.

3 Michael Rothmann. *Die Frankfurter Messen im Mittelalter*. Stuttgart: Steiner, 1998.

4 Peter Beyer. Leipzigs Auseinandersetzung mit Frankfurt am Main (1706–1726). Symptom des Aufstiegs zur führenden deutschen Messestadt. In *Leipzigs Messen 1497–1997. Gestaltwandel. Umbrüche. Neubeginn, vol. 1: 1497–1914*, Hartmut Zwahr, Thomas Topfstedt, Günter Bentele (eds.). Cologne, Weimar, Vienna: Böhlau, 1999, 193–204.

https://doi.org/10.1515/9783111621296-017

fairs of the Byzantine period[5] which, in turn, had their roots in the regular markets of the Roman Empire. The Ottoman market and fair system extended from the Balkans (the so-called "Balkan fairs"[6]) far into Anatolia, but only reached its greatest development in the eighteenth and nineteenth centuries. Until the end of the seventeenth century, there were rigid trade restrictions between the Ottoman Empire and the Habsburg Empire, which were not conducive to the development of an international trade fair system on the Balkan Peninsula. The great annual markets and the fairs of the southern Russian-Ukrainian region and Siberia did not experience their peak until the eighteenth and especially the nineteenth century, when these economic areas were given much greater economic value than had ever been the case before.

Thus, Poland and Muscovy (as well as Hungary, which will not be the subject of this study[7]) remain the areas of study for supra-regional-international trade fair activities in the later Middle Ages and the early modern period, both of which will be examined in the following sections from their medieval origins to the seventeenth century. The seventeenth century was a time of significant changes in both Poland and Muscovy, so that this caesura lends itself as the end point of the research to be given here. At the end of the article, there will be some reflections on the comparison of the Polish and Muscovian great markets with the western European fairs, which will also lead to a conceptual classification of the various market opportunities.

---

5 Basilike Papoulia. Jahrmärkte in Byzanz. In *Messen, Jahrmärkte und Stadtentwicklung in Europa/Foires, marchés annuels et développement urbain en Europe*, Franz Irsigler, Michel Pauly (eds.). Trier: Porta Alba, 2007, 41–49; Mihailo St. Popović. Jahrmärkte im europäischen Teil des Byzantinischen Reiches und deren neuzeitliches Nachleben. In *Europäische Messegeschichte, 9.–19. Jahrhundert. Forschungsstand und Forschungsperspektiven*, Markus A. Denzel (ed.). Cologne, Weimar, Vienna: Böhlau, 2018, 43–53; Klaus-Peter Matschke. Commerce, Trade, Markets, and Money: Thirteenth-Fifteenth Centuries. In *The Economic History of Byzantium, from the Seventh through the Fifteenth Century*, vol. 2, Angeliki E. Laiou (ed.). Washington, DC: Dumbarton Oaks Research Library and Collection, 2002, 771–806.

6 Suraiya Faroqhi. The Early History of the Balkan Fairs. *Südost-Forschungen* 37 (1978): 50–68. For Moldova, see Arno Mehlan. Die großen Balkanmessen in der Türkenzeit. *Vierteljahrschrift für Sozial- und Wirtschaftsgeschichte* 31:1 (1938): 17–18; for Macedonia, see Mihailo St. Popović. New Insights into the History of Balkan Fairs in the Historical Region of Macedonia (13th–19th Centuries). *Bulgaria Medievalis* 2 (2011): 757–776.

7 Boglárka Weisz. *Markets and Staples in the Medieval Hungarian Kingdom*. Budapest: Research Centre for the Humanities, 2020; Norbert Spannenberger. Märkte im Königreich Ungarn, Kroatien und in Siebenbürgen. In *Europäische Messegeschichte*, Denzel (ed.), 267–283; András Kubinyi. Die Märkte Ungarns im Spätmittelalter. In *Messen, Jahrmärkte und Stadtentwicklung*, Irsigler, Pauly (eds.), 253–262.

1 The emergence of a "network of great annual markets" in Poland

In the Kingdom of Poland, a first annual market system emerged during the era of the founding of cities in the thirteenth and fourteenth centuries which then expanded southwards and eastwards until the sixteenth century. According to Maria Bogucka and Henryk Samsonowicz, 340 annual market privileges were issued between 1320 and 1530: 19 in the fourteenth century, 72 in the fifteenth century, and 249 in the first three decades of the sixteenth century, whereby the dates of the individual market events were in each case aligned and adjusted with those of neighbouring markets.[8] This first Polish annual market system was characterised by a prominent role of the Crown, which was instrumental in establishing these market events, and the weighty importance of the *szlachta*—the magnates and the small landed nobility—as privileged agricultural 'entrepreneurs' and landowners within the trade events, who became increasingly important in the grain and cattle trade from the middle of the fifteenth century onwards.[9]

The most important annual markets were those in Thorn, Gniezno, and Poznan, then Warsaw and Łęczyca (exactly on the border of the Wielkopolska and Mazovian Lowlands). The markets in Wrocław provided a link to Leipzig and the central German (great) annual markets and thus to the west of Europe. In addition, in the Grand Duchy of Lithuania, there were Vilnius and Grodno (Hrodna) in Lithuania in the north-east, as well as the village of Mohylew (Mogiljow, today Mahiljou on the Dnjepr) in present-day Belarus as a border market to Muscovy. After the annexation of the Republic of Novgorod in 1478 and the Russian expansion to the west, the standard of living had risen in Muscovy, and trade between western Europe and Moscow had expanded. This allowed a system of annual and cattle markets to develop in Belarus, among which Mohylew, Szkłów, and Vilnius were the most important. In the south, Wrocław, Kraków, Jarosław, Lublin, and Lviv were the most important annual markets. At least until the end of the fourteenth century, Lviv was only a cattle market and only became more important in the second half of the fifteenth century after the granting of the first stacking

8 Maria Boguczka, Henryk Samsonowicz. *Dzieje miast i mieszczaństwa w Polsce przedrozbiorowej*. Warsaw: Zakład Narod. im. Ossolińskich Wyd., 1986, 182–197.

9 Werner Scheltjens. North-Eurasian Fairs from the Late Middle Ages to the Nineteenth Century. In *Europäische Messegeschichte*, Denzel (ed.), 329–330; Henryk Samsonowicz. Die Handelsstraße Ostsee–Schwarzes Meer im 13. und 14. Jahrhundert. In *Der hansische Sonderweg? Beiträge zur Sozial- und Wirtschaftsgeschichte der Hanse*, Stuart Jenks, Michael North (eds.). Cologne, Weimar, Vienna: Böhlau, 1993, 27.

rights, and then replaced Wlodomierz and Volhynia as the gateway to the east.[10] The aforementioned markets were essentially located on the long-distance trade routes through Poland until the end of the fourteenth century, of which the first two in particular were of international relevance:

1. on the southern route from Wrocław via Kraków and Jarosław to Lviv and further east on the *via tatarica*;
2. on the central route from Gdańsk via Toruń to Kraków on the one hand and on the so-called *via nova* via Łęczyca and Sandomierz to Lviv on the other;
3. on the rather supra-regionally important, so-called Great Polish Road from Frankfurt an der Oder via Poznań and Gniezno to Toruń, where the route branched off to the Baltic port of Gdańsk on the one hand and via Grodno to Vilnius on the other; and finally
4. on the route from Toruń via Konin and Kalisz to Wrocław.[11]

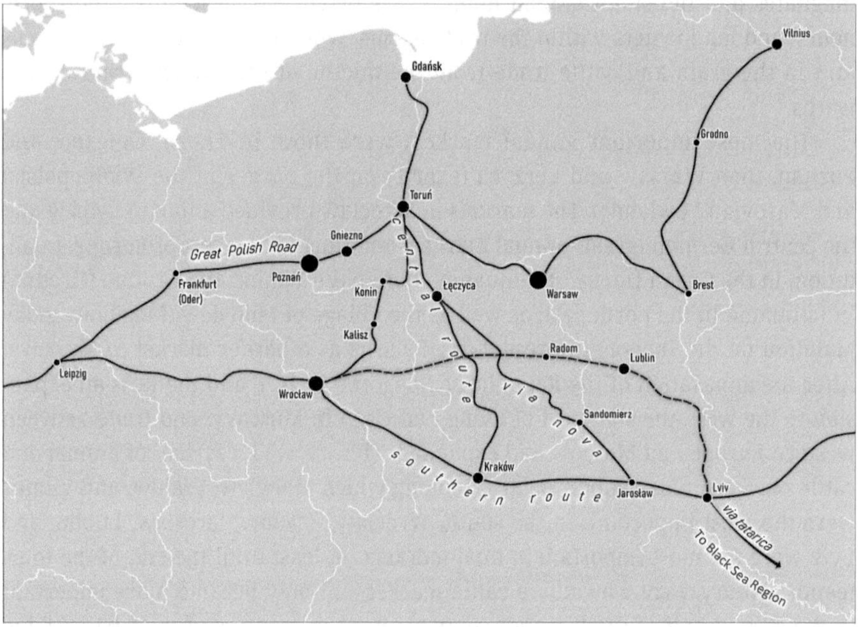

Fig. 1: Commercial routes through Poland at the end of the fourteenth century.

10 Scheltjens, North-Eurasian Fairs, 330–331, 334. On the Polish cattle markets, see Jan Baszanowski. Ochsenzuchtgebiete und Ochsenausfuhr aus Polen vom 16. bis 18. Jahrhundert. In *Internationaler Ochsenhandel (1350–1750). Akten des 7th International Economic History Congress, Edinburgh 1978*, Ekkehard Westermann (ed.). Stuttgart: Steiner, 1979, 129–130.

11 Antoni Czacharowski. Jahrmärkte und Messen im mittelalterlichen Polen. In *Messen, Jahrmärkte und Stadtentwicklung*, Irsigler, Pauly (eds.), 235.

In this context, the *via* nova—the main trade route between the Baltic Sea and the Black Sea, which was established as the 'newest' in the fourteenth century—was considered a distributor road to the *via tatarica*, and the abovementioned trading centres were all located at the crossroads of the *via nova* with main trade routes in the west-east direction.[12] In general, during the reign of King Casimir III/I the Great (1310–1370, reigned from 1333), Poland gained considerable importance in European transit trade between Silesia, Hungary, and Russia from the mid-fourteenth century onwards. Then, in the fifteenth century, grain, furs, and oxen as international merchandise were decisive enough that Poland "fut incorporée [. . .] dans l'orbite du développement de l'Europe."[13] This development strongly promoted the annual markets in Poland—and subsequently also in Lithuania—in the long term.

Among the numerous Polish annual markets, whose attendance ranged from two or three hundred to one or two thousand,[14] the following stand out in particular, as they were also frequented by foreign visitors and could therefore claim a kind of supra-regional or even international relevance. In this sense, they—or, at least, most of them—could with some probability be described as great annual markets, while the others were of more local or, at best, regional significance:

12 Samsonowicz, Handelsstraße, 24, 28–29. The *via nova* was thus part of the trade route from Danzig to Kaffa, on which trade was conducted in stages—from the Black Sea to Lemberg predominantly by Italians and Armenians, from Lemberg to Thorn by Germans with the participation of Ruthenians and Poles, and from Thorn onwards exclusively by German merchants.

13 Henryk Samsonowicz. Les foires en Pologne au XVe et XVIe siècle sur la toile de fond de la situation économique en Europe. In *Der Außenhandel Ostmitteleuropas 1450–1650. Die ostmitteleuropäischen Volkswirtschaften in ihren Beziehungen zu Mitteleuropa*, Ingomar Bog (ed.). Cologne, Vienna: Böhlau, 1971, 254–255 (citation at 255). See also Henryk Samsonowicz. Przemiany osi drozynch w Polsce późnego średniowiecza. *Przegląd Historyczny* 64:4 (1973): 711; Henryk Samsonowicz. Niektóre cechy charakterystyczne sieci jarmarcznej w Polsce późnego średniowiecza. In *Studia nad dziejami miast i mieszczaństwa w średniowieczu*, vol. I, Maria Bogucka, Antoni Czacharowski (eds.). Toruń: Uniwersytet Mikołaja Kopernika w Toruniu, 1996, 9–14.

14 Maria Bogucka. Fairs in early modern Poland. In *Messen, Jahrmärkte und Stadtentwicklung*, Irsigler, Pauly (eds.), 248.

Tab. 1: Great Annual Markets in Poland and Lithuania, twelfth to sixteenth centuries.[15]

Place	Starting at or around
Wrocław (3)	John (24 June), Bartholomew (24 August), Elizabeth (19 November)
Lviv (1)	21 January (only cattle)
Toruń (2)	*Trium Regum* (6 January), Exaltation of the Holy Cross (14 September)
Gdańsk (1)	Dominicus (8 August)
Kraków (2)	Jacob the Younger (3 May) or Stanislaw (8 May), Michaelis fair (29 September)
Lublin (3)	Candlemas (2 February), Pentecost, Simon and Judae (28 October)
Gniezno (2)	Adalbert (23 April), Bartholomew (24 August)
Poznań (4)	*Invocabit* (first Sunday of Lent), Johannes (24 June), Dominicus (8 August) or Michaelis (29 September; since the sixteenth century), Luciae (13 December; since the sixteenth century)
Warsaw (4)	*Misericordia Domini* (second Sunday after Easter), John (24 June), 1 August, 15 October
Łęczyca (2)	16 July, St. Nicholas (6 December)
Vilnius (3)	*Trium Regum* (6 January), 4 March, Assumption

In Polish cities, the existence of annual markets often competed with the staple right which, as in Wroclaw, was only suspended on the respective market dates. The holding of annual markets was often associated with guest trading—that is, the time of the fairs was the only time when merchants from outside the town were allowed to do business with each other without a resident merchant acting as an intermediary. It was possible for great annual markets to exist in two cities as comparatively close to each other as Poznań and Gniezno, because the trade at

15 Czacharowski, Jahrmärkte und Messen, 236–240; Bogucka, Fairs in early modern Poland, 246–247; Adelheid Simsch. Posener Marktzettel aus den Jahren 1579/80. Eine bisher unveröffentlichte Quelle zur Geschichte des Posener Handels in der zweiten Hälfte des 16. Jahrhunderts. In *Beiträge zur Stadt- und Regionalgeschichte Ost- und Nordeuropas. Herbert Ludat zum 60. Geburtstag*, Klaus Zernack (ed.). Wiesbaden: Steiner, 1971, 155. On the duration of the Polish great annual markets, which could range from two to three days to six weeks, see Bogucka, Fairs in early modern Poland, 247: "In practice the officially fixed duration was often prolonged by a longer stay in the city of some foreigners, who tried to conclude their business on the basis of fair's freedom." See also with some different information Hermann Kellenbenz (ed.) *Handelsbräuche des 16. Jahrhunderts. Das Meder'sche Handelsbuch und die Welser'schen Nachträge*. Wiesaden: Steiner, 1974, 63 (but only Wrocław, Poznań, and Lublin); https://fairs-in-history.huma-num.fr/collection/COL0041 (date of access: October 31st 2023).

the fairs was so extensive that both could profit from it in good cooperation, not in competition.

The expansion of the fair system of the fifteenth century was accompanied by the rise of Lviv to become the most important connecting place between the Orient and the west via the land route. From the first decade of the fifteenth century, the city endeavoured to enforce not only its ancestral staple right, but also the compulsory road traffic on the *via tatarica* and the road through Moldavia. Here, merchants from the west and north had to lay down their goods for a fortnight before they were allowed to travel further into Moldavia on the *via tatarica*. The Polish king had granted the city this right in the second half of the fourteenth century as well as the *Straßenzwang*, so that "for decades it would have a monopoly on the intensive exchange of goods between the West and the Orient and the significant income that flowed from it." For this reason, Lviv had no particular interest in a fair or annual market privilege.[16] Lviv thus became an important trading partner for Bessarabian, Moldavian, and Wallachian princes as far away as Kaffa (present-day Feodossija), the centre of the slave and grain trade on the Black Sea.[17]

According to Maria Bogucka, Poznań, Gniezno, Toruń, Gdańsk, Kraków, Brest-Litovsk, Jarosław, Lublin, and Zamość can be considered the most important and thus probably the largest annual markets in sixteenth-century Poland. They are characterised by the fact that they were all located on the borders of the Polish-Lithuanian state, while in the interior of the country, smaller annual markets served as intermediaries and local trading centres. A special concentration of great annual markets can be found in the south-east (Lublin, Zamość, Lviv, and Jarosław) and in the north-west (Poznań, Gniezno, and Toruń). Therefore, Gniezno, Poznań, and Lublin were particularly prominent within this market network, as the first two cities were located on important inland trade routes and close to western Europe, while Lublin was close to the 'border triangle' between Poland, Lithuania, and Ukraine. Lublin, like Wrocław, was a hub of exchange with the Belarusian markets as well as the Ukrainian ones. Gdańsk played a special role as a seashore market, where goods were transferred from sea to land and vice versa: the Dominicus Market, which was visited by more than 400 ships in the second half of the sixteenth century, can almost be classified as a kind of 'sea fair' (while the other

16 Czacharowski, Jahrmärkte und Messen, 236.

17 Scheltjens, North-Eurasian Fairs, 331–333. See also Maurice Lombard. Caffa et la fin de la route mongole. *Annales. Histoire, Sciences Sociales* 5:1 (1950): 100–103; Marian Małowist. *Kaffa—kolonia genueńska na Krymie i problem wschodni w latach 1453–1475*. Warsaw: Tow. miłośników historii, 1947.

annual markets held here were at best regionally relevant).[18] Gdańsk was thus considered the Polish gateway to the entire Baltic Sea region and integrated into the west European trade network.[19] For Lithuania, Vilnius and—on the route from Lublin to Smolensk—Mohylew and Szkłów (Shklow), less than 40 kilometres away, should be mentioned, of which Mohylew was the most important of the Belarusian and Lithuanian towns around 1600.[20]

Moreover, with the granting of an annual market privilege in 1528, Warsaw gained importance among the great annual markets of Poland, which should enjoy the same rights as the traditional markets in Poznań, Gniezno, and Lublin: "Il me semble que ces foires avaient une certaine analogie avec les fameuses foires de Champagne qui se tenaient dans plusieurs endroits et représentaient ensemble le centre principal des échanges entre le Nord et le Sud."[21]

All in all, the (great) annual markets in Poland-Lithuania in the fifteenth and sixteenth centuries essentially fulfilled two functions: first, they served to exchange local products; second, they were intermediaries on the land route between western Europe, Moscow, and Central Asia on the one hand and the Black Sea region on the other. On the northern route, mainly furs, skins, wax, and honey were traded for textiles, metals, and goods from overseas, while on the

---

18 Bogucka, Fairs in early modern Poland, 244, 246; Maria Bogucka. Jarmarki w Polsce w XVI–XVIII wieku. In *Studia nad dziejami miast*, Bogucka, Czacharowski (eds.), 25 (the overview map of Polish fairs is not included in the English version); Jerzy Topolski. Faktoren der Entstehung eines internationalen Jahrmarktnetzes in Polen im 16. und 17. Jahrhundert. *Studia Historiae Oeconomicae* 5 (1970): 107–108, 110.

19 Zsygmunt Pál Pach. Zur Geschichte der internationalen Handelswege und des Handelskapitals vom 15. bis 17. Jahrhundert. *Jahrbuch für Wirtschaftsgeschichte* 10:3 (1969): 179–192; Johannes Schildhauer. Zur Verlagerung des See- und Handelsverkehrs im nordeuropäischen Raum während des 15. und 16. Jahrhunderts: Eine Untersuchung auf der Grundlage der Danziger Pfahlkammerbücher. *Jahrbuch für Wirtschaftsgeschichte* 9:4 (1968): 187–211; Johannes Schildhauer. Der Seehandel Danzigs im 16. Jahrhundert und die Verlagerung des Warenverkehrs im Nord- und Mitteleuropäischen Raum. *Jahrbuch für Wirtschaftsgeschichte* 11:3 (1970): 155–178; Marian Małowist. Les produits des pays de la Baltique dans le commerce international au XVIe siècle. *Revue du Nord* 42:166 (1960): 175–206.

20 Topolski, Faktoren der Entstehung, 105–108, 113; Scheltjens, North-Eurasian Fairs, 334. The markets in Poland mentioned by Topolski (Faktoren der Entstehung, 108–109), which specialised in livestock trade (Jarosław in Lesser Poland, Łęczyca, Lowiez, Jarocin, and Kobylin in central and western Poland) are probably not to be regarded as great annual markets despite the high numbers of livestock traded. These Polish livestock markets were only connected with the Belarusian markets to a small extent, but much more strongly with the Ukrainian ones, because their existence was conditioned by the demand for meat from the Ukraine in western Europe. According to Bogucka (Fairs in early modern Poland, 247), larger cattle markets also took place in Warsaw and Lublin.

21 Samsonowicz, Les foires en Pologne, 256.

southern route—through Armenian, Greek, and Jewish merchants—primarily Oriental goods were traded. Gdańsk was connected to both routes via the Vistula. The annual markets were also the places at which the members of the *szlachta* obtained their central income from grain sales and bought luxury goods such as textiles, wine, fruit, or spices (as the Moscow nobles did further east).[22] Thus the international annual market network in Poland played a central role in the pan-European west-east trade over land until the early seventeenth century. Although the multitude of smaller and large annual markets does not allow a clear network and a stringent sequence of the individual markets to emerge one after the other, the Polish 'fair system' extended from the fifteenth century onwards from Leipzig in the west via Gdańsk in the north and Lemberg, the gateway to the Oriental trade, in the southeast to the markets in Vilnius in Lithuania, Mohylev in White Ruthenia, and Kamenec Podolski in the Ukraine. This close-meshed network of annual markets is virtually a characteristic of the Polish economy at the end of the Middle Ages and the beginning of the early modern period.[23]

The increase in the number of large annual markets and their rising turnover is also due to the fact that, given the growing income of the middle classes and peasants in the fifteenth and sixteenth centuries, many goods, although still expensive, lost the characteristic of being luxury products. This made larger markets all the more necessary, as there was not enough cash available. For here, on the one hand, there was the possibility of mutual credit for the time of a market; on the other hand, there was the cyrograph, "a kind of primitive bill of exchange," as a cashless payment medium in which the debtor undertook to pay the creditor the debt on a certain date and at a certain place—for example, at another market. To guarantee liability, such credit transactions were usually entered in the municipal official books.[24] According to Henryk Samsonowicz, 'classical' Italian-style bills of exchange could also have circulated and been used as credit papers at individual great annual markets—for example, by Italian and German merchants in Gniezno, Toruń, and Kraków.[25] In the sixteenth century, up to 60% of all transactions at the Dominicus Market in Gdańsk could have been financed by credit and, in addition, the various great annual markets were used by merchants not least to grant loans to members of the *szlachta* or to have their debts repaid.[26] In

22 Scheltjens, North-Eurasian Fairs, 333–335.
23 Topolski, Faktoren der Entstehung, 101.
24 Topolski, Faktoren der Entstehung, 102–103.
25 Henryk Samsonowicz. Jarmarki w Polsce na tle sytuacij gospodarczej w Europie w XV–XVI w. In *Europa—Slowianszczyzna—Polska. Studia ku uczczeniu Profesora Kazimierza Tymienieckiego*, Juliusz Bardach (ed.). Poznań: Uniwersytet Mikołaja Kopernika w Toruniu, 1970, 524.
26 Bogucka, Fairs in early modern Poland, 247.

contrast to the Polish great annual markets, the sixteenth-century annual markets in royal and ducal Prussia cannot claim more than regional significance.[27]

This extensive network of great annual markets in Poland rapidly lost both its importance and its function in the wake of the devastating wars between 1647 and 1667, neither of which could be revived despite the renewed economic boom in the eighteenth century. The Polish annual markets sank to local transshipment centres with agricultural and forestry goods, where trade was no longer primarily handled by city-based merchants, but by members of the *szlachta* with the support of their Jewish commercial agents. This process, which had already begun in the second half of the fifteenth century but intensified significantly from the seventeenth century onwards, hindered commercialisation in Poland in the long term, since the *szlachta* promoted the production and distribution of goods but not their trade. The nobles traded and consumed primarily for their own needs and increasingly displaced the merchants as the actual mediators of the exchange of goods until the eighteenth century. The previous nature of the Polish great annual markets as a kind of fairs thus changed significantly, so that they often degenerated into small markets.[28]

The decisive structural changes—indeed, the destruction of the previous system of Polish-Lithuanian great annual markets—occurred in the second half of the seventeenth century due to the military invasions of foreign powers in the Russian-Polish War (1654–1667) and above all in the parallel Polish-Swedish War (1655–1660), the so-called Swedish Deluge (*Potop szwedzki*), with its devastating consequences for the country and its population, its economy, and foreign trade, comparable to the Thirty Years' War in the Holy Roman Empire.[29] The available trade credit was no longer sufficient for further growth. Not least due to the years of war, land trade through Poland was severely impaired, and the sea route to Arkhangelsk and later to Saint Petersburg gained considerably in importance—to the detriment of the great annual markets in Poland.[30]

27 Piotr Paluchowski. Miejsca i terminy jarmarków na terenie prus królewskich i książęcych w końcu XVI wieku na podstawie wykazówz Gdańskich kalendarzy. *Czasynowożytne* 24 (2011): 37–59.

28 Bogucka, Fairs in early modern Poland, 248–249; Scheltjens, North-Eurasian Fairs, 334. On Thorn, see the dissenting opinion of Jürgen Sarnowsky. Märkte im mittelalterlichen Preußen. *Hansische Geschichtsblätter* 120 (2002): 60–61, who assumes a fully functioning annual market only after the Thirty Years' War and sees the first introduction by the Polish king in 1472 rather as a failed attempt.

29 See Hilmar Sack, Tomasz Łopatka. Thirty Years' War and Potop. Heroism and "barbarian savagery": Existential War Experiences in the 17th Century. In *Deutsch-Polnische Erinnerungsorte*, vol. 3: *Parallelen*, Hans Henning Hahn, Robert Traba (eds.). Paderborn: Schöningh, 2012, 147–165.

30 Scheltjens, North-Eurasian Fairs, 335. See also Topolski, Faktoren der Entstehung, 116.

Great annual markets or fairs in Muscovy

In the area of the later Tsarist Empire, the oldest annual markets on the banks of the Volga can be traced back to the early Middle Ages—that is, to pre-Russian times, especially in Itil, the capital of the Khazar Empire from the mid-eight to the end of the tenth century, and in Bolgar (or Bulgar), the capital of the Volga Bulgars between the eight and fifteenth centuries.[31] After the collapse of the Volga trade during the Mongol invasion in the first half of the thirteenth century, new annual markets were established between the mouth of the Mologa into the Volga and Sarai, the capital of the Golden Horde, at the latest in the fourteenth century. One of these annual markets was located in the immediate vicinity of what later became Nizhni Novgorod on the Balakhonskaia peninsula at the confluence of the Oka and Volga rivers, which has been documented since 1366 and was frequented by Muscovite, Tatar, Armenian, Bukharian, and Khiva merchants.

From 1257, a one-day market was held on 24 June (Saint John's Day) on the so-called Great Field (*arskoe pole*) near Kazan, the capital of the khanate of the same name. This 'Kazan Fair' was the most important and largest annual market in the area of the Russian rivers in the fifteenth and sixteenth centuries. Merchants from central Asia, China, Siberia, India, Moscow, Novgorod, Pskov, and numerous other cities came together here. However, their visit was very dangerous, especially for Russian merchants during this period of the Moscow-Kazan Wars (1439–1552). A massacre of Russian merchants and envoys in Kazan in 1521 prompted Grand Prince Vasily III of Moscow (1479–1533, reigned from 1505) to ban his subjects from attending the fair in 1524 and, at the same time, to establish a new competing great annual market at the outermost border of his fiefdom, in the small fortress of Vasilsursk at the confluence of the Sura and Volga rivers, which had just been conquered in 1523.[32] Vasilsursk lay a good 230 kilometres northwest of Kazan on the Volga and could thus have been seen as a staging post on the way from the Russian cities to Kazan, but these new annual markets were not visited by Oriental merchants and died out. Thus, there were no significant annual markets on the Volga in the late sixteenth and early seventeenth centu-

31 Anne Lincoln Fitzpatrick. *The Great Russian Fair. Nizhnii Novgorod, 1840–90*. London, Basingstoke: Palgrave Macmillian/New York: St. Martin's Press, 1990, 14; James Thal. Schifffahrt und Handel des russischen Reiches im Jahre 1849 nebst den neuesten statistischen Daten über Bevölkerung, Cultur und Industrie. In *Mittheilungen über Handel, Gewerbe und Verkehrsmittel, so wie aus dem Gebiete der Statistik überhaupt, nach Berichten an das k.k. Handels-Ministerium*, 2. Jahrgang, Direction der administrativen Statistik (ed.). Vienna: Kaiserl.-Königl. Hof- und Staatsdruckerei, 1851, 118–119.

32 Fitzpatrick, *The Great Russian Fair*, 14–15.

ries, not least because of the ongoing wars with the Tartarians, the uprisings of the Cheremisses against Russian rule, the so-called period of turmoil (*smuta*, 1598–1613) with the reign of the false Dimitri (Dimitri II, c. 1580–1606, reigned from 1605) and the trade monopoly of the English.[33]

When Kazan was finally conquered by Ivan IV the Terrible (1530–1584, reigned from 1533) in 1552, however, another place on the Volga became the most important market centre of this area in the long term—the annual market at Makarev Monastery, located about 500 kilometres northwest of Kazan. The monastery there, founded in 1439 by the monk Makarios (1349–1444), had been destroyed before the middle of the fifteenth century by Ulug Mehmed, Khan of Kazan (1438–1445, formerly Khan of the Golden Horde from 1419–1424 and 1427–1438) and was rebuilt by the monk Avraami from 1620–1624, thereby reviving the pilgrimage. At this supra-regional pilgrimage centre, an annual market was held on the anniversary of the death of St. Makarios (25 July), which in the first half of the seventeenth century was still a simple farmers' or local market to supply the pilgrims, but where linen, wooden goods, hats, and fur boots, furs, and devotionalia were also traded. Initially, the monastery had sole sovereignty over the market, which was confirmed in 1641 by Tsar Michael I (1596–1645, reigned from 1613) and whereby the monks received permission to collect a market levy. However, this annual market quickly acquired all-Russian significance and lasted for a fortnight as early as the 1660s, as it had become the meeting place for merchants from Moscow and Kazan, and the Kazan trade had been transferred here from the Great Field. In 1667, Tsar Alexei I (1629–1676, reigned from 1645) tried for the first time to exert more influence on the market by granting five days of free trade but then demanding a levy to the state. However, the Tsar failed because of Abbot Theodore's refusal. Makarev was ideally suited geographically as a fairground site, because in the late seventeenth century, shipping on the Lower Volga to and from the south began and ended there, and Oriental products came there on boats from as far way as Astrakhan, which on their return journey took with them European goods that had come into the country on the Upper Volga via Arkhangelsk and Vologda.[34] From 1666, the great annual markets used about 1,400 stalls or booths and 1,800 shops.[35] In the wake of the conquest of Siberia, the now great Makaryev annual markets continued to gain importance "in the hinterland of European Russia," becoming "a major vehicle" for trade with the cities of Siberia and with China and "a commercial intermediary between East

33 Thal, Schifffahrt und Handel, 119.

34 Fitzpatrick, *The Great Russian Fair*, 15–17.

35 Michal Wanner. The Russian-Chinese Trade in Kyakhta, its Organisation and Commodity Structure, 1727–1861. *Prague Papers on the History of International Relations* 18:2 (2014): 47.

and West, an important market in Russia's trade with Asia." Towards the end of the seventeenth century, the annual turnover of goods is said to have been about 80,000 roubles.[36] The great annual markets in Makarev lasted from 1 to 30 July.[37]

Arkhangelsk, built in 1584 on the Tsar's orders and belonging to the north Atlantic region, was the first Russian seaport. The Ostrog was originally called Novocholmogory after the nearby trading post Cholmogory and subsequently 'Archangel City' from 1613 onwards. Situated on the lower reaches of the Dwina, 40 kilometres from its mouth on the White Sea, Arkhangelsk was considered Moscow's port on the White Sea because the port, blocked by ice from October to May, was connected to the Volga and its tributary, the Kama via two canals, so that the city and port had a huge hinterland—ultimately as far as Moscow.[38] The decisive advantage of the Arkhangelsk route for the northwestern European trading nations was ultimately the greater security compared to the Baltic route and the elimination of the Sound tariff. Shipping to the White Sea started from the northwest European ports in April or July. With a sailing time of four to six weeks, they arrived in May or August, stayed for the time of the annual market there,[39] and returned south with the onset of autumn. There was also the so-called 'early voyage,' which was profitable because goods from the previous season that had been stored in Arkhangelsk over the winter could be bought more cheaply. Trade took place in Arkhangelsk in the form of fairs or great annual markets. Similar to Kaffa in the fifteenth century and Gdańsk in the sixteenth century, such maritime fairs were held in Arkhangelsk to handle foreign trade, the first being held when the ice melted on the Vistula or the Northern Dvina, the second at harvest time:

> Archangel'sk had maritime fairs which depended on the arrival and departure of foreign ships at the time when the White Sea was not frozen, on one hand, and on the arrival of commodities produced from the Russian interior, on the other.

36 Fitzpatrick, *The Great Russian Fair*, 17; Thal, Schifffahrt und Handel, 119.

37 Scheltjens, North-Eurasian Fairs, 336.

38 Walter Kresse. *Die Fahrtgebiete der Hamburger Handelsflotte, 1824–1888*. Hamburg: Museum für Hamburgische Geschichte, 1972, 13.

39 This was reported in the late seventeenth century by Johann Philipp Kilburger. *Kurzer Unterricht von dem russischen Handel, wie selbiger mit aus- und eingehenden Waaren 1674 durch ganz Russland getrieben worden*. Hamburg, 1769, chap. IV, quoted in Christoph F. Menke. *Die wirtschaftlichen und politischen Beziehungen der Hansestädte zu Rußland im 18. und frühen 19. Jahrhundert*. PhD diss., University of Göttingen, 1959, 379–380.

According to older literature, the fairs lasted until September or even longer.[40] While a positive boom of the Arkhangelsk fairs could already be observed in the first half of the seventeenth century, the protectionist-oriented New Trade Statute (*Novotorgovyi ustav*) of Tsar Alexei I of 1667—the year of the great city fire—fixed a new, economically even more important role for Arkhangelsk and its seashore fairs. The Trade Statute of 1667 established Arkhangelsk's position on the White Sea as the gateway to the west and the orientation of the other markets towards its seashore fairs whereby, with a few exceptions, foreigners were forbidden to trade within Russia.[41] At the Arkhangelsk seashore fairs, arriving Russian and foreign merchants tried to sell everything they had with them. This trade was largely conducted as a barter transaction (*baratto*), but those who paid cash received more favourable prices.[42]

In 1667, when Ukraine east of the Dnieper became part of Russia with the Treaty of Andrusovo, the most important annual markets of the entire southern Russian-Ukrainian area were held at the Svinsky or Svensky Monastery, at the confluence of the Desna and Svin rivers, three miles from Bryansk. In the early years of the Great Northern War, Tsar Peter I the Great (1672–1725, reigned from 1682) forbade 'Greeks' and the inhabitants of southern Russian towns to travel to Moscow, to the Svinsk or other fairs, and to trade among themselves (1701). A fair was held for them in Azov for the first time from 20 August 1701, and at the same time, the Svinsk fair was discontinued. The Polish merchants were 'diverted' to the fair in Smolensk for their Russian trade. However, this measure was not successful in the long term, for the Svinsk fair was restored on 25 June 1711, as Azov had proved unsuitable for its intended function as a gateway to the west, and Peter I had also turned increasingly to the north-west. To this end, in addition to the founding of Saint Petersburg in 1703, the great annual markets of Riga (20 June–10 July), which had been interrupted for several years, were re-established for merchants from land and sea. Indeed, as Werner Scheltjens has observed, "a shift towards the Baltic Sea coast was undeniable in the North-Eurasian system of fairs of

40 Scheltjens, North-Eurasian Fairs, 335–336 (citation at 336). See also Topolski, Faktoren der Entstehung, 116.

41 Stefan Troebst. Isfahan—Moscow—Amsterdam. Zur Entstehungsgeschichte des moskauischen Transitprivilegs für die Armenische Handelskompanie in Persien (1666–1676). *Jahrbücher für Geschichte Osteuropas* 41 (1993): 195–205.

42 Troebst, Isfahan, 77; Hermann Kellenbenz. Marchands en Russie aux XVIIe–XVIIIe siècles. In *Europa, Raum wirtschaftlicher Begegnung. Kleine Schriften I*, Hermann Kellenbenz (ed.). Stuttgart: Steiner, 1991, 213.

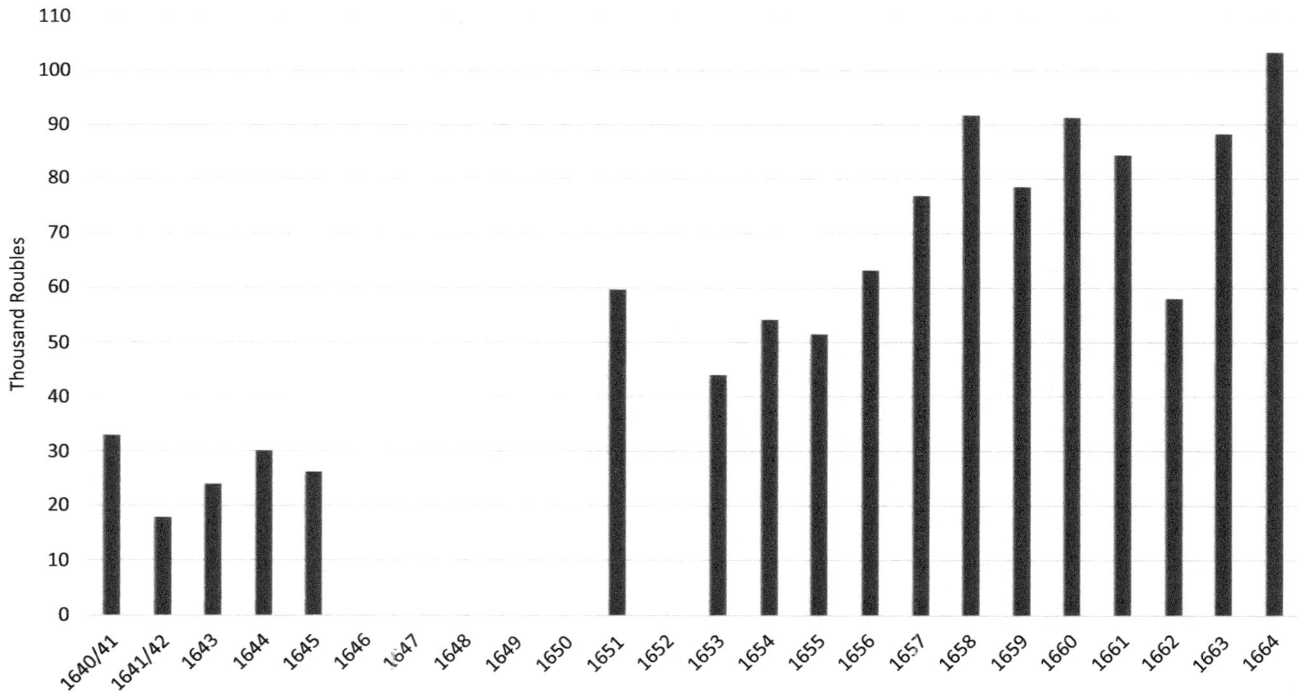

Fig. 2: Toll revenues at the Arkhangelsk Fairs, 1640/41 to 1664, per thousand roubles.[43]

43 Stefan Troebst. *Handelskontrolle, "Derivation", Eindämmung. Schwedische Moskaupolitik 1617–1661*. Wiesbaden: Harrassowitz, 1997, 535.

the early eighteenth century."[44] This fair policy, which was primarily oriented towards the Baltic Sea region, was also directed by a magistrate's ordinance of 1721 to further increase the number of fairs in the country, especially in those places where it was necessary to transfer from water to land transport and vice versa. As a result, it should be noted that due to the rise of Saint Petersburg and the economic expansion of its hinterland, Makarev became the largest Eurasian fair in Russia even before the end of the Great Northern War (1700–1721). When the Vyshni Volochok canal between the Msta and Tverza rivers north of Tver and the Volga and Neva river systems was completed in 1722, goods from the Urals or Astrakhan could reach Saint Petersburg by water via the Makarev fairs, which further increased the already significant importance of these fairs.[45]

In the late seventeenth century, in addition to numerous locally or at best regionally important fairs, a good half dozen can be considered great annual markets or even fairs. In addition to the fairs in Makarev, these were the 'maritime fairs' in Arkhangelsk, then the great annual markets at the Svinsky Monastery or in Azov, in Tikhvin, Irbit, and Smolensk, which were particularly singled out due to their high relevance in Tsarist tax legislation between 1684 and 1700 or through privileges. In this context, the two fairs in Tikhvin (13 January–13 February and *velikij post* in Lent), which were privileged in 1607 and 1622, and the one in Smolensk were seen as exchange points for contact with neighbouring Swedes and Poles respectively, while Svinsk and Azov were seen as gateways to central Asia. Makarev and Irbit were regarded as starting points for trade with Siberia and China, especially since the Russian-Chinese Treaty of Nerchinsk (27 August 1689) had provided for the establishment of regular trade relations, as a result of which trading posts were then established on both sides of the Russian-Chinese border in Kyakhta and May-Ma-Chen. Further, the network of annual markets in Siberia, where local markets had been held along the land and water routes since the Russian land seizure in the sixteenth century, became increasingly dense in the course of the seventeenth century and especially after 1689.[46]

44 Scheltjens, North-Eurasian Fairs, 337.

45 Scheltjens, North-Eurasian Fairs, 338–339.

46 Scheltjens, North-Eurasian Fairs, 336–337. The Treaty of Nerchinsk is discussed in detail in C. Bickford O'Brien. *Russia under two Tsars 1682–1689: The Regency of Sophia Alekseevna*. Berkeley, Los Angeles: University of California Press, 1952, 105–124 (trade relations, in particular, are discussed at 119). See also Michal Wanner. First Russian-Chinese Doplomatic and Business Relationship 1689–1728. *Prague Papers on the History of International Relations* 17:2 (2013): 66–76.

The specific nature of annual markets and fairs in eastern Europe

The overview of Polish and Muscovite market opportunities shows a certain variety of types, which would be even richer if one were to include the markets of the Ottoman Empire, which extended far to the south. The functionality of the east-central, eastern, and southeastern European markets was in many respects similar to that of the western European markets and fairs: the catchment area of the individual markets could be local, regional, supra-regional, or international, and they served as trans-shipment centres for goods, money, and information, as centres of communication and cultural exchange, and as points of attraction for a usually comparatively large number of people of different origins, cultures, and religions. However, common to the large market opportunities of western Europe, the fairs of eastern Europe also had their border market function, which also played an essential role here in all centuries for the topographical location of larger markets. They functioned as border markets between economic areas of different levels of development, and as such contributed in the long term to the rapprochement and integration of these economic areas. They could also function, albeit not regularly, as credit markets for merchants and other private individuals, albeit to a much lesser extent than was the case in western Europe.

However, there is another specific aspect: the eastern European markets or fairs, however large they might be and however many people they might attract, were not centres of cashless payment transactions or extensive state financing, at least not until the late eighteenth century. They were and always remained commodity markets or commodity fairs. Commodity trade in whatever goods constituted the core business at all these markets, while money and credit transactions had at best an accompanying function—that is, supporting commodity trade. This is a (if not *the*) fundamental difference with the western European fairs where, starting with the Fairs in Champagne and culminating in the Bisenzone fairs, an increasing specialisation towards cashless payment transactions and international credit business in the sense of a European high finance can be observed.

Nevertheless, the question remains to be discussed whether the larger of these markets were fairs in the full sense of the word, which is the assumption of previous literature, especially in the English language. How can these periodic markets of eastern Europe be defined terminologically? Market events in eastern Europe generally lack two essential characteristics of fairs: firstly, there is no cashless payment system pointing beyond the market, so that the markets, however large, would not have represented a money or capital market or even a central element of state financing; secondly, in none of these markets was trade between merchants the dominant one, but rather between wholesalers and retailers or even end consumers. This also explains the very large numbers of visitors to these fairs as compared to western European markets or fairs, which could reach several tens of thousands, even hundreds of thousands of people per event at the great annual markets in this region. Therefore, the range of goods on offer was not limited to long-distance trade or commercial goods, but also regularly included livestock and agricultural products from the immediate surroundings. Further, this finding applies not only to the many small annual markets, but also and especially to the large fairs, which were often referred to as 'commodity fairs' in the habitual language use of the nineteenth century in order to characterise their rather limited function compared to the western European fair tradition. Examples include the Polish annual markets of the eighteenth century, where the minor nobility sold their agricultural products or had them sold and stocked up on consumer goods. In addition, a high degree of internationality can be postulated for fairs, at least in the western European tradition, which can be regularly proven at the large fairs from Champagne to the Bisenzone.

In order to escape the terminological difficulties resulting from these considerations, Manfred Straube proposed the term 'great annual markets' (*Große Märkte*) primarily in the case of Leipzig[47] (which until the eighteenth century had only a rather small number of international guests) in order to emphasise not only the supra-regional relevance of the Leipzig markets on the one hand, but on the other hand also to refer to their (still) non-existent internationality and their lack of function as an international capital and financial market. The concept of a great annual market seems extremely suitable to characterise this intermediate position between regionally important markets, which existed in abundance in almost all European countries, and the large fairs with their international visitor, goods and payment traffic, and the resulting capital and financial market. Understood in this way, however, the supra-regionally important markets of eastern Europe in particular can be characterised as great annual markets. At best, the term 'fair' seems appropriate for the markets of Makarev in the late seventeenth century and the sea fairs of Arkhangelsk. Makarev developed into a centre of 'international' exchange between European Russia and the central Asian countries in the last decades of the seventeenth century—not before!—and thus had by far the widest catchment area of all the Muscovite great annual markets, but remained a genuine commodity fair throughout. As a seaport, Arkhangelsk was

47 Manfred Straube. *Geleitswesen und Warenverkehr im thüringisch-sächsischen Raum zu Beginn der Frühen Neuzeit*. Cologne, Weimar, Vienna: Böhlau, 2015, 11; Manfred Straube. Aktuelle Fragen der deutschen und internationalen Messegeschichte. In *Europäische Messegeschichte*, Denzel (ed.), 19–20.

per se a place of international exchange, but its 'fairs' were not the typical, precisely timed, periodically held market events, but extended over the entire summer months, as long as shipping across the White Sea was possible. Thus, the term 'fair' seems to be of rather limited use for these two fairs and only partially comparable to western European market events of this type.

Perhaps this differentiation, which the German language in particular allows—or even provokes—may be perceived as artificial and subtle, and it may not be so decisive for the understanding whether a large market of supra-regional relevance is called a 'trade fair' or only an 'annual market.' However, such a differentiation can sharpen the view of the different types of fairs and make it clear that a pure commodity fair (such as Makarev) had a very different character than a highly specialised exchange fair of high finance (as was the case in Bisenzone). There were many mixed forms in between, at which the different branches of business were represented in diverse combinations and which made up the individual character of the respective fair.

Conclusion: The trade fair system east of Leipzig and Leipzig's function in it

While the 'long' sixteenth century in western Europe marks the climax of the international fair system with several innovations in the money and credit sector, in eastern Europe, the actual phase of the upswing and heyday of the great annual markets only began in this century, initially in the area of the Polish-Lithuanian Union (since 1569) with its connections to Russia and the Black Sea region. This topographical concentration shows a new geographical orientation of the European annual market and fair trade: if the medieval annual market systems and the later fairs in western Europe mediated primarily between south and north or vice versa—between Italy or Spain and northwestern Europe—the main axis of the annual market and fair trade in eastern Europe changed from west to east and vice versa from the sixteenth century onwards. In the south-north traffic between the Mediterranean region and the emerging region of northwestern Europe, fairs and great annual markets had become more and more obsolete after the level of economic development of the different economic areas had converged and the commercial intercourse had been increasingly taken over by sea transport between the Mediterranean ports and those of the Atlantic coast or the North Sea, not least in the wake of the numerous land wars of the sixteenth century in this region. Even though in eastern Europe, in the Baltic Sea region, sea transport between west and east was also increasingly common, this only applied to the northern route which, if one wanted to sail to the Atlantic, was also made more expensive by the Sound toll. As a result, land trade in eastern-central Europe, which was conducted via fairs and markets, was able to survive even over long distances into the nineteenth century and for much longer than was the case for most goods in western Europe.

Thus, "[the] early modern trade fair and annual market system [. . .] was characterised by a renewed east-west shift,"[48] and this development is closely linked to Leipzig's rise in becoming an international trade fair city. With the reorientation of European trade routes in the sixteenth century and the increasing importance of Polish annual markets as transit hubs, Leipzig began to replace Frankfurt am Main as the western starting point of this trading system. In this function, Leipzig became the most successful commodity fair in Germany until well into the nineteenth century and survived much longer than its German competitors in the Holy Roman Empire. However, Leipzig was not only the western gateway to trade via Warsaw, Brody,[49] and Berdichev into the vastness of the Russian area, but from the eigteenth century onwards, increasingly also to the southwest via Vienna and then Belgrade or Brašov (Kronstadt) into the regions of the Serbian, Wallachian, Moldovan, and Bulgarian merchants trading in Leipzig under the name of 'Greeks,'[50] as well as occasionally even the Armenian diaspora in the western Balkans[51]—that is, in the broadest sense, into the Ottoman sphere of influence, be it to either Skopje and Salonika or to Bucharest, Rusčuk (Ruse), and Constantinople and from there further into the Levant or as far as Egypt (Cairo).[52] Via Leipzig, the great annual markets of eastern Europe in particular were connected to the central European trade routes and structures. The connec-

48 Michael Rothmann. Überall ist Jahrmarkt und Entwicklungstendenzen der Institution des periodischen Marktes in Zentraleuropa vom 14. bis zum 17. Jahrhundert. In *Fiere e mercati nella integrazione delle economie europee, secc. XIII–XVIII*, Simonetta Cavaciocchi (ed.). Florence: Le Monnier, 2001, 106.

49 Katharina Middell. Brody, Leipzig, Lyon: Europäische Handelsbeziehungen und ihre Träger (1770–1820). In *Leipzig, Mitteldeutschland und Europa. Festgabe für Manfred Straube und Manfred Unger zum 70. Geburtstag*, Hartmut Zwahr, Uwe Schirmer, Henning Steinführer (eds.). Beucha: Sax, 2000, 531–533.

50 Virginia Paskaleva. Economic and Cultural Relations of Bulgaria with the City of Leipzig from the End of the 18th Century to the Russo-Turkish War of 1877/78. *Yearbook of History of the USSR and the People's Democratic Countries of Europe* 6 (1962): 392, note 13. See also Gheron Netta. *Die Handelsbeziehungen zwischen Leipzig und Ost- und Südosteuropa bis zum Verfall der Warenmessen*. Zürich: Univ. Diss., 1920, 41.

51 See Olga Katsiardi-Hering. Commerce and Merchants in Southeastern Europe, 17th–18th Centuries: 'Micro-Districts' and Regions. *Études balkaniques* 51:1 (2015): 19–35.

52 Paskaleva, Economic and Cultural Relations, 394.

tion of the larger periodic markets of eastern Europe via the Leipzig fairs was thus one of the decisive criteria of the European trade fair system since the sixteenth century and reached its peak in the later eighteenth and early nineteenth centuries.

Bibliography

Primary Sources

Kellenbenz, Hermann (ed.). *Handelsbräuche des 16. Jahrhunderts. Das Meder'sche Handelsbuch und die Welser'schen Nachtrage*. Wiesbaden: Steiner, 1974.

Kilburger, Johann Philipp. *Kurzer Unterricht von dem russischen Handel, wie selbiger mit aus- und eingehenden Waaren 1674 durch ganz Russland getrieben worden*. Hamburg, 1769.

Thal, James. Schifffahrt und Handel des russischen Reiches im Jahre 1849 nebst den neuesten statistischen Daten über Bevölkerung, Cultur und Industrie. In *Mittheilungen über Handel, Gewerbe und Verkehrsmittel, so wie aus dem Gebiete der Statistik überhaupt, nach Berichten an das k.k. Handels-Ministerium*, 2. Jahrgang, Direction der administrativen Statistik (ed.), 109–140. Vienna: Kaiserl[ich]-Königl[ich] Hof- und Staatsdruckerei, 1851.

Literature:

Baszanowski, Jan. Ochsenzuchtgebiete und Ochsenausfuhr aus Polen vom 16. bis 18. Jahrhundert. In *Internationaler Ochsenhandel (1350–1750). Akten des 7th International Economic History Congress, Edinburgh 1978*, Ekkehard Westermann (ed.). Stuttgart: Steiner, 1979, 125–136.

Beyer, Peter. Leipzigs Auseinandersetzung mit Frankfurt am Main (1706–1726) . Symptom des Aufstiegs zur führenden deutschen Messestadt. In *Leipzigs Messen 1497–1997. Gestaltwandel. Umbrüche. Neubeginn, vol. 1: 1497–1914*, Hartmut Zwahr, Thomas Topfstedt, Günter Bentele (eds.). Cologne, Weimar, Vienna: Böhlau, 1999, 193–204.

Bickford O'Brien, C. *Russia under two Tsars 1682–1689: The Regency of Sophia Alekseevna*. Berkeley, Los Angeles: University of California Press, 1952.

Bogucka, Maria. Fairs in Early Modern Poland. In *Messen, Jahrmärkte und Stadtentwicklung in Europa/ Foires, marchés annuels et développement urbain en Europe*, Franz Irsigler, Michel Pauly (eds.). Trier: Porta Alba, 2007, 243–251.

Bogucka, Maria. Jarmarki w Polsce w XVI-XVIII wieku. In *Studia nad dziejami miast i mieszczaństwa w średniowieczu*, vol. I, Maria Bogucka, Antoni Czacharowski (eds.). Toruń: Uniwersytet Mikołaja Kopernika w Toruniu, 1996, 15–26.

Bogucka, Maria, Henryk Samsonowicz. *Dzieje miast i mieszczaństwa w Polsce przedrozbiorowej*. Warsaw: Zakład Narod. im. Ossolińskich Wyd., 1986.

Czacharowski, Antoni. Jahrmärkte und Messen im mittelalterlichen Polen. In *Messen, Jahrmärkte und Stadtentwicklung*, Irsigler, Pauly (eds.), 235–241.

Faroqhi, Suraiya. The Early History of the Balkan Fairs. *Südost-Forschungen* 37 (1978): 50–68.

Fitzpatrick, Anne Lincoln. *The Great Russian Fair. Nizhnii Novgorod, 1840–90*. London, Basingstoke: Palgrave Macmillian/New York: St. Martin's Press, 1990.
Irsigler, Franz, Michel Pauly (eds.). *Messen, Jahrmärkte und Stadtentwicklung in Europa/Foires, marchés annuels et développement urbain en Europe*. Trier: Porta Alba, 2007.
Johanek, Peter, Heinz Stoob (eds.). *Europäische Messen und Märktesysteme in Mittelalter und Neuzeit*. Cologne, Weimar, Vienna: Böhlau, 1996.
Katsiardi-Hering, Olga. Commerce and Merchants in Southeastern Europe, 17th–18th Centuries: 'Micro-Districts' and Regions. *Études balkaniques* 51:1 (2015): 19–35.
Kellenbenz, Hermann. Marchands en Russie aux XVIIe–XVIIIe siècles. In *Europa, Raum wirtschaftlicher Begegnung. Kleine Schriften I*, Hermann Kellenbenz (ed.). Stuttgart: Steiner, 1991, 205–283.
Kresse, Walter. *Die Fahrtgebiete der Hamburger Handelsflotte, 1824–1888*. Hamburg: Museum für Hamburgische Geschichte, 1972.
Kubinyi, András. Die Märkte Ungarns im Spätmittelalter. In *Messen, Jahrmärkte und Stadtentwicklung*, Irsigler, Pauly (eds.), 253–262.
La foire. Brussels: Édition de la Librairie Encyclopédique, 1953.
Lapeyre, Henri. *Une famille de marchands: les Ruiz*. Paris: S.E.V.P.E.N., 1955.
Lombard, Maurice. Caffa et la fin de la route mongole. *Annales. Histoire, Sciences Sociales* 5:1 (1950): 100–103.
Małowist, Marian. *Kaffa—kolonia genueńska na Krymie i problem wschodni w latach 1453–1475*. Warsaw: Tow. miłośników historii, 1947.
Małowist, Marian. Les produits des pays de la Baltique dans le commerce international au XVIe siècle. *Revue du Nord* 42:166 (1960): 175–206.
Matschke, Klaus-Peter. Commerce, Trade, Markets, and Money: Thirteenth-Fifteenth Centuries. In *The Economic History of Byzantium, from the Seventh through the Fifteenth Century*, vol. 2, Angeliki E. Laiou (ed.). Washington, DC: Dumbarton Oaks Research Library and Collection, 2002, 771–806.
Mehlan, Arno. Die großen Balkanmessen in der Türkenzeit. *Vierteljahrschrift für Sozial- und Wirtschaftsgeschichte* 31:1 (1938): 10–49.
Menke, Christoph F. *Die wirtschaftlichen und politischen Beziehungen der Hansestädte zu Rußland im 18. und frühen 19. Jahrhundert*. Göttingen: Univ. Diss., 1959.
Middell, Katharina. Brody, Leipzig, Lyon: Europäische Handelsbeziehungen und ihre Träger (1770–1820). In *Leipzig, Mitteldeutschland und Europa. Festgabe für Manfred Straube und Manfred Unger zum 70. Geburtstag*, Hartmut Zwahr, Uwe Schirmer, Henning Steinführer (eds.). Beucha: Sax, 2000, 531–544.
Netta, Gheron. *Die Handelsbeziehungen zwischen Leipzig und Ost- und Südosteuropa bis zum Verfall der Warenmessen*. Zürich: Univ. Diss., 1920.
Pach, Zsygmunt Pál. Zur Geschichte der internationalen Handelswege und des Handelskapitals vom 15. bis 17. Jahrhundert. *Jahrbuch für Wirtschaftsgeschichte* 10:3 (1969): 179–192.
Paluchowski, Piotr. Miejsca i terminy jarmarków na terenie prus królewskich i książęcych w końcu XVI wieku na podstawie wykazówz Gdańskich kalendarzy. *Czasynowożytne* 24 (2011): 37–59.
Papoulia, Basilike. Jahrmärkte in Byzanz. In *Messen, Jahrmärkte und Stadtentwicklung*, Irsigler, Pauly (eds.), 41–49.
Paskaleva, Virginia. Economic and Cultural Relations of Bulgaria with the City of Leipzig from the End of the 18th Century to the Russo-Turkish War of 1877/78. *Yearbook of History of the USSR and the People's Democratic Countries of Europe* 6 (1962): 389–409.

Popović, Mihailo St. Jahrmärkte im europäischen Teil des Byzantinischen Reiches und deren neuzeitliches Nachleben. In *Europäische Messegeschichte, 9.–19. Jahrhundert. Forschungsstand und Forschungsperspektiven*, Markus A. Denzel (ed.). Cologne, Weimar, Vienna: Böhlau, 2018, 43–53.

Popović, Mihailo St. New Insights into the History of Balkan Fairs in the Historical Region of Macedonia (13th–19th Centuries). *Bulgaria Medievalis* 2 (2011): 757–776.

Rothmann, Michael. *Die Frankfurter Messen im Mittelalter*. Stuttgart: Steiner, 1998.

Rothmann, Michael. Überall ist Jahrmarkt und Entwicklungstendenzen der Institution des periodischen Marktes in Zentraleuropa vom 14. bis zum 17. Jahrhundert. In *Fiere e mercati nella integrazione delle economie europee, secc. XIII–XVIII*, Simonetta Cavaciocchi (ed.). Florence: Le Monnier, 2001, 91–108.

Sack, Hilmar, Tomasz Łopatka. Thirty Years' War and Potop. Heroism and "barbarian savagery": Existential War Experiences in the 17th Century. In *Deutsch-Polnische Erinnerungsorte*, vol. 3: *Parallelen*, Hans Henning Hahn, Robert Traba (eds.). Paderborn: Schöningh, 2012, 147–165.

Samsonowicz, Henryk. Die Handelsstraße Ostsee–Schwarzes Meer im 13. und 14. Jahrhundert. In *Der hansische Sonderweg? Beiträge zur Sozial- und Wirtschaftsgeschichte der Hanse*, Stuart Jenks, Michael North (eds.). Cologne, Weimar, Vienna: Böhlau, 1993, 23–30.

Samsonowicz, Henryk. Jarmarki w Polsce na tle sytuacij gospodarczej w Europie w XV–XVI w. In *Europa—Slowianszczyzna—Polska. Studia ku uczczeniu Profesora Kazimierza Tymienieckiego*, Juliusz Bardach (ed.). Poznań: Uniwersytet Mikołaja Kopernika w Toruniu, 1970, 523–532.

Samsonowicz, Henryk. Les foires en Pologne au XVe et XVIe siècle sur la toile de fond de la situation économique en Europe. In *Der Außenhandel Ostmitteleuropas 1450–1650. Die ostmitteleuropäischen Volkswirtschaften in ihren Beziehungen zu Mitteleuropa*, Ingomar Bog (ed.). Cologne, Vienna: Böhlau, 1971, 246–259.

Samsonowicz, Henryk. Niektóre cechy charakterystyczne sieci jarmarcznej w Polsce późnego średniowiecza. In *Studia nad dziejami miast*, vol. I, Bogucka, Czacharowski (eds.), 9–14.

Samsonowicz, Henryk. Przemiany osi drozynch w Polsce późnego średniowiecza. *Przegląd Historyczny* 64:4 (1973): 697–716.

Sarnowsky, Jürgen. Märkte im mittelalterlichen Preußen. *Hansische Geschichtsblätter* 120 (2002): 51–72.

Scheltjens, Werner. North-Eurasian Fairs from the Late Middle Ages to the Nineteenth Century. In *Europäische Messegeschichte*, Denzel(ed.), 325–352.

Schildhauer, Johannes. Der Seehandel Danzigs im 16. Jahrhundert und die Verlagerung des Warenverkehrs im Nord- und Mitteleuropäischen Raum. *Jahrbuch für Wirtschaftsgeschichte* 11:3 (1970): 155–178.

Schildhauer, Johannes. Zur Verlagerung des See- und Handelsverkehrs im nordeuropäischen Raum während des 15. und 16. Jahrhunderts: Eine Untersuchung auf der Grundlage der Danziger Pfahlkammerbücher. *Jahrbuch für Wirtschaftsgeschichte* 9:4 (1968): 187–211.

Simsch, Adelheid. Posener Marktzettel aus den Jahren 1579/80. Eine bisher unveröffentlichte Quelle zur Geschichte des Posener Handels in der zweiten Hälfte des 16. Jahrhunderts. In *Beiträge zur Stadt- und Regionalgeschichte Ost- und Nordeuropas. Herbert Ludat zum 60. Geburtstag*, Klaus Zernack (ed.). Wiesbaden: Steiner, 1971, 153–171.

Spannenberger, Norbert. Märkte im Königreich Ungarn, Kroatien und in Siebenbürgen. In *Europäische Messegeschichte*, Denzel(ed.), 267–283.

Straube, Manfred. Aktuelle Fragen der deutschen und internationalen Messegeschichte. In *Europäische Messegeschichte*, Denzel(ed.), 15–42.

Straube, Manfred. *Geleitswesen und Warenverkehr im thüringisch-sächsischen Raum zu Beginn der Frühen Neuzeit*. Cologne, Weimar, Vienna: Böhlau, 2015.

Topolski, Jerzy. Faktoren der Entstehung eines internationalen Jahrmarktnetzes in Polen im 16. und 17. Jahrhundert. *Studia Historiae Oeconomicae* 5 (1970): 101–116.
Troebst, Stefan. *Handelskontrolle, "Derivation", Eindämmung. Schwedische Moskaupolitik 1617–1661.* Wiesbaden: Harrassowitz, 1997.
Troebst, Stefan. Isfahan—Moscow—Amsterdam. Zur Entstehungsgeschichte des moskauischen Transitprivilegs für die Armenische Handelskompanie in Persien (1666–1676). *Jahrbücher für Geschichte Osteuropas* 41 (1993): 180–219.
Wanner, Michal. First Russian-Chinese Doplomatic and Business Relationship 1689–1728. *Prague Papers on the History of International Relations* 17:2 (2013): 66–76.
Wanner, Michal. The Russian-Chinese Trade in Kyakhta, its Organisation and Commodity Structure, 1727–1861. *Prague Papers on the History of International Relations* 18:2 (2014): 35–49.
Weisz, Boglárka. *Markets and Staples in the Medieval Hungarian Kingdom*. Budapest: Research Centre for the Humanities, 2020.

Chapter V: **Presentation of the CoMOR website/ database**

Noémie Lacroix, Jean-Paul Rehr, Leif Scheuermann

Fairs in History: the public database of the CoMOR project

Throughout the high to late Middle Ages and up to the modern period, fairs played an important role in the development of the European economy and especially in the trans-regional exchange of goods. In order to understand the radical expansion of money markets and the transformation of exchange that occurred in the late Middle Ages and the first centuries of the early modern period that made the role of fairs so important in the economy, the CoMOR project focuses on the period between the decline of the classic fairs at Champagne beginning around 1350 and the emergence of fairs dedicated to finance and money exchange in the seventeenth century, with a particular emphasis on the fairs of France, Germany, and the north of Italy. Funded by the French *Agence nationale de la recherche* and its German equivalent, the *Deutsche Forschungsgemeinschaft*, the principal investigators Jean-Louis Gaulin and Susanne Rau made an online, collaborative database to record and support the research central to the project. This database needed to respond to the goals of the project and its various contributors, as well as providing a platform for future collaboration. This article presents the database—hosted at http://fairs-in-history.huma-num.fr— together with the decisions taken to respond to the project, the contributor requirements, and the opportunities that it offers to users.[1]

The requirements of the CoMOR project

The multidisciplinary quality of the project team quickly led to the question of each team member's particular requirements for the database, with respect to both subject area and methods. Indeed, the long history of European fairs between 1350 and 1600 is one so rich that it can be approached in numerous ways, with numerous methods, as evidenced by the articles in the current volume.

1 For a technical explanation of the workings of the database, including how the project assures the long-term viability of its data, see the Data Management Plan of the project in Jean-Paul Rehr, Jean-Louis Gaulin, Susanne Rau, Ulf Christian Ewert. *The CoMOR Data Management Plan*. 2019–2023. DOI: 10.34847/nkl.8ceekn2a. See also the forthcoming data paper by the same authors with Leif Scheuermann. The CoMOR project would also like to recognize and thank Marjorie Burghart for her early contributions to the digital conceptualization of the project.

https://doi.org/10.1515/9783111621296-018

To effectively study the itineraries of merchants or those places in which the fairs were conducted (spatial analysis), the database needed to capture the place names with their locations encoded according to modern geographic reference systems (these names often differing according to the period and to the language of documentation). Similarly, studying the relations and networks of merchants required that the database could act as an index of personal names, as well as groups and organisations which they frequently constituted (from consulates and chancelleries to banking institutions and families), as well as being able to link these "entities" in relations and networks. The latter, in particular, demanded that a given person represented across different sources would be referenced as a single entity in the database (with a normalisation of each name). A third interest of the project is the study of goods bought and sold at the markets as well as the related flow of money and credit, and as such obligated the database to manage the type, quantity, and value of merchandise traded at an international level.

The above elements are already challenging enough. However, this was compounded by another effect of the extensive spatial and temporal dimensions of the project—the diversity of historical documentation. Sources for research include merchant manuals, fair almanacs, contracts, wills and testaments, consular deliberations, fairs privileges, old maps, merchants accounts and registers, tolls and customs ledgers—to name just a handful of types. These diverse sources are held in archives and libraries across Europe. They may be original parchment or paper documents, printed materials, or sources already issued as a critical edition. Beyond the contents of the sources, the CoMOR database also needed the capacity to describe the sources and their metadata, even where these could radically change from one document to another.

One further challenge arises from the heterogeneous nature of the project sources: some are exceptionally lengthy, containing much detail that interests the project research goals (for example, account record and fairs privileges), while others are very short and terse (such as consular deliberations and credit notes). The CoMOR database needed to be structured in such a way as to accept this diversity of sources while being capable of bringing the relevant datapoints together—whether greater or lesser in quantity—in a way that provides useful analytical outcomes.

Other demands were made on the design of the database. Firstly, the database should not be a simple deliverable at the end of the project timeline, but rather a database operational as early as possible in the project so that it would be used by project members from the moment they began their research. This would assure data coherence with respect to all information about fairs found in the archival sources, thus permitting validation, improvement, and reuse from their very inception as data records. Moreover, the database was built to be collaborative: all members of the project team could contribute together and in dynamic fashion, as well as invite other collaborators and students to join the project. Finally, the database should not only serve as a repository of data, but as a point of distribution for the group's research. The data would need to be accessible to all and at all times. Consequently, the stored data needed to be easily accessible and interrogable by other users and machine-readable by internet search engines and other systems. The response to these requirements was an online database constructed with an app-like interface—the website *Fairs in History*. This website offers a single interface which allows both access to—and entry of—data from sources. As such, all researchers associated with the project are able to access it from anywhere and anytime, and—another important goal for the project—permits access for the general public.

The online database, with its app-like interface, requires no particular technical skill in order to create well-ordered, reusable data, permitting researchers to work completely independently without need for recourse to a programmer or technical specialist. Further to the goal of ease of use, the site interface is available in French, English, German, and Italian, facilitating use by a multilingual, international research community. The ease of use, however, does not mean that there is no quality control of the data. It was important that the work product of researchers, even those of students, be protected and assured of their value. The response to this was the creation of a publishing process within the database that depends on roles and privileges assigned to users. The first level of privilege is a "contributor" who may enter their own new records, but who may not modify the records of other users. These new records, which are not yet visible to the public, are validated by an "editor" who evaluates the quality and integrity of the data and authorises their publication to the public. At times, a researcher may wish to enter data with the goal of using the database tools to analyse it, but they do not yet want to make the data available to the public (perhaps to protect forthcoming work)—this is considered an 'embargo' of data, and to facilitate this, a date of future publication can be applied to records in the database.

From a broader perspective, the CoMOR project obligated itself to principles and practices of Open Science and FAIR data (Findable, Accessible, Interoperable, and Reusable).[2] Among the chief concerns of these principles are that the data should be made available to the public in open formats with the least restrictive license possible, supported by proper documentation. Data should be deposited in

2 FAIR data (as well as the acronym) was first defined in Mark D. Wilkinson et al. The FAIR Guiding Principles for Scientific Data Management and Stewardship. *Scientific Data* 3:1 (2016): 160018, https://doi.org/10.1038/sdata.2016.18 (14 January 2024). the present-day iteration of FAIR principles can be found at https://www.go-fair.org/fair-principles/ (07 October 2024).

repositories that can assure their persistence and access over time, while providing a normalised perennial identifier. The team made a number of technical decisions to facilitate this, the most important among them storing the data in TEI-XML files,[3] constructing the database using Open Source technology,[4] and hosting it on the Huma-Num infrastructure.[5]

The database *Fairs in History*

The requirements of the project and of the team members having been defined, the *Fairs in History* database was developed and put into service within the first year of the project. The following describes in greater detail the type of data being gathered, how they are put into relation with each other, and the tools offered to researchers by the web application.

The CoMOR project does not have in its mandate the publication of philological or diplomatic editions of sources subject to research, but rather the extraction of data identified by the project scope from those sources. At the highest level, the database indexes instances of fairs in the sources and the terminology used to describe them (*nundinae, forum, foire, fiera, messe,* etc.), the dates and places related to them (the fairs themselves, the commercial agreements implicated in them, the itineraries of merchants who journey to them), the names of those people and groups associated with them (merchants, political entities, banks), the interactions between them, and finally, the merchandise, monies, and quantities transacted. As mentioned above, the database also captures the metadata of sources: the date and place a document was created, the name of the person or entity who created it, the typology of document, and archival references.

To establish links between various data points, the latter have been normalised and organised in a cascading set of structures created especially for the project, based on a custom-controlled vocabulary specific (see Fig. 1). The database is composed of "collections" which act as containers for a series of "sources" judged by its editor to be somehow coherent. The "sources" themselves are singular documents—perhaps privileges, letters, or sequences of entries from ledgers—adapted to the form required by the database. That form is an "event," which is a method of describing a single conjunction of people, places, dates, and objects

3 TEI-C is the acronym for the Text Encoding Initiative Consortium (https://tei-c.org/), a body responsible for maintaining a long-standing schema for encoding texts and their metadata.
4 eXist-db, an XML database (https://exist-db.org/).
5 Huma-Num. https://www.huma-num.fr/ (07 October 2024).

found in those archival records which pertain somehow to the study of fairs and merchants from the late medieval to the early modern period.

This flexible structure can thus be adapted to any of the diverse types of documentary sources that make up the corpus of the CoMOR project. Metadata is also flexible, with minimal requirements. Certain components of them—such as the date and place of production of the source, the entity responsible for it, the archival reference, and at least a single date reference for an "event"—are required, and even then, it is possible to indicate a degree of certainty about the data.

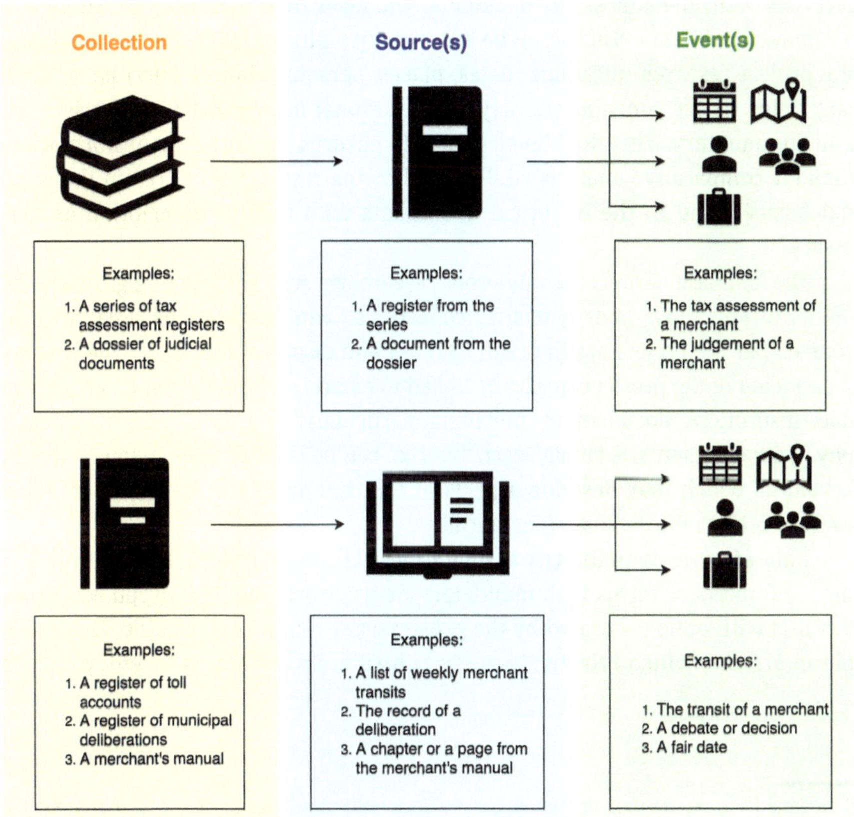

Fig. 1: Examples of the relationships of *Collection*, *Source*, and *Event* in the CoMOR database. Graphic by Noémie Lacroix.

The structure of the data model also facilitates the various queries that respond to the research questions of the CoMOR project and the individual researchers. The analysis of networks of merchants may be interrogated through the passive links between people (for example, certain people found together in a single source) or through the links of actions that connect them in a form of a "predicate." The "predicate" is the label of an action of or between actors in an "event." In this fashion, the links between merchants may be explicitly described, even in complex transactions. To take an example, one can record the fact that in April 1423, Petrus de Aquiano and Aymonetus Regis transported, on behalf of magistro Symundo, certain merchandise which originated at the Geneva fair and for which the transporters paid a toll at Villeneuve to a certain Jaquemet Medici, the toll collector.[6]

Such flexibility, minimally constrained but providing a controlled vocabulary, can welcome almost any document, whatever their gaps may be. So long as a minimum of data exists, it can be entered. Virtually all fields directly related to the project research questions (dates, places, persons, objects, fairs) have auxiliary fields where contributors may add additional data, extracts of the sources, and commentary. This dual-level structure ensures the integrity of normalised data for comparative analysis while still allowing researchers to retain the original forms found in the historical documents with further description as necessary.

The database permits the numerous researchers who work with digitised documents to add those images to the "collections" with annotations (assuming, of course, that the project has the right to reuse and display the images). The core research data of the project can also be linked to exterior references, whether individuals, institutions, documentary metadata, particularly to a standardised bibliography,[7] with commentary. Finally, each "source" can be labelled with Themes—that is, keywords which may describe aspects of the content of the "source" and allow users to browse the database thematically.

Data entry is done directly through the website interfaces, each of which is made of masks or forms with mandatory fields clearly marked, dropdown or select lists with options curated by the project team, and free-text fields. These simple interfaces, which effectively guide contributors in their data entry, assure

---

6 Noémie Lacroix. Archivio di Stato di Torino Sezioni Riunite, Inventario 69, folio 31, mazzo 9, compte du petit péage de Villeneuve (1423–1424) (COL0095). In *Configurations of European Fairs: Merchants, Objects, Routes (ca. 1350–1600).* Jean-Louis Gaulin, Susanne Rau (eds.). https://fairs-in-history.huma-num.fr/collection/COL0095 (31 December 2023). See also Franco Morenzoni. *Marchands et marchandises au péage de Villeneuve de Chillon: (première moitié du XVe siècle).* Lausanne: Université de Lausanne, 2016, 166–167.

7 The project bibliography is open and public, managed at https://www.zotero.org/groups/2476769/comor/ (07 October 2024).

data normalisation for comparative analysis between different sources while still permitting the researcher to describe their sources as fully as they need.

Beyond acting as a database for recording data, *Fairs in History* is a platform for accessing the records. The entirety of the data published is accessible directly on the website as well as made available in a number of formats for download (PDF or the TEI-XML source files). All data is made available under the Creative Commons Attribution-NonCommercial-ShareAlike License (CC BY-NC-SA 4.0),[8] a license facilitated by the project's use of stable identifiers and structured citation reference.[9]

The site offers numerous methods for exploring the data: dynamic indexes and browsable lists, a variety of search engines, and numerous options for filtering data. The indexes facilitate quick access to names, places, objects, and merchandise found in the sources, or exploration by keywords. Certain content is enriched with external references, such as the place index which provides maps for locating a place and sub-lists of historic names.[10]

Three search engines offer different methods for accessing site data. The full-text search engine provides a way to search data in the free text fields (commentary and source extracts).[11] An advanced search tool permits a multi-faceted search of all data from "collections" down to the components of "events."[12] This engine, in particular, gives users maximum control over the parameters of their search to obtain completely refined results. Finally, a third search engine is narrowly focused on exploring the fairs themselves, presented in something of the fashion of a calendar.[13]

Example use cases of *Fairs in History*

The *Fairs in History* database has been in production for the greater part of the formal life of the CoMOR project and by the end of the project funding phase,

---

8 That is, users may reuse the data so long as they cite the source, use the data for non-commercial purposes, and in turn impose the same license conditions on their redistribution of the data. See license details at https://creativecommons.org/licenses/by-nc-sa/4.0 (07 October 2024).

9 Each "collection" has a unique, permanent project identifier as well as a DOI.

10 This enrichment has, in particular, been affected through reference to old maps indexed and geolocated by Leif Scheuermann, allowing a dual historic and modern view of CoMOR project data.

11 Simple Search, CoMOR. https://fairs-in-history.huma-num.fr/simplesearch (07 October 2024).

12 Search, CoMOR. https://fairs-in-history.huma-num.fr/search (07 October 2024).

13 Fair Explorer, CoMOR. https://fairs-in-history.huma-num.fr/fair_explorer (07 October 2024).

over 100 collections were created. The site is ready and able to take in new data from the current team and new contributors interested in fairs and merchants, and provides a standardised set of tools for analysis and visualisations. Among the latter are five different, ready-built data exports which gather datasets automatically according to specific criteria.[14] Four datasets are structured around the *Events* ('fair calendar,' 'fair references,' and 'trade data,' with or without merchandise) with the fifth dataset assembling relational data for various applications of network analysis.[15] All of the data exports are formatted to comply with specific open protocols used by most open source software. The 'fair calendar' and 'fair references' take advantage of the underlying geo-encoding to output as geoJSON for easy import to GIS systems.[16] The datasets aimed at network analysis are exported as CSV files containing nodes and edges accepted by most network analysis packages. The 'trade data' is output in both CSV and geoJSON formats, providing multiple possibilities for interrogating the data. The datasets are exportable by 'collection'; however, due to the fact that they all follow the same data models, datasets can be easily combined, allowing one to effectively map the geo-encoded elements of the entire CoMOR project data or analyse the networks contained in it. What follows below are two examples, from two different collections, demonstrating the possibilities with CoMOR data.

---

14 Downloads, CoMOR. https://fairs-in-history.huma-num.fr/downloads (07 October 2024).

15 The variety of applications of network analysis to historical studies has exploded in the last 15 years, extending far beyond sociological origins of social network analysis. The literature has grown with it, although a key starting point for historians would now be Claire Lemercier. Formal Network Methods in History: Why and How? In *Social Networks, Political Institutions, and Rural Societies*, Georg Fertig (ed.). Turnhout: Brepols, 2015, 281–310. https://doi.org/10.1484/M.RURHE-EB.4.00198. For another comprehensive overview, see K. Patrick Fazioli. Modeling the Middle Ages: A Review of Historical Network Research on Medieval Europe and the Mediterranean World. In *Social and Intellectual Networking in the Early Middle Ages*, Michael Kelly, K. Patrick Fazioli (eds.). Binghamton, NY: Gracchi Books/Punctum Books, 2023.

16 In the last twenty years, geographic information systems have been used in numerous projects of spatially oriented historical scholarship, although a comprehensive introduction is still a research desideratum. For this reason, only two fundamental—albeit somewhat older—edited volumes by Anne Kelly Knowles shall be mentioned here: Anne Kelly Knowles. *Placing History: How Maps, Spatial Data, and GIS Are Changing Historical Scholarship*. Redlands, CA: ESRI Press, 2008; Anne Kelly Knowles. *Past Time, Past Place: GIS for History*. Redlands, CA: ESRI Press, 2002. For spatio-temporal analysis of the CoMOR data, see Ulf Christian Ewert, Susanne Rau, Leif Scheuermann. Räumliche Konfigurationen des Messehandels im frühneuzeitlichen Europa. Gedruckte Messekalender des 16. und 17. Jahrhunderts und ihre computergestützte Analyse. *Vierteljahrschrift für Sozial- und Wirtschaftsgeschichte* 110:4 (2023): 494–541.

The first example comes from the *Collection* “Biblioteca Riccardiana di Firenze, Pegolotti, La pratica della mercatura (COL0018).”[17] In the middle of the fourteenth century, the Florentine merchant Franceso Balducci Pegolotti composed *La pratica della mercatura*,[18] a treatise providing rare, precious insights into merchants, commerce, and trade of the late Middle Ages. Marta Gravela, researcher with the CoMOR project, studied the manual and from it entered the fair and exchange data into *Fairs in History*. Using *Fairs in History*'s automated network analysis datasets imported into Gephi (a popular open-source software for analysing and visualising network graphs),[19] one can quickly visualise the mercantile links which existed between the towns cited by Pegolotti in the fourteenth century, and in so doing understand quickly the depth of the networks he described and his vast worldview. Fig. 2 represents a general overview of the trade networks described by Pegolotti. In this typical network graph, the towns are represented by circles (‘nodes’) with their size reflecting their ‘importance’ in Pegolotti's tables of trade: the more the town is cited, the more the trade recorded for them by Pegolotti and the larger the node. At a glance, we can see that Pegolotti focused on Venice, Florence, Famagusta (Ammóchostos), Genoa, and Bruges as centres of trade (whether in reality they were such centres or not is another matter for analysis).[20] The four node colours in this graph indicate another tendency in the data—the effect of sub-networks emanating from hubs. In network analysis terms, this is ‘community’ or ‘modularity’ analysis and uses an algorithm to attempt to segregate the graph into smaller, local networks according to the intensity of connections between groups of nodes. For this high-level view, we have set the algorithm to a fairly low ‘resolution’ to distinguish the broadest tendencies. As mentioned previously, all locations in the *Fairs in History* database have been geo-encoded with latitude and longitude. This allows network analysis applications such as Gephi to ‘read’ the coordinates and place them in relative geographic position. The result in Fig. 3 shows how the ‘hubs’ or ‘local networks’ from Fig. 2 follow a certain geographic logic—albeit not exclusively! In this representation, we see that the four sub-networks are roughly demarcated by zones of interaction (again expressed in modern geographic terms): the Adriatic Sea, the

17 Marta Gravela. Biblioteca Riccardiana di Firenze, Pegolotti, La pratica della mercatura (COL0018). In *Configurations of European Fairs*, Gaulin, Rau (eds.). https://fairs-in-history.huma-num.fr/collection/COL0018 (01 January 2024).

18 Francesco Balducci Pegolotti. *La pratica della mercatura*. Allan Evans (ed.). Cambridge: Medieval Academy of America, 1936.

19 Gephi. The Open Graph Viz Platform. https://gephi.org/ (07 October 2024).

20 The names of the towns in the graphs based on Pegolotti's manual have been standardised into modern English. They are not the city names as written by Pegolotti in the fourteenth century.

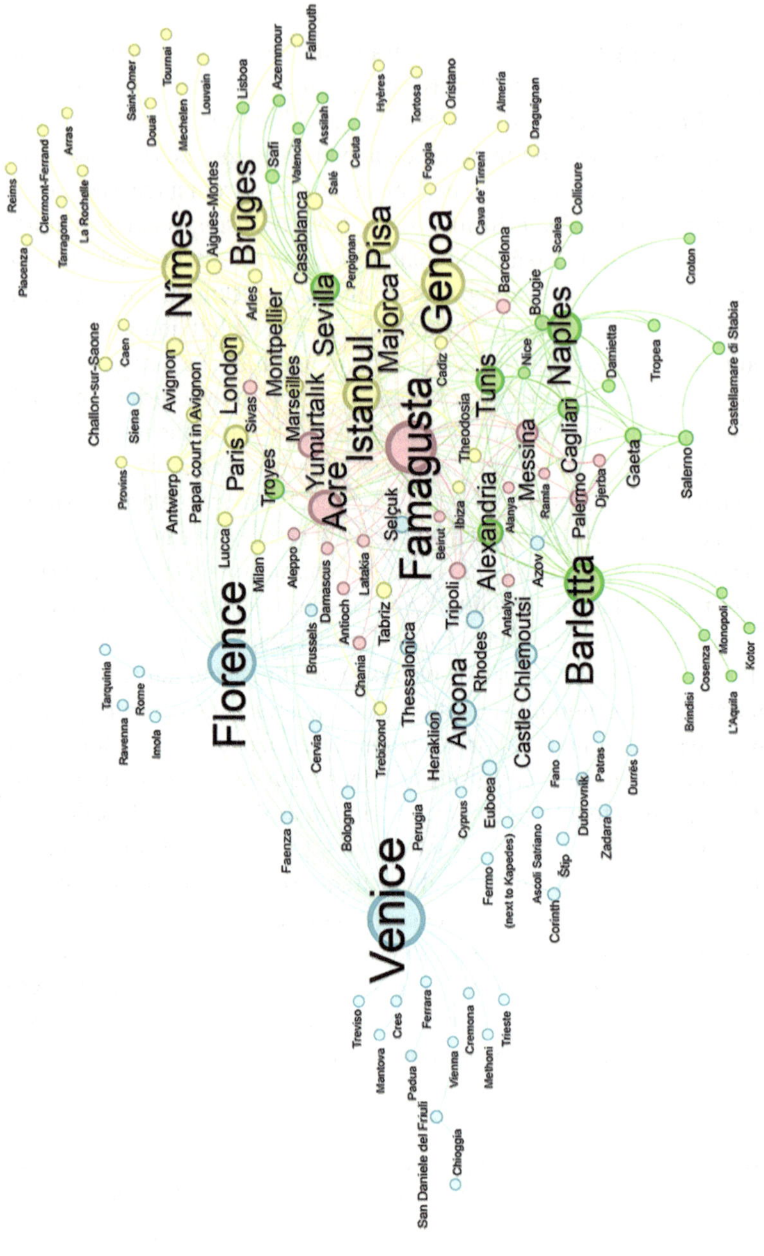

Fig. 2: Network of mid-fourteenth century trade in Pegolotti's *La pratica della mercatura*. The node size reflects the frequency of mentions of a given place, combining imports and exports—the larger the circle, the more frequently a place appears in Pegolotti's lists. The four colours represent 'communities' or 'groups' of intensive inter-trade. Graphic by Jean-Paul Rehr and Noémie Lacroix.

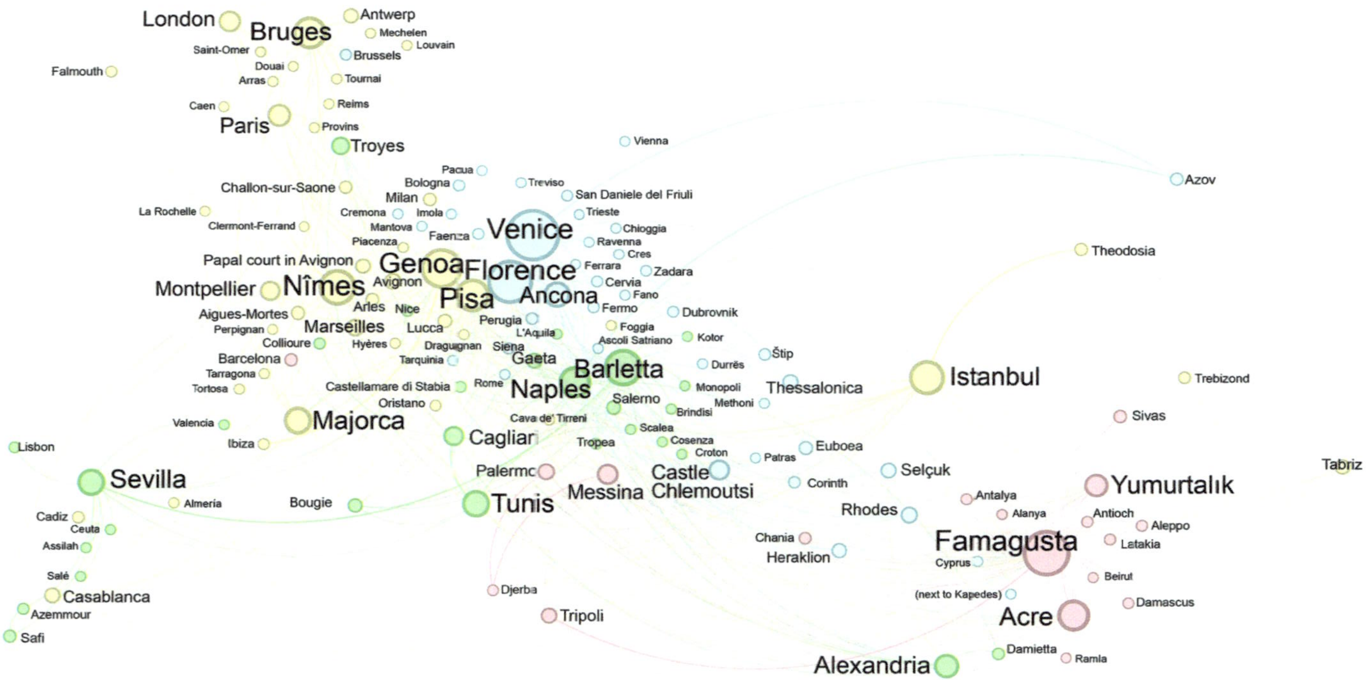

Fig. 3: Network of mid-fourteenth century trade in Pegolotti's *La pratica della mercatura*, with the same criteria as Fig. 2, except that it is displayed according to geographic coordinates. The colours represent the same 'communities' or 'groups' of intensive inter-trade. Graphic by Jean-Paul Rehr and Noémie Lacroix.

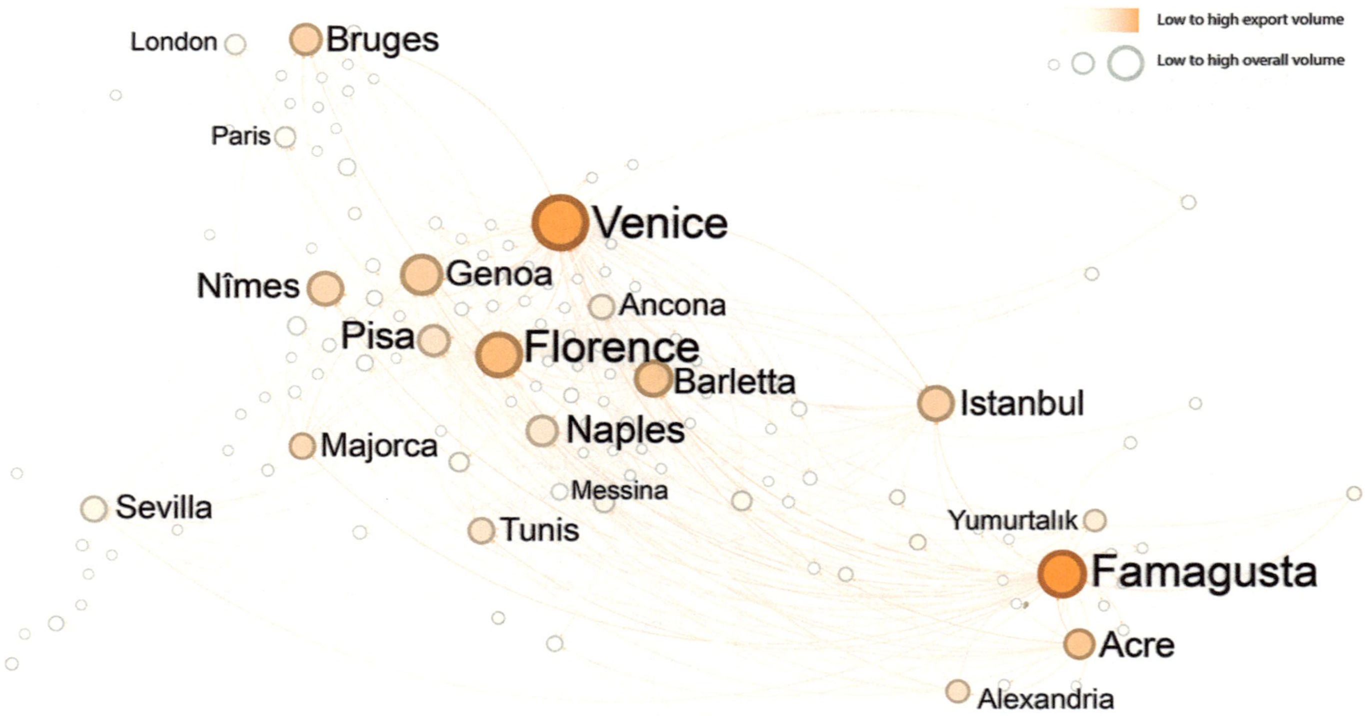

Fig. 4: Network of mid-fourteenth century trade in Pegolotti's *La pratica della mercatura*. with emphasis on exports. The node size reflects the frequency of overall mentions of a given place, the intensity of orange node color represents greater export volumes. Graphic by Jean-Paul Rehr and Noémie Lacroix.

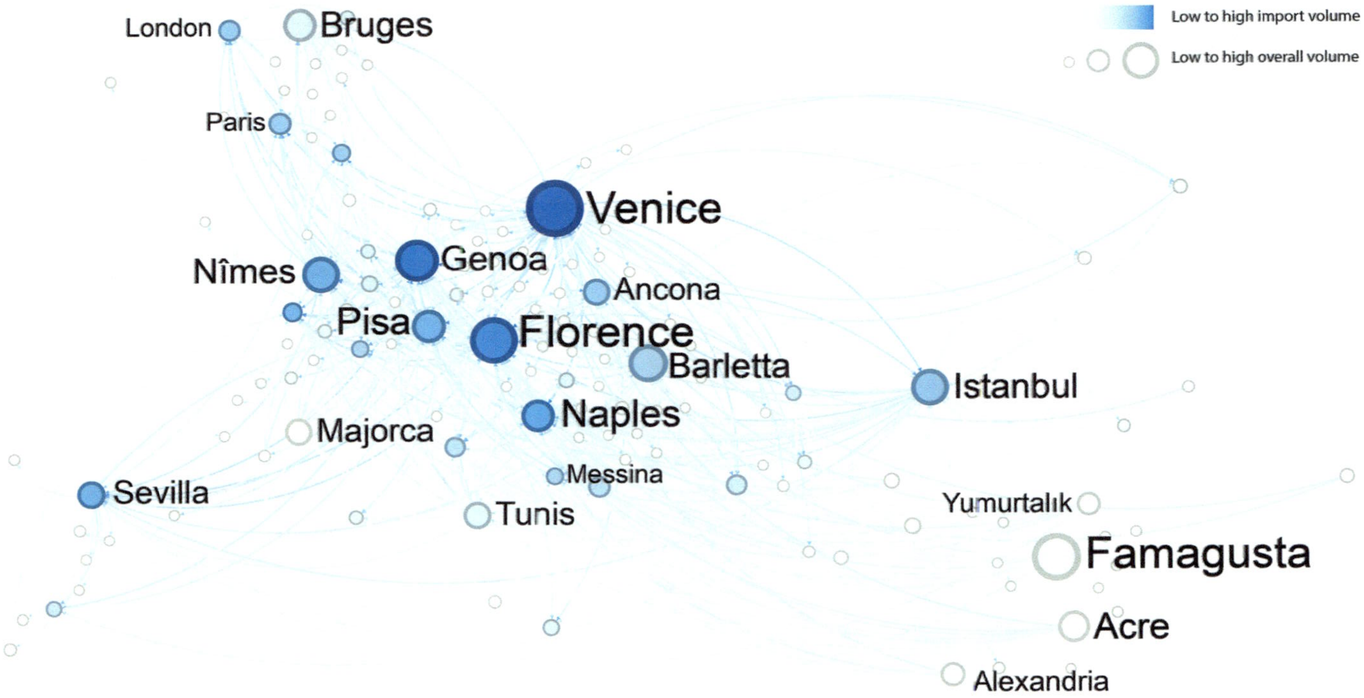

Fig. 5: Network of mid-fourteenth century trade in Pegolotti's *La pratica della mercatura*, with emphasis on imports (to compare with exports in Fig. 4). The node size reflects the frequency of overall mentions of a given place. The intensity of the blue node colour represents greater import volumes. Graphic by Jean-Paul Rehr and Noémie Lacroix.

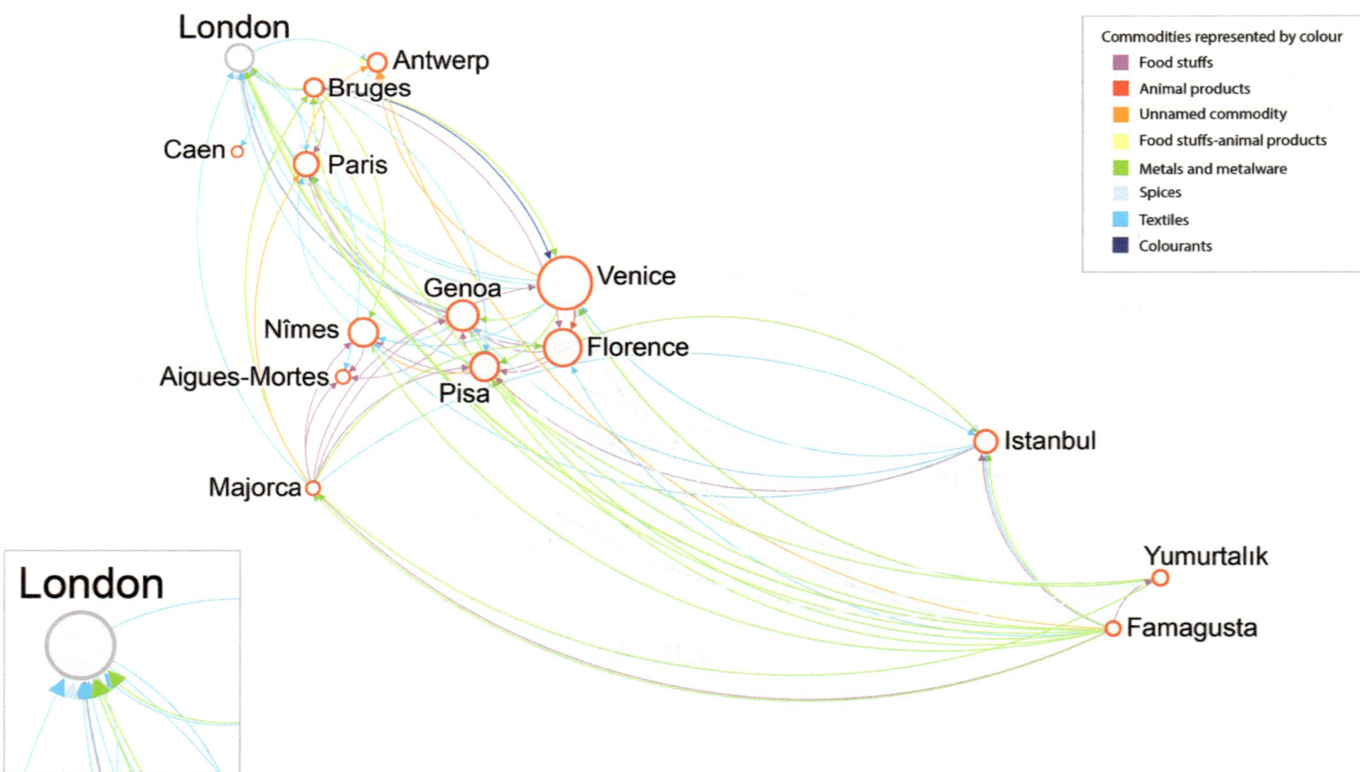

Fig. 6: Network of trade with London in Pegolotti's *La pratica della mercatura*. The edge colour equates to a type of textile, as indicated in the graphic legend. Graphic by Jean-Paul Rehr and Noémie Lacroix.

eastern Mediterranean, the western Mediterranean, and a broad axis between Genoa, Pisa, and northwestern Europe, extending up to England. However, these are not neatly contained: Brussels, Alexandria, Istanbul, Troyes, and Barcelona all appear as significant breaks in the apparent geographic continuity.

Pegolotti's tables of town trade actually contain directionality, or imports and exports. This directionality is captured in *Fairs in History* and exported with the data, allowing us to explore the movement of merchandise. Figs 4 and 5 present the trade direction, with Fig. 4 depicting the importance of towns in exports and Fig. 5 focused on their relative position as importers. Comparing the two side by side, we see that certain towns like Venice are true "hubs," with merchandise flowing in and out, while "hubs" like Famagusta are really centres of export.

The same Pegolotti dataset can produce other insights too. Although *Fairs in History* is not meant to be an 'accounting system' per se, all trade can be encoded for commodity, volume, and value. Marta Gravela encoded all the commodities traded between the towns recorded by Pegolotti. In Fig. 6, the commodity data is rendered from the point of view of trade with a particular town, called an 'ego network' in network analysis. The exchanges between towns ('edges') are coloured according to the category of merchandise (foodstuffs, textiles, metal, etc.), demonstrating the reach of the commercial network of the English trade centre in the fourteenth century as seen by this Italian merchant.

The second example comes from the *Collection* "Museum Plantin-Moretus, PK.OP.21317 (Jost Amman's allegory / fair calendar) (COL0104)."[21] In 1585, the draughtsman and engraver Jost Amman created an allegory of commerce represented in the form of the town and port of Anvers (see Fig. 7). In the upper part of the engraving, he included a calendar of European fairs. This calendar provides an overview, month by month, of the principal fairs with the name and coat of arms of the host towns. As with other fair calendars, the names of the towns and the dates of their fairs were entered into *Fairs in History* so as to see all fairs of the same epoch together. That data can be downloaded in geoJSON-format to be imported into a cartographic or geographic information system (GIS) in order to produce a simple map that allows one to understand the geographic coverage of Amman's calendar (see Fig. 8).

21 Ulf Christian Ewert, Noémie Lacroix. Museum Plantin-Moretus, PK.OP.21317 (Jost Amman's allegory/fair calendar) (COL0104). In *Configurations of European* Fairs, Gaulin, Rau (eds.). https://fairs-in-history.huma-num.fr/collection/COL0104 (06 January 2024).

Fig. 7: Allegory of commerce, Jost Amman, 1585.[22]

22 Jost Amman, *Eigentliche Abbildung deß ganzen Gewerks der loeblichen Kaufmannschaft/Samt etlich der nahmhafft und fuernehmsten Handelstaedt Signatur und Wappen zum Theil fuernehmlich die Maerckt und Messen begriffen seyn/so deß Jahr ueber in jedem Monath einfallen/auch hin und wider in Europa zu unterschidlichen Zeiten gehalten [. . .]*, wood engraving (on paper), ca. 1585, 95 cm x 64 cm, Antwerp, Museum Plantin-Moretus, PK.OP.21317. Photo credit: Peter Maes.

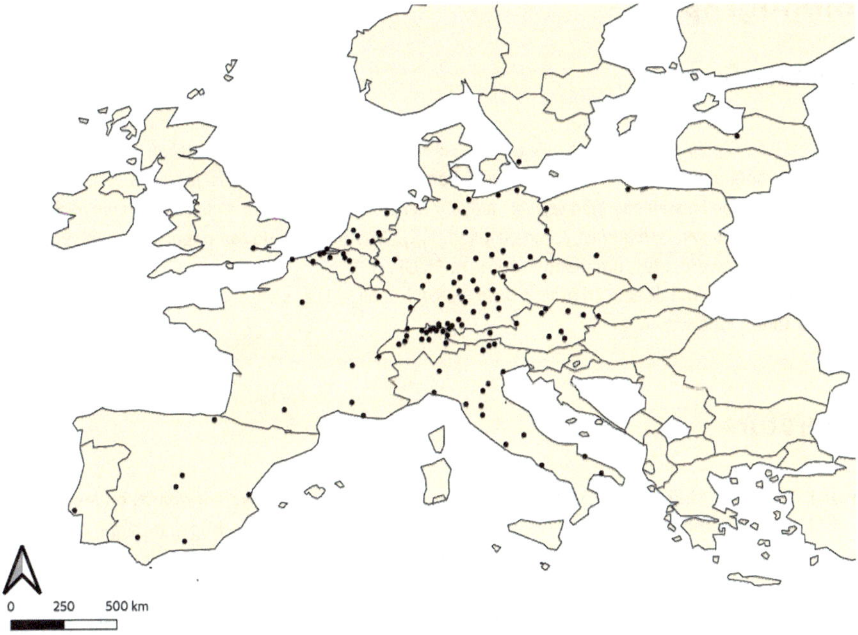

Fig. 8: Fair locations cited in Jost Amman's calendar projected on to a modern map of Europe. Map graphic by Noémie Lacroix.

This tour of the CoMOR database, *Fairs in History*, only touches briefly on its potential. The opportunities are three-fold for researchers. The first is the data already present, as entered by the first members of the CoMOR research team, which demonstrates the possibilities of a database that unifies heterogeneous sources. The second are the tools, ready to use, for exploiting the data through both quantitative and qualitative methods. The third opportunity is an expression of the founding idea of the project: the database is not simply a container of final project data as some fixed deliverable; it is a living entity that invites other researchers and their students to not only reuse the existing project data, but to join in a collaboration that continues to seek, through the ongoing contribution of a variety of sources, more insights into the fundamental reshaping of markets that occurred in the transition from the Middle Ages to the beginning of the modern era.

Bibliography

Primary Sources

Amman, Jost. *Eigentliche Abbildung deß ganzen Gewerks der loeblichen Kaufmannschaft/Samt etlich der nahmhafft und fuernehmsten Handelstaedt Signatur und Wappen zum Theil fuernehmlich die Maerckt und Messen begriffen seyn/so deß Jahr ueber in jedem Monath einfallen/auch hin und wider in Europa zu unterschidlichen Zeiten gehalten [. . .]*. Wood engraving (on paper), ca. 1585, 95 cm x 64 cm. Antwerp, Museum Plantin-Moretus, PK.OP.21317.

Pegolotti, Francesco Balducci. *La pratica della mercatura*. Allan Evans (ed.). Cambridge: Medieval Academy of America, 1936.

Literature

Fazioli, K. Patrick. Modeling the Middle Ages: A Review of Historical Network Research on Medieval Europe and the Mediterranean World. In *Social and Intellectual Networking in the Early Middle Ages*, Michael Kelly, K. Patrick Fazioli (eds.). Binghamton, NY: Gracchi Books/Punctum Books, 2023, 37–68.

Knowles, Anne Kelly. *Placing History: How Maps, Spatial Data, and GIS Are Changing Historical Scholarship*. Redlands, CA: ESRI Press, 2008.

Knowles, Anne Kelly. *Past Time, Past Place: GIS for History*. Redlands, CA: ESRI Press, 2002.

Lemercier, Claire. Formal Network Methods in History: Why and How? In *Social Networks, Political Institutions, and Rural Societies*, Georg Fertig (ed.). Turnhout: Brepols, 2015, 281–310. https://doi.org/10.1484/M.RURHE-EB.4.00198.

Morenzoni, Franco. *Marchands et marchandises au péage de Villeneuve de Chillon (première moitié du XVe siècle)*. Lausanne: Université de Lausanne, 2016.

Rehr, Jean-Paul, Jean-Louis Gaulin, Susanne Rau, Ulf Christian Ewert. The CoMOR Data Management Plan. 2019–2023.

Wilkinson, Mark D et al. The FAIR Guiding Principles for Scientific Data Management and Stewardship. *Scientific Data* 3:1 (2016): 160018. https://doi.org/10.1038/sdata.2016.18 (14 January 2024).

List of authors

Matthias Baumgartl, Dr., Archivist at the Bayerisches Hauptstaatsarchiv

Markus A. Denzel, Dr., Professor of Social and Economic History at the University of Leipzig

Ulf Christian Ewert, PD Dr., Research Associate at the Historical Commission at the Bavarian Academy of Sciences and Humanities

Jean-Louis Gaulin, Professor of Medieval History at the Department of History, University Lyon 2, member of the CIHAM-UMR 5648 (Lyon-Avignon); CoMOR project leader France

François Gipouloux, Directeur de recherche émérite at the Centre National de la Recherche Scientifique – École des Hautes Études en Sciences Sociales, Centre d'études sur la Chine moderne et contemporaine-UMR 8173

Pauline Gomes, PhD student at the University Lyon 2 and University of Turin, member of the CIHAM-UMR 5648 (Lyon-Avignon)

Marta Gravela, Dr., Associate Professor of Medieval History at the Department of Historical Studies, University of Turin and principal investigator of the ERC project DemAlps: "Democracies of the Alps. Issues, practices and ideals of politics in mountain communities, 1300-1500" (Grant agreement no. 101077793)

Armand Jamme, Directeur de recherche in Medieval History at the Centre National de la Recherche Scientifique, member of the CIHAM-UMR 5648 (Lyon-Avignon)

Noémie Lacroix, PhD student at the ERC Project DemAlps, University of Turin and University of Lyon 3

Heinrich Lang, PD Dr., Research Fellow at the Department of Social and Economic History, University of Leipzig, associated fellow at the Centre for Advanced Studies "Religion and Urbanity", University of Erfurt; co-investigator of the CoMOR project

Clément Lenoble, Chargé de recherche in Medieval History at the Centre National de la Recherche Scientifique, member of the CIHAM-UMR 5648 (Lyon-Avignon)

Claudio Marsilio, Dr., Associate Professor of Economic History at the Department of Economics, University of Verona, and Associate Researcher at the Institute for the History of Mediterranean Europe of the Italian National Research Council (ISEM)

Ezio Claudio Pia, Dr., member of the CoMOR project, associated researcher at the CIHAM-UMR 5648 (Lyon-Avignon)

Susanne Rau, Dr., Professor of Spatial History and Culture at the Department of History and Fellow at the Max Weber Centre, University of Erfurt; CoMOR project leader Germany

https://doi.org/10.1515/9783111621296-019

Jean-Paul Rehr, Research Fellow at the ERC Project DemAlps, University of Turin, and associated member of CIHAM-UMR 5648 (Lyon-Avignon)

Nicolas Sarzeaud, Fellow at the Académie de France à Rome - Villa Médicis

Leif Scheuermann, Dr., Professor of Digital Historical Heritage at the University of Trier, principal investigator of the ERC Project "Simulation of transport between the Adriatic Sea and the Danube" (Grant agreement no. 101001835), and Chair of the Institute for Historical Regional Research of Rhineland-Palatinate

Boglárka Weisz, PhD, Senior Research Fellow, Head of the Medieval History Department, Institute of History of HUN-REN Research Centre for the Humanities